Socialist Agriculture
in Transition

DATE DUE FOR

About the Book and Editors

Because of altered investment priorities, policymakers in socialist countries can no longer increase the resources devoted to agriculture as they have in the past. Instead, they must seek alternative means of improving agricultural performance. One approach has been to change the structure of socialist agriculture and to foster organizational changes within agricultural units.

The contributors to this volume evaluate such reforms and weigh their implications for agricultural output and trade. They examine the normless links being introduced in the USSR and compare Soviet experiences with the successes of Chinese and Hungarian reorganizations; describe and analyze the changes being implemented in the German Democratic Republic, Yugoslavia, and Vietnam; and pay particular attention to the role of Polish agriculture in the production crisis and to agriculture's potential for improving Poland's overall economic performance. The contributors also address issues of infrastructure development, the incentives being developed to foster more efficient allocation of resources within the agricultural sector, and the likely growth of East-West and intra-socialist agricultural trade.

Josef C. Brada is professor of economics at Arizona State University. He is the former editor of *Comparative Economic Studies* and the current editor of the *Journal of Comparative Economics* and *Soviet and East European Foreign Trade*. **Karl-Eugen Wädekin** was professor of international and East European agrarian policies, Justus-Liebig-Universität, Giessen, and researcher at the Zentrum für kontinentale Agrar- und Wirtschaftsforschung, Giessen. He is currently teaching and conducting research at the Department of Economics and the Slavic Center at the University of California, Berkeley. His books include *Agriculture in Eastern Europe and the Soviet Union: Comparative Studies*.

Socialist Agriculture in Transition

Organizational Response to Failing Performance

edited by
Josef C. Brada
and Karl-Eugen Wädekin

Westview Press / Boulder and London

322278

Westview Special Studies on the Soviet Union and Eastern Europe

Published in 1988 in the United States of America by Westview Press, Inc.; Frederick A. Praeger, Publisher; 5500 Central Avenue, Boulder, Colorado 80301

Library of Congress Cataloging-in-Publication Data
Brada, Josef C., 1942–
  Socialist agriculture in transition.
  (Westview special studies on the Soviet Union and
Eastern Europe)
  1. Agriculture—Economic aspects—Europe, Eastern.
2. Agriculture—Economic aspects—Communist countries.
3. Agriculture and state—Communist countries.
4. Agriculture and communism. I. Wädekin, Karl Eugen.
II. Title. III. Series.
HD1917.B73 1988   338.1′0947   86-28995
ISBN 0-8133-7344-1

Composition for this book originated with conversion of the editors' word-processor disks. This book was produced without formal editing by the publisher.

Printed and bound in the United States of America

The paper used in this publication meets the requirements of the American National Standard for Permanence of Paper for Printed Library Materials Z39.48-1984.

6   5   4   3   2   1

Contents

SECTION 8
ALLOCATING RESOURCES TO PROMOTE EFFICIENCY AND STRUCTURAL CHANGE IN AGRICULTURE

SECTION 9
INTERNATIONAL TRADE AND THE AGRARIAN SECTOR

Introduction

Karl-Eugen Wädekin

At one time agriculture and agrarian policies in the USSR were an almost unexplored part of the little explored field called Soviet Studies. No more than a handful of people were interested in it, partly because the sources and data for research were extremely scanty after Stalin's collectivization. Prior to that shattering event, even Soviet publications gave detailed and competent information on the state and development of Russia's agriculture, and non-Communist observers had opportunities to see the countryside and to obtain information from various sources, among them even highly placed officials. It was this pre-collectivization period when western studies of Soviet agriculture started.

The first scholarly and comprehensive book on the revolutionary change and new state of Soviet agriculture was published by the Russian emigre Boris Brutskus in the series of the Osteuropa-Institut at Breslau.[1] Soon such early studies of Soviet agriculture in Germany were carried out also by non-emigres. They found a main publication outlet in the monthly *Osteuropa*. Among those observers Otto Auhagen is to be named in the first but not the only place with his timely reports from Moscow during 1925–31. He was followed by Otto Schiller, who for a number of years had directed model state farms of German-Soviet joint ventures and then continued Auhagen's reporting. Schiller published two books on the subject in 1933 and 1943, which include the collectivization period.[2] The second one, however, already suffered from the deteriorating information situation, though not, it has to be emphasized, from Nazi influence on its contents.

Very soon, studies of Soviet agriculture gained importance in other western countries, too. Books like those by Fisher, Robinson, Timoshenko and Hubbard at once come to mind,[3] not to speak of a number of important articles by those and other authors.

During the Second World War and the early post-war years there was public interest in the West in objective studies on the socio-economic internal affairs of the Soviet ally, whereas no such research was possible in Germany for reasons of political warfare and subsequent destruction. This is not to say that such work was wholly stopped in the West. Naum Jasny's monumental book of 1949 and Lazar Volin's equally important, though less voluminous, work of 1951 bear witness to the continuation of research during the intervening years.[4]

After 1948, not only did the psychological impact of the anti-Hitler alliance subside, but the expansion of Soviet dominance over most of Eastern Europe, including East Germany, and Stalin's policy of collectivizing agriculture in those countries in imitation of the Soviet model gave research on this agrarian system a new impetus of public interest in the West, including the western part of Germany.

After Stalin's death in March, 1953, even the Soviet leaders more or less admitted the weaknesses of his agricultural system, but they denied that these were an inherent part of the Soviet system in general. Similarly, the collectivization drive temporarily stopped in most, though not all, of East Europe after Stalin's death; its methods were admitted to have been wrong, but here, too, it was denied that something was wrong with collectivization in itself. Thus there was ample room for East-West disputes over the merits of socialized agriculture and for underpinning the western point of view by research on the true state and development of agriculture under the various Communist regimes. An increasing number of research publications by other authors during and after the mid-1950s followed Jansny's and Volin's earlier work. The field of relevant studies became so wide and manifold and the number of authors and publications so great that an outline of the development during and since that time would require a long article, if not a book in itself.[5]

The years of temporary political and lasting socio-economic change in the Communist world after Stalin's death brought with them also a growing amount of official and semi-official economic information, including that on the agrarian sectors of the various countries concerned. The Soviet authorities, after a lapse of 17 years, in 1956 and 1957 published two small volumes of statistics, which were followed by a more voluminous and informative one in 1959 (with data up to 1958). These annuals have continued to be published up to the present, with changes in the details covered and the statistical methods applied. For agrarian studies, the special statistical volume *Agriculture of the USSR,* which appeared in 1961, was a benchmark; its sequel was published in 1971, but no new edition has come out since then. Those of us who worked in the field at that time will remember the speeches of Nikita Khrushchev, who was responsible for Soviet agrarian policy during 1953–64. They were colorful and often uncouth, but nevertheless contained more factual information than those of his successors.

More information, statistical and other, became available during those years on the East European countries as well. Although the extraction of meaningful bits out of the available and often purposefully incoherent and distorted information still was an important part of western research on the Soviet Union and East Europe, it was no longer as important as it was during Stalin's time and the first years after his leadership. This was simply because the mass of information from which to select had grown so much and also had improved in quality. Competent interpretation became a rewarding task.

If the 1950s saw the rapid expansion of studies of Soviet and East European agricultural affairs, the subsequent decade was one not only of their further intensified development, but also of another change in emphasis. By the beginning of the 1960s, collectivization was basically completed in most of East Europe with the two exceptions of Yugoslavia and Poland where it stopped during the preceding decade and remained only a long-term goal. Thus the collectivization process as such became a subject of recent history, not one of analysis of current events. The most topical field of interest now was the functioning of socialized agriculture. At the same time, Khrushchev's reorganization of Soviet agriculture influenced also the ways in which agriculture developed in the East European countries.

Against the background of Moscow's hegemony and the Soviet model of agricultural organization, a number of national peculiarities emerged. Studying the Soviet model alone no longer yielded sufficient insight into the state and development of collectivized agriculture in East Europe, not to speak of the two Communist countries with still predominant small-peasant farms. This made scholarly work in the field both more interesting and more demanding, but also brought the danger of losing sight of the common features which still persist along with the national peculiarities. The variety of languages adds another dimension of difficulties, although it is somewhat diminished by the publication of a common periodical and a common statistical annual by the countries of the Council of Mutual Economic Assistance (CMEA). (Albania does not belong to the CMEA; with its little known language, its restrictive publication practice and its still being very much Stalinist, Albania presents special obstacles to research and therefore is unduly neglected.) Fortunately, some of the countries have developed publication activities in Russian and even more in western languages, most notably Yugoslavia, Hungary and Poland. Still, a broad picture of the agrarian sectors and policies in East Europe and the Soviet Union as a whole is difficult to obtain, and a picture of all the current events and trends in detail is beyond the possibilities of an individual researcher.

For these reasons, cooperation and mutual exchange of knowledge have become imperative for scholarship in the field. The First Conference on Soviet and East European Peasant Affairs, organized in 1962 by Roy D. Laird at the University of Kansas, marked this new stage. Since then, such conferences have become an institution of sorts without developing a formal organization, membership and secretariat. They are held at irregular intervals on the initiative of individual scholars and with the help of the institution to which they belong. One reason why such informality works is the smallness of the scholarly community of those working in this specialized discipline. In the western world they number less than one hundred, and almost all of them know each other and keep in contact.[6]

The present volume of papers of the Seventh Conference held at Grignon, France, in July, 1984, mirrors, as did its predecessors, the need to combine the work of a number of scholars if a comprehensive picture for the whole of Eastern Europe and the Soviet Union is sought. Such a picture can never be complete, and its constituent parts unavoidably will have varying emphases. The conference organizer has to take into account not just idiosyncrasies of the contributors but each one's topical and linguistic competence and the focus of his or her current work. Exactly because a formal organization for Soviet and East European studies does not exist, not to speak of a central authority for assigning tasks, the topical gaps in the proceedings are natural. Such imperfection seems a low price for the flexibility and research productivity of so small a community as described above.

All the same, an effort was made at Grignon to give emphasis to those aspects which are most important in general and with those of greatest present-day interest. As a common background to the various contributions, G. Lazarcik's basically statistical paper continues and updates the painstaking research done by the Research Project on National Income in East Central Europe. Those who have done similar work can appreciate these results, even though there will always remain disputable data as far as validity, comparability and additional data are concerned.

Polish agriculture stands out in today's public interest. This is so because of the crisis it is going through together with the Polish economy and society at large. The two authors from Poland frankly admit that it will take a number of years if not longer until Polish agriculture's performance can come close to its natural and labor potential, and that this depressing fact is to a large degree due to the mistaken policies of the past. The same point is made by the two western observers, although with sharper wording. Nevertheless one must not overlook the fact that after the low of 1980, Poland's grain harvests have been increasing year after year up to 1984. Moreover, probably no one, not even the Polish statistical administration and planning commission, knows exactly how much meat and other food is really produced and marketed beyond the officially known quantities. In any case, with the higher prices the disparity of consumption between different population segments must have grown between 1979 and 1985 due to disparities not only in legal labor incomes but in those from other sources as well, including western valuta. Through such influences the consecutive price increases for food and other consumer goods in the public retail trade system lose much of their dampening effects on overall demand, and inflation in the national currency continues.

Discussion of policies toward producer prices, particularly those policies seeking to come to grips with rising producer costs and at the same time to provide incentives for output increases, looms large in other countries of the CMEA system as well. The contributions to the present volume do not deal with this issue in the case of the USSR, where producer price policy plays an important role, as has become obvious in the large increase of Soviet state procurement prices in 1983 and on earlier occasions. But the recent producer policy for Yugoslavia and the GDR is the subject of the contributions by E. Schinke and I. Loncarevic (Giessen).

These are two contrasting country cases. In Yugoslavia's still predominantly small-peasant agriculture the state influences only part of the food market directly and moreover has to fight inflation in all spheres of the economy, including the foreign sector. The likelihood is not great that Yugoslav inflation can be halted, the less so because in agriculture its impact is compounded by the existence of a long-standing, though not publicly stated, policy of discriminating against the private peasant or at least of making the peasant bear the brunt of a mistaken socio-economic policy. The contents and effects of this policy are the subject of R.F. Miller's contribution to the Grignon conference.

East Germany has a totally socialized agriculture and a moderate inflation rate. The main goal of its agricultural price policy is to change the input mix by changing the cost structure. In the first place it aims at reducing energy consumption, including the energy embodied in industrially produced inputs, as well as the use of non-agricultural raw materials, most of which the GDR is forced to import. As has recently been pointed out by Karl Hohmann, this rather bold and also costly price policy had to be watered down in 1984. The connection with energy consumption is especially grave in the GDR, as on the one hand this country has to import considerable quantities of petrol fuel and on the other hand has developed its agriculture along very energy-intensive lines. As shown in K. Hohmann's contribution to the Grignon conference, considerable savings of energy consumption in agriculture were achieved, yet it is questionable whether these can continue without depressing the productivity on farms.

Hungarian agriculture is the success case among the European countries under Communist rule. This is not to say that it is without problems. Apart from the external factor of deteriorating prices of agricultural exports, the production cost problem looms large and is combined with that of labor productivity. Although the latter is quite good by socialized agriculture standards, it is not sufficient for a country which very much depends on agricultural exports and therefore has to compete on the world market. The other countries, including those of Western Europe, simply protect their agricultural labor incomes by levies and subsidies, a thing which Hungary cannot afford to do beyond a certain level.

On the large-scale socialized farms of Hungary a still too numerous labor force is employed in relation to the relatively great capital inputs on those farms. At the same time, roughly one third of the total gross output of Hungarian agriculture from household plots and other auxiliary mini-farming or gardening is produced with enormous inputs of self-employed labor per unit of output. Because the combined labor income per worker from both kinds of production equals or exceeds that earned in industry, despite lower hourly wages in agriculture, labor costs in agriculture are higher than Hungary can afford in view of the level of development of the economy. The other source of excessive costs is inefficient capital inputs, which stem from the heavily subsidized and therefore not sufficiently economically planned investments made in recent years. It is true, of course, that some of the past overinvestment has also been due to unforeseen changes in export markets, which, among other things, have caused a number of large and modern livestock operations to stand partly idle. It is important to note that Hungarian economists by now clearly see that the main task of agriculture in Hungary, in contrast to the other CMEA countries, is not a further increase in production but rather a lowering of its cost.

For Soviet agriculture, a number of crucial issues have been raised at Grignon without trying to cover all its aspects. Among them, the inadequate rural road network can hardly be overemphasized, although it has been merely mentioned by most observers. Elizabeth Clayton made it the subject of her paper.

The new organizational ventures may be expected to figure prominently under the new leadership of M. Gorbachev: the "contract brigade" together with the "normless link" and the RAPO (county agro-industrial association). N. Radvanyi shows the development and function of the latter in the Union Republic of Georgia, where it originated more than ten years ago under specific local conditions. After further experimenting in Estonia and Latvia, the RAPO was introduced throughout the USSR. Whether it will be equally successful in the rest of the country remains to be seen. From the mere formation of super-bodies integrating the whole food complex of the given territorial units from county up to the all-Union level, it does not follow that these organizations will turn out to be more than an additional bureaucratic structure superseding the existing ones without sizably reducing them. It may be possible somewhat to diminish interference of central authorities such as economic branch ministries and the *Selkhozktekhnika* association, but this would not in itself eliminate friction between the interests of the producing farms, the procurement organization, the state and so-called consumer cooperative network and the industrial forward and backward linkages. The fact that the local leading cadres of all those organizations and enterprises are represented in the new agro-industrial association councils is no guarantee that they will cooperate better in the common interest than they did before. Most of the not directly agricultural organizations and enterprises remain under their own super-local hierarchy and thereby still are under a "double-subordination" (*dvoinoe podchinenie*), which has been an administrative device known to the Soviet system almost from its earliest inception and which has not worked too well up to the present time. Finally, the scheme does not eliminate the possibility of conflicts of interest between the local units (county, province, Republican or all-Union associations), which are natural under any system.

The approaches of the four renowned authors of the chapters about the contract brigades or normless links are different, but they seem to concur on one conclusion: if this new form of labor organization is to work economically, it will have to be applied in ways which so far are not discernible in Soviet reality and are not likely to become so under the present overall system without some genuine changes of its parameters. A. Pouliquen makes the remarkable point that their purpose is very much one of social engineering. However, he does not thereby deny that their purpose is as much an economic one, namely to achieve higher labor productivity through more performance-oriented remuneration and, as a result, greater total output.

Growing consumer demand as a consequence of rising incomes, not of physiological deprivation, on the one hand, and the inefficiency of the livestock industry as manifest most of all in low feed conversion ratios, on the other hand, undoubtedly form the central problem of the Soviet food complex. I. Stebelsky demonstrates the great disparities of consumption among the major regions of the country. B. Severin gives a concise analysis of feed production and consumption in Soviet animal farming. It helps us to better understand the reasons for the huge Soviet grain imports in spite of a total domestic grain output of 0.65–0.75 ton per head of the population plus great availabilities, at least potentially, of non-grain feed.

Even without grain imports, the USSR in 1983 would have had 300–310 million barley units of feed for producing a total of about 36 million meat units, i.e., an average of 8.5 tons of barley units for 1 ton of meat units.[7] And this almost incredible ratio so far has not been sufficient for making feed imports dispensable. Rough as the above calculation is, even with a wide margin of error it permits the conclusion that better performance of the Soviet livestock industry would totally change the present shortage situation.

It clearly emerges that the shortcomings of Soviet animal production lie at the heart of the import needs. Dealing with the foreign trade aspects of the Soviet food economy, P. Raup in his contribution points at some more causes of overconsumption of grain in the USSR, among them exaggerated seeding rates. These, however, are derived from calculations by the U.S. Department of Agriculture (ERS division) based on Soviet handbooks for farm managers and reveal a kind of norm and not necessarily the reality. According to a recent article in the official Soviet daily for agriculture, total grain seed spent is 20 million tons per year less than assumed in the grain utilization balances calculated by the USDA.[8] Yet even these seeding rates are higher than the American ones under comparable conditions, as demonstrated by Professor Raup.

J. Hajda and P. Kelley both deal with the international aspects of the agricultural foreign trade of Communist countries. Naturally, they devote much space to the USSR and United States as the biggest grain importers and exporters, respectively. This especially applies to Professor Hajda's discussion of the policy implications of that trade, while Professor Kelley also takes the overall world market trade into account, including the European Community and the less developed countries. Both envisage continued large Soviet imports, though not at the level of most recent years. But they take a guarded view concerning their importance of the United States and its share in them. That Moscow diversified its grain and other food imports is an established fact by now. It remains to be seen what will happen when the total volume of Soviet imports will diminish to the level of, say, 1978–80.

Papers on China and on Vietnam were also presented at Grignon in spite of the title of the conference referring to European Communist countries only. If only for the sheer size of China, C. Aubert's contribution on Chinese agriculture and agrarian policy would deserve interest for some time to come in spite of the breathtaking changes of the recent past and present time. The reason is the author's profound knowledge and analytical ability. In addition, the comparison with Vietnam reveals a fascinating fact: this ally of Moscow, after having collectivized agriculture in a Soviet-inspired way, changed over to a system of small group production within the large collectives which resembles the Chinese reform. If Soviet ideologists had inhibitions, they did not reveal them in public, and they also seem to take rather an indulgent attitude towards the changes in the Chinese countryside. A possible explanation might be that both countries are similar insofar as they suffer from rural overpopulation or minuscule land endowment per worker, under conditions of a low level of economic development. An Asian variant of NEP (Lenin's New Economic Policy) could very well be considered appropriate by Moscow and not against an adapted form of Leninism.

In a similar trend of thought the present writer contributed a paper comparing the recent organizational approaches in the socialized agricultures of the USSR, China and Hungary. He reviews the differences of size of the countries in combination with the communications and transport network, and of the natural and historical endowments (labor abundance or relative shortage, stage of industrialization) as an explanation for the emerging differences of policy in spite of a common Marxist-Leninist ideology. This is not to deny that other factors such as political culture, national homogeneity and foreign policy constraints also have played an important role.

It would be easy to point out the gaps in the proceedings of the Grignon conference. Geographically, Rumania and Bulgaria were completely missing from the agenda, mainly because those who were invited from the two countries did not come. By subjects, the coverage is not uniform for the various regions, although it has to be added that in most cases those topics were covered that seemed of greatest interest for a given country. Still, the role of the private sector is dealt with only at random, except for the non-collectivized countries, Hungary, as well as, indirectly, China. Yet such criticism would be beside the point. The important fact is that at the Grignon meeting equally as at the preceding conferences scholars with thorough knowledge and experience in the field of studies of agriculture under Communism were brought together and shared their research results and views for four days in a way and with an intensity that hardly could have happened on a different occasion.

Some people argue that Communist agrarian policy is primarily oriented toward socio-political and developmental goals and only in second place at production goals. Whether it has indeed been more successful in building a new society may be disputed but shall not be dealt with here. Instead the undisputable fact has to be pointed out that in their own plans Communist governments have for decades put great emphasis on production and in practice have accorded it priority over other goals. Any political system may be judged by its own goals, and by this token the record of Communist agrarian policy is anything but brilliant.

There remains the question whether all this is of interest to more than that small community of specialists described above. It may be argued that in western countries, not only in those which export agricultural products, there exists quite some interest in information about the prospects of exports to the socialist counties, most of which have to buy such commodities. More than that, their activities may greatly influence the prices on the world food market. However, such a narrowly defined interest inevitably has its ups and downs and does not form a satisfactory basis for a long-term research strategy and for the education of the appropriate specialists. On the other hand, the subject is too involved and manifold to be handled by "crash course" researchers. Truly specialized research is needed for specialists of other disciplines to draw on, and together they provide generalized information to the communication media and to decision-makers in many fields.

The question why Communist agriculture shows poor results is at the same time the question of whether and when its performance may be expected to improve. There is no simple answer to this. Factors of socio-political structure, of public investment and other economic policy, of natural endowment and availability of industrially produced inputs, of historical and national tradition, and many more, come in. For example, why does the Communist agrarian system work more or less satisfactorily in Hungary and East Germany (which differ significantly in their practical application of Marxism-Leninism) and why does it not perform well in either Romania and Yugoslavia, which also are very different from each other?

It would be too utilitarian an approach if the justification of such studies were based solely on considerations of gaining thorough information with a view to the international food market. Whether the socialist countries are considered enemies or friends or detached partners, they form too big a part of this world to be ignored. Agricultural performance is an important aspect of their weakness or strength. Lack of information about it in the West would be self-defeating, not to speak of the fact that intellectual curiosity is part of being a civilized nation.

Notes

1. Boris Brutzkus, *Agrarentwicklung und Agrarrevolution in Russland* (Leipzig: 1925).

2. *Die Krise der sozialistischen Landwirtschaft in der Sowjetunion* (Berlin: 1933); *Die Landwirtschaftspolitik der Sowjets und Ihre Ergebnisse* (Berlin: 1943).

3. Harold H. Fisher, *The Famine in Soviet Russia, 1919–1923. The Operation of the American Relief Administration* 1st edition (New York: 1927); Geroid T. Robinson, *Rural Russia Under the Old Regime*. 1st edition (New York: 1932); V.P. Timoshenko, *Agricultural Russia and the Wheat Problem* (Stanford, Calif.: 1932); L. E. Hubbard, *The Economics of Soviet Agriculture* (London: 1939).

4. Naum Jasny, *The Socialized Agriculture of the USSR* (Stanford, Calif.: 1949); Lazar Volin, *A Survey of Soviet Agriculture* (Washington, D.C.: 1951). Volin had published a number of articles on the subject before the war.

5. The by far not exhaustive bibliography of only English-language titles on the subject in the present writer's *Agrarian Policies in Communist Europe* (Totowa, N.J., The Hague, London: Allanheld, Osmun and Martinus Nijhoff, 1982) covers some 50 printed pages.

6. For a Soviet observer such informality seems hard to imagine. Thus, in his recent article "Bourgeois Conceptions of the Development of Agriculture in the USSR," *Voprosy ekonomiki*, No. 3 (1985), (in footnote 1 on p. 123), E. Keselman mentions the "permanently functioning Conference" as "one of a whole network of services researching the agriculture of the USSR and the other countries of Socialism"; his "network" consists of a total of three, the other two being the Giessen Center (which he erroneously places under the writer's direction—"v kotorom rukovodit") and the "programme of comparative agrarian changes" under A. Nove (whom he wrongly places at Edinburgh—in "England"). For the rest, Keselman does not really argue with Western authors in the field, but rather "proves" their being wrong by most of the time quoting Marx, Engels, Lenin, the USSR statistical yearbook and some other Soviet publications. Generally, one gets the impression that Keselman was given excerpts and not the original western publications for criticism.

7. The calculation is based on the Soviet statistics of oat units (recalculated at 100 for 85 barley units) consumed and of meat, milk, eggs and wool produced, both according to *Narodnoe khozyaistvo SSSR v 1983,* Moscow 1984, pp. 262 and 271 (1 kilogram of meat taken at unity, or at 0.667 kgs of milk, or 20 eggs or 0.28 kgs of wool).

8. *Sel'skaya zhizn,* January 1984, p. 1 (leading article).

The Normless Link: A New Era in Socialist Agriculture?

1

Labor Incentives
in Soviet Kolkhozy

Alec Nove

This paper has a cause: the appearance in the *Journal of Comparative Economics* of an article by L. Israelsen, in which it was argued, *inter alia*, that labor incentives are more effective in a kolkhoz than in a capitalist enterprise; the latter pays its employees the equivalent of their marginal product, whereas in a kolkhoz the pay of members equals the hours they work divided into the net product, and extra effort would earn somewhere between average and marginal product, which, on conventional assumptions, must be more than the marginal product.[1] Since any kolkhoz member can increase his share by working more, this would particularly benefit him/her in a large kolkhoz. The specific conclusion is then drawn that those who argue that kolkhoz labor incentives are in principle ineffective, and "that the large size of collectives exacerbates the problem" are in error.

There can scarcely be any observer of the Soviet kolkhoz, in and out of the Soviet Union, who doubts that labor incentives are notoriously poor. It seemed to me that there were some clear fallacies in Israelsen's argument. But the editors of the *Journal of Comparative Economics* were unconvinced by my rebuttal, and indeed refused to publish it. On reflection, my rebuttal did take too many things for granted. This encourages me to try to formulate the argument step by step, more carefully.

One point is surely worth making at the very start. If we are discussing the eliciting of *extra* labor effort in realistically envisageable situations, the assumption of diminishing marginal productivity can be a misleading simplification. One has to ask: what is the reason for which the work is wanted? This is a particularly important point in agriculture: thus in winter there may be little work to do, whereas it is vital to secure extra effort at harvest time. Industrial firms too, may require additional labor, or extra hours from their existing labor force, to meet specific requirements, such as agreed delivery dates, or to ensure that the product reaches a port in time for loading, or a variety of similar reasons. In these conditions, a capitalist firm or farm would pay overtime rates or a bonus to elicit the extra effort, a situation not envisaged in a simple world of smooth curves and diminishing marginal productivity, in which overtime pay would make no sense at all. (In fact, increasing returns are by no means rare in real life, despite their inconvenience for neo-classical model builders, as Kaldor, among others, has been pointing out.)[2]

It is essential to distinguish between two different questions: the *offer* of work to the labor force, and that labor force's *willingness* to work. Also essential is the correct specification of the incentives of management. Let us accept the simple assumption that the capitalist is interested only in profit. What, then, is the kolkhoz management interested in? This question is of key importance. Suppose it were democratically elected, as it would be if it were a genuine cooperative. Suppose further that it was free to decide what to produce and how much to sell. Management would then be charged by the members with maximizing net revenue per member. This would bring us close to the "Illyrian" model, or to some variant of "Yugoslav" self-management, a world explored by many economists: Ward, Domar, Meade, Vanek. . . . It is generally agreed that this sort of cooperative would tend to employ fewer people than would a capitalist firm. So we may find some who were willing to work denied the opportunity to do so for as many hours as they wished, because it would not "pay" the cooperative to use additional labor if the effect would be to reduce the average "dividend" per member, even when this is significantly above the marginal product, as management would seek, on behalf of the members, to limit the number of hours worked. On the face of it, then, in this situation the member would have better incentives for work when work is offered, than his equivalent in a capitalist firm, for the reasons advanced by Israelsen, though allowance would have to be made for seasonal and other peak requirements for labor. The point about requirements is important. It is neither sensible nor remotely realistic to assume that work is necessarily available for anyone who wishes to work at any time, any more than its converse: that peasants will necessarily be ready to work whenever they are required. Tasks are finite and are not regularly spread through the year; they have to be undertaken in sequence. To abstract from this means that one is abstracting from agriculture when writing about agriculture.

However, even in this imaginary picture there is one very important difference with the worker in a capitalist enterprise. The latter is a *wage*-earner, who knows in advance the wage-rate (or overtime rates for any extra work), and so, whatever the marginal product might be (of which the worker has no idea and cares less), he knows what he will receive for his additional efforts. The kolkhoz member cannot know this in advance. Even if the peasant fully trusts the management, even if the latter is free to decide what to do, even if agricultural prices are fixed at acceptable levels, the peasant can know in advance neither the size of the net revenue nor the total number of hours worked by his fellow-members, and therefore the dividend per hour is a question-mark. There may be a guaranteed minimum payment, as there is in kolkhozy today, but, if the cooperative is to be solvent (as many kolkhozy today are not), this minimum must be significantly below the average. This would also affect the distribution of time and effort between collective work and private activities, since the kolkhoz member has a private plot, of which more in a moment. So the relative effectiveness of incentives must be affected by uncertainty as to what the income might be, even on these favorable institutional assumptions. But those assumptions are, of course, quite unreal.

Kolkhoz management is not genuinely elected by or responsible to the peasants. Nor is it free to decide what to produce or what to sell. It has its own success criteria, which are not linked with peasant incomes at all, but with plan fulfillment. This totally changes the interest and attitude of management to the use of labor. Suppose that output or sales are below plan. Then, management would seek to utilize additional labor which produces increase in output, even if the marginal product was small, and even if its utilization would diminish the "dividend" per hour and per peasant. Therefore management would be willing to "employ" labor in circumstances in which no capitalist (or self-managed firm) would do so. For management the marginal cost of the extra labor is zero or close to zero; the total size of the net product divided by the hours worked is what determines the total "dividend." More hours worked simply reduces the pay per hour. The peasants know this, and also that plan-orders from above may, and frequently do, require an increase in output of some product which it is plainly unprofitable to produce, and this further affects their morale and commitment to collective work. They are also painfully aware that procurement quotas may be arbitrarily varied, that machines may break down, that there may be power cuts, that deliveries of fertilizer and pesticides may or may not arrive, that some tractors will be out of action at harvest time for lack of spare parts. They also know that the outcome depends on the quantity (and quality) of the labor of fellow-peasants, which may or may not be forthcoming. All this, and the weather too.

In Israelsen's model there is no guaranteed minimum, which makes his conclusions totally untenable. The introduction of a guaranteed minimum does reduce the disincentives to work. In the actual Soviet experience of recent years, the combination of high costs, lavish use of labor, the priority of plan-fulfillment and the guaranteed minimum have led to serious losses and a very rapid increase in state credits granted to farms, many of which have had to be written off.[3]

In the present instance we cannot assume perfect foresight. The peasant members cannot know in advance what they would receive for their work. To assume that they do would be an example of illegitimate use of an otherwise legitimate simplifying assumption. If an essential difference between a wage-earner and member of a kolkhoz is precisely that the wage is known in advance and the "dividend" is not, one cannot usefully eliminate this essential difference by assuming that is does not exist.

Furthermore, there is another piece of knowledge which each peasant cannot have, especially in the *large* kolkhoz which Israelsen is discussing.

Suppose for a moment that each member has the "rational expectation" that his/her labor will be well remunerated (he/she will have no notion of either the average or the marginal product of labor, before or even after the event). The same knowledge must be assumed to be in the possession of all the other peasants. In a large kolkhoz (say with 500 members, scattered over several villages) he cannot possibly know how many others will offer additional labor with the same expectation. Yet, on the posited assumption, their hourly remuneration is determined by the total hours worked divided into the total net product. The expectation of additional earnings is in some degree dependent on the others abstaining from increasing the total number of hours worked, if this would reduce the pay per hour. One cannot meaningfully introduce perfect knowledge into this model. It is almost as if it was known that a particular horse would win the race at odds of ten to one: the odds would then not be ten to one.

It may be useful to cite two examples of the lavish use of labor by kolkhoz management. One of these dates back to the early 1950s, the other is from 1983, thereby demonstrating that these habits are of old standing and persist. The first was used in an article I wrote together with Roy D. Laird that appeared in *Soviet Studies*.[4] We noted then that a Soviet source singled out for praise the following phenomenally labor-intensive way of using a threshing machine: two shifts of 70 persons each, working almost round the clock. Commenting on this and on similar examples of the lavish use of labor, Laird and I remarked that since "the total distributed to kolkhozniki is in any event limited to what is left over after all other commitments are met . . ., if labor days are wasted the only result is to reduce the payment per labor-day" (p. 442). So, as can be seen, we drew the conclusion at the time that marginal cost of labor must appear (to the management) to be zero, given the method of payment then in force. Many have been the changes since the date; prices, peasant incomes, investments, are now much higher. But certain habits do persist. Thus *Pravda* (July 7, 1983) reported on the excessive use of urban "mobilized" labor on kolkhozy in harvesting cotton in Turkmenistan. They kept this labor on even when the extra amount of cotton that could be harvested was quite small, and in no way justified the extra expenditure involved; furthermore, delays in ploughing adversely affected the next year's harvest. The article gives this as one reason (the others related to machinery, seed, lack of effective herbicides) to explain the fall in net kolkhoz revenue by 25 percent in five years. Why, then, was there such waste of labor? The article explains: because of the "struggle to fulfill the plan." These examples support the view, for which plenty of other evidence exists, that the kolkhoz management does not give priority to achieving a high level of remuneration per hour, as compared with reporting plan fulfillment or over-fulfillment to higher authority.

But it is time to introduce the private plot. Peasants can divide their time between collective work and private production and marketing. Let us look at the many variables which could determine this division.

a. The minimum time which must be devoted to collective work, either because of a regulation to that effect, or in order to avoid informal sanctions which could be imposed by a hostile chairman.
b. The expected rate of pay for collective work, and thus the amount likely to be foregone by choosing not to do it.
c. Free market prices.
d. Distance to the market, means available for the journey (bus, train, hitch-hiking), cost of journey, number of fleas (if any) in a hostel (if any) in town, and so on.
e. Opportunity to shop in town, contrasted with the availability of goods in the village store.
f. The labor actually required on the (small) plot, the number of private animals, and so on. The seasonal nature of agricultural labor must also be borne in mind. One cannot plant private or collective onions in February, or gather fruit in March. Peak labor requirements for the harvesting and marketing of private produce tend frequently to coincide with peak labor requirements for the kolkhoz.
g. The opportunities available to sell private produce (e.g., to cooperative trade) without having to take it to urban markets.
h. The family's needs for food, and its availability from sources other than the private plot.

In 1952 the average rate of pay for collective work was miniscule. Private plots supplied almost all of the family's food, other than bread-grains, and most of the cash as well. There is clearly no need to explain further why incentives for collective work were ineffective at that time. It is quite a different situation today. We now have to explain the inadequacies of incentives when average pay is much higher. It is only right to add that acute problems in respect of labor incentives are encountered in *sovkhozy* (state-farms), which do pay a more regular wage,[5] which sets up the presumption that the element of uncertainty ("what will my pay per hour in fact be?") has been somewhat reduced. Other negative factors may be more important.

This must bring us to another of Israelsen's arguments: the one which concerns the size of the kolkhoz (sovkhozy tend to be, on average, even larger). It is by no means only a question of not knowing how many hours will be worked by fellow-peasants or what pay per hour will be. It is also very important to know how well the work will be done. Agriculture requires that a number of tasks be performed in sequence. When these tasks are divided among different persons or groups, it becomes particularly difficult for management or rank-and-file peasants to relate the final outcome to the quality with which each task is performed. Good ploughing can be wasted if sowing is poorly done, or weeding is neglected, or if the harvesting begins late because the combine-harvesters are out of order. Tractor-drivers given a ploughing plan in hectares may increase their "output" by refraining from ploughing deep or carefully enough, but the disappointing harvest could also be the result of poor work somewhere else along the chain of sequences.

Add the well-known difficulty of supervising work in scattered fields, and we see several different forms of diseconomies of scale. Incentives become detached from the desired end-result, and sometimes (as in the case of tractor-ploughing) have the perverse effect of rewarding poor quality work.

These defects are common to state and collective farms, and critical articles in the Soviet press tend to cite examples "impartially" from each. Thus, for instance: "Sometimes the harvest is many times lower but the pay is higher. Why? Because it is not based on final output. . . . If one has carried out additional tasks, recorded a larger number of hectares, then one gets more pay. With such a system of rewards, why should a 'mechanizer' bother with the size of the harvest? . . . In the old days, did the peasant ever try to calculate separately how much he would earn for ploughing, then sowing, then harvesting? It is the final outcome he had in mind." The author, a kolkhoz brigadier, concludes that the contract brigade or the zveno is the answer (*Pravda*, January 9, 1983). Later the same year, the director of an efficient State farm complains that though yields are much lower and costs higher on neighboring farms, they earn more than the workers on his farm because earnings depend on plan-fulfillment and plans depend on past performance (*Pravda*, August 15, 1983). As Stefan Hedlund says in an unpublished paper, "the system fails to motivate the peasants to work well, to relate quality as well as quantity of work to the final result."

The Merits of the Autonomous Work-Group

This is why, in kolkhozy and sovkhozy, it has long been proposed that there be autonomous work-teams (beznaryadnoye zvenya or brigady, now often referred to under the designation of kollektivnyi podryad). The principle is simple: a small group of anywhere from four to thirty peasants contracts to carry out all the sequences and tasks in respect of some crop or livestock, over one or several years; in some instances the group is given a "crop rotation" for several years; they keep the same land, but change the crop (e.g., *Ekonomicheskaya gazeta* No. 31 (July 1983) p. 15). The farm undertakes to supply the needed equipment and other material inputs, and to pay this small team previously agreed sums which are directly related to the harvest, the milk yield or whatever the product may be. There is a long and frustrating history to this solution of the labor-incentive problem. It was already being discussed and experimented with in the 1960s. At the international congress of agricultural economists held in Minsk in 1970, Roy Laird asked the then minister of agriculture, Matskevich, if he favored the beznaryadnye zvenya, and got the short answer: no. The sad fate of one of the experimenters, Khudenko, has been documented several times: he died in prison. As he undoubtedly ignored a number of rules and regulations, his fate was perhaps not due directly or solely to his experiments with the beznaryadnoye zveno. Nonetheless, the issue disappeared for several years from the public press, to re-emerge at the end of the 1970s. *Pravda* and other official publications began to publish articles in praise of those who organized such *zvenya* (for instance, *Pravda,* November 25, 1979; July 14, 1980; March 25 and 26 and May 25, 1981). But until May 1982 there was no official party pronouncement, for or against. In the May 1982 decree, in Brezhnev's last year, there is a positive mention of the kollektivnyi podryad, but a more definite and strongly positive note was struck by Gorbachev in *Pravda* of March 20, 1983. Before analyzing these policies, let me make one last reference to Israelsen's article. Were he right, then, as already pointed out, not only is Gorbachev wrong to back the small work-unit, but the Chinese are also mistaken in introducing the "household responsibility" system, which has the same objective: to relate effort more directly to result, and relate incentives to both. Gorbachev's article insists that the group is to elect its own leader, and to determine its own work assignments. Clearly its members would see directly what cannot be observed in the larger unit: who does what, when and how. There would be no need for supervisory personnel. One Soviet source gave this as one reason for the opposition to the proposal among petty officials.[6] Members can jointly regulate their labor inputs in relation to the task at hand with some confidence that success will be rewarded. True, they have to contend with weather hazards (the standard contract does provide for a minimum reward in the event of natural disasters). As will be pointed out in a moment, severe practical problems still remain, but at least in this model it does seem rather self-evident that, *pace* Israelsen, peasants will have better incentives than in a large kolkhoz. Surely it is unnecessary to seek formal proof for the proposition that any incentive scheme involving payment by results loses its effectiveness if these results depend on the work of a large number of scattered individuals. Economists in general do have an unfortunate tendency to treat labor as a species of homogeneous robot, and to neglect quality as well as work-motivation. It is true that such unquantifiable considerations as pride in work well done, conscientiousness, a sense of responsibility, do not lend themselves to mathematical treatment and cannot be fed into a computer. The question of work morale and commitment is a key one in Soviet agriculture. One cannot but echo the heartfelt words of Fyodor Abramov: "The old pride in a well-ploughed field, a well-sown crop, well-looked-after livestock, is vanishing. Love for land, for work, even self-respect, are disappearing. Is this not a cause of absenteeism, lateness, drunkenness?" (*Pravda* November 17, 1979). It became urgently important to find a remedy.

So let us return to the autonomous work-group (whether the term zveno or brigada is used is immaterial; these days some brigady are small). Why was its introduction so long delayed? Will it now be introduced throughout Soviet agriculture? With what effects?

. . . and the Obstacles to Its Viability

Among the obstacles to overcome was a long-established belief in the existence of organizational and technical economies of scale in agriculture. The Marxist roots of this belief have been well analyzed by Michael Ellman.[7]

These ideas have doubtlessly been reinforced by considerations of a more practical kind: planners prefer a smaller to a larger number of units to whom to send their orders, and the notion of autonomy (no imposed work-assignments, which is what the word beznaryadnyi means) runs counter to a habit of mind which stresses hierarchical subordination. Uncontrolled spontaneity, samotyok, is a word of pejorative connotation. It should be recalled that kolkhozy were greatly enlarged in the years following 1950, through successive waves of imposed amalgamation. Petty supervision requires petty supervisors, whom such a reform threatens with unemployment.

Then there is the long-ingrained distrust of peasants and concern for the rebirth of private-property instincts. This too is linked with practical con-siderations: if an area of land is assigned to a work-group for too short a period, it may have no interest in its longer-term fertility; if for a long period (many years) then they may come to regard it as "their own" the more so as there are now "family zvenos" (semeinye zvenya) and "their numbers are growing" (A. Vyugin, *Pravda,* January 9, 1983). But we must also be aware of problems of a totally non-ideological kind. It so happens that I discussed them with a Soviet official at the Minsk conference in 1970. The official (unlike Matskevich) was favorably inclined to the idea, but pointed to serious frictions and conflicts which could result among the peasants themselves. Not all tasks are divisible into small groups of the zveno type, many tasks undertaken by a zveno could be seasonal, with little to occupy the members the rest of the time. There would, on the other hand, be periods of peak demand for labor in which the zveno would have seasonal "non-members" or part-time members. Members may well be chosen who have skills (e.g. to operate tractors, etc.), and they could earn much more than the less skilled general-purpose workers. Nor is it an easy matter to negotiate a contract with each that would be regarded as fair by others. There would most likely be very wide disparities in earning, some predictable, others not, which could give rise to protests and discontent.

The same point struck me in China during my visit there in 1983. The "household responsibility system" is also based on contract; the household had (up to 1985) delivery obligations, at fixed prices. Much depended, therefore, on the prices and the obligations. As one Chinese official said to me: "no one will get rich growing rice." When I then asked him what was raised in his district by those who do get rich, he replied: ducks. It was admitted that it could well be that what the household is ordered or allowed to do, rather than the skill and energy they show in doing it, which will have a decisive bearing on their income.

To estimate the possible results of the autonomous group system in the Soviet Union it is important to examine carefully the type of contract which is to be made.[8] Gorbachev and others have rightly stressed that one must show care and imagination in drafting such contracts (there must be "eco-nomically soundly based tasks"), and that the mutual obligations must be strictly observed if the new system is to function smoothly. There have been instances reported of such zvenya falling apart when the conditions necessary for their functioning are not observed (e.g., *Pravda,* January 9, 1983). Here it is necessary to stress a vitally important difference between the Soviet Union and China. Chinese agriculture is still using traditional techniques, with relatively little mechanization and few industrial inputs apart from mineral fertilizer. Soviet agriculture, however, is now capital-intensive, with production depending on a wide range of supplies from industry. The autonomous groups are to be issued with the needed machinery and equipment, and will require regular and reliable supplies of fuel and other inputs. No doubt the regular supply of these will figure in the contractual obligations of the kolkhozy and sovkhozy. But, with the best will in the world, will they be able to carry them out, bearing in mind the notoriously poor record of the agricultural machinery industry and of Sel'khoztekhnika in supplying the farm's requirements?

Attempts to introduce forms of brigadnyi podryad in the building industry have foundered on this very same rock: how can workers be expected to accept payment by results if these results are repeatedly affected by non-arrival of the needed materials, or the non-repair of equipment?

So a precondition for success is a drastic overhaul of the system of material supply, of the links between industry and agriculture. Will this be achieved by the "agro-industrial-complex" approach? We will have to wait and see. Decrees have been adopted before now which changed little. After all, the shortage of spare parts has figured in satire, song and story for at least forty years, and has so far proved incurable. Similarly, decrees on the production of small machines have been frustrated by the priority given to plan fulfillment in aggregate terms, which turns industry's efforts towards the large-scale machines. So cautious scepticism is not out of place.

There is, furthermore, another obstacle of a more psychological kind, and which also was mentioned in China. A reform of this sort requires officials (sovkhoz directors, kolkhoz chairmen and others) to negotiate and observe contractual obligations with their own subordinates, those to whom hitherto they had the power to give orders. A big change in approach is needed, complicated by the fact that these officials will themselves be under pressure from above to fulfill production and delivery plans. Gorbachev in his speech stated that the autonomous groups must be "given the fullest autonomy (samostoyatel'nost') for the carrying out of their assignments (zadaniya)." Let us assume that he is sincere. But a number of times party and state officials have been urged, or even ordered, to cease petty interference with, and tutelage over, farm management, yet it has continued. Thus despite the decision published in May 1982 on this subject, a kolkhoz chairman (Y. Ipatenko) bitterly complained about the flood of peremptory orders: "when to spread manure, when to connect up the spraying machines, even how to combat mice" (*Pravda,* January 3, 1983). Nor is this surprising, bearing in mind that decrees of various sorts, such as that criticising the work of the Saratov obkom of the party (*Pravda,* July 7, 1983), urge and instruct party officials to ensure that various agricultural problems are resolved, and holding them responsible if they are not. Another decree (*Pravda,* August 20, 1983) orders officials to take priority measures with regard to sugar-beet, etc. This cannot but impel them to interfere with farm management and with the new "agro-industrial-complex" organs which, in their turn, are all too likely to issue orders to farm management. Complaints on this score have already appeared, see *Pravda*, December 17, 1983. For all these reasons, the smooth functioning of the kollektivny podryad system is hard to envisage. At the very least there must be acute growing pains in the first years. Particularly vulnerable will be that part of the reform relating to the obligation to ensure the regular supply of industrial inputs of all kinds. However, the idea of reform is surely along the right lines, and it is even possible that the efforts to implement it will lead to closer links between the needs of agriculture and the providers of industrial inputs, and thereby force industry at long last to "turn its face to the village customer" (litsom k derevnye, to recall a slogan-phrase of the 1920s) and, who knows, the much-needed practice of producing for the customers' needs might "infect" all of Soviet industry. Far-fetched? Yes, but not impossible.

Let us therefore withhold judgement and observe events.

Notes

1. L. Dwight Israelsen: "Collectives, communes and incentives", *Journal of Comparative Economics,* Dec. 1980, pp. 99–124.

2. For example see N. Kaldor: *Further essays in applied economics,* London: Duckworth, 1978, p. 237.

3. Suslov: "Kolklozy v sisteme narodnogo khozyaistva", *Voprosy ekonomiki,* No. 12, 1982, pp. 23–29.

4. A. Nove and R. D. Laird: "A note on labour utilization in Soviet kolkhozy", *Soviet Studies,* April 1953, pp. 434–442.

5. The sovkhoz pays a minimum wage equal to 80 per cent of the normal (tariff) wage. The remainder is paid in proportion to plan fulfillment, though the system is now being modified.

6. P. Rebrin: "Yacheika khozraschyota", *Novyi mir,* No. 4, 1969, p. 159.

7. M. Ellman: "Agricultural productivity under socialism", *World Development,* Sept./Oct. 1981.

8. Various kinds of contracts have been publicized, for instance in *Ekonomicheskaya gazeta,* No. 15, 27, 31, 36 (1983).

2

Contract Brigades and Normless Teams in Soviet Agriculture

Michael Ellman

A contract brigade (*podryadnaya brigada*) or normless team (*beznaryadnoe zveno*) is, in principle, a small, voluntarily formed group of workers (or collective farmers) in a state or collective farm who are paid according to their output and not according to their input (e.g., hours worked or planned tasks fulfilled) and who have complete freedom in organizing their work. They are allocated a certain quantity of means of production (e.g., fields, tractors), a contract between them and the farm management specifying the agreed output is signed, and they are left to get on with production. Their final income depends on the extent to which they fulfill their contract. The contract should be based on long term norms and not be revised adversely if hard work generates a high income for the members. They normally receive a regular monthly advance, often equivalent to the wages they would formerly have received, plus an end of the year bonus equal to their entitlement under the contract for the amount actually produced, less the total advance already paid. For each member of the contract unit, the bonus is normally proportional to the advance.

The organization of state farm labor in this way is an important break with the Taylorist tradition, that up until now has been dominant in the USSR, and that seeks to raise labor productivity by close supervision and direction of work and by the division of labor. The widespread use of contract brigades and normless teams is analogous to group piecework in a factory. In principle it makes sense for activities where the output of a small group can be readily identified, where the quality of the work done (i.e. the skill, effort and enthusiasm of the workers) has a big influence on the output, and where close supervision is impossible because, for example, the work is spatially scattered. It has the big advantage of providing incentives for output rather than for the use of inputs.

The organization of collective farm labor in this way is a complete break with Soviet traditions in view of the small size of the normless teams (often between 5 and 10 persons, compared with several hundred households in a collective farm) and the complete independence with which they may organize their work.

Since the apathetic attitude of the labor force is a notorious cause of the difficulties of Soviet agriculture, this potentially radical innovation in labor organization and incentives might lead to a significant improvement in the performance of Soviet agriculture. Whether or not this will happen depends largely on whether the innovation will actually be implemented in its original form or whether what will actually be implemented will be only a heavily watered down version.

The team as a unit of agricultural labor has had a long, but chequered, history in Soviet agriculture since collectivization (Pospielovsky 1970). It emerged in the 1930s, was officially sponsored at the 18th Party congress (1939) and was in practice extended to large-scale grain farming after World War II and advocated by Politburo member A.A. Andreev. It was backed again by Khrushchev (in 1964) and by the post-Khrushchev leadership (at the May 1966 Plenum). On the other hand, it was strongly attacked in a famous and very influential article in *Pravda* the 19th of February 1950. Similarly, one of its best known advocates during the 1960s, I.N. Khudenko, encountered extensive and influential opposition and died in a prison hospital. The main reason for the opposition appears to have been the fundamental conflict between the *modus operandi* of a small group making decisions for themselves in response to their own interests and wishes, and the Soviet economic environment and the natural desire of officials in the administrative economy to ensure that all economic activity takes place in accordance with official procedures and that all unplanned activity is suppressed.

The current campaign for the contract brigade and the normless team dates from the March 1983 Politburo decision and the March 1983 Central Committee conference in Belgorod. Belgorod was chosen as the site for the conference because it already had a long and successful experience with contract brigades (Kuznetsov 1984). The campaign for contract brigades in agriculture is part of a wider campaign for similar units throughout the economy. Along with the national drive for discipline and the foundation of the agro-industrial associations, it was part of the reaction of the leadership to the economic stagnation and food shortages of the late Brezhnev era.

The method of campaigns is a common method for introducing innovations in the USSR. It overcomes bureaucratic inertia by pressure from above through all the channels of hierarchy and control combined with widespread publicity. Although the innovation concerned may be a sensible and useful one, the method of campaigns is itself a cause of inefficiency (Nove 1964, pp. 203–204). The innovation will be applied too widely and/or other important tasks will be neglected so that good results can be reported in the latest campaign. Well known examples are Khrushchev's maize campaign of the 1950s and Brezhnev's industrialized livestock complexes of the 1970s. Both of these led to both positive and negative results. Maize is a useful crop in some places, but not everywhere. Industrialized poultry production was a success, but industrialized red meat production turned out to be very costly. The adverse effects of the campaign method tend to be particularly serious in agriculture in view of the weak political position of individual farms (as opposed, for example, to major heavy industrial plants) and the role of *administrirovanie* in Soviet agriculture.[1]

The purpose of using this new system of organizing agricultural labor widely is to raise labor productivity. According to V. Bashmachnikov (1984, p. 16), a deputy director of the All-Russian Scientific Research Institute for Agriculture Economics, farm Labour and Farm Management (VNIIETUSKh), contract units enable labor productivity to be increased by 15–20 percent, land productivity to be increased by 10–15 percent, and material input (e.g., machines, chemicals) productivity by 6–8 percent. This is a result of two factors. First material incentives increased by linking the income of the farmers to their output, rather than to some indicators of their input, such as hours worked. Secondly, mutual control in a small group is strengthened. This is achieved by making the income of each member of the contract unit dependent on the output of the unit as a whole. This gives each individual a direct material interest in and influence on the productivity of his/her colleagues. This combination of material incentives and mutual control is widely stressed in the Soviet literature and is fully in keeping with Soviet traditions.

Bashmachnikov has explained the situation as follows. "To a considerable extent (in the contract units) personal interests can be successfully realized only as a result of conscientious work by all members of a collective. Hence there arise relations of mutual economic dependence, which manifest themselves in the strengthening of mutual control and mutual demands, fulfilling the function of so-called 'group incentives' for high quality work. For this, various methods of socio-psychological influence are used, reprimands, persuasion, collective discussion, etc." Using the workers to check and spy on each other (who is shirking/drinking/absent? When?), if it works, is unlikely to be very popular with those deemed to be slackers. This may be an important cause of the fact, widely reported in the press, that after a time many of the contract units dissolve.

The current campaign is being implemented quickly. By January 1984, about one-fifth of all the brigades and teams in the arable sector worked according to the 'new' method and it is intended that by the end of 1985 45–50 percent of all those working on state or collectives farms in the arable sector will be working according to the 'new' method (Kostin 1984, p. 10). According to V. Zhurikov (1984b, p. 10), Head of the Chief Administration for Labor and Social Questions of the USSR Ministry of Agriculture, in an article published in May 1984, contract units were then responsible for about 20 percent of all arable land in the USSR, growing 17 percent of the grain (excluding maize), about 40 percent of the grain maize, more than 38 percent of the cotton, 5 percent of the sugar beet, 28 percent of the sunflowers, 26 percent of the flax, almost 22 percent of the fodder crops, 16 percent of the potatoes and more than 10 percent of the vegetables. This wide dispersion by crop indicates that the contract system, given the present technological level in Soviet agriculture, can more easily be introduced in the production of some crops than others.

It has been repeatedly explained in the press that it is undesirable to impose a uniform pattern across the country and that the system should be adapted to the specific features of particular kinds of production and particular areas. There is scope for a wide variety of forms. The USSR is a huge country with a wide variety of natural conditions, infrastructure, labor availability, and degree of mechanization. Combined with the official stress on avoiding the imposition of a uniform system and the need to adapt to local circumstances, this is likely to lead to numerous differences between the operation of different contract units. Bashmachnikov (1983, p. 134) has confirmed that this is the case. The variations effect the extent of specialization, the size and composition of the units, the method of distributing the collective earnings, and their management. The contract units may well work better in parts of the Transcaucasus than in much of Russia or the Ukraine.

In the minds of some of their keenest advocates, the new units should be virtually independent enterprises, the members of which should have the feeling of being owners of, and hence responsible for, the land and other means of production that they use. On the other hand, in practice the new arrangements appear in general to be closer to group piecework than to labor-only subcontracting. The 'complete independence' with which the members of the contract units do their work must, of course, be understood in a Soviet context. It certainly does not mean an absence of bureaucracy. Even when the organization of the work really is left to the workers themselves (subject to the contract), they are often obliged to keep detailed records (with respect to hours spent and material inputs used) in accordance with official procedure. The monthly advance that they receive, and their record keeping with respect to hours worked, emphasize their employee status. The chief economist of the state farm Meleuzovskii in the Meleuz district of the Bashkir republic has explained (Nasyrov 1983, p. 13) how each member of a contract team on his farm must fill in a form each day indicating the inputs used. Similar forms are issued to the heads of the fodder store, fuel stocks, central store, and energy chief, for control over the forms submitted by the team members. In addition, the contract units are often only responsible for part of the tasks necessary to fulfil the contract. Specialist services often have to be provided by the farm management or even a district agency (e.g., for plant protection). The relationship between the contract unit and the specialist services is often one of hierarchy and subordination. The extent to which the contract unit can fulfil the contract itself, and the extent to which it must rely on specialist services, has turned out to be an important factor in the success or otherwise of the contract units. Reliance on specialist services means losing control over part of the organization of the work necessary for the fulfillment of the contract and losing part of the payment for the crop. By and large, unless the contract units are responsible for a high proportion of the work, they are not a success. Similarly, the voluntary nature of the contract units, which are being organized on a mass scale in response to an official campaign, must be understood in the Soviet, or army, sense of the word 'voluntary.' The method of calculating the advance, and its size, are often imposed on the contract units (Zhurikov 1984a, p. 71).

How much has actually changed? Where the formation and composition of the contract units is decided by the local party committee, the records of the hours spent and the relative weighting to be attached to the different individuals is made by the farm management, the results-based bonus is small relative to the monthly advance, the contract units do not themselves do the great majority of the work necessary for the fulfillment of the contract, and production is disorganized by supply failures, the new system probably seems to many workers simply a way of transferring from the farm management to them the burdens of enforcing labor discipline and dealing with bureaucratic arbitrariness and supply failures. Many workers no doubt prefer a definite wage for fulfilling instructions without any responsibility, to the doubtful privilege of possibly earning a little more in exchange for long and frustrating struggles. There are plenty of articles in the Soviet press discussing the frustrations that were experienced, prior to the present campaign, by activists in the normless team movement. As one such activist has explained (Glotov 1982, p. 15) "hardly a day passed by without conflicts." The incentive effect of the final bonus is, of course, undermined by shortages, the difficulty of allocating credit within a contract unit in accordance with real contributions, and when the bonus is small relative to the advance.

Bashmachnikov and Bersenov (1983, p.4) note that "many units transferred to collective payment for work do not achieve an improvement in their production indices. As before there are frequent cases of the dissolution of such collectives or their rejection of collective payment." They argue (p.7) that success of the contract system requires that:

a. The contract units should be specialized,
b. their size should be small (if possible not more than 10 persons),
c. the tasks and equipment assigned to the contract units should be such that at least two-thirds of the work can be done by the contract unit itself,
d. the composition of the contract units should be determined in a voluntary way, taking into account the wishes of the workers concerning with whom they want to work.

"The results of sociological research of contract collectives enable us to state that, where the above requirements are ignored, as a rule in place of the positive features of mutual requirements and mutual assistance, mutual lack of confidence, conflicts, apathy and passivity develop in the collective."

The old *trudoden'* system on the collective farms was also in principle a results-based system. It gave notoriously bad results because of the low size of the payments, the uncertainty about their magnitude and the incentive for farm mangement to use labor until its marginal product was zero. The conditions necessary for the success of group piecework are, substantial payments on the basis of results,[2] a direct relationship between individual effort and individual rewards, substantially higher rewards for pieceworkers than for timeworkers, and no increase in the work norms when incomes are 'too high.' It is doubtful if those conditions will be met in most contract units in Soviet agriculture. In fact there are probably many contract units in which none of them will be met.

The input based system of rewards has in fact retained its supremacy. For each contract unit as a whole, ouput affects total income, but for any individual total pay is proportional to labor input as measured by hours spent (or tasks fulfilled) times the grading coefficient used by the contract unit. Hence, for any individual within the new system, getting a more favourable grading coefficient (i.e., receiving more credit per recorded hour worked) will produce bigger benefits than harder work on the current grading coefficient.

At the present time the Soviet press is full of reports about the favourable working of the new system. The general picture painted is one in which the introduction of the contract brigade or normless team raised productivity significantly. As is well known, however, such articles, which can be read in files of Soviet newspapers and economics journals about all the failed panaceas of the past, from collectivization to large scale cattle complexes, are evidence not of the success of the policy concerned, but of the effectiveness of the agitprop department of the Central Committee. For employees in the media, the current official campaign for contract units is simply "the latest economic-political campaign" (Bazarov 1983, p.19) and they react accordingly. What is the real experience of the contract brigades and normless teams?

In a thorough study of the experience of the contract brigades and normless teams, Wadekin (1984) has argued that they have not achieved, and will not achieve, "a real break-through towards higher output and more efficient utilization of inputs."[3] The fundamental reason for this is that the introduction of contract brigades and normless links in a fundamentally unaltered planning, administrative and behavioural system, is based on a one-sided diagnosis of the causes of low productivity in Soviet agriculture. The current changes in the organization of agricultural labour are based on the idea that this is the fault of the collective and state farmers who do not work as hard and as efficiently as they should and the lack of incentives for them and of adequate control over them. In fact, as is well known (Ellman 1981, Johnson & Brooks 1983), although poor labor incentives are an important problem, another cause of low productivity is the in many respects counterproductive planning and management system to which farms are subject. Hence an effective reform must also tackle the administrative system in which farms are enmeshed. A modern agriculture relying heavily on industrial inputs must be able to obtain these inputs when, where and in the quantities and qualities required, something notoriously difficult for farms in the administrative economy. Furthermore, if they are to work as intended, the members of the contract units must be able to take and implement their own decisions regardless of instructions from higher up, something also notoriously difficult to do in the administrative economy.

The introduction of contract brigades and normless teams is an attempt to obtain a major increase in efficiency by means of a partial change within a complex interrelated economic mechanism. Such attempts are very common in the USSR and normally ineffective. The reason for this was long ago explained by Kornai (1959, pp. 225–226).

> One cannot exchange a cog in an integrated, functioning machine for another one of quite a different type. The latter may be new, but it will obstruct the working of the machine nevertheless. . . . A solution can only be found by taking a comprehensive view of both centralization and decentralization and by renouncing the idea of piecemeal tinkering with the economic mechanism in the course of efforts to change it. . . . The reforms we need are of a kind which will improve all the major methods and institutions of our economic mechanism in a systematic, parallel and harmonious manner. In other words, the job of transforming the system of plain index numbers should be matched by an overhaul of the system of incentives and of prices, as well as of the functioning of the monetary and credit systems etc.
>
> It is not necessary that all these changes should be brought about all at once in every sphere; this would probably create too much of an upheaval. It is possible to carry out the reforms that are needed in a number of stages. What is essential is that the changes brought about in various spheres should complement one another in an organic manner. They should consitute parts of a thoroughly thought out, centrally coordinated series of reforms based on a uniform conception.

As Bashmachnikov (1984, p.17) has noted, "many collectives, which are formally contract units, work inefficiently. This is explained by a whole number of interconnected reasons of an objective and subjective character. The most fundamental is the imperfection of the general economic mechanism of the management of agricultural production."

The laziness and poor work of the peasants has long been a problem for the rulers of Russia. In the nineteenth century, the standard argument of progressives was that this was the fault not of the peasants but of the land tenure and social system in which they were entrapped. In *The development of capitalism in Russia* Lenin agreed with the well known narodnik A. N. Engel'gardt that "the usual accusations about the laziness and slackness of the workers are a result of the 'stamp of serfdom' and forced labour 'for the landlord,' that a new organization of agriculture requires also that the boss display entrepreneurship, knowledge of people and ability to deal with them, knowledge of the work and of its stages, familiarity with the technological and commercial aspects of agriculture, i.e., those qualities which did not and could not exist in the Oblomov serf countryside." It is as true today as when Lenin wrote, that the work effort of the Russian farmers is determined by the economic and social environment in which they find themselves. Furthermore, in the Soviet countryside as in the Oblomov countryside, entrepreneurship by the bosses for socially useful objectives is conspicuous by its absence. How could it be otherwise when the bosses are judged by plan and campaign fulfillment, and initiatives to improve the position of a farm and its inhabitants that are not in the plan/current campaign may be treated as serious criminal offences?

How long will the current campaign continue? Will it peter out, or be completely reversed, within a few years? Past experience is not encouraging. At the end of the 1960s there were about 10,000 contract units in the RSFSR but in the mid-1970s a decline began and by 1980 there were many fewer (Bashmachnikov 1984, p. 17). For decades now the *zveno* has been an institution that has been officially supported when the agricultural situation is difficult and criticized when it improves. Current official support for it reflects the unfavourable agricultural situation of the late seventies and early eighties. When this improves, how solid will the support for contract units be?

The material published in the Soviet press makes it abundantly clear that the 'new' system has run into numerous problems. Even before the campaign began, Zaslavskaya (1980) drew attention to the difficulties caused by shortages of consumer goods. Cash loses its incentive effect when there is nothing to buy. Under these conditions the extra work involved ceases to be attractive and the normless teams dissolve. This is an example of the problems caused by "piecemeal tinkering." Bazarov (1983) too, has drawn attention to the number of contract brigades that dissolve after a time. Furthermore, the brigades and teams remain part of the farm, the management of which can, and does, arbitrarily remove personnel and materials from it when convenient to the management (Glotov 1982, Artishchev 1984, Popkov 1984). There is a contradiction between paying the labor force according to results and rewarding the farm management and specialists for plan fulfillment (Zhurikov 1984a, p. 74). Because the organization of contract brigades and normless teams is an official campaign, many of them that appear in the statistics are purely paper organizations (Starukhin 1984). In many cases the 'new' contract brigades are simply the former brigades with a purely fictitious autonomy and only small results-related bonuses. The suppliers of inputs often fail to meet their commitments so that the agreed contracts cannot be fulfilled for reasons outside the control of the contract unit. Although the contract is supposed to be binding on both sides, the management sometimes ignores it if a favourable outcome would produce 'too high' an income for its members. The organization of contract units is a matter that is supervised by the relevant party committee. One raikom secretary has described (Artishchev 1984) the process by which participants in normless teams are chosen. "Each one was spoken to on the farm. Then the list was confirmed at a meeting of the district committee executive (*raikom buro*)." This is a typical example of the conflict between the campaign method and the voluntary principle.

The ultimate aim of the introduction of contract brigades and normless teams is to overcome the shortages of food products that plague the USSR. The Soviet leadership is well aware of the existence of shortages and of their economic, social and political consequences. On March 27, 1984, *Pravda* (p.1) stated that, "The food problem is the central problem, both economically and politically, of the current decade." Similarly in his speech during his visit to a Moscow metal factory in April 1984, Chernenko observed that (*Pravda*, 30-4-84, p.2) "To be honest, in a number of regions there are still interruptions in the availability of livestock products. It is still necessary to make a big effort to improve the supply of food products to the population. . . ." Shortages, however, will never be eliminated by changing the organization of labor in production since they are not generally caused by lack of production. The existence of shortages is a general problem of the administrative economy (Kornai 1980). No one consciously plans for them. As Ellman (1983, p. 12) has noted, "In fact they plan to overcome them. Nevertheless they persist, since they result from definite forms of behavior generated by the given social relations and institutional conditions." Since the shortages are not in fact caused by inadequate production then even if the introduction of contract brigades and normless teams raised production significantly it would not overcome the shortages. Maintaining retail food prices well below equilibrium levels is certain to generate shortages. Of course significant food price increases would be problematic from a political point of view, but the significant price increase for vodka, widely regarded as a necessity in the USSR, in 1982 seems to have passed off peacefully. A factor that plays an important role in exacerbating food shortages in the USSR is the poor distribution and processing system. Losses between the point of production and the point of consumption are known to be very high (Markish & Malish 1983). Improvements here would be very useful and would enable a given level of production to satisfy more needs.

The whole idea of overcoming Soviet food shortages simply by raising production is absurd in a country where so much agricultural output and food is wasted and where retail prices are significantly different from the market clearing level.

Conclusion

It is too early to make a definite assessment of the attempt, officially launched in March 1983, to alter the organization of labor in the Soviet farm sector. The aim of this attempt is to raise productivity by combining material incentives for high levels of output with a strengthening of social control over the quality of work. The system currently being disseminated has a long and controversial history in the USSR. Its stress on small groups and allowing the workers themselves to decide on the organization of the labor process, are radical policies in the USSR. Because of the diversity of the Soviet farm sector, it is being introduced more quickly in the production of some crops than others, and taking different forms in different places.

Preliminary indications suggest that it is yet another official campaign, like Khrushchev's maize and Brezhnev's industrialized livestock complexes, that like its predecessors, will have some positive effects but also negative ones and will not be a panacea. The 'new' units have experienced numerous problems and in many cases they suffer from spontaneous disintegration. How long the campaign will run, and whether or not it will one day be reversed, are uncertain.

Whatever happens to agricultural productivity, food shortages will persist. Their intensity will fluctuate in accordance with developments affecting wages, the distribution of the national income, agricultural output, prices, and processing and distribution.

Notes

I am grateful to G. Bos for research assistance and to the participants in the Grignon conference for helpful discussion.

1. *Administrirovanie* means bureaucratic decisionmaking in accordance with the laws of hierarchy and subordination. It has no exact English equivalent. It is variously translated as "a system of management based on coercive measures, used by the bureaucracy" (Lewin) or "rule by fiat" (Joravsky).

2. According to research carried out at VNIIETUSKh (Bashmachnikov 1984, p. 18) the minimum amount of the result based final payment necessary to produce an incentive effect differs in different places. In the steppe region, for skilled workers it is about 600 roubles, i.e. 30 percent of annual earnings.

3. For a similar conclusion see Dyker (1984).

References

E. Artishchev. Shchedrost' podryada, *Pravda,* 10 March, 1984.

V. Bashmachnikov. Kollektivnyi podryad na proizvodstvo produktsii v sel'skom khozyaiste, *Voprosy ekonomiki,* no. 4, 1983.

V. Bashmachnikov. Novyi tip vnutrikhozyaistvennykh sotsial'no-ekonomicheskikh otnoshenii, *Sotsialisticheskii trud,* no. 5, 1984.

V. Bashmachnikov & V. Bersenov. Sotsial'nye istochniki ekonomicheskoi effektivnosti kollektivnogo podryada, *Ekonomika sel'skogo khozyaistva,* no. 6, 1983.

E. Bazarov. Brigadnyi podryad, *Zhurnalist,* no. 8, 1983.

D. Dyker. The collective contract and the "link" in historical perspective, *Radio Liberty Research Bulletin,* January 20, 1984.

M. Ellman. Agricultural productivity under socialism, *World Development,* vol. 9, no. 9/10, 1981.

M. Ellman. Changing views on central economic planning: 1958–1983, *The ACES Bulletin,* vol. XXV, no. 1, 1983.

V. Glotov. Chto zemledel'tsu nuzhno? *Sel'skaya nov',* no. 8, 1982.

D.G. Johnson & K.M. Brooks. *Prospects for Soviet agriculture in the 1980s* (Bloomington, Indiana, USA), 1983.

J. Kornai. *Overcentralization in economic administration* (Oxford), 1959.

J. Kornai. *Economics of shortage* (Amsterdam), 1980.

L.A. Kostin. Stanovlenie brigad, *Ekonomicheskaya Gazeta,* no. 3, 1984.

A. Nove. *Was Stalin really necessary?* (London), 1964.

G. Kuznetsov. Raspredelenie po trudu v usloviyakh razvitogo sotsializma, *Ekonomika sel'skogo khozyaistva,* no. 1, 1984.

Yu Markish & A.F. Malish. The Soviet food programme, *The ACES Bulletin,* vol. XXV, no. 1, 1983.

F.G. Nasyrov. Rezul'tatov analiziruem ezhemesyachno, *Ekonomicheskaya Gazeta,* no. 23, p. 13, 1983.

M. Popkov. Mnozhit sily podryad, *Pravda,* 9 June, 1984.

D. Pospielovsky. The link system in Soviet agriculture, *Soviet Studies,* no. 4, 1970.

A. Starukhin. Litsom k ekonomike, *Pravda,* 9 April, 1984.

K.E. Wadekin. "Contract" and "normless" labour on Soviet Farms, *Radio Liberty Research Bulletin,* February 8, 1984.

T.I. Zaslavskaya. Ekonomicheskoe povedenie i ekonomicheskoe razvitie, *EKO,* no. 3, 1980.

V. Zhurikov. Material'noe i moral'noe stimulirovanie rabotnikov pri kollektivnom podryade, *Ekonomika sel'skogo khozyaistva,* no. 3, 1984a.

V. Zhurikov. Podryadnye metody plyus sovremennye formy upravleniya, *Sotsialisticheskii trud,* no. 5, 1984b.

3

The Zveno and Collective Contracts: The End of Soviet Collectivization?

Roy D. Laird and Betty A. Laird

[The zveno is] a throwback to private-property instincts [that] . . . represent a fallacious nonsocialist path.

—A. Strelyany
Komsomolskaya Pravda, October 15, 1965

The Politburo . . . endorsed the experience of collective farms, state farms and other state agricultural enterprises that are employing the collective contract.

—*Pravda*, March 11, 1983, p. 1

Each hectare will get a proprietor, and signposts will appear across our land: "S. S. Zhelebrovsky's Land," "V. I. Bolotov's Land," "V. Ye. Rashchupkon's Land" and "A. F. Uvarov's Land."

—Leonid Shinkarev
Izvestia, March 28, 1983, p. 2

Carried to its logical extreme, the wholesale adoption of the collective contract scheme in Soviet agriculture would result in the decollectivization of the Soviet countryside in the sense that the huge permanent brigades would be abandoned and production decision making would be in the hands of those actually doing the work.

What Is a Collective Contract?

To a very large degree, the endorsement of the collective contract by the Politburo in March of 1983 represented a victory for the pro-zveno advocates in a battle that has raged, with varying degrees of intensity, since the end of World War II. However, even though the beznaryadnoye zveno (unregulated link) has provided the prime model for the (*kollektivnyi podryad*) (collective contract), the descriptions of the collective contract schemes that have been adopted suggest that they differ widely from the zveno experiments of recent decades. To say the least, the collective contract scheme covers a multitude of sins and virtues. The voluminous literature published on the contracts in the Soviet press in recent months reveals that, within certain restrictions, the contract groups come in many forms and sizes. Thus, whereas the contract groups are said usually to range in size from five to twenty-five members, one Soviet author even points out that they may consist not only of entire brigades, but also of single families, or "even separate individuals."[1]

The essence of the scheme is that a specific group of kolkhoz (or sovkhoz) workers is recognized as a legal entity, within the jurisdiction of the farm, and assigned the responsibility for crop production on a specified number of hectares of the farm's land, or for the husbanding of a portion of the farm's livestock herd. The contract group and the farm management sign an agreement identifying the production unit for which the group is responsible, indicating the obligation of each party to the agreement, and spelling out the terms of remuneration. Thus, given the availability of needed inputs, such as the right kind of fertilizer in the needed quantity, the level of the workers' income will be determined primarily by the group's successes or failures on that portion of the farm's enterprise for which they are responsible.

For example, if the Stromas team has been assigned the 600 hectares on the southwest corner of the farm, their part of the bargain will be to deliver to the farm at harvest time specified quantities of the crops that they are designated to produce. For its part, the farm management agrees to provide the team with essential inputs such as fertilizer and machinery and to pay an agreed-upon price for the produce as well as a bonus for above-contract production. The management probably also agrees to pay the team a portion of their wages in advance. The quantity of various crops to be delivered by the team is based upon a projected yield figure. Apparently, the widespread practice is to set a yield based upon the average yield on the farm in recent years. Thus, if the agreed-upon yield figure for wheat were 1.5 metric tons per hectare and the team succeeded in producing 3.0 tons per hectare, the team members would have increased their income considerably over what they would have earned under the old brigade-piece-work system, if everything else were equal.

Clearly, in the eyes of the proponents of the collective contract, moving to such a system should alleviate many of the problems of Soviet agriculture. On balance the present authors accept most of these arguments. Indeed, from the first article we published on Soviet agriculture, with Alec Nove in 1953, through many later articles and books on Soviet agriculture and its problems, we have repeatedly made most of the points now promulgated by the Soviet proponents of the collective contract.[2] In a section below "Advantages and Problems Associated with the Collective Contract," we attempt to summarize those arguments. However, before turning to that enterprise, a short look at the zveno controversy is called for.

The Zveno Controversy[3]

The opening and closing paragraphs of our 1966 article on the zveno read as follows:

> Pressures to adopt the zveno . . . as the basic work unit in the kolkhozy and sovkhozy may well represent the most momentous force for fundamental change in the Soviet political system since the drive to forced collectivization in the early 1930s.

> Perhaps the Soviet leadership would agree with the assertion contained in the opening paragraph of this paper. Surely the widespread substitution of independent teams for brigades would constitute much more than a Liberman reform for agriculture. Perhaps the revival of the controversy is a forerunner of some future major reorganization, but as of mid-1966 the Stalinist agricultural system seems to have received a stay of execution. From the political point of view, Stalin had been right in condemning the zveno, and, as reported by the latest advocates of the teams, the present day opponents of the move seem to agree with Stalin. Thus, the zveno are seen as "a throwback to private-property instincts [that] . . . represent a falacious, nonsocialist path."

Although zveno-like groups are known to have been in operation in the 1930s following on the heels of collectivization, the first major battle in their favor came in the immediate post–World War II years. A.A. Andreev, the Politburo's agricultural specialist, became the major proponent of their widespread adoption. The leadership and the Party had been preoccupied with pursuing the war, and controls over the farms had been relaxed. As a result, real "kolkhoz democracy" came into play, in the sense that there was a widespread reordering of the work arrangements according to the desires of the farm workers. Nevertheless, until the Politburo's action in 1983, the large permanent brigade remained the officially sanctioned way of organizing the farm work. Prior to the amalgamations of the 1950s the average field brigade numbered probably 20–30 peasants; since the amalgamation the number has been 100 or more. In contrast, the typical zveno established during the war years included a half dozen or so individuals, often from the same family. As in the case of the zveno championed by Andreev in the early 1950s, the pattern was to assign a portion of the farm's production to the zveno members, and their earnings depended upon the fruits of their labor.

Andreev had traveled about the countryside and, drawing upon his observations, he argued that the wholesale adoption of the zveno, even in grain growing regions, would help solve the problems of Soviet agriculture. Unfortunately for Andreev, unlike for his current successor Gorbachev, the time was not ripe for the zveno idea. Khrushchev led the counter attack, championed the *agrogorod* (agricultural city) scheme which, while abandoned as too costly, came to be interpreted as the amalgamation of the smaller farms into the huge farms of today. Khrushchev won the battle and replaced Andreev as the Politburo's agricultural spokesman, while lesser advocates were silenced and/or imprisoned. As Leonard Shapiro was to observe, for the time being the zveno was in effect outlawed in 1949 because "from the point of view of party control, the brigade system had considerable advantages over the link system."[4] Still, the scheme was not to die, and favorable articles extolling the virtues of the zveno reappeared in the 1960s. Not only were the zven'ya said to be more efficient than the permanent brigades, but data were cited to support the claim that they were more productive.[5] However, the major battle was not won by them. New data were published, purporting to prove that the permanent brigade system was superior after all.[6]

One of the long-time champions of the link concept is academician V. Tikhonov. While participating in the International Conference of Agricultural Economists in Minsk in 1970, we had the opportunity to speak with Tikhonov about the zveno. Our assertion was that if universally adopted, both labor productivity and output would increase. Our notes indicate that while he emphatically agreed with the former advantage, he did not believe that yields would increase. Thus we find a report on an April 1983 interview with him most interesting.[7] The bulk of his answers to the questions put to him reveal that he still stresses increased labor productivity. Reading between the lines one might conclude, because at no point does he directly speak of increased output, that he still has his doubts that the new system will increase production significantly. Indeed, the closest he comes to implying that increased production might result is in his answer to a question concerning the applicability of the scheme to livestock raising. Here is part of his answer: "This system of wages is simply universal. If administrative obstacles are not put in its way or labels hung around its neck, but instead the links are attentively followed up and aided, then excellent results would be attained."

Why Now?

Given the potentially enormous implications for change that going over to the collective contract system has for the Soviet Union, why has the leadership endorsed a system which, in effect, has been so roundly damned for so long?

From the beginning, Soviet collective agriculture suffered from two major flaws, lagging investment and what we have referred to repeatedly as "system costs." From Lenin through Stalin, and part of the time under Khrushchev, agriculture was worse off than just a neglected poor cousin of the Soviet economy. Much of the time, capital was drained from an impoverished countryside to finance urban industrial growth. However, under Brezhnev's leadership all that changed; unprecedentedly enormous amounts of capital were spent on agriculture, although not always wisely. Still, the result was as expected, increased productivity, but certainly not a proportionate increase. Furthermore, a point of diminishing returns was reached in the mid-1970s. Indeed, looking back, the turning point probably was 1976. All-crucial grain production reached an unprecedented 224 million metric tons in 1976. However, in the last eight years, based on official figures and USDA estimates (including the 1984 crop), even counting the bumper year of 1978 (a new record of 237 mmt.), annual grain production has averaged less than 190 mmt. Given Soviet needs and goals there have not been just four bad grain years, there has been a period of eight years of poor performance consisting of seven poor years and one bumper year when weather conditions may have been the best in this century. Certainly weather conditions have deteriorated, but the Soviets themselves implicitly, sometimes explicitly, admit that far from all the problems can be blamed on the weather. Thus, referring to "the last four years" Voskresensky states: "Much depends on climatic conditions. . . . But not everything. No wonder the Russian proverb says that the weather is the weather but work is work."[8]

Yield increases have stagnated and the effort to convert the individual farms to economic accountability (*khozhraschet*) has failed miserably. In 1980 only 8% of the teams and brigades on the farms were on a cost-accounting basis. More seriously, between 1970 and 1980 many of the farms came to be dependent upon state financing. In that period farm indebtedness increased more than tenfold, from 2.4 to 25.7 billion rubles, and short-term indebtedness increased more than threefold, from 10.3 to 34 billion rubles[9]— this at a time when the state has been paying higher prices for produce, and huge amounts of hard currency have been spent on imported grains.

Meanwhile, however, the Soviets have been observing their Hungarian neighbor make major adjustments in agricultural policy, throw out bulky centralized controls, institute independent teams and profit motive, and by doing so, increase production, yields, and efficiency enormously. Soviet independent team advocates are coming out of their closets in droves and pointing their fingers at success. This time they are being allowed to speak. They are emphasizing system costs, that is, the built-in inefficiency of a system that imposes centrally-taken decisions from above on farm workers and managers, depriving them of initiative and the critical advantages gained from timely, on-the-spot decision making. The Soviet imposition of factory-type organization on the countryside with its living plants and animals has been costly. Looking hungrily at Hungarian success, M.S. Gorbachev seized the independent team banner, and the Politburo, undoubtedly frustrated by agriculture's inadequate showing and increasing costs, backed him. Article after article has appeared in the Soviet press extolling the virtues of the "collective contract" in its various forms and urging widespread adoption of the scheme.

Advantages and Problems
Associated with the Collective Contract

From a myriad of recent successes and failures in instituting the collective contract, a prescription for standardizing the contracts has emerged. This was enunciated by Gorbachev, who was the featured speaker at the all-Union conference held on the collective contracts, in Belgorod March 18–19, 1983. According to the reporters he "specified a number of basic requirements which, in the opinion of scientists and experts, must be met when introducing the collective contract system":

- voluntary joining in regular work collectives (brigades, detachments, sections), and full autonomy of those collectives in performing their production targets;
- regular long-term assignment, as a rule, to the contractor collectives of such activities as crop rotation or the growing of a set of crops, the operation of agricultural equipment or the raising of a livestock herd, so as to keep their members busy with contract work on a year-round basis, insofar as possible;
- assignment to contractor sub-units of economically justified and cost-effective tasks with allowance for attained levels of output, progressively rising norms for the consumption of raw and other materials and resources and the assurance of proper bookkeeping;
- basing remuneration on stable—over a number of years—higher or progressively rising rates payable for output depending on the levels of crop yields and livestock productivity as well as on bonus rates for increase in labor productivity and output, improvements in quality of output and reduction of production cost;
- paying guaranteed wages in poor harvest years as based on rates payable for the volume of operations performed;
- the incentive pay system for final production should be maximally simple and easy to grasp and it should provide for a substantial proportion of extra pay allowances and bonuses in the overall earnings of workers.[10]

Why Are the Collective Contracts Superior?

The arguments for the collective contract add up to claimed economic improvement by almost any measure. Voskresensky sums them up as follows:

> No matter what indicators we use to compare the collective contract with piece work, the contract's advantages leap to the eye. Here are generalized results for the country as a whole: the collective contract groups are systematically obtaining 20–30 per cent more produce from each hectare of land allotted them than the groups doing piece work and, moreover, and this is especially important!—they do this with less material resources, which means at a lower production cost. Labour productivity in these groups is 15–20 per cent higher and output per unit of fixed assets—5–8 per cent more. And this is true for *any year,* whether favorable or unfavorable for crops, *for any type of farming*—raising crops or livestock—and *everywhere*[11] (Voskresensky's italics).

As stressed by Gorbachev and his fellow conferees at the Belgorod meeting, the bottom line is increased worker incentives. Although the "piece-work" system supposedly went out with the abandonment of the *trudoden* (labor-day system) and the institution of guaranteed minimum wages, there is now an open admission that this was not really the case. The bonus-brigade system still required measures of work performed, which meant that if a machine operator strained his equipment by moving too fast, tearing out plants in the process, or did not plow to the necessary depth, he might be credited with more piece units, which brought him more wages than he would attain through increased yields, even though the price would be costly repairs and lower yields.

According to Academician Tatyana Zaslavska, an economist and sociologist, "sociological research . . . revealed that (under the old system) many . . . are working without any interest in the results obtained. . . . Hence [there is] rampant absenteeism, violation of work schedules, careless handling of costly machinery and fertilizers which leads to damage, etc." Further, she asserts that 26 percent of the tractors are operated in violation of the most elementary maintenance rules. Again, according to a poll taken in 10 rayony in Siberia, only 4 percent of the administrators and 22 percent of the workers believe that the workers "work as hard as they can."[12] Ideally, under the contract system, the collective team is responsible not only for the output but also for the input. Thus, if fertilizer is not wasted, machines are properly cared for, and weeds are truly kept from the fields, team members profit personally. Their income at the end of the season is "directly dependent on results." Further, since the ideal is for the teams to be permanently responsible for both the fields and the equipment, there is an appeal to a sense of "proprietorship." Knowing that extra work put into terracing fields will reduce erosion, team members perform such tasks in the off seasons.[13] Similarly, knowing that they must pay out-of-pocket for tractor repairs, they watch for deterioration and make minor repairs themselves thereby avoiding costly major repairs and extensive down-time in the repair shop.[14]

Furthermore, we learn:

> The microclimate in the collectives is better. People trust one another. They are constantly helping each other out. Both mutual demands and responsibilities are higher. No one is indifferent to violators of labor discipline or to the land. Machine operators pick up trash from the fields without being reminded, "overhaul" the fields, and plow up forest edges and unneeded roads. And if they are hauling organic fertilizer, for example, they prepare it carefully and apply it evenly.[15]

Thus the collective contract holds great promise for its advocates.

Start-Up Problems

No published commentary we have seen has anything but high praise for the collective contract system itself. However, many Soviet observers worry about serious problems related to bringing the new system on-line. Gorbachev and his fellow conferees at the Belgorod conference also worried about failures to fully live up to the "basic requirements" for their success as outlined above. Specific concerns included:

- Failure on the part of management to live up to its part of the bargain;
- A reluctance on the part of managers to relinquish much of the power they now hold;
- The tendency for farm managers to divert team members to non-group tasks must be resisted;
- Since a major key to the success of the system is that of developing a sense of "proprietorship" among the workers, temporary assignment of either land or workers must be resisted, permanent long-term commitments are vital to success;
- The arrangements for payments to the teams must not be complex, they should be kept simple, and the team members must be allowed to divide their earnings in their own way;
- A failure to adhere to the principle of "volunteerism" must be avoided. If the workers do not genuinely wish to join a collective contract group, the scheme won't work;
- There should be no imposition of rigid patterns, each contract should be tailored to fit the particular farm and its needs.[16]

Although Gorbachev's reasons for failure of contracts are the ones that are most often cited in the Soviet press, one finds occasional references to the following as well: disagreement among the contractors over wage distribution, conflict between the team leader and the farm manager, wage distribution, conflict between the team leader and the farm manager, confusion over the terms of the contract, failure of the manager to pay the team as agreed, cheating by contract workers, bad weather (which oftentimes penalizes contract teams), and unsatisfactory team leaders. Thus, although each year thousands of new contract teams are formed, many disband. Interestingly, on one wealthy state farm in Western Siberia a contract team of machine operators disbanded when their earnings had doubled because there was nothing in the local shops that they wanted to spend their money on. Thus they preferred making 250 rubles per month and working less for it. The author concludes, "The organization of teams, with their opportunities for increased earnings, should be accompanied by growth in the supply of goods and services in rural localities."[17]

Conclusions

The post-Brezhnev leadership has signalled a recognition that Soviet agriculture is in a new "time of troubles," and nothing short of drastic change in the management of the farms will correct the situation. Obviously, the Stalinist agricultural system is being much more seriously challenged this time around. Whereas the Stalin Politburo rejected Andreev's zveno, the post-Brezhnev Politburo has sanctioned the collective contract scheme as championed by Gorbachev. Still the stakes are as high as ever.

Although, this time there is no indication of high-level opposition to the change, and everyone who has put pen to paper favors the collective contracts, as we have reported, there is a recognition that serious impediments exist to their successful adoption. Many Soviet commentators mention the need for changes in attitudes, but Voskresensky goes the farthest by almost stating that such a change must start in Moscow itself.

> The contract system is unthinkable without high overall standards in economic thinking at all levels of the country's economy—from the central planning organs to . . . the accounting clerk at a collective or state farm.

The obvious question arises, does not the proposed change add up to a return to private farming? Voskresensky meets the question head on:

> If we say that the use of the collective contract system, on a mass scale, was and is still hindered by the force of inertia, by the long tradition of doing piece work, by conservatism in economic management thinking and dogmatic fears (And doesn't this look like a step backwards, a return to the pre-collective farm period?), then it would be the truth. But, alas, not the whole truth.[18]

In our view it is 95 percent of the truth, but still believing that the Soviets can have their socialist cake while eating the advantages of private farming, the author makes the point that fundamental differences will exist between Soviet and Australian or American agriculture. He stresses three points. First, there will be no change in the "ownership system." The state will continue to own the land, and the machinery will remain the property of the collective or state farm. Second, although hard work should result in higher income for the members of the team, they will not be allowed to make "super profits." If they are blessed with a bumper crop one year, the whole farm will share in the benefit. Third, unlike the American farmer, if there is a crop failure, the Soviet farmers will not be ruined; the state will provide a "guaranteed" payment.

One wonders whether the author knows that some one-third of the land farmed in the United States is rented land (and many banks, in effect, own a lot of the agricultural machinery), if he knows about United States crop insurance and federal disaster loans and payments, and that most American farmers use the profits from bumper years to reduce their loans. Of course, in the points raised there are some differences, but they are not as great as Voskresensky implies.

Furthermore, Voskresensky fails to mention a number of differences that have long plagued farm production in the Soviet Union that will continue even if the collective contract system becomes widespread, differences that will diminish any benefits that such a system can effect. For example, the contracts do not include the right of the farmers to decide which crop to grow. That decision is made at higher levels. Furthermore, they will have little control over the application of fertilizer and pesticides if the kolkhoz does not receive adequate supplies of appropriate chemicals and make them available to the teams. Nor will teams be able to plant and harvest at the proper time if the machinery is not available or parts are missing.

There is no doubt that this time around the Soviet leadership is intent upon rectifying some of the nation's most serious agricultural problems. However, the impediments to implementing the scheme and, most of all, the political price that must be paid if it succeeds are so great that we will be surprised if the success envisaged is achieved. Clearly, there is much dragging of feet. Yet, given that the Politburo has blessed the scheme, we will not be surprised to learn that in the next year or two "all" Soviet farms have adopted the new system. What will surprise us is if the vast majority of the schemes are really worth any more than the paper on which the contracts are drawn.

All through the post-Stalin era volumes have been written on the need to achieve the advantages of economic decentralization. This, of course, was what the Liberman reforms were all about. Where are they now?

The Soviet Union is the most politicized system in the world. The bottom line of the system is the perpetuation of the incumbent leaders in their position of power, and thus the rewards to the rank and file of the party, whose loyalty is essential to continuing the system, are virtually assured. Consequently, however genuine the past calls for decentralization have been, the left hand of party control has taken away what the right hand of economic rationality has given.

The point made by Shapiro in 1960 still applies in the mid-1980s. What finally emerges in the countryside will be governed by what the leadership judges is best "from the point of view of party control. . . ."[19] Again, genuine wholesale adoption of the scheme would spell the end of collectivization in practice, if not in name, and the central leadership would no longer control agricultural production. Moreover, if such a scheme works for the farmers, why cannot the urban workers reap the benefits of free-enterprise and work for themselves? Gorbachev and his followers have opened the lid of communism's Pandora's box. Surely, when they see what is emerging, there will be a frantic effort to slam it shut.

Notes

1. Lev Voskresensky, "From 'Piece Work' to 'Contract'," *Moscow News*, Nos. 14 & 15, 1983. Ironically, since *Moscow News* is not available to the ordinary Soviet reader, of the scores of reports and articles read by the authors in the preparation of this paper, Voskresensky's two-part article is by far the best, most clear, and quite detailed single account of what the collective contracts are and are not.

2. A. Nove and R. D. Laird, "A Note on Labour Utilization in the Kolkhoz," *Soviet Studies*, Vol. 4 (1953) pp. 434–442.

3. Much of the material presented here is drawn from Roy D. Laird "The New Zveno Controversy," *Osteuropa Wirtschaft*, Vol. XI, No. 4 (December, 1966), pp. 254–261.

4. Leonard Schapiro, *The Communist Party of the Soviet Union* (New York: Random House, 1960), p. 515.

5. A. Strelyany, *Komsomolskaya Pravda*, October 15, 1965, pp. 2–3.

6. V. Borovsky, "Organization of Labor in the Kolkhoz and Sovkhoz," *Ekonomika Sel'skogo Khozyaistva*, No. 10 (October, 1965), pp. 37–51.

7. Kapitolina Kozhevnikova, "Master of the Field," *Literaturnaya Gazeta,* April 20, 1983, p. 13. For the Western student of Soviet agriculture, perhaps the most interesting revelation in the interview is his statement as follows: "Our country now has nine consumers for every one producer of agricultural output." The implication is that including part-time workers and those who work on the private plots, in the 1980s the USSR still has some 30,000,000 farmers.

8. *Ibid.*

9. I. F. Suslov, "The Kolkhozy in the System of the Peoples Economy," *Voprosy Ekonomiki,* No. 12 (December, 1982), pp. 23–29.

10. G. Martyshkin and Yu. Proskurin, "For a Broad Introduction of the Collective Contract System," *Ekonomika Sel'skogo Khozyaistva,* No. 5 (April, 1983), pp.72–77.

11. Voskresensky, *op. cit.*

12. *Ibid.*

13. Martyshkin and Proskurin, *op. cit.*

14. N. Bagretsov, "The Grain Grower Took a Contract," *Pravda,* March 12, 1983, p. 2.

15. *Ibid.*

16. Martyshkin and Proskurin, *op. cit.*

17. Leonid Shinkarev, "One's Own Land," *Izvestia,* March 28, 1983, p. 2.

18. Voskresensky, *op. cit.*

19. Shapiro, *op. cit.*

4

The Contract Brigades:
Towards a Neo-collectivism
in Soviet Agriculture?

Alain Pouliquen

The title of this article is not a provocative joke. Moreover, although it inverts the interrogative statement of Roy and Betty Laird in the present volume it does not attempt a point by point critique of their analysis, nor of those of Alec Nove and Michael Ellmann. Rather, I propose here a different view of the problem and of the way of dealing with it. So my critique will be conceptual rather than textual, and leads me to an alternative hypothesis regarding the future of contract zvenos or brigades.

The interrogative form of Roy and Betty Laird's title is essential. Indeed, like Nove and Ellmann, they understand perfectly that the large scale development of the contract collectives is encountering serious brakes and obstacles of ideological and systemic origin, particularly if one considers it, as they do, as an economic decentralization (which is a crucial point, as will be shown below). The dirigiste economic logic, i.e. that of "economics of shortage" of Janos Kornai, continues to prevail in the Soviet Union at all levels of agriculture and associated sectors. Now it is precisely this logic that, through various channels, seems to prevent the agricultural collectives from settling down to work on a large scale and in true conformity with a logic of economic autonomization, by which I mean market or quasi-market relations between the sub-units and the rest of the system.[1] Therefore, Roy and Betty Laird cannot, at the moment, go beyond conjecture concerning the possible beginnings of the decollectivization of Soviet agriculture.

Meanwhile, much like Alec Nove, they do not exclude such a scenario for the future, since according to them, the logic of contract zvenos goes precisely in this direction and, implicitly, no other remedy is conceivable today for the current "sickness" of Soviet agriculture. This implies that they consider as conceivable the following development: an at least partial and gradual "infection" (cf. Nove) of the upper levels of the sector's management by the dynamics of economic decentralization. This approach, whose internal consistency I do not contest, fits in well with the dominant view of western observers, and also with the argument of Soviet researchers who initially promoted this reform.

According to this view, because the origin of the economic sickness is the traditional centralized Soviet system, the basic remedy can only be found in economic decentralization. However, to be effective and efficient, the latter must be generalized, which leads to the dilemma of all or nothing: either historical rupture, possibly gradual but nevertheless complete, with the existing economic mechanism, or continued floundering in stagnation and crisis. However, as will be argued below:

- it is not certain that economic decentralization, in the strict meaning of the term,[2] is the only way available to the Soviet leadership for mobilizing hidden reserves and moving on to more intensive growth;
- it is even less certain that this choice is really open to the leadership because it is not consistent with the basic features of the Soviet social order;
- unlike first appearances, the present development of contract zvenos or brigades is, at least potentially, the bearer of another logic in response to the economic problem. This alternative is perfectly consistent with the existing social order and does not involve any upheaval of the traditional economic mechanism.

At this point, I must make a fundamental statement without being able to develop it here, for reasons of space. However, it is illustrated below on the subject of the future of contract collectives in agriculture.

The essential social relations that structure the Soviet system are not of a socio-economic kind.[3] Above all, they are relations of submission, control and integration of persons and groups as such, and not directly as economic agents. It is only through the mediation of these direct interhuman relations (i.e., quite specific mechanisms of personal and collective submission and more or less paternalist and bribed integration, but also active collaboration of individuals in the Soviet social order), and not through market exchange relations,[4] that the Soviet system has long since ensured its global economic reproduction and growth.

The word "kollektiv" in the Soviet Union, at enterprise and brigade levels, cannot be reduced to a functional salaried staff who are "sellers" of labor and passive executors of orders, plus their supervisors.[5] Above everything else, it is a vital, probably the main, mechanism for reproduction of the Soviet social order:

- it is penetrated by the Party, and more generally, by all the organs of social control and mobilization (the Komsomol, the trade union, the women's union, the groups of innovators, police informers, etc.);
- at least in a first stage, the "kollektiv" plays a dominant role in the selective allocation to its members, in a simultaneously hierarchical and

collectively self-managed way, of various material and moral prerequisites or approval/sanctions of crucial importance: privileged and semi-gratis access to essential goods and services (housing, vehicles, "vouchers" for "cures" and holidays, etc.), possibility of foreign travel, of training, of geographic or professional migration, access to subsidiary private activities (in agriculture—household plots and all the associated goods and services), promotion in social organizations and the professional hierarchy, various medals (useful in everyday life), sanctions of the "comrades' court", etc.

All this distribution, outside wages and the market, of essential advantages and rewards broadly reduces the importance of classical (western-type) wage-earning in its role of control and stimulation of the work-force. Moreover, it is far from being reducible to an automatic and detailed application of legal regulations. Above all, it creates relations of personal and collective subordination that are radically different from those of the salaried employee type. The former consist of "clientism", paternalism and favoritism, and of conformist and personal (unconditional and non-contractual) submission to the local and global social order. All this greatly transcends the mere imperative of economic efficiency of work. It is above all as a person, in all his aspects, and not as a salaried worker, that the individual thus tends to be controlled, integrated, confined, but also mobilized by the basic kollektiv.[6] The horizontal aspect, collectively self-managed, spontaneous, but at the same time guided from higher levels of the hierarchies, of this integration in a collective whole must also be stressed. The struggle between individuals for the advantages distributed operates first inside the collective. It thus focusses on this micro-social scale the strategies of mutual submission, neutralization, collaboration, rivalry, exclusion, surveillance, denunciation and correction (in official terms: "fraternal mutual aid").

At the same time, the members of the kollektiv make a common cause, materially, towards the outside, to obtain from it by any means the maximum of material and human resources and to supply it with the minimum of goods and services produced and information.

All these mechanisms, both horizontally self-managed and vertically guided, in which ideology also plays an important part,[7] make this "community" a blended whole, effectively barring any conscious and organized individualism, any self-legitimation of personal authority, even if it is founded on local economic success.[8] Every social position can only be conceded and legitimized from and by upper levels of the hierarchy. The kollektiv tends to be a kind of collective person, and the "true basic subject of the Soviet system".[9] It functions according to logical and foreseeable laws that are irrelevant to those of western micro-economics. On this point, official Soviet rhetoric is not always as surrealistic as many western observers think, provided that one decodes it as the rhetoric of power. It is full of confirmations and illustrations of these social realities and mechanisms, though it distorts them from the terminological point of view.

However, this micro-social mechanism of reproduction of the Soviet social order is not safe from degradation and, for economic use, from contradictions, even though it is increasingly vital for global economic and social reproduction.

First, the wage aspect of social relations at work seems to have acquired increasing importance during the Brezhnev era in a spontaneous manner obviously unwanted and ill-controlled by the Center:

- the continuous aggravation of the shortage of labor has allowed certain categories of workers like the "mekhanizatory" in agriculture to develop a high mobility of employment, to make their various employers compete for their services, and to escape towards the "second economy" between two successive employments;[10]
- even in the case of employed workers, the development of the "second economy" is increasing the amount of competition and shortage on the labor market, compelling the directors of enterprises to use often illegal increases of wages, bonuses and various allowances;
- in agriculture, industrialization of the organization of work by means of extreme division of tasks, increased distance between workers and managers, irregularity of effective employment, large size and temporary nature of the labor collectives has reduced the efficiency of the specific mechanisms of social integration and control by the kollektiv;[11]
- on the other hand, the increased shortage of consumer goods relative to the distributed purchasing power acts in two opposite directions. It strengthens the influence of selective allowances in kind by the kollektiv, but it also steps up the workers' flight towards the "second economy" and the mere "work" of searching for goods on the various markets (white, grey, black, etc.).

Finally, a tendency towards the "liberation of the workforce", in the Marxist sense, has appeared during the last twenty years. Workers have tended to escape from the confining control of the kollektiv and to become, as Zaslavskaia says, autonomous "subjects".[12] However, it will be noticed that this escape is particularly difficult for the huge army of agricultural manual workers.

At least at first, this compels the enterprises to reply to this challenge in a "wages" or "quasi-wages" way. Even the numerous allowances and favors in kind tend to play indirectly the role of a part of the total wages, which weakens their role of integration and submission to the kollektiv. However, the Soviet system is, by nature, poorly equipped to manage and check this type of answer in an efficient manner at the macroeconomic level. Among other reasons, this results from the weakness and the decrease of the attractiveness of money, but also from the anti-economic rationality of the production units and their sub-units. The tendency to maximize inputs and minimize outputs is only thwarted, from outside these units, by upper economic, administrative and "political" organs.

Although the mechanism of integration, submission and control of the individual by the kollektiv remains relatively efficient for the reproduction of the social order itself (hierarchies and norms of behavior), its efficiency is relatively poor as regards its economic use. This contradiction, which remains paradoxical for many western observers, is inherent to the Soviet social order in its present state and worsened during the second part of the Brezhnev era because of the above-mentioned spontaneous process.

Taking up this fundamental challenge by a logic of economic decentralization-stimulation in the strict sense would mean, for the Soviet authorities, submitting to these spontaneous social processes and actually amplifying them. It would be a political adventure, if not suicide, overthrowing the very bases of the Russian variant of Soviet social order, which is not the Hungarian one, in this respect. That is one of the reasons why I think that as soon as it reaches a mass scale, the contract brigades movement, both in industry and in agriculture, is no longer relevant to this logic but to an alternative one, directed against market relations, and neo-kollektivist towards the rank-and-file workers. Above all, this logic thwarts their "escape" and their economic "liberation", in the Marxist sense. First appearances are misleading in this respect, for the successful local experiments that have preceded, and in principle inspired, the present campaign profited from special local conditions. These often gave them some features of true microeconomic decentralization. Moveover, the appealing "economic" rationalization of these experiments by the Research Institutes that have promoted and studied them has fostered this impression among western observers.[13] The observation that it is impossible to generalize such conditions should not lead us too hastily to expect failure or a purely fictitious development and the economic failure of the contract brigades in agriculture.

Indeed, the whole of the preceding analysis, and also study of the reports of economic and administrative officials in the Soviet Press, foster the following hypothesis. Once it has reached a mass scale, the logic of this restructuring will no longer be a delicate economic autonomization and stimulation by money (logic I), but the following (logic II) (which does not require the meeting of such delicate conditions—the actual purposes of the contract brigades (zveno) are both):

1. Tightening up and making economically operational the old Soviet social mechanism of the kollektiv.

There is no question of giving it up, or replacing it by a purely microeconomic mechanism with the corresponding spontaneous social structure. In this respect, we must avoid too exclusively an economic reading of the Soviet literature that initially defined and promoted the philosophy of the contract brigades. Indeed, beside economic chapters or excerpts, there are more sociological ones in these books: they recall the crucial importance of the social control and blending implemented in the new "kollektiv" by the Party group and other organs (Komsomol, Union organization, etc.).[14] Even on the highest level, M.S. Gorbachev made the point that "the new forms of labor organizations" have "great importance for the solution not only of economic but also of social and educational tasks".[15] The Soviet press is also full of officials' reports stressing above all the superiority of the new brigades or zvenos in work-discipline, the struggle against absenteeism, and above all the excessive mobility of workers.

2. Reconfining into permanent "kollektivs" workers who had a tendency to escape them in a simultaneously individualist, parallel and purely wage-earning way.

3. Transferring from officials and directors to workers the greater part of production responsibilities and risks, and the burden of adjustments to make up for failures in supply of the means of production.

In this perspective, it matters little whether the wages in proportion to production, are "stimulating" or not. The essential point is that workers should be confined in a position, without any alternative, that compels them, for their mere survival, to concern themselves with a final product.[16] In any case, in remote country areas it is doubtful whether money wages are very "stimulating" because of the particularly acute shortage on the official market of manufactured consumer goods. This is why the present partial return to the old system of payment in kind, in the form of a share of the harvest, seems logical. Moreover it has the advantage of inciting the kolkhozniks to increase their private animal production, and thus to bind them more strongly to the land. It is significant that this practice concerns in particular the "mekhanizatory" and mid-level specialists, especially "scarce" and having professional and territorial mobility.

For the same reasons, failures to provide means of production are not as critical an obstacle as is often claimed. It can probably be assumed that those supplies will not be obtained any worse at brigade or zveno level than they now are at kolkhoz or sovkhoz level. Moreover, as soon as they become a vital necessity for the workers themselves, the authorities probably expect the latter to exert increased pressure in this respect on the management of the enterprise to use the means supplied less wastefully and, above all, to make up for these failures by more work and a spirit of responsibility and initiative.

4. Collectivizing the productive responsibility of the workers, then of their work itself, through the collectivization of wages. Up to now, the collective social control already described used only the "carrot" and the "stick" of the non-wage allowances. Henceforth members of the kollektiv will be both in mutual rivalry for wages themselves, through the "work participation coefficient" (K.T.U.), and in forced community.[17] Henceforth, everybody will pay for the indiscipline, laziness, absenteeism, alcoholism or carelessness of others. Moreover, each person is explicitly incited to watch over, re-educate, denounce, etc. the others, or in official language, to "aid" them. But simultaneously, everybody competes to obtain a good K.T.U. from management.

All this is more an indication of a strengthening and an extension of the traditional mechanism of collective social control, and an economic operationalization of this mechanism, than an economic logic of enterprise.

It is in precisely these terms that mid-level officials and managers praise the superiority of the new collectives.

This social form of organization seems to have no equivalent in the economic history of non-collectivized agriculture in market economies. If, however, one looks further for historical analogies, the division of the feudal estates into sub-units ruled by the metayage system comes to mind. This analogy is misleading, however, for share-cropping lacks the internal "collectivism" of each sub-unit.[18] There is more of the logic of the territorial brigades of the Stalin era with, however, three important differences:

- higher level of specialization and mechanization,
- maintenance, so far, of the minimum guaranteed wage (the monthly "advance"),
- less traditionally authoritarian and more strictly "kollektivnye" social relations at work.

On the whole, we are led to considering the contract brigades campaign as the beginning of a re-collectivization of agricultural work at a point in time when such work was tending to change into an individualist wage-earning system. That is to say, contrary to conventional wisdom, the growing size of kolkhozy and sovkhozy and thus the creation of "factories in the fields" was the main source of a weakening of the social fabric in agriculture because it strengthened the role of wages while weakening the role of cohesiveness and mutual control among agricultural workers. The monetarization and specialization of work made possible by large agricultural units thus produces a form of alienation that did not exist in smaller units.

This view of the matter has the great advantage of being quite consistent with the fundamental features of the Soviet social order. On the other hand, the whole economic history of the Soviet Union reveals the total incompatibility of this order with the decentralizing logic of the economic spirit, that is, decentralization in a market or quasi-market manner. Unlike market-oriented reforms this neo-collectivist scenario does not limit Soviet leaders to the alternative of "all or nothing" (in the special case of the USSR, the eventuality of "all" would mean a quite unlikely revolution). Although it is a profound distortion of its prime economic inspiration, it can be imagined that this pseudo-reform could achieve positive economic results in agriculture, but for reasons and in ways that are not those usually given by western analysts.

Nevertheless, I will remain interrogative in my conclusion, as do Alec Nove, Roy and Betty Laird, but for different reasons:

1. Although extensive economic decentralization can be considered to be very unlikely,[19] it seems, at the moment, that this logic is still present in local variants of contract brigades.[20] In other words, it is sometimes compounded with neo-collectivist logic in a contradictory manner.[21] Perhaps the debate among top Soviet leaders on the exact

content and the tempo and extent of implementation of the reform has not yet been quite settled. This could explain the relative slowness of the formation of contract brigades in agriculture, at least at the beginning of the campaign: such brigades accounted for about 8 percent of the total collectives in 1982,[22] 20 percent in crop production in 1983 according to Ellman.

2. In addition, uncertainty persists as regards the ability of agricultural workers to resist efficiently a restructuring that hardly seems to correspond to their spontaneous inclination. This reticence tends to confirm our analysis, although a truly decentralizing logic would probably receive their active support. It is rather at the level of the workers, and not in the "conservative reluctance and opposition of mid-level management" (the traditional scapegoat used by official Soviet rethoric as regards economic reforms) nor in the dysfunctional behavior of higher and lower administrative levels of the sector, that I would see the main origin of a possible economic failure or abortion of the reform.

Inversely, if the neo-collectivist logic becomes the ascendant one, which cannot be avoided in case of a general adoption of the reform, there would be no fundamental reason for the local party and state officials and for the managers of sovkhozes and kolkhozes to oppose it on a long-term basis. On the contrary, they would gain from it due to the greater submission of the workers to their power and from reduction of the officials' own direct responsibility for agricultural production. Besides, one cannot see why their worries would notably increase as regards the supply of means of agricultural production, which would only be the case if the economic logic were to prevail.

Therefore, I remain open to the possible surprises that the contract brigades or zvenos may hold in store for us. However, the preceding analysis and the proportion of about one-fifth of crop production collectives already concerned cause me to imagine the "surprise" of their considerable extension, achieved in a "neo-collectivist" manner, and without a decentralizing "infection" of the Soviet system as a whole, as the technical particularities of agriculture can make it profitable to give back the direct responsibility of entire biological cycles to little groups of workers or at least of "mekhanisatory": the economic results may turn out to be somewhat positive, for their principles are relatively well founded from the agronomic point of view.

Notes

1. Shortcomings in the supply of means of production, low attractiveness of money for workers, especially in the countryside; reluctance (quite logical) of the mid-level officials, because of the rules of the game they continue to have to play.

2. Transformation of economic units and sub-units into autonomous factors linked with the global system by money and commodity exchanges of a market or quasi-market type.

3. And certainly not "state" or "etatic" capitalist type as seen in France by Charles Bettelheim and other scholars. Cf. C. Bettelheim, *Les luttes de classes en URSS; Les domines* (Paris: Seuil Maspero, 1982). See also his three other volumes.

4. On the markets of material commodities and labor. Nor through "central planning", considered in itself as a socially empty and purely "rational" mechanism, as a kind of Deux ex machina.

5. Cf. Pouliquen (A.) "L'organisation du travail agricole collectif et le controle social de l'activite economique en URSS". INRA Economie Sociologie Rurales. Montpellier, 1982, 46 pp. See also (without the appendices): *Revue d'Etudes Comparatives Est-Ouest*, V. 13, No. 3 (1982), pp. 5–48.

6. Cf. Pouliquen, *op. cit.*

7. Which it is impossible to dwell on here for reason of space.

8. Russian notions of "kollektivnost" or "splotchenost".

9. Cf. A. Zinoviev, for instance in: *Le communisme comme realite,* Julliard L'age d'homme. Paris: (1981), p. 333. These notions and formulations are also very present and explicit in official Soviet rhetoric about basic labor. Collectives: see, among many examples: pp. 11–18 of V.A. Tikhonov: "Pervichny trudovoi Kollektiv v seljskom khoziaistve", *Ekonomika,* 280 pp., Moscow, 1979. See also the 8th clause of the Soviet Constitution, and comments on it by L.I. Brezhnev during the 24th Party Congress. Western economists are often too quick to consider these aspects as "pure ideology" or "pure propaganda".

10. At least on a local and regional scale. Administrative control is more effective for geographical than for inter-enterprise or inter-sector mobility.

11. Cf. Pouliquen, *op. cit.*

12. Cf. the "Report from Novosibirsk".

13. Cf. V.F. Bashmachinkov (pp. 8–90 and 247–275) in Tikhonov, *op. cit.*

14. Cf. for instance I.G. Alexeiev (pp. 161–195) in Tikhonov, *op. cit.*

15. Speech at Smolensk, reported in a slightly condensed version in Pravda, June 28, 1984, p. 2.

16. In this respect, K.E. Wadekin clearly shows the strongly constrained and submitted character of the new brigades (or zvenos): deep assymetry of the actual "contractual" duties; non-respect of the principles of voluntary adhesion and of inviolability of the means controlled by the collective; total dependence of the brigade for its inputs and the outflow of its outputs, etc. These features result broadly, in practice, from mere official regulations and not only from their "local deformation". See Wadekin (K.E.) "Contract" and "normless" labor on Soviet farms. R.L.R. Bulletin; February 8.

17. This key to the distribution of the collective wages is collectively worked out at brigade (zveno) level. However, it is significant that it can be distorted by the enterprise management. This rule, quite typical of the logic of collective control, was introduced precisely to thwart the worker's spontaneous leaning to egalitarian distribution (taking only working time into account).

18. It seems more consistent with the "responsibilities" system on a household basis in China, cf. C. Aubert in the present volume.

19. Since it would require an incredible upheaval of the social basis of Soviet power, and since this power still has alternative logic II at its disposal. Through an economic approach, Wadekin and Ellman seem to come to the same scepticism on this point.

20. For instance, the "Guektarchiki" family group in Azerbaidjan (which is also relevant to a patriarchal logic).

21. The spontaneous practice of local managers and officials seems to be "neo-collectivist" (authoritarian creation of the brigades, etc.).

22. Cf. p. 288 in "Narodnoe Khoziaistvo USSR, 1982".

References

1. Bashmachinkov, pp. 116 and 247–275 in *Tikhonv, op. cit.*
2. C. Bettelheim, *Les luttes de classes en URSS. Les domines* (Paris: 1982).
3. B. Chavance, *Le systeme economique sovietique* (Paris: 1983).
4. G. Duchene, *L'officiel et le parallele dans l'economie sovietique. Libre no 7* (1980), pp. 151–188.
5. A.I. Katorguin, *Organizacia Trudovikh kollectivov v rastenievodstve* (Moscow: 1979).
6. B. Kerblay, *La societe sovietique contemporaine* (Paris: 1977).
7. J. Kornai, *Economics of Shortage* (Amsterdam: 1980).
8. A. Nove, *L'economie sovietique* (Paris: 1981).
9. A. Pouliquen, "L'organization du travail agricole et le controle social de l'activite economique en URSS". INRA/Economie et Sociololgie Rurales, Montpellier, 1982, republished without appendicies in *Revue d'Etudes Comparatives Est-Ouest* (September: 1982), Vol. 13, pp. 5–48.
10. M. Rakovski, *Le marxisme face aux pays de l'Est* (Paris: 1977).
11. J. Sapir, *Travail et travailleurs en URSS* (Paris: 1984).
12. L. Schapiro and J. Godson, *L'ouvrier sovietique Illusions et realites* (Paris: 1983).
13. E. Teague, "The USSR law on work collectives: worker's control or workers controlled?" RFE/RL 184, Munich, 1984, 16 pp.
14. V.A. Tikhonov, Editor, *Pervichnyi trudovoi kollectiv v seljskom khoziaistve* (Moscow: 1979).
15. K.E. Wadekin, "Labor remuneration in the socialized agriculture of Eastern Europe and the Soviet Union". RFE/RL 8, February 1984.
16. K.E. Wadekin, " 'Contract' and 'normless' labour on Soviet farms". RFE/RL 8, February 1984.
17. T.I. Zaslavskaya, "Ekonomicheskoe povedenie i economicheskoe razvitie", *EKO.*
18. A. Zinoviev, *Le communisme comme realite* (Paris: 1981).

5

Agrarian Structures and Policies in the USSR, China, and Hungary: A Comparative View

Karl-Eugen Wädekin

Introduction

The paper argues that the present differences of agrarian structures and policies among the three countries are to be explained, largely though not wholly, by differences in their factor endowment and levels of economic development. Therefore, despite their common adherence to Marxist-Leninist ideology, differences have developed among these countries in the specific way that this ideology is applied to agriculture. Where recent changes in labor organization and in local administration show seeming similarities, their actual contents and effects may differ widely, just as formerly a uniform Soviet-type model was forced upon them all, despite widely differing socio-economic conditions. The present organization of agriculture in China and Hungary does not preclude the possibility that one day the current appeals to private income incentives may lead to a situation where not only the application of Marxism-Leninism will be changed, but some of its basic tenets may also be infringed upon.

Leaving aside Yugoslavia and Poland, where collectivization has been renounced for the time being, the diversity among countries with socialized agriculture has been increasing during the past quarter of a century, while at the same time retaining the label of Marxism-Leninism. The present paper deals with the USSR, China and Hungary, three among which the differences have become most conspicuous. It argues that the diversity stems mainly from practical economic policy rather than from ideological orientation. Therefore, it is the socio-economic setting in its recent development which is subsequently investigated in order to find out whether it has sufficient explanatory power with regard to the differences of agrarian policies and performance in these three countries.[1]

For the present purpose the differing levels of industrial development are assumed to be known, and merely illustrated inversely, in Table 5.3, by the

55

share agriculture contributes to the national income (socialist definition). The relevant data show China on the expected much lower level of non-agricultural development, and Hungary on about the same level as the USSR.[2]

Differences in Factor Endowment
and Productivity

The most important difference is that of agricultural land per head of the total population.[3] By that indicator the Soviet Union is almost eight times and Hungary three times better off than China. If the number of people working each 100 hectares of "land units"[4] is examined, one finds that the differences are yet greater. They reflect only in part the stage of industrial development, i.e., the amount of labor-saving inputs supplied to agriculture. However, output per worker, measured in grain, meat and milk, mirrors the greater labor productivity caused by the intensity and quality of land use as well as of work. The number of workers per land unit is double in Hungary compared to the USSR, but in recompense each worker in Hungarian agriculture produces 11.9 tonnes of grain, 1289 kilograms of meat and 2308 kilograms of milk, whereas its Soviet counterpart's output was only 5.4 tonnes and 485 and 2856 kilograms, respectively, in 1982.[5] Thus, the smaller number of workers per land unit in Soviet agriculture is mainly due to a more extensive type of land utilization, not to a higher technological level. The number of workers per unit of land in China is 20 times greater than in the Soviet case, but output of grain and meat per worker is not 20 times, but only 6–7 times smaller, while hardly any milk is produced on Chinese farms.

Land productivity differs in similar ways, although here the climate and quality of soils have an additional impact. While in Northeast China many farms suffer from disadvantages of nature comparable to those under which much of Soviet grain is produced, the share of such areas is greater in the USSR. More of Chinese farming is carried out on irrigated land under a warmer climate. Such land accounts for nearly half of the total arable land and very often permits double-cropping. This is part of the reason for the higher Chinese hectare yields. It has to be added, though, that they may be lower to the degree that the actually sown area is larger than the official statistics tell, as American satellite photos seem to indicate. Hungary has little irrigation but also little land under a harsh climate. That her grain yields were about double those of Soviet yields during most of the 1960s may be attributed mainly to this fact. However, for the fact that, since then her grain yields have risen to three times the Soviet level and now exceed the Chinese level by one half, there is hardly any other explanation than just better farming methods and organization.

The density of livestock holdings per land unit is greatest in China, and the meat output per livestock unit[6] surpasses that of Soviet animals by more than one third, while Hungary keeps almost as many animals per land unit.

But their productivity is in Hungary more than double that of the Chinese, and trebles the Soviet level. Leaving aside the traditionally insignificant role of milk production in China, which is carried out on a very low level of productivity, one finds Hungarian production of milk definitely superior to that of Soviet cows; again, these higher yields were achieved only during the past ten years, starting from a level roughly equal.

It is not possible to quantify the input of capital in a comprehensive and comparable way. To a degree, irrigation installations are a capital asset, independent from their incorporating traditional or modern technology, and Chinese agriculture is richly endowed with them. Recently, their total value was estimated at roughly 100 billion yuan.[7] Available and at the same time roughly comparable indicators for other capital inputs are few, the most general and prominent among them being numbers of tractors and combine harvesters for machinery in general and fertilizer quantities supplied for current inputs from industry. In view of the shorter distances between farms and fields, Hungarian agriculture seems to be on about an equal level of tractor and harvester availability with Soviet farms.[8] By another measure, which is not available for China, the level also was almost equal in 1982: 372 kWh of electrical energy consumed in agriculture per hectare in the Soviet Union, and 394 in Hungary.[9] In view of the greater output per hectare as well as per worker, capital productivity must be higher in Hungary. Chinese productivity of capital is high for the mere fact that not much of it is put in; if one relates the tractor and harvester numbers to the hectares without regard to double-cropping, then the irrigation part of capital is indirectly taken into account in the calculation. If one does not do so, the machinery outfit and fertilizer application looks yet poorer, particularly because most Chinese tractors are very small and are used largely for transportation because of the shortage of trucks.

The overall impression thus gained is unequivocal: Chinese agriculture produces with immense labor inputs and very intensive land use, i.e., on a level of traditional agriculture with little capital and low labor and animal productivity, but with high capital and medium-high land productivity. The productivity of Soviet agriculture is low by any measure, even for labor, the latter being applied on amply available land resources. Hungary leads on all accounts: in land, animal and capital productivity she comes close to a good West European level, while her agricultural labor productivity still is low by Western, yet high by Eastern, standards. Put in other terms, all this means that, in both Chinese and Hungarian agriculture, the productive factors in short supply are land and capital. As land cannot be augmented in either country or else only at high cost of land improvement, it is capital which has the greatest potential for increasing productivity and thereby output. On the other hand, labor is abundant in China and in sufficient supply in Hungary, so that in both cases labor-saving farm organization or devices should range only second in priority. In the Soviet Union, too, labor shortage is not an urgent problem, except in some regions.[10] So the low Soviet land and animal productivity should be increased in the first place while utilizing available capital more efficiently. This can be achieved without great additional capital inputs until productivity approaches, though not equals, because of the less favorable natural endowment, the level of Hungarian agriculture.

Since this has not been achieved so far, there must be other influences that in Soviet agriculture prevent the basic production factors from coming to bear. Apparently, those influences could likely be overcome by moderate reforms without fundamentally changing the Marxist-Leninist system of planning and directing the economy.

With all this, one has, of course, to bear in mind that regional differences exist in countries as vast as the USSR and China. Yet if in some regions the above conclusions do not apply, they must be, against the background of statistical averages, all the more relevant for the remaining regions.

The Development of Demand
and Supply of Food

It is an established truth that the performance of agriculture has been unsatisfactory up to the present in the USSR, and that it has greatly improved during the past fifteen years in Hungary, and during the past six years in China. It is also generally known that this statement has to be made against a background of rapidly rising demand in the Soviet Union and China, which results from income as well as population increases. In contrast, income and population increases have been moderate in Hungary. Part, though not the whole, of the Soviet food imports and of the Hungarian export surpluses are due to this differing development of demand. Assuming an income elasticity of demand for food of 0.6 for the Soviet Union and 0.5 for Hungary, one may roughly estimate the increase of overall demand for food during 1970–82 at roughly 30–35 and about 10 per cent, respectively.[11] At the same time, overall Hungarian agricultural output, according to FAO indices, increased by 43 per cent and that of the USSR by only 15 per cent. Even with a considerable range of error, the expanding export capacities situation in the one, and the deteriorating supply situation in the other case, become obvious. Moreover, the Soviet development has to be seen against an excess demand existing already at the beginning of the period.

For China, less data of this kind are available, but a great excess demand is unmistakable during the period dealt with here although against a background of markedly growing food output per head. Overall real purchasing power, as implied by a Chinese source, has increased by 73 per cent during 1978–82,[12] which no imaginable growth of food production can match. However, most of the increase, 84.9 per cent, was among the rural population where it consisted to a large extent in own consumption of food in kind. The income growth in urban areas was said, by the same source, to have been only 25.6 per cent. In addition, the supply of nonfood consumer goods was stepped up. As to the preceding first half of the

1970s, it may be assumed that income growth was negligible, but that total Chinese population still increased by about 2 per cent p.a., so that the FAO index of per head food consumption showed modest growth of 0.35 per cent on the annual average 1971–77, probably not changing the already existing demand excess.

Thus, demand for food has greatly intensified in China and the USSR during the 1970s and into the 1980s. With a view to agrarian policy, the question emerges whether a Marxist-Leninist regime is, and feels, forced to yield to such pressure. The course of events has shown that both Moscow and Peking did feel they had to act under its impact, though they did so in different ways. Hungary did so at an earlier stage, through changing her agrarian policy, beginning in the mid-1960s, and therefore is not under a similar pressure now.

Food Imports as a Way Out

One possible shortcut to relief consists of importing the quantities needed to satisfy demand. Exactly during the time span with which we are dealing here, Moscow began spending large and increasing sums of hard currency for food imports, mainly to create a sufficient feed basis for the domestic livestock sector. It is obvious that China, in view of its population numbers and its limited capacity for non-agricultural exports, is not able to import enough for appreciably narrowing the gap between supply and demand for food, except for a few urban agglomerations. Although quite impressive in absolute value, the net imports have been negligible per head of China's total population. Even with grain, which accounts for most imports, they figured at a modest net 17 kilograms per head on the annual average 1980–82 (see Table 5.4). The Soviet Union, whose imports have become sizable on a per head basis apparently hoped that the foreign trade shortcut would be needed only for the short or medium term. After that period Soviet domestic food production was expected to be up to its task, mainly through greatly increased investment in agriculture and the food sector as a whole. China could not hope, for obvious reasons, to overcome the situation by heavy investment.

Restrictions on Domestic Solutions

Only when it turned out that added investment alone could not achieve the needed output growth did the Soviet leaders begin serious consideration of another (the abortive attempt of 1965 being the previous) restructuring of the organization of their socialist agriculture, because in spite of the capital inputs, neither labor nor land productivity had risen sufficiently under the existing system. As to land, all three countries are in the same situation of more or less exhausted reserves. In China, mobilization of her immense labor numbers has been the obvious option for solving the problem.

Hungary had earlier, and rather successfully, undertaken moderate reforms of her agricultural organization and labor incentives in combination with as much investment as she could afford, including a sizable contribution from Western technology and know-how. In principle China as well as the Soviet Union by now are trying a basically comparable course, though in very different ways and degrees. The differences are greatest in the methods of planning, managing and remunerating agricultural production on the farm and local level. Before looking at them more closely, two points of difference among the three countries must be mentioned.

One of them is the way of restricting consumer demand, particularly its growth. Up to the present, the Soviet leadership has not been willing to let prices for food rise in public retail outlets. These prices have been kept stable since 1962, when Khrushchev's raising of them led to great dissatisfaction among the population and to local riots. This price stability has lasted so long that by now consumer price increases of a magnitude that would appreciably relieve the pressure of demand are so great that they may be politically and economically unwise, or feasible only over a number of years and with concomitant considerable wage increases.

The post-Mao Chinese leaders resorted to consumer price increases in state retailing only to a small degree, but did tolerate and openly admit a moderate inflation and stimulate growth of the non-agricultural consumer good production and services. Hungary with some caution applied all these means. Food prices were raised in consecutive steps, some inflation has been tolerated and admitted, and the production of non-food consumer goods and services was increased. In the Hungarian case, the achievement of an approximate balance of supply and demand for food, as distinct from the imbalance up to the period in question, is due to this demand side policy as much as to the enlarged and improved supply. In China, imbalance continues to exist in the non-food, and regionally also in the food sphere, but less so than a decade earlier, and on an appreciably rising standard of living. In the Soviet Union, the imbalance has become greater instead of smaller, and a feeling of stagnation in consumer goods supply per head seems to be widespread, although it may not be wholly justified numerically in the non-food sphere.

The second factor is the sheer size of a country, which is of more than quantitative importance. It implies not only distances but also greater regional differences and natural impediments to transport. Where an economy has not yet reached a high level of development, the transmission of informations and directives is also made more difficult. The ease of making a telephone call from Washington to Los Angeles or to a small town in Oregon is in sharp contrast to the time-consuming difficulty of doing the same between Moscow and Tashkent and the near-impossibility of putting in an ordinary quick call to the manager of a large farm in Kazakhstan. The problem is still more formidable in China, while it is small in comparison in Hungary. Nationality problems may compound these difficulties, and a regional inclination towards self-assertion may make information and control still more difficult between center and periphery. While problems with nationalities may be less in China because of the overwhelming majority of the Han people, transportation and communications between the regions of that country may be assumed to be even more difficult than in the USSR.

Size has also an international aspect. The role of a super-power not only puts a heavy burden on the economy, but also makes Soviet economic change more risky, especially with a view to preserving some degree of uniformity of economic structure and political intent within the orbit of Moscow's hegemony. It seems that for the time being China bothers less about that aspect and gives priority to improving her economy and food supply.

For a small and nationally almost homogeneous country like Hungary, such problems matter less. Not only has balancing food supply and income become less of a problem there, but, more important, decentralization of decision-making is less of a threat to control by the central government. There are other reasons why the agrarian "Hungarian model" can hardly be transferred as a whole to other countries under Communist rule, but the above factors alone clearly represent serious barriers to such an effort.

Mobilization of Labor Reserves— Mao's and Deng's Approach

Already Mao's "Great Leap Forward" (1958–59) with the People's Communes replacing the collective farms of the Soviet type can largely be explained in terms of socio-economic, not ideological goals within already established politico-ideological parameters. Veiled Soviet criticism of them was directed at their being premature, not at their being a deviation from Marxism-Leninism. In essence, it was an effort to overcome existing economic and organizational difficulties by mobilizing the abundant mass of Chinese rural labor for agriculture proper as well as for infrastructural works, including large-scale water management and non-agricultural economic activities in the countryside without paying an adequate remuneration for such work. What was needed for this purpose was strict, quasi-military discipline (instead of incentives) and control over those masses. For enforcement and control and for productive use of mass labor, ideological-political, administrative-political and technical-economic cadres were needed. These were too few in number to be spread over nearly 700,000 collective farms and they were concentrated on 26,578 People's Communes by the end of 1958. The cadres oversaw production, capital construction and local administration. In addition, the large size of People's Communes made it easier, though not more efficient, to concentrate the investment means gained by holding down consumption.

We do not know whether Mao thought in these terms, and what else was on his mind, but it seems evident that extreme mobilization of the abundant labor factor on gigantic farms, which at the same time were administration units, was the dominant feature of the venture. Within a few years it became obvious that neither the enforced work discipline nor the unit size were economically effective, and very likely they did not even bring the necessary administrative control over as vast and variegated a country as China. Yet it took many years of setbacks and turmoil, including factional strife after the death of Mao, until Deng Xiao Ping was able to put his concept into practice. Under his leadership present-day Chinese agriculture and rural organization turned into the opposite of the Maoist and the Stalinist models in many respects. All the same, one basic idea is common to both: to mobilize that factor of production, labor, which is amply available.

The new organization, which has extensively been dealt with in Western publications, is based on motivating peasants to more and better work through incentives that appeal at their individual, rather than collective, income aspirations and even their ownership instincts. At the same time it provides for only limited mechanization, mainly of an overhead character and of work processes where machines are not labor but time-saving or intensify land use.

Reform or Organization?

Applying Morris Bornstein's characterization of the post-Stalin model of a socialist economy,[13] and adding large farm size to his point 2, one finds that in Chinese agriculture, up to 1983, these points were not wholly abandoned. Even concerning point 2, collective land ownership continues juridically, although actual land use has become private and small-scale, yet with strong state influence. Four of the points were still wholly valid (Nos. 1, 3, 6, and 9), and the remaining four continued to apply at least in parts. Point 4: Output for local consumption was no longer planned in detail, but procurements/deliveries of main products were, up to and including 1984. Point 5: Control of wage funds had been substituted by contracts, but most of the means of production still were produced and in part also distributed, thereby rationed, by administrative orders. However, it is hard to define how much of the control over distribution remained with the center, and what share of inputs, e.g. building materials now was produced privately. Point 7: Money was no longer passive, but did not yet play a decisive role on its own. Point 8: At least that part of earnings which derives from sales to the state, was determined by quantities of produce.

Thus, in the light of these nine points, the Chinese deviation did not seem to be a fundamental one in ideological terms, especially so as in some East European countries, points 3 through 6 are not strictly adhered to either, not even in the USSR. The reorganization of China's agriculture has been aimed mainly at mobilizing within the existing overall system the available great labor resources by appealing to the interest and initiative of the smallest social unit after the mass mobilization through the People's Communes and their brigades failed. Still one correctly tends to consider the new organization a real reform because of the important second point, namely the abandonment of large-scale production as an essential feature of a socialist agrarian economy.

Outside agriculture, small-scale, in part even private enterprise clearly is tolerated only in a subsidiary function in all these countries, but in agriculture its role is appreciable in the USSR, important in Hungary and predominant in China. It is China that has gone farthest towards small-scale organization of agricultural production under what is called the "household responsibility system". It would be saying too much, however, if one called it wholly privatized. Not only the land, but also what Lenin during the NEP period called the "commanding heights" of the economy, have remained under control of the state and its organizations ("the society").

One may make the point that the Chinese economy still is similar to that of the Soviet Union during most of the 1920s, and therefore Lenin's NEP model more appropriate than Stalinist collectivization. In this way, present-day Chinese agrarian policy would still be truly Leninist-Marxist. Be that as it may, it still is something special to retreat from socialization once it has been achieved, whether prematurely or not, to a less collectivist stage. Such reversing of "the course of history" must look questionable to a Marxist-Leninist. Together with the partial deviations pointed out above, it really is a bold and unorthodox undertaking. Yet it does not necessarily follow that it means an abandonment of Marxism-Leninism or even a long-term course in a direction leading away from it, even if factual socio-economic life may bring about such a development as time goes by.

For Hungary, reviewing the nine points shows that in the economy as a whole, in Hewett's words, "they have barely begun to take measures to attack the basic expectations listed above" and that the country "has not yet fully embraced the radical reform option".[14] Yet in collective and private agriculture things look somewhat different. Points 4 and 8 have wholly been abandoned, and more or less significant inroads were made on three other points. The means of production are not fully rationed since a considerable part of investment does not depend on central funds (point 5); prices, although set centrally for their more important part, are changed quite frequently, and reflect more the supply-demand relationship than costs (point 6); money flows continue to be adjusted centrally but are allowed some active role on their own (point 6). Thus, less than half of the nine points are fully retained. As distinct from China, large-scale farming has been retained, but in a flexible combination with private small-scale production.

The essence of the change in Hungarian agriculture consists of its being controlled in an indirect and partly decentralized way. On this account, the smallness of the country seems to play a significant role, whereas for both China and Soviet Union, their immense size is an important factor working in favor of retaining central management and decision making, not only in the political but also in the economic sphere. Concerning availability of capital, Hungarian agriculture has not been in an ideal, but surely in a much better position than its Chinese counterpart. Labor was amply available only up to the early 1960s, but less so at the time when the reform was conceived. At that time, the problem became one of activating hidden labor reserves, such as those under or above working age, the housewives, etc., not of mobilizing a surplus, at least not a surplus in relation to the existing level of mechanization of work and to the availability of capital in general.

This was effected quite successfully in those fields where the degree of mechanization was lowest: livestock, fruit, wine, vegetable production, in the beginning also row crops, and it was done by tolerating private plot activities as well as the formation of small groups of manual workers in the plantations and fields, who received a fixed share of the output in kind (Nadudvar system), and combining private and collective work in the animal sector. The approach had its economic rationale and did not contradict basic tenets of Marxism-Leninism. And, of course, it happened to be handled skillfully. Where and when field or livestock operations became more mechanized, the Nadudvar System was dropped or changed, but bonuses according to productive performance and the combination of private and collective production activities remained.

In most of Soviet agriculture and its research and decision-making centers, it is realized that the sector has to become more efficient. The change in methods, though not in principle and in structure, was already great from Stalin's last years to the end of the era of Khrushchev. After his demise, even "reform" was an official notion, although less for the collective than the state farm sector. During the 1970s it was rather reorganization, integration, technical modernization and improvement of the existing system that was propagated, together with the greater priority for agricultural investment and remuneration that had started earlier. Decentralization hardly entered into the debates.

Of the three basic factors of production, none has been in surplus in the USSR since the New Lands were opened up (1954–56), and labor reserves dwindled steadily. Given the overall parameters with no single factor in surplus for mobilization, one might conceive of a reform of Soviet agriculture which resembles the Hungarian. However, the example of the other East European countries shows that even reforms of the moderate Hungarian type require an unusual audacity and skill under a Communist regime with its paramount interest in interior political stability. The force of inertia must be particularly great in the Soviet Union with its size and national diversity, with its super power demands on the economy and its social element of a bureaucracy which was established half a generation earlier than in the other countries, including China. There was some movement in the Soviet Union, all the same, but it was clearly the least among the three countries under scrutiny. The capital means of production, having become available more amply than previously, today are rationed less strictly, and some leeway was given for decentralized investment by leaving a percentage of profits with the farms for the corresponding decisions (Bornstein's point 5). It has to be added that point 2 also no longer applies fully. Not collective but state farming today is dominant in Soviet agriculture. Yet this does not, and was not meant to, signify a change of structure. It may be considered a deviation from Marx's, but not from Kautsky's or Lenin's Marxism. All the other points have remained basically unchanged since their overall relaxation after Stalin's death.

Decentralizing Labor Organization
Within the Farm

The formation of smaller units of labor within the huge farms (concerning our addition to point 2) and their remuneration according to productive performance instead of by fixed work norms deserves closer scrutiny. Are there parallels between recent Soviet, Hungarian and Chinese practice of remunerating farm teams according to output? Discussing this question one first has to state that it boils down to the decision-making power and size of the unit, whereas remuneration according to productive performance, instead of work norms fulfilled, is not new in any of the countries of "really existing socialism". Such remuneration in fact has been the essence of collective farming since Stalin. It was somewhat weakened during the 1960s in East Europe and the Soviet Union on collective farms by introducing a guaranteed minimum basic payment for work done, whereas on state farms with their fixed wages the bonus and premium element in wages was strengthened. The size of the wage fund in collective and of the bonus/premium fund in state farms for a given year still largely depends on that farm's profits of the year. The recent change then lies in measuring and remunerating the productive performance, not of the whole labor force of the farm but of its subunits, yet the basic idea of the payment system remains the same.

In practice, productive performance, as far as it is influenced by humans, depends not only on the efforts and skill of the labor unit, but also on the rationality of the set tasks and the supply of inputs needed to fulfill them. If task and inputs are not adequate, the efforts and skill will come to naught, and the incentive character of payment according to output will be lost or even turned into a disincentive. Therefore, in order to make such payment effective, the labor unit and its management should have the right to reject unreasonable tasks and to demand the inputs it needs. It should also be able to ask for other tasks and to reject inputs which it does not need, because the cost of inputs received is deducted from the value of the overall output delivered. It is self-evident that, under such conditions, the subunits will perform badly where the tasks are fixed from above without regard for or detailed knowledge of the local conditions, and will perform better if it has some real bargaining power with regard to the setting of the tasks. Similarly, adequate, in quantity, quality and assortment, supplies of inputs (fertilizer, plant protection chemicals, machinery, feed, building materials, repair and maintainence services, etc.) will *ceteris paribus* enhance or jeopardize the incentive effect of the payment system. Because nowadays not production but rather procurement or sales tasks are set from above, much also depends on how great a share of output has to be earmarked for such compulsory sales. If that share is high, it effectively predetermines the production program.

The small group system was chosen as the unit of reference for remuneration assignment, because the whole collective farm had proven too large to make effective a performance-oriented system. Five hundred workers on 5000 hectares of land of unequal quality and with different functions of the labor subunits make it impossible for the individual worker to assess how much of his own effort goes into his final remuneration and how much is made useless by the laziness or inefficiency of the others; or else, how lazy and inefficient can he be and still get a good wage because of the efforts of the others. The smaller the unit, the more he can see of the interdependencies of efforts, the extreme being the single individual who alone decides and assesses his efforts and their reward.

It does not necessarily follow that the smallest team or the individual and his family always is the optimal labor unit. Optimality may depend on a number of factors, such as the kind of product, of work and its mechanization not only because of economies of scale, but also because of the given field and herd sizes under an inherited or prescribed socio-economic setting, whether economically rational or not. The important point is that each group member can observe and judge the performance of the others as to their influence on his own efforts. Thus, payment according to productive performance does not mean much in itself, as long as its productivity-increasing effect depends on a number of factors external to the labor unit. Any comparative assessment of the recent forms of labor organization and payment in the three countries under review has to take these factors into account.

In China the quantity of available industrially produced inputs is generally (with some exceptions) very low. Abstracting from the question of the rationality of the set tasks, productivity of labor therefore depends almost exclusively on workers' efforts. The small size of the teams, mostly families, makes the effort put in easily observable by each member, and the connection with remuneration easily visible. In addition, it seems fairly evident that, in order to invite such effort, the team (family) should have autonomy in planning and organizing its own work. To the degree that more inputs become available, their adequate and timely supply will become a factor influencing productive success, in dependence of which the labor effort may have greater or smaller effect. This may already gain importance for the "specialized households", which are given priority in the supply of inputs. But for the great majority of Chinese farm households this is a matter of the future.

It is hard to judge, however, whether the small team in Chinese agriculture has bargaining power in fixing its tasks, that is, whether it is a partner with equal rights when the procurement contracts with the production brigade, farm section, or other superordinated organization are concluded. Reports indicating the government has difficulties in getting enough of those products produced and procured for which the price structure is unfavourable, seem to imply that the teams are not simply fulfilling orders, or that the requested sales leave them some leeway for producing beyond the quantities stipulated by the contracts. Vice versa, some products with favorable prices have been produced in surplus in recent time. On the whole, the growth of Chinese agricultural production in recent years is an indication that this "responsibility system" works well under the given circumstances and overhead management and apparently includes some indulgence towards private interest. The actual pattern is still developing with some flexibility and regional variants.

In Hungary, the Nadudvar system of the early 1960s has not been the most conspicuous feature of agricultural organization under the reform, although in a sense its basic idea is preserved in the combination of private and collective production. For example, a great number of pigs are owned by the collective farm and fattened on private premises and by private labor but with feed purchased in part from the public sector. Or there is fruit and wine growing with division of labor involving manual work by individuals or small teams and mechanized work by the farm brigade. In addition there is private plot farming and many possibilities exist for selling its output on the free market as well as to the public sector. Most important, however, is the fact that rigid planning in physical quantities was abandoned, and thereby much bargaining and decision-making power given to the large farm. The farm management on its side distributes or contracts tasks to the smaller units, from the brigade down to the family, very much on terms of commercial partners. What seems typical for Hungarian collective agriculture is the fact that, on the basis of a common pattern, there are various forms, and that their application is flexible, depending on product, kind and quantity of available capital inputs, market access and other local conditions. Moreover, they are compatible with or complementary to private sideline production. It is this overall setting and only in part the form and size of group organization of labor that have made such arrangements work towards the known Hungarian production success.

The Soviet application of product-oriented labour remuneration for "normless teams" or "contract brigades" on farms is characterized by a number of restrictions. The group must not be too small, consisting of either a whole brigade (a few dozen people including seasonal auxiliary workers) or a *zveno* (rarely less than a dozen people, if seasonal workers are included)[15]; it has very limited bargaining power as to what tasks it is assigned and which inputs it receives at what time; in practice, though not on principle, its workers are sometimes ordered to do other than the contracted work; finally, from the almost permanent non-fulfillment of the production plans of Soviet agriculture as a whole it follows that, more often than, not these labor units will not fulfill their plans and therefore get only the basic minimum wage. As long as they represent only a minority, as they did up to 1984, examples of successful teams cannot serve as reliable predictors of the viability of such organizations once they are introduced throughout Soviet agriculture. In all this, the rigid and cumbersome planning system as well as the eagerness not to let things get out of control will play an important role. A recent press report by the chairman of the trade union council of Orenburg province put it very clearly that this remuneration system in itself has little effect: "One has only, it is being said, to bring people together in the corresponding brigades and links (*zven'ya*), to fix formally in a document their task, assign them land and machinery, sign a contract, and then things work out by themselves. *Practice tells a different story.*[16] (Emphasis added. —K.-E.W.) And that author goes on saying that "educational work" to arouse "the sense of collectivity" and "social activity" has to accompany the introduction. In other words, he advocates an element of "moral" incentive, which *per se* is independent of a possible reform of the organization of farming and its material incentives.

As long as those circumstances are not changed, the Soviet venture neither promises an appreciable incentive effect, nor can be considered as more than a purely formal parallel to its Hungarian and Chinese counterparts. One thing is sure, however, the Chinese "responsibility team" recently has gone farthest towards making the individual peasant family the basic unit of production. The Hungarians, too, ascribed an important role in the production process to the individual, but more selectively and with some restraint. Moscow gave the existing subunits of the large farms a production-oriented remuneration system, it is true, but did so in ways that made it unlikely to provide appreciable incentives. (Cf. the contributions of M. Ellman, R. and B. Laird, A. Nove and A. Pouliquen in the present volume.)

The present organization of collective labor in Hungarian and Chinese agriculture tends to blur the previous dividing line between the public and the private sector by intensifying their symbiosis. In Soviet agriculture the two continue to be kept more distinctly apart. Moscow tries to take advantage of some untapped labor reserves of the private sector by giving the citizen more opportunities to produce food from his plot and animal holding but attaches a number of strings to such activities. Other than in Hungary and China, exceeding the former upper legal limits on private livestock holdings is conditioned upon delivery contracts with public procurement organizations or with the collective and state farms. Great emphasis is put on channelling private produce into public marketing outlets instead of the free market with its higher prices and less than full control. The contrast of the form and the results with those of Hungary as well as of China is obvious to any visitor of those countries.

A word has to be said about the fact that the Chinese People's Communes were abolished. The previous People's Communes may be seen also as a vehicle for integrating rural agricultural and non-agricultural production, services, procurement, administration, education, social security, militia-territorial defense, and Party and propaganda work on the county (hsiang) level. Such Communes had been previously weakened by transferring much of the actual farm management to the brigade and team level. Now they have lost also their public administration and related functions, which were assigned to what again is the county, in most cases also called a township. What remained is an association for some overhead functions of farming and for rural non-agricultural economic activities of more than a certain size. It may well be that by abrogating the name of People's Commune, verbal expression was given for what since 1980 has been happening in many places.

It is a striking contrast that, at the same time, Soviet agricultural organization made a move in the opposite direction, towards amalgamation of functions through the "Agro-Industrial Association", first on the lowest, the *raion,* level then also on the provincial and republican level. Although it is directed at unifying the food complex only (agriculture and its backward and forward linkages), not the other public functions, the RAPO (raionnoe agro-promyshlennoe ob"edinenie) is designed for managing within one comprehensive local complex many functions, which formerly were under the jurisdiction of various branch ministries. Whether it will work satisfactorily may be doubted but cannot be discussed here.

Conclusion

It may safely be assumed that in the three countries dealt with above, Marxist-Leninist ideology has been and continues to be taken seriously by those in power. Divergences in its application in practical policy therefore may be explained mainly by the different conditions under which the ruling Communists have been acting after collectivization was completed. The impact of the personality of the various leaders, can not be denied, yet one has to keep in mind that the given conditions exert great influence on who comes to and stays in supreme power, and what kind of policy he is able to pursue realistically.

The historical heritage of a nation and the political culture based on it surely also have an influence, and moreover very much contribute to what kind of politicians will rule a country. But while such factors can hardly be quantified, they are to a considerable extent reinforced by the socio-economic conditions of the present time and recent past. As a consequence, the above comparative analysis of those conditions indirectly takes into account, if only in part, such no-quantifiable factors.

The present paper has sought to demonstrate the socio-economic basis of the differing agrarian structures and policies in the Soviet Union, China and Hungary with regard mainly to two aspects, the factor endowment, which urged though not forced upon the Communist leaders certain measures in the food sector and, secondly, that, even where recent measures of labor organizations and of administration on the local and farm level seem rather similar, their actual contents and effects may differ quite widely. This argument may be taken to the higher administrative structure as well, but limits of space prevent this. It has been shown that the basic forms of local or central management of agriculture (and of the economy at large) may conform to pre-established political notions without revealing much about the reality underlying them. The differences may be of some other dimension, e.g., the role of plan tasks, input supply, etc., in the product-oriented labor remuneration. These are established truths in the West, but so far not sufficiently taken into account with regard to Communist regimes. It is, of course, also true that the conditions for applying a socio-economic system may differ widely and a uniform policy be forced upon them all the same, usually with dire results, as in the not-too-distant past of Communist agrarian policies.

Simply to speak of "socialist" for characterizing what the production modes of agriculture in countries under Communist rule have in common, is less and less meaningful. By the same token, the word "capitalist" may convey an idea of the principles governing the western economies at large, but would give only a very vague notion about how the agricultural sector works within, say, the European Community or North America or Japan. "Typical" features of Communist agrarian policy such as fixed administrative prices, procurement quotas, even some central planning, are not alien to much of "capitalist" farming (e.g. the British marketing boards). Apart from the overall economic setting in socialist countries, their farm sectors have basically one major trait in common, namely they start from the Soviet model, which calls itself Marxist-Leninist and was established by Stalin half a century ago. Up to the early 1950s, this model was authoritative from East Germany to North Korea and China. It has left an imprint on the subsequent development of all these agricultural sectors since then, even where explicit or implicit deviations from that model came about. But it also has developed and diversified to a remarkable degree since then. Even the Soviet system underwent some modification.

One important question remains, though. Even with the basic Marxist-Leninist tenets still taken for granted among all Communist leaders, one may suspect that the present Chinese indulgence towards the family unit of labor organization and private small-scale production and trade could unfold with an unwanted momentum of its own. A stage might be approached then, where those tenets are seriously endangered by a kind of capitalist development which the leaders cannot stop or reverse at will. Or the Hungarian economy might reach a stage of efficiency and sophistication when further growth will be impeded by the existing political system, and retaining that system will lead into an economic decline. It seems, however that such problems will not arise during the current decade. Up to now, Moscow has agreed to the agrarian policy of Budapest and has not yet accused Beijing of being anti-Marxist. The scope for tolerated differentiation within the Communist world has become much wider than one could expect in Stalin's and even in Khrushchev's time.

Notes

1. Whenever available, the statistical base for the present article was derived from FAO data because they are thought, in spite of some inherent deficiencies and of their not always being identical with those of the national statistics, to be computed with a view to comparability, including the many estimates which FAO statisticians had to make. Thus, the calories consumption per head (see Table 5.2) seem overstated by them in the case of China. Where FAO data were lacking, CMEA data were used for the USSR and Hungary, rarely Western data, with the one exception of labor, where FAO as well as CMEA and Chinese data are thought to be less informative than those compiled by the CIA in its *Handbook of Economic Statistics*.

2. Taking into account the recent setback of the Soviet food sector and the good performance of its Hungarian counterpart, the approximately equal position of the two countries holds true also for the early 1980s.

3. If one considers that 45 per cent (in 1981) of arable and permanent crop land in China is irrigated, and therefore almost always double-cropped or, not too often, triple-cropped, the actually cultivated area appears greater. The correspondingly changed man/land, man/machinery and fertilizer/land ratios for China in 1981 are added in parentheses in Table 5.1.

4. The land unit applied here is a synthetic measure where one hectare under arable and permanent crops is taken at unity, and other land, basically untilled pasture, at one fifth of its physical dimension. Thereby the great difference of the two kinds of agricultural land in productive potential is approximately taken into account.

5. Derived from FAO output data (*Production Yearbook 1982*, Tabs. 15, 94, 96) and labor numbers in *Handbook 1983*, op. cit, p. 53.

6. The definition of livestock unit applied here equals 1 unit to 1.25 heads of cattle (including calves), or 4 pigs, or 10 goats/sheep, or 100 fowl.

7. *China Daily*, October 8, 1984, p. 3.

8. The corresponding figures for Canadian agriculture: 77 and 320 ha.

9. Derived from *Statisticheskiy ezhegodnik stran-chlenov SEV 1983* (Moscow, 1983), p. 47.

10. It has to be spelled out at this point that labor shortage or abundance is not an absolute notion, but always a function of the availability and utilization of fixed as well as turnover capital.

11. The estimate is based on the official data for average non-agricultural wages times the number of employed (*Statisticheskiy ezhegodnik stran-chlenov SEV 1983*, pp. 381, 383, 393, 395) deflated by the consumer prices index as estimated in the *Handbook of Economic Statistics 1983* (CIA), p. 51.

12. I am indebted to Dr. Bernd von Sydow, Beijing for information on the Chinese source.

13. Morris Bornstein, "Economic Reform in Eastern Europe", *East European Economies Post-Helsinki* (U.S. Congress, Joint Economic Committee), Washington, D.C., 1977 pp. 103–194 (cf. p. 125). His 9 points were recently rendered by Ed. A. Hewett in his paper for the NASEES annual meeting at Cambridge, March 24–26, 1984, in the following shorter version: "1. All significant means of production outside agriculture are nationalized. 2. In agriculture the dominant pattern is [Large-scale production and—add K.-E.W.] collectivization, with nominal cooperative ownership. 3. The economic organization is hierarchical, and decisionmaking concentrated near the top. 4. Output and its distribution are planned in detail in physical units. 5. Means of production are rationed by administrative orders: labor is controlled through controls on wage funds; capital is controlled through the central distribution of investment funds, and through controls on construction materials and the distribution of the machinery and equipment. 6. Prices are set centrally and are changed infrequently. These are cost-plus prices which generally allow the various branches to cover current costs and earn a small profit. 7. Money is passive; planners adjust financial flows to planned physical flows through taxes, subsidies and credits. 8. Incentives to managers and workers emphasize the fulfillment of quantitative targets. 9. Multiple exchange rates (effected through the tax/subsidy system) separate domestic and foreign trade prices."

14. Bornstein, according to Hewett, *op. cit.*

15. At the time of writing, family groups seemed rather the exception. This began to change during 1985, together with increasing emphasis on farm, but not small group autonomy. It remains to be seen, however, whether the parameters of the groups' production activities, as outlined below will also change.

16. *Sel'skaya zhizn'*, May 25, 1984, p. 2.

Table 5.1

The basic parameters of farming, 1970 and 1981

	Soviet Union 1970	1981	Hungary 1970	1981	PR of China[++] 1970	1981
Arable and permanent crop land[+], mill. ha	233.8[+++]	232.2[+++]	5.6	5.3	<125.8	100.9
of which irrigated (%)		7.8		3.5	< 65(?)	45
Other agr. land[+]	374[+++]	373.6[+++]	1.3	1.3	>209.2(?)	285.7
Total population	242.8	267.7	10.3	10.7	838.4	1007.75
Land units[+] per head of total population	1.26	1.15	0.54	0.52	0.2(?)	0.16(20)
agricultural workers per 100 ha land units[+]	12.2	10.2	21.5	20.6	>158	204(130)
Fertilizer (eff. nutrient) supplied per ha land unit[+], kgs.	34	66	143	274	> 18	84(65)
Ha land units[+] per tractor	155	118	81	102	<1000	199(256)
ha grain sown area per grain combine harv.	183	159	254	226		2965

[+] The land unit used here is a synthetic measure, where one hectare of arable and permanent crop land is taken at unity, and one hectare of other agricultural land at one fifth of its physical extension.

[++] The data for China are not very reliable, least so those for 1970; thus land in the 1970 by FAO seems sizably to exaggerate actual cropping of the time, and labor numbers are interpolated between those of 1965 and 1978 as given in Handbook of Economic Statistics 1983, p. 53. Fertilizer supplies are from a Japanese paper for the OECD, Paris. For the man/land and land/inputs ratios added in parentheses for 1981, see footnote 3.

[+++] The FAO data on land used here deviate considerably from those in official Soviet statistics.

Sources: On principle, the data are taken from FAO statistics for comparability, i.e., from Production Yearbook 1976, Table 1 (land) and 1982, Tabs. 1, 2, 3 and 115. However, labor data in Handbook of Economic Statistics, 1983 (CIA), Washington 1983, p. 53, although not beyond criticism, were considered being closer to reality, and therefore used here. Fertilizer, tractor and harvester numbers in the USSR and Hungary in 1970 are from Statisticheskiy ezhegodnik stran-chlenov SEV, Moscow 1983, pp. 186, 221, 223.

Table 5.2

Growth and performance indicators of agriculture in 1971 and 1981

	Soviet Union		Hungary		PR of China	
	1971-72	1981-82	1971-72	1981-82	1971-72	1981-82
Production indices (1974-76 = 100) for:						
Total agricultural	91.6	101.0	90.5	117.3	89.4	124.4
Livestock produce	92.1	105.5	89.4	121.8	86.4	133.9
Grain (excl. legumes)	94.4	92.2	86.1	112.7	86.2	120.3
Food per head	94.5	95.5	91.6	115.2	96.1	112.6
	1969-71	1978-80	1969-71	1978-80	1969-71	1978-82
Consumption of kilo-calories per head of which:	3286	3389	3275	3533	2112	2472
from animal products	782	891	1054	1258	177	254

Source: FAO Production Yearbook, 1982, Rome 1983, Tabs. 5, 7, 8, 9 and 103.

Table 5.3

Development and productivity indicators, 1970 and 1982

	Soviet Union		Hungary		PR of China	
	1970	1982	1970	1982	1972	1982
Share of agriculture in overall national income produced (%)[+)]	22.0	15.3	21.7	18.7	.	about 27 (1983)
livestock unit[++)] per land unit[++)]	0.36	0.44	0.71	0.83	>0.94	1.03
milk, kg per cow	2210	2052	2252	3610	533	699
meat per livestock unit[++)]	0.11	0.11	0.25	0.34	0.09	0.15

[+)] National income socialist definition, i.e., excluding part of the services and not deducting amortization.

[++)] Land unit as in Table 1; the livestock unit applied here equals 1.25 head of cattle, 4 pigs, 10 goats or sheep, 100 fowl.

Sources: For the shares in national income in Hungary and the USSR - Statisticheskiy ezhegodnik ... 1983, p. 41. For China - derived from China Daily, September 15, 1984. p. 2, which indicates "about 35 percent" for agriculture's gross domestic product, obviously including forestry, fisheries and non-agricultural side-line activities. All other data from or derived from FAO Production Yearbook 1982, Tabs. 15, 86, 87, 88 and 96, and ... 1974, Tabs. 108, 109 and 110.

74

Table 5.4

Foreign trade in agricultural products, 1969-71 and 1980-82 (three-year averages)

	Soviet Union		PR of China		Hungary	
	1969-71	1980-82	1969-71	1980-82	1969-71	1980-82
Balance of foreign trade in agricultural prod. (million US-$)	- 720	- 16699	+ 229	- 4120	+ 179	+ 1199
Per head of total population ($)	- 3	- 62	- 0.3	- 4	+ 17	+ 112
Net imports (-) or exports (+) of grain (in million US-$)	+ 373	- 6389	- 99	- 3407	+ 1	+ 219
in thsd. tonnes	+ 5498	- 35955	- 3187	- 17586	+ 37	+1283
in kilograms per head of total population	+ 23	- 134	- 4	- 17	+ 3.6	+ 120
Net imports (-) or exports (+) of oil-seeds (in million US-$)	+ 3	+ 264	+ 2	+ 35	- 34	- 179
in thsd. tonnes	+ 30	- 1014	+ 32	+ 184	- 321	- 582
in kilograms per head of population	+ 0.1	- 3.8	- 0.04	- 0.2	- 30	- 54

Grain comprises SITC 041-045.2, 045.9 and 9-046; oilseeds SITS 081.3 through 081.39.

Sources: FAO Trade Yearbook 1974, Tabs. 5, 36, 78; ...1982, Tabs 5, 36, 8.

Problems of Soviet Agriculture

6

Did the Kolkhoz System Really Fulfill the Initial Aims of the Party in the 1930s?

Stephan Merl

Introduction

In retrospect Soviet collectivization may seem a "strategy" by which agriculture had to contribute to industrialization. But had such a strategy been formulated when collectivization started at the end of 1929? Did the kolkhoz system actually fulfill the expectations in social, political and economic regard? There obviously is a wide-spread consent in the literature that collectivization generally produced the kind of political and social results which the Party had expected.[1] On the economic aims opinion is divided. We find the view that collectivization did play an important role in industrialization,[2] while others argue that in this respect it at least fell far short of expectations.[3]

In spite of the fact that the Party leadership in general seemed to be content with the kolkhoz system in the 1930s, I doubt that it met any of their expectations. The outcome had little to do with the initial aims. Although the Party in fact did not control the social and economic processes, its leadership, in its voluntaristic way of thinking, was convinced that it did and appraised the outcome in a pragmatic manner as socialism. In this paper I will put forward some arguments to support the view that the kolkhoz system in the 1930s failed to reach its initial aims and that forced collectivization was not started in 1929 primarily for economic reasons. First I shall raise the question of what the expectations of the Party were and whether economic arguments played a role in the decision to collectivize. I shall then examine the situation during the 1930s by discussing the use made of the kolkhoz labor force and finally try to sum up the outcome of collectivization in regard to the social, political and economic aims.

Expectations of the Party

A comprehensive formulation of aims underlying the collectivization policy is nowhere to be found. Therefore we have to look at the whole context of the debates up to 1930.

The main political aim consisted of extending state control over the peasantry and agricultural production, as well as over commodity exchange. To put it briefly, this meant finishing with peasant intractability and the threat of a capitalist restoration, a threat that the Party thought to be inherent in the very existence of small scale peasant production. Concerning the social aims, the Party wanted to end "exploitation of man by man", and this presumably meant abolishing the private ownership of the means of production and diminishing social differentiation among the peasants.

In economic terms collectivization was supposed to organize mechanized large-scale production units. From the construction of "socialist forms of production" in agriculture the Party expected a revolution in the forces of production and thus a significant increase in output. Whether the Party saw further links between collectivization and industrialization is uncertain. But during the late 1920s there were further demands on agriculture, regardless whether in collective or individual structure. Agriculture was supposed to deliver industrial crops needed for the manufacturing sector, as well as grain, both for the supply of industrial workers and, perhaps even more urgently, as an export commodity needed to finance the import of industrial implements. If Stalin spoke of a "tribute" by the peasants to industrialization, this meant nothing more than that the transfer of capital, continuing throughout the 1920s, should not be stopped.[4] The transfer of workers from agriculture to industry did not become a political aim until 1930/1931, after forced collectivization had started.[5]

Motives Behind the Decision
to Collectivize

Forced collectivization obviously proceeded in an unplanned and haphazard manner. Was there a necessity for it? In the Western discussion the so-called "industrialization debate" is often taken as a rational background. But the debate is little more than a construction by Erlich.[6] It is interesting in a theoretical sense, but it has hardly any relevance to the actual decisionmaking process.[7] If there existed an economic necessity for collectivization at this moment, we should find evidence for it in economic planning. But even the optimal variant of the five year plan, approved by the Sixteenth Party Conference in April 1929, did not speak of collectivization as an impending task. As to solving the difficulties of grain supply, priority was given to the construction of state farms. In this context the plan thus saw one link: only industrialization, especially the construction of big tractor plants, would make collectivization possible.[8]

Obviously the planners did not see collectivization as a precondition for industrialization. They even argued that the state had to concentrate its means on forced industrialization and could not afford money to build large-scale production units and the state-farm project at the same time. The planners therefore did not want to start wholesale collectivization before the production of tractors within the Soviet Union reached the necessary amount, that is not before the mid 1930s.

What then pushed ahead forced collectivization in 1928/1929? I have treated this subject elsewhere at length and will therefore repeat only a few points of my arguments here.[9] The most important factor obviously was the political pressure exercised on the apparatus since 1927/1928. In the atmosphere of struggle against "bourgeois thinking" in the apparatus and the so-called "right opposition" within the Party, economic reasoning did not count.[10] Everyone had to fear for his job if he spoke critically about economic aims set by the Party or doubted the possibility of overfulfilling a planned target. Limitations existing in a capitalist economy were claimed to be no longer effective.[11] The reaction of people on all levels of the apparatus was characterized by fear and submissiveness. To cite Strumilin, a famous statistician close to the aims of the Stalin group, on the reaction of his collegues, they "preferred to stand for higher tempos rather than to sit [in prison] for lower ones".[12] This of course had consequences for the decisionmaking process. Nobody risked to openly oppose the central directives. Thus the Party leadership lost an important source of information for judging the risks of its directives.[13] Besides the political pressure on the apparatus another point has to be mentioned, the competition existing within the bureaucracy between different organizations. In spite of the strong centralization of the decisionmaking process the voluntaristic understanding of "planning" had the consequence that all projects were subject to an uncontrolled outcome. Not the fulfillment of the plan but its overfulfillment to the highest possible degree was required. Because of the restriction of the material resources this led to a continuous struggle between the different agencies of economic management and the regional authorities.

Under these conditions the starting point of forced collectivization was as early as May 1928. At this time the Party leadership discussed the first wave of founding of kolkhozes in the spring of 1928.[14] The Party gave a scathing judgement of these collectives. They were too small, combining only some poor peasants and about twenty hectares of land. These were not the mechanized large-scale production units, showing the peasants the future of agriculture of which the Party had dreamt. So the Party leadership ordered the enlargement of the kolkhozes; either by combining several existing kolkhozes or by directly founding large-scale kolkhozes. Although this was a general statement, without a concrete time set, the demand was taken up immediately by several institutions concerned with agriculture. Since the fall of 1928 "Kolkhoztsentr", the central association of the kolkhozes, and "Khlebotsentr", the central association of the grain cooperatives, started to build up large-scale kolkhozes in practice. They traced out one plan of collectivization after the other, one even more ambitious than the other, with the single purpose of getting some tractors. The founding of big kolkhozes with 2000 hectares and more, during which force was used against the peasants, became more and more widespread.[15] Thus the motive which should hold off founding big kolkhozes at this time, the scarcity of tractors and tractor implements, necessary for large-scale production in agriculture, due to the existing competition, became the main motive of pushing ahead with collectivization.

In the summer of 1929 even the wholesale collectivization of complete counties started. At this time the counties had to draft their regional "five year plans". After the Party proposed to equip a very few counties with tractors completely, a competition between the counties started and each tried to get the tractors by drafting plans to finish collectivization in ever shorter periods, starting at the same time to collectivize the peasants by force.[16] In late 1929 in the Lower Volga district, about 50 percent of the peasant farms were already "collectivized".[17]

Based on a vague directive from above, the existing competition between various agencies of the bureaucracy and the general pressure on the apparatus to overfulfill plans, forced collectivization had started long before there was a formal Party directive to do so. The apparatus got active anticipating Party policy, and by this contributed to the formation of Party policy. The Party leadership was not really in control of this process and proved to be incapable of recognizing the connection between the political pressure on the apparatus and its supposed submissiveness. It saw the outcome as a "movement from below", from the lower levels of the Party and Soviet hierarchy.

The final decision to start forced collectivization apparently fell in late 1929 in a mood of success. In his famous article, published in March 1930, Stalin spoke of "dizziness from success", trying to blame the local apparatus for the faults of collectivization in the winter of 1929/30. But in fact this was more a characteristic of decisionmaking at the top.

If judging in an uncritical manner, as the group around Stalin obviously was doing, in late 1929 there seems to be a lot of successes for the policy of a "socialist offensive":

a. Grain procurement was finished with an apparently excellent result as early as the anniversary of the October Revolution,
b. all reports from below seemed to prove that peasant opposition was easy to break and it was possible to push them into kolkhozes, at least in combination with a policy of "class struggle" in the countryside,
c. Stalin was celebrating a victory over "bourgeois specialists", who had claimed that the rate of industrial growth must decline. But in 1928/ 29 the planned rate of industrial growth had again been surpassed.[18]

In late 1929 the victory over bourgeois specialists and the "right opposition" in the Party seemed to be at hand; why not press further ahead with the socialist offensive? The group around Stalin came to the conviction that it would be possible to solve the problem of small scale peasant farms in one fell swoop. In this process the leadership group lost all sense of their original purpose for collectivization.

If collectivization was aimed at supporting industrialization, there should have been ideas about how this should work in practice. But neither the internal organization of the kolkhozes nor the mechanism to extract "surpluses" were planned in advance. The existing internal organization of the old kolkhozes, which until 1928 were truly collectives in our understanding, i.e., they primarily served the interests of their members, was not suitable for kolkhozes dominated by state interests. Although in late 1929 a commission had discussed questions of organization, a model statute was not published until March 1930, when the Party was already in retreat on the question of collectivization.[19] Even after March 1930 it took years, in some cases until 1934, to develop an operating, if not necessarily successful, kolkhoz system in practice. Throughout 1930 there were a lot of often contradictory directives on questions of organization and in the kolkhozes a great variety of methods, more or less in contradiction to state interests, were practiced.[20]

To name only some points: the final decision to keep tractors and tractor implements outside the kolkhozes fell not before the end of 1930. The use of the MTS as a mean of central control over the kolkhozes was decided even later.[21] The famous system of distribution within the kolkhozes by "trudodni" (labor units) had only a trial run in 1930 and it took until 1933 to put it fully into operation.[22] No less confusion existed in the kolkhozes over the organization of labor and the obligation or the right to take part in kolkhoz work. Even the low state prices for agriculture products were not yet in effect in this moment, for at first they were a result of the unplanned and uncontrolled process of inflation. Only from 1933 did they constitute an intentional element of official price policy.[23]

For lack of space I will not go further into detail on these points. But there is little evidence to support the view that forced collectivization had been a strategy to secure industrialization. In practice the mechanism that served to extract "surpluses" from the kolkhozes developed only as a consequence of the economic failure of the whole policy of the "socialist offensive" in the early 1930s.

Use Made of the Kolkhoz Labor Force

To exemplify the working of the kolkhoz system in the 1930s I will now discuss the use made of the kolkhoz labor force. The selection of this part of kolkhoz life is primarily for pragmatic reasons: the available data on this issue are comparatively better than on other questions of kolkhoz life.

Some data are available to judge the effects of migration to cities during the 1930s. During the 12-year period from 1927 to 1938 about 18.5 million people migrated to the cities from agriculture.[24] This means a yearly average of 1.5 million people. Nearly the same migration had been reached already in 1927 to 1929.[25] Most of the newcomers to cities were men.[26] This unbalanced migration strongly affected the structure of the peasant household by sex.

During the 1930s the ratio between men and women in peasant households shifted due to the male rural-urban migration. The decrease in the total number of household members was partly caused by the strong losses due to starvation and epidemic diseases between 1932 and 1934.[28]

What was the influence of "planning" on migration? While during the 1920s migration increased steadily, in the first half of the 1930s strong fluctuations are to be found. Due to totally unrealistic expectations of industrial growth and widespread rumors of shortages in the supply of industrial labor, net migration to cities in 1931 reached a peak of more than four million persons. Beside the chaos and the loss of political control caused by this process in the cities, it obviously surpassed the real need for labor in industry.

In 1932–1933 the Party tried to get things under control and abruptly stopped migration to town by introducing the passport system. Many former peasants were sent back to the villages by force.[29] Only in the mid-1930s was there a need for additional labor from the countryside again and labor shortages became a problem for some branches of industry during the late 1930s.[30] Already these rough data show that the kolkhoz system did little for a planned, steady supply of workers to industry. But this was not the fault of the kolkhoz system alone. The contemporary Soviet concept of "planning" and the whole political system contributed to these problems.

Concerning the use of labor within the kolkhozes the available data reveal some interesting facts. The process of mechanization was quite strong during the mid-1930s. Even harvesting machinery was widely used for grain by the second half of the decade. One should keep in mind that mechanization set free a lot of workers in the kolkhozes and should have mitigated the problems arising out of strong seasonal fluctuations in agricultural work. Nevertheless, the data prove that mechanization in fact had little influence on the use of labor within the kolkhozes. It is clear that the kolkhoz system managed to keep the number of days worked on a high level without any considerable increase in agricultural production. The failure to increase productivity thus withheld a lot of surplus workers from the labor market.

While the annual number of trudodni (labor units) earned for work in the kolkhoz per household increased throughout the 1930s, the total number of days worked increased only until 1934 (to 350 days a year per household), then stayed at the same level for the rest of the 1930s.[31] But kolkhoz work did not lose its seasonal character. This can be gleaned from the evaluation of kolkhoz household budgets for 1937. While in July there were 44 working days per kolkhoz household, during winter time there were only 17 without regard to the duration of the working day.[32] Only 20 percent of all able-bodied kolkhoz members had something like a full-time job in the kolkhoz earning more than 300 labor units a year, i.e. they worked about 230 days and more. More than 60 percent of all able-bodied earned less than 200 units, working less than 150 days.[33]

While the kolkhoz labor force consisted to an important part, about 60 percent, of women and adolescents, their share in the number of days worked was significantly lower, about 40 percent. Obviously the adolescents and most of the women in the kolkhoz were used only as temporary help. Old men in general had a permanent job. Only 36 percent of the kolkhoz workers were adult men, but their share in the days worked was above 50 percent. Table 6.2 shows that the use made of the kolkhoz labor force was highly differentiated by sex and age. While those men who stayed on the kolkhozes generally held a permanent job, women had little chance to work full time. Work by children and adolescents during times of peak demand for labor still was widespread in the kolkhozes.

What types of permanent occupations existed in the kolkhozes? Field work made up more than 60 percent of all days worked and this was seasonal work. Productive and draught animals throughout the 1930s required only a modest share of total labor input, less than 20 percent. Therefore most permanent jobs in the kolkhozes were to be found in administrative and service functions. Even the "mechanizatory", the drivers of tractors and harvesters, formally kolkhoz-members, worked only for several months each year in the M.T.S. and then were set free. For women there were only very few permanent jobs in the kolkhoz, such as nurse, milk maid and tending the cattle. For men, work in the fields had less significance. They filled jobs like accountant, kolkhoz chairman, coachman, brigadier, guard, "head of department", construction worker, blacksmith, tending the horses, etc. Thus in the kolkhozes work in agricultural production was done mostly by women and adolescents, while men filled administrative and service functions.[35] Before trying to explain this state of affairs, we should first look at Table 6.3 to see what other occupations the kolkhoz members had.

For lack of space I cannot comment on the limitations for the comparison here.[37] The data for 1925 are representative of all the remaining years of the 1920s, the data for 1937 for the whole period 1934 to 1938.

The comparison produces some interesting results. Kolkhoz labor in the 1930s was still used to an important extent outside the kolkhoz. While during the second half of the 1920s about three to four million persons annually left the peasant farms for seasonal work outside agriculture (average: 5 months; most important jobs: wood-cutting, floating, construction work), during the second half of the 1930s about four million kolkhoz members temporarily absented themselves from the kolkhoz for similar reasons.[38] More than 80 percent of the absentees were men, most of them aged 16 to 30. In fact even by 1939 the situation had not changed considerably. In this year a lot of these seasonal workers were excluded from the kolkhozes because they did not achieve the minimum of labor units prescribed in the kolkhoz.[39]

Another finding is that more extensive use of the labor force seems to have been made in the 1930s. But this is to a good part due to the different way of counting. Probably kolkhoz work was also less efficient. Table 6.3 further demonstrates that men hardly took any part in the work, including livestock raising, on the private plots. This was done by women.[40]

While the distribution of labor in the kolkhoz has suggested that the surplus labor consisted mainly of women,[41] it always has been evident that women also worked to a large extent in the private economy, on the private plot as well as in the household. In fact their working day throughout the 1930s was significantly longer than that of male kolkhoz members.[42]

The data show that probably a significant part of the kolkhoz labor force, especially men, were not used economically. It is obvious that the kolkhoz economy, with its single minded concentration on field production, badly needed areas of production that made it possible to use surplus labor outside the peak of field work in July–August. But the low state prices for most agricultural products blocked the integration of livestock, horticulture, etc. into kolkhoz production. If a shift of production towards these sectors had been undertaken, the kolkhoz population would have lost their most important means of survival within the kolkhozes, which depended upon their producing these products on private plots for their own consumption and marketing them on the kolkhoz markets. To make better use of the kolkhoz labor force (and to increase agricultural production), the Party would have had to raise state agricultural prices dramatically. The low state prices also made the integration of supplementary processing activities into the kolkhoz impossible. If the state had allowed industrial production within the kolkhozes, this would have become the main money income and the kolkhoz members would have lost interest in agricultural production. Thus all projects of 1929/30 to build up agro-industrial combines ended and the kolkhozes even lost an important source of income which the peasants still had in the 1920s.[43]

The displacement of men from agricultural production to administrative and service work was also due to the kolkhoz system. Only young men had the chance to leave the kolkhozes for industry, others were lucky if they found a job outside the kolkhoz in the villages. The other men had to look for a permanent job in the kolkhoz. The specialization of jobs by no means corresponded to the needs of the generally small kolkhozes. If a man found a permanent job in the kolkhoz, he would not take part in production work. Even if he only had to work one or two hours a day these would earn him full labor units because of the kind of work men usually were assigned. Many kolkhoz jobs owed their existence to the state's interest in control and suppression. Armed guards in the fields, supervisors, etc. had little to do with production work. Thus the state got the work it paid for: low incomes led to sloppy and bad work, an expression of the lack of interest in the results of kolkhoz production.

Probably the surprisingly high level of peak work loads during harvest time was due to state pressure too. To get the grain under its control as quickly as possible, the state forced the kolkhozes to do everything at the same time: to harvest, to thresh and to deliver the crop to the state. This hindered other urgent work in the kolkhoz economy and inevitably caused permanently high losses in the fields. Evidently an organization of work more attuned to economic necessities would have increased the proportion of the harvests brought in and made the forced deliveries to the state easier to bear.

The kolkhoz system thus by no means abolished surplus labor in the countryside. And, although this may look contradictory at first glance, it even sharpened labor shortages during harvest time. Because the kolkhoz system did nothing to overcome the low attractiveness of life in the countryside, it fostered the migration of young men to industry, and hence contributed to the scarcity of qualified labor in agriculture. The negative effect of surplus labor, low incomes, was felt more strongly in the kolkhozes than it had been in the small peasant farms of the 1920s. Thus the kolkhoz system did not make national use of the available labor within the kolkhozes. On the other hand, it did not allow the Party to put the labor supply for industry on a regular, controlled footing. Actually, the scarcity of labor set free for work outside agriculture had not been the problem of the 1920s.

The Political Aim: Control

What precisely does state "control" mean? If we understand by "control" the power to remove any person at any time from any post and cast this person into prison or labor camp, it is beyond doubt that the Party did exercise control. But below I shall use the term "control" in the sense of "making people effectively do or not do certain things".

Did the Party control the kolkhozes? It is beyond doubt that the Party, i.e. the county Party committees (Raikomy), nominated and discharged the kolkhoz chairmen. The assembly of kolkhoz members was forced to agree. Thus the Party attempted to frighten both kolkhoz management and kolkhoz members. But such a system could function only if it was used cautiously. Otherwise it became destructive for any economic goals. In fact, even during the second half of the 1930s, fluctuation of kolkhoz chairmen was incredibly high. Each year, in about 45 percent of all kolkhozes, the chairman was on his post less than one year, in others the chairmen were exchanged up to six times a year.[44]

The discharge of a kolkhoz chairman generally happened during specific campaigns (grain procurement etc.). County administrations and kolkhoz chairmen partly had the same interests in opposing state demands, for example by hiding as many agricultural products as possible from the central organizations. We have knowledge only of those cases in which they failed to do so; their overall frequency and extent, however, is unknown. The raikomy therefore would seldom start any repression against a kolkhoz chairman on their own. Generally they would intervene actively only when put under pressure from above, i.e., during campaigns, when the Oblast' committee sent its plenipotentiaries to the counties.

The discharge of a kolkhoz chairman as well as the purges throughout the 1930s are to be seen as evidence for lack of control by the Party leadership. The high fluctuation in leading positions on all levels is one of the most important features that distinguishes the Soviet industrialization period from industrialization in other countries. This policy obviously was responsible for a great part of the economic failures. There was a strong correlation between the economic success of a kolkhoz and the number of years its chairman stayed in office.[45]

Did the state control the decisions of the kolkhoz management? I do not think so, if we understand control in the sense defined above. In fact there were no common interests. The state did not respect the needs for development of the kolkhoz economy. If the kolkhoz chairman did not fulfill the state plan for delivery he would be discharged. But he would also be discharged if his kolkhoz was in a desolate condition. A successful kolkhoz chairman at once had to make the state think he complied with state demands and at the same time deceive the state as much as possible. The chairman respected state demands only if there was a special campaign. Otherwise it would be sufficient to keep good relations with the county party committee. Official reports were falsified. I will present some examples for this. State laws demanded that the kolkhoz chairman should select suitable young men for work in industry and sent them to work by a contractual agreement with an industrial plant. In fact throughout the 1930s the kolkhoz management, often supported by county party and state organizations, did its best to hinder seasonal or permanent migration into industry. Of course the kolkhoz needed skilled labor, and that meant especially young men, and the practice to hoard labor for times of peak work loads was widespread since the late 1920s. Anybody who wanted to leave the kolkhoz was regarded as a deserter. He had trouble getting a passport; the kolkhoz management would try to frighten him by throwing his family out of the kolkhoz; in extreme cases this could be an equivalent to a sentence of death by starvation.[46] This was against state law, apart from the period 1933 to 1934, and the chairman could be sent to prison for it. But if there was no special campaign, no one would take interest in it. If the chairman did not frighten the members into staying on the kolkhoz, he might lose most of his better qualified workers and might be sent to prison for sabotaging the state plan for agricultural production. Control did not function well, because it did not respect economic necessities. Therefore it created uncontrolled processes over and over again.

Let us take another example. To keep the administrative and service apparatus small, the kolkhozes were not allowed to spend more than 8 percent of all man-days for these tasks. Formally the kolkhozes respected these limits, but in fact they were doing nothing else but window-dressing. Most kolkhozes used up to 20 percent of all labor units on service and administrative work, declaring most of it as "field work".[47] To follow state demands, kolkhozes falsified their reports. To enforce its demands the state had to start a special campaign and at times mobilized tens of thousands of controllers. To diminish the apparatus in the kolkhozes, such a campaign was started in 1940. About 30 percent of all administrative and service workers were "freed for productive work".[48] But such campaigns had only temporary effects, already in 1933 there had been such a campaign, for they did not tackle the real causes of the dilemma. Probably only recruitment into the army in 1941 kept these people from returning into their "jobs" in the following year.

The measures of state control (discharge, trial, purges, etc.) were only suitable for frightening persons in management positions. They had little effect on a simple kolkhoz member on the lowest level in the social hierarchy. Obviously even among simple kolkhoz members fluctuation, i.e., going from one kolkhoz to the other ("letuny"), was quite frequent, up to 10 percent, during the late 1930s.[49]

Such measures were by no means suitable to improve agricultural production. The zveno (team) propagated by Gorbachev today, which is to be paid according to the actual results of its work, was proposed as early as the late 1930s.

Did the state control the production and marketing of agricultural products by administrative measures, as is widely accepted in the literature? In fact this form of control had only limited effects, even with respect to grain. Here the state dictated a low price, which stood in no relation to the costs of production. It seems to be more precise to speak of a tax in kind on grain in this respect. If we take into account that the M.T.S. invariably worked with high losses, which the state had to pay, the rationality of this price policy is quite doubtful. Concerning industrial crops, administrative measures failed. To increase production, the state had to use economic incentives. The prices for industrial crops were significantly increased in 1935. In fact the state even paid high premiums to the kolkhozes in addition. If we look at animal products, fruits, vegetables, etc. the state in fact did not exert control at all, neither by political nor by economic means. The state prices for these products were low, but they hardly had any meaning. These products did not go into the public procurement system, but were sold on the free kolkhoz market, where the state did not control the prices. The Party failed to abolish private markets because the state trading sector was not able to provide the necessary food supply for the population. A pure administrative control thus was executed only on grain. The administrative fixing of prices had narrow limits, for the state had to respect the costs of reproduction to increase production.

From this evidence it seems clear that we have to rethink the question as to what extent state control was effective over members, agrarian production and commodity exchange of the kolkhozes.

Social Goals

The main social goal, the abolition of private property of the means of production, failed. Forced by the uprising of peasant women in early 1930[50] the Party had to tolerate private plots and private property of some implements of production in the kolkhozes. Because the kolkhozes proved unable to provide sufficient food for their members, private production even became a precondition for the survival of rural families during the 1930s. The kolkhoz system thus did not end petty bourgois thinking but perpetuated and strengthened it.[51] This was a great failure of Bolshevik ideology.

The Party also did not succeed in ending "exploitation of man by man". Hiring of day-laborers by the kolkhozes was still widespread. During the harvest private peasants and kolkhoz members from neighboring kolkhozes, all paid with money wages, were hired. For lack of qualified members, most kolkhozes were forced to hire construction workers, accountants etc.[52]

Social differentiation obviously sharpened during the 1930s. While in the 1920s there were primarily two different regions (black soil, non-black soil), within which the economic conditions were comparatively similar, in the 1930s this intraregional homogeneity disappeared. In general we find in every district kolkhozes with good results, while the great majority was in poor condition.[53] This seems to be due only in a very small measure to the working morale of the kolkhoz members or the general economic conditions set by the state. Rather, much of this varying performance can be explained by chance elements, such as the qualification and experience of the kolkhoz management, repression hurting the kolkhoz, relationship to the raikomy etc. State "control" thus by no means created equal chances for the kolkhozes.

I would like to make some remarks on the income of the kolkhoz households. After the increase in the prices for industrial crops in 1935 the distribution of money income among the kolkhoz households became even more unequal. In 1937 the mean monetary income distributed by the kolkhozes in Uzbekistan amounted to above 3000 Rubles annually per household, while in the Upper Volga district it was only 336 Rubles.[54] But the distribution from the kolkhoz made up only 20 percent to 50 percent of the total income.[55] The income from the private plot was very important. It is of great interest that about 20 percent of the money income of a kolkhoz household was from work outside agriculture, earned in general without separation from the kolkhoz household.[56] Just as peasants in the 1920s, the kolkhoz members thus at least partially participated in the increase of money income outside agriculture. For lack of space I shall not go into more detail on these questions. But social differentiation within and between the kolkhozes is a topic of great significance that has been neglected in research until now.

Economic Aims and Contribution to Industrialization

Both unquestionable economic goals, the introduction of large-scale production units in agriculture and the raising of agricultural production, failed. The average kolkhoz until 1949 did not reach the "optimal size" in the understanding of the Party. Most of the big kolkhozes of late 1929 had fallen apart in the beginning of 1930. Comprising less than eighty previous peasant farms and only about 500 hectares of cultivated land, the average kolkhoz lagged far behind the production units of several thousands of hectares which the Party had envisioned. It was Khrushchev, starting the amalgation of kolkhozes in 1950, who got them closer to the initially planned size.

The "socialist form of production" did not prove its superiority over small peasant production in practice. Although the "grain problem" was claimed to be solved, in fact the harvest data were only artificially pushed up by introducing the so-called "biological harvest" in 1933, which hid the real grain shortage throughout the 1930s. It was Khrushchev who put an end to this fictitious victory.

What about the kolkhoz system's contribution to industrialization? Of course it is methodologically difficult to ascertain the difference between what agriculture would have contributed under any conceivable circumstances, that is at least the supply of labor for industry, and what was the special contribution of collectivization. To add further confusion, we even have to take into account that there was a radical change in agricultural policy, especially in the system of procurement, just before collectivization started. It would be wrong to attribute developments connected with this change to collectivization. In this context it seems necessary to remember that only from 1931 onwards the grain came predominantly from the kolkhozes.

The arguments generally put forward in favor of collectivization are:

- that it was easier to collect grain from kolkhozes than from individual farms,
- that collectivization raised the amount of marketed grain,
- that collectivization secured the food supply of workers and employees at the cost of the peasants,
- that collectivization intensified the transfer of capital from agriculture to industry.

Was it easier to get agricultural products from the kolkhozes? Unfortunately this argument missed an important development just before forced collectivization started. Since the spring of 1929 grain procurement was based on the "Ural-Sibirian-Method",[57] which placed the obligation to deliver a certain amount of grain on the land community, with great success, as grain procurement in the fall of 1929 and 1930 proved. This method had an old tradition and was exactly the way collection of taxes took place in pre-revolutionary Russia. So the real question is, whether it was easier to collect grain from kolkhozes than from land communities. In fact it did not become easier to collect grain after 1931. Throughout the 1930s the state had to struggle to get agricultural products, although they were in the hand of the kolkhozes.[58] To this end the Party had to organize a special campaign each year and to mobilize the whole State and Party apparatus.

There is no question that the amount of market production of grain increased from 1929 onwards (i.e., already since before collectivization started and before the kolkhozes delivered the greatest amount of marketed grain). Karcz named the main reason for it, the decline in the number of cattle and horses.[59] But other factors were also important. The liquidation of security grain stocks in the countryside, the decline in the number of peasants as a consequence of famine from 1932 to 1934, and the decline in peasant consumption. That we have to reckon the decline in the marketing of animal products against the increase in grain marketings is not the only objection. Obviously the Soviet data on state grain procurements considerably overstate the increase in the total amount. While in the 1920s grain consumed in the villages was counted as peasant consumption, in the 1930s the data are on gross marketing of kolkhozes and state farms.[60] In fact already during the 1920s there had been a lot of non-agricultural households in the villages. If we look at figures on gross grain marketings by peasants for the years 1923 to 1927, this was about 33 percent of the harvest (25 to 26 million tons),[61] and in such a comparison the increase in gross grain marketings in the 1930s appears even less impressive, if we also take into account the high losses due to transportation and storage in the state trading sector. The chaos in railroad transportation during the first half of the 1930s was at least partly due to unnecessary grain transportation to the center and back to the grain areas.[62]

The composition of the food rations of city workers had been qualitatively better than that of peasants since 1924, especially because of the higher consumption norms of animal products in the cities. That it stayed better throughout the 1930s is therefore not yet proof for the success of collectivization. In this context it seems to be more important that the food situation in the cities deteriorated in spite of rationing. Until the outbreak of the war the 1927 quality level was not reached again.[63] The workers suffered more from the shortage of animal products, since these have had a greater significance in their food ration, and the increase in the consumption norms of grain products and potatoes always has been a sign for the deterioration of food supply. In fact the state was more concerned with getting raw materials from agriculture for industrial processing than with feeding the workforce.

Only party members and stakhanov-workers received all the food they needed for life. The other workers received, for reasonable prices, communal feeding in the factories as well as bread, but had to buy at least some animal products and vegetables on the kolkhoz market. They spent a significant part of their wages for these products, and in this way the state indirectly financed the kolkhoz members through diverted non-agricultural incomes. Workers and employees living in the countryside since the mid-1930s even had to produce themselves part of the agricultural products they needed.

Concerning the transfer of capital to industry, it is now widely accepted, as the result of the Barsov discussion, that collectivization did not raise the share of agriculture in accumulation in industry during the first five year plan.[64] I want to add only one argument here. It may be considered the major prerequisite for a contribution by the agricultural sector towards industrialization, to take advantage of the available supplies of peasant implements and horses as long as possible. But the Party managed to destroy this prerequisite in the very beginning of the 1930s. Thus an important possible contribution was lost and, as a consequence, the state had to import most tractors and related machinery in 1930 and 1931. There is some ground for assuming that, had the traditional tools and sources of traction been maintained, the better employment of the means of production in collective farms might have made possible an increase of production without requiring new, industrially produced inputs at this time.[65] In fact, field work, measured in sown area excluding that which involved sowing fields so late in the season that a harvest could not reasonably be expected, decreased during the early 1930s only by less than 10 percent while total horse power of horses and tractors combined decreased by 50 percent between 1929 and 1934.[66]

The specific contribution of collectivization to industrialization thus is much more difficult to ascertain than is often thought. Although it is certain that there was a contribution of agriculture to industrialization in the 1930s, it is very likely that this contribution would have been higher without this form of forced collectivization. If we remember how little the Party leadership in its collectivization policy took into account necessities of industrialization, this outcome should not be surprising. Nove argues that, in 1929, there was no political alternative to collectivization.[67] He might be right. But there were alternative ways of collectivization in this period, based more on peasant implements for a certain period, probably better suited for the necessities of industrialization.[68]

Conclusion

The kolkhoz system in the 1930s did not fulfill the initial aims of the Party. Most of these had to be abandoned in the very process of collectivization (1930–1934) in connection with the economic failure of this policy. The kolkhoz system of the 1930s was much more stamped by pragmatic compromises between ideological aims and basic necessities of life against the general background of a desperate situation in the supply of food.

There is no contradiction in the fact that the Party leadership during the 1930s in general seemed to be content with the kolkhoz system. Based on the firm conviction that all failures were caused by personal faults and the incapacity of people in the Party and State apparatus, they did not blame the system. In its voluntaristic way of thinking the Party leadership sought to control social and economic processes, while only discharging and frightening persons in leading positions. Throughout the period, the Party leadership was far more concerned with short-run problems of agricultural production and procurement policy than with the long-run results of its policy. It was not before 1939 that a new attempt towards the implementation of initial aims was started, directed primarily against the private plots. This attempt came to an end with the German attack on Soviet Russia in June 1941.

The criticisms and reforms of Khrushchev, starting with the amalgamation of kolkhozes in 1950, were all based on the discrepancy between initial aims and outcome. In its neglect of critical analysis and its incapacity to understand basic economic necessities Khrushchev's agrarian policy sometimes reminds of the shortcomings of collectivization policy. But this is not the place to go into further detail on this question.

92

Stephan Merl

Notes

1. R. Miller, R.C. Stuart, and K.-E. Waedekin, in P. Dorner (ed.), *Cooperative and Commune: Group Farming in the Economic Development of Agriculture* (Wisconsin UP: 1977), pp. 355–356.

2. E.H. Carr and R.W. Davies, *Foundations of a Planned Economy 1926–1929*, vol. 1.1 (London: 1969), pp. 237 ff.

3. Michael Ellman, "Did the Aricultural Surplus Provide the Resources for the Increase in Investment in the USSR During the First Five Year Plan?", in *The Economic Journal*, vol. 85 (Dec. 1975), pp. 844–863; Jerzy F. Karcz, "Soviet Agriculture: A Balance Sheet," in *The Development of Soviet Economy, Plan and Performance* (New York: 1968), pp. 108–146; same author, "From Stalin to Breshnev: Soviet Agricultural Policy in Historical Perspective," in J.R. Millar (ed.), *The Soviet Rural Community* (University of Illinois Press: 1971), pp. 36–70; James R. Millar, "Mass Collectivization and the Contribution of Soviet Agriculture to the First Five-Year Plan. A Review Article," in *Slavic Review*, vol. 33 (Dec. 1974) 4, pp.750–766; same author, "Soviet Rapid Development and the Agricultural Surplus Hypothesis," in *Soviet Studies*, vol. 22 (July 1970), pp. 77–93. (Cf. A. Nove's comment and J.R. Millar's reply in *Soviet Studies*, vol. 22 (1970–71), pp. 394–401, and vol. 23 (1971–72), pp. 302–306; same author and Corinne A. Guntzel, "The Economics and Politics of Mass Collectivization Reconsidered," in *Explorations in Economic History* 8 (1970), pp. 103–116; Ljubo Sirc, "Economics of Collectivization," in *Soviet Studies*, vol. 18 (1966–67), pp. 362–370.

4. Stephan Merl, *Der Agrarmarkt und die Neue Oekonomische Politik. Die Anfaenge staatlicher Lenkung der Landwirtschaft in der Sowjetunion (1925–1928)* (Muenchen, Wien: R. Oldenbourg Verlag 1981), pp. 305–309.

5. The first five-year plan even wanted to diminish migration to towns. See *Piatiletnii plan narodno-khoziaistvennogo stroitel'stva SSSR*, Tom 2.2 (Moskva: 2nd Ed., 1929), pp. 160 ff.

6. Alexander Erlich, *The Soviet Industrialization Debate, 1924–1928* (Cambridge, Mass.: Harvard UP 1967).

7. See for a critique J.F. Karcz, "Agriculture and the Economics of Soviet Development," in same author, *The Economics of Communist Agriculture. Selected Papers*, ed. by A.W. Wright (Bloomington, Ind.: 1979), pp. 441–480.

8. *Plan*, tom 2.1, pp. 273–277; Stephan Merl, *Die Anfaenge der Kollektivierung in der Sowjetunion. Der Uebergang zur staatlichen Reglementierung der Produktions- und Marktbeziehungen im Dorf (1928–1930)* (Wiesbaden: Otto Harrassowitz Verlag: 1985), pp. 370–380.

9. Merl, *Kollektivierung*.

10. On this point see Moshe Lewin, "The Disappearance of Planning in the Plan," in *Slavic Review* (1973), No. 2, pp. 271–287; Stephan Merl, "Handlungs-spielraeume und Sachzwaenge in der sowjetischen Wirtschafts- und Sozialpolitik der Zwischenkriegszeit," in W. Fischer (ed.), *Sachzwaenge und Handlungsspielraeume in der Wirtschafts- und Sozialpolitik der Zwischenkriegszeit* (St. Katharinen: Scripta Mercaturae Verlag 1985), pp. 175–229.

11. See for example Stalin's argumentation in favor of the state farms, in I.V. Stalin, *Sochineniia*, Moskva 1953, vol. 11, pp. 190–193.

12. S.G. Strumilin, "O tempakh nashego razvitiia," in *Planovoe khoziaistvo*, 1929, No. 1, p. 109.

13. See for example the report from Kolkhoztsentr to the Politburo of September 7, 1929, which listed every difficulty but gave everything a generally optimistic

outlook, in: *Materialy po istorii SSSR,* tom VII: *Dokumenty po istorii sovetskogo obshchestva* (Moskva: 1959), pp. 203–270.

14. *Izvestiya,* May 16, 1928.

15. See Merl, *Kollektivierung,* pp. 331–343.

16. *Ibid.,* pp. 356–365.

17. V.K. Medvedev, *Krutoi povorot. Iz istorii kollektivizatsii sel'skogo khoziaistva Nizhnego Povolzh'ia* (Saratov: 1961), pp. 81, 130.

18. On this point see N. Jasny, *Soviet Industrialization 1928–1952* (Chicago: 1961), pp. 54–56.

19. *Sobranie zakazov,* 1930, No. 24, Art. 255. On the commission see B.A. Abramov, "O rabote komissii Politbiuro TsK VKP (b) po voprosam sploshnoi kollektivizatsii," in *Voprosy istorii KPSS* (1964), No. 1, pp. 32–43; M.L. Bogdenko, "K istorii nachal'nogo etapa sploshnoi kollektivizatsii sel'skogo khoziaistva SSSR," in *Voprosy istorii* 38 (1963), No. 5, pp. 19–35; N.A. Ivnitskij, "O nachal'nom etape sploshnoi kollektivizatsii (osen' 1929- vesna 1930 gg.)," in *Voprosy istorii KPSS* 4(1962), No. 4, pp. 55–71.

20. R.W. Davies, *Industrialization of Soviet Russia,* vol. 2: *The Soviet Collective Farm 1929–1930* (Chatham: 1980).

21. See R.F. Miller, *One Hundred Thousand Tractors. The MTS and the Development of Controls in Soviet Agriculture* (Cambridge, Mass.: Harvard UP, 1970), pp. 36 ff.

22. N. Dem'ianova, "K istorii kolkhoznogo trudodnia," in *Problemy ekonomiki,* 1940, No. 5–6, pp. 191–203.

23. Ulrich Weissenburger, *Monetaerer Sektor und Industrialisierung der Sowjetunion (1927–1933). Die Geld- und Kreditpolitik waehrend der ersten Phase der Industrialisierung der UdSSR, ihre externen und internen Rahmenbedingungen und ihre Auswirkungen auf das gesamtgesellschaftliche Gleichgewicht* (Frankfurt/M.: Haag und Herchen Verlag 1983), pp. 396 ff.

24. M.A. Vyltsan, *Zavershaiushchii etap sozdaniia kolkhoznogo stroia* (1935–1937 gg.) (Moskva: 1978), p. 192.

25. *Sotsialisticheskoe stroitel'stvo SSSR. Statisticheskii ezhegodnik* (Moskva: 1936), p. 545.

26. *Trud v SSSR. Statisticheskii spravochnik* (Moskva: 1936), p. 8.

27. L.E. Mints, *Agrarnoe perenaselenie i rynok truda v SSSR* (Moskva, Leningrad: 1929), pp. 10 ff.; *Proizvoditel'nost' i ispol'zovanie truda v kolkhozach vo vtoroi piatiletke* (Moskva, Leningrad: 1939), p. 128; Merinov in: *Sotsialistisheskoe sel'skoe khozjajstvo,* 1941, No. 3, p. 18.

28. This is evident from the regional numbers of household members, see *Proizvoditel'nost',* p. 128.

29. *Sobranie zakazov,* 1932, No. 84, Art. 516. For the decrease in the total number of workers by branch see *Sotsialisticheskoe stroitel'stvo 1936,* pp. 508–509.

30. See for example Moskatov, in *Bol'shevik,* 1941, No. 7–8, pp. 37–50.

31. *Kolkhozy vo vtoroi Stalinskoi piatiletke. Statisticheskii sbornik* (Moskva, Leningrad: 1939), pp. 36, 43; trudodni counted into days worked by data from Babynin in *Problemy ekonomiki,* 1940, No. 2, p. 68.

32. *Proizvoditel'nost',* pp. 85 ff.

33. *Kolkhozy vo vtoroi piatiletke,* pp. 38–39.

34. *Proizvoditel'nost',* p. 126.

35. *Proizvoditel'nost',* pp. 97, 110, 123–124.

36. Mints, *Agrarnoe perenaselenie,* p. 66; *Kolkhozy vo vtoroi piatiletke,* p. 56; Merinov in *Sotsialistisheskoe sel'skoe khoziaistvo,* 1941, No. 3, p. 18.

37. I will do it at length in my present study "The system of Soviet collective farms in the 1930s. Productivity, stability, share of industrialization."

38. See V.P. Danilov, "Krest'ianskii otkhod na promysly v 1920-kh godakh," in *Istoricheskie zapiski* 96, Moskva 1974, pp. 55–122; M.A. Vyltsan, "Trudovye resursy kolkhozov v dovoennye gody (1935-1940 gg.)," in *Voprosy istorii*, 1973, No. 2, pp. 22–24.

39. Two thirds of the male kolkhoz members, not achieving the minimum of labor units, were workers and employees of state enterprises, see Merinov, in *Sotsialistisheskoe sel'skoe khoziaistvo*, 1941, No. 3, p. 17.

40. For data on the work in the private economy by sex and age see Shekhter in *Plan*, 1935, No. 19, p. 27.

41. See for example Merinov, in *Sotsialistisheskoe sel'skoe khoziaistvo*, 1941, No. 3, pp. 16–24.

42. *Plan*, 1935, No. 15, p. 37; Babynin in *Problemy ekonomiki*, 1940, No. 2, pp. 70–71.

43. R.W. Davies, "The Soviet Rural Economy in 1929–1930: The Size of the Kolkhoz," in C. Abramsky (ed.), *Essays in Honour of E.H. Carr* (London: 1974), pp. 255–280; Merl, *Kollektivierung*, pp. 365–369.

44. *Sputnik kommunista v derevne*, 1936, No. 17, pp. 13–16; *Kolkhozy vo vtoroi piatiletke*, p. 60; *Pravda*, December 10, 1940; A.P. Teriaeva, *Trud v kolkhozakh vo vremia velikoi otechestvennoi voiny* (Moskva: 1947), p. 25.

45. *Problemy ekonomiki*, 1936, No. 3, p. 63.

46. See for example *Sotsialisticheskoe zemledelie*, April 8, 1937; *Sobranie zakazov*, 1938, No. 18, Art. 115.

47. Chuvikov/Safroshkin in *Sotsialisticheskoe sel'skoe khoziaistvo*, 1941, No. 2, pp. 33–36.

48. *Ibid.*, p. 36; *Izvestiya*, January 15, 1941.

49. N.Ja. Gushchin, E.V. Kosheleva, V.G. Charushin, *Krest'ianstvo zapadnoi Sibiri v dovoennye gody (1935-1941)* (Novosibirsk: 1975), pp. 50, 61 ff; *Kollektivizatsiia sel'skoe khoziaistva Zapadnoi Sibiri (1927-1937 gg.)* (Tomsk: 1972), pp. 267–276.

50. See Merl, *Kollektivierung*, pp. 151–153; P.G. Chernopitskii, *Na velikom perelome. Sel'skie Sovety Dona v period podgotovki i provedeniia massovoi kollektivizatsii (1928-1931 gg.)* (Rostov na Donu: 1965), p. 101.

51. Moshe Lewin, "The Kolkhoz and the Russian Muzhik" in *Peasants in History: Essays in Honour of Daniel Thorner* (Calcutta, Oxford UP: 1980), pp. 55–68.

52. Chuvikov/Safroshkin, pp. 33–34; *Proizvoditel'nost'*, pp. 97, 110, 123–124.

53. See for example V. Dmitriev in *Sotsialistisheskaya rekonstruktsiia sel'skogo khoziaistva*, 1939, No. 1, pp. 45–51; M.I. Kubanin, *Proizvodstvennye tipy kolkhozov. Protsess rosta proizvoditel'nosti truda v kollektivnom zemledelii* (Moskva, Leningrad: 1936).

54. *Kolkhozy vo vtoroi piatiletke*, pp. 117–118.

55. M.A. Vyltsan, "Biudzhety semei kolkhoznikov v 1933–1940 gg.," in *Ezhegodnik po agrarnoi istorii vostochnoi evropy 1966 g.* (Tallin: 1971), p. 601.

56. M. Nesmii, *Dokhody i finansy kolkhozov* (Moskva: 1940), p. 59.

57. See Yuzuru Taniuchi, "A Note on the Ural-Siberian Method," in *Soviet Studies* 33 (1981), pp. 518–547.

58. Moshe Lewin, " 'Taking Grain': Soviet Policies of Agricultural Procurements Before the War," in C. Abramsky (ed.), *Essays*, pp. 281–324.

59. Karcz in *The Soviet Rural Community*, pp. 42–46. A recent challenge of this view by Morrison (David Morrison, "The Effect of Falling Livestock Numbers Upon Soviet Grain Marketings and Procurements in the 1928–38 Period," in *Jahrbuch der*

Wirtschaft Osteuropas, vol. 10, 1. Halbband, (Munich: 1982), pp. 239–251) is the result of misunderstandings of Soviet data on the number of livestock and on the consumption of fodder.

60. For comparable data on gross and net marketings of grain for the period of 1925–1932 see Karcz in *The Soviet Rural Community,* p. 44.

61. Merl, *Agrarmarkt,* pp. 445–451.

62. *Ezhegodnik khlebooborota,* No. 4–5 (1929/30 i 1930/31) (Moskva: 1932), pp. 26, 32.

63. Arcadius Kahan, "The Collective Farm System in Russia: Some Aspects of Its Contribution to Soviet Economic Development," in C. Eicher/L. Wilt (eds.), *Agriculture in Economic Development* (New York: 1964), pp. 258 ff. The view that collectivization was necessary for feeding the workers is recently to be found in Mark Harrison, "Why Was NEP Abandoned?," in Robert C. Stuart (ed.), *The Soviet Rural Economy* (Totowa, N.J.: Rowman & Allanheld 1983), pp. 63–78.

64. See Ellman, "Agricultural Surplus," in *The Economic Journal,* vol. 85 (1975), pp. 844–863; Millar, "Mass Collectivization," in *Slavic Review,* vol. 33 (1974), pp. 750–766. There is still a dispute on the reliability of the Barsov data. But the recent contribution by Morrison suffers from the onesideness of its critique, concerning only the data of industrial deliveries to agriculture, see David Morrison, "A Critical Examination of A.A. Barsov's Empirical Work on the Balance of Value Exchanges Between the Town and the Country," in *Soviet Studies,* vol. XXXIV (1982), pp. 570–584.

65. For similar findings see the result of linear programming by Hunter; Holland Hunter, *Modeling Alternative Developments, 1928–1940* (Unpublished conference paper, SSRC Conference on Soviet Economic Development in the 1930s, University of Birmingham, June 16–19, 1982).

66. Rough estimate based on data in *Sotsialisticheskoe sel'skoe khoziaistvo 1936,* pp. 249, 354: *Sel'skoe khoziaistvo SSSR. Ezhegodnik,* 1935 (Moskva: 1936), pp. 347, 351 f.; Auhagen, Der erste Fuenfjahrplan in der Landwirtschaft, in *Osteuropa 1933/34,* pp. 262–264.

67. See for example in "A Debate on Collectivization: Was Stalin Really Necessary," in *Problems of Communism,* vol. XXV (1976), No. 4, pp. 49–62.

68. Merl, *Kollektivierung,* pp. 318–330; same author, "War die Kollektivierung wirklich notwendig," in *Osteuropa,* vol. 34 (1984), pp. 329–343.

Table 6.1

NUMBERS AND SEX OF PERSONS BELONGING TO

PEASANT HOUSEHOLDS[27]

	men	women	all	women for each 100 men	women for each 100 men in total population
1926					
all persons	2.41	2.53	4.94	105	107
14 to 60 years	1.40	1.51	2.91	108	
1937					
all persons	1.85	2.14	3.99	116	(109)*
16-59 years	0.91	1.10	2.01	121	
1939					
16 to 59 years	0.92	1.21	2.13	132	

*1939

Table 6.2

PARTICIPATION OF THE KOLKHOZ MEMBERS IN THE KOLKHOZ

ECONOMY 1937 BY SEX AND AGE (IN PERCENT)[34]

	men (16 to 59 years)	women (16 to 59 years)	old people (above 59 years)	adolescent (under 16 years)
Workers	36.4	43.1	5.8	14.6
Days worked	52.6	36.9	5.9	4.5
Labor units	55.8	35.5	5.1	3.5

Table 6.3

USE OF THE LABOR FORCE** IN PEASANT FARMS (1925) AND

IN THE KOLKHOZES (1937, 1939) IN DAYS WORKED/YEAR[36]

	All Labor Force			Men		Women	
	1925	1937	1939	1937	1939	1937	1939
Days worked in the Kolkhoz	N/A	134.2	152.9	169.6	212.3	101.7	107.9
Days worked in the M.T.S.	N/A	3.7	4.1	7.2	8.9	0.6	0.4
Days worked on the private plot	N/A	44.1	49.0	16.4	18.8	69.4	71.9
Days worked in private and kolkhoz agriculture together	131.5	182.0	206.0	193.2	240.0	171.7	180.2
Days worked outside private/ kolkhoz agriculture: in industry, construction, on state farms etc.	35.5	50.1	22.2	78.3	35.6	24.5	11.9
1. Days worked in production	167.2	232.1	228.2	271.6	275.6	196.1	192.1
2. Days not worked in production (including days worked in the household)	112.8	55.9	59.8	16.4	12.4	91.9	95.9
3. Days worked in the household (as part of 2.)	52.9	(50)*	(50)*	(5)*	(5)*	(90)*	(90)*
	280	288	288	288	288	288	288

* Author's rough estimate
** 1937, 1939: able bodied kolkhoz members 16-59 years, days worked: without regard to length; 1925 all able bodied over 10 years, converted into man-workers; days worked: man working days.

7

Food Consumption Patterns in the Soviet Union

Ihor Stebelsky

Introduction[1]

Food consumption in the Soviet Union is by no means homogeneous. Its spatial variation is affected by the widely-varying traditional dietary habits of the many peoples in the USSR, by variations in environmental conditions conducive to the production of different commodities, by different levels of development of distribution systems, and by the regional differences in the relative affluence and hence the ability to pay for the income elastic commodities, such as meat, milk, eggs, and fish.

The purpose of this paper is to examine, at the macro-regional scale, patterns of food consumption in the Soviet Union, to compare the observed differences to Soviet scientifically established norms of consumption, and to explain the variations of consumption with a number of independent variables. Regional food consumption patterns in the Soviet Union have not been studied before. In the West, analysts at the United States Department of Agriculture (USDA) (Schoonover, 1974) and the Organization for Economic Cooperation and Development (OECD) (Slater, 1975) have used food consumption trends of the Soviet Union as a whole to project Soviet demands for meat and, coupled with an estimate of the Soviet capacity to increase its domestic meat supply, to predict the magnitudes of future Soviet grain imports. Presently, a team at Radio Liberty-Radio Free Europe (Parta, 1982) is conducting a study of regional and seasonal food availability in the Soviet Union, based on interviews of recent emigres, but it does not attempt to measure the disparities of food consumption *per se*. Soviet researchers have focused either on nutrition and the question of establishing scientifically-based food consumption norms that its population should attain (Mel'nikov, 1976; Petrovskiy, 1964) or on the economic relationships between income, prices, and the demand for food commodities, so that predictions in changing demand can be improved (Baranova and Levin, 1978; Karapetyan, 1980; Komarov and Chernyavskiy, 1973; Levin, 1969; Sarkisyan and Kuznetsova, 1967). Only recently an article on the geography of food consumption in the Soviet Union appeared in *Vestnik Moskovskogo Universiteta* (Nikol'skiy,. 1981, translated in *Soviet Geography,* 1982), but the treatment of the subject was brief and descriptive, rather than analytical. The only study of any depth, conducted by Karchikyan (1977), was published in Yerevan in only 500 copies. This dearth of analytical work reflect the rather sensitive nature of the topic of regional disparities and stems from the fact that information on food consumption for the union republics is scarce, incomplete, and has appeared in published form only recently and sporadically.

The Data

Fundamental to this study is the reliability and availability of Soviet food consumption data. The official Soviet food consumption data are based on a variety of sources, principally on balances of the supply and uses of agricultural products and on periodic family budget surveys. The absolute levels in any one year must be used with great care for international comparisons because of definitional problems. For example, Soviet milk consumption data, unlike the FAO, the OECD or the USDA milk consumption indicators, include not only fluid milk but also other dairy products, such as cheese and butter, converted to the fluid milk equivalent. Nevertheless, the data are considered reliable in trend. The economists Gertrude Schroeder and Elizabeth Denton (1982), who computed an index of consumption in the USSR, found them consistent with statistics for production, immediate uses, changes in inventories and net imports. For a regional analysis of food consumption in the Soviet Union, the details of the definitions are not problematic; the availability of data for the union republics, however, poses a constraint. Although food consumption data for the Soviet Union as a whole have been published on a regular basis since 1965, for some union republics they appeared regularly only more recently, for others only sporadically, and for still others not at all. For the purpose of this study all available republican yearbooks have been searched in the Library of Congress and elsewhere to compile the most comprehensive data base on regional food consumption in the Soviet Union.

Analysis

As the first step in the analysis, the compiled data were plotted on graphs. A separate graph was made for each of the nine commodity groups: meat, milk, eggs, fish, sugar, vegetable oil, potatoes, vegetables, and grain products. The graphs revealed not only the generally known trends of improvement in food consumption for the Soviet Union and the year to year fluctuations, but also the absolute and relative levels of food consumption for each of the eleven union republics for which data were published. Over some ten to fifteen years, the relative positions of the eleven union republics have changed very little.

The recent regional food consumption patterns can be summarized with 1975 data (Table 7.1). Their regional differences can be compared even more readily when the per head consumption values of each republic are transformed into percentages of the U.S.S.R. average (Table 7.2).

Patterns of food consumption observed among the eleven union republics may be generalized into three major regional groupings. The Baltic republics stand out as areas of high per head consumption in descending order of fish, milk and milk products, meat, eggs, and potatoes, near average in the consumption of sugar, mostly below average for vegetable oil, and below average for consumption of vegetables and grain products. The Slavic republics are above average in the consumption of nearly all commodities, except for vegetable oil and vegetables in Belorussia, eggs and fish in Ukraine, and vegetables and grain products in Russia. The Caucasian and Central Asian republics are dramatically below the USSR average in the per head consumption of fish, potatoes, eggs, vegetable oil, sugar, meat and (except for Armenia) meat products, near (some above and some below) the average consumption of vegetables, and consistently above average in the consumption of grain products. Although fruit consumption data for republics generally are not published, one study (Nikol'skiy, 1982), at least, suggests that the southern regions, including the Caucasian and Central Asian republics, enjoy higher than average per head consumption levels of fruit and melons in the Soviet Union.

When food consumed by the population is converted into calories as the lowest common denominator, disparities among the republics remain (Table 7.2). The Slavic and Baltic republics register, in general, an above average intake per head, whereas the Caucasian and Central Asian republics register a below average caloric intake. The food consumption per head in the Caucasus and especially in Central Asia is thus lower not only in the quality of its mix (i.e. fewer animal products) but also in the quantity of caloric intake.

Human physiological needs for food consumption are not uniform, however. The needed caloric intake depends on age, sex, and physical occupation of individuals, as well as on the climatic conditions of their habitat. The scientifically established norms of food consumption, established by the Institute of Consumption of the Academy of Medical Sciences of the USSR, were designed to reflect the different demographic, social and economic characteristics and environmental conditions of each republic, and the specific commodities adjusted so as not only to satisfy the physiological needs of that population but also its cultural preferences for certain foods. For this reason, in the republics with aged, urban population structures and colder climate, higher levels of consumption per head were recommended, especially in meat, milk, eggs and fish (Table 7.3). Conversely, for republics with young, rural population structures and warmer climates, lower levels of consumption were recommended, especially in animal products. Differences in consumption among different animal products or among different plant products that can be readily substituted for one another were recommended in a way that would reflect primarily cultural preferences (Donskova and Ibragimova, 1981, p. 42).

When Soviet-recommended norms for each republic are used as measures of adequate food consumption, and the 1975 levels of consumption are expressed as percentages of their respective recommended norms, a clear regional pattern emerges (Table 7.4). Only the Baltic republics have levels of meat consumption close to their recommended norms. Republics in the Caucasus and Central Asia lag far below their recommended norms of meat. Milk consumption is inadequate in nearly all republics, but the shortfall is particularly glaring in Central Asia. Egg consumption appears inadequate everywhere, but remains particularly acute in the Caucasus and Central Asia. Fish consumption more than satisfies the needs in Estonia and Latvia, appears nearly adequate in the RSFSR and Belorussia, but falls below the needs of Lithuania and Ukraine, and much below the needs of the Caucasus and Central Asia. Sugar consumption, by contrast, is more than adequate in most republics. Vegetable oil consumption appears more than adequate in two Baltic and two Slavic republics, but far below the norms in Central Asia and especially in the Caucasus. Potato consumption exceeds the norm in the Slavic and Baltic republics but falls short in the Caucasus and Central Asia. Vegetable consumption is very inadequate everywhere, whereas grain is consumed beyond the recommended norms everywhere, and especially in Georgia and Ukraine. Indeed, were it not for this high level of grain consumption, Belorussia, Georgia, and Ukraine would not have managed to attain a total caloric consumption above the recommended norm (Table 7.4). Meanwhile, unless the Soviet-recommended norms for its republics are too rich or food consumption underreported, the consumption patterns in Central Asia and also in Azerbaydzhan suggest caloric undernourishment and possible protein deficiency (Table 7.4).

What are the factors that appear to influence the patterns of consumption in the Soviet Union? It is thought that the per head consumption of any republic is related to the production of food commodities, to the strength of the market system as reflected in the retail trade turnover per head, and to the affluence of the population as expressed in average wages per person in a household. In order to establish the strengths of these relationships, several sets of correlations were calculated between a number of independent variables and the per head consumption of each union republic.

The first set of correlations was calculated between the average per head production of each food commodity (Table 7.5) and its respective food consumption. The closest relationship (Table 7.6), in descending order, was observed for the production of eggs, followed closely by meat, potato, and then by milk, fish and vegetables. Highly refined and processed products, such as sugar and vegetable oil, indicated very low correlations, whereas the transportable grain products displayed an inverse correlation between production and consumption. Perhaps constraints in the production, transportation and storage systems coupled with republican rather than union-wide procurement of all food products except grain contributed to such close positive relationships.

The level of retailing was more closely correlated with the per head consumption of some food commodities than was per head production (Table 7.6). Highest relationships were observed with respect to fish and meat, although the correlations were also high for eggs, grain products (negative), and milk, and significant for potatoes, vegetable oil and even sugar. Vegetable consumption appeared spatially unrelated to retail trade, possibly because, in some republics, much of that commodity bypassed state retail trade and, in any case, could be bought for less during its longer growing season. It has to be borne in mind, that retail trade, its network as well as its turnover, is much greater in urban than in rural (with their higher degree of producers' own consumption) areas of the Soviet Union, while cash incomes are also generally higher in urban areas. Thus, the correlation is also one of the regional variations of the degree of urbanization.

Affluence of the population, measured in terms of average monthly wages of workers and employees per person of an average household, provided the highest correlations for fish and meat, very high correlations for eggs and grain products (negative), high for vegetable oil, and significant for potoatoes, milk, and sugar. An attempt to relate food consumption to average monthly wages alone was less effective, although the strongest relationship in this instance proved to be a negative one with the consumption of grain products (Table 7.7).

Conclusions

In conclusion, the inter-republican variation in the food consumption per head not only reflects cultural preferences but also has implications from the standpoint of proper nutrition. The factors responsible for the inequitable food consumption levels appear to be, in order of importance, 1) inadequate republican production, especially in the case of eggs, potatoes, milk, and vegetables, 2) disparities in affluence, especially in the case of fish, meat, vegetable oil, and sugar, and 3) poorly developed retail trade, which corresponds with high per head consumption of grain. The announced Soviet food program, aimed at improving food production, processing and distribution, has the right thrust, but it will have no impact on the disparities of affluence which are related, primarily, to the variation in the average number of children in the household.

Notes

1. The author thanks the Social Sciences and Humanities Research Council of Canada for the research grant, and the Kennan Institute for Advanced Russian Studies in Washington, D.C. for the fellowship and assistance that made this study possible. Constructive comments from many helpful colleagues on earlier drafts of this paper are gratefully acknowledged.

References

Baranova, L. Ya., and Levin, A. I. 1978. *Modelirovaniye i prognozirovaniye sprosa naseleniya.* Moskva: "Statistika."

Donskova, S. V., and Ibragimova, N. Ya., eds., 1981. *Ekonomika pishchevoy promyshlennosti.* Moskva: "Legkaya i pishchevaya promyshlennost'."

Karchikyan, O. Kh. 1977. *Proizvodstvo i protrebleniye sel' skokhozyaystvennykh produktov.* Yerevan: Izdatel'stvo AN Armyanskoy SSSR.

Karapetyan, A. Kh. 1980. *Dokhody i potrebleniye naseleniya SSSR.* Moskva: "Statistika."

Komarov, V. Ye., and Chernyavskiy, U. G. 1973. *Dokhody i potrebleniye naseleniya SSSR.* Moskva: "Nauka."

Levin, A. I. 1969. *Sotsial'no-ekonomicheskiye problemy razvitiya sprosa naseleniya v SSSR.* Moskva: "Mysl'."

Mel'nikov, Ye. B. 1976. *Osnovy fiziologii pitaniya, sanitarii i gigiyeny.* Moskva: "Vysshaya shkola."

Nikol'skiy, I. V. 1981. Vzaimosvyazi geografii potrebleniya i geografii torgovli, *Vestnik Moskovskogo Universiteta. Seriya 5. Geografiya.* No. 2, pp. 33–38. Translated version: Nikol'skiy, I. V. 1982. Linkages between the geography of consumption and the geography of food retailing, *Soviet Geography: Review and Translation,* Vol. XXII, No. 9, pp. 640–646.

Petrovskiy, K. S. 1964. *Gigiyena pitaniya.* Moskva: "Meditsina."

Parta, R. E. 1982. Food Supply in the USSR: Worsening Trend, First Semester, 1982. N. P.: Radio Free Europe—Radio Liberty, Soviet Area Audience and Opinion Research, AR #10–82.

Sarkisyan, G. S., and Kuznetsova, N. P. 1967. *Potrebnosti dokhod sem'i.* Moskva: "Ekonomika."

Schoonover, D. B. 1974. The Soviet feed–livestock economy: preliminary findings on performance and trade implications, in *Prospects for Agricultural Trade with the USSR.* Washington, D.C.: U.S. Department of Agriculture, Economic Research Service.

Schroeder, G. E., and Denton, M. E. 1982. An index of consumption in the USSR, in *USSR: Measures of Economic Growth and Development, 1950–80.* Washington, D.C.: U.S. Government Printing Office, pp. 317–401.

Slater, J. 1975. Soviet Union: Factors affecting the availabilities of major food products to 1985. Paris: Organisation for Economic Co-operation and Development, Directorate for Agriculture and Food. Mimeographed. Restricted.

Table 7.1

Levels of Food Consumption, 1975
In specified units per person per year.

	Meat kg	Milk kg	Eggs eggs	Fish kg	Sugar kg	Vegetable oil kg	Potatoes kg	Vegetables kg	Grain Prod. kg
USSR	57	316	216	16.8	40.9	7.6	120	89	141
Es SSR	80	442	258	27.6	41.3	8.2	140	79	104
La SSR	77	484	239	23.5	43.8	6.7	138	73	106
Li SSR[a]	76	447	234	15.4	36.9	5.0	186	84	108
Be SSR	62	385	260	17.2	39.5	5.7	215	75	141
Uk SSR	60	335	210	15.9	45.4	8.5	143	118	151
RSFSR	60	332	252	21.1	43.6	8.0	131	84	131
Ge SSR	42	286	109	6.8	38.1	3.8	35	63	189
Ar SSR	42	392	125	3.5	28.5	1.9	55	110	147
Az SSR	32	290	122	3.7	38.1	1.9	24	56	158
Tu SSR	47	154	75	4.1	26.0	5.9	26	89	159
Ki SSR	38	178	101	6.0	30.5	5.6	65	81	145

[a]1974 data.

Table 7.2

Republican Levels of Food Consumption as Percentage of the USSR Average, 1975

	Meat	Milk	Eggs	Fish	Sugar	Vegetable oil	Potatoes	Vegetables	Grain Prod.	Caloric Consumption
USSR	100	100	100	100	100	100	100	100	100	100
Es SSR	140	140	119	164	101	108	117	89	74	101.7
La SSR	135	153	111	140	107	88	115	82	75	104.4
Li SSR	133	141	108	92	90	66	155	94	77	99.5
Be SSR	109	122	120	102	97	75	179	84	100	107.8
Uk SSR	105	106	97	95	111	112	119	133	107	109.2
RSFSR	105	105	117	126	107	105	109	94	93	100.3
Ge SSR	74	91	50	40	93	50	29	71	134	100.4
Ar SSR	74	124	58	21	70	25	46	124	104	91.2
Az SSR	56	92	56	22	93	25	20	63	112	88.6
Tu SSR	82	49	35	24	64	78	22	100	113	81.1
Ki SSR	67	56	47	36	75	74	54	91	103	80.7

[a]According to Karchikyan (1977), p. 68.

Table 7.3

Recommended Norms of Food Consumption
In specified units per person per year.

	Meat kg	Milk kg	Eggs eggs	Fish kg	Sugar kg	Vegetable Oil kg	Potatoes kg	Vegetables kg	Grain Prod. kg
USSR	75	434	292	18.2	36	7.3	97	146	120
Es SSR	80	515	292	21.9	42	6.5	137	146	95
La SSR	80	515	292	21.9	42	5.5	137	146	95
Li SSR	77	515	292	18.2	40	5.8	146	146	95
Be SSR	77	439	328	18.2	33	7.3	146	128	120
Uk SSR	71	410	328	18.2	36	7.3	93	164	119
RSFSR	78	472	306	21.5	40	7.3	105	138	115
Ge SSR	69	319	220	11.0	29	6.9	58	150	148
Ar SSR	69	319	220	11.0	29	6.6	58	150	142
Az SSR	66	319	220	11.0	31	6.6	55	146	139
Tu SSR	64	319	146	11.0	24	7.7	55	164	146
Ki SSR	77	422	182	7.3	31	7.3	64	142	140

According to Donskova and Ibragimova (1981), pp. 40-41.

Table 7.4

Consumption as Percent of Recommended Norm, 1975

	Meat	Milk	Eggs	Fish	Sugar	Vegetable Oil	Potatoes	Vegetables	Grain Prod.	Caloric Consumption
USSR	76	73	74	92	114	104	124	61	118	98
Es SSR	100	86	88	126	98	126	102	54	109	96
La SSR	96	94	82	107	104	122	101	50	112	98
Li SSR	99	87	80	85	92	86	127	58	114	94
Be SSR	81	88	79	95	120	78	147	59	118	104
Uk SSR	85	82	64	87	126	116	154	72	127	108
RSFSR	77	70	82	98	109	110	125	61	114	96
Ge SSR	61	90	50	62	131	55	60	42	128	102
Ar SSR	61	123	57	32	98	29	95	73	104	93
Az SSR	48	91	55	34	123	29	44	38	114	83
Tu SSR	73	48	51	37	108	77	47	54	109	85
Ki SSR	49	42	55	82	98	77	102	57	104	80

[a]According to Karchikyan (1977), p. 68.

Table 7.5

Food Production, 1971 - 75
In specified units per person per year.

	Meat kg	Milk kg	Eggs eggs	Fish kg	Sugar kg	Vegetable Oil kg	Potatoes kg	Vegetables kg	Grain Prod. kg
USSR	56	350	206	29.3	304	9.4	359	91	727
Es SSR	115	832	329	211.1[a]	-	-	945	97	688
La SSR	97	713	254	174.7[b]	104	10.1	675	89	551
Li SSR	137	840	258	104.9[c]	261	1.7	817	114	731
Be SSR	85	622	247	0.7[c]	120	2.3	1405	81	600
Uk SSR	68	421	232	14.4	951	23.4	435	135	827
RSFSR	54	352	226	39.0	157	9.5	355	75	776
Ge SSR	25	109	100	17.1[d]	27	3.4	49	76	146
Ar SSR	24	149	114	0.4[e]	45	4.7	74	122	97
Az SSR	19	105	91	12.5	-	6.4	21	97	152

[a]1971 and 1972, averaged.
[b]1971 and 1975, averaged.
[c]1965 to 1969, averaged.
[d]1971 to 1973 and 1975, averaged.
[e]1970 and 1975, averaged.

Table 7.6

Correlation Between Some Independent Variables and
Per Person Food Consumption, 1975

Independent Variable	Meat	Milk	Eggs	Fish	Sugar	Vegetable Oil	Potatoes	Vegetables	Grain Prod.
Food Production kg per person	.924	.798	.958	.762	.278	.357	.923	.681	-.646
Retail Trade rub. per person	.928	.786	.826	.939	.598	.623	.675	.002	-.837
Affluence av. mo. wages of worker per person in av. household	.941	.644	.833	.956	.625	.796	.689	.120	-.809
Wages av. mo. wages of worker	.480	.066	.205	.416	-.122	.522	.082	.265	-.562

Table 7.7

Other Independent Variables Used for Correlation With
Per Head Food Consumption, 1975

	Retail Trade rub. per head	Affluence av. mo. wages of worker per person in av. household rub.	Wages av. mo. wages of worker rub.
USSR	827	39.4	145.8
Es SSR	1171	51.5	159.8
La SSR	1169	45.8	146.4
Li SSR	924	41.9	142.3
Be SSR	795	34.9	125.5
Uk SSR	754	39.3	133.5
RSFSR	912	43.8	153.2
Ge SSR	650	29.0	118.9
Ar SSR	655	27.7	138.6
Az SSR	488	24.5	125.1
Tu SSR	579	31.3	162.6
Ki SSR	595	29.2	134.2

APPENDIX A

Sources for Table 7.1:

Ekonomika i kul'tura Litovskoy SSR v 1975 godu. Statisticheskiy yezhegodnik. Vilnius: "Mintis," 1976. P. 234.

Kirgizstan za gody Sovetskoy vlasti. Yubileynyy Statisticheskiy yezhegodnik. Frunze: "Kyrgyzstan," 1977. P. 193.

Narodne hospodarstvo Ukrains'koi RSR u 1979 rotsi. Statystychnyy shchorichnyk. Kyiv: "Tekhnika," 1980. P. 254.

Narodnoye khozyaystvo Armyanskoy SSR v 1976 godu. Statisticheskiy yezhegodnik. Yerevan: "Ayastan," 1977. P. 182.

Narodnoye khozyaystvo Azerbaydzhanskoy SSR za 60 let. Yubileynyy Statisticheskiy sbornik. Baku: Azerbaydzhanskoye gosudarstvennoye izdatel'stvo, 1980. P. 233.

Narodnoye khozyaystvo Belorusskoy SSR 1980. Statisticheskiy yezhegodnik. Minsk: "Belarus,'" 1980. P. 195.

Narodnoye khozyaystvo Estonskoy SSR v 1979 godu. Statisticheskiy yezhegodnik. Tallin: "Eesti raamat," 1980. P. 219.

Narodnoye khozyaystvo Gruzinskoy SSR za 60 let. Yubileynyy Statisticheskiy yezhegodnik. Tbilisi: "Sabchota sakartvelo," 1980. P. 208.

Narodnoye khozyaystvo Latviyskoy y SSR v 1978 godu. Statisticheskiy yezhegodnik. Riga: "Liesma," 1979. P. 174.

Narodnoye khozyaystvo RSFSR v 1978 g. Statisticheskiy yezhegodnik. Moskva: "Statistika," 1979. P. 217.

Narodnoye khozyaystvo SSSR v 1979 g. Statisticheskiy yezhegodnik. Moskva: "Statistika," 1980. P. 432.

Narodnoye khozyaystvo Turkmenskoy SSR v 1980 godu. Statisticheskiy yezhegodnik. Ashkhabad: "Turkmenistan," 1981. P. 137.

Data for Table 7.5 calculated according to:

Ekonomika i kul'tura Litovskoy SSR v 1974 godu. Vilnius, 1975. P. 93.

Narodne hospodarstvo Ukrains'koi RSR u 1973 rotsi. Kyiv, 1974. P. 164.

Nar. hosp. Ukrains'koi RSR u 1975 rotsi. Kyiv, 1976. P. 143.

Nar. hosp. Ukrains'koi RSR u 1979 rotsi. Kyiv, 1980. P. 114.

Nardnoye khozyaystvo Armyanskoy SSR v 1977 godu. Yerevan, 1978. Pp. 60–61.

Nar. khoz. Azerbaydzhanskoy SSR v 1974 godu. Baku, 1975. P. 96.

Nar. khoz. Azerbaydzhanskoy SSR za 60 let. Baku, 1980. Pp. 93–94.

Nar. khoz. Estonskoy SSR v 1972 godu. Tallinn, 1973. Pp. 102–105.

Nar. khoz. Gruzinskoy SSR k 60-letiyu Velikogo Oktyabrya. Tbilisi, 1977. Pp. 66–67.

Nar. khoz. Gruzinskoy SSR v 1973 godu. Tbilisi, 1974. Pp. 98–99.

Nar. khoz. Kirgizskoy SSR. Yubileynyy statisticheskiy sbornik. Frunze, 1973. Pp. 41–42.

Nar. khoz. Kirgizskoy SSR v 1975 godu. Frunze, 1976. P. 60.

Nar. khoz. Kirgizskoy SSR v 1979 godu. Frunze, 1980. P. 56.

Nar. khoz. Latviyskoy SSR v 1971 godu. Riga, 1972. Pp. 100–101.

Nar. khoz. Latviyskoy SSR v 1978 godu. Riga, 1979. P. 72.

Nar. khoz. Litovskoy SSR v 1978 g. Vilnius, 1979. P. 63.

Nar. khoz. RSFSR v 1975 g. Moskva, 1976. P. 130.

Nar. khoz, RSFSR v 1980 g. Moskva, 1981. P. 105.

Nar. khoz. SSSR v 1968 g. Moskva, 1969. P. 305.
Nar. khoz. SSSR v 1969 g. Moskva, 1970. P. 269.
Narodnoye khozyaystvo SSSR v 1922-1972 gg. Yubileynyy statisticheskiy yezhegodnik.
Moskva: "Statistika," 1972. Pp. 499, 503, 504, 516, 518, 519, 531, 533, 534,
544, 546, 556, 558, 569, 571, 581, 583, 584, 594, 596, 597, 607, 608, 609,
619, 621, 631, 632, 633, 644, 645, 646, 656, 658, 659, 669, 670, 671, 681,
682, 683.
Nar. khoz. SSSR v 1975 g. Moskva, 1976. Pp. 10, 298-303, 360, 371, 372, 381,
398-399.
Nar. khoz. SSSR v 1980 g. Moskva, 1981. Pp. 193-196.
Nar. khoz. Turkmenskoy SSSR v 1980 g. Ashkhabad, 1981. Pp. 42-43.

Sources for Table 7.7:

Itogi vsesoyuznoy perepisi naseleniya 1970 goda. Tom VII. Moskva, 1974. Pp. 234-237.
Nar. hosp. Ukrains'koi RSR u 1979 rotsi. Kyiv, 1980. P. 222.
Nar. khoz. Armyanskoy SSR v 1975 godu. Yerevan, 1976. P. 178.
Nar. khoz. Azerbaydzhanskoy SSR za 60 let. Baku, 1980. P. 205.
Nar. khoz. Belorusskoy SSR. 1980. Minsk, 1980. P. 174.
Nar. khoz. Estonskoy SSR v 1979 godu. Tallinn, 1980. P. 199.
Nar. khoz. Gruzinskoy SSR za 60 let. Tbilisi, 1980. P. 184.
Nar. khoz. Kirgizskoy SSR v 1980 godu. Frunze, 1981. P. 205.
Nar. khoz. Latviyskoy SSR v 1978 godu. Riga, 1979. P. 159.
Nar. khoz. Litovskoy SSR za 40 let. Vilnius, 1980. P. 168.
Nar. khoz. RSFSR v 1978 g. Moskva, 1979. P. 197.
Nar. khoz. SSSR v 1975 g. Moskva, 1976. P. 619.
Nar. khoz. Turkmenskoy SSR v 1980 godu. Ashkhabad, 1981. P. 117.

8

The Experiments in Georgia, 1974–1984: Quest for a New Organization in the Soviet Agricultural System

Jean Radvanyi

In 1974, the first RAPO (agro-industrial district union) was established, on an experimental basis, in Abasha district (rayon) of Georgia. From 1978 to 1982, this new form of management of the agricultural complex was progressively generalized to all districts in Georgia. An all-Union standard by-law for RAPOs, published in late 1982 (Izvestiya 9/12/82), took the generalization beyond the borders of that Republic. In March 1983, a Georgian State Committee for agricultural production was created regrouping the functions of three ministries—agriculture, land improvements and technical supply (*Zarja Vostoka [ZV]* 12/3/83). While Georgia was not the only Republic to experiment along those lines, parallel schemes were launched in Estonia from 1975 onwards, and soon after also in Latvia, it became a kind of testing ground for new agricultural strategy, a status which became nearly official under a resolution of the CC of the CPSU (*Pravda* 25/12/83). The aim of this paper is to show what was at stake in these Georgia experiments with emphasis on the main innovations and on the obstacles encountered.

Local Level: Abasha and the Setting Up of the RAPOs

The Abasha agro-industrial union was created in October 1974. Its by-laws, modified in 1978, serve as the basis for the drafting of the standard by-laws for RAPOs in the Republic, as published in *ZV* (24/1/84). The basic principle, and the main innovation compared to Soviet rules, was the reuniting in a single body of all the agents of the agro-industrial complex represented on the territory of a district, regardless of the administration they may be subordinated to, including farm units (kolkhoz, sovkhoz, interunit groupings); technical services (input supply, land improvements, chemicals); transport and building services; processing firms. Some of these firms, those under the jurisdiction of the State Committee for Agriculture at the level of the Republic, were under the direct responsibility of the RAPO. The others were ruled by the principle of dual subordination. They remained subjected to the norms of their administration (Federal or joint Federal-Republican). Directives and plans, however, must compulsorily pass through the RAPO management which coordinates the whole body.

The Georgian RAPO by-laws rest of course on the standard Soviet by-laws of December 1982, but also are inspired by the Abasha experience and differ in various aspects from the Soviet standard, particularly with regard to subordination relationships and the definition of links between the RAPOs and central administrations. See for instance the end of article 3: "It is only with the agreement of the RAPO that bodies exerting their tutelage over firms under double subordination may decide upon matters concerning the agro-industrial complex." This is not in the standard Federal by-laws.

All firms entering the RAPO pay a levy. The proceeds go into a common fund managed by the RAPO management which thus has real means to get things done. In Abasha the levy is 12 rubles for every 1,000 rubles of turnover. It finances RAPO staff and 20 percent of the proceeds go into four funds: productive investments (30 percent), bonuses (16 percent), sociocultural purposes and housing (50 percent), reserves (4 percent).[1] The total amount of those levies varies greatly among districts: 90,000 rubles in Abasha in 1979 when a number of firms refused to pay their share; seven million rubles in Maharadze, a rich tea growing district (*Izvestiya* 19/1/83). The sum of these decentralized funds exceeded 50 million rubles in 1983 for the whole Republic (*ZV* 7/4/84); this is 10 percent of all agricultural investments. In addition to those amounts, which it preferentially directs towards local weak points, the RAPO can redistribute part of the firm's own financial and capital resources in order to correct certain disparities.

The advantages of a unified territorial authority and management are obvious, and their desirability had long been expressed in the press (*Zemle odin khozyain*). To implement it, the experiences in Bulgaria and Hungary, which Abasha leaders visited were specifically taken into account.

The standard organizational chart, Figure 8.1, which is dated after the reform of the ministries (which will be commented upon later), is interesting on several counts. In principle, coordination between activities long separated under different and ultimately opposed administrations is ensured: crop production and chemicals; livestock raising and fodder base; land improvements, crop production, processing. In Abasha, in 1973 there were eight supervisory administrations for 18,000 hectares of arable land. Technical supply services are regrouped directly under the authority of the president. The shadow of the MTS is thus revived, although in a quite different context, and the Georgian leaders do not hesitate to complain about "their overhasty suppression." The management has means of its own to further self development including: planning services, intersectoral links services, and technical innovation that should allow it also to fight to remove obstacles that are still numerous in practical operations.

The first obstacle is to really regroup all the firms concerned under a single authority. It is a simple matter for kolkhozy and sovkhozy which are under the jurisdiction of authorities at the Republic level. As early as 1974, in Georgia, the Ministry of Agriculture, covering kolkhozy, and the Ministry for Sovkhozy had been merged. In an interview in 1983, Mgeladze emphasized the flexibility of the kolkhoz system and expressed regrets that, in certain districts and for certain production sectors, this form of production should have been too hastily abandoned for sovkhoz. It can in fact be observed that a part of the difficulties come from the administrations exerting authority over the specialized sovkhoz, such as the Ministry for Fruits and Vegetables and specialized Unions like Gruzchai for tea or Samtrest for grapes. These administrations are either Federal or joint Federal-Republic and sometimes refuse to enter the RAPO. In certain districts like Mtskheta they hold the majority; 10 firms out of 15 refused to join (*ZV* 2/7/81). In other cases, those administrations tried to avoid transfering part of their funds or their prerogatives to the district level. From this point of view, dual subordination is a complex issue. Most of the governing bodies at the level of the Republic considered, at the outset, that this dual subordination was a source of security ensuring a certain flexibility. In fact, the higher administrations that were not at the level of the Republic were very reluctant to apply this principle and often went on ignoring the very existence of this new territorial echelon in their instructions to their firms. From their side, RAPO leaders more and more openly criticized this principle to the point of requesting its abandonment (*Pravda* 2/5/84). It is in fact an element of uncertainty that slows down the move towards more autonomy in decisionmaking and investments and maintains an intense level of exchange of administrative circulars. To give a measure of this, it can be noted that, before the reform of the ministries, the RAPO in Abasha received yearly, from the three main agricultural administrations, up to 5,240 documents per year or 14 per day (*Pravda* 21/1/82).

The generalization of RAPOs to the whole of the Soviet Union in May 1982 and the merger of the three Georgian ministries was a first step towards removal of those structural obstacles. One of the essential features of this whole process must be emphasized. It is first through an administrative type of integration that the global cohesion of the Agro-industrial Complex (AIC) is striven for. In order to be efficient, a Soviet livestock raising complex must also own its fodder base. A RAPO must have direct control not only over the production sectors but also over the entire chain of services related to them. This originates from the weakness of the economic mechanisms that in practice exclude the possibility of resorting to market relationships. The Georgian theoreticians of the reform did not at all consider the weakness or absence of those market relationships a theoretical necessity. On the contrary, the practice of exchanges of services within the RAPO has made it necessary to experiment with accounting prices (raschetnye tseny) decided upon jointly at RAPO level, probably a decisive aspect of the reform (*ZV* 18/5/82). Delays and blockages in those matters, particularly in the operation of the administration and on account of the infinite variety of operational rules, were, however, such that it was not possible to consider going further towards what could be a more radical solution to those problems. It is not surprising, however, that those experiments served as a starting point for the raising of questions concerning the need for more open economic mechanisms: free choice of partners; adoption of commercial points of view (kommercheskiy podkhod); greater decentralization of the funds through the creation of a single budgetary package placed under RAPO's responsibility, etc.

Labor Teams and Private Plots in the Case of Abasha

The second field of experiments begun in Abasha concerns the organization of farm labor and relationships with the private sector. Those are not in a strict sense innovations but rather the revival of experiments launched in the early sixties and subsequently harshly criticized. As early as 1975 the zveno system of the self-managed zveno or brigade was generalized in Abasha district. Part of the land, for instance 40 hectares of corn (maize), and part of the equipment was alloted for a few years to a self-managed brigade that maintained contractual relationships with the farm unit (kolkhoz or sovkhoz) or directly with the RAPO. Concrete forms of these arrangements vary a great deal in accordance with the nature of the soil and the types of production. Some brigades are complex and take over all operations on a mixed farming area; others are specialized along product lines or by function, such as mechanization or land improvement. Two aspects are worth noting. Incentives through wages and bonuses are noticeably increased. In Abasha, in addition to the normal wage, the zveno or brigade gets 10 to 20 percent of the crop returns if the Plan is fulfilled and 50 to 70 percent of production outside the plan. For fruit and vegetables these premia are calculated in state purchase prices and paid in cash. For grain and fodder, they are paid in kind, which is important. This provides farm families with a higher consumption level and, more important, ensures supplies essential for their small plot livestock raising operations. It eliminates the need to engage in complex centralized storage operations. Another aspect is that a zveno may be a family unit. This form is rather extensively developed in Georgia. It is justified by the special characteristics of the production, such as citrus groves, the small size of plots due to regional topography, by the special mountainous environment and by the dispersed forms of settlement. In certain cases, it is the kolkhoz itself which is transformed along these lines. "In Mestia district kolkhozy ran deficits for years. At last, we reached the conclusion that it was foolish out there to have 400–600 person farms. Now the livestock and plots are allocated to the peasants, they are helped with loans, equipment, fertilizer and contracts for sales of output at pre-fixed prices are drawn. The kolkhoz exists but it is not the same; it has no brigade leaders, no farm manager, no comptroller; only the indispensable remains."[2]

It is significant that a parallel evolution was observed in the relationship between the collective and the private sector, essentially for livestock production. In this case, also, various types of contracts are utilized between the collective units and the farmers, individually or grouped by families or neighborhoods. The farm unit sells young calves or sows, and fodder and commits itself to provide free technical assistance. The animal husbandryman commits himself to sell, at a determined price, a fixed part of the production. In essence, such *kontraktatsiya* is not new, only its terms were defined in a narrower sense, the upper limits of livestock in private ownership had to be observed, and the practice was less widespread and not generally advocated.[3] Entered into Abasha on more liberal terms and in great volume in 1979, this system spread rapidly to the whole Republic. From 1981 onwards there were strong pressures so that each family entered into such a contract and kept at least one cow. There was thus a conjunction between increased shortages of meat and milk in a Republic which, during a whole period, had neglected livestock production in favor of special crops, and a strategic turning point with regard to the private sector.[4] We have for too long misestimated this form of production, say the Georgians. It should be put back into its rightful place but with close integration with the collective production system. Under the new contracts, individual plot production is more dependent on inputs and technical services provided by the collective sector and it is requested that the price for those inputs be in line with State prices. Even labor is more integrated: the labor days supplied on the plots to provide fodder for stock under contract are counted towards the minimal work time that each farmer owes to the collective sector, and that is the only obligation demanded when the contracts are signed. All this reminds one very much of the Hungarian methods, which have frequently been mentioned in the Georgian press (e.g., *ZV* 16/10/81), and at a Soviet-Hungarian conference on such questions that was held in Tbilisi in October 1981 (*ZV* 25/10/81). Mgeladze himself began to advocate such a policy for Abasha district soon after his return from a trip to Hungary in 1981.

Financial conditions seem, on the other hand, favorable enough to gain peasant participation. In Abasha, in 1982, 4,350 pig raising contracts were signed out of a total of 9,700 families (dvor). This allowed for deliveries amounting to 4,200 tons of meat providing 3 million rubles additional receipts for farmers and 1.9 million for the collective units that centralize deliveries (*Pravda* 7/2/83). In Abasha the private plots provide 47 percent of meat deliveries and 7 percent of fruit deliveries.[5]

Should one refer to a decollectivization process? It should be noted that production in the family zveno or that of plots remains fully planned and controlled by the collective sector which rules on the allocation of land, controls most of the seeds, young stock, fodder and technology. To prevent a surge of speculation, free market channels appear to have been more strictly controlled during recent years. This did not prevent a rather lax interpretation of the new rules from occurring in certain districts which brought about official clarification: "collective units were and remain the main producers; they are the hub of the rural economic mechanism" (Shevardnaze *ZV* 7/4/84). However, in spite of "the occurrence of misunderstandings and differences in appreciation," "cooperation with the population must be developed and strengthened." Shevardnadze also insisted on the need to reject dogmatic formalism on those matters. Collective forms must be more flexible and adjust to local conditions and the auxiliary economy must be redefined; "it should be said bluntly that it is not at all a private sector but a real variety of the collective sector of the collective production and economy (*ZV* 26/11/81). At the same time, he insisted on the fact that, during the tenth Plan, growth had been faster in the collective than in the private sector, 40 percent compared to an overall growth of 34 percent. The latter sector was, however, able to rapidly cover a part of the food deficit and with smaller State investments.

On the whole, RAPOs are credited with a large share of the significant improvements in the economic indices for the agro-industrial complex of Georgia during the tenth and early eleventh Plans. Their role is felt to be particularly important in all traditionally weak links: mechanization, use of chemicals, transport, storage, first processing. A large share of their means was, in fact, concentrated there, one of the top objectives being to reduce losses officially estimated, in Georgia, at 20 to 25 percent of production (Shevardnadze, *ZV* 27/3/81). This experiment was made possible only because the party took direct control of those matters. The RAPO president is, by law, vice-president of raiispolkom and de facto member of raikom. Above all, the leaders of the Georgian party controlled the operations from start to finish. It is the raikom secretary who launched the Abasha experiment with the support of the party leadership, and this support was vital when the reluctance of State administrations, at the Federal or Republic level, had to be countered. The blockages then encountered clearly showed the need for the later stage of the reform.

The Restructuration of the
Republic Level Machinery

The generalization of the Abasha experiment beyond the local level rapidly made contradictions visible at the Republican level. Like other small Union Republics, Georgia has no intermediate *oblast'* administration, which is the basic intermediate level in the large republics and generally is considered corresponding to the Republican level in the small Republics. It is true, the Republican level with its intricate administrative machinery, offices and ministries, has its own specifics in any case, but for the rest, the parallel to the Georgian development is that on the *oblast'* level.

In a first stage, the RAPOs in Georgia had been placed under the authority of the Council of Ministers of the Republic. It was considered that the authority of the Minister of Agriculture was not sufficient to solve problems involving other administrations, usually Federal-Republican ones. This meant that most of the final decisionmaking passed to the Central Committee of the Georgian CP itself. As mentioned above, the various administrations existing at the level of the Republic went on operating without real coordination in spite of the fact that their local representatives formally joined the RAPO. Finally, under the joint request of the representatives from Georgia and Estonia, the CPSU Politburo decided (*Pravda* 19/2/83) to extend the experiment by regrouping the ministries of Agriculture and Land Improvements and the State Committee on technical supply in a new body, the Federal-Republic State Committee on agricultural production.[6] In May 1984, it was announced that the rural construction organization Kolkhozstroi and all the agricultural research institutes up to then belonging to the Lenin Academy of Agricultural Sciences and those under the branch ministries would be subordinated to this new committee. It became the body that directed all RAPOs and covered all the essential technical services that were the major weak point of the existing system. Simultaneously, most dual subordination links were to be severed (*ZV* 15 and 17/3/83). The local branches of the three administrations were reorganized as well apparent on the RAPO organizational chart presented in 1984. The State Committee organization chart, see Figure 8.2, shows the tightening of responsibilities. All administrations specific to kolkhozy and sovkhozy are disbanded. Compared to the previous organization, twelve of the previous 24 vice-ministerial posts were done away with, the three first vice presidents retained their ministerial rank, and 400 posts out of 1200 were suppressed. Most of the cadres concerned were assigned to the RAPOs. It should be noted that the vital technical services, such as transportation and technical supply, economic matters and cadres are directly under the President.

This reshuffling at the Republican level is the first instance of a tightening of the Soviet State machinery after years of increasing fragmentation, the last instances being the creation, in 1980, of the Ministry of Fruits and Vegetables and that of Fertilizers. The reorganization exerted a very favorable role on the operation of the Agro-Industrial Complex (AIC) in the Republic, but it raised two unresolved questions. Firstly, parts of the agricultural production system still remained outside the new body. This is particularly sensitive in Georgia where a number of the sovkhozy specializing in products managed at the Federal level, such as wine and citrus, were under the authority of Federal or joint Federal-Republican administrations, Samtrest, Gruzchai, Fruits and Vegetables Ministry, etc. Many articles criticized the fact that, when this last ministry was created, 61 sovkhozy were separated from their parent authority at the Republic level, which made coordination and production equilibrium more difficult to obtain.[7] Similarly, the Ministry of Rural Building and other important bodies were not integrated.

It should however be noted that, at the Republic level, there are some coordinating structures. They may operate within the AIC itself, in Estonia, for example, the president of Agroprom (State Committee for Agro-Industry) is also president of the AIC, or at the level of the Council of Ministers where an intersectorial coordination council headed by the vice-chairman of the Council of Ministers in charge of agricultural matters has been operating since the end of 1981. On the other hand, a large concentration effort has been implemented within various parts of the AIC with the creation, at the Republic level, of production unions (PO) and scientific production unions (NPO), for instance for specialized transport equipment, farm machinery, and food industry machinery. These are crucial aspects since those new unions that regroup factories and institutes from different ministries and different Federal services are able to coordinate the production of these diverse units and adapt it to the specific needs of the Republic.

The second question is of a quite different nature and is relative to Republic-central organ relationships. The new State Committee on Agricultural Production now had no less than four administrations supervising it. These are the Georgia Council of Ministers, the two joint Federal-Republic Ministries of Agriculture and Land Improvements, and the USSR State Committee on farm technology. In addition, it must maintain relationships with numerous other central administration organs that were sometimes non-cooperative. *Pravda* (16/2/84) reported that some of these central organs merely severed all contacts while others went on sending directives without taking into account the changes that had taken place.

Some Aspects of Center-Periphery Relationships

Georgian leaders did not fail to emphasize that the generalization of their experiment (according to Mgeladze, July 83, the same structures were to be adopted by three other Republics) required a stronger effort to implement equivalent changes at the Federal level. Certain structural defects have become evident, including center-periphery relationships. Two trips to Georgia by Gorbachev were probably not trivial. The first took place at the end of 1982 before the merger of ministries was announced. The second, at the end of 1983, when the RAPO by-laws were finalized (*ZV* 8/1/83 and 20/1/84). Still, conflicts with central administrations remained numerous. In some cases, it is mostly a matter of administrative rigidity that leads to prolonged application of outdated and inadequate norms. Fertilizer allocation rules are a telling example. There is a common base quota for the whole Union per sown hectare. Georgians have criticized this method of computation which discriminates against the planting of orchards on arable land which takes place extensively in their Republic. Price policy and services to and supplies for farm units raise much graver problems. Georgia, like other Republics, has obtained some changes in Federal policy. For instance, to encourage quality vineyards and wine, part of the grapes were purchased at prices five times higher than the norm (1.5 rubles against 0.3 to 0.4 rubles in 1983). This type of adjustment was only obtained after long negotiations, and it caused major discrepancies in profitability levels between farms in different regions. For a set of typical farms, the average level of profitability, however defined, is said to be around 75 percent for citrus, 40 to 80 percent for tea, 50 to 80 percent for vineyards but only 2 to 10 percent for grain and potatoes, 7 to 15 percent for animal husbandry.[8] So the claims of leaders at the Republic level were much broader: "the Minister (of Agriculture) is convinced that Republic level bodies must have the possibility of regulating prices taking into account concrete conditions in the area and the interests of the economy at large."[9]

A significant instance of the difficult debates between bodies at Republic and Federal levels is given by the extraordinary adventure of "small mechanization." The Georgians take great interest in this for three reasons: small sized equipment is indispensable, as it is in the rest of the Soviet Union, for tilling the plots; it is also needed for cultivating orchards and vegetable crops which are important in Georgia; it is required in all steep fields and 70 percent of the agricultural area of the Republic, including tea gardens and most citrus orchards, are in mountain or piedmont zones. Complaints about lack of suitable equipment have been voiced for many years. A resolution of the CPSU Central Committee of February 1947 on the development of agriculture visualized that, in 1948, gardens should be mechanized and small tools produced. At an important conference in Baku in 1961, this matter was at the heart of the debates since it was noted that, in spite of a new resolution of 1953, the situation had not changed. In December 1964, at the supreme Soviet of the USSR, Chikovani, a representative from Georgia, after having thanked the Minister for his 1959 answer promising the delivery of small tractors from a factory in Volgograd, asked what had become of them. Then, in two articles in *Izvestiya* (12/1/77 and 15/8/79), Isvashchenko noted that a whole small tractor factory (at Pavlov on the Oka) has "vanished" being "spirited away" by the Minister while the Kutaissi factory does produce small tractors of which farmers can make no use. In 1974, the Georgians obtained the creation of a factory specialized in those small tractors, but again this factory was "forgotten" by the federal Ministry (*ZV* 21/6/81).

It appears that this last incident caused a scandal and the Georgians obtained not only the start of construction on this factory in Kutaissi but the creation of a whole specialized sector with a Federal research institute, a drafting office and three factories, two of which existed but are to be rebuilt and specialized, in order to cover the needs of the Republic and neighboring areas. The Kutaissi factory should have a capacity of 35,000 one-axle tractors, 15,000 small tractors and 15,000 sets of implements.

At stake here are the general problems of Soviet economic planning, and the case of Pavlov proves that they do not occur only in peripherial Republics. This instance shows that regional and republic level bodies must, in addition to correcting their own inadequacies, lead a watchful fight against central organs prone to revising downwards production plans for the farm units and factories under their authority or changing without warning their specialization and jeopardizing the plans at the Republic level and ruining regional consistency. Georgian leaders have insisted on several occasions on the fact that the sovkhozy and firms that were not under Republic jurisdiction were more systematically in deficit or failing in Plan fulfillment. For instance, between 1971 and 1980, agro-food firms under Federal authority registered a deficit compared to the Plan of 376 million rubles, 24.4 percent of the Plan, a deficit that was covered by firms under Republican authority (*ZV* 19/6/81). Here again the Georgians made themselves conspicuous by innovating a fundamental point, though the actual effects of their move are hard to evaluate. Georgians requested that an audit be made on numerous central administrations in order to measure their failures to meet their obligations (*ZV* 19 and 21/6/81). Following this they passed a decree prohibiting administrations at the Republic level and firms under Federal authority located in Georgia, from modifying their plans without previous agreement by the Council of Ministers and the Central Committee of the Republic Party (*ZV* 17/3/83).

Even though many points could not be covered,[10] this analysis shows that the experiments in Georgia since 1974 have had effects on the whole agricultural system.[11] The theoreticians of this reform emphasized that it involved no rupture in existing structures but attempts to change these structures through adaptation. Preventing events like those of the Khruschev era is an obvious concern. Many of the propositions formulated during his regime are, however, being revived, as are several of the innovations in agricultural organizations of various more advanced socialist countries. Maybe the great signficance of these developments is precisely that they create no rupture while, at the same time, allowing by stages rather extensive changes in the rules of the game.

Notes

1. G. Mgeladze (et al.), *Abashskij opyt upravleniya: rezul'taty, perspektivy.* Tbilissi 1982. This is a characteristic example of the role of the Party in such matters. Mgeladze, previously on the Republican Party *apparat,* was sent to Abasha as First Raikom Secretary in 1972. Thus it was the Party Central Committee of Georgia who through him organized the experiment. Afterwards, when it turned out to be successful, Mgeladze was appointed Minister of Agriculture in 1981 and President of the new State Committee of Georgia in 1983.

2. E. Shevardnadze: Iskat', deystvovat', utverzhdat'. *Izvestiya,* 12/1/84. Although Mestia, which Shevardnadze mentions as an example, is a mountain district, where such forms are most numerous, and in practice existed already before, it is clear from the context that he wants them to be applied in other districts as well.

3. For details of the Khrushchev and early Brezhnev period, see K.-E. Wadekin, *The Private Sector in Soviet Agriculture.* Berkeley, London etc., 1973.

4. E. Shevardnadze publicly announced the introduction of rationing by coupons for city people for those commodities (normirovannoe snabzhenie) (*ZV,* 26/11/81). Rural people therefore must cease their purchases in town which increases the pressure to generalize private livestock raising. In 1980, 30 percent of rural families with a plot had no cow, 60 percent no pig, 84 percent no sheep and therefore purchased through trade channels. Shortages were increased by the decision to put a ceiling

on Federal deliveries to the Republic at the previous level of 65,000 tons of meat and 840,000 tons of milk products, 46 percent and 126 percent of local production. This decision emphasized the wish that the Republic becomes rapidly autonomous in basic commodities.

5. For Georgia as a whole plots produced 89 percent of meat production in 1940, 70 percent in 1970 and 59 percent in 1979; for milk for the same years, 89, 58 and 54 percent; for grapes, 61 percent in 1966–70 and 56 percent in 1979; for citrus, 64 and 78 percent for the same years. See also, on those matters: J. Stadelbauer, *Studien zur Agrargeographie Transkaukasiens,* Giessen, 1983 and J. Radvanyi, Traditions et modernizations de l'agriculture caucasienne. In Societe et espaces ruraux dans les pays de l'Est. Montpellier, 1984.

6. In Estonia it was named "agro-industrial association" (agro-promyslennoe ob'edinenie), which was the name also for the corresponding organizations on the *oblast'* level, where such level exists. There seemed to be reluctance, however, in some Republics. In November 1984 the author was told by an Azerbaidzhan economist that this experiment will not be realized in the Azerbaidzhan Union Republic.

7. V. Kadulin, "Gruzija, eksperiment nabiraet silu." *Kommunist,* 1982, No. 7, p. 74.

8. *Rekomendatsii po sistemam vedeniya sel'skogo khozjajstva Gr. SSR.* Tbilissi, 1982.

9. Kadulin, *Loc. cit.*

10. Among complementary experiments particular mention should be made of attempts to computerize grape harvest operations at the level of a whole district (Telavi) and even to computerize production, transport and distribution operations for the whole of farming activities in the suburban district of Gardaban on the outskirts of Tbilissi.

11. A decision of the Central Committee of the CPSU and the Council of Ministers (*Pravda,* 23/11/1985) extended the Georgian and Estonian reforms to the entire Soviet Union by establishing Gosagprom, the State Committee for Agro-industry at the Federal and Republic levels. Gosagprom subsumes six ministries, Agriculture, Fruits and Vegetables, Meat and Milk Industry, Rural Construction and the State Committee on Technical Supplies. In the Summer of 1986 the author was informed that a further reorganization could place the Ministry of Land Improvements under the aegis of Gosagprom.

Figure 8.1

STANDARD ORGANIZATIONAL CHART OF A RAPO

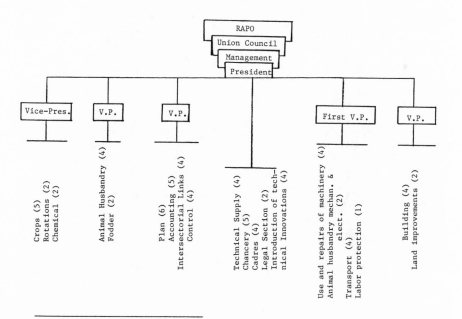

RAPO = Rayonnoe Agro-Promyshlennoe Ob'edinenie
Figures in brackets indicate the optimal staff numbers

Source: <u>Zarja Vostoka</u> 24/1/84

Figure 8.2

ORGANIZATION CHART OF GEORGIA STATE COMMITTEE FOR AGRICULTURAL PRODUCTION
(as of July 1983)

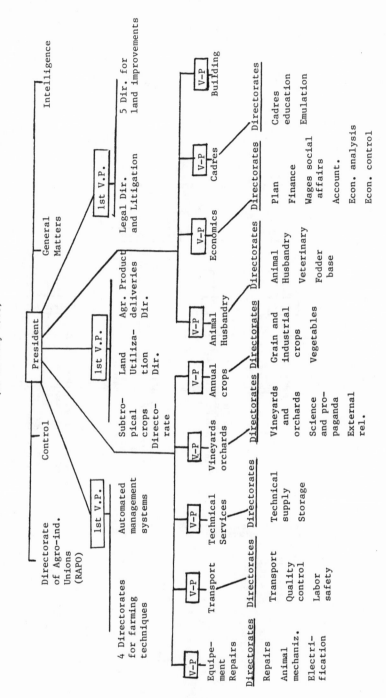

The Role of Agriculture in the Polish Economic Crisis and Recovery

9

An Overview of the Role of Agriculture in the Polish Economic Crisis

Zbigniew M. Fallenbuchl

After a period of rapid economic growth in the first half of the 1970s, the rate of growth of Net Domestic Material Product (NDMP or "produced national income") in Poland started to decline in the middle of the decade. It dropped from above 10 percent in 1972–74 and 9.0 percent in 1975 to 6.8 percent in 1976, 5.0 in 1977, 3.0 in 1978, −2.3 in 1979, −6.0 in 1980, −12.0 in 1981 and −5.5 in 1982. A positive rate appeared again in 1983 (4.0–5.0 percent), but the economy has not yet been stabilized. The crisis is extremely severe because it is composed of several overimposed elements, of which the state of agriculture is one. This sector of the economy has been adversely affected by a combination of institutional reorganizations, based on doctrinal and systemic concepts and not on pragmatic approach, the application of a development strategy that was based on the exploitation or, at least, neglect of agriculture, an inefficient and corrupt bureaucratic control and various short-run political considerations. In every decade agriculture was faced with a new drive to impose some institutional changes, each of which created instability, imposed costs and left some long-term consequences.

The 1940s witnessed a mass resettlement, post-war reconstruction and an agrarian reform that accepted the average area of new farms of 6.9 hectares (together 5.6 million hectares allocated), as compared with the average 9.3 hectares (total of 1.5 million hectares allocated) and the average enlargement of 2.0 hectares (500 thousand hectares allocated) of the 1918–39 reform, which had as its objective the creation of stronger individual farms. Larger farmers were regarded as a capitalist element in rural areas. Land transactions were restricted and the obligatory deliveries and taxation were strongly progressive according to the size of the land holding. Some liberalization appeared after 1956, but at the same time the maximum area of the holding was reduced in 1957 below the limit allowed by the agrarian reform legislation.

New restrictions were introduced in the 1960s. They were followed by a relaxation at the beginning of the 1970s, when obligatory deliveries were abolished, selling and buying of land encouraged and preferential treatment was given to larger farms producing a high proportion of their output for the market. Some de facto limitations appeared again in the second half of the decade, and some new relaxation in the early 1980s, including a return to the maximum of private holdings specified in the reform and a constitutional guarantee of the role of individual farmers.[1]

The reverses in the policy and inconsistencies in its implementation were responsible for no improvements in the agrarian structure until the beginning of the 1980s. Although some improvements were induced by recent policy changes, the unfavourable agrarian structure remains one of the main obstacles to modernization, improvement in productivity and expansion of production.[2] An interesting discussion has appeared in the economic press as to whether the authorities should now support the larger farmers, who are not only more productive but also less numerous and, therefore, easier to control and to integrate into socialist economy through contracts for deliveries of crops, linkages between the allocation of inputs and deliveries, and credits, or on the contrary, the medium farmers.[3] There are also warnings that the acceptance of one or another strategy may become another drive, supported by administrative pressures, and that changes in the agrarian structure must be gradual to be effective.[4]

At the beginning of the 1950s a collectivization drive destabilized agriculture. The number of collective farms increased from 635 with 16.9 thousand families and an area of 190.3 thousand hectares in 1950 to 9,076 with 188.5 thousand families and an area of 1.9 million hectares in 1955. At the same time the area of arable land in the state farms increased from below 2 million hectares to 2.8 million, or from 9.6 to 13.5 percent of total arable land. When decollectivization was allowed in 1956 the number of collective farms dropped to 1,534 with 27 thousand families and an area of 260.1 thousand hectares.[5]

Harvests of crops and livestock that had been increasing from one year to another in the preceding period stagnated in 1951–56. In addition to various dislocations the collectivization drive itself was capital-intensive.[6] As a Polish economist pointed out in 1958, "investment outlays in cooperatives during the first period are not directed for the expansion of production but for the transformation of the ownership relations" and "the transfer of cow from an individual to a collective barn does not result immediately in an increase in production and incomes which could cover those outlays."[7]

Ever since the decollectivization of agriculture, the policy towards the private sector was inconsistent. Political leaders, on the one hand, have needed its output, especially because this sector has a lower capital- and material-intensity and is more productive. On the other hand, they have expected it to disappear. The socialist reconstruction has always been accepted as a long-run objective and the private sector should therefore not be allowed to become too successful. It has not only suffered from underinvestment but also has been subject to many restrictions, heavy taxation and, until January 1, 1972, obligatory deliveries. The average income of individual farmers fluctuated between 15 to 26 percent below the average income in the socialist sector during the 1970s. In order to eliminate this lag, which was about −5 percent in 1979–80, prices were adjusted and the difference changed to +15 percent in favour of individual farmers in 1981.[8] However, despite policy declarations, farmers' incomes dropped again below that parity in 1982 and 1983.[9]

The legacies of the unsuccessful collectivization drive that was followed by discrimination against private agriculture includes mistrust of the authorities and uncertainty about the future. Incentives to invest, innovate and modernize have been undermined and no political declarations can now repair the situation.

The decade of the 1960s brought an attempt to accelerate "socialist reconstruction of agriculture" by the creation of state farms. The collective farms were considered a relatively primitive institution that perpetuates the backwardness of agriculture.[10] The modern, highly specialized and mechanized state farms were viewed as the main agrarian form of the future. They received priority allocations of fertilizers, building materials, fuels, tractors and other agricultural inputs. Their harvest of crops and the numbers of livestock per unit of land were, however, lower than in the private sector.

A reform of the state farms was introduced in July 1981. They were to become fully efficient, autonomous and self-financing economic units. Although considerable improvements have been recorded, about 15 percent of all state farms are still operating at loss, they enjoy special privileges and subsidies and, as the agricultural inputs are allocated by administrative methods, they have priority allocations.[11]

The policy has resulted in the allocation of scarce investment resources and agricultural inputs to the less efficient sector of the economy. Capital- and material-intensity of agricultural production have been increasing while the production effects have been unsatisfactory. Moreover, pressed to maximize production in order to show their superiority, the state farms have not been able to function as experimental farms, to improve plants, animals and agrotechnical methods, the task which the state farms are destined to perform in most nonsocialist countries.

During the 1970s a new drive was introduced. This time the stress was on the development of "agricultural circles" which proved to be the most expensive and the least efficient of all agricultural institutions.

These various drives have weakened agriculture and absorbed a large proportion of resources that were allocated to this sector of the economy. However, these allocations have been limited as the accepted development strategy has consistently given priority to industrialization and called for, at first, a drainage of resources from agriculture and, subsequently, for its relative neglect.[12] Agriculture received only 10.2 percent of total investment outlays in 1951–55 and 12.5 pecent in 1956–60.[13] The allocation somewhat improved later. It represented 15.0 percent in 1961–65, 17.4 in 1966–70,

14.9 in 1971–75 and 16.3 in 1976–80. While the average decline in total investment in 1981–82 was 20.8 percent, investment outlays in agriculture declined by 25.5 percent[14] despite the official policy described by the slogan "everything for agriculture."

The weakness of agriculture also has been reflected in foreign trade. The negative balance in trade in the products of agriculture and the food industry increased rapidly during the 1970s and was responsible for a very large proportion of the total negative balance in visible trade. The appearance of a very deep balance-of-payments disequilibrium in the middle of the 1970s, the growing indebtedness that it created and the attempts to cope with this situation by arbitrary cuts in imports by administrative commands were the immediate cause of the overall economic decline. External problems still destabilize the economy and prolong the crisis. The agricultural crisis has contributed to these difficulties.

It is now widely accepted in Poland that the difficulties experienced with trade in the products of agriculture and food industry are mainly caused by mistaken decisions regarding the expansion of the production of cattle, pigs and poultry by large-scale modern methods based on substantial imports of feeds. For this reason the official policy is now that of increasing the country's agricultural self-sufficiency. Morever, it has been decided to reduce also the dependence of agriculture on imported nonagricultural producers' goods.[15] This is a very dangerous policy, especially the planned attempt to effect a "conversion" of industry so that it could supply all the producers' goods needed by agriculture. This policy would petrify backwardness and would likely deepen stagnation at the time when every effort should be made to modernize Polish agriculture and to make it compatible with the level of development that has been achieved in other sectors of the economy.

The usual argument in favour of self-sufficiency is that Poland cannot now expect to obtain new credits and that it cannot, therefore, expand imports of feeds and nonagricultural producers' goods for agriculture. However the choice is not between expanding agricultural and various agriculture-supplying imports on credit or trying to achieve self-sufficiency in this field. The real problem is that of expanding the production of sufficiently attractive and efficiently produced manufactured goods and high quality foodstuffs for export in order to be able to pay for the necessary imports. Here, unfortunately, the Polish economists still seem to think in terms of a closed and not of a modern open economy. Instead of trying to effect a very expensive and time-consuming conversion of existing productive capacities, or to produce producers' goods for agriculture with capacities which have been built for other purposes, the whole effort should be directed to the expansion of the production of those exportables which the existing capacities can produce best. This would, however, necessitate a serious reform of the foreign trade sector and, indeed, of the whole economy. Despite all announcements and declarations about economic reform, a mass of legislative documents and continuous changing of various "instruments of reform", not much has actually been achieved, certainly not as much as is needed in order to expand the export of modern, high quality manufactured goods and foodstuffs to the West.

The crisis has already had some serious adverse effects on agriculture. The decline of the imports of feeds and nonagricultural producers' goods contributed to the catastrophic situation in respect of livestock, although, as often before, wrong price relations with the help of which the planners attempt "to steer" agricultural production were at least partly responsible.[16] If, as the result of the crisis, the policy of self-sufficiency in agriculture and in the production of industrial goods for agriculture were to be implemented, the adverse impact on the state of agriculture would be enormous.

Notes

1. B. Klepacki, "Warunek modernizacji rolnictwa" (A Condition for the Modernization of Agriculture), *Zycie gospodarcze*, No. 17, 1984, p. 10.

2. A. Szemberg, "Co nowego w gospodarce ziemia" (What Is New in the Use of Land), *Zycie gospodarcze*, No. 11, 1981, p. 6; A Szemberg, "Obraz przemian agrarnych" (The State of Agrarian Changes), *Zycie gospodarcze*, No. 18, 1982, pp. 1, 11.

3. A. Wos, "Strategia polaryzacji" (The Strategy of Polarization), *Zycie gospodarcze*, No. 4, 1984, pp. 6-7; M. Rakowski, "Poprzec sredniaka" (Support the Medium Size Farmer), *Zycie gospodarcze*, No. 14, 1984, p. 12; E. Bejgrowicz, "Wokoe strategii polaryzacji" (About the Strategy of Polarization), *Zycie gospodarcze*, No. 16, 1984, p. 10.

4. R. Manteuffel, "Jeszcze o strategii ale takze o taktyce" (More About Strategy But Also About Tactics), *Zycie gospodarcze*, No. 12, 1984, p. 11.

5. G.U.S., *Rolniczny rocznik statystyczny 1945-65* (Agricultural Statistical Yearbook 1945-1965), Warsaw, 1966, pp. 156-7, 185.

6. Z.M. Fallenbuchl, "Collectivization and Economic Development," *The Canadian Journal of Economics and Political Science*, v. XXXXIII, No. 1, February 1967, pp. 1-15.

7. W. Herer, "Niektore problemy wzajemnych proporcji miedzy rolnictwem i przemyslem" (Some Problems of Proportions Between Agriculture and Industry), in O. Lange (ed.), *Zagadnienia ekonomii politycznej socjalizmu* (Problems of the Political Economy of Socialism), Warsaw 1958, p. 123.

8. L. Zienkowski, "Parytet dochodow ludnosci rolniczej i nierolniczej" (Parity Between The Incomes of Agricultural and Non-agricultural Population), *Gospodarka planowa*, No. 6, 1982, p. 215.

9. J. Kozioe, "Postscriptum", *Zycie gospodarcze*, No. 10, 1984.

10. B. Galeski, "Kierunki zmian spolecznych wsi i jej perspektywy" (The Directions of the Social Changes in the Countryside and Their Perspectives) in W. Brus et al. (eds.), *Materialy do studiowania ekonomii politycznej socjalizmu* (Sources for the Study of the Political Economy of Socialism), Warsaw 1964, pp. 144-5.

11. A. Leopold, "Granice wyboru" (The Limits of Choice), *Zycie gospodarcze*, No. 9, 1984, p. 6; S. Piwowarczyk, "Wiecej prawdy o PGR" (More Truth About the State Farms), *Zycie gospodarcze*, No. 12, 1984, p. 10.

12. For more detail see Fallenbuchl, *op. cit.*

13. F. Kolbusz (ed.), *Rolnictwo w Trzydziestoleciu Polski Ludowej* (Agriculture in the Thirty Year Existence of People's Poland), Warsaw, 1974, p. 34.

14. G.U.S., *Rocznik statystyczny 1981* (Statistical Yearbook 1981), Warsaw, 1981, p. 182 and *Rocznik statystyczny 1983* (Statistical Yearbook 1983), Warsaw, 1983, p. 156.

15. "W strone samowystarczalnosci" (In The Direction of Self-sufficiency), *Zycie gospodarcze*, No. 7, 1983, pp. 1, 4; G. Pisarski, "Program rozwoju rolnictwa i gospodarki zywnosciowej" (The Programme of the Development of Agriculture and Food Economy), *Zycie gospodarcze*, No. 27, 1983, p. 2; "W kiernunku zywnosciowej samowystarczalnosci" (In the Direction of Self-sufficiency in the Production of Food), *Zycie gospodarcze*, No. 9, 1982.

16. Z. Kasprzyk, L. Wisniewski, "Po dwoch latach" (After Two Years), *Zycie gospodarcze*, No. 6, 1984, pp. 1, 4.

10

Prospects for Polish Agriculture in the 1980s

Edward Cook

Introduction

Since 1980 Polish agricultural production has fallen below levels of the previous decade. Food supplies have tightened and the quality of the diet has declined. Prospects for anything but a gradual and protracted recovery are dim. The reasons for the agricultural decline are tied to developments in the economy as a whole and to agricultural policies of the seventies.

Those policies were built around the notion that a program of state-fostered expansion of socialized agriculture could solve Poland's agricultural development problems. State and collective farms were allowed to operate in an increasingly lenient financial environment. Investment projects for socialized farms were decreed by the State and the resources for their implementation were guaranteed. Socialized agriculture was given priority access to purchases of land and other inputs.

Among private farmers, the State attempted to discriminate between farms considered to be commercially viable and those that were not. Furthermore, the network of private farmer cooperatives, the agricultural circle organizations, was fully integrated into the state administration. The impact of these policies was decidedly negative.

The State attempted to cover the weaknesses of domestic agricultural policy by steadily increasing the net imports of agricultural commodities. When the economic crisis arrived, therefore, food supplies were in a particularly vulnerable position. Between 1980 and 1983 agricultural imports were cut by more than half in an effort to balance agricultural trade. The long lines for food that were common in 1981–82 were in part the result of a sudden drop in food supplies, but, more than this, also a result of pricing and distribution shortcomings. Overall, food supplies remained adequate to meet the needs of the population. However, consumption of quality food items, particularly of meat, fell sharply and is much lower now than in the late 1970s.

The prospects for recovery of agricultural production are not bright. Investment in agriculture in the eighties will average well below that of 1976–80 and imports of intermediate agricultural products, such as grain and feed for livestock, will recover only slightly. A number of reforms have been implemented to correct the errors in agricultural policy of the previous decade. However, these reforms have come at an economically inopportune time. It is questionable if they will have a positive impact on production as long as agricultural living standards remain depressed. Furthermore, the reforms have failed to deal with a central problem of agricultural policies of the seventies, bureaucratic interference in local affairs, and have left private farmers still skeptical of the longer-term policy preferences of the State.

Agricultural Policies

Poland's failure to successfully collectivize agriculture in the 1950s meant that private ownership continues to play a predominant role in its agricultural sector (Table 10.1). This makes Poland unique among CMEA nations and seemingly contradicts Marxist-Leninist theory on agricultural organization in a socialist state. Poland's fragmented land structure also poses problems for policymakers. The scattered land holdings and small average size that typify Polish farms have made the introduction of much conventional modern technology for crop and livestock production economically unfeasible. Furthermore, many private farmers have needed to rely on non-agricultural income sources to guarantee themselves an average standard of living. The Government has often expressed doubt that land utilization on such "dual professional" farms is as intensive as it could be.

Experience of the Seventies

During the seventies, agricultural development policy in Poland was based on the notion that state-fostered expansion of socialized agriculture could successfully deal with the perceived economic and political problems. It was believed that the forced expansion of socialized agriculture would not harm the performance of private agriculture.[1] Socialized agriculture was given priority in the distribution of resources and in purchases of land from the State Land Fund, received increasingly large operational subsidies from the state, and often had its bank debts forgiven.[2] The state took an active role in developing long-term guidelines for land socialization, and in making investment and other managerial decisions for individual socialized farms.[3]

Though certain actions favorable to private farmers were taken, particularly in the first years of the seventies when compulsory deliveries were abolished and prices paid to farmers increased significantly, the second-class status of private farming combined with a general disdain for small-scale agricultural production on the part of many policymakers led to a deteriorating environment for private agricultural production.

This approach had a negative impact on agricultural performance. The growth of net final production in agriculture, measured in constant zlotys, slowed considerably throughout the seventies and actually declined in 1976–80. Value added in agriculture, after increasing only 3 percent in 1971–75 relative to 1966–70, fell 12 percent in 1976–80 compared with 1971–75.[4] Though both sectors were affected, the economic performance of socialized agriculture was hindered more than that of private agriculture. The high costs of the state's strategy of bolstering socialized agriculture caused a serious decline in the financial health of that sector. By 1980 value added per hectare of agricultural land in socialized agriculture had declined to just 1,235 zlotys compared with 11,323 zlotys in private agriculture.[5] Though one would expect higher value added per hectare in private agriculture because of that sector's higher labor intensity, such a discrepancy is startling. Between 1971 and 1978 the losses of the state farms increased almost seven-fold to 28.3 billion zlotys (nearly \$1 billion).[6]

The major harm done to private agriculture by the policies of the seventies was to reduce interest among young people in farming as a profession. Uncertainty about the long-term prospects for private farming, a less than average income from such work, and growing employment opportunities elsewhere in the economy, caused a four-fold increase in the outmigration from agriculture of labor in the 19–44 age bracket in the seventies compared with the sixties.[7] By 1980, the agricultural policies of the Gierek regime had become too costly to pursue further. As a result, the state was ready to listen to the demands for policy changes voiced by farmers following the rise of Solidarity.

Agricultural Policy: Reforms and Their Prospects

Between September 1980 and July 1981 the general agricultural policies of the 1970s were greatly revised. The changes aimed at improving the treatment of and prospects for private farmers and at increasing the managerial autonomy of socialized farms. The major points of reform affecting private agriculture were:

1. Guaranteeing the right of ownership and inheritance to private farmers and the permanent status of private agriculture in Poland.
2. Giving private farmers priority in purchasing land from the State Land Fund and reducing legal limitations on land sales.
3. Equalizing terms of access to credit for all sectors of agriculture and increasing the independence of banks lending to farmers.
4. Increasing supplies of machinery and spare parts to private farmers, including a shift in production from large to small machinery and an increased share of agricultural investment for the private sector.
5. Insuring profitability for farming and a living standard equal to that of urban workers through more favorable prices and an improved pension system for farmers.
6. Developing small-scale local industries and services for agriculture.

The reform of socialized agriculture, drafted in the fall of 1980, aimed at greatly reducing operational subsidies paid for the state budget and increasing the role of cost-accounting criteria at the farm level.[8] Credit policies, which had been quite lenient for state and collective farms during the seventies, were to be tightened up considerably. In part to cushion the shock of this new financial self-reliance, major farm price increases for agricultural commodities were enacted in April and July of 1981.

The major economic contraction and the resulting decline in the amount of real resources available cast a dark cloud over the reforms from their inception. Farmer aspirations for an improved standard of living seemed to have very slim chance of being realized by late 1981.

Politically, there was major disagreement over the shape of self-government in the countryside. The state was extremely reluctant to grant legal status to Private Farmers' Solidarity and unwilling to surrender bureaucratic control over local affairs. On October 8, 1982 Private Farmers' Solidarity and other independent farmers' organizations were outlawed.[9] During its brief legal existence, Private Farmers' Solidarity had difficulty maintaining unity among its regional branches and there were serious differences over strategy and purpose within the farmers' movement. In spite of the call to greater economic efficiency, the State remained politically committed to preserving the socialized sector more or less intact. Such a commitment meant the continued privileged treatment of this sector, though not to the extent characteristic of the seventies.

Despite the economic and political constraints, implementation of many of the agricultural reforms has continued since the declaration of martial law. Though the last few years have brought more equal operating conditions between private farmers and socialized agriculture and better financial performance of socialized agriculture, doubts clearly remain about the longer term policy preferences of the state. In July 1983 a constitutional amendment guaranteeing the permanence of "private family farms of working peasants" was adopted.[10] Though it is a stronger guarantee than anything private farmers had in the 1970s, serious doubts apparently remain in the minds of farmers concerning the long-term prospects for private agriculture.[11]

Following the banning of Private Farmers' Solidarity, the agricultural circles are now the sole "social-trade organizations" for farmers. Though their new guidelines allow them to be more responsive than they were in the past to the needs and interests of member farmers, they remain in reality extensions of the state administration and are provided little recourse in case of conflicts with other organizations. Their effectiveness in representing farmers, therefore, will be strictly dependent on the good will and full support of the state. However, it is unlikely that the state will allow the viewpoints of farmers to interfere with its management of the economic crisis.

The reforms have been more successful in balancing the share of investment between private and socialized agriculture. By 1983 investment shares were roughly equivalent to the relative share of land farmed by the respective farm types (Table 10.2). Similarly, sales of machinery to private farmers of most major types have actually increased since 1981 despite the overall decline in industrial production.[12]

Since 1980, private farmers have finally been given fair access to land purchases from the State Land Fund. In 1981, 1982 and 1983 the share of land in the private sector actually showed a modest increase, as did the size of the average private farm. The recent burst in sales from the State Land Fund fell off in 1983 and is not expected to revive during the next few years, as the best situated and highest quality land has been sold and less land is now coming into the Fund. Without increased private sales among farmers, slower improvement in the land structure is likely. A law simplifying the terms of such private transactions came into effect in the fall of 1982, but it is too early to assess its impact.[13]

The longer term development plan calls for roughly a doubling in the number of farms over 10 hectares in size and increases in the number of mini-farms of under 2 hectares. The aim of this approach is to have farmers currently in the 2–10 hectare range commit themselves either to full-time agriculture or agriculture as a secondary source of income. It is questionable whether current policies will be sufficient to achieve these goals even over the course of a number of decades. In the shorter term, expansion of farm size may be constrained by a lack of inputs. Currently, per hectare production is higher on the smaller farms. Until sufficient capital is available to increase per hectare production of larger farms, development of such farms would actually tend to retard recovery of agricultural production.

The reform of socialized agriculture, introduced on state farms on July 1, 1981, and extended to collective farms and the agricultural circle cooperatives on January 1, 1982, has resulted in improved financial performance. State farms, after running up a 22 billion zloty deficit in the 1980/81 fiscal year, registered profits of 28 billion zloty in 1981/82, 29 billion in 1982/83, and 50 billion in 1983/84.[14] Increased decision-making autonomy at the farm level is one of the key features of the reform of socialized agriculture. Farm managers took advantage of this increased authority by reducing unprofitable livestock production, particularly of beef cattle, and improving the crop sowing pattern.

Some serious problems, however, continue to surround the reform of socialized agriculture. Socialized farming enterprises now face the prospect of taking financial responsibility for poor investment decisions that were forced upon them in the seventies under the directive-subsidy system of management. A prime example is livestock housing, a good portion of which has no prospect of being profitably utilized in the next few years. There is evidence that the state has bolstered the financial performance of socialized agriculture by only partially enforcing the principle of financial autonomy. In 1982/83, the latest year for which data are available, subsidies to state farms of the Ministry of Agriculture more than doubled from the previous year and totaled 40.8 billion zloty.[15]

During the first three years of the reform of socialized agriculture, there was little improvement in labor productivity on state farms. Without improvement in this indicator, it is hard to imagine the eventual attainment of full financial health by these farms. Thus far the reform has not effectively linked worker remuneration with performance, nor has the process of nominating and recalling farm managers succeeded in eliminating poorly qualified management personnel.[16] Without solutions to these problems, socialized agriculture will remain incapable of competing equally with private agriculture, which in turn will require continued preferential treatment for state and collective farms.

The economic crisis has also made it impossible for the state to meet farmer expectations of an improved living standard. The state did increase average farmer income in 1981 by boosting prices paid to farmers roughly 60 percent while severely limiting price increases for inputs and services. This brought farmer income into rough parity with average non-farmer income for the first time in post-war Poland. The state failed to provide, however, sufficient quantities of either producer or consumer goods to the countryside to guarantee market equilibrium. Because of this, the higher procurement prices paid to farmers provided little incentive for higher production or sales of agricultural commodities to the state, but rather led to growing disruption of rural markets.

Since the imposition of martial law, farmers' real income has declined drastically, as prices farmers pay for inputs have increased more rapidly than prices they receive for their commodities.[17] Estimates of the Institute of Agricultural Economics and Food Economy and one given by the Deputy Director of the Planning Commission, place average farmer income once again below that of non-farmers.[18] A new law on private farmer pensions was adopted on January 1, 1983, which will allow the basic farmer pension to gradually rise to the minimum for industrial workers by 1986.[19] Nearly all the increase in benefits and coverage over the old system is to be financed by farmer contributions to the Farmers' Social Insurance Fund.

The prospects for farmer income, ruling out an unforeseen burst in productivity, are not bright. The state is more or less committed to limiting further growth in subsidies to the agro-food complex while at the same time retail food price increases remain highly unpopular. If the urban workforce continues to win wage raises in excess of planned guidelines, as happened in 1983 and 1984,[20] some of this excessive inflationary pressure may be relieved by further reducing the relative income of private farmers.

Investment and Input

Agriculture and the food economy have been designated as priority areas for investment in the eighties. Their share of total investment is planned to reach 30 percent by 1985 and maintain this level through the rest of the decade. In comparison, their actual share of investment during 1976–80 was 21.8 percent.[21] The decline in economy-wide investment between 1978 and 1982 has been so drastic, however, that despite the food economy's higher share, actual investment in the food complex in 1981–85 is officially expected to total just 80 percent of the amount achieved in 1976–80.[22] Average annual investment in agriculture alone in 1981–83 was only 70 percent of the 1976–80 average level.[23] This points up the seriousness of the resource constraints facing Polish planners as they attempt to revive agricultural production. Furthermore, preliminary plan guidelines for 1986–90 indicate only a modest recovery in anticipated investment in the food economy in the latter half of the decade.

Investment in agriculture alone, which accounts for 70–75 percent of investment in the food complex, therefore, is likely to be well below record levels in real terms for the rest of the eighties. Some savings can be realized in investment in livestock housing during the next few years, due to large unutilized capacity in both the private and socialized sectors. Also, the reform of socialized agriculture should allow state and collective farms to reduce their investment needs in the eighties. However, serious investment constraints are anticipated in areas such as land improvement, agricultural chemicals, infrastructure improvement, and small-scale machinery.

Fertilizer use is planned to increase strongly through 1990, reversing the recent decline (Table 10.3). Fulfillment of this plan is highly problematic. The Polish fertilizer industry is in serious need of capital overhaul simply to maintain current production levels,[24] and only one new production facility is expected to come on line by 1990.[25] There will also be problems importing needed raw materials, particularly phosphate ore. Furthermore, because of major retail price increases, farmers will probably not find it profitable to purchase the planned amounts of fertilizer even if they are available.

Poland ranks near the bottom in Europe in the use of plant protection chemicals (PPCs), such as herbicides and pesticides. Attempts to increase supplies in recent years have been based on production of older sulfur and copper-based mixtures that can be manufactured from domestic raw materials. However, supplies of most required PPCs are dependent on the import of raw materials and ready preparations from the West.[26] The continued import restraint, therefore, will hamper efforts to improve PPC availability. Furthermore, there is a shortage of small container packaging for distribution of chemicals to private farmers and many farmers lack the knowledge and experience to properly utilize these chemicals.[27]

Production and sales of agricultural machinery have generally received high priority since 1980. Despite the economic contraction, deliveries to farmers of many types of machinery have actually increased (Table 10.4). However, these deliveries remain well short of requirements and of delivery rates projected in 1981.[28] There is as yet little evidence of the development of new small-scale machinery, such as micro-tractors, appropriate for use on private farms.

For the rest of this decade Polish agriculture will continue to be plagued by machinery related problems that can only be moderately alleviated. These include an over-dependence on horses and tractors for agricultural transportation, the lack of an effective machinery repair network for private farmers, and a shortage of certain critical spare parts.

Large investment outlays are required to improve the rural infrastructure, in particular to increase storage facilities for agricultural products, to improve farm access to clean water supplies, and to improve the rural electrical network. Investment resources for these needs, as well as for land improvement work, will remain seriously short for the rest of the decade. In fact, actual land improvement work during the 1980s may not be sufficient to maintain total improved land area at its 1983 level of 6.3 million hectares.[29]

Prospects for Agriculture and Food Consumption

In 1983 the Polish government ratified a program for economic recovery, focusing on 1983–85 and containing plan guidelines for 1990. This program provides the outline of the strategy for reversing the recent decline in the quality of the diet, while eliminating the negative balance of trade in agricultural commodities. Though the plan targets are more realistic than those of the past ten years, they will prove difficult to realize.

Production and Trade Prospects

The agricultural portion of this program contains production goals for both 1985 and 1990 and represents a major downward revision in official expectations from guidelines developed in December 1981.[30] Agricultural production is not expected to reattain the pre-crisis peak it set in 1978 until 1985 or 1986. Meat production is expected to take even longer, until 1990 or 1991, to recover its previous record level. Despite the relatively modest growth rates in the plan for many agricultural commodities, an even slower recovery seems more likely. The main reason for pessimism is the anticipated continued shortage of resources both for agricultural investment and for import of intermediate agricultural products such as livestock feed. Investment plans will prove difficult to realize. Furthermore, many of those plans are probably inadequate for supporting officially anticipated agricultural production growth rates. An examination of recent policy developments in agriculture leaves little hope for significant improvement in the efficiency of Polish agricultural production.

Plan targets for major crops appear realistic. Some shortfall from plan is anticipated for grain production (Table 10.5), despite a continued rise from 1981 through 1984. A more significant shortfall is expected for oilseeds, which are used as raw material for vegetable oil production and also serve as a protein source in livestock feeds.

The plan targets for livestock, both in terms of inventories and meat production, appear out of line with the crop targets and beyond attainment (Tables 10.6 and 10.7). By the end of the 1970s between 25 and 30 percent of Polish meat production was dependent on imported feed. With a severe import constraint and anticipated modest expansion of domestic feed production during the 1980s, feed supplies by 1990 are likely to remain below record levels. In the last few years livestock holdings on socialized farms have been reduced as a result of the new emphasis on profitability and the drastic cutback in feed imports. Without more favorable farm prices for meat and a successful conversion to more self-sufficient feeding practices, livestock production will be slow to recover on socialized farms. In the private sector, the opportunity for improved living standards may be essential to convince farmers to once again expand livestock inventories, particularly of hogs, to previous record levels. However, such opportunities are expected to remain slim for the rest of the decade. Recent farm price increases for hogs have stimulated interest in hog raising for on-farm consumption, but not for the market.[31]

Milk production is projected to be close to plan in 1985. In the latter half of the decade more emphasis is expected to be placed on reducing the very high losses in milk processing and handling than on further large increases in production. Though production is projected to grow slowly between 1985 and 1990, supplies of milk and milk products to the consumer should increase somewhat faster. Egg production is projected to remain below the record 1980 level because of continued limitations on feed imports.

The Polish agricultural trade deficit grew tremendously during the 1970s, increasing from $100 million in 1972 to $2.3 billion in 1981.[32] This trend reflected both the policy of improving the Polish diet despite below-plan growth in domestic production, and attempts to maintain living standards in the initial years of the economic crisis. In 1982 and 1983 the agricultural trade deficit was pared substantially, largely through reduced imports.

The recovery program calls for balanced agricultural trade by the end of the 1980s. Consumption targets, particularly of meat, will likely have to be sacrificed to achieve this. Agricultural imports, at $1.3 billion in 1983, have probably been cut to the minimum allowable, given the State's intention to arrest further declines in the quality of the diet by 1985. Agricultural exports can be expected to generally continue the gradual uptrend of 1981–83 as a result of some increases in sugar, meat, fruit and vegetable exports.

Net imports of grain are expected to continue declining to 2.4 million tons in the 1985/86 July–June year. However, as recovery of meat production occurs during 1985–1990, they are projected to rebound to 3.4 million tons by 1990/91. Imports of oilseed meal (including oilseeds, all converted to soybean meal equivalent) should begin rebounding before 1985/86, but remain well short of the previous record.

Consumption Prospects

The outlook for a return of per capita meat consumption to the levels of the late 1970s is extremely dim. This is so because of reduced feed imports, projected slow growth in domestic feed production, and the need to increase meat exports. On the demand side, much higher real prices of meat introduced since early 1982 and the likelihood of further increases mean that Polish consumers cannot afford to purchase the levels of meat consumed in the late 1970s even if they were available.

Poland has traditionally enjoyed one of the highest caloric diets in the world. Despite the marked decline in the quality of the diet between 1980 and 1982, consumption levels, particularly of carbohydrate foods, remained adequate to meet daily caloric requirements (Table 10.8). Consumption of major protein foods such as meat, milk, eggs, and fish all declined, however.

The strategy for improving protein supplies during the rest of the 1980s is to shift reliance away from meat and fish toward milk, peas, and beans. Targets for per capita consumption originally published in October 1982 (under heading A in Table 10.8) were apparently revised downward in December 1982. However, revisions are available for 1985 goals only. The revised figures appear more realistic. The unrevised 1990 targets are probably on the high side for meat, eggs, and animal fats. It will prove difficult to reattain per capita meat consumption of 60 kilograms by 1990, which would leave it some 20 percent below the record level of 74 kilograms.

In addition to problems of increasing production of agricultural commodities, growth in food consumption will be retarded by weakened demand. In 1982 food prices increased an average of 136 percent while nominal income per capita increased by less than half of that—66 percent.[33] Despite declining levels of real food consumption, the share of disposable income devoted to food purchases increased, from 34 percent in 1981 to 47 percent in 1982 in worker-headed households.[34] This declined slightly to 43 percent in 1983.[35] Despite the major food price increases of 1982 and further increases in 1984 and early 1985, state budgetary subsidies to agriculture and the food economy remain large. If these subsidies are to be reduced in coming years, which has frequently been cited as official policy, then real prices for food may have to be increased further.

Notes

1. Wos, Augustyn, "Socjalistyczne przeobrazenia rolnictwa", in *Procesy rozwojowe polskiego rolnictwa*, PWRiL, Warsaw, 1979, p. 290.
2. Andrzejewicz, Jerzy, "Zreformowany system ekonomiczno-finansowy PGR", *Wies wspolczesna*, No. 3–4, 1982, p. 85.
3. Dabrowski, Przemyslaw, "Planowanie rozwoju rolnictwa w swietle badan nad przestrzenno-sektorowym zroznicowaniem produkcji rolniczej", *Zagadnienia ekonomiki rolnej*, No. 5, 1981, pp. 24–5.
4. Using the Polish definition of "produkcja czysta", which is gross final production minus material costs. *Rolnicza produkcja globalna, koncowa, towarowa i czysta w latach 1976-79*, GUS, Warsaw, 1980, and *Rocznik statystyczny*, GUS, Warsaw, 1982.
5. Ibid.
6. Andrzejewicz, Jerzy, "Produkcyjne i finansowe wyniki PGR", *Wies wspolczesna*, No. 10, 1980, p. 68.
7. Frenkel, Izaslaw, "Zmiany zatrudnienia w rolnictwie polskim (II)", *Wies wspolczesna*, No. 11, 1981.
8. "Uprawnienia terenowych wladz i wieksza samodzielnosc PGR", *Trybuna ludu*, 11/27/80.
9. For an English language copy of this law see Foreign Broadcast Information Service, *Daily Report: Eastern Europe*, 10/28/82, "Law on Farmers' Organizations Published", p. G19.

10. "Ustawa o zmianie Konstytucji Polskiej Rzeczpospolitej Ludowej", *Trybuna ludu*, 7/23–24/83, p. 3.

11. Farkowski, Czeslaw, "Polityka wobec rolnictwa indywidualnego", *Wies wspolczesna*, No. 6, 1983, p. 36.

12. Szalajda, Zbigniew, "Zadania przemyslu w rozwoju rolnictwa i przetworstwa rolno-spozywczego", *Wies wspolczesna*, No. 4, 1983, p. 30.

13. Szemberg, Anna, "Gospodarka ziemia a struktura agrarna", *Wies wspolczesna*, No. 9, 1983.

14. "Fakty przecza wrozbem", *Trybuna ludu*, 10/24/84.

15. *Rocznik statystyczny*, 1984, p. 302.

16. Bala, Jozef, and Wisniewski, Leszek, "Reforma gospodarcza a zarzadzanie w PGR", *Wies wspolezesna*, No. 8, 1983.

17. Sadowy, Eugeniusz, "Zmiany cen rolnych", *Wies wspolczesna*, No. 3–4, 1982, pp. 75–6.

18. "Warianty koncepcji planu 3-letniego a gospodarka zywnosciowa", *Wies wspolsczesna*, No. 10, 1982, p. 12, and "Wszyscy patrzymy w strone wsi", *Zycie gospodarcze*, No. 24, 6/12/83.

19. Martyniuk, Zbigniew, "Realizacja celow systemu emerytalnego rolnikow", *Wies wspolczesna*, No. 5, 1983.

20. "Wszyscy patrzymy w strone wsi", *Zycie gospodarcze*, No. 24, 6/12/83.

21. *Rocznik statystyczny*, 1981, p. 184, 1979, p. 117, 1977, p. 104; and *Rocznik statystyczny rolnictwa i gospodarki zywnosciowej*, 1982, p. 112.

22. "Podstawowe zalozenia programu rozwoju rolnictwa i gospodarki zywnosciowej", *Trybuna ludu*, 10/21/82.

23. *Rocznik statystyczny*, 1983, p. 156, 1982, p. 143.

24. "How Much Mineral Fertilizer Will There Be?" *Dziennik ludowy*, 2/18/83; translated in Joint Publication Research Service, *East Europe Report: Economic and Industrial Affairs*.

25. "Czy chemia nie nadaza", *Trybuna ludu*, 9/13/82.

26. *Zycie gospodarcze*, 3/7/82, op. cit.

27. "Pestycydy sa czy ich brak", *Zycie gospodarcze*, No. 31, 7/31/82.

28. "Wytyczne Biura Politycznego KC PZPR i Presidium NK ZSL w sprawie wezlowych problemow polityki rolnej, rolnictwa i gospodarki zywnosciowej", *Wies wspolczesna*, No. 4, 1981.

29. "Melioracja: trudny start", *Trybuna Ludu*, 12/14/83.

30. Struzek, Boleslaw, "Refleksje nad programem rozwoju rolnictwa i gospodarki zywnosciowej w latach 1981-85", *Wies wspolczesna*, No. 2, 1982.

31. "Czy musi byc mniej miesa?" *Trybuna ludu*, 11/6–7/82.

32. In addition to including the Polish categories of trade in agricultural raw materials and food products, this also includes trade in cotton which is placed under light industry in Polish foreign trade statistics.

33. *Rocznik statystyczny*, 1983, pp. 100 and 368.

34. This excludes expenditures for alcohol and tobacco. *Rocznik statystyczny*, 1983, p. 117, and 1982, p. 100.

35. *Rocznik statystyczny*, 1984, p. 130.

Table 10.1

Agricultural land by farm type[1], 1970, 1975 and 1980

	1970	1975	1980
	Million Hectares		
Total	19.5	19.2	18.9
Private	15.8	15.2	14.1
Socialized	3.7	4.0	4.8
of which:			
State farms	3.0	3.3	3.7
Collective farms	0.2	0.3	0.8
Agricultural			
circle farms	0.1	0.2	0.3
	Percent Of Total		
Private	81	79	75
Socialized	19	21	25
of which:			
State farms	15	17	20
Collective farms	1	2	4
Agricultural			
circle farms	1	1	1

[1] In terms of land utilization.

Source: Rocznik statystyczny 1981, p. 303.

Table 10.2

Share of investment in agriculture by farm type;
1978 and 1980-83 annual[1]

	1978	1980	1981	1982	1983
	--percent--				
Private farms	31.2	36.5	48.0	59.2	62.9
State farms[2]	34.7	33.8	25.6	20.2	18.5
Collective farms[3]	13.5	12.4	10.6	5.7	4.9
Agricultural circles	15.0	11.6	9.1	6.0	6.0
Agricultural service organizations	5.5	5.7	6.8	9.1	7.8

[1] Does not include investment in land improvement, electrification, and veterinary services.

[2] Includes investment in on-farm processing plants.

[3] Includes investment for both farming and service operations.

Source: Rocznik statystyczny, 1983, p. 284, 1984, pp. 305-6, and 1980, p. 257.

Table 10.3

Use of agricultural chemicals, 1970, 1975,
1980 and 1982-84 annual, and 1985 and 1990 plans

	1970	1975	1980	1982	1983	1984	1985 plan	1990 plan
			--kilogram of active matter per hectare--					
Fertilizer[1]	123.6	181.9	192.9	178.4	169.7	182.5	214	230
Plant protection chemicals[2]	0.39	0.58	0.49	0.86	0.78	0.59	1.0	1.5-2

[1] Data are for split years, i.e. 1970 represents use in 1969/70.

[2] Estimates based on annual deliveries to agriculture.

Source: Rocznik statystyczny, 1983, p. 288 and 1984, p. 310; Trybuna ludu, 10/21/82 and 2/4/85.

Table 10.4

Sales of tractors and main types of machinery to
agriculture, 1975, 1978, and 1980-83 annual

	1975	1978	1980	1981	1982	1983
			--thousands--			
Tractors	42.0	58.5	59.9	59.4	60.5	64.1
Grain combines	2.8	4.0	4.5	4.2	4.4	4.2
Fertilizer spreaders	4.7	6.1	6.6	14.3	25.0	43.5
Grain sowers	1.4	8.5	13.4	13.9	15.7	17.1
Mowers	19.2	16.4	13.2	18.6	23.0	25.3
Threshers	13.6	10.9	11.8	10.5	11.0	11.4

Source: Rocznik statystyczny, 1984, p. 308.

Table 10.5

Production of major crops, 1976-80 average,
and 1985 and 1990 plans and projections

	1976-80 avg.	Plan		Projection	
		1985	1990	1985	1990
	--Million Tons--				
Grain	19.5	23.0	24.6	22.0	23.9
Potatoes	42.7	45.2	44.0	44.0	44.0
Sugarbeets	14.1	16.5	17.0	16.0	17.0
Oilseeds	0.6	0.9	1.0	0.7	0.8

Sources: Rocznik statystyczny, 1983; Trybuna ludu, 10/21/82; and
ERS/USDA projections.

Table 10.6

June livestock inventories, 1980, 1984, and
1985 and 1990 plans and projections

	1980	1984	Plan		Projection	
			1985	1990	1985	1990
	--Million Head--					
Cattle	12.6	11.2	12.5	14.5	11.5	12.2
of which						
cows	6.0	5.8	5.9	5.9	5.8	5.9
Hogs	21.3	16.6	20.5	23.0	17.5	21.5

Sources: Rocznik statystyczny, 1983; Trybuna ludu, 10/21/82;
Rzeczpospolita, 7/25/84; and ERS/USDA projections.

Table 10.7

Production of meat, milk, and eggs, 1980, 1982,
and 1985 and 1990 plans and projections

			Plan		Projection	
	1980	1982	1985	1990	1985	1990
Meat, million tons liveweight	4.4	3.5	4.0	4.5	3.6	4.15
of which pork	2.2	1.8	2.2	2.5	2.0	2.3
beef & veal	1.4	1.3	1.25	1.55	1.2	1.35
poultry	0.6	0.27	0.3	0.3	0.25	0.3
Milk, billion liters	16.0	15.7	17.0	18.5	16.8	17.5
Eggs, billion	8.9	7.6	9.0	9.5	8.0	8.6

Sources: Rocznik statystyczny, 1983; Maly rocznik statystyczny, 1984,
p. 178; Trybuna ludu, 10/21/82; and ERS/USDA projections.

Table 10.8

Per capita food consumption, 1980, 1983, and 1985 and 1990 plans

			Polish Projections		
				1985	1990
	1980	1983	10/'82	12/'82	10/'82
			--kilograms--		
Meat & meat products	74	58.3	58	55.5	63
Milk & milk products, liters	262	275	275	268	285
Eggs, pieces	223	200	222	215	225
Fish	8.1	7.4	5.6	6.3	5.6
Fats & Oils	24.8	22.0	23.4	22.9	25.1
Grain products (flour equiv.)	127	122	127	132	125
Sugar	41.4	45.5	39.8	na	40.8
Potatoes	158	154	160	160	160
Fruit	37.7	38.0	45	39.8	50
Vegetables	101	103	120	118.6	125

na= not available.

Sources: Rocznik statystyczny, 1984, p. 122; Trybuna ludu, 10/21/82;
and Wies wspolczesna, No. 5, 1983.

11

Polish Agriculture and Martial Law, or What Happened to the Smychka?

Andrzej Korbonski

Introduction

For forty years, and especially since October 1956 which marked the collapse of the collectivization drive, the official policy toward agriculture has been textbook example of the schizophrenic nature of the Polish political system. Throughout the entire period, governmental policy consisted of pragmatic and rational thinking interspersed with dogmatic, irrational and, occasionally, plainly foolish ideas. On the one hand, Communist regimes attempted to introduce into the decision-making processes sound economic calculus; on the other, the same policy makers succeeded in offsetting the anticipated gains by disregarding not only some basic economic laws but also the elementary rules of political and social behavior. Major socio-economic reforms intended to improve the overall situation in the farm sector were frequently frustrated, if not sabotaged, by the middle-ranking and local *apparatchiki* entrusted with the implementation of the new policies. The ultimate result was that Polish agriculture, despite substantial increases in the amount of farm inputs and the volume of capital investment, as well as several major concessions granted to the peasants by the government, did not fulfill its goals, and its overall performance fell short of expectations.

It is not surprising, therefore, that agriculture continued to be blamed in some quarters as the culprit responsible for the persistent shortages and rising prices of basic foodstuffs, while both the peasants and large segments of the remaining population perceived the farm sector as the chief target of highly irrational and frequently nonsensical policies conducted by successive Communist regimes. One of the major victims of these policies was the *smychka,* the worker-peasant alliance, which until recently had formed one of the ideological foundations of the Polish communist system.

The purpose of this paper is to examine certain features of Polish agricultural policy since the imposition of martial law in December 1981.

It will be necessary, now and then, to refer to the pre-1981 policies but, since they have been rather extensively discussed in the literature, there is no need to repeat the various arguments.[1] The main focus will be on the private farm sector which still accounted for the lion's share of total farm output and employment in the early part of the 1980s.

Although it must have pained it greatly to do so, the Polish government had to admit that the performance of the farm sector in recent years has been dismal.[2] The Government singled out three principal reasons for this situation: the mistakes in Poland's overall economic strategy that favored industry while giving short shrift to agriculture; the erroneous agricultural policy that gave highest priority to the farm sector despite the fact that it was private farming that was still responsible for the bulk of agricultural output; and, to no one's surprise, bad weather.

While one cannot easily argue with the above diagnosis, there is little doubt that the various difficulties faced by Polish agriculture in the past forty years were above all political rather than economic. The generally unimpressive economic performance of the farm sector was clearly the outcome of faulty political decisions made by the Polish ruling oligarchy. The incontestable conclusion that emerges from an examination of the official policy followed in the 1970s and 1980s is that the Polish leadership essentially had reverted to its traditional stance of regarding agriculture as a marginal sector that had to be tolerated as a necessary evil. To put it differently, the private sector in particular was officially viewed as a cow that could be milked indefinitely without receiving much in return. This attitude was, of course, not new: it had strongly influenced the Polish party's collectivization policy in the 1940s and 1950s and it has also permeated the more benign policy toward the private sector during Gomulka's rule. The only real break in the adversarial relationship between the Party and the peasantry occurred in the early 1970s, but it proved to be short-lived.

Toward the end of the 1970s it became fairly obvious that the official policy toward agriculture had met with complete failure and that on the eve of the 1980s, the regime headed by Edward Gierek found itself in a difficult situation. Its ambitious plans to raise agricultural production and increase food supply lay in shambles and its inept policy managed to antagonize just about every segment of the population, but especially the workers and peasants. Until then, the dismal failure of the agricultural policy was to some extent offset by increasing the import of food stuffs. There had been, *per se,* nothing wrong with importing grain and fodder, especially when the value of Polish food exports more than paid for these imports. However, beginning in 1972, Poland ceased to be a net exporter of agricultural commodities and the growing cost of imported grain began to swell the already heavy burden of Poland's hard currency debt.

By the summer of 1980 the economic situation on all fronts was rapidly approaching a crisis and some drastic measures were necessary. In desperation, disregarding the lessons of December 1970 and June 1976, the regime turned once again to raising food prices. The official announcement of a price raise was followed by a series of strikes that ultimately led to the signing of a "social compact" between the government and the strikers, to the creation of an independent, self-governing labor movement, "Solidarity," and to the eventual imposition of martial law.

The Polish Peasants
and the Crisis of 1980–1981[3]

It may be argued that one of the reasons responsible for the highly discriminatory treatment of individual peasants by the successive Polish regimes has been the absence of an authentic, institutionalized pressure group that would be able to articulate peasant interests. The industrial workers had their unions which, albeit ineffectively, at least pretended to protect their interests; the farm laborers employed on state farms, agricultural circles, and other socialized farm enterprises were also represented by a government-controlled union. Yet, despite their large number, the private peasants were deprived of a formal representation.

The peasants' participation in the ruling Communist party has always been low and, in fact, their relative membership has been declining.[4] Officially, it was assumed that peasants' concerns would be represented by the satellite political party, the United Peasant Party (*Zjednoczone Stronnictwo Ludowe*), which, especially since the collapse of the collectivization campaign in 1956, has often been consulted with great fanfare by the ruling party. There is little evidence, however, that it has ever amounted to anything more than a traditional transmission belt used as a window dressing to make official policies more palatable to the peasants. As a result, its membership between 1970 and 1980 increased by only 12 percent which could be taken as a testimony of low peasant interest in the party.[5]

It also appears that the peasants have not been widely involved in the dissident activities that arose in Poland in the wake of the June 1976 crisis. This, in itself, was not greatly surprising since, until the explosion of the summer of 1980, the political opposition was almost entirely monopolized by members of the urban intelligentsia whose efforts to build bridges to the blue collar workers and the peasants remained largely unsuccessful. Thus, except for a few spontaneously formed groups protesting the government policy of land transfers to the state sector, the peasants appeared largely uninvolved and outside the mainstream of the dissident movement.[6]

It may be assumed that individual peasants were as surprised by the July–August 1980 strikes as the other segments of Polish society. Little is known about formal and informal contacts between worker and peasant activists, possibly because there were none. Despite frequent official declarations about the continuing importance of *smychka*, whatever contacts have existed must have been few and far between. During the worker riots in December 1970 and June 1976, the peasants remained on the sidelines and the same appeared true for their behavior in the summer of 1980. The peasants' indifferent attitude did little to establish close links with the workers some of whom were heard to complain that the peasants were being pampered and spoiled by the government and that they were only interested in squeezing the urban consumers by charging exorbitant prices for their products. Nonetheless, these must have been the views of the minority since, interestingly enough, one of the 21 points in the "social compact" signed in Gdansk on August 31, 1980, included a demand for the creation of favorable conditions for the development of family farming which the workers viewed as a permanent core of Polish agriculture. Additional demands were made for an equal treatment of all farm sectors with regard to acquisition of land and means of productions; and for the rebirth of a genuine peasant self-government.[7]

There is no doubt that the dynamic growth of the workers' Solidarity provided an impetus for the creation of similar movements by the peasants. Less than a month after the signing of the Gdansk agreement, three separate rural Solidarity groups applied to Warsaw court for a formal registration. After several legal maneuvers Poland's Supreme Court ruled in February 1981 that since individual peasants were not employees but owners, they could not form a labor union. Finally, with the active help of the Catholic Church, the peasants won their battle with the government which in April agreed to allow the formation of Rural Solidarity that became formally legalized in May 1981.[8] According to its own estimates, within a few weeks of its formation the new organization managed to enroll 1.8 million members, representing about half of all individual peasants.[9] Its elected leader, Jan Kulaj, a 23-year old peasant from southeastern Poland, appeared to be highly popular with the rank and file and the union also enjoyed the strong support of the Catholic Church.

The government's tactics vis-a-vis Rural Solidarity resembled those used against the industrial union. In both cases there were lengthy delays in the implementation of the respective agreements and also attempts to minimize the role of Solidarity by supporting the old "official" unions which were thoroughly discredited, yet were artificially maintained with the help of generous governmental subsidies. In the case of agriculture, the regime attempted to resurrect the agricultural circles as a form of peasant self-government, clearly intending to disrupt the unity of individual peasants.[10]

At the same time, however, there were signs that the ruling party, headed since September 1980 by Stanislaw Kania, was going to pay increasing attention to agriculture. One illustration of this concern was a relatively large number of peasants elected by secret ballot as delegates to the Extraordinary Ninth Congress of the Polish Communist Party which met in July 1981 to discuss and approve various reforms aimed at democratization of the party. As a result, there was a striking increase in the number of individual peasants elected to the party's Central Committee. Whereas only a single peasant sat on the Central Committee nominated by the Eighth Party Congress in February 1980, there were 29 peasant-members of the Central Committee elected in July 1981, representing, after the industrial workers, the second largest socio-economic group in that important body.[11]

The new concern for agriculture was also reflected in a programmatic resolution approved by the July, 1981, Congress.[12] The resolution emphasized the permanent character of individual farming as an integral part of Poland's socialist economy and guaranteed equal treatment for all agricultural sectors. It promised a major increase in farm investment and a large expansion in industrial production earmarked for agriculture. Finally, it came out in favor of greater self-government in the countryside with the participation of Rural Solidarity. For once the program contained no references to "socialist reconstruction of agriculture" which until now has been the main focus of all party declarations dealing with agriculture. It was, without a doubt, the strongest official endorsement of individual farming since the dissolution of the collective farms in 1956.

In the meantime, however, the economic situation in the country was going from bad to worse. The disastrous harvest of 1980 further reduced the available food supply and there was growing fear of widespread famine. The latter was averted by emergency food shipments from the United States, the European Community and some of the East European countries, including the Soviet Union. These shipments, however, did not prevent the introduction of meat and butter rationing. Fortunately, the weather cooperated for once in 1981 and that year's harvest turned out to be better than its predecessor. Nonetheless, the improved harvest did not result immediately in larger market supplies. On the contrary, the government reported that both grain and livestock deliveries in the second half of 1981 lagged considerably behind those of the previous year, despite higher output. Individual peasants appeared reluctant to part with their output because of the rapidly growing inflationary pressures, the declining value of money and the increasing shortage of basic farm inputs. Paradoxically, instead of stimulating deliveries, the increase in farm prices reduced procurements because the peasants were not interested in hoarding worthless currency and viewed both their crops and livestock as capital assets whose value appreciated daily.

The peasants' demand for cash was largely satisfied through their direct food sales to urban consumers. For all practical purposes the socialized food distribution system ceased to perform its basic functions which, to a large extent, were taken over by individual peasants. Prohibited from selling some of their products such as meat on the legal open market, the peasants engaged in widescale black market operations, charging prices well in excess of the official ones, and frequently demanding payment in hard currencies.

Nothing exemplified better the depth of Poland's agricultural malaise than this process of "primitivization" of food distribution which continues until today. The regime attempted to increase the volume of procurements by introducing the so-called tied sales whereby the peasants delivering certain foodstuffs would be entitled to purchase scarce household durables and other manufactured goods. The campaign fizzled out when it turned out that the peasants were much more interested in acquiring farm implements than in buying color television sets and the urban consumers began to resent the preferential treatment given to the peasants.

The latter reaction reflected the growing conflict between the farm and non-farm segments of the Polish population. Faced with progressive scarcity of basic foodstuffs, blue collar workers in particular again began accusing the peasants of deliberately withholding food and of trying to enrich themselves at the expense of the urban working class. There were growing demands, even among Solidarity members, for the reintroduction of compulsory deliveries as the only means of ensuring a steady supply of basic foodstuffs. The regime did little to mollify the conflict although it refused to reimpose the quota system, presumably in the hope that various other measures would persuade the peasants to deliver the necessary amounts to the state procurement agencies.

Peasants Under Martial Law

The imposition of martial law on December 13, 1981, accompanied by the arrest of the leadership of Rural Solidarity affected the Polish agriculture and the peasants much less than it did their industrial counterparts. In fact, right from the start the military junta began to flirt with the peasants, hoping to induce them to increase the deliveries of badly needed foodstuffs.[13] Thus, a few weeks after the coup, the Polish Communist Party, together with the puppet United Peasant Party, issued a proclamation reaffirming their support for the continuous existence of the private farm sector. In a well publicized press conference in January 1982, the Minister of Agriculture strongly defended the private sector against hostile criticism of other East Europeans who blamed private agriculture for Poland's food crisis.[14] In March 1982, when General Jaruzelski made his first official visit to Moscow since the imposition of martial law, he was accompanied by Vice Premier Roman Malinowski, the head of the United Peasant Party, which was clearly a bow in the direction of the peasants. Also in March, a *Sejm* (parliament) committee began drafting bills guaranteeing the permanence of the private farm sector and regulating, once and for all, the question of individual land titles, some of which had remained unsettled since the land reform of 1944. In April, Jan Kulaj, the leader of Rural Solidarity, was released from jail and appeared on television, praising the military government's agricultural policies and promising to cooperate with the authorities "for the good of my country and for the farmers."[15] Everything was being done to assuage peasants' fears and to convince them that the military regime was their staunch friend and supporter.

It soon became clear that the governmental campaign to gain peasants' confidence was meeting with little success. Various programs intended to increase the supply of grain failed rather dismally and United States sanctions, announced by President Reagan on December 23, 1981, closed off a major source of grain, further contributing to the existing difficulties.

By late 1984, it had become obvious that the success or failure of Polish agriculture in satisfying the demands put on it by the military regime, ultimately depends on the following four closely intertwined factors:

1. the final, unconditional recognition of the private farm sector as a permanent component of Polish agriculture and society as a whole;

2. the ability and willingness of individual peasants to raise their productivity and output;
3. the ability and willingness of the government to provide the farm
   sector with the necessary inputs and capital goods; and
4. the willingness of the consumers to accept higher food prices.

Insofar as the sanctity of private ownership of land is concerned, the
military government and its successor have tried on several occasions to
come up with legal provisions guaranteeing the permanence of the private
sector. Finally, after a lengthy discussion, a constitutional amendment (*zapis
konstytucyjny*) was passed by the Polish *sejm* in 1983.

Whether the absence of constitutional guarantees has had a major impact
on the economic performance of the private sector in recent years is not
entirely clear, but available evidence suggests that the Polish peasants in the
early 1980s were not particularly concerned with the threat of losing their
land to a state or a collective farm. Thus, demand for agricultural land has
been growing in recent years (as has its price) and between 1978 and 1981
close to a quarter of a million young peasants embarked on farming as a
career, presumably attracted by rising monetary and non-monetary advantages
generated by agriculture, especially when compared with non-agricultural
employment.[16] It may be assumed that even though the Polish parliament
amended the constitution in favor of individual peasants, the impact of this
new legislation may not be significant, considering the fact that the peasants
traditionally distrust the government and do not put much credence in the
supposedly ironclad character of communist constitutional law.

There is no doubt that individual peasants as well as the socialized farm
sector are capable of increasing agricultural production. All that is needed
is a rational farm policy which, on the one hand, would provide the necessary
farm inputs and, on the other, proper economic incentives for the peasants.
The potential of Polish agriculture is quite considerable and has not yet
been fully utilized. In this context it is worth citing a report on Polish
agriculture prepared by American farm experts who visited the country in
1982:

> Unlike many countries of the world, one cannot view Polish agriculture without
> being impressed with the long-term productive potential. Further, achievement
> of much of that potential does not pose an overwhelmingly formidable task.
> The natural resource base and climate are good, the state of scientific and
> technical knowledge is relatively high, and adequate infrastructure exists, and
> the human resource base is excellent. With these necessary conditions already
> existing, one can conclude that government policies, perhaps foremost, have
> stymied development in the past and that policies present the greatest impediment
> to developmental progress in the future.[17]

Apart from questions of policy, it is clear that; until and unless Polish
industry can provide the Polish agriculture with the necessary inputs, the
chances of a major expansion of farm output are slim. It is a matter of

record that the contemplated economic reforms, intended to reduce the extent of central planning, especially in industry, have not stimulated the output of farm implements, chemicals and other agricultural inputs and as a result the government was forced once again to put pressure on industrial branches to supply agriculture with the necessary means of production, thus delaying the implementation of reforms. Another possible source of inputs was to be an endowment or a foundation, controlled by the Catholic Church, which would provide financial and other aid to individual Polish peasants. The Jaruzelski regime apparently agreed to the establishment of the foundation in the aftermath of Pope John Paul's second visit to Poland in June 1983. The foundation was to channel funds in the form of grants with funds raised by Catholic church agencies in western Europe and, possibly, the United States.[18] For a variety of reasons the implementation of the initial agreement proved difficult and little progress was reported in the execution of the project during 1984.

One of the factors contributing to the current economic crisis in Poland has been the inability or unwillingness of successive Polish regimes to raise the level of retail prices of foodstuffs, many of which have remained largely unchanged for fifteen years. The failure of the previous three attempts at adjusting retail food prices was due, above all, to lack of proper preparation and consultation, especially with the industrial working class, which on three separate occasions rose up in protest against what it considered to be an unjustifiably high price increase. This, in turn, was caused by the lengthy delay in price reform which was largely responsible for the huge discrepancy between food and non-food prices and the rapidly growing agricultural price subsidies. The result was a sharp increase in food subsidies that gradually distorted the price differentials between food and non-food items, and that also greatly stimulated demand for some foodstuffs, particularly meat, which soon became a "political good." Consumption of meat became the chief determinant of the standard of living and popular welfare, and successive regimes, eager to acquire a modicum of popularity, opted for large imports of fodder which enabled the authorities to expand meat consumption but increased balance of payments deficits and used up valuable hard currency credits. The military junta has raised food prices sharply several times since December 1981, for once without violent popular reaction, in the hope that the price increase would reduce demand for such items as meat and thus lessen the pressure on livestock production, perennially the major bottleneck within Polish agriculture. This did not happen, mainly because the government, fearful of the workers' reaction, countenanced simultaneous wage increases which largely vitiated the effect of higher food prices and helped to maintain high demand for food. If attractive manufactured consumer goods had been available to absorb the additional purchasing power, the pressure on food would have been less extreme. In the absence of satisfactory alternatives, most if not all of the wage increases were spent on food.

Thus, while demand for food remained high, its supply stagnated. The reasons for this disequilibrium were simple and resembled those that had existed a few years earlier: state purchase prices remained considerably below black market prices; high inflationary pressure, enhanced by a shortage of farm inputs and consumer goods, made hoarding of cash highly unprofitable; and absence of feed concentrates forced the peasants to feed grain and even bread to livestock, the price of which remained high. Once again the peasants behaved in a highly rational fashion, frustrating the efforts of the government which, despite declarations to the contrary, continued to treat the peasants as simpletons.

This was clearly the crux of the matter. The Polish regime could pass constitutional amendments, promise the peasants a new deal, and declare its undying support of the private sector without eliciting an increase in farm output. What was needed was a fundamental change in the official attitude toward the peasants who for once had to be treated not only as full fledged citizens, but also as producers whose contribution to the country's output was now (and was bound to be in the future) of great importance to the state. The peasants could no longer be treated as second-class citizens but as *homines economici,* capable of rational economic calculation. As such they had to be allowed to organize their production in the most efficient fashion so that they could earn a reasonable return on their effort and investment.

It is interesting to note that all of the above issues became a major object of discussion in the Polish press which in the past two years has begun to pay increasing attention to the "peasant question." The seriousness and high quality of the discussion carried on in both the general and specialized press greatly resembled similar discussions that had taken place in the aftermath of de-collectivization in the late 1950s.[19] It appeared that both the government and the agricultural economists once again attempted to find a "model" that would satisfy the various protagonists: the peasants, the government, the economists, the workers and, last but not least, the ideologues. Inevitably, in the course of the discussion, the notion of the *smychka,* the peasant-workers alliance, became subjected to a thorough scrutiny.

What Happened to the Smychka?

As suggested at the outset, the *smychka* formed the cornerstone of the official policy in Poland toward agriculture between 1948 and 1956, the period that represented the heyday of collectivization until its collapse in October 1956. The notion of *smychka* was enshrined already in Russian Bolshevik ideology as an instrument to resolve the seemingly non-antagonistic contradictions between the workers and the peasants. Following the expropriation of the landowning class by means of the radical land reform of 1944 and the elimination of the capitalist elements, kulaks, from the countryside, the remaining "middle," "small" and landless peasants were viewed as the natural allies of industrial proletariat, bound to it by the *smychka.*

To be sure, the notion of the worker-peasant alliance was never fully explicated. It was one of the minor dogmas in the Communist vocabulary and as such it presumably required no elaboration. It hinted rather broadly that as long as a substantial share of the agricultural land remained in private hands, even though the hated kulaks no longer dominated the countryside, there were bound to be some antagonisms between the peasants and the workers, if only because of the different nature of their work. It was only with the total success of the socialization drive and the replacement of private holdings by first the collective and then by the state farms that the antagonisms were to disappear forever.

Since both the workers and the "working" peasants were seen as sub-species of a broadly defined working class, the underlying assumption was that of an equal treatment by the Communist regime. The concept of equal treatment included not only an attempt to equalize income and consumption per head for both classes but also an effort to improve the rural infrastructure in order to bring it closer to the urban one and to open educational opportunities for the peasants so as to allow them to augment the country's ruling elite.

It is clear that successive Polish regimes, from Bierut to Kania, never seriously intended to fulfill the promise of equal treatment and that the notion of *smychka* remained an empty slogan, to be resurrected infrequently on the occasion of solemn joint declarations on farm policy issued by the Polish Communist Party and the puppet United Peasant Party. In practice, the worker-peasant alliance implied unequal rather than equal treatment, with the peasants carrying more than their share of the burden of rapid industrialization, defense buildup and of the other components of postwar economic development.[20]

This is not the place to estimate in detail the individual peasant's contribution to socialist construction in Poland. Suffice it to say that this contribution was quite substantial even after the collapse of collectivization and the return to private farming after 1956. One of the indicators of anti-peasant bias which had characterized the governmental policy during the last twenty five years was the disparity between farm and non-farm incomes which has remained practically unchanged since the mid-1950s. Even though the available figures show peasant per head incomes between 1960 and 1980 to be only from 5 to 20 percent below comparable figure for non-farm incomes, it must be recognized that, whereas a very large share of non-farm income is spent on personal consumption, farm incomes represented the most important source of farm investment, suggesting not only that the actual disparity between workers' and peasants' disposable incomes was much larger than the data indicate but also that the respective shares available for household consumption favored the workers at the expense of the peasants.[21] If one considers, in addition, the abysmal state of rural infrastructure, the peculiar status of worker-peasants and the low enrollment of students of peasant origin at universities and other academic institutions, it is obvious that, at the beginning of the 1980s, communist Poland was a good example of a country of "two nations" in which one of them, accounting for close to one-third of the total population, was subjected to gross discrimination on all counts. This, in other words, was the *smychka,* the workers-peasants alliance, in practice,. in which one of the so-called allies appeared to pay a disproportionately heavy share of the costs of the partnership.

Paradoxically, the last three years have witnessed the process of *smychka arebours,* with the peasants for the first time since the war actually earning more than those employed in non-agricultural occupations.[22] The process of adjustment began in 1980 and accelerated in 1981–82, the last year for which reliable figures are available.[23] The improvement in peasants' terms of trade, resulting in higher real income of the farm populations, was due to a variety of factors, economic and non-economic. One of them was the fact that, whereas non-farm incomes were most likely estimated on the basis of official wage data, a large share of farm incomes was derived from black market operations, the revenue from which could not be easily calculated.

As suggested earlier, the crisis of 1980-81, culminating in the imposition of martial law, was at least partly due to a serious deterioration in food supply. Successive governments, faced with a multiplicity of problems, including the mounting hard currency debt, had a very few options at their disposal. Insofar as food supply was concerned, they had to curtail the import of grain and of other feedstuffs. At the same time, in order to stimulate domestic output, they had to provide meaningful incentives for the peasants by offering them higher delivery prices. While industrial prices rose as well, their increase was not nearly as high as that of farm delivery prices, and thus the price scissors for once opened in favor of the peasants. At the same time, the exodus from villages to cities continued, which meant that the farm population has declined somewhat in recent years, automatically raising the per head income figures. The latter were also supplemented by revenue from black market sales, mostly of meat, which also benefited the peasants.[24]

Politically, there was no other way. It may be said that, as mentioned earlier, the peasants came into their own only under the Jaruzelski regime. The military regime was desperately seeking even a modicum of legitimacy and it decided to pursue a kind of dual track policy: increasing the food supply of the urban population and cultivating the peasants. While the regime mistrusted the workers and probably feared them, it had to feed them in order to defuse continuing dissatisfaction and to prevent strikes and demonstrations. It was generally assumed that the Polish farm sector still had considerable reserves that could be mobilized if the peasants were to be given additional stimuli not only through money but also through actual availability of inputs. Additional incentives in this case meant, above all, higher farm purchase prices. The government did not hesitate to raise farm prices and it did so to the growing chagrin of the industrial workers.

The situation in Polish agriculture in 1984 is in a state of flux. There is no doubt that the Jaruzelski regime has favored the peasants, at least on the surface, but the question whether there is some real substance behind the pro-peasant rhetoric still remains to be answered. There is also no doubt that the peasants as a group have been doing quite well, especially when compared with the rest of society. The bountiful harvests in the last three years were clearly a factor that, together with high delivery and black market prices, helped to raise peasant incomes well above those of non-peasants. In fact, it was the impressive performance of the farm sector that most likely helped to keep the Polish economy afloat; a poor performance by Polish agriculture would create another serious political and economic crisis.

The Jaruzelski regime must be satisfied with agriculture's performance and perhaps because of this it has allowed some frank discussions concerning the future of the farm sector. The candor of these discussions has been quite surprising. The leitmotiv of the discussion was the future structure of private agriculture. Interestingly enough, only some isolated voices still advocated socialized agriculture as the answer to all ills affecting the agricultural sector.[25] The overwhelming majority of agricultural economists argued the merits of supporting the middle peasant as against those who favored the policy of polarization of the farm sector.[26] In contrast to the past, no one has questioned the sanctity of private ownership and the main point of contention concerned the most promising economic solution of the perennial problem of land fragmentation and differentiation.

As of now, it is difficult to say which option has attracted the attention of the regime. Whatever final solution is chosen, it is clear that there are still some strong opponents of any reforms aimed at strengthening the private sector. Still, it is clear that regardless of the outcome, the old notion of *smychka* has been thrown out the window and that the regime, instead of hailing the worker-peasant alliance as the foundation of socialist society, decided to throw its support behind the peasants rather than the workers. Whether this represents a fundamental change in course, whether it is only a temporary expedient, or whether it is simply an attempt to plant seeds of discord between the peasants and the workers in the well-tested manner of *divide et impera,* in the hope of polarizing Polish society and achieving its ultimate submission, remains to be seen.

Notes

1. For an extensive bibliography on Polish agriculture, see Andrzej Korbonski, "Agriculture and the Polish 'Renewal,' " in Jack Bielasiak and Maurice Simon, eds., *Polish Politics: Edge of the Abyss* (New York: Praeger, 1984), pp. 75–95.

2. For a good example, see J.S. Zegar, "Problems of Polish Agriculture in the 1970s and Expected Development in the First Half of the 1980s," in Karl-Eugen Wadekin, ed., *Current Trends in the Soviet and East European Food Economy* (Berlin and Munich: Duncker and Humblot, 1982), pp. 95–116.

3. This section is largely based on my "Polens Landwitschaft in der Krise von 1980/81," *Osteuropa,* Vol. 32, No. 7 (July 1982), pp. 576–587.

4. Individual peasants accounted for 11.1 percent of Communist party membership in 1970 and for 8.7 percent in 1978. *Rocznik Statystyczny 1980,* p. 25.

5. *Ibid.,* p. 23.

6. For a brief history of peasant dissident groups, see Radio Free Europe Research, "Chronicle of Peasant Dissidence," *Situation Report Poland/8,* October 3, 1980, and

Peter Raina, *Independent Social Movements in Poland* (London: London School of Economics and Political Science—Orbis Books, 1981), pp. 115–180.

7. See "Protokol porozumienia," *Polityka* (Warsaw), No. 36, September 9, 1980.

8. For a detailed chronology of events leading to the formal establishment of Rural Solidarity, see Radio Free Europe Research, *Situation Report Poland/7*, April 24, 1981, pp. 2–5.

9. John Darnton in *New York Times*, March 10, 1981.

10. For an interesting discussion of the relationship between the government and the individual peasants since the summer of 1980, including the question of proper representation of peasant interests, see Leon Bojko, "Czas chlopow," *Polityka*, No. 13, March 28, 1981; Krzysztof Komornicki, "Wszystko od poczatku," *ibid.*, No. 19, June 19, 1982: and Michal Monko, "Machlop kolko," *ibid.*, No. 10, March 3, 1984.

11. Zygmunt Szeliga, "Naprawde nowa ekipa," *ibid.*, No. 30, July 25, 1981.

12. *Nowe Drogi*, No. 8, August 1981, pp. 139–142.

13. In his address on December 13, 1981, proclaiming the imposition of martial law, General Jaruzelski specifically urged "brother peasants" not to "allow [their] fellow countrymen to starve" and to "take care of the Polish soil so it can feed us all." *New York Times*, December 14, 1981.

14. Harry Trimborn in *Los Angeles Times*, February 4, 1982.

15. Michael Dobbs in *Washington Post*, April 29, 1982.

16. *Report to the Rockefeller Foundation and Rockefeller Brothers Fund by the Agricultural Mission to Poland, December 1982*, pp. 30–31.

17. *Ibid.*, p. 175.

18. Dan Fisher in *Los Angeles Times*, June 29, 1983. See also "Der Westen und Polens Landwirtschaft," *Frankfurter Allgemeine Zeitung*, September 1, 1984.

19. See, for example, "Strategia rozwoju polskiego rolnictwa," *Wies Wspolczesna*, No. 10, October 1982, pp. 13–18, and several articles by best known Polish farm experts in *Polityka* and *Zycie Gospodarcze* throughout 1984.

20. Leszek Klank, "Nie tylko dochody," *Zycie Gospodarcze*, No. 47, December 12, 1982.

21. Lech Ostrowski, "Dochody rolnikow," *ibid.*, No. 14, April 25, 1982, and Wieslaw Gawron, "Bogatemu diabel dziecko kolysze," *Polityka*, No. 10, March 5, 1983.

22. Leszek Zienkowski, "Parytet—Liczby i interpretacje," *Zycie Gospodarcze*, No. 47, December 12, 1982.

23. Ostrowski, *op. cit.*

24. For a revealing account of illegal meat sales, see Marek Przybylak, "Slonina, schab spod serca," *Polityka*, No. 49, December 8, 1984.

25. See, for example, the two articles by Konrad Bajan, "Rolnictwo a kryzysy spoleczno-polityczne w Polsce," *Nowe Drogi*, No. 1–2, 1982, pp. 168–186, and "Kontrowersje wokol polityki rolnej," *Polityka*, No. 48, December 1, 1984.

26. Mieczyslaw Rakowski, "Poprzec sredniaka," *Zycie Gospodarcze*, No. 14, April 1, 1984; Lech Ostrowski, "Rolnicy a przyszlosc," *ibid.*, No. 40, September 30, 1984; and Augustyn Wos, "Permanentna przebudowa," *Polityka*, No. 49, December 8, 1984.

12

The Development Strategy of Agriculture in Poland[1]

Franciszek Tomczak

Introductory Remarks

Polish agriculture is undergoing a rapid transformation. In Poland as in other countries the scale and nature of those transformations are defined by the industrialization process, the evolution of social relations, the scientific revolution and international cooperation. The Polish transformation bears some distinctly specific features caused by natural conditions, the history of the economic and social development of Poland, and its unique demographic situation. This chapter shows some problems concerning the development of agriculture and food production determined by the above.

During the entire post-war period 1944–1985 a characteristic of the Polish agriculture has been the search for ways and means of rapid growth and the reconstruction of traditional agriculture. Agriculture had different tasks at each stage of the economic development of Poland, and the means by which those tasks were carried out were also different. Nevertheless, the essential quality of Polish agricultural policy has always been the same and has always been carried out. The main assumption was that there was a need to carry out two basic aims: the growth of production and the transformation of agriculture. As far as the realization of those two aims is concerned considerable progress has been made, manifested mainly by the growth of agricultural production, the expansion of the productive assets of agriculture development of agricultural education and technological progress, establishment and consolidation of the state sector including state-owned farms, state machine centers, etc., the development of trade and credit cooperatives, food processing enterprises and services for agriculture. The scale of the above mentioned progress has been reflected by the relatively high growth rate of agricultural production, 2–3 percent per year, by the modernization of production assets and facilities, the socialization of almost the entire volume of turnover between agriculture and the national economy, which has radically changed the nature of that part of agriculture composed of small private farms, the socialization of agriculture credits, and the development of the state and cooperative sector of services and the food processing industry. The character of the economic bonds between agriculture and the national economy, as well as between the rural and urban populations has changed entirely. Unfortunately these processes have not been going on in a harmonious way and due to the widespread violation of economic principles throughout the entire national economy towards the end of the 1970s, they became a factor deepening the crisis in the countryside.

Intensification—The First and Main Problem of the Polish Agriculture

Intensification of agricultural production is a necessity for Polish agriculture. This is so because Poland is running out of uncultivated arable land. At present, arable land per head in Poland is constantly diminishing not only because of the increase in population but also because of industrialization and urbanization. Besides, we must remember the need for further improvement in people's diet. If we only maintain the present level of nutrition, agricultural production must grow by 1-2 percent yearly. The need for intensification is also caused by the constant growth of food consumption per head, which, in turn, requires an increase in the overall volume of production despite the decrease of the area of arable land per head. In addition due to the high marginal capital-labor ratio in industry, agriculture has to provide employment for a large part of the increasing population in the countryside.

All these factors play their role in establishing directions for the Polish agricultural development. The lack of uncultivated land, the large rural labor force and the need to increase agricultural production in order to satisfy the growing demand for food, create conditions in which the intensification of the Polish agriculture is a necessity. Besides the above mentioned facts, attention should also be given to two factors that additionally cause the level of intensification to be relatively high. These are, first, relatively poor soil, and, second, relatively poor weather. Poor natural conditions require that much effort be put into land cultivation and result in very intensive efforts to improve on the natural environment.

The supply of agricultural labor also shows a decreasing tendency for two reasons. First, rural residents leave villages for work outside agriculture, second, the quality of agricultural labor is diminishing, the result of workers getting old and of the increased number of women employed in agriculture. The decrease of both land and labor volume reduces the productive potential of agriculture and these negative effects must be offset by the growth of capital resources. Thus investment and technical and organizational progress are the only sources of the growth of agricultural production in Poland.

It should be emphasized here that the present urgent need for the intensification of Polish agriculture is historically justified by the conditions of its development. Developed countries have undergone the stage of intensification much earlier. Tasks connected with the mechanization of agriculture, the transformation of agrarian structure, the increased use of fertilizers, etc. must be carried out in Poland precisely at the present stage of the country's economic development. As a result of the implementation of the intensification process, what will be manifested mainly is high production growth and complete satisfaction of the demand for foodstuffs, the basic emphasis in its implementation will be put on different aspects. The emphasis on the growth of production per unit of land will be replaced by one on the growth of labor productivity. This will mean that Polish agriculture will enter a new stage of technical and production development. The present economic situation directly underlines the importance of production problems in our agriculture.

The Food Deficit in Poland— Reasons and Results

The main problem at the present stage of agricultural development in Poland is the unsatisfactory level of redundant production. The food economy and agriculture are in crisis. Despite various efforts taken to increase agricultural production, the production of industries supplying inputs to agriculture, and the capacity of the food processing industry, the general level of efficiency of the entire economic system does not remotely match the present needs of the economic development of Poland. Agriculture and the food economy are now facing the need to radically reconstruct themselves technically, and to introduce widespread improvements in organization and management in order to become a branch of the national economy with high production, high efficiency and good equipment and facilities so that it can fully satisfy social needs.

In the 1970s Poland ceased to be self-sufficient in food production. If we take as an index of self-sufficiency the balance between agriculture production and food purchases, then the deficit was about 2 billion dollars yearly, and the imports of grain amounted to over 12 quintals per hectare of the grain cultivation area in Poland. With such a level of grain imports this country's minimal needs were satisfied with great difficulty, showing the extent of regress in the productivity and utilization of arable land.

The deficient food balance has a number of negative economic, social and political consequences. The main one is its impact on macroeconomic stability. Food plays an important role in shaping society's living standard and expenditures on food and food related products amount to about 50 percent of society's expenditures. In such conditions even a small food deficit is deeply felt by society and stimulates it to defend its past levels of consumption. This is manifested by the demands to maintain stabilized food prices and as a result most of the prices of basic foodstuffs have remained constant for the fifteen years prior to 1982 despite considerable growth of production costs and wages.

The main reasons for the food deficit in Poland as well as all its negative consequences are population growth, the change in employment structure, and income increases combined with the constant prices of foodstuffs. Since 1946 the Polish population has grown from 23.6 million people to 37. The Polish population is fed at a better level now than it was in the post-War period despite the decline in arable land area from 20.4 million hectares in 1946 to 18.8 million hectares. The number of people employed outside agriculture has been growing faster than the Polish population. Incomes have also grown fast. The change in employment structure and the increase in incomes expanded the demand for food, creating a large market for agriculture products. As a result, Polish agriculture has been operating in the entire post-War period in the condition of excess demand for agricultural products, a condition favourable for the intensification process. Because of their stable prices, the main foodstuffs are getting cheaper in relation both to people's incomes and to other consumer goods. Hence demand is constantly growing and affecting the market in such a way that it promotes waste in consumption.

Decisions taken before 1982 further increased people's incomes, mainly of individuals with lower incomes, which caused further increases in food demand. The increase of food prices did not cover this gap. Because the production situation in agriculture is difficult and there are no possibilities of improving the market supply, a further aggravation of the market imbalance is unavoidable.

From the point of view of the food market the situation in the market for other consumer goods and services is also unfavourable. The great shortage of industrial consumer goods, their high prices and frequently low quality are the reasons why those goods and services do not provide proper competition for food articles, and thus they can not balance the purchasing power of people on the market or suitably shape people's consumption patterns. So in order to maintain the present food market balance it would be necessary to achieve an agricultural production growth rate amounting to 3–4 percent yearly.

Ways Out of the Crisis

The supply of food depends on the extent of its production which in turn is a function of the quantity of land at the disposal of agriculture and its productivity. As the area of land per head is diminishing rapidly, the only possibility for increasing the food supply is to increase land productivity. This, however, requires an increase in expenditures for the intensification of agriculture. The internal possibilities of agriculture are rather small, there is no chance or need to increase employment, there are hardly any possibilities to expand the quantity or improve the quality of inputs manufactured in agriculture directly. At present agriculture intensification is based on industrial inputs, but in Poland for the last twenty years only about 10 percent of industrial production has been used for producing food, and only 6–7 percent for agricultural inputs. That share of industrial production which is used in agriculture has not been and is not enough to sustain technical improvement or the increase in agricultural production. The process of industrialization in our country is being carried out at the expense of resources and labor drawn from agriculture to such an extent that it has started neglecting agriculture's needs and interests. One of the essential conditions for the development of agriculture in Poland is to introduce suitable changes in direction of this country's industrialization and especially to expand industries working for the agriculture.

As far as the course of the present crisis is concerned, moves must be taken to make the entire society realize that the main producers of agricultural goods are family farms and to adjust economic and agricultural policy to this fact. Economic policy has for many years emphasized the importance of the state and cooperative economy, has promoted the taking over of land from agriculture in the process of industrialization. All this has led to the collapse of the production by private farmers. But if policy treats private agriculture as the main producer of food without making changes in its possibilities for development, then private agriculture's possibilities for development will constantly be limited and unable to satisfy social needs.

There is an urgent need to reformulate the basic foundations of agricultural policy so as to combine the growth of production with the reconstruction of agriculture. This principle matches fully the needs of both agriculture and society. It constitutes the general theoretical and practical output of Polish agrarian thought and is of great importance for both our country and for the development of contemporary socialist thought. Unfortunately this principle has not always been properly interpreted and realized by agricultural policy makers. Recently stress has been put on the second part of the above principle and that is why the Polish agriculture was being reconstructed in a primitive way. This was a harmful policy. At present the social development of the whole of agriculture is a new strategic aim of agricultural policy in Poland.

Polish agricultural economists are changing their stand concerning the transformations to occur in agriculture. They are beginning to justly adopt the opinion that internal structural changes in the private sector of agriculture, the technical and organizational progress it is undergoing, the increase in technological equipment, improvement of agrarian structure, etc. should be treated as an important element of the social and economic transforming of agriculture.

Private Agriculture as an Integral
Element of the Socialist Economy

The economic role of private agriculture can be shown by means of selected synthetic indices. Private (family, individual, peasant) farms produce about 80 percent of the global agricultural production in Poland, about 76 percent of market production, and the average value of agriculture production per hectare is higher in the private sector than in other sectors of agriculture. Private farms have become an integral, stable and developing element of the agricultural economy in Poland.

The need to assure the stable character of private agriculture points to the need to formulate the agricultural and economic policy concerning family farms in order to create suitable conditions for utilizing all their possibilities. This requires an answer to the question of linking the private sector of food production to the entire food sector and the country's national economy. Despite their family nature, private farms can properly function as an economic and production system in the conditions of a socialist economy. It is commonly accepted that private farms, if they cooperate with other social and economic systems and forms, can develop and consolidate their production and social role. The private sector of agriculture can fully adjust itself to the general economic interests of country.

Links between the private sector of agriculture and the entire national economy in Poland are constantly becoming tighter. The exchange of goods between agriculture and other branches of the economy is practically fully socialized, and the process of accumulation and reproduction in agriculture is defined by the national economic plan and is carried out in accordance with social needs. Fulfilling their own tasks private farms also promote the implementation of the entire society's aims. The purpose of private farmers' activity is to achieve the highest possible incomes as a result of their own work and the use of their own and collective means of production. This is the purpose of agriculture, and this is the task included in the economic policy adopted by Poland. The proper implementation of private aims turns out to be beneficial for the entire society. There are no contradictions between private and social point of view on these questions. An understanding of this fact is of great importance both as a theoretical concept and for the practical implementation of the present agricultural policy which essentially assumes a positive and continuing coexistence between the private sector of agriculture and the socialist economy.

The development and evolution of the private sector of the economy in the socialist system yield a considerable amount of experience. Based on such experience we can see that there are great possibilities for the development of that sector and that it can properly fulfill various economic and social functions posed by the state, despite its retaining of private property. Agriculture adjusts itself to the needs of society and satisfies those needs, while society should create means and conditions to make that possible. The essence of the adjustment processes in the private sector of agriculture is that it creates economic and social mechanisms to reconstruct agriculture and to evolve such forms of farming as are suitable given the existing economic conditions. Hence in Poland we can build strong, developed agriculture successfully only by developing the most modern, intensive and highly specialized family farms. Neither now nor in the future can any theoretical concepts and justifications be viewed as correct if they make full utilization of the productive potential in any form of agriculture difficult. This also concerns practical measures. An understanding of these realities has not been common in Poland. The prevalence of oversimplified ideas concerning the process of industrialization and the resulting neglect of the needs of agriculture are among the most important mistakes that have been made so far in Polish planning and economic policy. They are still an important obstacle to overcome on the road to the dynamic development of agriculture.

Determinants of the Development
Strategy of Polish Agriculture

All that has been said above determines the conditions for a new formulating of the development rules for Polish agriculture. The following questions are of first importance in its current and long-term development of agriculture. So far, there is no clear concept of the future model of the agricultural enterprise or farm that would ensure maximum food production, and that would be in line with the conditions of the present form of government. In particular, the future position of peasant agriculture is essential and important for the current and future development of agriculture, especially from the viewpoint of the individual agricultural producers, and of the sense of stability in farming. Up until now, the development strategy of agriculture has been shaped by the post-war land reform, and subsequently by the changing economic and political situation of the country. The lack of an adequate vision, apart from the formal-legal vision of socialization or cooperative forming, and of a mechanism of constant implementation of agricultural development programs were the weakest point of agricultural policy. In the discussions on the choice of the future model of agriculture there occurred two criteria: the production-economic and the socio-political one. Opinions on the subject of agriculture depended on the preference for one of them. The acceptance and full realization of the rule of stability and development of individual family farms solves the dilemma and can be a prerequisite for a new, original agricultural system in Poland.

Second is the aim of achieving a rational self-sufficiency in agricultural production. Food self-sufficiency is to be the result of effective operations in the sphere of the food economy. The degree of self-sufficiency cannot be assumed in advance for it changes with time and is of a relative nature. Self-sufficiency does not mean autarky since it is also necessary to take advantage of the benefits of the international exchange of commodities as the expression of social division of labor.

Third is the motivation system in agriculture. In Poland it is the most vital and, simultaneously, the weakest element of the functioning of the national economy, agriculture included. A faulty motivation system wrecks the initiative and restrains the development of agriculture. The motivation system for agricultural producers includes the system of agricultural prices, credits, taxes, stability of agricultural policy, guarantee of ownership of the means of production, observance of rights and obligations, production and trade services, etc. Each of these elements still leaves much to be desired.

Fourth is the rational use of productive resources in agriculture, the anti-waste campaign, and the reduction of production losses. These can be achieved by the following:

- a better sectoral and spatial allocation of productive resources, primarily of capital;
- higher interest among agricultural producers in the economic and rational management of productive factors;
- higher qualifications of agricultural producers;
- higher prices for food and more rational relative prices for productive resources;
- development of agricultural processing, storage and transport facilities, and improvement of agricultural products' turnover, from the producer to the consumer.

Fifth, improvement of the grain-feed balance. The essence of food production is the production of raw materials of plant origin as the basis of animal production, particularly under the circumstances of Polish agrarian structure. The problem of a plant raw material deficit, mainly feed raw materials, occurs, with different intensity, over the entire post-war agricultural development.

Sixth, the revival of the agricultural market and restoration of market equilibrium. The attempts to solve the problems of the agricultural market by a poorly organized system of supply contracts for agricultural products or the rationing of food supplies reduce the value of money. The restoration of market equilibrium and of the value of money will be the consequence of providing agriculture with productive resources and consumption goods.

Seventh is foreign trade in agricultural products. The advisable policy is a limit on the monopoly of central institutions in trading agricultural products, and the increasing of the exports of agriculture in line with the growth of production and processing.

Eighth is the relationship between agriculture and economic reform. It is a truism to say that agricultural development depends on the entire national economy, especially as regards providing a specified quantity and quality of inputs energy and raw materials. The economic reform must create conditions for appropriate production of those items. The development of agriculture depends on the solution of the most urgent and high-priority problems in the entire national economy. These include the following:

- the necessity of changes in the understanding and in implementation of the full-time employment rule; full-time employment is to be considered as a certain objective we are aiming at, and therefore, it cannot mean full-time employment at every time and place;
- maintaining a stable relationship between labor productivity and the level of incomes;
- improvement of the financial economy of the state, especially as far as money circulation is concerned, which also is a prerequisite for proper functioning of the market;
- restoring, to a specified degree, the rules of the market game, and thus, consolidating initiatives and the motivation system.

The focal point of the strategy for agricultural development should be to promote free economic choices regulated by prices and incomes. The starting point of this argument is simple: so long as agriculture is poor, the state will be poor. This thesis was fought against bitterly once. Now, agricultural economists and political parties are ever more plainly asked the question: what to do, how to act, so that agriculture is not poor? Agricultural poverty can be eliminated only by raising the level of production and, consequently, all the elements linked with it, including structural changes, increases of technical equipment and of other means of production, and the elements that concern the economic policy of the state. As economists, we declare that we have one basic aim in the strategy of agricultural development namely, agriculture must be highly productive and effective, and the agricultural population must be affluent. Any other strategy, in which we might see a continuation of, let us call it plainly, the economic discrimination against agriculture, justified by all sorts of social and political arguments, is simply unacceptable. Regardless of how radical the motto of affluence may be seen, we rest on this strategic thesis: a good farmer is a good and affluent producer.

We recommend a technocratic approach to the entire matter of agricultural development: food is to be available, and the economic policy must determine how production is to be realized, for how much and in which way. Thus, the development strategy of the food economy is reduced to one statement: food is to be available. Just that, and nothing more. In Poland, food is to be available according to the requirements of market equilibrium and the nutritional needs of society, and that is the answer apart from all kinds of discussions. Economic policymakers, on the other hand, are responsible for the determining of how much food is to be made available, how to produce it in the cheapest way, where and by what inputs, etc. All activities should aim at finding the optimal way of realizing this strategic rule, which is now determined as food self-sufficiency of the country. It is not only the problem of self-sufficiency as such but also the awareness that Poland can have plenty of food, regardless of fluctuations due to the laws of nature.

In this connection, let me make some comments. First, what does the strategy of agricultural development mean? I think it is the formulation of general objectives, which we are aiming at, a definition of a certain priority of those objectives, and setting up of mechanisms, by means of which the goals can be achieved. Naturally, these objectives cannot be determined in a model way. Nobody can say whether 10–15 years from now the agricultural goal will be identical. For the time being, these goals can be formulated within the concept of self-sufficiency, and, of course, everything we are saying here is of direct significance for determining the ways of implementing this self-sufficiency. This is essential since it offers a chance for a broad understanding of food and agricultural problems in the entire national economy, and a chance for a certain stabilization of the rules of action. This concerns, primarily, the production goal. If we assume self-sufficiency as a strategic goal, it is obvious that we shall not be able to abandon this goal even in a situation where we might be tempted to do so, for instance when the possibility appears to import 15 million tons of grain on credit. As it appears from this rule, it will be necessary for us, as regards grains and feeds, to have always in relation to our needs, 90–95 percent self-sufficiency. Any surplus over and above that is to be considered as a chance to be used, without disturbing the domestic market as was the case in the past. Our present-day experience plainly indicates that any connection with the western market must be carefully thought over, and, in most cases, it should be considered to be an extra possibility and not a fundamental factor.

Second, since, according to the above thesis, the weakest element of agricultural policy, as well as of the whole economic policy in Poland, is the faulty motivation system, the question arises how to find and formulate the mechanism of a better system. Some elements of the economic reform, see Wiktor Herer's paper, particularly the price and income policy, must create such a motivation system. This system would resolve questions connected with employment, agrarian structure, retaining of small holdings, etc. We thoroughly believe that money and the market will be of great significance there. It is becoming a general opinion that a full economic system can be created only by a food market, a good price and good money. Therefore, all that can be done in order to have a good stable market, functioning according to the rule of the law of value, and all that is defined as good money in the sense of shaping the market, will determine the setting up of such a motivation system. The farmer must be able to make a living, that is the basic motive, while the other one is the chance of achieving all the benefits resulting from earned profits. If the motivation reaction is hindered by poor functioning of the market, particularly by shortages in the market, it affects production decisions unfavorably.

Third, the author has frequently and firmly professed the thesis supporting the theory of subserviance of individual agriculture to the needs of the society, the consistence of this agriculture with the social interests, etc, emphasizing the special role of linking peasant agriculture with the state through trade, and co-operative and service institutions. Of course, we have treated all the advances in this respect favorably. Now, the time has come to verify this theory, not so much for theoretical as for practical respects. The system of subordination of peasant agriculture to the state became so bureaucratic, passive and inflexible that it is an obstacle to the development of the whole of agriculture and to the evolution of its production. This subordination of agriculture to institutions and organizations which seek to implement their own objectives, is ever more frequently a factor disorganizing and slowing down agricultural development.

Fourth, strategic questions linked to the agrarian structure are most essential. Undoubtedly, there are no chances whatever for determining the strategy of agricultural development, the objectives of that development, the ideas running ahead of time, without answering the question of what the agrarian structure will be like. One of the two recurring aspects is the relationship between peasant agriculture and the other sectors, and the other one concerns the internal situation in peasant agriculture. It is a vital problem, and we have to find the answer to the question of how individual farming is to be included in the system of a state which will no longer be passing through a crisis, but rather be a normally functioning, fairly up-to-date socialist state. There is only one possibility: the process of concentration must follow. Meanwhile, this necessary concentration process is contradictory to the current agricultural situation. At the present time, all the farms, regardless of their area, have to produce to a maximum, and thus influence the development of the entire food economy. For the future, however, the main possibilities stem from the need for concentration, and all favorable elements occurring in this connection.

It must be emphasized that the problem of agricultural income parity, so ardently raised in Poland now, cannot be solved with today's agrarian structure. It is simply impossible to ensure income parity to the great number of small-scale and non-specialized farms by means of prices. Attempts to realize such a levelling of incomes will always bring about a rise of food prices, and income increases mainly due to price rises, which is contrary to the needs of the whole economy. The solution to this problem is known, and West European countries have been through that stage 30–50 years ago. Industry and the whole economy controlled the mechanism of migration and of economic growth, whereas in Poland the migration process of the seventies became a slowdown factor of economic development. The economic sense of the mechanism was lost, and it became one of the factors of economic crisis.

Last, there are some important conclusions concerning the increasing of productive resources in agriculture. It must be stated that up till now, due to supply conditions, we are emphasizing primarily the problem of increasing productive resources, capital in the first place. The time is coming, however, when there will have to be stressed more strongly another aspect, namely the effectiveness of using those means, and the degree of their rational use. We are searching for a marked acceleration of rationalization of using those means, simply by better organized and better trained manpower, that is to say, by better work organization.

Notes

1. Part of this paper was presented at the Confederation Internationale du Credit Agricole Central Committee meeting held in Warsaw and published by CICA (Zurich, 1981), No. 64.

13

Planning the Development of Agriculture Under the Conditions of Polish Economic Reform

Wiktor Herer

Since this chapter concerns management and planning problems in agriculture, I will first explain briefly the fundamental principles behind the reform of the management and planning system for the whole Polish economy. They can be summarized under three points.

1. State and cooperative firms have been granted autonomy. Their management must be based on the three S principles: samodzielnosc—autonomy; samorzadnosc—self-management; samofinansowanie—self-financing. Only in certain cases, provided for by the law, may State bodies take decisions in the field of activity of a State firm.[1]
2. Firms manage their activity within the framework of a central State Plan. Adjustment of the firms' activity to the objectives of the plan must be obtained by the economic policy of the State which must influence the firm through economic instruments. Administrative orders, defined in their scope by the law, may be used only exceptionally.[2]
3. Workers of the firm participate in its management through bodies such as the general assembly of workers of the firms and the workers' council designated by this assembly. This council has broad prerogatives. In particular, it decides on the firm's annual plan. The workers' council has the right to stop the execution of a decision of the manager of the firm when such a decision is contrary to a workers' council resolution on a matter on which it holds sole competence.

Summing up, it may be said that market mechanisms should assume an essential role in the Polish economy. The central Plan's tasks must be achieved not through directives but through the creation, by the State's economic policy, of economic conditions suitable to the fulfilment of those tasks. The system of management and planning thus sketched will be referred to as

170

the reformed system as opposed to the traditional system that was in operation for close to 40 years and was based on directives and rationing.

Having thus sketched the general principles of the reform, we turn to the problems of agriculture and consider first private farms which provide 80 percent of agricultural output. Most of the rest comes from the State farms. Their planning and management system will be discussed separately.

Economic Reform and
Individual Peasant Farming

Poland is probably the only example of the durable coexistence of an individual agricultural economy producing the bulk of farm output and central planning system covering the whole of the economy.[3] The result of this situation is that, throughout all the post-war period, the market has always played in our economy a very important, though varying, role. After the abolition of the compulsory deliveries in 1971, the market has become the sole economic link between the private agricultural sector and the non-farm sector that is almost entirely nationalized and ruled by a directive planning system. The role of the market, which should be stressed, is however fundamentally different from that found in Western Europe.

Market demand for food originates almost entirely from wage earners in the non-agricultural socialized sector. The global supply of industrial inputs and consumers' goods is produced by the state industrial sector and sold to farmers by the cooperative and the state trade sector. The state has a monopoly on foreign trade. Marketing firms that purchase the farm output are either state owned or cooperative. Outside the state trading channels, there is always, in Poland, development of free trading relations between farmers and the non-farm population. There are also private food shops retailing farm products purchased directly from farmers, but their number is minute. These non-state channels play a marginal role in disposal of farm output and in supply of the urban population.[4] Their economic importance is, however, essential since every farmer is entirely free to market all his output on the free market. We will return to this later.

In order to study these rather peculiar market relationships within imperative central planning and the way in which individual farms operate in this system of dirigisme in the non-farm sector, we will first indicate the principles of this coexistence then the deviations between principles and reality.

In accordance with the principles of the system, individual farms are not subject to any administrative pressures with regard to the structure of production or the quantities of output to be supplied. They are thus free to dispose of their production and to buy their means of production. The influence of the central plan on the production pattern of individual farms, on its dynamics and on the distribution of output was therefore mostly felt through price policy.[5] It led to the adjustment of the farm production to the needs of the whole economy. Another important tool by which the central Plan influenced individual farming was industrial policy which determined the production of farm inputs by state industrial firms.

Within this system, a unity of objectives between the central planner and the individual farmer tended to create itself. Both tended to maximize the value added of the farm. One can thus assert that the private farmer who does not hire wage labor, the typical case for Poland, does not maximize profit but rather value added. He is therefore willing to spend in the zone of decreasing returns, which are often felt in agriculture, in order to maximize simultaneously his family's income and the country's national income. The barrier that limits the maximization of this income is his preference for leisure. By expending more labor the farmer chooses in general between the marginal product he can obtain and a consequent loss of leisure. In the course of this process of choice, he does not fear overproduction since he enjoys the guarantee of fixed prices. The system of land taxes also reinforced the tendency to maximize value added. In contrast to an income tax, the land tax did not increase as production rose. Rather, when the latter increased, the tax was spread out over a greater income.

It is only during brief periods that the above principles operated in their pure form. Specifically during 1971–1973, which can be considered as a sort of honeymoon period for the coexistence between autonomous individual farms and the non-agricultural sector operating under the traditional principle of central planning.

What are the difficulties in the coexistence of the two sectors? The basic condition is the smooth operation of the market that links private agriculture to state industry. The essence of this operation is expressed by equilibrium on the market which means, in simplified form, continued sale of industrial goods bought by farmers. Practice has shown that this condition was only partially fulfilled. Industry and trade, managed from the center through directives coming from above, were too rigid and unable to suitably adapt their supply to the neeeds of agriculture. Adjusting to this demand depended not only on the production capacities of national industries, but also, to a large extent, on the ability to import from capitalist markets a number of inputs used directly or indirectly by agriculture. Particularly important were high protein content feeds like soybeans or groundnuts which cannot be produced under our climate. This lack of flexibility stems from the fact that the non-farm sector, including foreign trade firms, managed by centralized directives, was not able to react directly to the impulses coming from the farm market. It was rather in an indirect way that farmers' needs were satisfied as the central planners studied the needs of the farm market. On the basis of these studies planners expressed their demands in the form of directives to industrial and foreign trade firms. This system was indeed rather rigid and caused continuous disequilibria in the various segments of the farm market. These disequilibria showed up on shortages along marketing channels that weakened the effectiveness of the central plan in its actions to influence the pattern of farm production through market mechanism. Prices ceased to be a sufficient instrument of regulation.

Under the continued influence of those causes, and particularly during 1975–79, the Polish economy was thus kept in an uneasy and constantly perturbed balance. This induced the planners to use, with regard to farms, various non-market measures, mostly rationing in the sale to farmers of industrial inputs. This often implied giving up the pure conditions of free monetary sales by setting up additional rules. Within the framework of the sales contract for his production, the farmer was given not only the price but the right to buy certain well defined industrial goods which were subject to regulation.[6]

Several reasons explain the conditions just described. The main one, as mentioned above, is the contradiction between the market orientation of the peasant farms and the imperative system of planning in industry. Another essential reason is the fact that private farms were, to a large extent, considered as foreign bodies in the planned economy system and therefore they were, in a certain way, discriminated against with regard to their supply of inputs which were allocated preferentially to state farms.

What Did Reform Change
in the Individual Farm Sector?

Reform did not bring any changes with regard to the principles of operation on private peasant farms.[7] The principles of autonomy and self-financing already existed for those farms before the reform. It is their political status that was changed. Individual farms, which were often considered as alien to the system of central economic planning, must presently become a fundamental element of the type of planned socialist economy being built in Poland. This is expressed, for instance, in the Constitution of the Polish People's Republic which stated that "the State takes care of the individual and family farms of working peasants and guarantees their permanent existence."[8] In accordance with this provision, the aspiration for the enlargment of farms is presently encouraged. Another principle, adopted at the same time, is that of the unity of agriculture: the individual sector and the state sector are on equal footing and neither of them may be discriminated against.

The economic links between the individual peasant sector and state industry will have to be modified according to the principle of the reform since industry will presently be composed of autonomous, self-managed and self-financed firms. Under the conditions described above, links between state industries and both private or state farming will be of a direct nature. Firms supplying the rural market must adjust the dynamics of their production on the basis of the signals they will receive directly from the agricultural market. Indirect links through the central plan will be restricted solely to major strategic investments such as, for instance, a fertilizer or tractor factory. The bulk of industrial products must be conveyed to agriculture under the principle of direct contracts between the rural trade network and the various autonomous firms of the state industrial sector. The role of private handicrafts in supplying agriculture with goods and services must increase. In accordance with the principles of the reform, all this should give more flexibility to the whole system supplying farmers with inputs and consumer goods as well as furthering conditions of market equilibrium. This should also be encouraged by the price setting system for goods sold to farmers. This system rests on two possibilities. Prices may be official, thus centrally fixed. Such prices cover basic farm inputs and a small number of staple consumption goods, mostly food. Alternatively prices may be contractual, set within the framework of contracts between trade organizations and industrial firms. Though they are referred to as contractual, these prices are set under the control of the central price agency, which limits the possibilities of price rises.

It can therefore be stated that the renewed importance of market relationships in our economy is linked simultaneously to the fact that the center retains a strong interventionist position with regard to price formation. This strong position has also been retained for setting prices paid to farmers for commodities they sell. Prices for staple commodities such as wheat, live animals, milk, sugar beets and rapeseed are fixed by the central price board. Only for fruit and vegetables is there a system with completely free determination of prices through free market operation.

When we say that prices paid to farmers for basic commodities are centrally fixed, we do not mean that the central planner has unlimited possibilities of fixing prices, nor should one believe that there would be a possibility for some professors to invent prices in their offices on the basis of cost of production studies. The practical situation is quite different. A dominant factor for the state policy with regard to prices is the fact that there exists a free market for farm products which is not a black market but a legal one. The share of this private market in total marketings is minute. The essential part of the farm goods move to the non-farm population through state and cooperative trading organizations.

However, the fact that the farmer has full freedom to dispose of his output in the way he sees fit and may always sell through the private market[9] is of major importance from the point of view of price policy. The free prices originating on the free market are a base reference, a real shadow market for the state prices. The latter only fulfill their role and really serve for purchases as long as they are not too different from the free market prices. State decisions with regard to prices are thus not fully administrative ones since they must take into account the free market price relationships and, in a way, adjust to them. The existence of an adjustment process does not mean that state pricing decisions are passively dominated by the market. The farm price setting process must be linked with a set of actions influencing all market relationships. The dynamics of wages in the non-farm state sector, the income elasticity of demand for food of the non-farm population, which influences the flows and prices of consumers' goods of industrial origin, are of fundamental importance for the price formation of food products in state retail trade and of inputs for agriculture. State organizations purchasing farm products are often threatened by competition from the free market because the latter offers more advantageous prices. Faced with situations of this kind, the planner can accept these higher prices but he can also attempt to stop their increase by slowing down wage increases in the non-farm sector, or by importing foods for which there is a deficit, or by stimulating farm production through additional imports of inputs, where, in the case of imports of feed, the effects can be quite rapid.

It is easy to notice that, among those instruments that can exert an influence on the market for farm products, non-farm wage policy has the main role. In the past, the efficiency of state policy concerning farm prices was improved by issuance of directives regarding wages and their readjustment, within the framework of the central plan, to conform with farm price policy. This had very positive effects on the stabilization of the farm market. At the same time, this had very negative effects on industrial production as it limited the possibilities of flexible stimulation of output in industry. This is why, within the framework of the planning system presently being reformed, a quite new form of regulation policy for non-farm incomes has appeared to serve the needs of farm market stabilization. For instance, taxes paid by industry are currently playing an increasing role in this regard.

Within the system just described it is obvious that the degree of freedom of the planner and the strictness of the need to adapt centrally fixed prices to those formed freely on the market will vary from commodity to commodity. Freedom is greatest for those products that must undergo industrial processing before they reach the consumer, such as sugar beets. Freedom is much more reduced for directly consumable perishables. Fruit and vegetables belong to that group. On that market, state firms must submit entirely to the market. They pay prices that may vary daily and compete with private traders. Our fruit and vegetable market is thus hardly different from those found in western countries; it has all its vices and advantages. It is the only segment of our market that experiences overproduction.

The system just described implies a central regulation by state action. It can, however, be referred to as a market regulation system because it differs in an essential way from the administrative form of regulation used until now in industry and which lacked any reference level in the form of a free market price.

Reform of the Management and Planning System on State Farms

Under the conditions of the traditional planning system with prescriptions and rationing, state farms operated under principles similar to those of industrial state firms. The production structure was patterned under the implacable impact of centralized directives that included rationing of financial means and inputs. Practice has shown that management under such conditions has very negative effects on efficiency. Production costs on state farms were considerably higher than those of individual units and important state subsidies were needed. In agriculture, the directive system produced worse results than in industry because it prevented state farms from adjusting their production structure to the very diverse natural and economic conditions they were subjected to.

Reform modifies this situation. State farms have obtained full freedom to organize their production and to purchase the inputs they need on the market. They must adjust to the same market conditions, that is they earn the same prices as the individual farms. They must also get their supply of inputs on the market on an equal footing. State farm activity must be based on the principle of self-financing and involves progressively giving up all subsidies.

Summing up, we may note that, in contrast to the case of individual farms where reform does not change the very essence of firm operation, change on state farms is of a fundamental nature. Reform in that sector was urgently needed and much easier to carry out than the reform of industrial firms. This stems from the non-monopolistic nature of farm production. Because of its specific character, agricultural production prevents, in all fields of production, the establishment of any monopoly position of firms. This of course, makes reform easier.

Barriers to Carrying Out the Reform

The objective of reform is to leave full freedom to both peasant and state farms in the choice of production structures, the tempo of their growth and the use of techniques on the basis of free access to all sorts of inputs purchased at equilibrium prices. A balanced market must create a demand barrier for low quality industrial goods and pull down costs of production in industries producing goods for the rural market. It should at the same time create economic barriers to price increases of products farmers buy and progressively eliminate administrative regulation of those prices although such regulations are, however, necessary in the first stage of the reform.

It is through the market that the central planner must influence the development of agriculture. He will also make use of other mechanisms such as prices, interest rates, allocation of certain inputs that embody technical progress such as seeds or improved livestock. It is the lack of equilibrium of the market, that we will briefly attempt to characterize, that prevents the fulfillment of those basic principles.

The fatal economic policy of the seventies brought disintegration of the industrial production apparatus and a fall in national income. This was accompanied by a very large rise in nominal incomes for both the farm and non-farm population. At the same time, state-fixed prices were increased but at a rate that was not high enough to attain market equilibrium under conditions of falling industrial and meat production. Socio-political constraints and numerous other factors prevented the attainment of market equilibrating price rises. This resulted in a situation of deep disequilibrium where the flows of money in the hands of farm and non-farm active population exceeded the value of the flows of goods supplying the market. What is called a money surplus was created. It can be represented by equation 1.

(1) $M_t = f(t) + b$

where:

M = the monetary surplus that the population holds in its quest for goods—excluding durable savings. It is this money surplus which exerts a pressure on the market.

t = independent variable designating time in years.

f(t) = the increase over time of the monetary surplus starting from the base period zero ($f(0) = 0$).

b = the monetary surplus at the start of the period studied ($t - 0$).

The above formula sheds some light on the mechanism by which the monetary surplus is formed and increased. Its source is in the positive difference between the value of the flow of monetary incomes that the population will devote to market purchases and the value of the annual flow of goods sent to markets. This difference creates an inflationary gap, the flow of money earmarked for purchases which, since it cannot find goods on the market, feeds the growth of the monetary surplus and causes it to increase, (the f(t) element in Equation 1). Since this monetary mass surplus increases at each period (e.g. year) it is for each year of a given time period equal to the starting or base period surplus (the b variable in formula 1) plus the cumulated value of later surpluses. The monetary mass surplus at the end of a period t is thus composed of two elements: its base value at the period of origin, and its increase over time (f(t)). These monetary surpluses are currently large and jeopardize the attainment of the principles of reform.[10] Price ratios fixed by the state can still, to a certain extent, influence the structure of farm production. Prices are, however, losing their strength as an instrument stimulating farm production increases. On many peasant farms, the positive price elasticity of supply is now in doubt. Disequilibrium on the input market reduces the choice of techniques and, therefore, the efficiency in the use of inputs.

Under such a situation, it is easy to note that the outcome of the reform will depend on market equilibrium being reestablished. The simplest solution would be to expand farm and industrial production to the point where they would match the excess money held by the population, calm down the market and transform "hot" money into reserves calmly sleeping in some bank vault. This would require a real upsurge of industrial production which is obviously impossible. I personally see a two stage solution. The first one would bring about the shrinking of the monetary surplus and enable the transition from the present situation, with both price increases and market disequilibrium, to a more classical inflation (price rises with market equilibrium). As even this second type of inflation, with market equilibrium, does not yet create favourable conditions for the development of agricultural production, a second stage would be needed during which stabilized but flexible prices would replace inflation in order to prevent market disequilibria from being created.

The most difficult step is from the present state to inflation with equilibrium. To cover it, a sharp increase in the prices of industrial goods is needed, as well as a certain increase for food prices, in order, among other things, to eliminate food subsidies. Rises in wages and prices paid to farmers cannot fully compensate for the cost of living increase caused by these price increases. A somewhat paradoxical situation is thus created: to prevent price increases in the future, it is necessary, in a first stage, to increase them now. The importance of the opposition a move of that kind will meet need hardly be explained. So we have before us a complex socio-political problem. The price rises, necessary for market equilibrium and to stop speculation have widely differing impacts on the household budgets of the various social groups. So actions designed to bring back market equilibrium must be combined with protection of the interests of those social groups that are economically weakest. This complex problem is currently the main theme of concern for numerous segments of the scientific community.

Notes

1. Law concerning State firms 25 September 1981, in Wladyslaw Baka. *Polska Reforma Gospodarcza* (Polish Economic Reform) Warszawa, PWE, 1982, p. 20.

2. *Kierunki reformy gospodarczej. Dokument komisji dla Spraw Reformy* (Economic Reform Orientation. Reform Commission Document), *Ibid.,* p. 89.

3. Over the past 40 years, this coexistence had its hard times (as well as the very bad 1951–1953 years). We are not happy about our agriculture's present stage of development, but we cannot forget that, during 1955–1975, under conditions of coexistence of private farms and central planning, agriculture developed rapidly. In the private sector, production levels per hectare are two and a half times higher than in the interwar period. Considering the unfavourable soil and climate conditions of our country, this is not a bad performance. In addition, it must be noted that private farming gives more production per hectare at less cost than the state farm sector.

4. It is only in the field of fruit and vegetables that the so-called free market plays a significant role in supplying the population.

5. Prices of all inputs purchased by farmers as well as prices of basic farm commodities sold by them were centrally set by the State.

6. The reader may be surprised to see that we only consider disequilibria through insufficient supply which cannot match demand. We ignore the case where supply exceeds demand. This is because an excess of supply very seldom occurs in centrally planned economies. If it were to happen it could be immediately absorbed by an adequate price decline, if such were deemed useful from the point of view of the whole economy. The case of demand exceeding supply is much more difficult to handle in centrally planned economies.

7. The situation in the state farming sector, to be examined later, is quite different.

8. Constitution of the 1983 People's Republic of Poland Art. 15–3. The four new words are "gwarantuje trwatosi tych gospoderstuv".

9. Suppressing meat trading hit mainly private trade intermediaries and it hardly affected sales of meat by farmers directly to consumers.

10. It is easy to note that the situation thus described differs essentially both from inflation processes observed in Western Europe and from hyperinflation as found, for instance, in countries like Brazil.

Hungarian Agriculture:
Evolving to Maintain Progress?

14

Hungarian Agriculture in the 1970s and 1980s

Ivan Benet

Because the subject of this chapter is very broad, I shall stress only the key questions regarding the development of Hungarian agriculture in the 1970s so that each question can be examined in adequate detail. As for the 1980s, I shall refer more to our problems and to the open questions of further development.

The Rate of Growth of Output in Hungarian Agriculture in the 1970s

Table 14.1 provides an international comparison of the rates of growth of gross agricultural production. Hungarian agriculture occupies fourth place among the 18 countries for the sample period. Only the agricultural output of the Netherlands, Romania and Spain grew faster than that of Hungary, and the annual growth rate of agriculture output surpassed 3 percent in only four countries among the 18 in course of the surveyed period.

The relatively rapid growth of output was accompanied by changes in the structure of production. Taking the average of the years from 1966 to 1970, crops accounted for 57–58 percent of gross agricultural production and animal production for 42–43 percent. This ratio changed to 53–54 percent and 46–47 percent for the years from 1976 to 1980. Within crop growing the share of horticulture dropped, and between 1966/70 and 1976/80 about 81 percent of the increase in agriculture production was due to 4 activities: wheat and corn growing, pig and poultry breeding. From the structural aspect this is an important characteristic of the growth of Hungarian agricultural production.

Another important characteristic of this growth is that the growth rate of 3.1 percent would be significantly higher if we were to take into account all activities realized within the farm sector. After 1968 the sphere of activity of Hungarian farms was broadened from crop growing and animal husbandry to include significant non-agricultural activities. As a result of this development the share of non-agricultural activities within all activities of the state farms and the collective farms of the cooperatives even surpassed 30 percent by 1982. This non-agricultural activities have become an interegral part of the business activities of Hungarian cooperative farms and state farms, and are developed in close interaction with agricultural pursuits.

The Results of Development

Among the most important results of development was that in the first half of the 1970s Hungary solved its cereal problem. The breadgrain supply of the country is ensured in the long term, and through the revolution in corn production the feed basis of pig and poultry breeding activities became consolidated. Industrial production systems came into general use in corn production and yielded significant results even when measured by international standards. It is worth mentioning that in the average annual corn production for the years 1966 to 1970, did not reach 4 million tons while it approached 6.4 million tons on the average for the years between 1976 and 1980. As may be seen from Table 14.3 average yields grew from 3.2 tons/ha between 1966 and 1970 to almost 4.9 tons/ha for 1976–1980. In the years between 1976 and 1980, Hungary reached the level of 1.2 tons/ha of grain production per head. In the course of the 1970s, the country thus became a net grain exporter in contrast to having been a net grain importer in the 1960s, while at the same time greatly increasing its meat production.

The Hungarian level of meat production was 133 kg/per head in 1980 which is quite high in comparison to other countries. As Table 14.4 shows, among the 18 countries surveyed, the 249 kg/per head meat production of Denmark is outstanding while Hungary occupied a remarkable third place (after the Netherlands) by that year.

Agricultural development achieved in the course of the 1970s also made itself felt in changes in food consumption. Table 14.5 shows that the consumption structure of fats significantly altered in favour of vegetable fats. The consumption of eggs grew by 109 percent, and that of poultry meat by 93 percent. Meat consumption grew by about 53–54, that of milk and dairy products by 47 percent. Attaining the annual 73 kg/capita meat consumption level was rendered possible by the rapid growth in pork and poultry consumption. Another favorable tendency is that the consumption of cereals declined.

A less welcome aspect of Hungarian food consumption revealed in Table 14.5 is that, in the course of the past 12 years, vegetable and fruit consumption grew only moderately. Food consumption can be seen also from another perspective. Of every 100 Ft. spent for commodities by the population, the share of foodstuffs represented about 29 Ft. and that of alcoholic beverages, tobacco, etc. 16 Ft.

For the evaluation of Hungarian food consumption in an international perspective useful information is furnished by the analysis of the Economic

Research Institute (Gazdasagkutato Intezet). By surveying the characteristics in structure and standard of Hungarian food consumption it may be concluded that the consumption of basic foodstuffs except milk, is significantly greater in Hungary than in other countries at a similar level of economic development. Regarding the total consumption of meat, fats, flour and sugar, the value of our annual surplus consumption could be estimated at world market prices to an amount of about 1 billion U.S. dollars in the middle of the 1970s.

Hungarian agriculture also made an important contribution to the maintenance of the equilibrium of the foreign-trade balance. It is well known that Hungarian agriculture exports exceed agricultural imports. We should like to make two points in this respect. One is that also the foreign trade balance of agribusiness as a whole is positive although it is negative in the sphere of its backward linkages since more than 50 percent of the means of production of industrial origin but agricultural in destination is imported. On the other hand, we must refer also to the fact that the positive trade balance of agribusiness increased in the 1970s and also at the beginning of the 1980s and played a positive role in creating the equilibrium of the foreign trade balance of the Hungarian economy at the beginning of the 1980s.

The Major Factors of Economic Growth

The rapid growth outlined above was undoubtedly motivated by several factors in Hungarian agriculture. The most important ones will be now described in brief.

Hungarian agricultural policy should be mentioned first. Since its analysis would require a book, or even several volumes, I stress here only two important basic principles of policy that proved correct. One was that policymakers considered state and cooperative property as equal, i.e., to be equivalent and thereby prevented a kind of reorganization. The second basic principle leads us to small-scale production. Through political support and the economic stimulation of small production, Hungarian agricultural policy maintained and even strengthened the multiorganizational nature of Hungarian agriculture. Policymakers regarded small-scale production as a lasting and organic aspect of Hungarian agriculture. Thus small-scale production was one of the factors contributing to rapid development in the 1970s. Its share remained significant, representing 40 percent of gross agricultural production (crop growing and animal husbandry) between 1966 and 1970, and 36 percent between 1976 and 1980. (See Table 14.6.) The share of small-scale production in national income generated by agriculture can be estimated near 50 percent. The weight and role of small-scale production, of course, differs among activities and this is true also for the changes in its role. This difference is already obvious even if we consider only the aggregates of the major activities since in the average for the years 1971 to 1975 the share within animal husbandry was distributed evenly between the large-scale enterprises and small-scale production, and on the average for 1976–1980 the share of small production was still 45 percent. The role of small-scale production is particularly important in pork production where its share was between 54 and 60 percent in the 1970s.

Although the share of small-scale production in crop growing can be estimated at "only" 25 percent, nevertheless, the role of small production in certain crop-growing activities was in fact equal to that of the large-scale enterprises for the 1970s. The fact, for example, that in the course of the 1970s somewhat more than 50 percent of the gross production value in vegetable growing, fruit production and vinticulture was produced by the small producers also is a reflection of the importance of small-scale production. Small-scale production, moreover, contributes with another "additional value" to economic growth as it gives time and opportunity for experimenting with and the propagation of large-scale technologies. This role can hardly be overestimated.

Finally, and in order to avoid misunderstandings, I emphasize here that to oppose small-scale production in favor of large-scale enterprises makes no sense. Hungarian agricultural policy endeavors to produce a synthesis of the two and I think the soundness of this effort was shown to be correct in Hungary.

Among the factors stimulating economic growth, production systems must be emphasized. Except for poultry meat (broiler chicken), they appeared in the course of the 1970s and rapidly gained ground in Hungarian agriculture. It is correct to say that in the decade of the 1970s the production systems formed the principal way of industrialization in Hungarian agriculture. The great importance of the systems consists essentially of the fact that they formed the framework for the organizing activity that permitted the coordination of the means of production at a high level. This led to production results that surpassed the average. In respect to the economic evaluation of the activities of production systems, the majority of them achieved a level of financial returns needed for to justify themselves in economic terms. They improved the level of yields and increased commodity output and the profitability of these activities. At the same time, it must be recognized that in the course of propagating the system in animal husbandry we also sometimes had failures.

When evaluating the production systems we must emphasize that in two activities, poultry and corn, where they produced a decisive turn, we had to import technology and resources.

Among the factors stimulating rapid economic growth the role of foreign trade must be stressed. It contributed in part by overcoming the restraints of a limited domestic market through the export of foodstuffs at rising prices. It also played an essential role in the satisfaction of the increasing import demands of agriculture. The total direct and indirect, import demand of the agricultural sector doubled between 1966/1970. Furthermore, this import demand increased in both dollar and ruble trade. These imports of course exerted a positive effect on technical development in agriculture.

It can hardly be disputed that one of the factors stimulating the rapid economic growth of Hungarian agriculture was the availability of energy inputs at relatively low prices until 1978. Hungarian agriculture exploited this opportunity as demonstrated by the fact that the annual average growth rate of direct energy consumption was 9.3 percent between 1970 and 1980. Behind the increase in energy consumption in Hungarian agriculture during the 1970s were such factors as the decline in the number of active earners by 18 percent, the slow response of domestic economic management to the world market price explosion of energy, as well as the extension of agricultural activities and the development of forward linkages and non-agricultural activities of the total agricultural consumption of the equivalent of 1.7 million tons of fuel in 1978, this last sphere of activity used the equivalent of about 0.4 million tons of fuel.

The energy dimensions of Hungarian agriculture significantly changed at the end of the 1970s. Energy consumption per 100 ha of cropland grew from the 500 kJ in 1970 to 1064 kJ in 1978 while energy consumption per capita of active agricultural earners increased at the same time from 28 to 73 kJ. In other words, in 1978 the share of agricultural energy consumption represented 7.3 percent within the total energy consumption of the national economy, and 5.4 percent when calculated for the purely agricultural activities only. The modification of agricultural energy dimensions was accompanied by the increased energy demand of total, including non-agricultural, farm production. These allow us to see the imperative need after 1978 within the sphere of technical progress for the kind of further development demanding less energy.

Hungarian Agriculture
and the Decade of the 1980s

The year of 1973 was very disadvantageous in Hungarian agriculture. We suffered a decrease of about 20 percent in our terms of trade. It became obvious only after several years that cheap and unlimited raw-material imports could not be maintained. For the decade of the 1980s, another important relationship is that national income consumed cannot be greater than national income produced. This made a structural transformation of the Hungarian economy necessary, and the demand for a more rational management of the factors of production intensified.

The development of Hungarian agriculture can be successful in the 1980s only if agriculture takes a new path of growth. I cannot undertake to outline in this paper all the related targets in a complex manner. I endeavour only to indicate the major differences between the old and the new paths of growth.

- The supply side of the market was decisive on the old path of growth. Hungarian agriculture had to confront demand limitations only rarely and these were of a temporary nature. On the new path of growth, in contrast, demand is dominant. This is a new and unusual situation for us and we must learn to adapt ourselves to it. For the agriculture of western Europe, of course, this is already an old issue.

- The increase of the volume of production was at the center of the old path of growth. Production-centricity was dominant. On the new path of growth, the market stands in the center and production figures "only" beside it, although more so for some products than for others.
- The old path of growth concentrated on the increase of gross production. The new one puts national income in the center: one must concentrate on the utilization of the whole bio-mass produced and the importance of the utilization of by-products and wastes is growing.
- The need to have a more rational management of the factors of production is now greater. Consequently, we are dealing with the more rational utilization of land, with the problems of better labor management, with the introduction of technologies demanding less capital, as well as with constraining the energy demands of production "within limits". There is full agreement that, while the old path of growth was energy-wasting, the new one should be energy-saving.
- Exogenous and endogenous factors determined and determine both the old and the new paths of growth. The difference lies in the fact that the role of the exogenous factors becomes intensified in the new path of growth. The success of Hungarian agriculture is much more dependent upon external factors in the course of the 1980s than in the 1970s. In this respect it is sufficient to mention only that we intend to market more than 50 percent of the increase in production abroad, 20 percent in the 1970s.

Beginning in 1979, Hungary's agriculture, in the new phase of the nation's economic policies, has taken several steps in the direction of adapting the new path. I would primarily mention here that, in terms of 1981 prices, during 1981–83 and as compared to the average for the years 1976–80, crop production and animal husbandry saw an annual increase of 2.7 percent, while the whole of agriculture, including non-agricultural activities, grew by 4.8 percent. The continuing rapid growth is all the more noteworthy because after 1979 the conditions of growth became less favourable for all sectors.

The price scissors opened wide. The price index of agricultural products in 1983 was 22 percent higher from in 1978, while during the same years the prices of industrial products used by agriculture grew by 46 percent. The economic management of agriculture had to become more budget conscious. A good example of this is in the area of energy conservation. Hungary's agriculture used up the equivalent of 1.7 million tons of oil in 1978 and this figure remained about the same for 1982–83. If we take into account the growth experienced since 1978, then the drop in energy demand per unit of output becomes evident.

My personal opinion is that the most important task is to accommodate the buyers' market better and more rapidly, which is no easy task given the fact that Hungary's agriculture produces for many different markets. It is quite clear that the foreign trade mechanism must be further developed. Hungarian agriculture proved to be a successful sector of the national economy in the 1970s. Will it continue to remain so in the 1980s? This is one of the most important questions for us.

Table 14.1

The rate of economic growth of Hungarian
agriculture in international perspective

Country	Yearly average growth of gross agricultural production at world market prices of 1971/75 between 1966/70 and 1976/80 (in percent)
Netherlands	4.1
Rumania	3.4
Spain	3.3
Hungary	3.1
United States	2.4
Jugoslavia	2.2
Soviet Union	2.0
Czechoslovakia	1.9
GDR	1.9
Bulgaria	1.8
Belgium	1.8
United Kingdom	1.8
France	1.7
Austria	1.5
Poland	1.5
FRG	1.3
Italy	1.3
Denmark	1.0

Source: Calculated on the basis of international data about
agriculture (42 agricultural products) at the Central
Statistical Office, Budapest.

Table 14.2

The structure of gross production in Hungarian
farmers' cooperatives and state farms
in 1980

Item	State Farms	Farmers' cooperatives
	Percentages	
Agricultural activity	71.6	71.2
Non-agricultural activity	28.4	28.8
Therein: food industry	14.2	5.1
other industry	8.0	12.1
building industry	3.1	6.4
transports	0.6	2.1
commerce	1.9	2.5
other	0.6	0.6
Total	100.0	100.0

Source: A Mezogazdasagi uzemek kiegeszito teiekenysegenek adatai
1970-1981.   (Data about the non agricultural activities of
the agricultural enterprises between 1970 and 1981).   Center
for Statistics and Economic Analysis of the Ministry for
Agriculture and Food, Budapest, 1982.

192

Table 14.3

Average crop yields

Item	1966-1970	1971-1975 tons/hectare	1976-1980
Wheat	2.4	3.3	4.1
Rye	1.2	1.5	1.6
Winter Barley	2.3	3.1	3.1
Spring Barley	1.9	2.7	3.0
Oat	1.4	1.8	2.4
Corn	3.2	4.2	4.9
Rice	2.0	2.4	1.5
Sugarbeet	32.5	33.0	33.6
Tobacco	1.2	1.1	1.3
Sunflower	1.1	1.2	1.6
Potatoes	10.5	11.8	14.1
Onions	13.6	14.5	15.3
Tomatoes	13.8	22.1	25.1
Red Pepper	6.5	6.3	7.6
Maize	17.9	19.3	19.0

Source: Based upon data published by the Ministry of Agriculture and Food and its Center for Statistics and Economic Analysis.

Table 14.4

The Development of meat[*] production in kilograms per head

Country	1970 kg per head	rank	1980 kg per head	rank	1980 1970
Austria	61.3	11	85.4	9	139.3
Belgium	86.4	5	110.2	5	127.5
Bulgaria	56.1	12	73.3	13	130.6
Czechoslovakia	73.5	8	90.1	8	122.5
Denmark	200.4	1	248.9	1	124.1
United Kingdom	48.1	14	53.9	17	112.1
France	75.4	6	94.0	7	124.7
Netherlands	105.8	3	149.6	2	141.4
Jugoslavia	37.3	17	63.9	14	171.3
Poland	65.9	10	83.8	10	127.1
Hungary	100.7	4	132.9	3	131.9
GDR	73.6	7	106.4	6	144.6
FRG	66.2	9	74.4	12	112.4
Italy	44.0	15	51.9	18	117.9
Rumania	42.2	16	79.7	11	189.3
Spain	37.1	18	60.7	15	163.6
Soviet Union	49.1	13	55.1	16	112.2
United States	110.2	2	116.7	4	105.9

*Beef, pork, mutton and poultry and goat meat.

Source: Computed on the basis of international data of agriculture, 1980, at the Central Statistical Office. Budapest.

194

Table 14.5

The Development of Food consumption
in Hungary in 1968 and 1980

Item	Per Capita annual food consumption/kg/		
	1968	1980	1980/1968
Meat total	53.8	73.0	135.7
of which: pork	29.1	40.1	137.8
poultry	12.1	18.1	148.8
beef	8.1	9.4	108.0
Milk, dairy products	110.6	162.5	146.9
Eggs	12.1	18.6	153.7
Fats, total	26.4	30.6	115.9
of which: animal	24.2	22.0	90.9
vegetable	2.2	8.6	390.9
Cereals	132.5	116.4	87.8
Sugar	31.7	35.0	110.3
Vegetables	82.4	85.5	103.8
Fruits	68.9	76.0	110.3
Consumer Goods: coffee dg/head	120.0	300.0	250.0
tea dg/head	7.0	9.3	132.9
wines	34.8	86.0	247.2
beer	51.2	35.0	68.4
spirits	3.9	9.0	230.8
Calories, total /kJ/	13305	13481	101.4

Source: Statisztikai Evkonyv 1983. (Statistical Yearbook, 1983)
(Budapest: Central Statistical Office, 1984), p. 252.

Table 14.6

The structure of gross production according
to social sectors (in 1968 prices)

Item	Percentage structure of the gross production value in the average of the years		
	1966/1970	1971/1975	1976/1980

Crop growing

Large-scale farms	67.9	72.0	75.0
Small-scale production	32.1	28.0	25.0
of which: State Sector	14.8	15.3	14.9
Collective of the cooperatives	53.1	56.7	60.1

Livestock Husbandry

Large-scale farms	49.6	50.5	54.7
Small-scale production	50.4	49.5	45.3
of which: State Sector	15.8	15.1	17.1
Collective of the cooperatives	33.8	35.4	37.6

Agriculture

Large-scale farms	60.1	62.5	64.4
Small-scale production	39.9	37.5	35.6
of which: State Sector	15.2	15.2	15.7
Collective of the cooperatives	44.9	47.3	48.7

Source: Based upon the data of the Center for Statistics and
Economic Analysis of the Ministry for Agriculture and
Food.

Promotion of Efficiency in the Agriculture of the German Democratic Republic

15

The Reform of Agricultural Prices in the German Democratic Republic

Eberhard Schinke

The agricultural price reform that came into effect in the German Democratic Republic at the beginning of 1984 resulted in a marked increase in the prices of agricultural products and inputs, which hitherto had only changed rarely, and then only by very small amounts. As a result of the increase in the level of both producer and input prices, and a change in the relative input and producer prices as well, price relationships between individual goods have been altered and consequently there has been a shift in price structures. The price of mineral fertilizers, for example, has more or less doubled, and similarly the price of a type E512 combine harvester has increased from M70,000 to M130,000. Producer prices for grain rose by approximately 50 percent to an average M630 per ton, fruit by an average 30 percent, milk from M1.05 per kg. to M1.70 per kg., and pigs for slaughter from M4.90 per kg. to M7.60 per kg.

Aims of the Price Reform

The price reform had two main objectives. The first was to remove, or at least reduce, the subsidies that have been paid from the state budget for agricultural inputs. The prices paid by the agricultural sector for industrial goods, energy and other inputs should in the future cover their production costs, as has long been the case for other sectors of the economy. The second aim is to improve the efficiency of the agricultural sector. Producers will therefore be granted an initial adjustment of their prices to compensate for the increased input prices and a further increase in order to stimulate production. The intention is to enable agricultural enterprises to accumulate the funds needed to finance their future expansion. It is also hoped that higher input prices will contribute indirectly to an increase in efficiency as a result of more economical use of funds and more efficient use of capital goods in the agricultural sector.

It is not intended that increases in producer prices be shifted forward onto retail food prices. As these had already been subsidized before 1984 by constantly increasing amounts, this will constitute an increased burden on the State budget. Since the abolition of the food rationing more than 25 years ago and the subsequent standardization of the retail prices of foodstuffs previously treated separately (rationed and unrationed), stable food prices have been one of the principal objectives of economic policy. Despite subsequent changes in both the level and structure of costs of production, processing and marketing, together with the increase in purchasing power and the changes in consumption patterns, consumer's food prices have remained substantially unaltered since 1960. Only in the case of a few products (e.g. potatoes, sugar, eggs) have there been minor changes in the basic consumer price; otherwise prices have only been raised when new types and qualities have been introduced. It is not our intention here to investigate the impact of this price policy on the consumption of foodstuffs. It should be noted, however, that there is a relatively high demand for processed animal products (meat, butter) and for high quality products.

Reasons for the Price Reform

Evolution of Producer Prices

Our attention will be focused above all on the relation between retail food prices and agricultural producer prices. In parallel to the separate lists of retail food prices mentioned above, for many years after World War II agricultural producer prices were determined by a two-level system: a lower price for quantities which, according to the Plan, had to be delivered, and a higher price for those goods which were produced over and above the requirements of the Plan.

These two price levels were brought together in a series of adjustments made between 1962 and 1964 for vegetable products and in 1969 for animal products. These prices then remained largely unchanged until 1983, and only in the case of a few products such as cattle and milk were producer prices raised significantly. However, whereas most basic prices remained stable, real profits per unit of output increased markedly in many cases. This apparent contradiction is explained by the fact that the basic price was increased by a series of adjustments, in part related to considerations of season or quality, and in part to policy goals such as the concentration and specialization of production in large units. Indices (1960=100) of prices actually paid reveal that the greatest increase was in the year in which the previous two-level price system for the good in question was replaced by a single level, but in many cases the figures also rose substantially in subsequent years.

Between 1960 and 1980, therefore, producer prices actually paid rose on average by 48 percent, prices of crop products increasing by 38 percent and those of animal products by 51 percent. The largest increases were in the prices of potatoes, fruit, vegetables, cattle and pigs for slaughter, and milk. Oil seeds and sugar beet have remained largely unaffected by price rises, cereal prices have been stable since 1965 and egg and poultry prices have only risen slightly after falling in the mid-1970s. The shift in the price structure in favour of animal products is a reaction to the steady growth of losses registered by the enterprises producing meat and milk. The reason for this is that technical progress has proved slower here than in the case of crop or, especially, cereal production, and as a consequence labor productivity in the livestock sector has increased less rapidly than in crop production. The modernization of the livestock sector calls for a high level of investment, which can be recouped only over a long period of time.

The result of this trend in producer prices has been an ever-increasing gap between the delivery prices of the processing industries on the one hand, and the stable food retail prices on the other. This gap has been bridged with subsidies, which by 1983 had risen to 12.1 billion marks. (See Table 15.2.) Nevertheless, producer prices were not high enough to guarantee the income level required to achieve the declared policy goals, especially of ensuring a steady accumulation of capital. Although revenues varied greatly from branch to branch, enterprises were bound by the directives embodied in the Plan and were in no position to abandon or at least reduce production in unprofitable sectors such as beef or milk production.

The authorities hope to solve both problems by raising prices and changing the price structure. At the same time, particularly attractive prices will serve as an incentive for farms to give priority to the production of those commodities considered vital for the economy, as far as this is possible within the framework established by the Plan.

Evolution of Input Prices

The increase in producer prices is also designed to compensate for the increase in agricultural expenditure resulting from the sharp rise in the prices of industrial inputs and energy. Until 1983 these input prices were kept low by means of subsidies which have now been removed. This is the second attempt to bring the agricultural sector into line with significantly higher industrial price levels and thus terminate the special treatment enjoyed by agriculture in comparison with other sectors purchasing the same goods.

An effort had already been made within the framework of the 1967 attempts at economic reform to make new industrial sales prices for machinery, vehicles and other production inputs applicable to the agricultural sector. In 1971 at the latest, when price increases for construction materials and work came into force and energy subsidies were reduced, it became clear that the agricultural sector would be unable to meet these increased prices for its inputs without a corresponding increase in the prices of its own products. It was decided to leave agricultural producer prices unchanged and instead to scale down the otherwise intended increases in the prices of inputs. In the following years not only was the dual price system (agricultural enterprises/others) retained for industrial goods, but industrial price increases introduced as a result of the increase in the prices of raw materials did not apply to the agricultural sector.

At the beginning of the 1980s there was a clear attempt to dismantle the privileges accorded to the agricultural sector in its dealings with industries supplying inputs. This trend was reflected in the fact that increases in the prices of spare parts were passed onto the agricultural sector, even if only in part and in small increments. Despite these efforts, however, expenditure in support of factor prices continued to rise, as may be seen in Table 15.1.

This continued expansion of input subsidies cannot be explained by increased spending by the agricultural sector. There has been a slowdown in the rates of increase recorded for the registration of new vehicles, for new construction, and for the consumption of animal feed, mineral fertilizers and energy, and in some cases there have even been decreases in purchases of industrial inputs. It is the declared aim of agricultural policy today not to allow any further reduction in the number of workers employed in the agricultural sector, that is to apply the brake to the substitution of capital for labor. The increased cost of subsidizing inputs can only be explained, therefore, by increased costs in the industries supplying the agricultural sector. These cost increases, in turn, reflect the increases in the prices of both imported and domestic raw materials and energy. On the other hand, however, there are grounds for assuming that agricultural enterprises fail to make optimal use of industrial inputs. This may, perhaps, be explained by the policy of subsidization, which considerably reduces both the cost of the sector's inputs and benefit the enterprise might derive from more economical use of these inputs. It must also be remembered that, as a result of the separation of animal husbandry and crop production, together with the excessive size of the restructured enterprises, unit costs in general, and unit transport costs in particular, have remained high.

The elimination of subsidies and the consequent rise in the cost of production inputs should result in more economical use and thereby in a significant increase in the productivity of capital. This effect will be reinforced by higher agricultural earnings, which the initiators of the reform do not intend to see eaten away in part by individual branches within the farm sector.

New Producer Prices:
Level and Structure

The consequence of the reform of agricultural producer prices has been the largest agricultural price increases in the history of the GDR. Wheat prices increased by 82.9 percent, rye by 46.7 percent and barley fodder by 66.7 percent. The hitherto profitable rape and sugar beet, on the other hand, will increase by a mere 25 and 37.6 percent respectively. The price of cattle for slaughter increased by between 76 (heifers) and 87.1 percent (cows), and of pigs by the relatively small margin of 55.1 percent. The basic price of milk, which was raised on several occasions in the past few years, was raised again by 63.8 percent, and the price of wool by as much as 117.7 percent. The varied price increases for different products reflect several overlapping trends, one of which is the equalization of hitherto very different rates of profitability. Thus, for example, the hitherto relatively high price (compared to production costs) of pigs is raised less than the prices of other slaughter animals. In the second place, the reform is intended to stimulate the production of those products for which demand has remained unsatisfied, such as beef and early potatoes. Third and closely related is a category of goods whose prices will rise very steeply in order to reduce the dependence of the GDR on imports: wheat, barley for industrial processing and wool.

As a result there have been shifts in the relationships between the prices of individual products. Thus, for example, the relation has narrowed between wheat, for which demand is great, and rye, which is less important, from 1:1.3 to 1:1; that between wheat and sugar beet has narrowed from 1:0.41 to 1:0.55; that between feed barley and cattle for slaughter has increased from 1:14.1/15.8 to 15.8/16.6, while the relation between feed barley and pigs for slaughter has narrowed from 1:14.8 to 1:13.8.

It is an open question whether these prices, which came into effect on January 1, 1984, will not be changed again in the near future. It is highly unlikely, however, either that there will be any significant deviation from the general principles established by the price reform, or that the general level of agricultural prices will suffer any alteration. It is possible, however, that recent shifts in the cost structure have not been taken into consideration by the new prices, which were calculated in 1983 and, in some cases, as long ago as 1982; or simply that in the new calculations various factors, including the reactions of agricultural enterprises were misjudged. Nevertheless, there is a good internal comparative basis for assessing the effects of the new price system, as enterprises were instructed to draw up their plans for 1984 on both old and new price bases. The resulting data will determine whether there will be any further corrections or not.

Subsidies for Retail Prices

The increased producer prices will result in much higher subsidies for retail food prices, as retail price levels are to remain unaffected by the reform of agricultural prices. There will be no direct relation between food prices and agricultural producer prices. The two price levels will be separated at the processing or wholesale stages. The agricultural sector will receive the producer price plus any supplements (or reductions) for quality, date of delivery, etc. Wholesale prices will also be fixed for any further trading in these products. These prices may be less than or exceed the delivery price plus processing, storage and marketing costs. Their level will be independent of both these costs and the delivery (producer) price, and will be determined solely by those criteria which are to be observed in setting consumer prices. If the producer price exceeds the costs plus the standard profit margin, any difference will flow into the State coffers as a product-related levy. Should the sales price be lower than the costs, as is the general rule in the case of food stuffs, the difference will be refunded by the State. Traders are allowed a fixed product-related mark-up, which will not result in any significant change in the price structure.

This system, which is applied throughout the economy of the German Democratic Republic, has long given rise to a high level of subsidization for agricultural products, because the sum of agricultural production costs and the processing costs of the food industry is usually well in excess of retail prices. Almost all important food prices are subsidized, most support going to animal products (e.g. meat, milk, butter), as well as to such products as bread, flour, potatoes, sugar and vegetables. In the past these subsidies have increased constantly, although the actual rates of increase have varied.

Judging from the current level of agricultural sales and the new basic prices for standard qualities, the author estimates that subsidies in 1984 will be twice the 1982 total. In absolute terms the increase in subsidies will thus be at least three times that of 1981 (M3312), which has been the highest up to now and the amount allocated for the support of foodstuffs as a percentage of the state budget will be well in excess of the previous peak, 8 percent in 1973.

It is a matter for debate whether the price support for foodstuffs should be regarded as subsidization of consumer prices, or wholly or partly as subsidization of the agricultural sector. Equally plausible is the view that neither of these interpretations is valid, but that subsidization in fact aids those industries supplying the agricultural sector. Those that benefit most are not such branches as the engineering or motor vehicle industries, but rather the basic industries supplying raw materials. In the latter sectors, delivery prices have been kept at a surprisingly low level, in view of the increased production costs. In a centrally-planned economy, such as the GDR, where prices at all levels in all sectors of the economy are determined by a central authority, the question is in any case of secondary importance, so long as it is not an objective of economic policy to use prices to obtain a true picture, at least in its broad outlines, of the costs and benefits involved.

The fixing of input and output prices and of the quantities, assortment and quality to be delivered to the State considerably reduces the scope for decision-making by enterprises. This is also true for agriculture, or more exactly speaking, for farms. In their power to set prices and determine quantities to be delivered, the central authorities possess an instrument that will permit the achievement of such objectives at the enterprise level as self-financing only when very specific relations between prices and delivery quotas prevail. A mechanism that would permit changes in costs to be reflected without delay in prices has not been introduced, allegedly for technical reasons, in fact, however, for political reasons. Instead this task has been allocated to a wide range of allowances, bonuses, levies, etc., that offer the central price authorities an additional advantage in that they allow differentiation according to such diverse criteria as product branch, region or even individual enterprises.

Table 15.1

Product-linked Support for Agricultural

Production Inputs (million marks)

1978	1979	1980	1981	1982	1983
4864	5156	6112	6366	6909	7836

Sources: GDR budget calculations for these years, as
published in Neues Deutschland, June 6, 1979; July 4, 1980;
June 27, 1981; July 3, 1982; October 28, 1983; June 16, 1984.

Table 15.2

Price Support for Foodstuffs (million marks)*

1970	1978	1979	1980	1981	1982	1983
4600	7720	7722	7848	11160	11668	12095

*Excluding the subsidies included in Table 15.1.

Source: Same as Table 15.1.

APPENDIX A

Appendix Table 15.1

Basic Purchase Prices of Farm Products
(Marks per 100 kilogrammes)

	1966	1969	1971	1976	1981	1984[a]
Wheat	35.00	35.00	35.00	35.00	35.00	64.00
Rye	40.00	40.00	40.00	40.00	45.00	66.00
Barley, for brewing	62.50	55.00	55.00	55.00	55.00	95.00
Barley, for other processing	38.00	38.00	38.00	38.00	38.00	70.00
Oats, for processing	48.00	48.00	48.00	48.00	48.00	78.00
Oats, for feeding	42.00	42.00	42.00	38.00	38.00	62.00
Barley, for feeding	33.00	33.00	33.00	33.00	33.00	55.00
Rape	104.00	104.00	104.00	104.00	104.00	130.00
Sugar beet	8.50	8.50	8.50	8.50	8.40	11.70[b]
Potatoes, early (c)	*	*	*	31.00	34.00	68.00
Potatoes, late	*	*	*	24.00	27.00	47.00
Cows, for slaughter	–	380.00	380.00	430.00	465.00	870.00
Heifers, for slaughter (d)	–	380.00	390.00	440.00	520.00	915.00
Pigs, for slaughter[e]	–	500.00	520.00	490.00	490.00	760.00
Broiler (f)	466.00	430.00	430.00	370.00	370.00	620.00
Milk (g)	–	76.00	81.00	84.00	105.00	172.00
Eggs (Marks per 100 pieces)	–	*	*	31.43	31.43	40.60
Wool (Marks per kilogramme)	62.00	62.00	62.00	62.00	62.00	135.00

a) Paid to all farms without small private ("individual") producers, for which there are different prices (as a rule something lower ones).
b) Up to a sugar content of 13.5 percent; for each 0.5 percent more additional charge of 0.70 Marks.
c) Mid of July price.
d) Live weight, quality class C.
e) Live weight, quality class IV (105-125 kilogrammes)
f) 1967-1968: 471.00 Marks.
g) Up to 1980 3.5 percent, from 1981 4.0 percent fat content.
– No uniform basic price.
* Data not available.
Sources: Statistical Yearbook of the GDR, different volumes; State price decrees.

Appendix Table 15.2

Average Prices Paid to Farms (Without Additional Charge For Production Increase, Including Revenue for Seeding Material)
(Marks per 100 kilogrammes)

	1960	1966	1969	1971	1976	1981
Wheat	30.65	36.06	36.95	38.87	35.42	36.61
Rye	32.42	41.21	41.25	42.32	40.11	44.18
Barley, for brewing	61.44	63.40	57.02	55.95	49.91	54.29
Barley, other	31.63	36.16	35.95	36.33	34.67	35.96
Oats	25.30	43.85	44.33	44.21	39.90	40.78
Oil Seeds	101.86	108.39	108.68	109.38	106.97	110.56
Potatoes	9.55	16.33	19.43	24.09	25.31	28.09
Sugar beet	6.54	8.00	8.60	9.00	8.30	8.40
Pigs	341.46	450.10	490.70	522.12	502.70	507.90
Cattle, sheep	281.80	330.37	437.27	451.43	516.30	563.80
Poultry, rabbits	500.00	519.29	516.61	531.12	503.60	515.70
Milk[a]	51.76	61.64	73.82	79.92	82.80	103.40
Eggs	29.29	31.75	32.55	33.33	32.50	32.70
Wool[b]	16.82	22.58	50.32	57.00	61.20	59.61

a) Up to 1980 3.5 percent, from 1981 4.0 percent fat content.
b) From 1968 washed.

Source: Statistical Yearbook of the GDR 1982, p. 257.

Appendix Table 15.3

Retail Prices of Selected Food Products and Beverages
(Mark per kilogram)

Wheat flour	1.32
Rye bread	0.52
Wheat bread	1.00
Potatoes	0.17
Sugar	1.55
Beef (for roasting, without bones)	9.80
Pig meat	8.00
Fresh milk (1 litre) (bottled, 2.5 percent fat content)	0.72
Butter	10.00
Margarine (cheapest)	2.00
Eggs (piece)	0.34
Chocolate (milk)	38.50
Beer (lager) (1 litre)	1.44
Coffee	70.00
Russian tea	24.00

Since 1960 prices for almost all products remained without
alteration. Only prices of potatoes, sugar, and eggs have
changed: in 1965 prices of potatoes and eggs rose (from
0.60 to 0.85 Marks for potatoes, and from 1.50 to 1.55 Marks
for sugar), price of eggs declined (from 0.37 to 0.34 Mark).

Source: Statistical Yearbook of the GDR 1982, p. 260.

16

Energy Consumption
in the GDR's Agriculture

Karl Hohmann

Energy Consumption in the
Agriculture, Forestry and Food Sector
of the GDR During 1970-1980

The agriculture, forestry and food sector[1] (AFF) as a whole is the third largest energy consumer in the GDR, topped only by the chemical industry which consumes 25 percent and the metallurgy, ore mining and potash industry which consumes 21 percent. Of the directly used energy sources, AFF receives 18 percent followed by the transport sector.[2] Nearly 31 percent of this consumption is in the food sector, equalling 5.6 percent of all energy directly used in the GDR for fuel and heating processes.[3] Of this share, 40 percent (2.3 percent of the total energy consumption in GDR) is used in sugar refineries.[4] Because the data on energy consumption in the East German food sector are deficient, and because in western economies this sector usually is not incorporated organizationally and statistically in the food industry, thus restricting the comparability of these data across countries, such comparisons will be made at random.

Direct Energy Consumption

Table 16.1 demonstrates that the structure of the energy sources used in the AFF has changed markedly from 1970 to 1980. In particular, the use of fuel oil and gas, from gasworks and natural gas, and of electric energy has been increased much more than that of solid fuels and diesel oil. Unfortunately, no data are available on the quantities of gasoline consumed in the AFF, but on the basis of available data on some collective farms[5] it appears that at least 45,000 tons of gasoline were consumed in agriculture. Part of that quantity, namely 20,000 tons can be assigned to animal production and the remaining 25,000 tons to crop production, including irrigation and sprinkling.

The rapid rates of increase of electric energy, gas and fuel oil consumption are due to the forced industrializing of animal production and to the installation of machines for technical drying of green fodder and the pelletization of straw.

Investigations in 120 livestock farms showed that their energy consumption increased from 4.2 × 10⁹ J to 7.1 × 10⁹ J per cattle unit from 1975 to 1979.[6]

This increase was caused by the mechanization of important work processes by means of electric energy as well as by the increased energy consumption for ventilation and air-conditioning of stables. Animal production in total consumes 60 percent of the electric energy supplied to agriculture,[7] and for fuels it is second to the consumption by green houses. From research results from 23 industrial pig rearing farms and 28 industrial pig fattening farms as well as from 200,000 partly mechanized stable boxes it emerges (Table 16.2), that the specific energy consumption in industrial farms is nearly twice as high as in stables holding smaller animal numbers. This is due to the higher consumption of heating energy for maintaining a stable atmosphere, and for warm water preparation.[8]

There are no comparable data on the energy consumption in industrial cattle farms at this time, but it may be assumed that it also is twice as high as in smaller stables. The reason is that here, too, the energy requirement for stable heating (10 percent of cow, 35 percent of calf, 40 percent of breeding pig and 25 percent of pig fattening places have heating installations)[9] and for warm water preparation is large. This has led to an energy consumption in industry-type animal production of about 40 percent of total animal production, though only 22 percent of the livestock of the GDR is concentrated there.[10]

The increased humidity of the grains harvested in the 1970s as well as the production of dried green fodder, root-crops and straw pellets in a total of 400 agricultural drying and pelletization systems, which was increased from 380,000 tons to 946,000 tons for dried green fodder, from 99,000 to 358,500 tons for root crops and from 24,500 to 1,363,600 tons for straw pellets,[11] have more than doubled the share of the drying systems in the energy consumption of AFF.[12]

By reducing the volume of pelletization and green fodder and root crop drying during the years after 1978, the share of these systems in the energy consumption of total agriculture decreased until 1980. In spite of improved technology of drying, the thermal efficiency of the systems used in the GDR is 20 to 30 percent below international standards which reduces the economic efficiency of these methods in spite of subsidies for the energy consumed.[13]

The consumption of diesel fuel increased by about 26 percent during 1970–1980 due to the doubling of intra-farm transport distances through the concentration of crop production on about 1,200 farms and the associated orientation of labour organization according to products and technologies. As a result, the diesel consumption for transport, turnover and storage increased 2.2 fold despite an only 20 percent rise in the volume transported.

The share of diesel consumed for transport in the AFF increased from 30 percent in 1972/73 to about 50 percent in 1980.[14] As an additional factor, the expected expansion of the share of trucks in total AFF transport from 30 percent to 50–70 percent could not be achieved. Moreover, the state of the intra-farm road system also restricts the energy advantage of trucks over tractor transport. Up until now, the improvement of the intra-farm road system and a sizeable numerical expansion of the number of trucks which is desirable for saving energy, "has not been possible for macro-economic reasons."[15]

Measured in primary energy units and in relation to one hectare of total (including non-arable) agricultural area, the direct energy consumption for driving and heating processes of the AFF in GDR increased by 50 percent from 24×10^9 J/ha to 36×10^9 J/ha. Of this consumption, roughly 30 percent is that of the food part-sector, whereas 70 percent is consumed by agriculture (including greenhouses and technical drying) and forestry during the whole period. Table 16.3 clearly shows the transition from solid energy sources such as crude brown coal and brown coal briquets, to fuel oil, gas and electric energy for heating energy, and the decrease in the share of diesel fuel among the energy sources used in the AFF of the GDR.

Indirect Energy Consumption

Energy sources are used not only for driving and heating, but agriculture in any developed economy also demands significant amounts of energy for machines and yield-increasing technologies. As far as the amounts of energy used for industrially produced inputs can be calculated, given the lack of sources on GDR agriculture, they are summarized in Table 16.4. The quantities of fertilizers and plant protectives supplied to agriculture and the machines and equipment of the GDR'S agriculture (as far as calculable) are evaluated according to the primary energy units required for their production and maintenance and are related to one hectare of agricultural area. The energy spent on the production of the machines and equipment needed for the production of these agricultural production goods remains unaccounted as are the energy amounts represented in human work and animal draught power and those embodied in farm buildings.

The following coefficients from GDR-literature are applied for calculating the energy equivalents of fertilizers, machines and equipments:[16]

Nitrogen fertilizer $\quad\quad\quad\quad\quad$ 75×10^6 J/kg N
Phosphate fertilizer $\quad\quad\quad\quad$ 14×10^6 J/kg P_2O_5
Potash fertilizer $\quad\quad\quad\quad\quad$ 9×10^6 J/kg K_2O
Lime fertilizer $\quad\quad\quad\quad\quad\quad$ 5×10^6 J/kg CaO
Plant protectives $\quad\quad\quad\quad\quad$ 100×10^6 J/kg agent
Self-propelled machines
$\quad$ (tractors, trucks etc.) $\quad\quad$ 85×10^6 J/kg production expenditure $+$ 25% a year for maintenance[17]

Trailers and interior
fittings of stables   68 × 10⁶ J/kg production
                                                             expenditure + 20% a year for
                                                             maintenance

The relative shortage of machinery causes a correspondingly long utilization time each year. Therefore several East German scholars have argued that the energy equivalents for maintenance of machines as quoted in international publications are not applicable to the situation in the GDR.[18] Self-propelled machines therefore are assessed at 29.8×10^6 J/kg (8.5×10^6 J + 21.3 $\times 10^6$J) of energy consumption a year during a ten years period, and trailers and stable equipment at 20.4×10^6 J/kg (6.8×10^6 J + 13.6×10^6J). The calculation of the overall weight of the machines used in GDR agriculture was made on the basis of the tractive power available in agriculture in 1970, 1975 and 1980 and of the technical data on the weight/power ratio of self-propelled machines used in the GDR, which are 55 kg/h.p. for tractors, 35 kg/h.p. for trucks and 70 kg/h.p. for self-propelled harvesters. The total weight of the trailers (ploughs, harrows, drawn harvesters etc.) was assessed at 1.5 times the weight of all self-propelled machines. In calculating the energy equivalents of stable fittings it was assumed that the steel expenditure as quoted for industrial dairy cattle farms of about 235 kg/animal place[19] is typical for the expenditure per cattle unit on modern livestock farms. For partly mechanized stables, 50 percent of this steel expenditure was assumed per cattle unit and under conditions of manual work only 25 percent per animal unit. In connection with the increased mechanization of animal production, steel expenditures of 106 kg/cattle unit (1970), 121 kg/cattle unit (1975) and 144 kg/cattle unit (1980), respectively resulted.

This expenditure was recalculated for the total number of cattle units per hectare of agricultural area, and the result is shown in Table 16.4 together with the other prefabricated industrial inputs. As with the consumption of energy sources for driving and heating processes (Table 16.3) the energy equivalent of production goods from other sectors of the economy supplied to agriculture increased by about 50 percent between 1970 and 1980. Simultaneously the share of machines increased from 41.9 percent of the indirect energy use to 48.5 percent (excluding buildings and imported feed).

To summarize one may state that the energy consumption of GDR agriculture, including feed imports (Table 16.5) which are assessed at 14.2 $\times 10^9$ J/t,[20] increased continuously from 40.55×10^9 J/ha in 1970 to 59.65×10^9 J per hectare in 1980. As during the same period the yield level of vegetable and animal production (food production in t of grain units per hectare of agricultural area) increased only from 18.85 million t grain units (2.99 t g. u./ha agricultural area) to 23.94 million. (3.80 t g. u./ha agricultural area), the specific energy consumption increased by 16 percent (from 13.6×10^9 J/t to 16.7×10^9 J/t).[21]

It emerges that in 1970 the energy consumption in agriculture still was less than the energy amounts contained in the agricultural products (calculated in grain units) but that by 1980 the energy consumption exceeded the energy contained in agricultural output.

As the calculation methods used in the GDR differ from those of western authors or publications[22] for the energy equivalents of electricity and machinery parks, the energy expenditures of GDR agriculture as calculated in the present paper are not comparable with data for other countries or of other authors. The energy expenditures calculated in the present paper are much higher than those of GDR authors. Partly with reference to western sources, the latter assess the energy equivalents for electric energy at 3.6 × 10^6 J/kWh, and those for machines and equipment at 52 percent of the diesel fuel consumed, and attribute to agriculture only 60 percent of the direct energy consumption of the whole AFF (i.e., they exclude the technical drying of green fodder and straw-pelletization). In this way they arrive at an energy efficiency of agricultural production of about 1:1.53.[23]

Changes After 1980

The increases in world market prices for crude oil and raw materials of 1973/74 and 1978/79 were mirrored only with some delay in the prices which the GDR had to pay for Soviet crude oil, because these price increases were postponed due to the mechanisms of price formation in the intra-CMEA trade of the GDR. In this way increased energy and raw material prices became a central problem for the economic growth of the GDR much later than was the case for the western industrialized nations. Only after the share of export earnings of GDR trade with the USSR spent on paying the Soviet crude oil deliveries increased from an average of 11 percent in 1971/75 to 18.3 percent in 1976 and then to 32.8 percent in 1980,[24] were drastic reductions made in all branches of the GDR economy in the use of liquid energy sources, and a reduction of the crude oil quantities received from the USSR was negotiated. All the same, the share of the export earnings of the GDR spent on crude oil purchases from the USSR reached in 1982 the record level of 41.7 percent.[25] The agriculture, forestry and food sector (AFF) was assigned the task of reducing its energy expenditure in absolute terms for 1985 by at least 7 percent compared to 1980,[26] or, in other words, given planned increases in output to reduce the specific energy expenditure by about 4.0 to 4.5 percent per year between 1981 and 1985.[27] In particular, all liquid energy sources used for heat production were to be replaced by domestic brown coal[28] and the consumption of diesel fuel for transportation of agricultural products was to be decreased by about 25 percent.[29]

By changing 45 drying systems to gas, and 40 more from fuel oil to brown coal between 1981 and 1983, the fuel consumption of the agriculture, forestry and food sector was to be decreased by about 157,000 t.[30] Moreover, it seems that 56 drying systems, which worked on brown coal briquets or hard coal will change over to the use of crude brown coal.[31] Also, fuel oil for heating on animal farms and in the food sector should be replaced by gas or crude brown coal by the end of the 1981–1985 five-year plan. These measures will not cause a decrease in energy consumption, but they will reduce the need for oil imports from the Soviet Union.

A reduction of energy consumption for heating is to be achieved through an increased use of alternative energy sources and by a more economical use of traditional energy sources. On animal farms the consumption of warm water is to be reduced to a minimum, existing stable ventilation systems to be replaced by "free ventilation", and "full air-conditioning" eliminated, because "energetic aspects" require the acceptance of a sub-optimal climate stability and lower productive performance of animals.[32]

In the AFF the utilization of alternate energy sources, which are to save an equivalent of 9 million tons of crude brown coal in the GDR by 1985,[33] is at present restricted to heat reclamation systems. In early 1983, the AFF in GDR used 87 large and 128 small heat reclamation systems, 1227 installations for heat reclamation from milk, 43 low temperature generators for heat reclamation from air and 17,971 m^2 of radiation surfaces. All these should have an energetic effect during 1983 of a total of $2,960 \times 10^{12}$ J, i.e., about 365,000 tons of crude brown coal equivalents.[34] In addition, 4 wind power plants were in operation at that time for draining agricultural land or supplying pastures with water and electricity and also 5 sun-collectors with a collecting surface of 210 m^2.[35] In December 1982 the first large-scale technical biogas system (reactor volume of 500 m^3) has been put into operation.[36]

The drastic reductions of diesel fuel and gasoline[37] supplies available after 1981 forced the farms to change their labor organization. The earlier enlargement of farms through the separation of vegetable and animal production and the orientation of labor organization according to products and technology had more than doubled the distances of the transport of workers and goods in agriculture, which must be considered the main reason for the roughly 26 percent increase of fuel consumption between 1970 and 1980. Now these distances are to be reduced through a labor organization in crop farming designed to take account of the territorial structure of the villages and to the adaptation of territorial labor units or brigades to the actual locations of animal farms. Within three years the share of farms with "territorial organization" of workers brigades increased from 48 to more than 60 percent.[38] Moreover, where technology and organization permitted more of the transportation of sugar beet, cereals, fertilizers and building materials was transferred from road to railway or inland water transport. In spite of these and other measures, among which a change of tractor and truck motors to woodgas or to horse-drawn transport also deserve mention, some farms had to restrict particular work processes of cultivation and machine use on the land.[39]

According to available publications specific energy consumption of transportation and heating processes in agriculture and forestry was reduced by about 3.3 percent in 1981 as compared to 1980,[40] and in 1982, including the food sector, even by 9.5 percent compared to 1981.[41] The reduction by 6.2 percent envisaged for 1983, was not achieved.[42] The reduction of specific energy consumption per unit of output achieved in 1981, was caused less by economical use of energy than by yield increases of about 5 percent. It seems that in absolute terms the consumption even continued increasing in 1981, as otherwise the specific energy expenditure should have decreased. It was only in 1982 that energy consumption decreased in absolute terms. This in part was due to the particularly good weather conditions in the summer and autumn of that year. Compared to the years 1977–1981, 310,000 tons less of water had to be removed from cereals by drying[43] and the dirt on harvested sugar beets was also sizably less at 16.2 percent while in 1980 and 1981 it was 28.6 percent.[44] This fact alone reduced the transport volume by 1.1 million tons compared to the preceding years. Moreover, because of the reconstruction of the agricultural drying systems and the related capacity reductions, only about 310,000 tons of technically dried dry-fodder were produced,[45] only 40 percent of the quantities produced in previous years and only half of what is considered necessary for supplying the livestock herds.

In view of the measures ordered in the beginning of the decade for energy saving in the agriculture, forestry and food sector, which also included the reduction of fertilizer and tractor deliveries by about 20 percent in 1982,[46] it deserves mentioning that in GDR agriculture no drastic production declines have been reported and that in 1982 and 1983 so far the biggest quantities of grain are said to have been harvested in the GDR.

By now, most of the energy economies easily achievable along organizational lines are likely to have been achieved. The volume of energy sources refined from crude oil and in 1983 directly used in GDR agriculture were 46 percent of the gasoline, 84 percent of the diesel and 39 percent of the heating oil the GDR agriculture had consumed in 1980.[47] In individual districts the consumption of diesel fuel is said to have been lowered by as much as 27 percent since 1980.[48] Therefore future success in this field will depend more than ever on the technical innovations and material inputs that the GDR economy will be able to provide for purposes of energy savings. For 1984 it is envisaged to employ 1,000 systems of heat reclamation, 900 heat pumps and 1,500 installations for heat reclamation from milk in the whole national economy, thereby economizing an energy equivalent of 2 million tons of crude brown coal equivalents,[49] and to step up by all means the research on the utilization of alternative energy sources such as biogas, wind and solar energy.

The present paper only seeks to reveal the reasons and results of the increasing energy consumption in GDR agriculture. Therefore the comparative aspects are neglected. A comparative examination of the structure and tendency of energy comsumption in the agricultural sector of CMEA countries, published by Adamovicz in 1980, however points out that in 1977 the agricultural sector of the GDR accounted for the greatest amount of direct and indirect energy consumption per hectare of agricultural area in the CMEA.[50]

Notes

1. The food part-sector, Nahrungsguterwirtschaft in the East German meaning of the term, consists of the first stages of the treatment and processing of agricultural products. Among establishments included are mills, slaughter yards and meat processing plants, dairies, sugar and starch refineries, plants for the production of mixed feeds, refrigeration and storage facilities, fresh-water fisheries and egg and poultry processing.

2. Gunther Zaschke, Wolfgang Reichert, "Engergie sparen—eine Forderung auf Dauer". *Kooperation,* Berlin (Ost), Heft 6/1981, pp. 263–266.

3. E. Manzke, "Moglichkeiten zur Senkung des Energieverbrauchs in der Zuckerindustrie", *Lebensmittelindustrie,* Leipzig, Heft 11/1982, pp. 489–492.

4. *Ibid.*

5. Joachim Kuhlewind et al., "Territoriale Arbeitskollektive bestanden Bewahrungsprobe", *Kooperation,* Berlin (Ost), Heft 9/1983, pp. 400–402; Jurgen Hennig et al., "Mit den verfugbaren Fonds and Material und Energie mehr und effektiver produzieren", *Kooperation,* Berlin (Ost), Heft 1/1983, pp. 10–12, W. Hoffmann, "Rationeller Energieeinsatz in der Beregnung", *Melioration und Landwirtschaftsbau,* Berlin (Ost), Heft 4/1982, pp. 170–172.

6. G. Flachowsky et al., "Uberlegungen zum effektiven Einsatz technischer Energie bei der Erzeugung von verzehrbarem Tierprotein", *Internationale Zeitschrift der Landwirtschaft,* Moskau/Berlin (Ost), Heft 2/1982, pp. 121–126.

7. *Ibid.*

8. Otto Siegl et al., *Losungsvorschlage zur rationellen Energieanwendung in der Schweineproduktion, Agra-Buch,* Markkleeberg, 1982.

9. G. Hutschenreuther, "Energieokonomisches Bauen in der Landwirtschaft", *Melioration und Landwirtschaftsbau,* Berlin (Ost), Heft 1/1982, pp. 15–18.

10. Richard Heinrich et al., "Vervollkommnung der Produktionsbedingungen in der Tierproduktion durch Rationalisierung und Rekonstruktion", *Wirtschaftswissenschaft,* Berlin (Ost), Heft 11/1980, pp. 1311 ff.

11. Karl Hohmann, "Zur Entwicklung wichtiger Inputs im Agrarsektor der DDR", *FS-Analysen,* Berlin, 6/1981, p. 44.

12. Walter Berndt, "Qualitatsentwicklung unter besonderer Berucksichtigung des Nahrungsgetreides aus der Sicht der der Getreidewirtschaft", *Forschungsergebnisse zur Zuchtung und Produktion von Getreide unter Berucksichtigung spezifischer Gebrauchswerte* (Tagungsbericht der Adl Nr. 195), Berlin (Ost), pp. 27–34.

13. K. Keller, und D. Keller, "Rationeller Energieeinsatz bei der Trocknung von Futter und beim Einsatz von Rohbraunkohle in landwirtschaftlichen Trocknungsbetrieben", *Feldwirtschaft,* Berlin (Ost), Heft 4/1983, pp. 167–169.

14. Kunibert Muhrel, "Moglichkeiten zur Einsparung von Dieselkraftstoff bei Transport- und Umschlagsprozessen in der Landwirtschaft", *Agrartechnik,* Berlin (Ost), Heft 6/1979, p. 248; Hartwig Angermann et al., "Aspekte fur einen sparsamen Einsatz von Dieselkraftstoff", *Kooperation,* Berlin (Ost), Heft 11/1981, p. 501.

15. K. Algenstaedt et al., "Zur effektiven Nutzung von Energie und Energietragern in der Landwirtschaft der DDR", *Internationale Zeitschrift der Landwirtschaft,* Moskau/Berlin (Ost), Heft 2/1982, pp. 112–115.

16. D. Knuppel, "Zur Effektivitat des Energieeinsatzes von Massnahmen zur Reproduktion der Bodenfruchtbarkeit", *Feldwirtschaft,* Berlin (Ost), Heft 1/1984, pp. 23–25; Werner Grosse, "Der spezifische Energieaufwand des Produktionsverfahrens Getreide", *Wissenschaftliche Zeitschrift der Technischen Universitat Dresden,* Heft 6/1981, pp. 73–76.

17. Werner Grosse, "Zum energetischen Herstellungsaufwand von Landmaschinen", *Agrartechnik,* Berlin (Ost), Heft 1/1984, pp. 21-23.

18. Werner Grosse, "Der spezifische Energieaufwand . . .", p. 73; D. Knuppel, "Zur Effektivitat . . .", loc. cit.

19. R. Thurm, "Gestaltung der Verfahren der Rinderproduktion bei optimalem Einsatz von Energie, Material und Arbeitskraften", *Agrartechnik,* Berlin (Ost), Heft 7/1981, pp. 319-321.

20. Adolf Weber, "Langfristige Energiebilanz in der Landwirtschaft", *Landwirtschaft—Angewandte Wissenschaft,* Heft 221, Munster—Hiltrup 1979.

21. Konrad Merkel, "Landwirtschaft und Agrarpolitik der DDR unter Unsicherheiten und Risiken", *FS-Analysen,* Berlin, Heft 6/1983, pp. 31-49.

22. G. Leach, *Energy and Food Production* (Guildford: 1976); FAO, "The State of Food and Agriculture" (Rome: FAO, 1976); "Agrarwirtschaft und Energie", *Berichte uber Landwirtschaft* (195. Sonderheft), Hamburg und Berlin, 1979.

23. Werner Isbaner, Rudolf Huwe, "Probleme der effektiven Energieverwertung in der Land- und Nahrungsguterwirtschaft der DDR", *Wissenschaftliche Zeitschrift der Universitat Halle,* Heft 1/1983, pp. 121-129.

24. Maria Haendcke-Hoppe, "Spezifische Probleme der Aussenwirtschaft", *Wirtschaftsstrategie der DDR fur die achtziger Jahre,* FS-Analysen, Berlin, Heft 7/1981, pp. 39-61.

25. Maria Haendcke-Hoppe, "DDR-Aussenhandel im Zeichen schrumpfender Westexporte", *Deutschland—Archiv,* Koln, Heft 10/1983, pp. 1066-1071.

26. J. Stein, "Technische Losungen der Warmeruckgewinnung aus der Milchkuhlung und ihre Anwenderergebnisse", *Agrartechnik,* Berlin (Ost), Heft 2/1982, p. 56.

27. G. Andres, "Ergebnisse und Entwicklung der Einzelteilinstandsetzung in der landtechnischen Instandsetzung", *Internationale Zeitschrift der Landwirtschaft,* Moscow/Berlin (Ost), Heft 2/1982, p. 189.

28. Bruno Lietz, "Bessere Instandsetzung bei sinkenden Kosten", *Neue Deutsche Bauernzeitung,* Berlin (Ost), Nr. 50/1982, pp. 3-5.

29. "Rationelle Energieanwendung", *Kooperation,* Berlin, Heft 12/1983, p. 532; L.M., "Noch kurzere Wege fur LKW und Traktoren", *Bauern-Echo,* Berlin (Ost), Nr. 240/1983, p. 3.

30. H. Kittlauss, "Zur Projektierung der Substitution von Heizol durch Rohbraunkohle fur den Betrieb von landwirtschaftlichen Trocknungsanlagen", *Melioration und Landwirtschaftsbau,* Berlin (Ost), Heft 7/1982, pp. 324-326.

31. K. Keller und D. Keller, "Rationeller Energieeinsatz bei der Trocknung von Futter beim Einsatz von Rohbraunkohle in landwirtschaftlichen Trocknungsbetrieben", *Feldwirtschaft,* Berlin (Ost) Heft 4/1983, pp. 167-169.

32. Otto Siegl et al., "Losungsvorschlage zur rationellen Energieanwendung in der Schweineproduktion", *Agra-Buch,* Markkleeberg 1982, p. 16.

33. H. Muller und K. Schroder, "Zur Warmeruckgewinnung in landwirtschaftlichen Trocknungsanlagen", *Agrartechnik,* Berlin (Ost), Heft 10/1983, p. 468.

34. G. Zaschke, "Neue Losungen zur rationellen Energieanwendung und Stand der Sekundarenergienutzung in der Land-, Forst- und Nahrungsguterwirtschaft", *Melioration und Landwirtschaftsbau,* Berlin (Ost), Heft 9/1983, pp. 410-411.

35. *Ibid.*

36. G. Breitschutz et al., "Inbetriebnahme einer grosstechnischen Biogasanlage in der Landwirtschaft", *Agrartechnik,* Berlin (Ost), Heft 11/1983, pp. 508-510.

37. R. Voss, "Erfahrungen des Jahres 1982 und die weiteren Aufgaben der Forstwirtschaft bei der Einsparung von flussigen Energietragern", *Sozialistische Forstwirtschaft,* Berlin (Ost), Heft 7/1983, pp. 201-203; Hans Zacharias, "Landwirtschaft

und kommunistische Erziehung", *Polytechnische Bildung und Erziehung*, Berlin (Ost), Heft 10/1982, pp. 353–361.

38. Arnold Juschak, "Eine Plane unterm Kutschbock", *Neue Deutsche Bauernzeitung*, Berlin (Ost), Nr. 9/1984, p. 9; R. Voss, "Erfahrungen des Jahres 1982 . . .", *op. cit.*

39. Wilfried Stephan, "Dichte Reihen bis zum Rain", *Neue Deutsche Bauernzeitung*, Berlin (Ost), Nr. 10/1983, pp. 4–5.

40. Gerald Schmidt, "Im Ringen um hohere Effektivitat in der Landwirtschaft", *Einheit*, Berlin (Ost), Heft 9/1982, pp. 904–906.

41. G. Zaschke, "Neue Losungen . . .", *op. cit.*

42. "Im Karl-Marx-Jahr Schopferkraft der Bauern auf hohe Ertrage gerichtet", *Neues Deutschland*, 22/23,1,1983, Berlin (Ost), p. 3.

43. H. Jacobi, "Zu einigen Ergebnissen der Getreide- und Olfruchternte 1982", *Getreidewirtschaft*, Berlin (Ost), Heft 12/1982, pp. 267–270.

44. P. Mehlhase, "Transportoptimierung fur Zuckerruben", *Feldwirtschaft*, Berlin (Ost), Heft 1/1983, pp. 394–396.

45. Fritz Berg, "Stand und Tendenzen der Trockengrobfutterproduktion aus volks- und betriebswirtschaftlicher Sicht", *Kooperation*, Berlin (Ost) Heft 5/1983, pp. 232–234.

46. *Statistisches Jahrbuch der DDR 1983*, Berlin (Ost), p. 189; *Statisticheskii ezhegodnik stran-chlenov SEV*, 1983, Moscow, p. 222.

47. Werner Felfe, "Der Beitrag der Land- und Meliorationsbauer fur den bewahrten Kurs der Hauptaufgabe", *Melioration und Landwirtschaftsbau*, Berlin (Ost), Heft 6/1984, pp. 226–233.

48. Wilhelm Jahn et al., "Rationelle Betriebsorganisation durch betriebswirtschaftliche Projektierung", *Kooperation*, Berlin (Ost), Heft 10/1983, pp. 453–455; Klaus Jentsch, "Rationeller Einsatz von Dieselkraftstoff—grundlich analysiert, straff geleitet und geplant", *Kooperation*, Berlin (Ost), Heft 4/1983, pp. 182–186.

49. Willi Stoph, "Anspruchsvoller Plan orientiert auf hohen Leistungsansteig im 35. Jahr unserer Republik", *Neues Deutschland*, Dec. 9, 1983, Berlin (Ost), pp. 3–5.

50. M. Adamovicz, "Energieverbrauch und—produktion in der Landwirtschaft der Mitgliedslander des RGW", *Internationale Zeitschrift der Landwirtschaft*, Moskau/Berlin (Ost), Heft 2/1980, p. 193; Victor Merkin, "Energy Consumption in East European Agriculture: Barrels vs. Bushels", *ACES Bulletin*, No. 2/1982, p. 21.

Table 16.1

Energy consumption in the agriculture, forestry and food
sector of the GDR in 1970, 1975 and 1980

Energy sources	Consumption			Index 1970=100	
	1970	1975	1980	1975	1980
electricity (GWh)	2,682	3,766	5,000	140	186
gas total (Mill. m^3)	67	193	235	288	350
crude brown coal (1000 t)	2,194	2,380	3,041	109	139
briquets (1000 t)	2,398	2,746	2,667	115	111
fuel oil (1000 t)	173	445	547	257	316
diesel oil (1000 t)	918	1,015	1,157	111	126

Source: G. Zaschke, W. Reichert, op. cit., p. 263

Table 16.2

Energy consumption in industrial and traditional pig rearing
and fattening stables in the GDR

Energy consumption	rearing farms industrial/traditional		fattening farms industrial/traditional	
electric energy (kWh/animal place)	139.5	130.5	90.0	34.7
heating energy (10^{6}J/animal place)	1,515.7	780.5	552.9	308.3
total energy consumption[1] (10^{6}J/animal place)	2,017.9	1,250.3	876.9	433.2

1) 1 kWh electric energy = 3.6 x 10^{6}J

Source: Otto Siegl et al: "Losungsvorschlage ..." pp. 3 - 7

Table 16.3

Direct energy consumption of the agriculture, forestry and food
sector of the GDR in 1970, 1975 and 1980

energy sources	energy consumption[1] in 10^9 J/ha agricultural area			structure of energy use in %	
	1970	1975	1980	1970	1980
fuel oil	1.18	3.02	3.73	4.9	10.4
gas	0.33	0.94	1.15	1.4	3.2
electric energy	5.55	7.78	10.37	23.1	28.8
crude brown coal	2.82	3.05	3.92	11.7	10.8
brown coal briquets	7.52	8.59	8.38	31.2	24.6
diesel	6.24	6.88	7.88	26.0	21.8
lubricants[2]	0.40	0.44	0.50	1.7	1.4
total	24.01	30.70	35.93	100.0	100.0
of which:					
food processing	7.68	9.82	11.14	32.00	31.00
agric. and forestry (incl. greenhouses & drying systems)	16.33	20.88	24.79	68.00	69.00

1) Energy equivalents:
   fuel oil and diesel = 42.7×10^9 J/t;
   gas (technical and natural) = 30.7×10^3 J/m^3;
   electric energy = 13.0×10^6 J/kWh;

   brown coal briquets = 19.7×10^9 J/t;

   crude brown coal = 8.1×10^9 J/t;

2) on the assumption that a consumption of lubricants accounts
   for 6.4 percent of consumed diesel fuel.

Source: Author's own calculation (based on Table 16.1)

Table 16.4

Energy consumption of GDR agriculture through industrial inputs
in the years of 1970, 1975 and 1980
(in kg material/ha agricultural area and in 10^9 J/ha agricultural area)

industrial inputs	kg material ha/ agricultural area			energy equivalent (10^9 J/ha agricultural area)		
	1970	1975	1980	1970	1975	1980
Nitrogen (N)	81,3	107,7	119,9	6,10	8,08	8,99
Phosphate (P_2O_5)	65,2	70,1	62,0	0,91	0,98	0,37
Potash (K_2O)	97,7	112,2	79,2	0,88	1,01	0,71
Lime (CaO)	186,8	206,3	197,8	0,93	1,03	0,99
Plant protectives (effective ingredients)	2,9	3,6	4,3	0,29	0,36	0,43
Self-propelled machines	79,8	99,0	141,0	2,37	2,94	4,20
Trailers	119,7	148,5	211,5	2,44	3,03	4,31
Equipments of livestock stables	87,0	107,7	135,4	1,77	2,20	2,76
total				15,69	19,63	23,26

Sources: Author's own calculations on the basis of the statistical
annuals of the GDR and other sources

Table 16.5

Energy expenditure (direct and indirect), energy yield and
energetic efficiency in GDR agriculture
in 1971, 1975 and 1980 (in 10^9 J/ha agricultural area)

		1970	1975	1980
a)	indirect energy use	15.69	19.63	23.26
	of which fertilizers and plant protectives	(9.11)	(11.46)	(11.99)
	machines and equipment	(6.58)	(8.17)	(11.27)
b)	direct energy use	16.33	20.88	24.79
c)	imported feed	8.53	9.44	11.60
	total energy consumption	40.55	49.95	59.65
d)	vegetable production (in t grain units/ha agricultural area)	(3.24)	(34.3)	(38.1)
	in 10^9 J/ha agricultural area	45.54	48.20	53.45
e)	food production[1] in t grain unit/ha agr. u.a.*	2.99	36.5	38.0
	in 10^9 J/ha agr. used area	42.04	51.30	53.31
f)	energetic efficiency			
	$\dfrac{a+b}{d}$	1: 1.42	1: 1.19	1: 1.11
	$\dfrac{a+b+c}{e}$	1: 1.04	1: 1.03	1: 0.89

1) crops and animal products (including production from imported feed)

Sources: see text

*dt = 0.1 metric tons

Yugoslavia: The Agrarian Sector in a Labor-Managed Economy

17

Recent Agricultural Policy in Yugoslavia: A Return to the Private Sector?

Robert F. Miller

Introduction

In several previous writings I have traced the evolution of Yugoslav agricultural policy and the changing relationship between the still dominant private sector (with 83% of the arable land) and the officially favored public sector.[1] Looking back over the past fourteen years, I am struck mainly by the lack of real change in this relationship despite numerous policy declarations. Most of the announced changes have been stillborn, and many opportunities have been missed.

The situation at the beginning of the 1980s was extremely complex. In the deepening economic crisis after Tito's death ideological and political rigidities continued to disfavor private agriculture in important ways, even though it has become increasingly obvious to many Yugoslav officials that the latter must remain for an indefinite period the principal basis for any expansion of agricultural output. On the other hand, an examination of Table 17.1 suggests that overall agricultural performance was not entirely dismal. Production of the main grain crops, wheat and corn, was at or near record levels, and state procurement targets were generally being met. At the end of 1983 it looked as if the long cherished goal of basic agricultural self-sufficiency could in fact be reached, and scarce hard currency would no longer be required for mass food imports. However, the longer-term perspectives for an agriculture-led export recovery program were decidedly less promising. Marketing and price policy and the generally chaotic state of agricultural decision-making were evidently not generating the atmosphere of confidence which all agreed was necessary to stimulate investment and commitment from the peasants to develop production in line with the ambitious official growth targets. In this paper I shall be looking at recent agricultural performance and the principal factors affecting the ability of the regime to carry out a viable long-term agricultural development policy. I shall be particularly concerned with problems of the private sector, which, I continue to believe, holds the key to any successful solution.

Recent Agricultural Performance

Although the absolute size and relative share of the active agricultural labor in the total active work force has continued its rapid decline (from 4,207,000 or 47 percent in 1971 to 2,487,646, or 25 percent in 1981), agricultural production has shown substantial, if uneven, progress in the period since 1975.

With the exception of poultry the large socialist sector farms, in which the Government has long placed so much faith, have not managed significantly to increase their share of total production in the 1980s. As Table 17.2 shows, the private sector, although steadily declining in many respects, has been able to maintain its share of total production and procurements. A few points are worth making in connection with the relative shares of the two sectors. First, with respect to tractor ownership the average horsepower of tractors in the socialist sector is substantially greater. While the great majority of private tractors is in the 35 horsepower category, seven out of eight socialist sector tractors were larger than this by 1983, and the average size has been steadily growing since the late 1970s, especially in the over-100 h.p. category.[2] Given the much greater size of the socialist sector fields this tendency is understandable, although private-sector tractors seem to be increasing in size also.

Second, with regard to mineral fertilizer consumption, the recent increase in the cost of such fertilizers and their decreasing availability because of shortages of imported chemical inputs have priced many private farmers out of the market. The result has been to reverse the positive tendency for private farmers to increase the application of mineral fertilizers. In any case, the Yugoslav consumption of fertilizers (95 kg per hectare in 1982 on a nutrient basis) is one of the lowest in Europe, and its disproportionately low use in the private sector (less than two times as much consumed on almost five times the area) suggests tremendous room for improvement. As the availability of such inputs increases, and their prices come to bear a more realistic relationship to the producer prices for farm products, one can expect private sector yields to continue to approach those of the socialist sector.

For the moment, however, the serious economic crisis plaguing Yugoslavia makes any such projection seem almost irrelevant. Although agriculture, and especially the private sector, have done rather better than most other branches of the economy, the shortages of hard currency for essential inputs and of dinars for working capital and commodity purchases have hit agriculture hard as well. Thus, for example, despite the fact that the private sector seems relatively well supplied with tractors (12.4 hectares of plowlands and gardens per tractor), shortages of tires and spare parts have conspired to keep a large proportion of peasant tractors out of service during peak periods (over 40% in the spring of 1984 according to one estimate).[3]

Harsh economic conditions, compounded by irrational governmental intervention in the market, have also had a serious depressant effect on the realization of production programs, particularly for industrial crops. The contracted acreages for sowing sugar beets, sunflower, and soybeans remain below official expectations. Despite steady, if moderate, increases in producer prices the peasants are reluctant to contract for these crops because of the intensive cultivation required, because of the unstable price relationships to other more favored crops, such as wheat and corn, and because of the monopoly position of the processor-buyers. With wheat and corn they can usually find an alternative purchaser at prices significantly higher than purchasing organizations are permitted to pay. As one commentator in the authoritative business journal *Ekonomska politika* put it:

> One is left to conclude that the resistance of farmers to industrial crops comes not only from their unfavorable prices, or from broader conditions on the market, but above all because there do not exist the usual mechanisms of a modern agricultural market, such as commodity reserves, terminal prices and shipments, etc., and because they are not accompanied by appropriate measures for differentiated credit policies, tax incentives, etc.[4]

Nor is there clear sailing for the more successful crops of wheat and corn. The good 1983 wheat harvest of 5,519,000 tons was accompanied by record state purchases of over 3.5 million tons. In fact this total was obtained by an aggressive procurement campaign reminiscent of Soviet practices. Local authorities exerted unusual pressure on the peasants to give up their "last grain" of wheat. For most private peasants wheat is only marginally profitable anyway. Its advantage in addition to ease of cultivation is that of cash-flow, since the banks always manage to supply the procurement officials with funds to pay up in full and on time, which is rarely the case for corn and animal products, even if the wheat price is not especially attractive. A deputy Federal Secretary for Agriculture told the present writer in Belgrade in March 1984 that excessive pressure on the peasants to part with their wheat in 1983 was one of the reasons for the cutback in wheat acreage by more than 200,000 hectares for the 1984 crop. The non-availability of fertilizers and tractor parts and tires and lower sub-surface moisture were compensated by excellent growing conditions, which kept total wheat production in 1984 at about the same level, about 5.6 million tons. Yugoslav efforts to achieve self-sufficiency in bread grains nevertheless still have some way to go, especially given the high costs of production.

For corn and meat production the situation is quite different. Corn has become truly a "golden crop" for Yugoslav peasants. Governmental efforts to maintain an agreed maximum price of 17 dinars/kg soon proved futile, as prices on the free market and in intra-village exchange quickly escalated to 25 dinars/kg and by the end of 1984 were reaching 35 dinars/kg. Pressure on prices came not only from semi-legal private traders but also from industrial firms, which, in the crisis of hard currency supplies, found that corn had become virtually a universal medium of exchange. It could be exported for cash to pay for needed imports or simply exchanged on a "compensation" basis.[5]

Thus the peasants found it more profitable to hold on to their corn than to sell it at official prices. Socialist sector livestock producers became desperate for it to feed their animals, but they were forbidden by law to pay the higher free-market prices. Meanwhile, the peasants themselves were continuing to turn away from meat and dairy production. Prices offered by socialist-sector processors were simply not high enough relative to corn to present an attractive proposition. While it is true that shops in the major cities are now well stocked with meat products, this is more a reflection of high retail prices and the decision of the peasants to unload their animals now rather than a sign of any progress toward solving demand in the longer run. Most Yugoslavs are simply unable to afford meat on a regular basis anymore, and the livestock industry is in serious trouble. In any case, Yugoslav livestock production has hardly been a model of intensive husbandry in recent years. A report published in late 1982 by a high-powered study commission on agriculture under the well known Krajgher Commission compared livestock holdings in Yugoslavia to those of leading West European producers. As Table 17.3 suggests, the vaunted socialist sector lags behind even the backward private sector in intensity of animal husbandry in Yugoslavia. More recent data, reflected in Table 17.4, show a potentially even worse situation. An article in *Ekonomska politika* published one year after the above report recorded very low levels of intensity of livestock holdings for reproduction purposes.

The author of the article expressed the fear that this decline portends a long-term trend, signalled by the massive livestock slaughter of 1983. The peasant farmer appears to be returning to the traditional pattern of non-specialization ('svastarenje') after the failure of governmental efforts to stimulate specialized production for the market, a failure largely attributable to perennial underfulfillment of investment programs.

> Agriculture, indeed, represents the most visible example of how with decreasing investment one cannot achieve anything but a decrease in production and even fewer available resources for the next round.[6]

Despite ambitious plans for an agriculture-led recovery in the 1980s, the current economic climate has made it impossible to fulfill investment programs in that sector. Indeed, the rate of investment as a share of social product in 1981 in agriculture was running at about half that of the economy as a whole. Table 17.5 illustrates the tendency for the rate of agricultural investment to stagnate or fall in recent years noted in the previous quotation and for private investment to decline as a share of the total. Data for an extension of these trends to the present time are unavailable, but a Yugoslav commentator has recently noted that the current plans for a significant increase in agricultural investment in current prices from 20.3 billion dinars in 1981 and 26.5 billion dinars in 1982 to 30 billion dinars in 1983 and 38–40 billion dinars in 1984 and 1985 was looking increasingly doubtful by the end of 1983 despite an inflation rate of 30–60 percent per year over the entire period.[7]

Thus, rather than leading the economy towards recovery, agriculture seems to be suffering the same fate as other sectors. Indeed, as the above commentator concludes, "Instead of defending the population against inflation, agriculture has been its generator."[8] The private sector, which most Yugoslav observers now recognize as the main basis for future agricultural growth, has been exacting its revenge for the previous decades of economic neglect and discrimination. It is "playing the market" with a vengeance, producing what it wishes to produce and selling to the highest bidder in total disregard of ambitious official plans for more balanced development and exportable surpluses. The question is, what remains to be done to bring the resources of the private sector into the battle for development. Is it too late to reverse the social, economic, and psychological damage to peasant agriculture, even assuming that the political will can be found to bring about the necessary policy changes? In the next section we shall be looking at some of the principal socio-economic changes in the Yugoslav village in recent years in order to be able to assess present and future capabilities more comprehensively.

Socio-economic Changes in the Yugoslav Countryside

Despite the continuing decline of the agricultural population (from 38.2% of the total population in 1971 to 19.9% in 1981), the number of individual peasant farms has actually increased in the past fifteen years. If from 1960 to 1969 the number of individual peasant farms declined from 2,623,000 to 2,602,000, by the 1981 census it had climbed back to 2,676,000.[9] The total currently in general use is over 2,700,000.[10] This seeming resurgence of the private sector is misleading, however, for the growth in the number of farms is partly a consequence of the further parcellization of peasant farms resulting from the egalitarian traditional inheritance laws still operating in Yugoslavia and the great rise in the price of land in recent years. Whether they intend to farm it or not, inheritors are taking up the land willed to them and setting up households in the village. When one considers that in the 1981 census only 46.5 percent of the population was recorded as urban, this phenomenon is not so surprising.[11] The Yugoslav industrial labor force is to a great extent, still made up of commuters from the village.

The vast majority of these commuter households continue to engage in agricultural production, often at a fairly high level of intensity and mechanization, but mainly for home consumption. These are the so-called "mixed farms" (*'mesovita gazdinstva'*), officially defined as farms in which at least one active member of the household is employed on a regular basis in an off-farm job. Opposed to these are the so-called "pure" agricultural farms, where all active members are employed on the household farm even though a substantial part of the household's cash income may come from outside activities such as transport and other services, handicraft sales, etc. The other two categories of farm recorded in the Yugoslav statistics—"non-agricultural farms", where no active member works on the farm, and "aged farms" (*staracka gazdinstva*), where all the householders are beyond an active working age—are of no concern to us here. Suffice it to note that in a 1975 survey these accounted for almost one-third of the total number of farm households.[12] One of the most important recent socio-economic trends in Yugoslav agriculture is the fairly steady decline in the share of "pure" agricultural households and the corresponding increase of "mixed" households. Table 17.6, which is based on the results of annual surveys of a representative sample of more than 3000 households from all over Yugoslavia, shows this shift during the late 1970s and early 1980s. Except in Croatia there has been a decided movement away from "purely agricultural" to "mixed" farming. One suspects that in Croatia the reverse pattern applies primarily to the rich agricultural plains regions of Slavoni and Baranje, bringing the proportion of purely agricultural farms there to approximately the same level as in the other main region of plains agriculture, the Vojvodina. In Macedonia, too, the movement away from "pure" farming has apparently ceased, at least temporarily. My very rough estimate from projections of recent trends is that of the approximately 2.7 million individual peasant farms presently in Yugoslavia only some 650,000 (or about 24 percent) may still be classified as "purely agricultural". About 1.25 million are now "mixed". These can probably no longer be relied upon as major sources of marketed commodities, except perhaps for specialized items for the local market.

This tendency does not necessarily mean that private agricultural commodity production is doomed shortly to disappear. It does suggest, however, a process of shaking out of the commercial producers. Generally, these are the larger private farms of more than 5 hectares with reasonably good land. The correlation between farm size and the "pure" vs. "mixed" categories of farming is far from perfect. For example, in Slovenia the majority of even the largest farms is now "mixed".[13] Nevertheless as a general rule it is only the largest farms that are, or have the capability to be, purely agricultural. Thus, in addition to the decline in the agricultural share of the total active Yugoslav labor force noted earlier, from 47.3 percent to 25 percent in the past decade or so, one finds the active peasants increasingly concentrated on a diminishing number of farms where agriculture is the chief means of livelihood.

Accompanying this "deagrarianization" process, to use the terminology employed in the Yugoslav literature, is a noticeable tendency for the "aging" and "feminization" of the agricultural labor force. It is important to emphasize that there are important regional variations in the pace of these changes. Slovenia, the most prosperous and heavily industrialized of the six republics, for example, had the lowest percentage of its total active population, 9%, working in agriculture in 1981.[14]

Of these, 56 percent of persons working on private farms were women. And 55.4 percent (both males and females) of the peasant farm labor force there were 45 years and over. Only Croatia, with 58.2 percent, had an older farming population.[15] By contrast, the Vojvodina, the main farming region, had a "feminization" level of only 35.3 percent on peasant farms in 1981.

On the other hand, persons aged 45 and over made up 55.1 percent of the agricultural population in the Vojvodina in 1981, and the rate of aging was higher there than in most other regions.[16] One of the most serious aspects of the aging problem in the Yugoslav private sector is the difficulty young adult male peasants are having finding wives. The attendant problem of reproducing the peasant farming population in the future is particularly acute in Slovenia, where even wealthy peasants cannot find brides.[17] The survival of the private farming population is not so acute an issue elsewhere, but the tendency is basically the same throughout Yugoslavia.

Nevertheless, as noted earlier, the situation is not quite desperate, nor is it necessarily irreversible. For one thing, in the current economic crisis agriculture is one of the only sectors where it is still possible to earn an income that roughly keeps pace with the rate of inflation. There are signs of an increased willingness of at least some young persons to remain on the farm in the absence of suitable employment alternatives in industry.[18] However, such cases are usually confined to the wealthier areas with good farmland. The poorer regions are, indeed, dying out as farming centers.[19] For the peasants this exodus is undoubtedly rational economic behavior, even if it is strategically troubling to the regime, which depends on an able-bodied population-in-being in the mountainous regions as a pillar of its territorial defense system. Nevertheless the process there is probably inevitable and possibly irreversible despite recent ameliorative measures.

A good indication of the continuing attractiveness of private agriculture in the richer plains regions is the sharp rise in the price of farmland. In Subotica on the northern border of the Vojvodina, for example, land was selling for as much as 480,000 dinars per hectare in early 1983,[20] and the price has continued to rise. The old individual farmsteads (*salashi*) once traditional in the area are re-emerging with a vengeance after years of government efforts to promote village-type settlements. I consider this further evidence of a renewed interest in private farming.

> "Why are people building *salashi* again?" asks one writer. "The answer is very simple: they want to be as close as possible to their fields, to their work place".[21]

Thus, while up to 1973 many peasants were anxious to get rid of their land, whatever the price, now the price is so high that the socialist sector cannot afford to buy it.

Another, related, symbol of the revival of private agriculture is the increasing tendency for people not necessarily connected with agriculture to buy or rent land and to farm it for profit with the aid of hired labor and/or intensive mechanization. Among those with sufficient capital to purchase land at current prices one finds doctors, lawyers, and other well heeled professionals; while among the renters one often finds agronomists and veterinarians employed on the socialist sector farms and combines. The political authorities are ambivalent toward this development, for it is difficult to square with the socialist foundations of the worker self-management system. One Yugoslav agricultural official told the author, however, that he did not see anything wrong with the practice of non-peasant farming, since the objective of current policy is to maximize output on all available land. And since most of the land in question was the property of aged or infirm peasants or non-rural inheritors unable or unwilling to work it, the new entrepreneurs were performing a useful function. Even when, as in several cases reported in *Borba* in the fall of 1983, officials of socialist sector farms rent public land and hire public machinery and employees to cultivate it for their own profit, such activity is regarded as an out and out theft of social property only in some regions.[22] In others it is tolerated and even condoned.

Although the official attitude toward private farming remains at best skeptical and at worst ideologically hostile (again with substantial regional variations), it is clear that the basic orientation is changing. Were Tito and Edvard Kardelj still alive, it is difficult to imagine their acceptance of this relative toleration. It is not inconceivable that in the future toleration may develop into active government support for the private sector. Such support is not yet evident, although the argument in terms of economic rationality is a powerful one.

A good example of the economic rationality of such a policy and the utility of encouraging the concentration of private farming on the larger farms is the relatively greater propensity of the latter to invest in production. Table 17.7 shows the recent investment patterns of these farms for selected republics and provinces. Investment as a percent of social product for the private sector as a whole for these years was as follows: 1978—10.6 percent; 1980—10.0 percent; 1981—9.9 percent.[23] For the largest farms (over 8 ha.) in the sample shown in Table 17.7 it is obvious that the rate of investment is substantially above these levels, with some notable regional exceptions. I would contend that this is a substantial argument for an easing of existing restrictions on farm size especially in the plains areas, where up to now that has been taboo. Meanwhile, continuing discrimination by political authorities at all levels, however inconsistently applied, is impeding the rational use of the productive potential already available on the peasant farms and discouraging investments in expanded capacity. At present the rather heavy application of machinery on peasant farms, especially in Slovenia, is being used merely as a labor saving device for mixed farms, rather than as a means of intensifying and expanding production.[24] That is certainly the case elsewhere in Yugoslavia as well, as any casual traveller in the countryside will attest.

Evidently a definite long-term commitment to a liberalization of operating conditions for the peasant farms is imperative if the private sector is to perform its desired role in production. In the next section we shall see that consistency of policy is still far from assured in the foreseeable future.

Changes in Official Policy

For several years now there has been no shortage of intelligent diagnoses of what ails Yugoslav agriculture. However, beyond the need for greater investment (upon which almost everyone agrees), the big difficulty lies in the prescription of appropriate cures. The ideological baggage of the past still burdens most of the solutions proposed to what remains the main problem: how to get the peasants to participate in official programs to expand agricultural output. Part of the problem is the composition of the decision-making apparatus. The main participants in the agricultural policy process can be separated analytically (and institutionally) into three basic functional groups: 1) the top political decision-makers, for whom agriculture is merely one troublesome component of the overall economic and social system; 2) the agricultural officials at various levels charged with the implementation of policies endorsed by the first group; 3) the academic economists and agricultural specialists who act as government consultants or otherwise lobby for their pet ideas through the media or by direct contacts with "influentials" from groups 1 and 2.

Ideological considerations seem to weigh most heavily in the thinking of the first group, at least in their authoritative public statements. Not so strangely perhaps, it is also evident in the policy prescriptions of the third group, possibly for opportunistic reasons to legitimize their proposals for presentations to the first group. In my experience it is the second group, the administrators and executive officials, who tend to be most pragmatic. In private conversation they often dismiss the policies and proposals of the other two groups as impractical or uninformed by direct experience with peasants and agricultural production.

The section on agriculture in the famous "Krajgher Commission" Report, "The Long-Term Program for Economic Stabilization" of 1983, is a good illustration of these tensions between diagnosis and prescription in current policy thinking.[25] Its authors were largely members of group three. Thus, after decrying the past neglect of agriculture and the resulting negative social, economic, and regional (read "defense") consequences, they call for a "strong dynamic development" (*dinamiziranje*) of agricultural production as the *sine qua non* for general economic stabilization and growth. Agriculture must in the future be treated "like any other economic activity" and no longer as a mere buffer. It must be able to determine its prices and levels of income and accumulation to ensure "simple and expanded reproduction" on the same basis as other sectors of the economy. Both the socialist and private sectors must be stimulated to seek greater production and higher yields in order to make agriculture a leading source of export earnings.

The report recognizes the need for a more rational social policy regarding food and agriculture, basically, a policy of cheap food for the workers, but warns that "the demands of social policy must not be satisfied through non-economic prices for agricultural products, that is, must not be a burden on the income of agriculture, but on the income of the entire economy". The socialist sector comes in for particularly strong criticism. It has the best land, yet in crop yields and intensity of livestock operations it lags far behind the advanced foreign competition. Nevertheless, the large socialist farms are still regarded as the only vehicle for improving agricultural productivity. Like the Soviets, the authors of the report are fascinated by visions of a nationwide "agro-industrial complex". The small-scale individual farms (both pure and mixed farms are mentioned) can participate in this project only by becoming formally linked to the socialist sector. Only then can they be provided with the expert advice, the investment resources, and the secure markets for their produce that long-term development requires.

In general, the vision presented is one of a totally organized system of agricultural production, procurement, processing, and sales. Commodity markets are a part of the proposed system, but one wonders just what role they would be allowed to play in regulating supply and demand. Thus, despite the new awareness of the importance of agriculture in overcoming the present economic crisis, the solutions offered differ little from those of the past. The main reliance is still on the socialist sector, which is projected to grow at the expense of the private. By the year 2000 the former is to account for 26.9 percent of the total arable land fund (55.4 percent in the Vojvodina).[26] Yet nothing is said about how the socialist sector is to be enabled to pay for its expanded acreage. A skeptical official told the author in 1984 that it would require 70 years for this target to be reached at the present rate of land purchases. The same criticism can be levelled at the program of agricultural investments as a whole. The investment rate for the "agro-industrial complex" targeted under the 1981–85 "Green Plan" (13 percent of total investments) has been fulfilled by less than 50% for the first three years of the plan.[27] The targets of 38–40 billion dinars for 1984 and 1985 seem no more likely to be attained.[28]

As so many times in the past, agricultural policy declarations connected with the "Long-Term Program" appear to be merely pious hopes. Greater effort is being made to provide material support for policy objectives such as, for example, the 1 percent levy on personal incomes for livestock development that was introduced in 1983, although the results so far show little improvement. What is needed is a long-term commitment, consistently adhered to and based on rational, attainable targets. The national track record up to now has not been encouraging on any of these counts: consistency, perserverance, rationality, or realism. Perhaps this time with the overall economy in such dire peril, the results will be better.

In addition to long-term economic measures, the Federal and Republic governments have undertaken a series of legislative and fiscal initiatives to stimulate agricultural production. The current debates on land-use policy are perhaps the most important and revealing. Since 1953, when the government finally gave up on Soviet-style forced collectivization, a universal 10 hectare maximum was set for individual households. The idea behind this inspiration of Edvard Kardelj was to prevent the development of really viable private farms, thus avoiding the "kulak danger" and inducing the peasants to band together in looser types of general farm cooperation (opste zemljoradnicke zadruge-OZZS).[29]

In many respects it was a return to the original "Lenin Cooperative Plan".[30] These cooperatives worked, after a fashion, but only with heavy public subsidies. Peasants joined them because they were the only channel for the large-scale purchase of inputs and sales of peasant produce. The peasants were reluctant to commit much of their own resources to the OZZs, fearing that they were a vehicle for the eventual resumption of collectivization, which is, of course, precisely what the regime intended them to be. Under the economic reforms of 1965 the OZZs were forced to sink or swim on their own earnings. Most of them sank, merging with the large agro-industrial combines, or reducing their activity to the procurement of peasant produce at the lowest possible prices. Peasants in remote areas suddenly found themselves left to their own devices, without access to farm inputs or agronomic services, and without a reliable market for their commodities. The memory of, first, collectivization and, then, abandonment has left among the peasants a legacy of suspicion and distrust of organizational forms bearing a governmental stamp. In addition to the lingering fear of collectivization and continual experience of discrimination as potential "kulaks" by both federal and local officials, the peasants have more recently had cause to complain of economic exploitation by the socialist sector.[31] Until they are permitted to form genuine cooperatives of their own, as they are nominally allowed to do under the Law on Associated Labor of 1976, the peasants will be very reluctant to tie their fortunes to the socialist sector, as most of the long-term development proposals continue to insist that they do.

In the meantime, legislative and fiscal measures are being debated and sometimes even enacted, to compel or induce peasants to use their privately owned land more intensively. On the one hand, efforts have been made, or are in progress, to raise the 10-hectare maximum in regions of nominally more difficult farming conditions. In Slovenia and Croatia, for example, land-holdings 600 meters or more above sea level may be expanded to 20 hectares. In Serbia similar measures are shortly to be applied to land above 400 meters.[32] At present the average farm has only 3.4 hectares of plowland, and only 6 percent of farms are in the over-10 hectare category. Yet such global figures, which have long been used as an argument against extending the maximum, are probably misleading. In my view, extending the maximum will be of benefit precisely where it is needed: in the purely agricultural farms. Moreover, for maximum productive effect it should be extended to the plains regions as well. Farms of, say, 10–20 hectares would be well within the range of the West European countries which have long been regarded as models of efficiency by the Yugoslavs.

The new legislation establishing a higher maximum usually contains provisions requiring inheritors who do not intend to farm the land they receive to dispose of all but a small portion of it (1 hectare in Croatia) to the socialist sector or to the communal land fund for sale or lease to whoever will farm it. In some places fines are imposed on landholders who do not cultivate their land.[33] Such legal compulsion rarely works and is hard to enforce. Changes in the inheritance laws to prevent fragmentation of already highly parcellized landholdings are undoubtedly necessary, but they will take time. Land is still a highly fungible commodity, and traditional inheritance customs die hard. Other legislative measures to overcome parcellization by aroundation and commassation of small plots have long been on the books. Their effect has been minimal, however, since local haggling over who gets what and who sacrifices what is an extremely acrimonious and costly process, especially when the socialist sector is one of the parties.

In the past several years fiscal policy has become another element in the discussion on improving land-use. Since 1952 taxes on peasant farms have been computed on the basis of a so-called cadastral income, that is, the potential income per hectare from land of equivalent quality according to a 5-point classification scale. Revaluations of the cadastral income have been rare (the last one was in 1977), with the result that the effective tax rate on the peasant farm has steadily declined. If, for example, in 1960 the tax burden on net income produced by the private agricultural sector was 12.6%, by 1979 it had declined to just over 2 percent. Adding in various assessments and contributions to local authorities, the total tax burden over the same period declined from 13.6 percent to 9.2 percent.[34] In the debates on tax policy it has been argued that this rate is substantially below that on workers in the socialist sector (agricultural as well as industrial) and that, accordingly, peasant taxes should be significantly increased. Among the proposals offered are either a large increase in the cadastral income basis, or a tax on actual farm income, or some combination of each. Under an inter-republican social compact laboriously concluded in February 1983 the first solution was adopted. In Croatia the cadastral income basis was raised by a factor of 4.9; in Bosnia-Hercegovina—4.7; Serbia Proper—4.3; and the Vojvodina—4. The others were still to be decided at the end of 1983. Bucking the tide as usual, the Slovenes opted for a new tax based on "actual income", with special incentive rebates for increased dairy production, land under cultivation, and crop yields.[35] The Vojvodina has similarly introduced rebates for increased cultivation of favored industrial crops and livestock.[36]

The discussion and final outcome of the debates on tax policy for individual peasant farms offer another good illustration of the differential attitudes among different groups participating in policy formation. Critics of the low tax rate on peasant incomes, mainly academics, conveniently ignored the fact that the peasants received very little for their tax dinar, no social security or health benefits and poor infrastructural or service assistance from the local authorities. Agricultural officials and the peasants themselves are all too well aware of this discrepancy and do not hesitate to say so in private conversation. The notion of taxing "actual income", a favorite of the academic economists, is similarly disparaged by the second group. That may work in Slovenia, I was told by one official. There they know how to keep books. Elsewhere, uncovering the records of annual household income would be an almost impossible task. The opportunities for falsification and evasion are too great. This official confided that he did not think it was necessary to tax the peasants at all, as long as they produce something for the market. According to another source, the peasants usually manage to avoid even the present low taxes: "No one makes losses because of taxes".[37]

Thus, the debates and policies on taxation, too, have a fantastic quality. Agricultural policy appears to be made in a vacuum, with little concern for the practicalities of actual implementation. A similar fate seems to be in store for the question of land rent, which is becoming a new favorite of the academic economists. The latter are ever willing to present innovative applications of Marxist agrarian theory to current problems, and the top political leaders, always anxious to be seen to be doing something, oblige them by enacting their proposals into laws and programs which have little chance of being successfully implemented.

Conclusions

To the extent that "market socialism" exists at all in Yugoslavia it is clear that it is present least of all in agriculture. There are, to be sure, free market elements at work in the individual peasant sector, in intra-village trade, on peasant markets in the cities, and in dealings between the peasants and various middlemen. But the point is that the regime has never accepted these elements as legitimate. To the extent possible, where the socialist sector is concerned and where state procurements are involved, it has always tried to regulate and administer agricultural production and sales by non-market means.

There are, of course, sound political reasons for the government to have done so, above all to keep food prices low for the poorly paid working class population. Nevertheless this policy has been disastrous for agriculture, and particularly for the socialist sector, which has refrained from producing those items, such as meat, whose prices are most strictly controlled. The result has been a low level of capital formation by agricultural enterprises in general. But the main reasons are ideological. The bias for the total organization of agriculture has left no room for the development of a genuine market which could assist in the allocation of resources and bring the tremendous potential of the private sector into play for the attainment of production objectives. Thus, correct diagnoses of the needs and problems of agriculture development are continually frustrated by the socialist organizational fixation which seeks to encompass all elements of production, both private and socialist, with an all-embracing regulative system.

One of the most cogent statements of this dilemma was made by a Yugoslav economist in the authoritative journal *Ekonomska politika* in April 1982. The author, Dragan Veselinov, after criticizing the regulated pricing policy and its consequences of over-consumption of food products by the population, explains its basis in the following terms:

What is the reason for this lack of funds? The conviction that the primary problem in the solution of the peasant question in Yugoslavia lies in the organization of economic relations, that is, in the forms of integration of the peasants,—this is an illusion of socialism the world over. It would seek first of all to create everywhere a communist collective of economic relations around the peasants, without establishing the strategic position of agriculture *vis-a-vis* industry. Thus in practice it has neither accepted the laws of peasant production nor supported those forms of integration which the peasants themselves have demanded. Socialism has everywhere devised its own historical concepts of peasant integration . . . without ever learning that no form of integration of the peasants can survive which the peasants themselves have not developed as their own.[38]

The message is clear. The private sector must be given leeway to develop its own forms of production and its own forms of integration. As we have seen the potential for expansion of the private sector exists. It remains to be seen whether the political will can be found to remove the ideological and organizational barriers to the realization of that potential. At present there is unfortunately not much basis for optimism on this score.

Notes

I should like to express my profound gratitude for the hospitality and scholarly cooperation of Dr. Ivan Loncarevic of the Zentrum fur Agrar und Wirtschaftsforschung of Justus Liebig University in Giessen, Federal Republic of Germany. His comments and the materials we exchanged were invaluable for the formulation of this paper. My special thanks are also due to Professor K.-E. Wadekin for helping to arrange my visit to Giessen. Last, but certainly not least, I wish to emphasize my boundless appreciation and admiration to Rose Di Benedetto and Mary Towle of the Russian Research Center, Harvard University, for the speed and skill with which they converted my scribblings into a readable paper.

1. For example, R.F. Miller, *Socialism and Agricultural Cooperation: The Soviet and Yugoslav Cases* (Canberra: Department of Political Science, RSSS, Australian National University, Occasional Papers, 1974); "Group Farming Practice in Yugoslavia", in Peter Dorner, ed., *Cooperative and Commune: Group Farming in the Economic Development of Agriculture* (Madison: Univ. of Wisconsin Press, 1979), Chapter 7; "Alte und neue Formen der Kooperation fur Jugoslawiens Bauern", *Osteuropa*, Vol. 30, No. 6 (June 1980), pp. 517–530; "Sozialistische Theorie und sozialer Wandel in Jugoslawiens Landwirtschaft", *Osteuropa*, Vol. 30, No. 10 (October 1980), pp. 1123–1138.
2. *Statisticki godisnjak Jugoslavije, 1983*, p. 238.
3. "Nece devize", *Ekonomska politika*, No. 1668, 19 March 1984, pp. 6–7.
4. "Bauk ugovaranja", *Ekonomska politika*, No. 1667, 12 March 1984, pp. 12–13.
5. *Ibid.*
6. "Rizik zaostajanja", *Ekonomska politika*, No. 1650, 14 November 1983, pp. 24–26.
7. "Put u ekstensivnost," *Ekonomska politika*, No. 1649, 7 November 1983, p. 18.
8. "Rizik zaostajanja," Loc. cit.
9. *Statisticki godisnjak Jugoslavije, 1983*, p. 493.
10. See, for example, "Sve je manje ratara", *Borba*, 22 November 1983, p. 1.

11. *Statisticki godisnjak Jugoslavije, 1983,* p. 114. The definition of "urban" population used for the 1981 census encompassed all residents of settlements officially registered as cities at the time of the census.

12. Vladimir Cvjeticanin, Josip Defilippis, *et al., Mjesovita domacinstva i seljaci—radnici u Jugoslaviji* (Zagreb: Institut za drustvena istrazivanja Sveucilista u Zagrebu, 1980), p. 37.

13. Joze Tavcar, "Individualni sektor u slovenackoj poljoprivredi", *Glasnik poljoprivredne proizvodnje, prerada* i plasmana, No. 2 (February 1984), p. 12.

14. *Saopstenje,* Saveznog zavoda za statistiku, No. 264, 26 August 1982.

15. *Ibid.* No. 192, 21 June 1983.

16. *Ibid.*

17. Tavcar, *op. cit.,* p. 16.

18. See, for example, D Lazic, "Sve vise zadruga", *Politika,* 20 March 1984, p. 8; and Bogdan Ibrajter, "Zadruge za 42 sela", *ibid.,* 17 March 1984, p. 8. The latter case is from Novi Pazar, a poor region of Southwestern Serbia, where alternative employment for the predominantly Muslim youth is not easy to find.

19. Dragan Jovanovic, "Sela bez seljaka", *NIN,* 24 April 1983, pp. 19–20.

20. Luka Ivkovic, "Njive ponovo na ceni", *NIN,* 27 February 1983, p. 22.

21. *Ibid.,* p. 23.

22. Hajrudin Suljicic, "Otpori 'mocnika", *Borba,* 19 September 1938, p. 4.

23. *Statisticki godisnjak Jugoslavije, 1983,* p. 227.

24. Tavcar, *op. cit.,* p. 12.

25. *Jugoslovenski pregled,* No. 7–8, July-August 1983, pp. 297–299.

26. "Dugorocni program razvoja agroindustrijske proizvodnje", *Borba,* 8–9 November 1982 (Supplement), p. 15.

27. *Yugoslavia: Agricultural Situation,* Attache Report, No. YO-4004, 15 February 1984, p. 24. I am indebted to Mr. Harlan Dirks of the U.S. Embassy, Belgrade, for making this report available to me.

28. "Put u ekstensivnost", *Ekonomska polititika, op. cit.*

29. Now the cooperatives are called simply "farmer cooperatives", or *zemljoradnicke zadruge.*

30. For a brief account of the "Lenin Plan" as applied to Yugoslavia, see Miller, *Socialism and Agricultural Cooperation,* 1974, *op. cit.*

31. "Crveni kulaci?" *Ekonomska politika,* No. 1658, 9 January 1984, p. 6.

32. Zaharije Trnavcevic, "Udarac uprazno", *NIN,* 11 March 1984, p. 20.

33. "Rizik zaostajanja", *op. cit.*

34. "Prinuda kao podsticaj", *Ekonomska politika,* No. 1636, 8 August 1983, pp. 16–17.

35. *Ibid.*

36. B. Gulan, "Za stocare laksi porez", *Borba,* 3 February 1984, p. 4.

37. "Prinuda kas podsticaj", *op. cit.*

38. Dragan Veselinov, "Kompleks o seljaku", *Ekonomska, politika,* 19 April 1982, pp. 11–12.

Table 17.1

PRODUCTION OF SELECTED AGRICULTURAL PRODUCTS, 1976-1983

(thousand tons)

Product	1976-80 crop	1980	1981	1982	1983
Wheat	5,306	5,091	4,270	5,239	5,519
Corn	9,144	9,317	9,807	11,126	10,688
Sugar beets	5,297	5,213	6,224	5,677	5,700
Sunflower	434	302	327	233	-*
Beef (live wt.)	966	979	1,038	1.018	-*
Pork (" ")					
Mutton (" ")	118	118	118	124	-*
Poultry (" ")	320	377	384	384	-*
Meat (sl. wt.)	1,180	1,226	1,253	1,300	1,280
Milk (mil. lt.)	4,101	4,352	4,478	4,594	4,682

Sources: Statisticki kalendar Jugoslavije, 1981, 1982, 1983; Valdimir
Stipetic, "The Agricultural Economy of Yugoslavia in the 1970s and
Prospects for the Early 1980s," in Karl-Eugen Wadekin, ed., Current Trends
in the Soviet and East European Food Economy (Berlin: Duncker and Humblot,
1982), p. 321.

*Not available.

Table 17.2

RELATIVE SHARE OF SOCIALIST AND PRIVATE SECTORS IN SELECTED AREAS
OF AGRICULTURAL PERFORMANCE
(in %)

	1980		1981		1982	
	Soc. Sector	Pvt. Sector	Soc. Sector	Pvt. Sector	Soc. Sector	Pvt. Sector
1. Arable land	17	83	17	83	17	83
2. Social product	27	73	27	73	29	71
3. State purchases	47	53	47	53	47	53
4. Wheat Production	37	63	37	63	35	65
5. Corn Production	16	84	17	83	17	83
6. Livestock herd	12	88	12	88	13	87
7. Tractors	6	94	6	94	6	94
8. Mineral fertilizer consumption	34	66	35	65	36	64

Source: Statisticki kalendar Jugoslavije, 1981, 1982, 1983.

Table 17.3

NUMBER OF LIVESTOCK PER HECTARE OF ARABLE LAND

	Beef Cattle	Pigs	Sheep
FRG	2.1	3.1	0.2
England	2.0	1.2	4.2
Italy	0.9	0.9	1.0
France	1.4	0.7	0.7
Yugoslavia			
Total	0.8	1.0	1.0
Socialized Sector	0.3	1.0	0.2

Source: "Dugoroncni program razvoja agroindustrijske proizvodnje," Borba, 8, 9
November 1982 (Supplement), p. 3.

Table 17.4

LIVESTOCK HOLDINGS IN YUGOSLAVIA IN MID-1983
(per Hectare of Arable Land)

	Total	Socialist Sector
Cows	0.20	0.07
Sows	0.10	0.10
Ewes	0.33	0.14

Source: "Rizik zaostajanja," Ekonomska Politika, No. 1650 (14 November 1983),
pp. 24-26.

Table 17.5

INVESTMENT IN AGRICULTURE BY PROPERTY SECTOR AND AS

SHARE OF SOCIAL PRODUCT ATTRIBUTED TO AGRICULTURE

(in percent)

Sector	1972-76		1977-79		1980		1981	
	(A)	(B)	(A)	(B)	(A)	(B)	(A)	(B)
Private Sector	48	7.9	52	12.2	52	10.0	51	9.9
Socialist Sector	52	25.9	48	33.5	48	25.4	49	25.7
Total	100	12.3	100	17.6	100	14.1	100	14.2

Sources: "Dogorocni program," op. cit,. p. 14; Statisticki godisnjak
Jugoslavije, 1983, p. 227.

(A) - Share of total agricultural investment.

(B) - Agricultural investment as share of social product attributed to
agriculture.

Table 17.6

DISTRIBUTION OF PRODUCING AGRICULTURAL
HOUSEHOLDS BETWEEN PURE AND MIXED FARMS
(in %)

	1978	1980	1982
All Yugoslavia			
pure	47.4	42.2	40.4
mixed	52.6	57.8	59.6
Bosina-Herzegovina			
pure	50.6	44.1	41.1
mixed	49.4	55.9	58.9
Montenegro			
pure	36.5	26.5	23.7
mixed	63.5	73.5	76.3
Croatia			
pure	37.5	40.7	43.4
mixed	62.5	59.3	56.6
Macedonia			
pure	61.1	50.5	52.4
mixed	38.9	49.5	47.6
Slovenia			
pure	21.4	20.5	20.0
mixed	78.6	79.5	80.0
Serbia Proper			
pure	56.2	45.6	43.6
mixed	43.8	54.4	56.4
Kosovo			
pure	46.2	39.4	25.3
mixed	53.8	60.6	74.7
Vojvodina			
pure	57.1	53.5	47.1
mixed	42.9	46.5	52.9

Source: Anketa o seoskim domacinstvima, 1978, 1980, 1981.

Table 17.7

INVESTMENT RATE ON LARGER PEASANT FARMS
IN SELECTED TERRITORIES
(IN CURRENT DINARS)

1978

Territory	Farm Size	Total Available Funds	Cash Investment In Farm	Investment As a % of Available Funds
Yugoslavia	5-8 ha	109149	10876	10.0%
	> 8 ha	145646	20913	14.4%
CROATIA	5-8 ha	94902	8144	8.6%
	> 8 ha	132784	17682	13.3%
SLOVENIA	5-8 ha	178473	29275	16.4%
	> 8 ha	169611	23529	13.9%
SERBIA (Proper)	5-8 ha	102417	9171	9.0%
	> 8 ha	123789	12769	11.1%
VOJVODINA	5-8 ha	149397	20286	13.6%
	> 8 ha	231683	52666	22.7%

1980

Territory	Farm Size	Total Available Funds	Cash Investment In Farm	Investment As a % of Available Funds
YUGOSLAVIA	5-8 ha	176992	13226	7.5%
	> 8 ha	239809	24447	10.2%
CROATIA	5-8 ha	149175	9070	6.1%
	> 8 ha	287536	33040	11.5%
SLOVENIA	5-8 ha	282905	34876	12.3%
	> 8 ha	287536	33040	11.5%
SERBIA (Proper)	5-8 ha	166662	13736	8.2%
	> 8 ha	205553	16350	8.0%
VOJVODINA	5-8 ha	274133	22206	8.1%
	> 8 ha	450744	18789	10.8%

Table 17.7 (Continued)
INVESTMENT RATE ON LARGER PEASANT FARMS
IN SELECTED TERRITORIES
(IN CURRENT DINARS)

1981

Territory	Farm Size	Total Available Funds	Cash Investment In Farm	Investment As a % of Available Funds
YUGOSLAVIA	5-8 ha	275110	23620	8.6%
	> 8 ha	346220	45397	13.1%
CROATIA	5-8 ha	231812	15534	6.7%
	> 8 ha	309930	29052	9.4%
SLOVENIA	5-8 ha	231358	20134	8.7%
	> 8 ha	325560	46323	14.2%
SERBIA (Proper)	5-8 ha	278776	31178	11.2%
	> 8 ha	303445	41613	13.7%
VOJVODINA	5-8 ha	449119	44201	9.8%
	> 8 ha	552620	104195	18.9%

Source: Anketa o seoskim domacinstvima, 1978, 1980, 1981

18

Price Policy and Price Formation in the Yugoslav Agro-Food Sector

Ivan Loncarevic

An Overview of Yugoslav Agriculture and Price Policy

During the development of socialist Yugoslavia, price policy and price formation, being an important component of economic policy, changed and were reformed at the same pace as there was change and reform in overall economic policies and systems.

The Early Post-war Periods

The first period from 1946–1952 was one of planning and central management following the Soviet model. Through compulsory deliveries of farm products at low fixed prices a policy of income distribution in favor of industry and of the socialized sector of the economy at the expense of the private farm sector was exerted. Only a small part of private farm production above compulsory deliveries was priced freely on farmers' markets. By means of low delivery prices, food processing industries got low priced raw materials enabling the urban population to be supplied with cheap food.

The second period, after 1952, brought more flexibility and even suppression of planning and central management of the economy. Worker self-management was introduced, compulsory deliveries abolished and some elements of market economy introduced, culminating with the economic reform of 1965. This was a period of dualism in price formation with some of them formed freely on the market and the remainder determined by various administrative means including State price setting. Through unequal prices (price disparities) price policy aimed at distributing income in favor of those sectors of the economy whose expansion was consistent with the concept of forced industrialization.

The most important farm prices, as well as those of raw material, investment goods and communal services, were kept at low levels by administrative regulations, particularly fixed or ceiling prices, while most of industrial and product prices were unregulated. Low prices for raw materials, including agricultural ones, were intended to induce rapid development of processing industries, particularly food industries. For social reasons, consumers' goods prices were kept low, particularly for certain basic foods like bread, fats, and sugar.

As early as 1956, there was a change in price policy as contractual price formation was, in principle, handed over to purchasing organizations while for grain guaranteed prices and for industrial crops minimum prices were introduced. However, in view of the great influence of the State on the purchasing organizations and of their monopoly position, the State price intervention machinery was hardly disturbed. According to Markovic (1974, p. 111) social sector firms subject to State price fixing under guaranteed or minimal prices handled 85 percent of purchases in 1965. Until 1970, these forms of price interventions only concerned deliveries from private producers under contract. In 1964, free sales on peasant markets represented about 13 percent of total sales by private farms (excluding trade between farms).

During this period, practically all the capital formation in the economy was financed through the State budget or investment funds. Only a very small marginal part of profits remained at the disposal of the firms. In the field of agricultural price policy, the dominant view was that private farms should not earn any profits since, according to Marx, their production does not go beyond obtaining "simple reproduction". The improvement in the economic situation of private farms between 1957 and 1961 was due mostly to yield improvements and to better input supply, fertilizers, improved seed, etc., rather than to price increases.

After the 1965 Economic Reform

It is easy to understand that a unilateral economic policy of that kind and a price policy which fails to take into account economic criteria necessarily led to structural distortions in economic development and brought about economic difficulties which increased the need for economic reform. So, with the economic reform of 1965, a third price policy period began. The reform was based on the principle that economic agents should operate on a rational economic basis and that the market should be the only criterion for guiding production. The main aim of price policies in the economic reform was to get rid of the price disparities, accumulated during the previous period, so as to equalize terms of trade between agriculture and industry. To reach this goal, new prices were set with different price increases for the various sectors. While the general price increase was 25 percent, farm products increased 33 percent and industrial products less than 14 percent. Among industrial goods, consumer goods prices increased 8 percent, production goods and raw materials 23 percent (Marsenic, 1982, p. 350).

World prices were generally used as a reference for price setting and, for some products, cost of production plus a reasonable profit margin was used.

It was recognized that, on account of the extensive disequilibrium existing on many markets, a single change in prices followed by free price fixing could not bring about balanced price tendencies or correct future structural disparities. So, in 1967, 1972 and again in 1980, laws were passed refining principles and criteria for price formation and modifying direct and indirect price controls. All these laws state as a principle that economic agents freely set the price of their products according to market conditions (i.e. according to the law of supply and demand). They are not to be subjected to administrative interference. In accordance with the self-management model for working of the economy, the laws concerning price formation put great emphasis on self-management agreements between economic agents and on social conventions which are considered as a substitute for State interventions and a means of reducing "unhealthy" market competition and market disorder. According to the law, the role of socio-political institutions within general economic policy is to indirectly further global and partial equilibrium between supply and demand on the markets. It is only in exceptional cases, for instance if prices stray widely from the general trend, if markets are perturbed or if living levels of the population are endangered, that socio-political institutions may exert direct control over prices.

The price law of 1972 introduced three new elements: social conventions concerning prices[1]; price compensation; partial delegation of authority to Republics, Autonomous Regions and municipal authorities. According to the 1980 law currently in force all agents and authorities that are concerned with price formation and control must take into account the following elements:

- supply and demand conditions on the domestic market;
- world market prices and their influence on domestic price levels and on incomes, income distribution and social development policies;
- labor and capital productivity trends for each good and service to reflect efficiency;
- income distribution among labor, capital and management.

In addition to taking these criteria into account, price formation should stimulate productive forces and control increases in the cost of living.

According to Marsenic (1982, pp. 358–9) such general criteria can be little more than a starting point; they do not provide sufficient specificity for quantitative price formation. Only the two first criteria, market conditions and world prices, lend themselves to concrete applications. Since all criteria should be used, a complex procedure for quantifying the other criteria would be required.

The Federal Price Council set conditions under which price changes may take place. Average productivity in the corresponding economic activity is used as a base level for applying the efficiency and income distribution criteria. According to the law and to conventions between the Federal Government and the Republics and Autonomous Regions, agricultural product prices may be fixed under special pricing methods such as guaranteed, floor or target prices. The aim is to provide stable production conditions and eliminate market perturbations. These methods of price setting will be examined in a later section.

Measures of the 1980s

To sum up, it appears that developments in the field of price formation and price control led to retaining, up to now, strong state intervention in the field of primary income distribution through prices. According to Marsenic (1982, p. 354), "with regard to prices what the law considered as the rule, i.e., free formation on the market, remained the exception and what should have been the exception, namely administrative price formation and control, was in practice the rule". The main reason for this situation was that, until now, general economic policy and indirect economic and political measures did not favor market equilibrium. Limited capital and labor mobility, oligopolistic and monopolistic market structures which limited competition, differences in regional development levels and the neglect of economic laws which is inherent in the system are some of the reasons explaining why administrative price formation and control continue to prevail in practice. Similarly, self-management agreements and social conventions have, until now, aimed at preventing market competition rather than at furthering economic equilibrium. A predominantly administrative price formation policy and the weak influence of the market were not able to eliminate the strong disparities in economic structure and to achieve goals of the 1965 economic reform. Even after the reform primary income distribution was still in favor of final industrial products and adverse to capital goods and raw materials, including farm products. During recent years this caused such difficulties in supply that rationing had to be introduced for a series of products.

According to a study by Kranjec (1983), the economic situation of agriculture improved in 1965–66 and in 1973 as the result of large increases in farm prices. But during 1967–72 and 1974–80 agriculture's terms of trade deteriorated and the economic situation of the sector was below that preceding the reform. After 1980, farm producer prices increased as never before and more than industrial producer prices, but only at roughly the same rates as overall inflation (according to Kesic, 1984, and general Yugoslav statistics):

Price Increases	Agriculture	Industry	Overall Inflation
1981/1980	53%	45%	50%
1982/1981	35%	25%	32%
1983/1982	52%	32%	58%

This, however, does not mean that the agricultural situation improved after 1980.

After 1980 the most important economic policy objective was reducing inflation. Some of the strong inflationary pressures originate from agriculture in the form of inadequate supply. So increasing farm output became a major stabilization goal.

Within the framework of the fight against inflation and for the third time, all prices were frozen, on December 24th, 1983, for a maximum period of six months. On the basis of amendments to the 1980 price law, the Federal Executive Council revoked the general price freeze and, in May, 1984 and with a view to gradual liberalization, set three groups of prices:[2]

1. For about 18–20 percent of commodities and services (luxury goods and tourism, but also shoes and clothing) the prices were to be those of the free market, but changes had to be reported to the corresponding socio-political authorities within a week.
2. 22–23 percent of prices were set by the government: energy, railway transport and public communication services, mineral fertilizer, vegetable oil, wheat flour, cigarettes and, on the Republic and regional level, water, heating fuel, laundries, local and road traffic, bread, pasteurized milk, flour components for mixed feeds and bran.
3. The prices for the remaining products, among them chemicals for agriculture with the exception of fertilizer, were to be set by agreements between self-administrative units within the corresponding sectors or economic branches, yet needed approval from the relevant socio-political institutions (Zajednice za poslove cijena) within a month.

On September 1, 1984, the liberalization of the price regulations was continued, so that since then 55 percent of the prices have been allowed to fluctuate in response to the market, 33 percent to be set by agreements between self-administration units, and only 7.5 percent have remained subject to direct government fixing.[3] In addition, the Parliment authorized the government to annual prices, if and when the latter deemed that they were rising in a way contradicting the approved economic policy.

A new law on the "social control of prices", replacing that of 1980, is in preparation and was enacted in January 1, 1985. It differed from the previous law only in that it eliminates the binding criteria to be applied in price formation, including the producers' target prices for agricultural producers, so that one would expect the interests of the economic agents and the market situation to remain the only factors in determining prices. However, the other principles of the law are likely to remain unchanged. Apart from the free price formation by economic agents, the possibility of indirect state intervention on the markets by means of monetary, credit, tax, and import policy and the laying in of state reserves continues to exist. Moreover, guaranteed prices in agriculture and fixed prices for public services and for staples such as flour, bread, vegetable oil and sugar will be continued.

The amendments of 1984 did not make any alterations in the basic policy of previous price legislation. The emphasis has been on the criterion of world market prices with adjustments according to domestic economic results and income distribution. As with past legislation, so with the law enacted on January 1, 1985, it remains to be seen whether market principles will be applied in actual practice. It was hoped in Yugoslavia that the price freeze and subsequent gradual liberalization of price formation would contribute to limiting the 1984 inflation to less than 40 percent. However, on the basis of partial and preliminary information, it rather seems likely that the rate will be in 1984 about 52 percent.

Principles of Official Price Policy and Formation in the Agro-Food Sector

Current principles in the field of price policy and formation are stated in the two last conventions between the Federation and the Republics and Autonomous Regions on the development of the agro-industrial complex within Yugoslav socio-economic plans for 1976–80 and 1981–85. Both conventions put much emphasis on price policy and formation within the framework of economic and political measures for developing the agro-industrial complex. Planned development should achieve the following goals:

- adequate food supply for the population;
- supply of raw materials for processing industries;
- building up of agro-food reserves;
- increasing agro-food exports.

According to the conventions, conditions should be created such that economic agents may independently form agro-food product prices on the domestic market according to market laws and in agreement with self-management agreements, social conventions and price prescriptions. Emphasis is specifically placed on the need to take into consideration the links and mutual dependence and responsibility between agriculture, processing and trade. Social control over prices aims at stabilizing production and reducing market disturbances. All taking part in price formation or even in price fixing must, according to the earlier convention covering 1976 to 1980, consider the following factors:

- development objectives of the socio-economic plan;
- trends in average labour productivity and in income on social sector farms and in production cooperation with private farms;
- price trends on external markets;
- supply/demand situation and its effect on food prices and the cost of living.

In the new convention for 1981–85 no criteria for price setting are given. However, reference is made to the fact that the 1980 law on price criteria applies to the agro-food sector. Thus costs of production, which previously served as the basis for price computations, have been complemented by more flexible criteria.

Social control over prices consists mainly of the setting of guaranteed or minimum prices and, from 1978 onward, of setting producers' target prices for the main agricultural commodities. (See Table 18.1.)

Producers' target prices apply to sales by social sector farms and to state purchases from private farms. They represent gravitation points around which market prices should fluctuate as little as possible. (Compare Tables 18.1 and 18.2.) At the same time they serve as a basis for setting the domestic wholesale and retail prices of commodities made from agricultural products. Guaranteed prices may not be more than 10 percent less than the current ceiling price; the previous difference was 15 percent. They thus represent a minimum price at which territorial bodies will purchase products that cannot be sold for higher prices on the market.

Guaranteed and producers' target prices are fixed at a uniform level for the entire country in the case of the following products which are viewed as being particularly important: wheat, corn, rice, sunflower seed, soybeans, rape seed, sugar beets, tobacco, cotton, wool, milk, meat, oxen, pigs, sheep and poultry. Because of chronic shortages the guaranteed prices have never been employed in practice. Prices for other agricultural products such as fruits and vegetables, some grain and forage crops, calves and lambs are freely determined by market forces unless Republics and Autonomous Regions exercise their right to set producers' target and guaranteed prices for them.

Prices for products of the food industry, wheat flour, milled rice, sugar, sunflower, soybean and rape seed oil and tobacco products, are also set by the Federal authorities for the entire country. Other processed product prices are under the jurisdiction of Republics and Autonomous Regions and thus may vary regionally. Regional authorities also set price limits for the wholesale and retail prices of essential foods such as bread, sugar, oils, meat and milk. If these limits fall below the ceiling price, compensatory payments to the seller are mandated although, in practice, not always paid.

Prices of all important inputs such as machinery, tractors, fertilizers and crop protection materials are subject, for the whole of the country, to price control at the Federal level. Wholesale and retail margins are prescribed by Republics and Autonomous Regions mostly in the form of maximum prices. In addition, delivery premia for certain commodities and subsidies for inputs (e.g., fertilizers) may be granted by Republics and Autonomous Regions. Prices of farm products and foods which are not under Federal or Republic control may be controlled by communes (opcina).

For the setting of guaranteed and producers' target prices, both price relations between farm products (internal parities) and between input and output prices (external parities) must be taken into account. Prices must be fixed at the latest by October 15 for the next year. Adjustment between guaranteed and market prices should be obtained by stock interventions rather than by imports as well as by monetary and fiscal policy.

Practical Aspects of Agro-Food Sector
Price Policy and Formation

Even though all official documents emphasize that economic agents play a decisive role in price formation, in practice, until now, the role of the State has not diminished. There was only a transfer of some Federal responsibilities to Republics, Autonomous Regions and communes. It is estimated that about 80 percent of total value of farm production is subjected to official price control. In addition to the general elements affecting farm production (its biological character, seasonal and year to year fluctuations, cycles in production, low price elasticity of supply, etc.) and to its importance for supplying the population, a series of specifically Yugoslav factors complicate price policy.

Price Theory Factors

According to Begu (1984) the debate continues among Yugoslav economists on whether there is still room in socialism for the market and for money to influence the production of goods. Most economists, the official political view and concrete action speak in favour of market economy under Yugoslav conditions, yet several economists deny that a market economy exists and argue that the current economic difficulties of instability and economic depression confirm their views. Although the 1965 economic reform stated that all economic agents, including those in agriculture, followed the principle of economic behaviour, no answer was given, according to Selak and Mulic (1979), to the essential question of the role of prices in maintaining agriculture's capacity to achieve appropriate levels of capital formation. This matter is closely linked to the fact that most of farm production (in practice 70 percent of gross social product of agriculture) comes from very small and medium peasant farms with a high level of subsistence production. Their development is constrained by land ownership ceilings (10 ha as a general rule). According to the agro-political concepts of socialization of all agriculture, the continued existence of this type of farm is only tolerable for economic reasons.

The Situation on Agricultural Markets

There is chronic, and at times acute, disequilibrium between supply and demand in the sense that there is a chronic shortage on agricultural markets. Until now, according to the Krajger Committee the disequilibrium was mostly due to lower growth of supply than of demand. Table 18.4 shows that supply growth rates were less than 50 percent of demand growth rates. As shown on Table 18.5, except for 1957–61 actual agricultural production growth rates were well below planned ones. They were one third below desired rates. Main causes of this were forced industrialization at the expense of agriculture and unfavourable treatment of the private farm sector. The relatively high rate of increase in demand for agricultural products is due to labor productivity increasing at a slower rate than income and to the high income elasticity of demand, estimated between 0.72 and 0.58 for the various time periods (Anon., *Borba*, 1982). Supply deficits concern particularly wheat, vegetable oils, meat and milk.

The organization of markets in Yugoslavia greatly reduces competition and the influence of markets on prices. Agricultural production is mostly atomistic, but it is faced with organized input markets and with processing firms and trade organizations belonging to the social sector which hold oligopoly or monopoly positions. Input producers and processing and marketing firms can, through their market power, impose harsh contracts on unorganized private farmers. They often do so in practice which has negative effects on peasant farms' ability to earn sufficient profits to finance investment.

There is a lack of independent farmers' organizations that would coordinate peasant farms' production and marketing and thus appear as an important seller on the market capable of strengthening the bargaining position of private farms. Existing farm cooperatives are not considered independent peasant organizations and the association of private farmers with economic units belonging to the social sector has remained very inferior to what had been hoped, particularly with regard to vertical integration. The only challenge to the monopoly position of social sector economic units in purchasing from private farms is provided by illegal middlemen. Their importance, which varies over time and by commodities, is hard to estimate. Nevertheless, their existence is proof of deficiencies in social sector purchases and a testimony of their ability (Gulan, 1983). If inter-farm purchases, mostly calves, piglets, seed and fodder, for which no reliable estimates exist, are excluded, only a small part of marketed output of peasant farms is sold on peasant's markets; about 18 percent of total farm sales. On those markets competition is pure (numerous buyers and sellers) and prices are higher. They handle mostly fruits, vegetables, dairy products, eggs.

The role of the market and competition are further reduced by regional differences in the importance of production and agro-food markets (Vojvodina and Slavonia have most of the production and processing), by heterogeneous economic conditions and by the price formation mechanisms (great development level differences, administrative decentralization down to the Republic Autonomous Region and Commune levels).

Price Formation Criteria

As already indicated, the essential problem is practicability of taking into account all criteria simultaneously. On this, Stojanovic, from the Economics Faculty of Belgrade (1984) writes: "To put this in practice, complete information on a set of economic data would be required which is unattainable even with the most modern computerization. So, in practice, nobody takes those criteria into account and it would not even be possible to do so. Practice beats the law". Under Yugoslav conditions, data collection to apply the various criteria is very difficult. There are also problems in applying the various criteria singled out in the official instructions.

Taking into Account Socio-economic Development Objectives

This criterion raises the question of the influence of prices on production patterns, i.e., prices as an instrument of development. It is generally believed (see Popovic, 1979) that despite the low price elasticity of agricultural production, farms do react to prices but temporarily and with inter-farm differences. Up to now, there have not been in Yugoslavia any studies on the effects of price changes on farm production that could be used for practical decision making. Sector dualism with the large social sector firms and the very small family farms complicates the problem since their reactions to price changes are different.

Orientating production through prices would only be possible if there were long term planning of prices within a consistent economic plan. This is unattainable under the unstable conditions of the Yugoslav economy. So in practice, the leading role of prices was used little in price policy and in the setting of guaranteed and producer's target prices. Proof of this is given by the fact that the deadline dates for price setting are often not adhered to and that there are price changes during the production year. One reason for these delays is differences of interest between Republics and Autonomous Regions.

In addition, the price formation system fails to include a system for safeguarding internal price parities (between farm products) and external price parities (between input and output prices). So, as shown in Tables 18.6 and 18.7 there are strong and irregular annual variations in those ratios which do not maintain the necessary relationships. These practices of short term price fixing, of changing prices, of ignoring price ratios have destabilizing effects on agro-food prices and their structure and create uncertainty for the producer. All this leads to frequent shortages, inadequate production patterns and maladjustment between raw material production and processing capacities. As a substitute to orientation through prices, decisions concerning major products are the object of political campaigns, for instance for sowing crops for processing (wheat, sugar beets, oil seeds), for corn purchases, against the use of wheat as feed. Popovic (1979, p. 94) rightly regards these as outdated methods.

Stimulation of Labor Productivity and Income Changes

Farm prices should take into account labor productivity and incomes on social sector farms as well as labor productivity and incomes arising from production cooperation between those farms and private farms. Farm prices should be in line with the socially necessary labor input (including material input costs) i.e. with cost of production (cost price). Individual costs are not considered; for each product, average costs of input goods and services, average labor costs and "socially accepted" profit rates are calculated.

The application of this principle raises almost insuperable methodological difficulties. According to Popovic (1979, p. 89–108), social sector farms usually do not have all the information and data needed. Cost computation methods on those farms are not uniform so costs are not comparable. Until now, all labor productivity studies concern social sector farms. They only take into account direct labor costs (for an enterprise). Joint (indirect) labor inputs and capital expenses for production are not considered. Land is anyhow not a cost item since social sector farms receive it free. In any case, studies made in the social sector cannot yield valid results for peasant farms which have a different cost structure. According to certain estimates the shares of labor and capital are 40–60 percent on social sector farms and 75–25 percent on private farms (Popovic, 1979, p. 91).[4] Even if similar studies existed for peasant farms, they would raise problems of sampling and lack of accounts, and their results would not be valid for social sector units on account of the very small size of private farms, their different production structure and the need to value family labor.

If labor productivity and income were measured on the cooperative production activities between social sector units and private farms, they could not validly be applied for peasant farms since those joint activities are not widespread.

Using cost of production data from one sector for the activities where it is dominant or from the other sector for the enterprises dominating there would be a compromise solution. It is, however, of doubtful value since peasant farms are highly diversified and individual farms of the social sector have different specialization patterns.

Price formation on the basis of productivity is still further complicated by interdependence between costs of production on farms, in processing industries and in agro-food trade activities. As mentioned earlier input prices are formed under monopoly conditions. Productivity increases in processing industries and marketing firms are very slow because of obsolete technology, excess capacity and excess labor. Since retail prices of basic foods are strictly controlled to protect living standards, the effects of cost changes in processing and marketing have been passed on to producer prices.

Summing up, it appears that the labor productivity or cost of production criterion rests much more on political than on economic grounds.

Taking into Account External Market Prices

World market prices must be taken into account since the Yugoslav economy increasingly participates in the international division of labor. This element has gained in importance over the past ten years due to continuous deterioration of the trade balance and increasing foreign indebtedness. Increasing farm exports are needed to help reduce the foreign deficit.

No concrete indications are given on the application of this criterion for price formation. Since there is no single world market price for commodities, three kinds of prices are referred to: Yugoslav import and export prices, commodity exchange prices, foreign farm level prices (*inodomicilna cijena*). Using those prices as target prices for Yugoslav products is seldom possible.

Until now, Yugoslav export prices have not been sufficiently analyzed. Over the past ten years annual volume and price fluctuations were considerable so no clear tendency in price evolution or relation with internal prices appears. This is also the case for import prices (Table 18.8). Because of frequent dumping, import or export prices are not well suited as target prices.

Commodity exchange prices depend on price policies of the main producer countries and of the main buyers; they are influenced by the international political situation. In part due to speculation, they are subject to broad fluctuations which make it difficult to use them as target prices.

Foreign producer prices i.e. farm level prices (including subsidies) in producing countries would be the best reference for target price fixing. Until now, world prices have not been used as a criterion for Yugoslav farm price formation and it cannot be expected that they will be for a long time.

Results of a Yugoslav study on relations between average domestic prices and world prices for agro-food products in 1981 and 1982 are given in Table 18.9. In 1981, all prices studied were higher in Yugoslavia than in her trade with other countries. Foreign producer prices were 14.3% lower while at the most relevant (for each product) stock exchange places prices were 31.3% lower. On account of inflation, and using the average yearly exchange rates, the differences increased in 1982. If exchange rates after the devaluation of October, 1982, are used, price differences narrowed or even were inverse.

Lastly it should be noted that—according to the investigation used for Table 18.9—exported commodities are usually of better quality than those sold domestically while imported goods are usually of the cheaper and therefore inferior quality.

Market Influence on Agro-Food Prices

Since agro-food prices influence, on the one hand, farm and food industry incomes and, on the other hand, cost of living, optimal prices would in theory be formed with an equilibrium between supply and demand and under conditions of unlimited market competition. It is in practice almost impossible to find an ideal situation of that kind, and market conditions in Yugoslavia are far from it. As explained earlier, there was and still is a chronic disequilibrium between supply and demand for basic foods.

The low level of consumer food prices compared to farm output prices was, until now, one of the causes of inadequate development of farm production as a source of raw materials for food industries. Even the strong price rises following the 1965 economic reform did not have significant effects on supply increase because of the general course of inflation, mostly after 1971, and of the low price elasticity of supply. The effects of these price increases are rather to be found in price rises in other economic spheres, particularly food industries and trade, causing in turn an increase in living costs (see retail food prices, Table 18.3).

During recent years, the already high share of food in household expenses increased as, under stabilization policies, wages increased slower than food prices (Table 18.10).

To correct supply demand disequilibria, socio-political institutions should have sufficient reserves of the commodities in question and use them for intervening on the markets. Those interventions were, until now, inadequate in volume and frequency. Building up of necessary reserves has become more important in recent years as resorting to imports was constrained by lack of foreign currency and the burden of the external debt.

Subsidies, Bonuses, Compensatory Payments

Until now, direct State subsidies to agriculture consist of input subsidies (mostly for fertilizers), bonuses intended to stimulate certain productions (like the milk bonus and compensatory payments to protect the standard of living of the population).

The 1965 economic reform brought about a suppression of all State subsidies which were reintroduced a few years later. They were supposed to gradually fade out by 1979 but, in fact, this has not yet taken place. From 1977 onwards, subsidy funds were transfered from the federal budget to those of Republics, Autonomous Regions and municipalities.

From 1971 to 1978, total agricultural subsidies did not have very great importance. In 1976, they reached 4.4 billion Dinar (D) (including 0.9 for fertilizer) or 4.8 percent of the value of farm production. By 1978 (last year for which statistics are available), they had fallen to 1.3 billion D (0.7 for fertilizer) or 1.2 percent of value of production.

Conclusion

Since Yugoslav policy chose the path of market economy socialism with worker self-management, economic agents should orientate more their policy and price formation according to the conditions and laws of the markets. State price policy should therefore limit itself to indirect regulatory measures.

These principles are also valid for agriculture with, however, some differences linked with the influence of the biological nature of agriculture on State regulatory measures.

This tendency gained in importance in recent years since increased economic difficulties, in all fields of economic policy and particularly in price fixing, led to increased State intervention.

In order to carry this out in practice, several conditions should be fulfilled:

There should be a rough balance between supply and demand through rapid increase of farm output. This would be possible in practice by effective use of private sector productive resources and legal equality for this sector.

Market competition should be favoured by disposing of socialist sector oligopolies and monopolies in the activities linked with agriculture as well as through creation of independent peasant organizations.

Capital, labor and land mobility should be encouraged by improvements in infrastructure, waiving of restrictions on private land ownership and of administrative territorial obstacles.

Since it is impossible to eliminate annual and cyclical production fluctuations, suitable stocks should be built up in order to enable adequate market interventions at the right moment.

Ideological barriers should be disposed of. For instance, one should stop identifying private profits with private enrichment; socialist illusions concerning associations between private and social sector as well as self-management agreements or social conventions as a substitute to State regulation or "unhealthy" market competition should be abandoned.

In that respect, Veselinov (1982, p. 11–12) suggests that the Yugoslav League of Communists should deal with agriculture and finance instead of promoting farmer's associations and campaigns of explanations concerning them.

Notes

1. Social conventions are signed between the Federal Executive Council, the Chamber of Commerce, and concerned economic and socio-political bodies (Workers League, Trade Unions).

2. *Zakon o dopunama zakona o osnovama sistema cijena i druztvenoj kontroli cijena, Slusbeni list*, No. 21/1984, pp. 615–616.

3. *Odluka o uvjetima i nacinu formiranja cijena i drustvenoj kontroli cijena u 1984. godini, Sluzbeni list*, No. 23/1984, pp. 671–685.

4. Large social sector farms also have an excess of labor because of pressures by socio-political local bodies, obstacles to dismissing employees which are part of the Yugoslav system and are in contradiction to technological progress. They cannot compensate for this by area increases which are quite limited.

References

Anonymous. *Dugorocni program razvoja agroindustrijske proizvodnje, Borba*, 8 et 9 Nov. 1982 (dokumenti).

A. Begu, *Sto i kako sa cenama, na izmene ne treba cekati, Borba*, 30, March 1984, p. 5.

B. Gulan, *Nakupci "poslovniji" od drzava, Borba*, 26, Aug. 1983, p. 3.

J. Kesic, Trocifrena Pretnja, *Borba*, August 9, 1984, p. 2.

Krajger Federal Commission on Problems of Economic Stabilization.

M. Kranjec, *Posledice jeftine poljoprivrede, Ekonomska politika*, No. 1607, 17 Jan. 1983, pp. 27–29.

P. Markovic, *Okonomische Rahmenbedingungen fur die Entwicklung des Genossenschaftswesens und der bauerlichen Landwirtschaft, Sozialer Wandel in Jugoslawien - Genossenschaften als Tragersozialistischer Reformpolitik auf dem Lande*, eds. Franz Ronneberger et Borislav Radovanovic, Wissenschaft und Politik, Koln 1974, p. 111.

D. Marsenic, *Ekonomska struktura i privredni rast Jugoslavije*, Belgrade 1982, p. 350.

S. Popovic, Problematika cena, *Ekonomika poljoprivrede*, No. 51, 1979, p. 65.

Dogovor o osnovama drustvenog plana Jugoslavije za razvoj agroindustrijskog kompleksa od 1976, do 1980, godine, Sluzbeni list, No. 34, 1977, pp. 1380–1393.

Drustveni dogovor o ostvarivanju politike razvoja agroindustrijskog kompleksa utvrdjen drustvenim planom Jugoslavije od 1981, do 1985, godine, Sluzbeni list, No. 58, 1982, pp. 1435–474.

S. Popovic, *Aktuelna pitanja agrarne politike na podrucju SR Srbije bez polkrajina,* Institut za ekonomiku poljoprivrede, Belgrade 1979, p. 94.

V. Selak et J. Mulic, *Ekonomska politika Jugoslavije u oblasti cijena poljoprivrednih proizvoda i sredstava za proizvodnju u poljoprivredi,* Simposium Novi Sad, 21 Nov. 1979.

I. Stojanovic, *Jedinstveno trziste najhitniji zadatak, Borba,* 10 April 1984, p. 5.

D. Veselinov, *Kompleks o seljaku, Ekonomska politika,* 19 April 1982, pp. 11–12.

Zakon o osnovama sistema cijena i drustvenoj kontroli cijena, *Sluzbeni list SFRJ,* No. 1, 1980.

Table 18.1

Guaranteed and Producers' Target Prices of Main Products
(Dinar per kilogram)

	1970	1978	1979	1980	1981	1982	1983	1984
Wheat[a]								
Guaranteed	1.08	3.00	4.40	5.00	6.80	9.70	13.00[f]	17.00[f]
Producers' Target Price	-	3.30	4.40	5.00	8.30	9.70	15.00[f]	17.00[f]
Corn								
Guaranteed	0.65	2.10	3.45	3.45	8.50	8.50	9.27	13.05[f]
Producers' Target Price	-	2.30	3.80	3.80	8.50	10.50	13.50	14.50[f]
Sunflower[b]								
Guaranteed	1.43	5.90	5.54	6.20	15.20	18.45	24.30	38.25
Producers' Target Price	-	5.90	6.10	9.40	17.00	20.50	27.00	42.50
Sugar Beets								
Guaranteed	0.18	0.58	0.58	0.64	1.26	1.98	2.60	3.83
Producers' Target Price	-	0.61	0.63	0.90	1.80	2.20	2.90	4.25
Tobacco								
Guaranteed	-	-	39.90	45.30	83.70	99.00	122.00	160.00
Producers' Target Price	-	-	43.97	48.00	93.00	110.00	136.00	177.82
Slaughter Animals								
Pigs[c]								
Guaranteed	4.80	18.72	18.72	23.40	32.76	45.74	100.25	131.50
Producers' Target Price	-	19.76	21.32	26.00	36.40	57.20	111.39	145.70
Young Steers[c]								
Guaranteed	6.20	23.36	25.30	31.50	43.20	58.50	149.60	195.80
Producers' Target Price	-	24.09	66.71	35.00	48.00	74.00	166.30	217.50
Sheep[c]								
Guaranteed	3.50	18.62	18.62	23.40	36.90	45.90	144.00	188.20
Producers' Target Price	-	19.62	21.15	26.00	41.00	62.60	160.00	209.10
Poultry[d]								
Guaranteed	5.00	21.74	21.74	23.40	31.50	-	82.00	113.80
Producers' Target Price	-	22.88	23.50	26.00	35.00	70.00	82.00	113.00
Milk								
Guaranteed[e]	0.90	3.17	4.99	4.99	8.00	8.00	14.24	20.80
Producers' Target Price	-	3.77	5.34	5.34	8.00	14.24	14.24	20.80

a) First class wheat.
b) 42 percent oil content.
c) During 1970-1982 live weight price, beginning in 1983 price for fresh carcass meat.
d) Live weight price.
e) 3.2 percent butterfat content.
f) Because of the big difference between producers' target and market prices, and in
   order to stimulate sales by private producers, the government in 1983 felt compelle
   to set the purchase price for corn at 17.00 Dinar/kg and in 1984 that for wheat at
   22.00 Dinar/kg (plus 2 Dinar premium) and for corn at 27.00 Dinar/kg.

Source: Sluzbeni list SFRJ, various issues.

Table 18.2

Producer Prices of Major Agricultural Products
(Dinar per Kilogram)

	1970	1975	1978	1980	1981	1982	1983[a]
Wheat	0,97	2,18	2,88	6,04	8,97	12,00	14,96[b]
Corn	0,76	2,31	3,11	5,14	8,28	10,68[c]	-
Sunflower	1,45	5,35	5,86	9,87	17,29	16,52[c]	-
Sugar Beets	1,18	0,50	0,66	0,97	1,84	1,87[b]	-
Potatoes	0,61	2,09	2,88	4,39	8,29	8,47[c]	11,83[c]
Beans	2,66	8,65	14,51	22,31	61,17	83,14[c]	97,08[c]
Tomatoes	1,20	3,08	5,87	13,25	11,98	49,57[c]	25,00[c]
Onions	1,11	2,79	3,43	9,76	7,34	14,71[c]	18,74[c]
Apples	1,33	4,31	6,59	10,15	11,39	14,49[c]	20,45
Apricots/Peaches	1,67	7,53	9,93	12,09	14,49	25,00[c]	29,00[c]
Plums	0,42	1,92	3,11	4,92	6,38	20,70[c]	21,50[c]
Wine grapes	1,13	4,33	5,95	7,95	9,53	10,50[c]	11,00[c]
Animals for Slaughter							
Pigs	7,53	15,61	22,16	38,61	61,82	75,11[b]	118,06[b]
Young Steers	8,16	15,90	27,15	44,89	64,76	119,05[b]	220,06[b]
Sheep	5,49	11,77	22,02	43,20	64,13	77,66[c]	-
Poultry	8,43	19,93	23,94	31,51	44,86	66,24[c]	-
Milk	1,10	2,85	4.09	6,63	9,93	13,57[b]	17,78[b]
Butter	19,19	53,18	76,56	134,52	210,92	-	-
Eggs	0,52	1,09	1,64	2,71	4,73	5,15[c]	6,75[b]
Greasy Wool	13,09	29,88	27,62	41,40	86,68	151,57[c]	-

a) Preliminary
b) Official sector price
c) Private sector price

Source: Statisticki bilten "Promet poljoprivrednih proizvoda"; Statisticki bilten "Cijene"; Attache report, USA Ambassy, Belgrade, le 15 Avril 1984.

Table 18.3

Main Retail Food Prices
(Dinar per Kilogram)

	1970	1975	1978	1980	1981	1982	1983[a]
Wheat flour (type 500)	2,60	5,26	7,62	11,59	16,33	23,52	-
White bread (type 500)	2,61	5,08	7,45	11,08	15,50	21,42	-
Rice	5,49	15,26	21,68	34,96	54,00	74,00	-
Sugar	2,79	12,49	13,02	15,84	24,29	33,00	-
Oil (par liter)	5,28	15,72	21,69	28,16	41,46	64,00	-
Potatoes	1,16	3,82	5,40	9,31	17,25	19,00	25,00
Beans	4,35	14,69	25,66	35,08	76,00	125,00	150,00
Tomatoes	7,40	10,18	12,92	22,00	25,00	156,00	72,00
Onions	2,86	6,85	7,21	22,12	18,00	34,00	35,00
Apples	2,45	8,12	13,96	19,53	21,93	32,00	41,00
Peaches	-	4,61	11,27	26,00	25,00	-	-
Raisins	4,63	10,94	16,47	24,99	30,00	54,00	51,00
Pork[b]	18,41	40,68	64,00	108,00	146,00	200,00	293,00
Beef[b]	14,90	33,16	51,00	83,00	114,00	152,00	124,00
Veal[b]	18,68	43,60	69,00	114,00	156,00	216,00	330,00
Mutton[b]	11,75	29,21	45,00	75,00	106,00	147,00	270,00
Poultry Meat	12,81	25,59	36,51	51,00	69,00	111,00	-
Milk (par liter)	1,62	4,45	6,05	9,92	13,69	18,31	25,60
Butter	23,34	53,72	80,00	136,00	206,00	270,00	-
Soft Cheese	9,61	29,07	45,24	76,00	116,00	156,00	-
Eggs	0,67	1,39	2,11	3,48	5,96	7,28	10,35
Wine (ordinary)	5,03	15,42	20,52	27,30	40,00	45,00	-

a) Preliminary
b) Including bones (carcass)
Source: Statisticki bilten "Cijene"; Attache report, USA Ambassy Belgrade, of avril 15, 1984.

Table 18.4

Aggregate Supply and Demand for Farm Products

Period	Supply Growth Rate	Demand Growth Rate
1953-1961	3.8	5.9
1961-1971	3.1	4.9
1971-1981	2.0	3.1

With regard to population growth, income increase and income elasticity of demand.

Source: Dugorocni program razvoja agroindustrijske proizvodnje, "Borba" du 8 et 9 Nov. 1982.

Table 18.5

Farm Output Growth Rates

Period	Plan	Actual	Actual/Plan
1961-1965	7.5	1.4	19
1966-1970	4.6	3.0	65
1971-1975	3.5	2.8	80
1976-1980	4.0	2.2	50
1981-1985	4.5	2.1[a]	47

a) Actual achievement during 1981-1982.

Source: Idem Table 18.4

Table 18.6

Farm Gate Price Ratios
(wheat = 100)

	1970	1971	1972	1973	1974	1975	1976	1977	1978	1979	1980	1981	1982[a]	1983[a]
Corn	78	88	86	78	85	106	92	79	108	94	85	92	108	113
Barley	93	102	101	104	93	110	103	93	111	115	94	111	–	–
Oats	90	99	101	114	110	108	94	97	122	124	91	93	–	–
Rice	227	192	206	260	286	319	305	290	290	232	250	246	221	180
Potatoes	63	53	79	119	57	96	156	84	100	95	73	92	–	–
Sugar Beet	18	19	20	26	20	23	24	21	23	16	16	20	23	19
Sunflower	149	179	189	196	150	245	235	209	203	146	163	192	211	180
Soy	–	–	–	–	–	–	231	196	192	158	201	215	222	180
Cotton	412	375	450	523	455	523	505	420	426	287	199	462	538	438
Tobacco	1040	1053	1368	1442	1284	1659	1573	1268	1429	1096	921	1123	1134	907
Slaughter Animals														
Young Steers	839	790	1015	1210	766	729	795	767	993	772	743	720	763	–
Meat Pigs	776	617	673	994	711	716	827	775	769	646	639	687	589	–
Mutton & Lamb	566	537	614	830	581	539	597	620	764	709	715	713	645	–
Poultry	869	811	890	1104	860	914	810	785	831	621	522	499	722	–
Milk	113	117	145	154	116	131	132	142	142	109	110	110	147	–
Wool	1349	1285	1442	1706	1285	1371	1270	969	959	714	685	964	–	–

a)Target (prescribed) prices.

Source: Statistique Yougoslave; Sluzbeni list SFRJ.

Table 18.7

Input/Output Price Ratios of Agriculture
(Dinar)

	1970	1971	1972	1973	1974	1975	1976	1977	1978	1979	1980	1981
For 1 kg of concentrate feed												
Pork kg	0.25	0.26	0.35	0.38	0.39	0.36	0.29	0.35	0.35	0.30	0.28	0.25
For 1 kg of mixed feed												
Young Steers kg	0.11	0.10	0.10	0.10	0.13	0.16	0.13	0.11	0.10	0.11	0.14	0.14
For 1 kg of compound fertilizer												
Wheat kg	0.80	–	0.78	0.91	1.00	1.19	1.27	1.09	1.11	0.79	0.70	0.92
Corn kg	1.03	–	0.91	1.16	1.17	1.12	1.38	1.38	1.03	0.84	0.82	0.88
Sugar Beet kg	4.33	–	3.79	3.74	4.90	5.18	5.25	5.25	4.83	4.96	4.35	4.09
For 1 Tractor (35 HP)												
Wheat m.t.	26.2	24.5	35.8	28.9	22.0	25.4	25.1	22.8	23.7	17.5	13.5	13.9
Corn m.t.	33.4	27.7	30.0	36.9	25.8	24.0	27.3	29.0	21.9	18.6	15.9	13.3
For 1 Combine Harvester												
Wheat m.t.	75.8	63.8	63.5	69.6	–	86.0	86.8	72.9	113.2	82.7	61.9	77.8
For 1 Litre of Fuel oil (wholesale price)												
Wheat kg	0.64	0.62	0.69	0.87	1.20	1.22	1.13	1.12	1.13	1.06	1.60	1.98
Corn kg	0.82	0.71	0.80	1.11	1.41	1.16	1.23	1.42	1.04	1.13	1.88	1.89
Sugar Beets kg	3.44	3.29	3.36	3.33	5.93	5.32	4.67	5.23	4.91	6.65	9.94	7.59
For 1 Litre of Fuel oil (retail price)												
Wheat kg	1.33	1.16	1.24	1.44	1.57	1.86	1.46	1.45	1.67	1.91	2.29	3.19
Corn kg	1.70	1.31	1.46	1.86	1.84	1.75	1.59	1.85	1.55	2.06	2.70	3.05
Sugar Beets kg	7.17	6.13	6.00	5.53	7.71	8.10	6.05	6.80	7.29	12.01	14.29	12.23

Source: Statistique Yougoslave

Table 18.8

Import and Export Prices in Percent of Farm Gate Price

	1970	1971	1972	1973	1974	1975	1976	1977	1978	1979	1980	1981
Wheat												
export price	-	-	-	-	-	-	-	137	101	62	127	80
import price	100	84	76	222	107	-	110	92	108	90	93	73
Corn												
export price	100	95	-	187	108	117	102	94	58	232	102	69
import price	389	99	85	92	133	-	-	-	67	66	82	-
Sunflower												
export price	114	93	135	131	212	111	107	105	222	115	470	433
import price	176	181	207	197	134	98	105	110	103	125	106	60
Tobacco												
export price	202	172	165	149	132	131	148	140	117	121	147	92
Slaughter animals												
Pigs												
export price	102	-	125	-	-	-	-	-	-	-	-	-
import price	-	-	-	-	-	-	-	68	-	-	63	57
Young Steers												
export price	109	102	111	121	120	128	142	151	107	101	117	113
import price	92	-	-	-	89	-	60	75	33	29	30	33
Milk												
export price	100	106	108	109	154	127	127	114	94	96	103	102
import price	83	82	72	-	89	-	-	-	-	81	98	89

Source: Statisticki bilten "Promet poljoprivrednih proizvoda" and Statistika spoljne trgovine, Various issues.

Table 18.9

World Market Prices in Percent of Farm Gate Prices

	1981	Indices	
		Average January–October 1982	
		According to the average exchange rate	According to the exchange rate as of October 22, 1982
Agriculture	100.0	100.0	100.0
Export Price	97.7	85.3	114.7
Import Price	92.6	75.5	106.6
Price of Foreign Production[a]	85.7	80.2	101.3
World Market Price[b]	68.7	59.3	77.3
Food Industry	100.0	100.0	100.0
Export Price	80.5	49.1	110.3
Import Price	64.6	53.4	70.7
Price of Foreign Production[a]	89.4	86.1	108.1
World Market Price[b]	96.1	53.6	75.2

a) The foreign product price is that of the producing country.
b) Prices on major world commodity exchanges.

Source: Pariteti domadih i svetskih cena, Jugoslovenski pregled, No. 4/1983,
         p. 54, Table 7.

Table 18·10

Food Expenditure in Percent of Total Household Expenses

	1973	1977	1978	1979	1980	1981	1982
Percentage share	39.5	38.7	38.3	37.7	38.3	39.1	42.0

Source: Statisticki godisnjak Jugoslavije 1980 and 1983;
         Statisticki kalendar Jugoslavije 1984.

Agricultural Policies and Reform in China and Vietnam

19

The New Economic Policy in the Chinese Countryside

Claude Aubert

Among communist countries, China long stood out as an exception. The "Chinese way" of the economy appeared atypical since it did not seem to suffer from the traditional illnesses of other Soviet-type economies. It was above all a model, and an exceptional one, because it gave priority to agriculture and because the achievements of its collectivization of the countryside succeeded in removing the spectre of former famines and in building the foundations of real development.[1]

It is hardly necessary to remind the reader that this rosy picture was painted in the Western world even though no systematic statistics were available and Chinese-language economic publications had almost disappeared. Mao Zedong's death in September 1976 and the coming to power of pragmatic leaders supported by Deng Xiaoping from December 1978 onwards (3rd Plenum of the 11th CCP Congress) coincided with the waiving of secrecy rules concerning economic data and information. Scores of social science journals are now published by Peking while all sorts of statistical abstracts have reappeared.[2] It now appears that the "Chinese way" was not what it was believed to be: agriculture's priority covered, in fact, large drawings from the farm sector through unfavorable terms of trade; collectivization ran into the same diseconomies of scale and wastage as elsewhere; the millions of deaths from famine during the Great Leap "Forward" are now common knowledge.[3]

At the very moment when China seems, from this point of view, to join the sad normality of "Eastern Countries", a New Economic Policy appears in the countryside and, again, the Chinese experiment becomes novel and the whole Chinese economic system adventurously moves along little explored paths.[4] This new policy looks very much like a real New Economic Policy (NEP) with its whole set of liberalization moves for the economy and its active minority of wealthy peasants. Contrary to the Russian precedent, this NEP does not come before collectivization, it follows it through a return to family farming. Far from leading to a "crisis in deliveries" or to "shortages of goods" it brings forth a revival of the rural economy and increases trade flows.

This does not mean that this kind of reverse NEP is sure to succeed. It means going through an evolution that is paradoxical in a Soviet-type system and its consistency with the Chinese political regime may be questioned. Will the communist machinery accept that the countryside be freed from the rigorous controls of the past period? Will a planned economy stand the strains of a relatively autonomous agricultural sector? These are not only essential theoretical questions; they are a grave concern for 800 million peasants who may be assumed to fear a retreat in policy, with a possible reactivation of past collectivization.

The Return to Family Farming

The disbanding of People's Communes and the return to family farming are probably the new policy's most spectacular features; hardly less than a real revolution in agricultural production structures.

The "Responsibility Systems"

The starting point was criticism of remuneration systems in the work collectives. They were rightly accused of not making peasants responsible, of encouraging laziness and egalitarianism. Remuneration was computed within production teams, thirty families or so, which were the real collectivization level, the team being both the labor organization unit and the accounting unit in charge of income distribution. The various systems of peasant remuneration through "labor points", the value of which depended upon the final results of the collective, were constantly oscillating between two ills: disincentive egalitarianism, or clumsy complexity. The egalitarian form was an allowance per day leading to being present rather than really working. It implied that end of year bonuses on the basis of work really done were marginal, in the poorer teams, compared to the rations allocated during the year. The complicated form was based on computation of norms since it was not work time but task performed that was paid. The diversity of tasks multiplied the number of norms and outran the limited accounting abilities of often illiterate peasant cadres.[5]

The leading idea of farm reform thus was to cease paying peasants for hard-to-measure work but to remunerate easily quantifiable final production.[6] This very simple idea was going to lead to a decollectivization of sorts. Practical measurement of this individualized final production could obviously only be handled by subdividing the labor collective and dividing the land. This is indeed what happened during the implementation of "responsibility systems linking remuneration to production" (*lianchan jichou zerenzhi*). Such was the name given to contractual formulae, intended to make the peasants responsible, and which, from 1979 onwards, were going to lead to de facto dissolution of collective structures.

Particularly during early times the responsibility systems were quite varied. Beyond their diversity and a certain confusion in terminology (sometimes wilfully maintained) three broad types of contracts have been operating in succession over the past few years.[7]

1979 was the year for "production contracts with the groups" (*baochan daozu*). Land was divided among small groups of five or six families with whom the team entered into a contract wherein the group delivered a specified volume of production that was paid for in labor points by the collective. The team usually handled certain essential tasks like plowing and supplied fertilizer and production means. The groups took care of tilling and harvesting. Group motivation for better work and more production rested on the fact than the group retained all or part of any production surplus above the quantity subject to contract.[8]

In 1980, appeared significant numbers of "production contracts with families" (*boachan daohu*).[9] These contracts were similar to those with groups, with the exception that land was allocated directly to individual families. On the whole, the number of operations handled by the teams shrank as draught animals were distributed among households. Under this type of contract it was more and more frequently specified that the whole of the production surpluses (above the contract) would go to the contracting family. These surpluses were left to the family or paid for by the team at a higher price (usually 50 percent above the state's quota price).

In 1981 there was progressive rise in "farming contracts with families" (*baogan daohu*) also called "integral farming contracts" (*da baogan*).[10] Land, which remains in collective ownership, is divided among families who commit themselves by contract to:

* pay the agricultural tax to the State;
* deliver to the State, at administrative prices, and for all main crops under the Plan, quantities of commodities fixed by the agreement;
* pay to the team flat levies to supply collective funds for accumulation and welfare as well as to pay for the cadres and employees of the collectives such as school teachers and health workers.

Once those obligations have been fulfilled, families may dispose at will of their production. Responsible for their profits and losses, within the constraints imposed by the contracted quantities and prices fixed for them, they organize their own work, pay for their inputs and for services like tractor plowing, irrigation, crop protection that are supplied by the teams, and they are thus autonomous in their management. Labor points are abandoned and the system is close to tenancy.

Analysis of data now available shows the extension of these responsibility systems as well as the progressive shifts in types of contracts as reform progressed. The various forms of contracts linking remuneration to output covered 29 percent of the teams at the end of 1979, 52 percent at the end of 1980, 81 percent of 1981, 92 percent at the end of 1982. Agreements with groups were found in 25 percent of the teams at the end of 1979, 24 percent in 1980, 11 percent in 1981. They were replaced by contracts with families (4 percent of teams end of 1979, 23 percent end of 1980, 65 percent end of 1981, 78 percent end of 1982). Among those, farming contracts, or quasi-tenancy, consistently increased. Almost nonexistent at the end of 1979, they concerned 5 percent of the teams by the end of 1980, 38 percent end of 1981, 70 percent by the end of 1982. These integral farming contracts are now generalized and 94 percent of Chinese teams applied them by 1983.[11]

This diffusion is in fact a decollectivization since both work organization and income distribution are now handled at the peasant family level. This decollectivization does not exclude, of course, the possibility that collective control can be maintained through the contracts signed with the teams.

The Double Logic of Breaking Up

All along this evolution, a double dynamic thus appears: reduction in farm unit size with the move down from the team to the group of families, then from the group to the individual family, and increased autonomy of family management as production contracts are replaced by farming contracts. The underlying logic of this dynamic can be clearly seen in the following sequence reported as occurring in a fair number of teams.[12] It usually started off by division of land between small groups. The egalitarianism that prevailed within the "big pot" of the team reappeared in the "small pots" of the groups while problems of authority were multiplied, with new "little bosses" in each group, without really solving the accounting problems. The next stage was an attempt to directly mobilize worker interest by entering into individual contracts with them for one of the crops of the year, generally not the most important one, corn for example, rather than wheat. Most frequently, the result was that peasants only took care of this crop, of which any surplus above the contract was theirs, and neglected the other crops grown collectively. So it was necessary to extend the range of individual contracts to the whole set of crops with the restriction that families would be granted only part of the surplus production (over contracted quantities) eventually arising. Of course peasants who handled the harvest individually were wise enough not to report the exact amount of production obtained and kept all the surplus. So it was necessary to apply in full the system of production contracts with families with only the collective accounting of labor points being kept. There again, however, the system was not satisfactory. Either the quantities of output which had to be handed over to the team for subsequent repartition among member families were important and peasants were dissatisfied with the payment in labor points they got because their value was reduced by the burden of collective expenses (for unproductive cadres or families with deficits . . .); or those quantities to be delivered were fixed at a low level, close to the rations eventually alloted by the team to each farming family member, in which case a computation of labor points became quite useless as most of the grain did not, in fact, leave the family farm. Separating the accounts of the various families and getting rid of labor points were the best solution and this is how "integral farming contracts" were developed.

The return to family farming, which has become general in China, follows therefore a logic of division of land and of accounts that puts forward the peasant family as the best suited entity both for efficiently organized farm work and for distributing incomes without problems. The strength of the peasant economy thus shown by the decollectivization movement in the Chinese countryside clearly underlines, in retrospect, how fragile and uncertain the collectivization equilibrium at the team level was. While it had succeeded in maintaining itself for about 20 years after the tragedy of the Great Leap Forward (1958–61), it just reflected an unstable equilibrium between the centrifugal forces of family interest and the will of political power to collectivize. Such a compromise was as unsatisfactory as the remuneration systems in use and which operated under a consensus of wastage: egalitarianism in distribution in return for second-rate individual work performance. As soon as the political pressure waned, and the need for collectivization faded, the compromise lost its importance and the equilibrium was broken.

A New Political Logic

The logic of breaking up the collectives and returning to family farming coincides with a new logic adopted by those in power. It is now clear that, although the current evolution was largely desired by the peasantry and was in line with the dynamics of a family-based peasant economy, it would not have been possible without the agreement of the authorities. Thus the history of the development of responsibility systems closely fits the phases of the fight for power between pragmatist reformers and conservative neo-Maoists.

As early as 1977, Deng Xiaoping, who had recently returned to the political scene, sent his trusted lieutenant Wan Li to the rather poor province of Anhui to engage there in an agricultural policy opposed, on every point, to that then defended, at the national level, by his rival Hua Guofeng. The latter wanted to limit private plots and family activities, close free markets, raise the level of collectivization from the team level to the brigade level (200 to 300 families) following the example of the famous Dazhai brigade.[13] Wan Li, on the other hand, protected small peasant freedoms and defended the rights of teams. As early as the winter of 1978, and even before the Third Plenum of December, which marked the victory of the pragmatists, led by Deng Xiaoping, over the conservative wing represented by Hua Guofeng, Wan Li allowed the first family contracts to be set up in order to counteract the effects of a drought affecting Anhui province.[14] This was but a revival of a method that had already appeared during the agricultural crises following, in 1956, land collectivization and, in 1961–62, the disrupting folly of the Great Leap.[15] It had not then been allowed to develop because Mao Zedong had opposed it, launching the People's Communes in 1958 and, at the end of 1962, the "Four clean ups" movement which preceded the Cultural Revolution.[16]

Deng Xiaoping's victory at the Third Plenum now gives the contractual system the opportunity to last. In 1979, reform opponents could not prevent the development of contracts with the groups, in spite of their repeated warnings about risks of deviating towards "division of land and individual farming" (*fentian dangan*).[17] In 1980, Wan Li returned to Peking to take over the direction of rural affairs. He extended the family contracts to the whole of the country by having the Central Committee adopt, in September 1980, document number 75 which in fact legalized this experiment. Conservatives managed to delay its publication until April 1981, but they could not stop the expansion of agreements with families which, at the end of the same year, held a majority position.[18] The opponents of the reform then changed tactics and tried to limit the application of those contracts solely to the poor areas of China where the material bases of farming collectives were relatively fragile.[19] For rich areas they advocated a counter-formula: "specialized contracts under unified management" (*tongyi jingying zhuanye chengbao*) that allocated contractual tasks to specialized groups or individuals while maintaining collective forms of distribution of remuneration and strict team control over individual activities.[20] This met with little success, never exceeding, in June 1981, 8 percent of the teams and then waning as farming agreements developed at full speed in 1981 and 1982. This progression was in step with the successive alignment of the various provincial leaders with the policy supported by Deng Xiaoping and Wan Li which was crowned, in September 1982, during the Twelfth Party Congress by the fall of the last conservative strongholds and self criticism by first secretaries Mao Zhiyong of Hunan and Bai Rubing of Shandong.[21]

The political logic guiding reformist leaders in their relationships with peasantry is really novel. Mao Zedong or his "heir" Hua Guofeng rested on authoritarian mobilization and strict control of the peasants within collectives. Deng Xiaoping, on the other hand, calls upon self-interest of individual families and leaves room, to a large extent, for the autonomous operation of the peasant economy. This reversal in political logic stems from recognition of a social reality and represents a strategic gamble.

Straight along the line of a pragmatic philosophy that adopted as its slogan, "search for truth in facts" (*shishi jiushi*), there is recognition that, in spite of nearly 25 years of collectivization, there had been little change in the traditional structure of village society. In contrast to the Soviet precedent, it does not appear that this society has been disrupted by the setting up of work collectives. On the contrary, the village society seems to have conquered from within the collective institutions. The new local communist leadership, while conforming formally to directives from the center, in fact kept close to the narrow interests of the village communities. Its power rested on family or clan solidarities and subdivisions while, in everyday life, the family retained its predominant role.

To a certain extent, it may even be argued that Chinese collectivization by slowing down trade flows, by fixing the population to the communal land had rather tended to reinforce certain archaic aspects of rural society.[22] Deng Xiaoping takes note of these facts and bets on faster modernization of this society by giving it more autonomy. His gamble is that these freedoms granted to peasantry will not endanger the political domination and the ideological monopoly exerted by the Party's machinery.

A New Chinese Way

The gamble was obviously daring. The political risks are commensurate with the economic stakes that the leaders assign to their new policy. These stakes, to use their own terms, are nothing less than the setting up of a new "socialist path of agricultural development (painted) with Chinese colors" (*Zhongguo tese de shehuizhuyi fazhan daolu*).[23]

The Rehabilitation of the Family Economy

This new path recognizes the fundamental role of the family economy.[24] Family level farm management henceforth appears best suited to the specific characteristics of agricultural production with its need for very flexible adjustments, for rapid decisions concerning living beings subject to unpredictable natural constraints. The family is considered best able to mobilize labor to take advantage of the diversity of its abilities and to adjust to the multiplicity of farm tasks. The fiction that the farm economy is "socialist" is, on the other hand, maintained by reasserting that land is collectively owned, with families only having its usufruct, that the major part of peasants' income originates directly from their work, and that, lastly, there is a "dual level of management" with team collective control topping daily family management.[25] The contractual farming agreements system is considered, by Chinese theoreticians, as sufficient to ensure the "cooperative" nature of Chinese agriculture and to integrate family activities into the global socialist economy.[26]

Claims that the path thus chosen is along the line of socialist continuity could be discussed; it must be recognized that the new and at last positive evaluation of family farms is courageous. These farms appear especially well suited to attain a diversification of farm production that has become one of the top objectives of the new policy. They can readily use to that effect the free time of a labor force which is employed in useful work on the crops only half the year. They can also mobilize in that direction family savings that, in the past, tended to be squandered in non-productive expenses in order not to have to put them at the collective's disposal.

The Specialized Households Model

The new recognition of the virtues of family farms goes with the more or less explicit abandonment of past views which favored a farming sector regrouping, in an undifferentiated way, large work collectives. On the contrary, the emphasis is on socialization of farm work through specialization and market orientation of production. The models are not, as in the past, brigades which, like the Dazhai one, proved their collective superiority through vast common infrastructural works aimed at promoting grain production. They are henceforth specialized households (*zhuanye hu*) devoting themselves to a specific enterprise with sale of most of the output.[27]

According to the official presentation of these households, they concern peasants who have been able to put to good use a particular ability or a keen trading or management skill, together with hard work, in order to set up particularly high performance specialized enterprises. They may specialize in livestock raising or fish farming which, even within the limited framework of a farm, allows for an increase in the scale of production, a rise in technical level and thus in labor productivity. These top farmers are considered, by the authorities, as presenting the future, to the extent that they prefigure a development stage where specialized production units will have become interdependent, thereby reaching an advanced level of agricultural work socialization. Specialized households are already dependent on others for their supplies. More important, they sell almost all of their output, a clear break from a mostly semi-autarchic type of agriculture.[28]

Those households cover a very wide range of activities. Some may specialize in livestock raising along with crop farming for which, like all others, they have signed contracts. Several hundreds of laying hens or tens of pigs for fattening are thus found. Others raise silkworms or rent a pond for fish farming or tend an orchard. All sorts of agricultural, "in the broadest sense", endeavors are present. The difference between the "specialization" of these households and the traditional "diversification" of peasant farmers' activities rests only in the fact that the specialized activity is the major source of income.[29]

Many rural households also specialize in non-agricultural pursuits while in the past peasants had no right to do anything other than farming (trade was a quasi-State monopoly and rural industry handled only by brigade or communal-level collective units). In addition to wide-spread revival of traditional handicrafts (iron or wood work, wicker-work . . .) there is now development, in certain villages, of small family workshops doing sewing, knitting, light mechanics.[30] These sometimes operate as sub-contractors for larger city firms. More significant still, private traders have reappeared. Once they have delivered what was provided for by their contracts, all peasants may now sell directly, on free markets, their production surplus, including grain. Certain specialized households dispose of their output through those channels and their trading abilities may be as important as their talents as producers. Some rural people are only traders. Provided they obtain a license and pay a tax, they are entitled to collect agricultural products not subject to deliveries, to rent transportation means such as railway cars or ships and to resell their goods in districts that may be quite distant.[31]

New Forms of Cooperation

Peasants have not only the right to trade and to engage in business, they may also freely join with others for operations exceeding the means of individual families. On the basis of free consent and for mutual benefit "new economic associations" (*xin de jingji lianhe*), as they are called for lack of a better name, may be set up. In contrast to the former collectives, with their single framework and similar size whatever the cooperative undertaking of villages, those new private associations allow for flexible combinations of individual labor, know-how or capital assets with quite varied modalities and at different scales. Thus two or three families with their own labor resources may set up an oil or a rice mill. Five or six of them may buy a truck with their savings and hire a driver. Several tens of families may get together to invest in a brick factory where a few of their members will work. Profits from those joint cooperative undertakings are generally redistributed between participating families on the basis of their inputs.[32]

Such an extensive liberalization of rural economic activities obviously competes directly with brigade and commune collective undertakings as well as with "purchasing and supply cooperatives". So both of these underwent a reform to enable them to resist the rise of individual firms and of petty private capitalism. Reform of the collective workshops in villages and small towns often appears to have consisted in leasing them out to individuals who are given full freedom to reorganize production and even to rehire individual staff members on the condition that they make profits and pay a lease, sometimes a high one.[33] For communal cooperatives, reform aimed precisely at reactivating their cooperative nature by giving back to the peasants the share they used to have, by selling new shares to rural households and by distributing dividends (in fact symbolic ones). Through this democratization of their management obtained by re-cooperativization (often with changes in the top staff after more or less spontaneous elections) an attempt is thus made to put more dynamism in the marketing policies of organizations which, for many years, had but handled the State's planified purchases and managed shortages.[34]

In certain branches this dynamization of state networks operating in post-farming activities involves the setting up of "joint agri-industrial and trade firms" (*nong-gong-shang lianhe giye*). They regroup the technical adminis-trations furthering relations among the producers, either collectives or individual families, industrial processing firms and state distribution networks. They can be created to launch certain products like mushrooms, or to expand pre-existing regional specialities like milk and fruits. The branches concerned are usually those where expansion is closely dependent on processing, marketing and even export facilities. Those firms attempt to associate producers with the profits obtained in those processing and marketing operations through the distribution of dividends on the shares they own or deliveries they make. This organic participation of very different bodies

such as administrations, firms, collectives and individuals, who may be under
the authority of various territorial units, aims at correcting the previously
existing situation of an agricultural economy where technical services were
not concerned about production, and where marketing agencies did not care
much for transactions not specifically provided for by the Plan.[35]

The Scuttling of People's Communes

More generally, the whole administrative services of the People's communes
had to be reformed to adjust to the changes that took place in the organization
of agricultural production. This reform implied that the communes, as
institutions, should disappear. They were progressively replaced by "township" (*Xiang*) governments, a move reaching all communes by the end of
1984. At least on the organizational charts, the separation between party
and government should then have been obtained and local administration
have regained its autonomy. At the same time, and it may be more substantial,
administrative services were deeply reorganized. The technical offices were
turned into "specialized companies" that provide supplies and direct technical
assistance to peasant households through "technical contracts". Thus seed
companies must spread the new varieties and compensate farmers for eventual
losses while they will collect royalties on production increments in order
to pay bonuses to the technicians in charge. Similarly, veterinary companies
will sign contracts with pig farmers. They will provide veterinary care for
animals with insurance in case of stock losses. Crop protection companies
operate in concert with households or groups who specialize in spraying
insecticides or pesticides. The companies supply them with equipment,
materials and advice.[36]

The move over from a collective to an individual type of farming led
also to a reform of the credit system to suit the new financing needs of
the family farms. The "credit cooperatives" went through a reform similar
to that of supply and marketing cooperatives, with sale of shares, distribution
of dividends, elections for management boards. They have been encouraged
to become more autonomous from the Agricultural Bank, of which they
were often only branches, by increasing their assets through deposits by
rural families and by better management of their loans. Above all, they
significantly reoriented their activities with loans to family farms now
exceeding agricultural loans to collectives.[37]

It is of course too early to evaluate the real extent of the application of
the new agricultural policy with regard to reform of administrative, commercial and financial services; bureaucratic pressures can hardly disappear
rapidly. It cannot be denied, however, that this whole new policy has a
consistency that contrasts with the attempts at farm reform of other centrally
planned countries. There has been not only a decollectivization of the
Chinese countryside, but, more important still, a whole set of measures
aimed at placing family farms, or at least the most efficient among them,
within a technical, commercial and financial environment favorable to their
development. Much remains to be done in order that all these measures be

carried out in daily practice. The fact that the approach to the problems has been systematic, covering all links and aspects of agricultural production, promises however in itself the ultimate success of the reform.

First Achievements and Pending Problems

The Rise in Output and Incomes

Decollectivization had immediate and spectacular effects in terms of production increases. Food grain production increased 23 percent between 1978 and 1983; an annual rate of increase of 4.2 percent against 3.5 percent on the average for the 1964–1977 period. The increase was particularly impressive in 1982 and 1983: 8.7 and 9.2 percent when the generalization of family farming agreements took place. For industrial crops, the increases were enormous between 1978 and 1983, 114 percent for cotton, 102 percent for oilseeds, 69 percent for sugar cane and sugar beets, 50 percent for tea, and meat production (excluding poultry) increased 64 percent.[38]

Most of those increases are explained by the use of productivity reserves through greater efficiency of labor within the family farms. For grain, all the incremental production was obtained through yield increases since harvested area fell 6 percent between 1978 and 1982. For industrial crops yield increases for the same period were high: 39 percent for cotton, 91 percent for rapeseed, 21 percent only for peanuts, +47 percent for sugar cane, 78 percent for sugar beets. The pig herd (supplying 94 percent of the meat, (poultry excluded) remained stable with about 300 million head but efficiency in husbandry improved as the ratio of annual slaughter to herd numbers increased from 53 percent to 69 percent with slaughter weights increasing from about 50 kg to 64 kg.[39]

These increments are also explained by improvements in input supply. Sales of chemical fertilizers increased 67 percent between 1978 and 1982 with a switchover to better quality (for instance urea produced in big newly started imported factories rather than ammonium bicarbonate, which is volatile and of low efficiency, produced in small rural factories).[40] Technical contracts appear to have been efficient; they explain the recent expansion of new hybrid rice varieties created by the Chinese that were used on 20 percent of the paddy fields area in 1983.[41]

Of course all those highly optimistic statistics are somewhat unreliable since decollectivization often implied abandonment of team level accounts. Production is now estimated rather than measured and the statistical services have only partly replaced the exhaustive enumerations of the past by sampling methods.[42] If, however, the exact magnitude of production increases is not certain, the global trends can hardly be questioned. Some indicators are significant: cotton imports fell in 1983 while urban rationing of cotton goods was waived early in 1984[43]; planned oilseed areas were reduced in 1983 as production exceeded processing capacity.[44] Gross grain deliveries increased from 62 million tons in 1978 to 120 million tons in 1983, their share in total grain production increasing from 20 to 31 percent.[45] As net deliveries for urban consumption remained at the same level (about 15 percent of production) the main share of incremental grain deliveries went to deficit rural areas thus encouraging the reorientations of households or even whole regions towards industrial crops.[46]

This unprecedented increase in grain deliveries as well as the considerable progress in industrial crops were also the result of increased outputs on family farms in response to spectacular rises in farm products' purchase prices. As early as 1979, the government decided to increase prices for compulsory deliveries in order to improve stagnating peasant incomes. Average price increases exceeded 20 percent. In subsequent years, as responsibility systems spread out, there were new price increases, not through increases in delivery quota prices but because the above quota share of procurement, paid at 50 percent higher prices, increased as well as sales made at "negotiated prices" (equivalent to free market prices). So the authorities were obliged to pay much more than forecast in order to maintain the flow of deliveries within the framework of the new contracts with families. In all, and cumulating all delivery types, average price increases between 1978 and 1982 were 49 percent for grains, 42 percent for cotton, 59 percent for oilseeds, 38 percent for sugar cane, 48 percent for tea and 66 percent for pigs (price per head).[47]

Since those price rises were only very partially passed on to state urban retail trade prices, (increases of 2 percent for grain, 16 percent for all food products[48]) the government was compelled to subsidize farm products purchasing organizations. Subsidies were 44 billion yuan for 1979 to 1981 including 20 billion for 1981 alone.[49] Since then, food subsidies should be around 20 to 25 billion per year or about 20 percent of budget appropriations. Chinese economists had estimated that, in 1978, unfavorable terms of trade caused a transfer out of the agricultural sector amounting to 25 to 35 billion yuan. So the price rises that have taken place since then ended a period of undervaluation of farm products causing a hidden transfer that, whatever the method of computation, could not have been lower than 20 billion yuan per year.[50]

These price increases caused a redistribution of national income in favour of peasants whose incomes increased greatly. According to a national sample survey of several thousand peasant families conducted by the national statistics office, income per person increased from 134 yuan in 1978 to 310 yuan, or about 150 US dollars, in 1983.[51] This is a 131 percent rise! From 1957 to 1978 and for the same sample, this average income only increased 84 percent in current yuans. In constant yuans, from 1957 to 1977, per capita income distributed by the collectives is only said to have increased by 19 percent.[52] Of course, part of this rise in peasant incomes is nominal since farmers still consume most of their production (the deliveries representing about 35 percent of output value). Yet it resulted in an increase of +111 percent from 1978 to 1982 (in current prices) of the volume of rural trade in comsumption goods. Annual sales of bicycles, mostly in rural areas, increased from 8 million in 1978 to 22 million in 1982. For both radio sets and watches there are identical figures: 14 to 36 million for the same years; for sewing machines the increase was from 4.4 to 11.4 million.[53] Thus the peasants' increased purchasing power took the form, at least in part, of purchases of consumption goods that industry was able to rapidly supply. Another part of the new rural wealth was absorbed by a wave of building that all travellers easily noticed. Instead of 100 million square meters of new buildings as in the late seventies, 500 to 600 million square meters, and even 800 in 1983, were built annually, a 10 billion yuan per year investment.[54] Finally rural savings absorbed a large share of peasant liquidity. The balance of rural deposits increased from 7 billion yuan in 1979 to 29 billion in 1983, an average annual increase of over 4 billion yuan, with more than 10 billion in 1983 alone.[55]

The first results of the new economic policy in the countryside are then extremely encouraging with regard to both production increases and income improvements. Undoubtedly rural living conditions have improved over the past two or three years. All direct witnesses confirm, on those matters, the official figures. The problem is whether observed rates of production increases can be maintained for a long time or whether they will very soon subside. Productivity gains, obtained through better input management as the result of decollectivization, are of a kind obtained at one stroke but hardly renewable. Similarly, the rise in farm prices seems already to have stopped and other sources of peasant income improvement will have to be found. It is unfortunately quite probable that the constraints characteristic of an underdeveloped economy will very soon reappear and hamper further agricultural progress. The possibility of sustained agricultural growth linked with a real development of the economy depends on whether solutions will be found to a number of problems that the reforms brought to light or left unsolved.

Tendencies Towards Privatization Versus Collective Controls

When reporting on the application of the new agricultural policy many western observers rather curiously emphasized problems that arose rather than the economic benefits obtained. In appraising those criticisms of the reforms one should attempt to separate the pro-Maoist prejudice of their authors from the real problems underestimated by Chinese authorities or even denied by the new official propaganda.[56]

A first set of problems originates from the hard-to-find equilibrium between evident tendencies towards privatization of agriculture and the upholding of collective forms of control safeguarding the "socialist" nature of the farm system.

Reflecting the concern of many members, Party ideologues attempted to show the socialist nature of the new farm structures by stressing the collective ownership of land. This point of view, of course, has little significance since private use right of the land is granted by lease for a relatively long period of time. In fact, the problem, at the beginning, was not so much privatization of land but rather convincing the peasants that the new systems would be durable and that their recently acquired right to till the land alloted to them could be upheld. Since farmers only benefited from short term contracts and were permanently threatened by eventual reallocation of land, they often tended to engage in a predatory type of agriculture rapidly exhausting soil fertility as the fields, very often, did not receive organic fertilizer or were not improved for fear it might benefit the neighbor.[57] The base length of contracts that, at the start, was three to five years was thus not long enough, and, in a recent directive, the Central Committee decided to increase it to 15 years or more.[58] This will protect the new "tenant's" interests and favor fertility conservation and proper land use. It will obviously weaken further the validity of the thesis that "socialist" agriculture on "collective" land is being practiced.

In reality, the essential aspect of collective land ownership is prohibition of sale or rental of parcels alloted to families. This prohibition raises problems as the absence of a land market hampers adjustments in farm scale to changing family size. At the outset land was divided quite equally among families according to the number of persons, including babies, and to their work force. Practically, allocation of parcels was handled by drawing lots to prevent any complaint.[59] In a few cases, some "mobile lands" were set aside, precisely to facilitate adjustments, and handed over temporarily under short term contracts to a few beneficiaries. More often, adjustments took place later through informal agreements; households that were short of labor could hire day-workers or convey their right to farm to neighbours or relatives. Those hidden arrangements were hard to prevent; they were a more flexible solution to the rigidity in land allocations than the "mobile lands". The same directive that extended leases to 15 years finally allowed these arrangements provided the teams approve them.[60]

The legalization of transfer in use of land alloted to a family, is often equivalent to a sublease that is usually only accepted against the guaranty of low-priced rations supplied by the farmer who takes over the lease. Together with the increase in contract length it follows the logic of tenure conditions implied by the setting up of the new accountability systems. This evidently is a move towards de facto privatization of farm structures. The same trend is at work with regard to the other factors of production. At the outset, draught animals had been allocated by rotation to families, since there were not enough for all. In 1982, statistics report 58 million animals used for plowing for 183 million peasant households. Farmers however were not individually responsible for those animals and tended to exhaust them. So it was necessary to allocate them to certain farmers under special contracts and against payment. Those farmers could then rent their services to neighbors. Generally, it ended up by selling the draught animals to those families who could buy them.[61] Privatization also concerns tractors and single axle tractors. At the end of 1983, out of 3.6 million units, no less than 1.5 million were in private ownership, mostly one axle tractors used for lucrative transport operations.[62]

There remains the matter of heavy collective equipment, particularly hydraulic installations, pumping stations or tube wells. At the beginning of the land division movement, it was reported that certain installations such as barns and silos had been dismantled or even pilfered.[63] These disorders do not appear to have been widespread. Usually general utility equipment was entrusted to teams or households of technicians who maintained and operated them. This is the case for hydraulic equipment. A few households in the village take care of the wells or pumps, and see to it that water reaches individual farmer's fields. They are usually paid directly by users on the basis of area or water flow time.[64]

If management of heavy collective equipment does not seem, in general, to have suffered much from the movement towards private farming, this does not apply to maintenance of infrastructure. It is true that contracts often provide that families should supply yearly a number of days of work for repairing small dykes or canals or for maintenance of rural roads. In practice, compliance is very difficult to obtain. Beyond this specific matter of local infrastructure, the general question raised is whether, in a decollectivized agriculture, labor can still be mobilized for collective tasks and the land improvements necessary for farm progress continued.[65] The matter is of acute importance because public appropriations and funds from rural firms earmarked for this are waning.[66]

It may be considered that tendencies towards privatization of agriculture are not, by themselves, an obstacle to agricultural development. The current success of the reforms may however, in the long run, be jeopardized by weakening of collective discipline in the field of land improvement investments and, more generally, anarchy in land use. Teams or villages are not, in this respect, without means of intervention and control. In spite of decollectivization and growing privatization, collective institutions still exist. Through the contracts they supervise, teams have their say in cropping patterns and retain certain duties in supply and, sometimes, in certain key operations. This theoretically gives them the means of insuring that collective discipline be obeyed. They also have authority over accumulation funds which gives them financial resources for common equipment and joint action. However, the odds are that these means will remain unused as long as a substitute is not found for the cadres, now lacking motivation since they have ceased being responsible for daily production management. This substitute could be a village-level body where community interests could express themselves and a common will for action shape itself.[67]

The official view is that the centrifugal forces of privatization will be balanced by maintaining institutional "unification" at the team level. It totally ignores the need for this social dynamics that, through participation and mobilization, would be the only way to provide again for collective control since coercion is not possible as it was in the past. In fact, if sharing the use of draught animals or teaming up of labor for certain field tasks now works, it is not through regulations but by families spontaneously organizing to revive past mutual-help customs. In a similar manner it would be most desirable that really autonomous village associations organize themselves, particularly for handling the necessary arbitration concerning access to water resources. Division of collectives has multiplied conflicts concerning sharing of water between family farms. Irrigation technicians certainly do not have the authority required to solve them. They may even encourage unfairness and operate rackets.[68] These village associations could probably also provide the framework for mobilization of families for land improvement tasks of common interest. In the past, particularly in southern China where they were powerful, certain clan organizations had been so able to carry out land investments of vital importance to the villages.

In the new farm policy, farmers are allowed to associate for economic activities. Will village communities be given the right to organize as such in order to really assume control over their destiny? It seems most doubtful that Chinese authorities consider even the possibility of such a move that would be alien to their logic with regard to institutional controls. They can accomodate individual initiatives but would hardly tolerate the emergence of collective counter powers.

Social Disparities and Economic Dualism

A second set of problems concern the appearance in the villages, as a consequence of the new policy, of increasing social disparities and income differentiation. The normal outcome of individualization of family farms and growing privatization of agricultural means of production is income inequalities linked to family labor resources, financial means and thus ability to buy an animal or purchase fertilizer. Increasing income differences are a hardly preventable corollary of management autonomy of farms and of the renewed dynamism of production.

In spite of declarations to the contrary by authorities and of corrective mechanisms invented by theoreticians, current policies tend to reinforce those inequalities.[69] The encouragement of specialized households clearly leads to the emergence of a new stratum of rich farmers. While the average peasant family does not earn more than 1000 to 1500 yuan per year, incomes of specialized households are, according to numerous examples presented in the Chinese press, in the 3000 to 5000 yuan range, and those are mostly in cash and therefore available for diversified forms of consumption and productive investments.[70]

The official thesis is that poorest farmers have not become poorer, which is plausible in the current context of general growth but warrants verification, and that the current minority of "rich before the others" farmers will pull the others along its path, which is more doubtful.[71] Early in 1984, there were about 24 million specialized households or around 13 percent of all peasant families.[72] Can this group, which in fact includes widely different cases, be rapidly increased? This raises the problems of limits to diversification and specialization in an agriculture which is bound to be mostly devoted to cereal growing, in a context of overpopulation and without any really important urban market as farming continues to occupy nearly 70 percent of the population.

Admittedly, a significant amount of diversification can be obtained by developing little used resources, particularly in mountain areas or by expanding ancillary family activities that were unduly neglected in the past. This diversification probably explains the new affluence felt everywhere in the countryside. On the other hand, generalization of livestock raising units for pigs and poultry would require feed surpluses vastly exceeding those currently available. Grain for feed (tubers included) only represents less than 20 percent of total grain production.[73] Large-scale pig-feeding specialized households who can purchase feed from outside bodies are, in that respect, in an exceptional situation. Similarly, the number of possible enterprises that appear profitable because they fill a gap neglected by a rather lethargic administrative economy, is relatively limited: all farmers cannot, for example, simultaneously start manufacturing soybean cheese or gathering medical herbs.

Of course, the ultimate capacity for development and diversification of the rural economy, particularly as concerns non-agricultural undertakings, should not be underestimated. Nor should the abilities of a peasantry with rich technical traditions and highly varied specialties be underrated. The matter is merely that access to profitable specializations is bound to be limited for reasons of the nature of the production involved or of scale. Those few families who can take advantage of them are thus in a privileged situation. Particularly advantaged are those specialized households who also have a priority for loans from credit cooperatives or for deliveries of supplies.[74]

A new category of specialized households has recently appeared, the presence of which may increase still more inequality in access to the means of production, since land itself is concerned. These are the "grain production specialized households". They benefit from a land concentration process and can thus market most of their grain crop. Their numbers are still very limited but strongly encouraged by propaganda. Their land comes from transfer of use rights from families unable to farm the land or who specialize in other activities. They also benefit from the "mobile lands" set aside in the allocation process. In certain districts, a few of the farmers thus manage to deliver more than half the whole grain quota deliveries. Not only is access to land highly unequal, but the high rate of marketing of a minority may push the others into damaging autarky.[75]

The crucial problem for future development of rural economy is thus to find driving mechanisms which can ensure that the majority of peasants be associated with the progress of the most advanced among them and to prevent that a minority retain at its profit the benefits of renewed growth. Chinese authorities, who elaborate at length on the merits of specialized households, are not very talkative, to say the least, about those driving mechanisms, which are, in fact, difficult to imagine. They are also very silent on the difficulties now confronting the poorest families who cannot, as in the past, benefit from collective rations. Officially team welfare funds should cope with the most dramatic cases. According to official figures of impressive accuracy 2,988,900 persons, ill, crippled, orphans, cannot provide for their needs and are guaranteed a minimal income by local authorities.[76] How is it possible to believe that rural poverty is of so limited extent when official estimates, at the end of the seventies, were that 100 million peasants were suffering from scarcity? It is also common knowledge that the teams have great difficulties in collecting money for the welfare fund. Moreover, this money is often used for other purposes if not directly pocketed by cadres.

Moreover, the power situation within the villages has not changed with decollectivization. A kind of collusion is found between cadres who take advantage of the new situation and the new elite of rich farmers that managed to emerge. The latter are often cadres who provided themselves with the best contracts (they are thus found among the "grain specialized households"). Conversely, it is often through their relations with local administration that specialized households manage to carry out their activities, obtain supplies and find outlets.[77] This collusion causes concern for the lot of the most disfavored. It is known that, in certain units, at least, and above a certain level in hierarchy, cadres used to take advantage of lax collective accounting to feast at the expense of their compatriots. Now they sometimes manage to double their wages or, worse, engage in various corrupt practices.[78]

Here again, and even if this type of practice does not exist everywhere, economic liberalization with no counterpart at the level of collective control may jeopardize the future of reforms and endanger the chances of obtaining a form of development that would be shared by many. Setting up control mechanisms at that level, attempting to redistribute incomes and reduce disparities is obviously a very difficult task. Whatever the solutions considered, none of them can be carried out without doing something about the possibility that local cadres may exert arbitrary power. This implies that some form of social organization representing village communities must be set up to obtain more effective control over application of the rules concerning farming agreements, allocation of contracts and, above all, use of collective finances. Of course, the chances that such organizations will be set up are very slim. Creation of true democracy in the countryside is still just an utopia.

No less utopian would be the aim of getting rid of the economic dualism that affects China as much as all other Third World peasant societies. It seems that Chinese reformers have accepted this dualism both between the specialized households engaged in modern agriculture and the mass of other traditional farms and between developed regions and those that hardly participate in national economic development.[79] The wager seems to have been made that the minority of advanced farms and the development centers in the richest agricultural provinces will be able, through an intensification of their trade with urban and industrial sectors, to give a new impetus to the industrialization and diversification of the whole economy. Thus later the jobs and outlets that are the only way of pulling rural population out of its present underdevelopment could be created. History will tell whether this wager was wise.

Can the New Rural Policy Last?

Early in the decollectivization movement some observers had expressed fears that more peasant autonomy could have negative effects on the supply of the cities. A specific risk was that, under less pressure from plan constraints, farmers would produce grain only for their own needs and switch over to more profitable activities. This fear was not justified; grain area did fall but grain production made a big leap while deliveries increased still more. So there was no "crisis in deliveries". But there was a massive redistribution of purchasing power in favor of the peasants as well as a heavy burden, for state finances, of farm price subsidies. Did this jeopardize the operation of the socialist economy and the industrialization process? The great increase in monetary supply of rural households does not appear to have caused grave disequilibria. Part of the purchasing power was absorbed in a real explosion of consumer's goods sales and in a wave of construction. The rest was on the whole absorbed by rural savings.[80] This analysis, however, underestimates inflation of which official figures can hardly give a true account.

The financial burden of subsidies, 20 to 25 billion yuan yearly, certainly explains the budget deficit that appeared after 1978. It reached 17 billion yuan in 1979, or 15 percent of budget resources; it is said to have been progressively reduced to 3 billion in 1982. However this excludes foreign borrowing and floating of Treasury bonds curiously counted as income in the budget. So, in fact, the 1982 deficit was 11 billion, 10 percent of budget resources.[81] This led the government to strongly cut down investment expenses from 40 billion yuan in 1979 to 27 in 1982. This was however compensated by increases in investments outside the budget financed by local governments, and retained firm funds. So total fixed capital formation, including firms' "renovation fund", increased from 67 billion yuan in 1978 to 85 billion in 1982 with state industry's share progressing from 39 to 47 billion.[82]

So, on the whole, it appears that the Chinese economy stood up well through decollectivization and the resulting change in terms of trade. There was a cost in terms of inflation, certainly higher than officially stated, and of persistent budget deficits, but deep changes in national income distribution finally did not really affect the rise in investments or lastingly disrupt industry financing. State industries, the heart of socialist economy, resisted quite well and after a few swerves came back to their previous growth rate. They found elsewhere the financing denied to them by the budget thus showing an autonomy in behavior that reflects the limits of the control planners exert on that part of industry they are supposed to control best. Light industries found new outlets on the peasant market while city food supplies improved with more deliveries of vegetables, milk, and eggs.

So according to the first results, which will have to be checked over a longer period of time, this economic success tends to indicate that the new Chinese economic model is viable. It is very like the neo-NEP model recently described by Berliner.[83] In both models there is co-existence, in a mixed system, of "commanding heights" with state industrial firms, that are at the heart of the system and remain subject to central planning, and a "neo-NEP" peripheral sector. In the case of China, the latter is mostly agricultural. There, the contractual economy and private initiative are dominant. They bring flexibility and dynamism to the whole system without questioning its foundations.

From this mostly "economic" angle the new Chinese farm policy can go on and last. It would even be a boon for the vitality of the economy as a whole, provided the new problems of dualism raised previously can be controlled, collective discipline can be preserved and social disparities reduced. The obstacles upon which farm reform may stumble are not so much economic as social and, above all, political. The social danger is not the risk, however real, of social dualism with the emergence of a minority of rich peasants. The revolt of poor peasants imagined by some authors is not for tomorrow. Nor is a demographic explosion the danger. Early critics of the accountability systems had stated that the lifting of controls in the countryside would increase the birth rate. This was not justified. The encouragement to large families due to the past system of minimum rations collectively distributed within the teams was much greater. True, there was an increase in births in the 1981 figures, but it was statistical readjustment linked to previous underestimation of birth rates that the July 1982 census had shown.[84] Anyhow, the authoritarian and sometimes brutal current family planning methods seem to have already caused a new decline in population increases.[85] The danger is elsewhere: in the rural exodus. Family contracts have liberated labor surpluses that were previously hidden within the work collectives. Out of more than 300 million farm workers it is officially estimated that 100 million are redundant and could be better employed elsewhere. Another indication of the magnitude of this rural over-population is the fact that there are now more than three active persons per hectare of cultivated land.[86]

The official thesis is that the rural exodus can be controlled and that there will only be movement out of agriculture with excess farm labor going to larger villages, township centers and market boroughs or, at most, to small towns where processing and service activities will develop. The migration to big cities, already confronted with unemployment problems, could thus be averted.[87] It is not certain, however, that authorities now have effective means of controlling migration flows. Even if peasants are administratively assigned to residence in villages where they are registered, nobody can, in practice, prevent them from moving freely, taking advantage of the waiving of past restrictions and monopolies. Already many of them leave to work on so called "temporary" building jobs in large cities.[88] The problem, if not controlled, runs the risk of being explosive since it threatens the workers' stronghold and their employment and social benefits. Before the farm reforms and its opportunities for relative peasant enrichment, the worker class was the main ally of the Party.

None the less, the main obstacle to the durability of the new farm policy is still political. Will the Party and state machinery accept the new freedoms given to peasantry? At the base level this machinery seems, in many places, to accept the new course of things, to take advantage of it rather than opposing it. They will attempt to tax the new peasant wealth or to participate within the "second economy".[89] It can, however, be imagined that many cadres, also threatened by the reform of the administration of People's Communes, will remain hostile to what they will perceive as a loss of power. Middle echelon members of the Party machine will probably be more sensitive to ideological arguments. Far from the rural base, they cannot benefit from some of the indirect consequences of the reforms. So they are hardly in favor of new policies. On the whole, reluctant cadres are probably the majority.

A reluctant machinery may, through inertia, slow down the implementation of rural reforms; but its inclinations carry little weight compared to decisions taken at the top. In that respect, and in contrast to what happens in the Soviet Union where leadership changes do not have much effect on the evolution of a limited choice system, changes in the leadership in China could upset the general orientations and turn current policies around.[90] The whole problem of continuation of the new economic policies for the countryside in the post-Deng Xiaoping era is thus raised. The victory of the reformist line over its conservative opponents owed much to the authority of Deng Xiaoping. His courage and exceptional political ability placed at the service of a deep feeling for national interest should be recognized. Zhao Ziyang and Wan Li are also full of determination in their will for reform, and peasants are grateful for it since they invented a popular saying: "To eat, go and get Ziyang, to get clothes, find Wan Li" (*Yao chi liang zhao Ziyang, yao chuan yi zhao Wan Li*). Is the present team assured of remaining in power after Deng Xiaoping has disappeared? Will it not be torn up by new dissentions? Will not a new majority and new equilibria emerge that could revise, at least in part, the reforms accomplished?

In final analysis, the sheer extent of the new rural policy may well be the safest base of its durability. Reform went so far that backward moves appear more and more impossible. A brutal recollectivization would certainly bring about a confidence crisis and a fall in production. This would be so grave that it would cause even the most ardent proponents of a return to Maoist orthodoxy to think the matter over.

Notes

1. This idealist approach is to be found in the studies of Charles Bettelheim and Helene Marchisio, *La Construction du Socialisme en Chine,* Paris (1965), or those of Jack Gray, "The Two Roads . . ." in Schram, Ed., *Authority Participation and Cultural Change in China,* Cambridge (1973).

2. Particularly noteworthy is the publication (first issue in 1980) by the Institute of Agricultural Economics (Chinese Academy of Social Sciences) of the monthly "Problems of Agricultural Economics" (*Nongye Jingji Wenti,* Abbrev. NYJJWT). In

1981 and 1982 began the regular publication of agricultural and statistical yearbooks, China's agricultural yearbook (*Zhongguo Nongye Nianjian*, Abbrev. NYNJ), China's Statistical Yearbook (*Zhongguo Tongji Nianjian*, Abbrev. TJNJ).

3. See my "Agriculture = la voie chinoise reste a trouver", in *Tiers-Monde*, April–June 1981, pp. 285–316.

4. See my "L'economie chinoise et le modele sovietique," in *Politique Etrangere*, 1/83, pp. 51–62.

5. Good examples of the diversity and complexity of norms' systems can be found in popularizing booklets; see Yuan, Ruofei, *Nongcun Renmingongshe Laodong Guanli* (Labour management in rural popular communes), Peking (1981); Hubei Province, Districts of Yingshan and Songzi, *Zhiding Laodong Ding'e Lanben Jinglian* (Model Experiments for the determination of work's norms), Commune Management Bureau, Ministry of Agriculture, Peking, 1981.

6. See Wu Xiang and Zhang Guangyou in *Renmin Ribao* (abbrev. RMRB, People's Daily), 9 April 1980. It is worth noting that in the Soviet wage reform of 1961–1962, a similar concern did not lead to decollectivization but to an over-complicated system of measuring piece-work in output terms, cf. Karl-Eugen Waedekin, *Die Bezahlung der Arbeit in der sowjetischen Landwirtschaft*, Berlin, 1972, p. 155 *et. seq.*, and *Agricultural Policies in Communist Europe*, 1982, p. 168 *et. seq.*

7. See my "Chine rurale = la revolution silencieuse", in *Projet*, September-October 1982, pp. 955–971.

8. Numerous examples of this system, combining the "five fixed" (manpower, land, quantity of product, costs, work-points) to the group and the "five unifications" (cultures planification, labor mobilization, distribution of revenues, gestion and compatability, use of big equipment) within the collective, have been presented in the Chinese media of 1979–1980, see RMRB 7 Oct. 1979 (Guanghan, Sichuan), 14 Nov. 1979 (Fengyang Anhui), 19 Dec. 1979 (Hanshou, Hunan), 15 Jan. 1980 (Guangchang, Jiangxi).

9. First justification of this system by Wu Xiang, in RMRB 5 Nov. 1980. Another version of this type of contract was called "production contracts to the laborer" (*baochan daolao*). The differences with the "family" contracts were only minor, and the change of name was often a subterfuge for concealing the reality of a de facto division of land between the families, see NYJJWT, 10/81, pp. 21–27 (investigation at Hancheng, Shaanxi).

10. Detailed description in NYJJWT, 9/81, pp. 17–22 (Yichun and Yongxin, Jiangxi), Ibid. 12/81, pp. 32–35 (Dezhou, Shandong), Ibid. 2/82, pp. 14–17 (Chuxian, Anhui). The introduction of this new system was widely discussed in specialized circles. See the summary of a conference in Kunming, in NYJJWT, 2/82, pp. 3–7, and the opinions of Xu Shiqi in NYJJWT, 3/82, pp. 3–7, Wang Kezhong, Ibid. 3/82, pp. 13–18, Zhang Guangyou, Ibid. 7/82, pp. 24–26.

11. Data for 1979, 1980, 1981, in Xing Su, in *Jingji Yanjiu* (Economic Research), 11/82, p. 6; for 1982 see RMRB 22, Aug. 82, 22 Jan. 83; for 1983, see Jingtang Shi, in NYJJWT, 4/83, p. 24.

12. See investigation in Henan, NYJJWT, 8/81, pp. 7–13; same observations at Xiaotan Commune by Yulin Zhang, in *Social Sciences in China* (Abbrev. SSC), 6/83, pp. 121 sq.

13. See our "Agriculture chinoise: recurrences", in *Mondes Asiatiques*, Summer 1978, pp. 33–70.

14. See report on Liu'an, Anhui, in NYJJWT, 3/82, pp. 3 sq.

15. See Dai Qingqi and Tu Zhan in RMRB, 23 Feb. 1982; in 1956 the system was called "the three contracted (work, production, finance) and one reward (surplus

of production)"; in 1962 first appeared the appellation of "production contract to the family" (*baochan daohu*).

16. See Parris H. Chang, *Power and Policy in China,* Pennsylvania State University Press, 1975.

17. See letter form Hao Zhang in RMRB, 15 March 1979, and subsequent debate and reports in RMRB of March and April 1979.

18. First publication of this document No. 75 in *Ban Yue Tan* (Abbrev. BYT) (Fortnight Talks) (8), April 1981, pp. 4–10. As the center legalized the contracts with the families, the peasants pressed locally for the application of the new dispositions, see report on a "strike" by villagers of Yongxing, district of Yuanping, Shanxi, in NYJJWT, 7/82, pp. 18–23.

19. This argumentation is reflected in the non-conclusive compte-rendu of a national meeting published in RMRB 6 April 1982; this point of view was also illustrated by conservative articles in the theoretical organ of the Party, see Du Runsheng in *Hongqi* (Red Flag), (19), 1981.

20. Examples in Jiangxi, RMRB 2 March 82, in Hunan, NYJJWT, 5/82, pp. 26–30. This model was sometimes forced upon the peasants, see RMRB, 16 Feb. 1982 (Jiangsu), 28 Feb. 1982 (Shanxi).

21. Self-criticism of Bai Rubing in *Xinhua* Agency (abbrev. XH), 3 Sept. 1982, of Mao Zhiyong in XH, 5 Sept. 1982, and RMRB, 28 Sept. 1982. Du Runsheng shows well this turning point by an eulogious article on *Baogan daohu,* in RMRB, 16 Sept. 1982.

22. See Claude Aubert and Cheng Ying, "Travail agricole et societe rurale en Chine", *Revue des Pays de l'Est,* Bruxelles (2), 1982, pp. 103–131.

23. See the long theoretical developments on this theme by Lin Zili in *Zhongguo Shehui Kexue* (Social Sciences in China, Abbrev. ZGSHKX, (2), 1983, pp. 107–128, and *Ibid.* (4), 1983, pp. 71–98.

24. The pivotal role of family economy in Chinese agriculture was emphasized by Zhang Yulin in JJYJ, 6/83, pp. 45–51; also Deng Zehui, *Ibid.,* 10/83, p. 48 sq.

25. See Tang Mingxi, in JJYJ, 12/83, pp. 42–47; see also Du Runsheng in RMRB, 7 March 1983, Zhang Yunqian, in NYJJWT, 1/84, pp. 18–21.

26. See Wu Xiang in NYJJWT, 2/83, pp. 3–10; Shi Jingtang, *ibid.,* 4/83, pp. 22–27; Jin Yao and *ibid.,* 10/83, pp. 31–34.

27. According to the process of their formation, the Chinese authorities distinguish the specialized families "by contract" (*chengbao*) from the "autonomous" ones (*ziying*). Following their degree of specialization and their rate of commercialization, another distinction is made between "key families" (*Zhongdian hu*) and "specialized families" (*zhuanye hu*). See definitions in RMRB, 14 June 1982, 25 August 1982.

28. Examples and analysis in NYJJWT, 2/83, pp. 40–46 (Shaanxi), *Ibid.,* 7/83, pp. 8–13 (Shanxi).

29. Concrete examples, with scales of production and revenues, have been published in the Chinese media, see RMRB, 1 Aug. 1982 (hens and chicken), 17 Aug. 1982 (pigs and toufu), 29 Sept. 1982 (oxen), 29 Jan. 1983 (ducks), etc. For a good discussion of diversification in the so-called "specialized households", see Huang Huanzhong NYJJWT, 12/83, pp. 27–31.

30. Examples of cottage industry in Liaoning (clothing) (Radio Liaoning, 3 Oct. 1982, in SWB, FE daily 7151), in Zhejiang, NYJJWT, 10/83, pp. 25–26, and RMRB, 8 Dec. 83 (plastics, cloth mills).

31. Regulations in Xh, 30 Jan. 1983, 26 Feb. 1983, and *New China News Agency* (Abbrev. NCNA), 9 Feb. 1983. The legalization of private commercial activities was

exemplified with the case of Wang Quanjing, see RMRB, 6 Jan. 1983, and editorial, *Ibid.*, 28 Jan. 1983.

32. First detailed description in Zhang Musheng, NYJJWT, 12/81, pp. 9–18 (associations in Jiashan district, Anhui). Other examples in E'Cheng, Hubei, NYJJWT, 9/83, pp. 11–14. For a general discussion see also Wang Guihuan, NYJJWT, 4/82, pp. 17–19.

33. Example of a small mechanics' enterprise in Pingyao district, Shanxi, RMRB, 8 Jan. 1983.

34. See this reform in Wangdu district, Hebei, report of Chen Jiliang in *Caimao Jingji* (Financial et Commercial Economy), 2/83, pp. 57–58; see also Zuo Mu and Wu Rong on Jiangdu district, Jiangsu, *Ibid.*, 4/83, pp. 41–45.

35. See for dairy-work in Heilongjiang, RMRB, 13 July 1983, for fisheries in Guangdong, RMRB, 20 July 1983, etc. For a general analysis of this form of joint management, see Zhang Xisheng in NYJJWT, 10/83, pp. 35–38.

36. Reform of the administrative system of the "popular communes", in *Nongeun Gongzuo Tongxun* (Rural work Bulletin, abbrev. NCGZTX), 4/84, pp. 8–10; *Ibid.*, 5/82, pp. 6–9. In October 1983, 12,786 "xiang governments had been already established in place of former "communes" (accounting for 20 percent of the total number of communes), see *Jingji Ribao* (Economic Daily, 26 Oct. 1983. Description of new specialized companies in the administration of communes, in NYJJWT, 6/83, pp. 9–13 (examples in Yichun district, Jiangxi).

37. Reform of the credit cooperatives in *Nongcun Jinrong* (Rural Finance) (abbrev. NCJR), 2/84, pp. 20–21 (example in Xiajiang district, Jiangxi). For general policy of rural finance, see *Zhongguo Jinrong* (Finance in China) (abbrev. ZGJR), 2/84, pp. 21–26. Agricultural loans to communes and brigades in 1982 were 3.5 billion *yuan*, to individuals 4.4 billion *yuan*, see TJNJ, 1983, p. 451.

38. Derived from NYNJ 1980 (p. 99 = 315.6 million t. grain, in 1978). TJNJ 1983 and statistical communique in NCNA, 29 April 1984.

39. TJNJ, 1983, pp. 171–172, 180.

40. TJNJ, 1983, p. 397.

41. NCNA, 30 Jan. 1984.

42. New sample methods described in Huang Liangwen and Wu Guopei, *Zhongguo Jingji Wenti* (Economic Problems in China), 1/84, pp. 56–62. See also concrete problems of sampling described by Wu Bofu in *Tongji* (Statistics), 3/84, pp. 23–24.

43. See NCNA, 22, 24 Nov. 1983.

44. See RMRB, 14 Dec. 1983, NCNA, 25 Jan. 1984, 29 April 1984.

45. TJNJ, 1986, p. 370.

46. TJNJ, 1983, p. 393.

47. Deduced from TJNJ, 1983, pp. 478–481.

48. *Ibid.*, p. 460.

49. Deduced from *Beijing Ribao* (Beijing Daily), 21 March 1982 and previous communiques of Finance Ministry.

50. Li Bingkun in Gongnongye Chanbin Jiage Qiandao Cha Wenti (Problems of Price Scissors between Industrial and agricultural Products), Peking, 1981, p. 50, estimates this transfer at 33.5 billions yuan for 1977. Using slightly different bases of calculation, Chen Jialiang in *Lun Caizheng Fenpei yu Jingji de Guanxi* (Relations between Financial Distribution and Economy), Peking, Chinese Association for Finance Science, 1981, pp. 102–127, estimates this transfer at 22.8 percent of budgetary revenues in 1978, i.e., about 25.6 billion yuan. All these estimates, based on differences between prices and "values" (material costs plus value added, with the social value

of one industrial work-day equivalent to about three agricultural ones . . .), are quite hypothetical. However the overevaluation of industrial prices compared to agricultural ones is beyond question.

51. TJNJ, 1983, p. 499, and NCNA, 29 April 1984.

52. See Zhan Wu, in NYJJWT, 8/80, p. 4.

53. TJNJ, 1983, pp. 367-379.

54. See NCNA, 20 Dec. 1981, 22 Dec. 1983, 14 Feb. 1984, and RMRB, 17 Sept. 1981.

55. TJNJ, 1983, p. 451, and XH, 1 Feb. 1984.

56. Representative of a pessimistic point of view on the "responsibility systems", see SINHA (Radha), "Le systeme de responsabilite de la production en Chine—ou la boite de Pandore", in *Reforme Agraire*, FAO, 1983, pp. 43-57. On the other hand, for a balanced and well informed analysis on the same subject, see Andrew Watson, "Agriculture looks for 'shoes that fit': The production responsibility system and its implications", in *World Development* (8) 1983, pp. 705-730.

57. See editorial, RMRB, 8 May 1983, and investigation at Jinhua, Zhejiang, in RMRB, 15 Aug. 1983.

58. See document No. 1 (1984) of the Central Committee of Chinese Communist Party, RMRB, 4 Feb. 1984, and XH, 11 June 1984.

59. Personal observations, trip report October 1981, and interview of Odile Pierquin, in *Aujourd'hui la Chine,* avril 1984, pp. 18 sq.

60. See Chen Zhiqiang and Tan Taifang in RMRB, 14 July 1983, Chen Fuchu in NCGZTX, 9/83, pp. 36-37 (investigation in Hunan).

61. See BYT (6), March 1982, p. 43, for previous formulae.

62. See NCNA, 27 Jan. 1984.

63. See NYJJWT, 6/81, p. 12, *Ibid.*, 1/82, p. 34.

64. See NYJJWT, 9/81, pp. 42-44, and RMRB, 22 Aug. 1983.

65. See Tong Zhongtian in NYJJWT, 10/83, pp. 58 sq.

66. Public investment for hydraulic facilities has decreased from 3.5 billions *yuan* in 1979 to 1.8 billion in 1982, and reinvestment of commune and brigade enterprises benefits for farmland infrastructure, from 1.2 billion yuan to 0.7 billion; see TJNJ, 1983, pp. 207, 325.

67. Most of the villages' cadres are now busy on their own plots and only interested by their own business; see RMRB, 9 Feb. 1982.

68. Irrigation fees are sometimes arbitrarily raised, as well as those for electricity, see RMRB, 6 July 1983.

69. Lin Zili has suggested that the payments to the collective, stipulated by the contracts, should be modulated in order to equalize the "standard revenues" of every agricultural worker, see RMRB, 16 Feb. 1983.

70. At Fuxin village, a farmer raises 1310 ducks; the sale of 750 ducks and of 5500 kg eggs yields a net profit of 6328 *yuan*. At Shucai village, two fellows contract a pond of about 1 ha for fish-breeding; with 500,000 fry, the expected (net) benefit is of 8500 *yuan*. A former medical orderly, returned to the Shuigui village, raises 100 fat pigs and expects a net profit of 4000 *yuan*. . . . See *Jingji Guanli* (Economic Management), 1/83, pp. 54-56 (investigation at Liuyang district, Hunan).

71. See Zhan Wu, Liu Wenbu, Zhang Houyi, in RMRB, 15 Aug. 1983, see also editorial of RMRB, 29 March 1984.

72. See RMRB, 14 Dec. 1983. Of these 24 millions households, there would be about 6 millions stock-breeders and 3 millions fish-breeders (but the definitions of these households lack clarity); see NCNA, 25 Nov. 1983, 4 Jan. 1984.

73. Personal estimation. Official sources give the round figure of 50 million t. of feed-grain, see RMRB, 16/4/83.

74. See regulations for specialized households in Anhui province, Radio Anhui, 3 June 1983, in SWB, FE daily 7353.

75. In Yangxin district (Hubei), 6 percent of families cultivate 10 percent of the agricultural surface and sell 40 percent of the procurement quota of the whole district, see Fang Jianzhong in NYJJWT, 8/83, pp. 48 sq. See also NYJJWT, 9/83, pp. 3–7 (investigation of Lin Zili and Tao Haisu, in Yanbei region, Shanxi). For preferential treatment of grain specialized households in Heilongjiang, see ZGJR, 2/84, pp. 27–28.

76. XH, 29 Jan. 1984. The Chinese media usually emphasize the progress achieved in the 241 poorer districts of China (50 *yuan* of collective revenue per head in 1978, more than doubled now . . .), see RMRB, 9 Aug. 1982.

77. In a sample of 50 specialized households in Xianyang and Chang'an (Shaanxi), 37 family heads are members of the Party or local cadres, see NYJJWT, 2/83, pp. 40–46.

78. The Chinese media regularly expose local cadres' abuses, resulting in heavy "charges" (*tanpai*) on their fellow villagers. The official policy is that the payments to the collective stipulated by the contract should be approximately 10 percent of the agricultural gross revenue of the families. The real amount is often the double of that figure, as cadres unnecessarily inflate collective funds (1/3 of the payments) and raise unduly their own subsidies (1/4 of the payments); see investigation in Shanxi, NYJJWT, 12/83, pp. 47–52; see also particular scandalous cases in RMRB 11 July 1983 (Mianyang, Hubei), 26 July 1983 (unwarranted fines).

79. See preferential investment in the rich areas of the "commercial grain bases", in 50 districts of 8 provinces (Liaoning, Jilin, Heilong-jiang, Jiangsu, Hubei, Jiangxi), in NCNA, 29 Dec. 1983, XH, 14 April 1984.

80. See forced sale of treasury bonds in rural areas, *Caizheng* (Finance), 10/83, p. 18.

81. TJNJ, 1983, pp. 445, 450.

82. Deduced from TJNJ, 1983, pp. 323 sq.

83. Joseph S. Berliner, "Managing the USSR economy: alternative models", in *Problems of Communism*, Jan-Feb. 1983, pp. 40–56.

84. See John S. Aird, "The preliminary results of China's 1982 census", in *China Quarterly*, Dec. 1983, pp. 613–640. The apparent natural increase rate was then 1.064 percent in 1980 and . . . 1.455 percent in 1981 (*Ibid.*, pp. 622–623).

85. Mass sterilizations campaign in Guandong, with quota assigned locally, see Radio Hainan, 25 May 1983, 16 Sept. 1983, Radio Guangdong, 29 June 1983, 8 Aug. 1983, 8 Oct. 1983 (in SWB, FE daily, 7374, 7444, 7380, 7419, 7463).

86. See our "Temps de travaux agricoles et sous-emploi dans les campagnes chinoises", Rapport d'enquete, Paris, INRA, October 1981.

87. See Zheng Zonghan in SSC, (4), 1983, pp. 164–190; Zhao Changzhi and Xue Fong in NYJJWT, 7/83, pp. 32, 35 (invest. in Jiangdu, Jiangsu); Yang Chenggang in *Renkou Yanjiu* (Population Research), 5/83, pp. 22–25.

88. Interview of Odile PIERQUIN, in *Aujourd'hui la Chine*, April 1984, p. 20.

89. A very common form of this "second economy" in rural areas is the embezzlement of chemical fertilizers by cadres of related departments who resell them, at high prices, on the black market. See letters of protest in RMRB, 29 Sept.

1982, 4 May 1983, 23 May 1983, and in-depth report by Wang Tai, Wu Si, Zhao Xiaohua in *Zhongguo Nongmin Bao* (China's Peasants Journal), 26 July 1983 (republished RMRB, 11 Aug. 1983).

90. See reports of Helene *CARRERE D'ENCAUSSE* and Marie-Claire *BERGERE* at CEPII meeting, 20 April 1984, Paris.

20

Specific Aspects of the Collectivization of Wet-Rice Cultivation: Vietnamese Experience

Adam Fforde

Introduction

This work forms part of an attempt to provide a wider perspective on the difficulties encountered in implementing agrarian policies in North Vietnam. The author's previous research has taken a detailed look at the political economy surrounding these issues, attempting to take explicit account of the complicated interactions between local incentive structures, the balance between collective and 'own-account' activities of cooperators, and the implications for the local power structure of the 'reform' strategies adopted by teams of outside experts in some cooperatives.[1] This approach was, in its basic assumptions and direction, far from being premised upon a 'technological determinism'. Yet the recent article by Francesca Bray (Bray, 1984) provokes a reexamination of the explanatory weight of the particular production conditions of wet-rice cultivation, and, specifically, the overall economic profitability (in the wider, non-pecuniary, sense) of large-scale collective production units in wet-rice growing areas. Such arguments are far from convincing: technology is a man-made creation, and its introduction the result of human decisions. Yet, although present day rice varieties are the result of many centuries of genetic engineering by humans and that the choice of rice as an object for that effort is a result of specific human needs, its innate qualities are part of the constraints presented by nature. The present work, therefore, should be taken as the author's reflections on the nature of those constraints and how they operated in the Vietnamese context, rather than an argument that in all circumstances and under all conditions, wet-rice cultivation is unsuited to large-scale organization. The experiences of Louisiana, Australia and the Camargue show that that is simply not the case.

298

A detailed examination of the institutional and incentive structures within which peasants in North Vietnamese cooperatives operated during the 1970s may be found elsewhere (Fforde, 1982; for a summary of the main results see Fforde, 1984b). The dominant ideology of the Communist leadership was, of course, Marxism-Leninism. This differed from Neo-Confucianism in that it was explicitly committed to economic and social advance; output had to grow, and the country had to be industrialised. In sharp distinction to the French colonial government, the leadership believed that this economic development should be based upon Vietnamese national independence. Thirty years of war had shown the commitment of the Communist leadership to both the nationalist and the socialist aspects of the Vietnamese socialist revolution.

From a comparative perspective, Vietnamese experiences with agricultural producer cooperatives appear highly conditioned by a number of inter-related factors. Among these the following seem to be of particular interest:

- The specific technical conditions of wet-rice cultivation both in the sense of supply conditions in the short-run, and in the sense of the changes possible during economic development.
- The historical familiarity of the Vietmanese peasantry with centralised nation-states.
- The particular circumstances of the post-World War II period: the two 'Resistance Wars' against the French (1946–54) and the United States backed Saigon government (ca. 1959–75).

Wet-Rice Cultivation from a
Northwest European Perspective

Francesca Bray (1984) provides an accessible and thought-provoking discussion of the different technical conditions under which northwest European and wet-rice based societies have tended to develop. To quote:

> The historical examples cited demonstrate that the dynamic underlying the development of the forces of production in wet-rice societies is very different from that manifest in the European transition from feudalism to capitalism. The model of technological progress accepted as generally valid is directly derived from the European experience; it postulates the superior efficiency of large units of production, culminating in the rationality of modern capitalism. (pp. 26–27)

In northwestern Europe the tendency for land-labor ratios to decline paralleled the profound and complicated changes in the pattern of property relations involved in the transition from feudalism to capitalism.

But, as Bray repeatedly points out, this pattern is not obviously of universal validity. To the degree that collectivisation policies are propagated as an attempt to reap the economic benefits of increased scale in European grain cultivation without the presumed political (and other) costs involved in land-concentration under some form of private property, then how can such policies be made effective in areas where such economic benefits are much reduced? A detailed examination of the changing technical aspects of wet-rice cultivation leads her to the conclusion that:

> . . . in wet-rice societies there is little trend towards the consolidation of holdings and the polarisation of rural society into managerial farmers and landless laborers. Units of management remain small, and the producers are not separated from control of the means of production. (p. 13)

It should perhaps be emphasised that her argument is not one of technological determinism, but, on the contrary, it stresses the importance of the social relations that accompany different methods of production. Crucially, increases in wet-rice output appear not to be accompanied by strictly economic pressures to increase the size of the production unit.[2] Adequate, in some sense, gains may be obtained from small-scale producers. And even if there are substantial increases in the degree of commercialisation of rice-farming, these do not appear to have resulted in capitalist production relations. Thus Bray writes, "We do not find the polarisation of rural society into large farmer-operators and landless wage-labourers . . ." (p.23).

Such arguments obviously have profound implications for the economic and political rationales behind attempts to introduce large-scale producer cooperatives into wet-rice cultivation in the Far East. The Vietnamese have argued for a long time that one fundamental aspect of their Revolution was that the transition from colonialism and 'feudalism' to socialism would take place without the country having to go through a capitalist stage. Collectivization provided a means for meeting that aim. The basic point here is that the supply response of wet-rice cultivation to the increased provision of inputs and the availability of a wider range of techniques typically could not be improved by an increase in the size of production unit, and, furthermore, would not be inhibited by the perpetuation of small-scale family production on plots of a size comparable to those of traditional rural organization.

The Vietnamese Historical Experience

The present author has discussed elsewhere the development of Vietnamese agriculture from the early 19th century to the start of collectivisation in the late 1950s (Fforde, 1983). Here it is important to appreciate the overall pattern of demographic growth as well as a number of other factors in the Vietnamese historical experience.

From at least the middle of the present millenium the Vietnamese 'heartland', the North (*mien bac*) or Tonkin, was an area of population saturation. Based upon wet-rice cultivation, the area supported a relatively homogeneous ethnic grouping that possessed a centralised nation-state operating according to established neo-Confucian principles (Woodside, 1971). Some form of long-run demographic equilibrium was maintained by the existence of an open border to the south. This process, the so-called 'March to the South', remains unfinished.[3]

The Vietnamese nation-state existed in competition with other states, most importantly China to the north, and the Cham and Khmer kingdoms to the south. The primary hydrological functions of social organization were two: first, the maintenance of the vital dykes around the Red River, which prevented floods; second, the management of local water-works that concentrated upon moving relatively small volumes of water over comparatively short distances (Chassigneux, 1912). There was very little evidence, in the North, of the sophisticated centralized control of water supply shown, for instance, by the Khmer. The activities of the State were correspondingly limited, requiring from its citizens taxes, corvee labour and military service.

The basic unit of rural life, the commune (*xa*), was corporately responsible for meeting these obligations. To this end, it was obliged to maintain records of its membership and land holdings. Because of its practical autonomy, however, these records were only one element in the negotiations over taxes etc, and did not therefore reveal the true situation. Communes did, however, keep their own record of land holdings. In addition, they established the important roll of the full members of the commune, (those whom the French called the *inscrits* (*noi tich*), who enjoyed access to various privileges. Others, whose names were not inscribed on the communal rolls (*ngoai tich*) had typically to live in the commune for three generations before attaining 'insider' status.

The formal head of the commune was chosen by the commune's leaders, so that the state had no agent of its own inside the commune. This man, known as the 'mayor' (*ly truong*), had responsibility for direct relations with the state. In recognition of the importance of controlling this interface, he was typically a young man who could be dominated by the "powers that be" in the commune. The importance attached to the role of the interface between the state and local interests still has strong echoes in present-day behaviour (Fforde, 1982, esp. pp. 288–291).

The commune was the focus for complicated local status rituals and also provided the basis for religious activities that were often explicitly nationalistic. In addition, it provided institutional insurance for individuals against two major areas of risk. These were, first, the impact of the unpredictable variation in precipitation and other natural phenomena; second, the unpredictable variation in family labor supplies. The basic units of the commune were families (*ho*) not much bigger than the typical modern Western nuclear family. These were usually organized geographically, into hamlets or villages. It has often been pointed out that the Vietnamese equivalent of the kin-based clan of South China was the administrative-geographical unit, whether at hamlet, village or commune level. It could be argued that this helped to increase the potential for political manoeuvering by increasing the alliance possibilities within the commune because the inherently unalterable links of kinship were less important.

Most peasants had some form of direct access to land, which was farmed either as private land (*tu dien*) or communal land (*cong dien*).[4] In principle, the commune's council of notables (*hoi dong ky muc*) had responsibility for the allocation of the communal land to those in need. This land took up around perhaps a quarter of the total acreage in the 19th century, and in some communes was far more extensive. It was an important check upon land concentration, since its presence ensured that the largest landholder in the commune was the corporate council of notables. The council was made up of the leading male members of the commune, who were not typically or necessarily the largest holders of private land. The commune tended to run its own affairs, without any functioning national system of property-rights in land. French investigators in the early part of this century found that local property rights were frequently strong enough to prevent those who were not members of the commune from buying land within it (Fforde, 1983, p. 51 et. seq.). As an institution, the commune was viewed by the court as a support to the status quo. Land concentration was therefore discouraged by officials, although not always with complete success. Too much should not be read into such court problems. During the early 19th century the situation was complicated by the need for the newly-established Nguyen dynasty to reinforce its authority over a country that had only recently been re-united after decades of civil war.

During the period of French colonial rule this relative balance of interests was disturbed. Higher and monetized taxes forced peasants to borrow funds from their patrons in the communes. In the absence of resources with which to increase commodity output this was the only way in which average producers in wet-rice areas facing demographic saturation could obtain the necessary funds (labor demand from the French plantations, mines and elsewhere was extremely limited). Thus the 1930s saw a process of land-loss familiar from elsewhere (Scott, 1976; Popkin, 1979), and gathering unrest in rural areas. In addition, there was a rapid increase in population, the origins of which are not fully understood. The lack of institutional support for families who were short of land or labor (e.g., a childless old couple) ran quite contrary to traditional sentiments.

These extremely unpopular trends were abruptly halted by the advent of the nationalist Vietminh administration in rural areas in the late 1940s and early 1950s. Indeed, it is extremely interesting to note that the larger proportion of all land re-allocated during the period 1945–56 was in fact given out in the period before the start of Land Reform proper in 1953. The nationalist movement appears to have responded to more traditional sentiments about the correct social role of local institutions, enforcing, inter alia, a more acceptable distribution of the communal lands. But, despite this, the Vietminh placed a radical emphasis upon opposing traditionalism in many other areas, for instance that of the role of women (Tran Nhu Trang, 1972).

Perhaps it would not be too far from the truth to suggest that, throughout the past few centuries, Vietnamese peasant families have expected their communes to provide an umbrella against the demands of the State for taxes, corvee and military recruits. In addition, local institutions were seen as a natural focus for the status rituals of everyday life, and a cushion against the vicissitudes of nature, both in the guise of bad weather and in the lottery of childbearing. This, then, would be their basic historical experience.[5]

Resistance War
and Socio-economic Development

Unlike the neo-Confucian dynasties and the French colonialists, the post-1954 government of North Vietnam (the Democratic Republic of Vietnam, or DRV) presented itself as a dynamic agent of progress and social change. Taxes were now not simply for the financing of administration, but, along with the other elements of state procurement, an integral part of the Vietnamese socialist revolution.

During the 1950s the DRV constructed the familiar apparatus of government in communist countries: state control over industry and trade coupled with a political hegemony based upon a Leninist Party and 'Front' organizations. In agriculture, cooperativization occurred in 1959-60. It appears that coercion was generally absent, and the rapid movement of peasants into 'lower-level' producer cooperatives resulted from perceptions of the balance of material benefits and costs (c.f. Wadekin, 1982, pp. 36–7). The steady trends from then until the late 1970s were for, first, a transition from 'lower-level' to 'higher-level' cooperatives (this was largely completed by the late 1960s) and, second, an amalgamation of cooperatives. Whereas the earliest coopertives were well below commune level, with an average membership of about 50 families, by the late 1970s the clear target was to have cooperatives coterminous with communes. By that time a typical commune would possess around 250–350 ha of wet-rice land and about 5,000 families. Agriculture remained dominated by rice mono-culture. Such strikingly high population densities were permitted by the adoption of double rice-cropping and the growing of a third crop of non-rice staples where and when possible.

At this time there still existed within the communes underlying territorial units that apparently played important social roles. These were the village (*thon* or *lang*) and the sub-village hamlet (*xom*). Amalgamation of cooperatives to commune level would often be from cooperatives at village level. The earliest cooperatives of the 1960s were apparently often based upon hamlets, which re-appeared within the commune-level cooperatives as the basis for the production brigades. Such cleavages, along with others based upon functional differences among brigades within the cooperative, provided the basis for conflicts within local rural society as higher authorities attempted to enforce official policies governing the way in which cooperatives should be managed. A vital ingredient of such conflicts was the balance of incentives acting upon cooperators when they allocated resources, most importantly their labor, between the collective and the so-called 'outside' economy, of which the legal so-called "5 percent land" given to them as private plots was an essential part.

During the very early 1960s state procurement prices were at times above those on the free market (the following is based upon Fforde, 1982, Ch. 2, and Fforde and Paine, forthcoming). Because of the extremely low level of industrialization achieved under the French, and because export-crop areas were largely in the South, this period saw a process of industrialization that was dependent upon aid-financed imports of means of production.

By the early years of the First Five Year Plan (1961–1965) familiar macro-economic problems resulting, inter alia, from the effects upon the overall balance of economic activity of the increases in state employment, the delays in increasing budgetary receipts and the lags in raising agricultural producer prices had their predictable results: free market food prices started to rise. In the absence of strict administrative controls, this led to an increase in the volume of sales by peasants on the free market, exacerbating the problems faced by policymakers in maintaining some form of macro economic balance.

For the next two decades such problems arising from the dynamic tension between the socialist and 'outside' economies would persist. But whereas the food "crisis" of the first five year plan saw de facto recognition of the role of the free market for food, it was not until 1967–68 that argument about the role of collective production per se in the Vietnamese revolution came to the surface. American bombing from 1965 onward both rapidly ran out of real targets and, by prompting increased assistance from other socialist countries, was somewhat self-defeating. It was estimated in 1968 that per head expenditure in the DRV had probably showed a net increase since the start of the bombing.[6] But it appears from official DRV data that aggregate food supplies per head were being pushed dangerously near subsistence by the late 1960s, so that by the end of the decade the area had become a food deficit region, dependent upon substantial food imports.

Despite, or perhaps because of, the food crisis of 1968–9 and its resolution by a shift to dependency on food imports, these years saw the central authorities reaffirm the need for collective production, and attempt to enforce collective organizational control over all the 95 percent of the collective acreage outside the 5 percent land. Despite the general evidence that substantial output gains were only forthcoming in exceptional conditions, primarily the provision of substantial supplies of industrial means of production which were by definition not available for all, the Vietnamese leadership did not abandon collective agriculture's important position within the overall frame-work of the Vietnamese socialist revolution. In practice, however, there arose in probably the great majority of cooperatives a balance between the superior economic attraction of own-account on outside activities and the need to have some form of collective production in order to avoid pressure from above.

Fforde (1982) examined a number of agricultural producer cooperatives in the North during the mid 1970s. The Thai Binh conference of August 1974 (Fforde, 1982, p. 134) had reaffirmed the central authorities' position. The correct way of organizing a cooperative was essentially collectivist, based upon Taylorist principles of the division of labour-processes into finite and supervisable steps (*khau*). The Management Committee of the cooperative was to control all activity within it, including distribution, and was to play a dynamic role in the development of production and the mobilization of economic surpluses outside the cooperative. In practice, however, the great majority of Management Committees were largely powerless; collective economic activity, if it occurred, was controlled by the brigades.

An important element of the so-called New Management System (NMS) presented at the Thai Binh conference was the attempt to increase the extent of the division of labour inside the cooperative by the use of specialized brigades. In the majority of cooperatives, where the cooperative itself had a largely nominal existence, such collective activity as occurred was under the control of the unspecialized rice-growing production brigades (*doi*). These had very strong usufruct to land they regarded as theirs. The pattern of landholdings appears to have been based upon the land-holdings of brigade members after the various land reallocations preceding cooperativization. It was therefore scattered, with 'near land, far land, good land, bad land' (*dat gan dat xa, dat tot dat xau*). Membership was typically based upon the constituent hamlets of the commune. In addition, brigades often had their own drying yards and other means of production. Even such a nominalized cooperative retained distributional functions, however, acting as the tax and procurement unit and as the conduit for any deliveries of consumer goods and means of production from the state. Such brigades therefore tended to use the cooperative as a manipulable interface between themselves and the state.

There is comparatively abundant evidence of the various conflicts induced by attempts to implement the prescribed management system (the NMS) into such cooperatives. The basic framework for local power struggles was derived from the three-sided set of relationships between the Management Committee of the cooperative, the production brigades, and the peasant families. The balance between collective and own-account activity tended to be set at a level where the risk of high-level intervention to end excess encroachment upon the cooperative's land offset the apparent gains from an increase in own-account activity. Thus the production brigades benefitted from the need to keep the nominalized cooperative as a protective intermediary between local interests and the State.

An incoming reform team would naturally base itself upon the Management Committee of the cooperative, and set about trying to implement the cooperative's rights to control production and distribution. Attempts to end irrational scattering of lands were usually resisted, as were attempts to unify the value of the work-point between brigades: both were seen as an attack upon brigade property. At the same time cooperators' own-account activities were more tightly controlled, with increases in labour-duties, obligatory supplies of pigs from the private herd, etc. At root, the widespread resistance to such technocratic groups derived from their disturbance of the local power balance. The previous implicit agreement between local cadres and cooperators typically tolerated excess own-account activity in return for behaviour on the part of the cooperators that was in the cadres' interests. This balance was disturbed by such impositions upon the cooperators as increased collective labour norms and a reduction in the permitted acreage of land farmed on their own account. Unless such efforts were supported by substantial deliveries of goods from above they had little chance of success.

The specialized production brigades, designed to curb the production autarky of the rice-growing brigades, had considerable difficulties obtaining resources. For instance, a major issue was the establishment of centralized collective pig herds. These were intended to produce pigs for export and manure for the cooperative's rice fields. In practice, they had problems obtaining piglets from the cooperators, and had often to expand vertically (e.g. by growing their own vegetables) in order to obtain feedstuffs. The specialized brigade or team responsible for the collective pig herd then usually found itself using the manure on its own fields to grow feed for its pigs. Competition for resources usually had to be solved by administrative measures such as the use of directives from the organs of the cooperative, since the balance of economic incentives was adverse.

In some cooperatives it was possible to observe apparently efficient collective activity along lines quite close to those prescribed by the central authorities. Here a possible explanation, in the absence of favourable resource endowments, was the presence of highly effective leadership that could override the problems of supervision and contract assurance involved in the use of collective methods of labor organization in such circumstances. In such cooperatives output benefitted from extensive direct accumulation in local waterworks and land levelling. This eased the introduction of new seed varieties, which, unfortunately, also tended to require additional inputs of fertilizer. Which usually were not available.

By the late 1970s it was clear that collectivized agriculture was performing well below expectations. Chronic dependency upon food imports was continuing, albeit to some extent as a result of bad weather. The 6th Plenum of August 1979 revealed a deep change in the policy atmosphere. Idle land belonging to cooperatives, it was said, could now be farmed by agents other than the cooperative itself. Among the list of such agents appeared the cooperators themselves, and from the winter of 1979–80 it was widely reported in the official media that peasants were enthusiastically responding to the spirit of the 6th plenum. During 1980 there was a striking public debate about the content of the new system, and by the autumn it was being presented as dependent upon the so-called output contracts (*khoan san—pham*) signed between cooperators and the cooperative. These effectively gave an area of land to the former in return for a fixed delivery of output to the cooperative. Collective control was maintained by the stipulation that certain parts of the production process (water supply, pest control, etc.) should be the responsibility of the cooperative. The rest, including most importantly the harvest, were to be carried out by the cooperator.

In the North agricultural output and state procurement rose in the early 1980s but subsequently appears to have stagnated. The relationship between this success and the changes induced by the 6th Plenum is, however, complicated. To begin with, it seems most appropriate to interpret the new policy as a somewhat ex post rationalization of events. There does not seem to have been a clear attempt on the part of the central authorities to respond to perceived economic difficulties by the introduction of a considered package of policy measures. The 6th Plenum appears more to have been a shift, albeit a major one, in the balance between the pressure from the centre for certain methods of economic organization in the rural periphery, and the various local interests' receptiveness to the attractions of own-account activity, the free market, the desire to avoid outside intervention and, above all, the economic possibilities of the various production methods on offer. Thus it is of great interest to observe Prime Minister Pham van Dong's visit to a district near Hai Phong in 1980. There a cooperative which was a model for the adoption of the new system was praised for having used the system secretly (*chui*) since 1972.[7]

An additional element is the effects of the 6th Plenum's emphasis upon mutually beneficial exchange on procurement policy, especially in the then still largely uncollectivized South. After 1980 some southern provinces showed themselves capable of delivering volumes of paddy to the state that exceeded the total obtained from the North in some years before 1975.

The outlook for Vietnamese agriculture remains crucially dependent upon the availability of inputs and the maintenance of a certain institutional flexibility. While the latter to some extent merely reflects past practice, the former will be determined by the development of such important sectors as industry, the area devoted to export crops such as tea, rubber and coffee and the export potential of Vietnamese light industry. These cannot be discussed here.

Conclusions

Three main conclusions can be drawn from the above discussion.

- The endogeneity of institutional content. The meaning and real functions of Vietnamese cooperatives were never determined entirely by elements outside the communes. Local interests were reflected in the extent to which cooperatives had any real meaning, and in the complicated balances and interactions between the so-called private and collective sectors.
- In such a system, the role of purely market relations is while marked, quite limited. Prices, or shadow prices, appear to be inadequate carriers of information in determining economic behaviour. Access to markets was itself endogenous, perhaps to be obtained by increasing the collective acreage in order to avoid outside interference. How should such a calculation be entered into some utilitarian calculus? This suggests that considerable care should be exercised when carrying out analysis of such systems, for the particular basis of individual decisions may not easily be open to direct observation.

- In the final analysis, basic economic and production conditions were of considerable importance. The problem here is that the effects of the relative inapplicability of large-scale production units to wet-rice cultivation acted parallel to those of the relative material disincentives for cooperators to participate in forms of collective activity. In some cases, both could apparently be overcome, either by exceptional leadership or by exceptional resource allocation. But in general it was true that most cooperators tended to avoid collective economic activity.

The basic problem with the above analysis is that, while collectivization was in practice reinterpreted by peasant actions in ways quite contrary to Party prescriptions, and that this was largely the result of peasants' beliefs that it was in their own interests to do so, this does not necessarily demonstrate the economic advantages of small-scale production. But this is what one should expect. Production is not carried out in a vacuum, with a neutral technology adopted on the basis of parametric prices and immutable institutions. Nevertheless, it is perhaps possible to conclude that, to the extent that wet-rice does have certain innate qualities, these were not sufficient to override the other elements in the equation.

Notes

Apart from stimulating discussion amongst participants at the conference, I owe thanks to Fiona Atkins, Tony Addison, Karl-Eugen Waedekin, Christine White and Francesca Bray for their comments on an earlier draft of this paper. Any remaining mistakes are, of course, my own responsibility.

1. A.J. Fforde (1982) bases itself upon a collection of both unpublished and published North Vietnamese studies of individual cooperatives collected during the author's stay at Hanoi University in 1978/79. The work is currently being revised for publication. A formal statement of the intended structure of agricultural producer cooperatives can be found in A. J. Fforde and a summary of the main elements of Fforde (1982) in Fforde (1984a). See also Vickerman (1984) for an analysis of agrarian change over a similar period based largely upon aggregate data. Studies of Vietnamese collective agriculture remain in their infancy. Research based upon detailed interviews (e.g. after the pattern of Parish and Whyte, 1978) has not yet been carried out.

2. The rapid summary presented here ignores the important difference between increases in land yields and increases in total output. Bray deals with this, emphasizing the tendency for wet-rice areas to arrive at situations of demographic saturation where the ability of additional labor inputs to provide further increases in land yields provides an important source of subsistence for the large population.

3. The Southern provinces in the Mekong delta carry approximately the same population as those of the North on around twice the cultivable acreage. Attempts to resettle large numbers since 1975 have, however, not been particularly successful.

4. The real meaning of such terms is highly debatable. Such issues are discussed in Fforde (1984a), passim.

5. The author does not wish to suggest that this experience was uniquely Vietnamese. Indeed, strong echoes from a quite different area and time can be found in the

analysis presented by Goran Hyden of the response of peasants in Tanzania to the Ujamaa policy and its subsequent difficulties (Hyden, 1980, passim).

6. See the Report of the Systems Analysis Group published in the *Pentagon Papers*, Gravel Edition, Vol. IV, pp. 225–7.

7. *Dai Doan Ket*, Hanoi, reprinted in *Doan Ket*, Paris, 18/4/1981. For a deeper discussion of policy debates in Vietnam see White (1982).

References

Francesca Bray, "Patterns of Evolution in Rice-growing Societies", *Journal of Peasant Studies*, No. 1 (1984).

E. Chassigneux, "L'irrigation dans le delta du Tonkin", *La Geographie*, 1912.

A. J. Fforde, *Problems of Agricultural Development in North Vietnam*, Ph.D. dissertation, Dept. of Economics, Cambridge (1982).

A. J. Fforde, "Law and Socialist Agricultural Development in Vietnam—The Statute for Agricultural Producer Cooperatives", *Review of Socialist Law*, 1984a.

A. J. Fforde, *Coping with the State—Peasant Strategies in North Vietnam*, Birkbeck College, Dept. of Economics, Discussion Paper no. 155, London, 1984b.

A. J. Fforde, *The Historical Background to Agricultural Collectivization in North Vietnam*, Birkbeck College, Dept. of Economics, Discussion Paper no. 148, London, 1983.

A. J. Fforde, with S. H. Paine, *The Limits of National Liberation*, London, forthcoming.

Goran Hyden, *Beyond Ujamaa in Tanzania—The Politics of an Uncaptured Peasantry*, London, 1980.

W. L. Parish and M. K. Whyte, *Village and Family in Contemporary China*, University of Chicago Press, 1978.

S. L. Popkin, *The Rational Peasant*, University of California Press, 1976.

J. C. Scott, *The Moral Economy of the Peasant*, Yale University Press, 1976.

Tran Nhu Trang, *The Transformation of the Peasantry in North Vietnam*, Unpublished Ph.D. dissertation, University of Pittsburgh, 1972.

A. Vickerman, *Agriculture in the DRV—The Fate of the Peasantry Under "Premature Transition to Socialism"*, Unpublished Ph.D. dissertation, Dept. of Economics, Cambridge, 1984.

K. E. Waedekin, *Agrarian Policies in Communist Europe*, London, 1982.

C. P. White, *Vietnam and the Chinese Model: A Comparative Study of Nguyen and Ching Civil Government in the First Half of the 19th Century*, Harvard University Press, 1971.

Allocating Resources to Promote Efficiency and Structural Change in Agriculture

21

Comparative Performance of Agricultural Output, Inputs, and Productivity in Eastern Europe, 1965–83

Gregor Lazarcik

Introduction

In the last eighteen years, the agricultural sectors in most East European countries have made tangible though uneven progress. This has occurred in the context of varying systems of management. In Poland and Yugoslavia, the ownership and management of farms remains overwhelmingly in private hands; less than one-fourth of agricultural land in each country is in state and collective farms. In Hungary, the New Economic Policy, put into effect in agriculture after the 1961–62 collectivization, has provided effective incentives to collective and individual farmers and decentralized management of collective farms. Bulgaria, the German Democratic Republic (GDR), Czechoslovakia, and Romania still operate under tightly centralized economic systems, although partly with private sectors. In recent years, all the East European countries have implemented policies intended to encourage better use of resources and to improve agricultural productivity, and most have explicitly announced incentives to increase output on farmers' personal plots and private farms.

In the following pages, the recent agricultural performance of Eastern Europe, excluding Albania, will be analyzed by country and for the area as a whole. Some comparisons will also be made with the Soviet Union, the Federal Republic of Germany, and the United States, in an attempt to better appraise the performance of recent years.

Agriculture's Role in East European Economies

Until the mid-1960s, agriculture, measured in terms of its share in total employment and its share in the gross national product (GNP), was the largest economic sector in several of the East European countries. Both its employment and GNP shares, however, have been declining steadily in all countries during the entire postwar period, due to rapid industrialization (see Table 21.1). By 1983, in all the East European countries, the share of agricultural labor had declined to below one-third of the total. In Czechoslovakia only 12.6 percent and in the GDR 10.0 percent of total employment remains in agriculture. The share of agriculture's contribution to total GNP also decreased substantially in all countries. It is interesting to note that in 1983 the GNP share of agriculture was larger than that of employment in the total for Czechoslovakia, the GDR, and Hungary.[1] Eastern Europe as a whole has a little less than one-fourth of its labor in agriculture and generates over one-fifth of GNP in agriculture.

Recent Growth of Output and Inputs

The various measures of output and expenses for Eastern Europe as a whole and for individual countries for the 1965–1983 period[2] are given in Tables 21.2 and 21.3. All measures in this study are independent estimates comparable with western agricultural measures.[3]

Official country sources publish on a regular basis measures of gross agricultural production which double-count, all intermediate products used on farms, in farm production.[4] Our agricultural output measures are independently calculated and they exclude the intermediate products. From 1975 to 1983 the greatest increase in agricultural output so measured was achieved by Yugoslavia with an increase of 23 percent, followed by Hungary, Romania, Czechoslovakia, Bulgaria, and the GDR, in descending order. Poland experienced a 3 percent decrease in output. During the period 1965–80, the output of animal products grew at a higher annual rate than output of crops on the average. In the 1970s, all the East European countries have put heavy emphasis on rapid increases in meat, eggs, and milk output in order to improve the quality of national diets. In 1981 and 1982, however, the animal output decreased sharply in the region as a whole due to decreased imports of feed, Bulgaria, Yugoslavia, and Hungary were exceptions.

The most spectacular rises in inputs from other sectors occurred in Bulgaria, with a more than two-fold increase, followed by Yugoslavia, Czechoslovakia, Hungary, Romania, and the GDR, while Poland experienced an actual decrease in inputs from 1975–1983.

Since operating expenses are subtracted from output to get the gross product, and gross product less depreciation to get the net product of agriculture, the higher cost increases in relation to increases in output are reflected in more sluggish rates of growth in gross and net product. In fact, the growth rates of gross and net product of agriculture were negative in Bulgaria and Poland for the 1965–70 and 1975–80 period and for Romania and the GDR for the 1965–70 period. There was a better performance in the 1970–75 and 1980–83 periods for both gross and net products in most countries. The interrelationship of total output, inputs, and gross and net product can be readily followed country by country in Tables 21.2 and 21.3.

Per Head Trends and Levels of Output

In general, the per head trends are similar to the total performance measures except that the rates of change are slowed down by increases in population. However, in the GDR the population declined by 1.9 percent from 1965 to 1983, while in other East European countries it increased to varying degrees which affected the differences in growth rates per head during the period under study. From 1965 to 1983 Hungary, Czechoslovakia, and Romania experienced the highest growth of per head output, 57, 43, and 42 percent respectively, followed by Yugoslavia, the GDR, and Bulgaria with 40, 36, and 26 percent growth respectively, while Poland experienced an increase of only 7 percent. In most countries, output of animal products per head increased at a higher annual rate than that of crops, in line with the effort to improve protein content in national diets.

Table 21.4 shows per head comparisons of levels of output, and gross and net product in agriculture in relation to the East European level, for individual countries in selected periods. These findings show that their level of agricultural output per head was lower in Czechoslovakia, Romania, Yugoslavia, and Poland (1981–83) than the average level for Eastern Europe, while Bulgaria, Hungary, and the German Democratic Republic were significantly above that level. Hungary has been and is the highest per head producer of agricultural output. Bulgaria and Hungary ranked highest in output of crops per head while the GDR, Hungary, and Czechoslovakia excelled in output of animal products.

Productivity of Land and Livestock

In most East European countries, the area of agricultural land[5] remained relatively stable during the period under study. In Czechoslovakia, the GDR, Hungary, Poland, and Yugoslavia, agricultural land declined by two to five percent, while in Bulgaria and Romania it increased by one and seven percent respectively in the same period.[6]

In comparison to Western Europe, per number of persons employed in agriculture per 100 hectares of agricultural land is greater in all the East European countries. By 1983, the number of hectares per person employed in agriculture ranged from 3.7 in Poland to 7.4 in the GDR, with 4.9 hectares the average for all Eastern Europe. Table 21.5 shows the trends of output measures per hectare of agricultural land by country and region. In general, the productivity of land increased in all the countries. However, the economically less developed countries, except Bulgaria, had the larger annual rates of increase because their production per unit of land was low in the earlier postwar years. In all countries the average annual rate of growth of output of animal products per unit of land exceeded that of ouput of crops except in Hungary for 1970–75 and the German Democratic Republic for 1975–80. In 1981–83, however, the animal output decreased in the region due to decrease in feed imports.

Relative levels of productivity of land in relation to the East European average as a base are shown in Table 21.6. Over the postwar period the differences among countries in productivity of land have been reduced, but in 1981–83 they were still very large, and they were greater in the ouput of animal products than in that of crops. In 1981–83, for example, the GDR produced more than three times as much animal products per hectare as either Romania or Yugoslavia, due partly to large feed imports. Levels of animal output were substantially higher in the more industrialized countries.

There have been even larger differences in inputs per hectare among East European countries. Czechoslovakia's and the GDR's levels were over 5 to 6 times as large as Yugoslavia's in 1981–83. The use of non-agricultural inputs per unit of land in the more advanced countries was far higher than in the less advanced countries. Differences in levels of gross and net product per hectare among countries of Eastern Europe were smaller than those of inputs, because those countries with higher output also had higher inputs.

In the last 20 years an effort has been made to improve the productivity of land, and in most of the East European countries yields of major crops have increased substantially. However, in the last eight years the improvement in yields slowed down. Overall, the yields were still substantially below those of the Federal Republic of Germany in 1981–83.

In the postwar period, the yields of meat per pig, milk per cow, and eggs per hen were increasing steadily from low levels. Hungary achieved the highest increases among the East European countries due partly to imports of high yielding breeding stock and of protein feedstuffs from the West. As of 1981–83, the yields per head of livestock remained substantially lower in all East European countries than in the Federal Republic of Germany, though higher yields per hectare and per animal in the Federal Republic are due partly to much greater inputs; thus on a net basis the differences are not as large.

Productivity of Labor in Agriculture

The quality of agricultural labor statistics varies from country to country. The GDR, Czechoslovak, Hungarian, and Polish labor data are more homogeneous, while those for the other East European countries are less standardized, and consequently the quality of labor units is less homogeneous. Concurrently with a steady decline in the agricultural labor force, output per unit of labor in agriculture increased sharply during the postwar period. Table 21.7 summarizes trends in the labor productivity by country and region from 1965 to 1983. Romania, Bulgaria, Hungary, Yugoslavia, and Czechoslovakia had the largest increases in output per unit of labor during this period (between 2 and 3 times); they were followed by the GDR and

Poland. In Eastern Europe as a whole agricultural output per unit of labor doubled from 1965 to 1983. The increases in inputs per worker in agriculture were very impressive in all countries. On the whole the East European growth performance per unit of labor has been impressive. It reflects largely the reduction of extensive disguised agricultural unemployment by transfers of labor to non-agricultural sectors of the economy, permitting better overall use of available labor resources.

Comparative levels of productivity of labor among the different countries in relation to the East European average are shown in Table 21.8. Very large differences in productivity of labor continue to exist among the individual countries. As of 1981–83, the Polish, and Romanian worker still produced only about one-fourth of the GDR output per worker. Czechoslovakia has been the second highest in output per worker, followed by Hungary, Bulgaria, Yugoslavia and Poland, on a rapidly descending scale. The differences in relative levels of inputs per worker have been even greater, because of much higher inputs per worker in more industrialized countries than in the less advanced ones. Relative levels of gross and net product per worker were approximately of the same order of magnitude as in the case of output.

Progress in Agricultural Technology

A widely used indicator of the extent of mechanization is the number of tractors or amount of tractor horsepower per unit of land and per unit of labor. Table 21.9 represents data on the available tractor horsepower per 1,000 hectares of agricultural land and per 1,000 workers in agriculture by country and by major region. Our findings show that in the 1979–82 period the extent of the use of mechanical power was still low, by West European standards, in most of the East European countries. Only Czechoslovakia and the GDR were close to West European levels. However, the level of West European mechanization was, in turn, low in comparison to that of the United States.

Most of the East European countries made rapid progress toward increased use of fertilizers in recent years. Table 21.10 shows that by 1979–82, consumption of fertilizers per unit of land exceeded the West European level in Czechoslovakia, the GDR, and Hungary. Bulgarian and Polish consumption per hectare were getting close to the level of Western Europe, and they were at about the average for Eastern Europe in the same period. The heavily increased application of fertilizers already has paid off with significantly increased yields in Eastern Europe.

The adoption of high-yielding crop varieties and livestock breeds helped to increase yields per unit of input in all the East European countries. Research on improvement of seeds has been stepped up by the agricultural research institutes, partly under the coordination of the CMEA (Council for Mutual Economic Assistance) Permanent Commission on Agriculture. The development of improved breeds of livestock has contributed to increased yields of milk per cow, eggs per hen, higher dressing rates of livestock, leaner types of animals, and higher daily gains in live weight for all livestock. New breeds of livestock are being imported from Western Europe and the United States, especially by Hungary and Yugoslavia.

Irrigation and drainage of agricultural land on a large scale is increasing the productivity of land in all Eastern European countries. The recent development in Eastern Europe of agro-industrial complexes is increasing the labor utilization through local processing of agricultural products, thus employing seasonally idle agricultural labor and diffusing technical knowledge in rural areas.[7]

Combined Factor Productivity in Agriculture

Knowing output, labor input, and estimated non-labor input indexes, we calculated the combined factor productivity in agriculture using a Cobb-Douglas production function.[8] Table 21.11 presents the combined factor productivity for the six East European countries individually and for the whole of Eastern Europe (excluding Romania, for which reliable data were not available) for the period 1965–83. The results show that, in all countries except Poland, combined factor productivity was increasing at a rate of about one percent or more annually, on the average, from 1965 to 1975. In Yugoslavia, however, the average compound rate of growth was over 2 percent while in Poland factor productivity decreased slightly in the same period. In Eastern Europe as a whole, combined factor productivity increased 11 percent between 1965 and 1975. This favorable progress could be explained by the positive effects of several "non-measurable" factors, such as improved technology, more efficient organization of production and better allocation of inputs, and above all, improved personal incentives to farmers via improved prices and incomes, and decentralization of decision making.

From 1975 to 1983, factor productivity increased rapidly only in Yugoslavia, by about 20 percent, while in Bulgaria and Hungary it rose marginally, by about 4 percent. In the other three countries factor productivity decreased noticeably after 1975: in Czechoslovakia by 3 percent, in the GDR by 6 percent, and in Poland by 13 percent. For the region as a whole, there was no improvement in factor productivity in the last eight years. The main reasons for lagging factor productivity were a slowdown in the application of new technology on farms, a sharp decrease in imports of feed and other inputs due to hard currency foreign exchange shortages, increases in the cost of fuel and other inputs, and a certain degree of recentralization in management and a consequent decrease in personal incentives to farmers. Last but not least, the adverse weather conditions in most European countries during the last several years also contributed negatively to factor productivity.

Size Comparisons of Output Between
Eastern Europe, USSR, Western Europe, and USA

In Table 21.12 we summarize our findings as to the comparative size of agricultural output in Eastern Europe, the USSR, Western Europe, the

United States and individual countries for selected periods in terms of international wheat units (totals and per head). The levels of agricultural output per head in terms of this standard indicate that the Soviet Union produced roughly 53 percent and Eastern Europe 61 percent of the output of the United States in the 1981–83 period; this is clearly inadequate if we consider 80 percent of the United States level to be the norm for an industrial society. However, levels of output per head in Eastern Europe in comparison to the Soviet Union were improving in the 1971–1983 period. Among individual countries, the highest level per head was in Hungary (94.2 percent of the US level in 1981-83), followed by Bulgaria (74.6 percent), the GDR (69.8 percent), Czechoslovakia (60.4 percent), Romania (57.5 percent), Yugoslavia (52.7 percent), and finally Poland (52.3 percent). International comparisons of output per head provide better measures of relative self-sufficiency than comparisons of total agricultural output. We may define "self-sufficiency" assuming that the United States level of output per head is about 25 percent above the norm of an adequate food supply.[9] Using this norm, only Hungary would seem to have about 10–15 percent of her output available for export, while providing more than adequate food domestically. All other East European countries would be considered to have 7 to 35 percent deficits in domestic output if they were to maintain roughly 80 percent of the United States norm. Western Europe seems to be the most deficient region in food supply per head, producing a little over one-half as much as the United States. Output levels per head show clearly that the domestic output of food in Eastern Europe and the Soviet Union was below even the reduced US norm by some 23 and 33 percent, respectively, in 1981–83, and this deficiency has been increasing in relation to US output per head since the mid-1970s.

Conclusion

Some tentative conclusions on the recent performance of East European agriculture are as follows:

1. Performance as reflected in our measures has been uneven. Agricultural output in the 1971–75 period grew at an average rate of 3.9 percent for the whole region, or more than double the rate for the previous five years. In 1976–1980, the average rate of growth was only 1.6 percent, and in 1981–83 it was 1.1 percent annually.
2. In gross and net product the best growth results in 1975–80 were achieved in Hungary, Romania, and Yugoslavia, the worst in Bulgaria and Poland. In 1981–83 the best results were obtained in Poland and Yugoslavia.
3. Progress in mechanization of agriculture has been good in Eastern Europe, but its level, except in Czechoslovakia and the GDR, is still signficantly behind that of Western Europe.
4. Considerably greater emphasis has been placed on animal output, in response to increasing demands for products of animal origin. However,

this effort has been slowed since 1980 by sharp decreases of animal feed imports.

5. All the East European governments put a stronger emphasis on increasing agricultural output and the productivity of land, capital, and labor. As a result, combined factor productivity increased in all countries except Poland from 1965 to 1974. Thereafter, factor productivity continued to rise only in Yugoslavia, while stagnating in Bulgaria and Hungary, decreasing in Czechoslovakia, the GDR, and Poland, and making no progress for Eastern Europe as a whole.

6. An international comparison of agricultural outputs shows that Eastern Europe as a whole accounted for about 56 percent as much output as the USSR and about 35 percent as much as the United States in 1981–83; output in the United States was about 60 percent larger than in the Soviet Union. In levels of agricultural output per head of the population, the United States ranks highest, followed by Hungary, Bulgaria, the GDR, Czechoslovakia, Romania, the USSR, Yugoslavia, Poland, and Western Europe, in descending order for 1981–83. These findings do not take into account country specialization or national priorities as to the allocation of resources to competing sectors of production.

With the purported trend toward rational use of resources in Eastern Europe, leaders there, as elsewhere, may want to ponder the influence of systems of management on productivity. Concern with agricultural efficiency has prompted improvements in motivation through higher producer prices, higher profit, more freedom of action, control of resources, and other personal incentives. To emulate the Hungarian success in agriculture, the governments in other East European countries have lately indicated more favorable policies toward private farmers and owners of private plots. They have started to help private farmers directly with incentives to increase output and productivity. It remains to be seen what impact these new policies will have on East European agriculture.

Notes

1. In Czechoslovakia, for example, the average agricultural labor income was 4 percent higher than the average nonagricultural labor income in 1982. (Calculated from *Statisticka rocenka 1982*, pp. 202, 210, 213, 537.)

2. Measures of performance for earlier postwar years are given in G. Lazarcik, U.S. Congress, JEC, *Reorientation and Commercial Relations of the Economies of Eastern Europe, A Compendium of Papers*, U.S. Govt. Printing Office, 1974, pp. 328–329, and *Ibid.*, pp. 594–595.

3. For definitions, see U.N., E.C.E., *Agricultural Sector Accounts and Tables: A Handbook of Definitions and Methods,* Geneva, 1956.

4. Poland is the only country in Eastern Europe that computes agricultural output measures (*produkcja koncowa* and *Produkcja towarowa,* i.e., first output and commodity output; the former includes the latter plus consumption in kind of their own production by farmers).

5. Agricultural land comprises all arable land, orchards, gardens, vineyards, permanent and temporary meadows, pastures, and grazing land.
6. See Soviet Ekonomicheskoi Vzaimopomoshchi. Sekretariat. *Statisticheskii Ezhegodnik Stran-Chlenov SEV. 1982*, Moscow, 1982, p. 178, and national statistical yearbooks.
7. See *Zemedelska ekonomika*, 1983, No. 7, pp. 495–496.
8. For explanation of this function, see sources to Table 21.11.
9. For the 1976–81 period, in the United States 86 percent of agricultural output was consumed domestically and the net balance was exported (see U.S. Dept. of Agriculture, *Agricultural Statistics, 1982*, pp. 430, 525). However, it is believed that the United States consumption level is more than adequate, and we reduce it to 80 percent as norm for illustrative purposes.

Table 21.1

AGRICULTURE'S SHARE IN PERCENT OF TOTAL LABOR FORCE AND GNP

	Labor force		GNP	
	1965	1983[1]	1965	1983[1]
Bulgaria	44.9	22.9	35.2	21.2
Czechoslovakia	19.5	12.6	17.6	14.7
GDR	14.0	10.0	15.6	12.6
Hungary	27.2	20.8	25.2	24.7
Poland	38.1	32.8	29.0	27.8
Romania	57.4	28.3	41.4	28.0
Yugoslavia	49.7	22.4	25.5	19.0
Eastern Europe	37.2	23.4	25.3	21.2
U.S.A.	6.9	3.0	3.5	2.2

[1]Preliminary

Sources: East European countries: Labor force: Agricultural employment is in terms of yearly averages or mid-year data of economically active persons in agriculture taken, or recomputed from statistical yearbooks of the respective countries. GNP: Calculated from Thad P. Alton and Assoc., OP-80, Tables 1-6. The shares were adjusted for forestry. Some data for 1983 were estimated from 1982 and the plan fulfillment reports for 1983 reported by the statistical offices of the respective countries. United States: Statistical Abstract of the United States, 1976, U.S. Department of Commerce, 1976, pp.356, 365, and 395, and Survey of Current Business, 1984, pp. 3 and S-9.

Table 21.2   GROWTH OF AGRICULTURAL OUTPUT

	Indexes, 1975=100											Average annual rates of growth*			
	1965	1970	1975	1976	1977	1978	1979	1980	1981	1982	1983¹	1965–1970	1970–1975	1975–1980	1980–1981¹
Bulgaria:															
Output	82.6	90.6	100.0	103.8	97.6	103.7	109.4	105.9	111.8	118.0	113.8	1.1	1.7	1.4	2.7
Crops	96.3	101.9	100.0	107.2	92.3	99.9	103.1	96.8	104.5	114.1	101.8	0.1	-0.4	-0.6	2.4
Animal products	69.5	79.8	100.0	100.5	102.8	107.3	115.4	114.6	118.9	121.7	125.4	2.4	4.0	3.3	3.0
Czechoslovakia															
Output	73.1	87.6	100.0	98.0	105.8	106.5	104.8	109.6	108.6	110.4	113.9	3.1	3.1	1.9	1.3
Crops	78.3	92.9	100.0	89.5	105.8	104.1	97.1	102.5	101.1	120.7	119.7	1.9	2.6	1.0	6.6
Animal products	71.4	85.9	100.0	100.8	104.8	107.3	107.3	111.8	111.1	107.1	112.1	3.6	3.3	2.2	-0.3
German Democratic Republic															
Output	79.9	84.9	100.0	99.9	103.3	103.4	105.7	107.2	108.8	102.8	106.4	1.0	3.6	1.5	-0.8
Crops	88.5	95.0	100.0	102.0	117.7	112.2	121.4	112.5	117.7	117.4	113.7	-0.2	1.3	3.1	0.3
Animal products	77.6	82.1	100.0	99.2	98.9	100.7	100.9	105.6	106.1	98.3	104.2	1.3	4.2	1.0	-1.2
Hungary															
Output	72.9	79.8	100.0	97.3	109.1	111.4	109.6	115.8	112.9	122.8	120.2	2.3	4.7	3.2	2.0
Crops	77.2	76.4	100.0	97.2	111.8	110.2	103.6	119.3	110.3	129.3	117.6	1.3	5.5	3.1	1.2
Animal products	70.0	82.2	100.0	97.4	107.3	112.1	113.6	113.4	114.7	118.4	121.9	2.9	4.2	3.3	2.5
Poland															
Output	77.7	84.8	100.0	98.1	99.7	106.3	105.3	96.3	89.3	94.2	96.6	1.4	4.1	0.2	0.6
Crops	89.4	100.1	100.0	110.0	100.1	106.0	106.0	84.1	102.7	98.7	104.6	1.4	0.4	-2.6	6.3
Animal products	72.9	78.6	100.0	93.2	99.6	106.4	104.9	101.2	83.9	92.4	93.4	1.4	5.8	1.4	-1.4
Romania															
Output	68.7	75.1	100.0	116.2	115.1	117.0	120.6	117.0	112.2	117.7	116.0	1.2	5.5	2.6	0.2
Crops	79.9	76.8	100.0	122.5	115.5	114.5	116.0	114.9	112.1	135.2	120.0	-0.7	4.5	1.5	3.2
Animal products	60.4	73.8	100.0	111.5	114.8	118.9	124.0	118.5	112.3	104.7	113.1	2.9	6.3	3.5	-2.1
Yugoslavia															
Output	74.5	85.3	100.0	108.1	113.7	111.0	112.4	113.9	116.3	123.5	122.7	2.4	3.8	2.2	2.5
Crops	79.3	91.6	100.0	114.4	117.5	107.5	110.4	112.3	113.3	128.3	126.5	2.7	2.4	1.1	4.9
Animal products	71.0	80.7	100.0	103.5	110.8	113.6	113.9	115.1	118.5	119.9	119.8	2.1	5.0	2.9	1.3
Total, Eastern Europe															
Output	75.7	83.8	100.0	102.5	105.6	108.3	109.1	107.3	105.3	109.1	109.8	1.7	3.9	1.6	1.1
Crops	84.4	90.2	100.0	108.5	108.5	108.1	108.9	104.3	108.7	119.0	114.3	1.0	2.1	0.6	3.7
Animal products	71.3	80.2	100.0	99.4	104.1	108.4	109.2	108.9	103.5	104.0	107.5	2.1	4.9	2.2	-0.3

¹Preliminary.

*Least squares fit of $I_n = I_0(1+r)^n$ was calculated for growth rates in all tables.

Sources: See appendix A. Indexes were calculated from physical quantities weighted by 1978 U.S. dollars.

Table 21.3 GROWTH OF OPERATING EXPENSES INCLUDING DEPRECIATION, GROSS PRODUCT, AND NET PRODUCT OF AGRICULTURE

					Indexes, 1975=100							Average annual rates of growth			
	1965	1970	1975	1976	1977	1978	1979	1980	1981	1982	1983[1]	1965–1970	1970–1975	1975–1980	1980–1983[1]
Bulgaria															
Expenses	57.6	90.9	100.0	107.1	134.7	158.0	152.1	204.9	216.7	229.0	241.2	9.4	1.9	14.7	5.6
Gross product	90.4	88.6	100.0	103.4	90.7	92.3	101.1	83.9	88.9	93.5	86.4	-1.4	2.0	-2.6	1.4
Net product	95.9	90.5	100.0	102.8	86.8	87.7	96.9	76.8	81.1	85.4	76.5	-2.1	1.5	-4.2	0.4
Czechoslovakia															
Expenses	64.0	84.2	100.0	104.4	104.3	114.2	115.9	119.3	134.7	130.6	135.9	4.4	4.1	3.7	3.7
Gross product	84.0	89.9	100.0	94.1	106.9	102.9	100.0	105.7	95.2	102.5	105.8	1.5	2.4	1.2	0.8
Net product	87.7	93.0	100.0	92.4	105.7	99.7	95.0	100.9	85.6	92.5	94.4	1.4	1.7	0.2	-1.2
German Democratic Republic															
Expenses	59.3	77.1	100.0	115.5	107.7	113.1	111.1	116.7	116.5	105.6	110.8	4.5	4.8	2.0	-2.5
Gross product	92.6	91.4	100.0	91.3	101.8	99.1	104.4	103.6	106.5	104.8	107.5	-0.2	2.7	1.6	1.0
Net product	99.1	95.0	100.0	89.0	100.2	96.6	102.0	100.6	103.3	100.8	103.4	-0.8	2.0	1.2	0.6
Hungary															
Expenses	48.4	69.4	100.0	101.3	111.0	120.4	122.9	128.6	125.0	133.9	139.6	7.8	7.8	5.6	3.2
Gross product	86.3	84.9	100.0	96.3	109.4	106.9	103.4	110.1	108.4	114.1	110.7	0.3	3.5	1.9	0.7
Net product	91.8	87.9	100.0	94.0	107.5	103.8	98.6	105.2	102.9	108.5	104.1	-0.2	2.7	1.0	0.2
Poland															
Expenses	46.9	70.3	100.0	92.3	99.0	105.2	112.4	107.4	83.3	88.2	88.7	11.7	8.8	2.9	-5.0
Gross product	99.1	95.2	100.0	102.3	101.5	108.2	103.4	93.5	97.7	102.5	106.0	-2.4	1.5	-0.7	4.3
Net product	104.2	97.4	100.0	101.8	100.2	107.0	100.7	89.1	93.1	98.1	101.7	-3.1	1.1	-1.5	4.6
Romania															
Expenses	39.0	59.0	100.0	103.8	106.3	105.4	112.9	124.5	118.7	124.5	124.2	8.5	11.3	3.9	0.4
Gross product	91.4	88.7	100.0	126.5	124.3	129.8	130.5	115.0	113.8	119.9	120.2	-1.0	1.6	2.4	1.9
Net product	100.3	92.2	100.0	129.3	124.4	129.3	128.8	108.9	105.4	110.4	107.3	-2.3	0.8	1.3	0.0
Yugoslavia															
Expenses	69.2	77.3	100.0	123.2	124.7	144.0	121.4	130.0	126.6	123.1	127.8	2.3	7.6	4.1	-0.8
Gross product	75.3	86.8	100.0	105.4	111.9	105.3	111.3	111.4	114.9	124.3	122.8	2.4	3.1	1.8	3.8
Net product	75.5	86.9	100.0	105.2	111.6	104.8	110.7	110.8	114.3	123.5	121.7	2.4	3.1	1.7	3.7
Total, Eastern Europe															
Expenses	52.0	73.1	100.0	103.4	106.9	114.1	116.3	121.9	115.8	118.0	120.5	7.6	7.1	4.1	-0.2
Gross product	89.6	90.3	100.0	102.7	106.1	106.7	107.5	102.3	103.7	108.7	109.2	-0.4	2.3	0.7	2.5
Net product	94.3	92.5	100.0	102.0	104.7	104.6	104.6	98.2	98.7	103.5	103.1	-1.0	1.8	0.0	2.0

Sources: See appendix A.

[1]Preliminary.

Table 21.4

PER HEAD COMPARISONS OF LEVELS OF OUTPUT, AND GROSS AND NET PRODUCT IN AGRICULTURE

[Eastern Europe=100]

	Agricultural output			Crop output			Animal output		
	1966-70	1976-80	1981-83[1]	1966-70	1976-80	1981-83[1]	1966-70	1976-80	1981-83[1]
Bulgaria	124.0	110.7	121.4	172.9	152.0	155.1	87.3	89.2	102.6
Czechoslovakia	92.6	92.5	97.2	68.0	62.6	67.8	111.1	108.1	113.6
German Democratic Republic	104.1	120.1	124.0	72.6	90.4	90.0	127.8	135.5	142.8
Hungary	128.3	128.0	140.4	140.4	150.7	159.1	119.2	116.2	130.0
Poland	103.6	101.2	90.9	87.9	85.2	80.0	115.4	109.4	96.9
Romania	87.4	91.5	88.3	109.3	113.6	111.9	71.0	80.1	75.2
Yugoslavia	83.8	78.6	82.9	105.5	97.7	99.8	67.5	68.6	73.6
Total, Eastern Europe	100.0	100.0	100.0	100.0	100.0	100.0	100.0	100.0	100.0

	Gross product			Net product		
	1966-70	1976-80	1981-83[1]	1966-70	1976-80	1981-83[1]
Bulgaria	121.6	128.4	120.9	123.2	125.0	114.6
Czechoslovakia	74.0	80.5	78.8	64.9	77.9	72.8
German Democratic Republic	104.7	115.2	123.1	103.8	111.9	121.8
Hungary	129.4	112.6	118.7	131.2	110.5	117.5
Poland	101.7	100.2	97.2	103.5	102.3	99.8
Romania	88.8	84.0	77.1	85.2	79.3	69.1
Yugoslavia	98.8	100.0	107.5	105.2	108.0	119.4
Total, Eastern Europe	100.0	100.0	100.0	100.0	100.0	100.0

Sources: Calculated from physical quantities weighted by 1978 U.S. dollars divided by population data (see appendix A).

[1]Preliminary.

Table 21.5 GROWTH OF AGRICULTURAL OUTPUT PER HECTARE OF AGRICULTURAL LAND

	Indexes, 1975=100											Average annual rates of change			
	1965	1970	1975	1976	1977	1978	1979	1980	1981	1982	1983¹	1965–1970	1970–1975	1975–1980	1980¹–1983¹
Bulgaria															
Output	84.9	89.8	100.0	99.7	93.7	99.3	105.0	102.0	107.8	113.7	109.6	0.2	1.9	0.9	2.7
Crops	98.9	101.0	100.0	103.0	88.6	95.7	98.9	93.2	100.7	109.9	98.0	-0.7	-0.2	-1.1	2.4
Animal products	71.4	79.1	100.0	96.6	98.6	102.8	110.8	110.4	114.6	117.3	120.8	1.6	4.2	2.7	3.0
Czechoslovakia															
Output	71.5	86.7	100.0	98.4	105.6	107.4	106.1	111.7	111.4	113.3	117.0	3.3	3.3	2.3	1.6
Crops	76.6	91.9	100.0	89.8	106.4	105.0	98.3	104.5	103.7	123.9	123.0	2.1	2.8	1.4	6.9
Animal products	69.9	85.0	100.0	101.2	105.4	108.2	108.6	114.0	113.9	110.0	115.1	3.8	3.5	2.6	-0.1
German Democratic Republic															
Output	79.1	85.0	100.0	99.9	103.4	103.6	106.0	107.7	109.4	103.4	107.1	1.2	3.5	1.6	-0.7
Crops	87.4	95.2	100.0	102.0	117.8	112.4	121.7	113.0	118.3	118.1	114.5	0.0	1.3	3.2	0.4
Animal products	76.8	82.2	100.0	99.3	98.9	100.9	101.1	106.0	106.6	98.8	104.9	1.6	4.2	1.1	-1.1
Hungary															
Output	71.0	78.6	100.0	97.5	109.8	112.6	111.6	118.3	115.8	126.3	124.0	2.5	5.1	3.7	2.3
Crops	75.2	75.3	100.0	97.4	112.5	111.4	105.5	121.9	113.1	132.9	121.3	1.6	5.9	3.5	1.5
Animal products	68.1	80.9	100.0	97.6	108.0	113.3	115.7	115.9	117.6	121.8	125.8	3.1	4.5	3.8	2.8
Poland															
Output	76.0	83.4	100.0	98.4	100.2	107.1	106.5	97.6	90.7	95.8	98.3	1.5	4.5	0.5	0.8
Crops	87.4	98.4	100.0	110.4	100.6	106.8	107.2	85.3	104.4	100.4	106.5	1.5	0.7	-2.3	6.5
Animal products	71.3	77.2	100.0	93.5	100.1	107.2	106.2	102.6	85.2	94.0	95.0	1.5	6.2	1.7	-1.3
Romania															
Output	69.5	75.1	100.0	116.1	115.0	116.9	120.4	116.8	112.2	117.5	115.9	1.0	5.5	2.6	0.2
Crops	80.8	76.8	100.0	122.4	115.3	114.3	115.8	114.8	112.1	133.0	119.9	-0.9	4.5	1.5	3.1
Animal products	61.1	73.9	100.0	111.4	114.7	118.8	123.9	118.4	112.3	104.6	112.9	2.7	6.3	3.5	-2.1
Yugoslavia															
Output	72.8	84.0	100.0	108.6	114.6	112.3	113.6	114.7	117.1	124.9	124.4	2.6	4.1	2.3	3.1
Crops	77.5	90.2	100.0	114.9	118.5	108.7	111.5	113.1	114.1	129.8	128.3	2.9	2.7	1.3	5.2
Animal products	69.4	79.5	100.0	104.0	111.7	114.9	115.0	115.8	119.3	121.3	121.5	2.2	5.3	3.1	1.6
Total, Eastern Europe															
Output	74.9	82.9	100.0	102.4	105.6	108.5	109.5	107.9	106.1	110.0	110.9	1.7	4.1	1.8	1.2
Crops	83.4	89.9	100.0	108.4	108.6	108.4	109.3	104.9	109.5	120.1	115.4	1.0	2.3	0.7	3.9
Animal products	70.5	79.4	100.0	99.3	104.1	108.6	109.7	109.5	104.3	104.9	108.6	2.1	5.1	2.3	-0.2

Sources: Data in table 21.2 were divided by acreage of agricultural land taken from statistical yearbooks of respective countries (see appendix A).

¹Preliminary.

Table 21.6

COMPARISONS OF LEVELS OF OUTPUT, EXPENSES INCLUDING DEPRECIATION, GROSS AND NET PRODUCT PER HECTARE OF LAND IN AGRICULTURE

[Total Eastern Europe=100]

	Agricultural output			Crop output			Animal output		
	1966-70	1976-80	1981-83[1]	1966-70	1976-80	1981-83[1]	1966-70	1976-80	1981-83[1]
Bulgaria	107.4	90.0	97.4	158.9	123.7	124.5	75.1	72.5	82.4
Czechoslovakia	117.6	115.2	121.5	83.0	77.9	84.8	139.4	134.6	141.9
German Democratic Republic	175.0	183.4	184.0	109.5	138.1	133.6	216.1	206.9	212.0
Hungary	105.5	116.8	127.0	122.8	137.5	144.0	94.6	106.0	117.6
Poland	113.4	106.3	97.0	98.1	89.5	85.3	123.0	115.0	103.5
Romania	68.7	76.5	73.8	86.7	95.0	93.5	57.4	66.9	62.8
Yugoslavia	67.7	68.8	73.0	85.8	85.6	87.9	56.4	60.1	64.8
Total, Eastern Europe	100.0	100.0	100.0	100.0	100.0	100.0	100.0	100.0	100.0

	Expenses including depreciation			Gross product			Net product		
	1966-70	1976-80	1981-83[1]	1966-70	1976-80	1981-83[1]	1966-70	1976-80	1981-83[1]
Bulgaria	101.1	73.0	104.9	107.8	104.4	97.0	110.3	101.7	92.0
Czechoslovakia	194.6	141.8	163.5	93.7	100.3	98.5	82.1	97.0	91.0
German Democratic Republic	178.1	201.5	188.4	175.2	175.9	182.7	173.6	171.0	180.8
Hungary	101.3	140.1	155.5	105.9	102.7	107.4	107.4	100.8	106.3
Poland	112.2	104.6	83.9	111.6	105.3	103.8	113.9	107.4	106.5
Romania	73.0	91.4	95.8	69.9	70.2	64.4	66.7	66.3	57.7
Yugoslavia	30.8	31.2	28.9	80.0	87.6	94.7	84.8	94.6	105.1
Total, Eastern Europe	100.0	100.0	100.0	100.0	100.0	100.0	100.0	100.0	100.0

Sources: Calculated from physical quantities weighted by 1978 U.S. dollars divided by hectares of agricultural land (see appendix A).

[1]Preliminary.

(continued)

Table 21.7

GROWTH OF AGRICULTURAL OUTPUT, EXPENSES INCLUDING DEPRECIATION, GROSS AND NET PRODUCT PER PERSON EMPLOYED IN AGRICULTURE

Indexes, 1975=100

	1965	1970	1975	1976	1977	1978	1979	1980	1981	1982	1983[1]	Average annual rates of change			
												1965–1970	1970–1975	1975–1980	1980[1]–1983[1]
Bulgaria															
Output	55.5	73.7	100.0	109.2	107.0	116.6	123.1	121.3	130.1	141.4	140.3	5.1	5.7	4.1	5.3
Expenses	38.7	73.9	100.0	112.7	147.6	177.8	171.1	234.8	252.2	274.2	297.2	13.7	5.9	17.7	8.2
Gross product	60.6	72.1	100.0	108.8	99.4	103.8	113.7	96.1	103.4	112.0	106.4	2.6	6.1	-0.1	3.9
Net product	64.4	73.6	100.0	108.2	95.1	98.7	109.0	88.0	94.4	102.3	94.2	1.8	5.6	-1.6	2.9
Czechoslovakia															
Output	59.4	76.2	100.0	100.1	109.7	113.4	112.4	117.7	116.7	119.5	124.2	4.6	6.2	3.5	1.9
Expenses	52.0	73.2	100.0	106.6	109.0	121.6	124.2	128.2	144.7	141.4	148.2	5.9	7.2	5.3	4.2
Gross product	68.3	78.1	100.0	96.1	111.7	109.5	107.2	113.6	102.2	111.0	115.4	3.0	5.5	2.7	1.3
Net product	71.3	80.9	100.0	94.3	110.4	106.1	101.9	108.4	91.9	100.1	103.0	2.9	4.8	1.7	-0.7
German Democratic Republic															
Output	60.1	75.6	100.0	101.8	105.9	105.6	108.2	109.5	110.5	103.9	107.6	4.6	6.1	1.8	-1.1
Expenses	44.6	68.7	100.0	117.7	110.5	115.6	113.6	119.2	118.5	106.7	112.0	8.3	7.3	2.4	-2.9
Gross product	69.7	81.5	100.0	93.0	104.4	101.3	106.8	105.8	108.1	106.0	108.7	3.3	5.2	1.9	0.6
Net product	74.6	84.7	100.0	90.7	102.8	98.6	104.3	102.8	104.9	101.9	104.5	2.8	4.5	1.5	0.2
Hungary															
Output	59.0	69.3	100.0	99.8	113.7	116.6	114.1	120.2	116.3	123.7	119.6	3.7	7.9	3.9	0.5
Expenses	39.2	60.2	100.0	104.0	115.1	126.1	127.9	133.5	128.8	141.0	138.9	9.3	11.0	6.3	2.1
Gross product	69.8	73.7	100.0	98.8	114.0	112.0	107.6	114.3	111.7	115.0	110.2	1.6	6.5	2.6	-0.8
Net product	74.3	76.3	100.0	96.4	112.9	108.7	102.6	109.2	106.0	109.4	103.6	1.1	5.7	1.7	-1.3
Poland															
Output	71.4	79.1	100.0	97.2	97.2	102.3	100.2	91.0	83.5	88.5	91.3	1.7	5.2	-0.9	0.7
Expenses	43.1	65.5	100.0	91.4	96.4	101.3	106.9	101.5	77.9	82.9	83.8	12.0	9.9	1.7	-5.0
Gross product	91.1	88.8	100.0	101.4	98.9	104.2	98.4	88.3	91.4	96.3	100.2	-2.1	2.5	-1.9	4.4
Net product	95.7	90.8	100.0	100.9	97.7	103.0	95.8	84.2	87.1	92.2	96.1	-2.8	2.1	-2.7	4.6

Table 21.7 (continued)

Indexes, 1975=100

	1965	1970	1975	1976	1977	1978	1979	1980	1981	1982	1983[1]	Average annual rates of change			
												1965–1970	1970–1975	1975–1980	1980–1983[1]
Romania															
Output	49.3	59.6	100.0	122.0	126.0	133.6	145.3	147.6	145.6	154.3	153.7	3.3	10.5	7.5	1.8
Expenses	28.0	46.8	100.0	109.0	116.4	120.4	136.0	157.2	154.0	163.2	164.6	10.7	16.6	8.8	2.0
Gross product	65.5	70.4	100.0	132.7	136.0	148.2	157.2	145.1	147.6	157.6	159.2	1.1	6.4	7.3	3.5
Net product	71.9	73.2	100.0	135.7	136.2	147.7	155.2	137.5	136.8	144.8	142.2	-0.3	5.6	6.1	1.6
Yugoslavia															
Output	56.9	71.5	100.0	112.8	124.2	127.2	135.4	144.5	156.0	174.3	182.3	4.3	7.6	7.1	8.1
Expenses	52.9	64.8	100.0	128.7	136.2	165.0	146.2	165.0	169.9	173.8	189.9	4.2	11.6	9.2	4.8
Gross product	57.5	72.8	100.0	110.1	122.2	120.6	134.0	141.3	154.2	175.4	182.4	4.4	6.4	6.8	9.0
Net product	57.7	72.9	100.0	109.8	121.9	120.0	133.4	140.6	153.3	174.4	180.8	4.3	6.8	6.7	8.8
Total, Eastern Europe															
Output	59.7	71.8	100.0	105.1	110.4	115.2	118.2	118.4	117.6	123.4	126.0	3.4	7.1	3.6	2.1
Expenses	41.0	62.7	100.0	106.0	111.8	121.4	125.9	134.5	129.3	133.6	138.2	9.5	10.3	6.1	1.0
Gross product	70.7	77.4	100.0	105.4	110.9	113.6	116.4	112.9	115.8	122.9	125.3	1.2	5.4	2.7	3.6
Net product	74.4	79.3	100.0	104.6	109.5	111.4	113.3	108.3	110.2	117.1	118.3	0.6	4.9	1.9	3.0

[1] Preliminary.

Sources: Data in table 21.3 divided by the indexes of agricultural employment of respective countries.

Table 21.8

COMPARISONS OF LEVELS OF OUTPUT, EXPENSES INCLUDING DEPRECIATION,
GROSS AND NET PRODUCT PER PERSON EMPLOYED IN AGRICULTURE

[Eastern Europe=100]

	Agricultural output			Expenses including depreciation		
	1966–1970	1976–1980	1981–1983[1]	1966–1970	1976–1980	1981–1983[1]
Bulgaria	104.1	106.3	123.7	98.6	86.6	133.3
Czechoslovakia	180.4	168.5	179.1	297.8	207.2	240.9
German Democratic Rep.	280.0	282.0	278.8	285.0	309.4	285.4
Hungary	155.1	161.7	168.1	148.8	193.7	205.8
Poland	110.3	91.0	72.2	108.9	89.6	62.5
Romania	51.0	68.5	75.1	54.3	82.0	97.6
Yugoslavia	62.9	69.7	85.7	28.5	31.5	33.9
Total, Eastern Europe	100.0	100.0	100.0	100.0	100.0	100.0

	Gross Product			Net Product		
	1966–1970	1976–1980	1981–1983[1]	1966–1970	1976–1980	1981–1983[1]
Bulgaria	104.3	123.2	123.1	106.7	119.9	116.7
Czechoslovakia	143.8	146.7	145.2	126.0	141.9	134.1
German Democratic Rep.	280.2	270.6	276.8	277.6	263.1	273.9
Hungary	155.8	142.3	142.1	158.0	139.8	140.7
Poland	108.6	90.1	77.2	110.9	91.9	79.3
Romania	51.9	62.7	65.6	49.5	59.2	58.8
Yugoslavia	74.4	88.7	111.1	78.8	95.9	123.3
Total, Eastern Europe	100.0	100.0	100.0	100.0	100.0	100.0

[1]Preliminary

Sources: Calculated from physical quantities weighted by 1978 U.S.
dollars divided by the number of employed in agriculture taken from
statistical yearbooks of respective countries. (See Appendix A.)

Table 21.9

Tractor Horsepower per 1,000 Hectares of Agricultural Land and per 1,000 Workers in Agriculture

	Amount of tractor horsepower			Eastern Europe = 100			Indexes 1973-76=100		
	1973-76	1976-79	1979-82[1]	1973-76	1976-79	1979-82[1]	1973-76	1976-79	1979-82[1]
Bulgaria									
Per 1,000 hectares	534	602	632	82	75	64	100	113	118
Per 1,000 workers	2,646	3,462	3,795	91	88	74	100	131	143
Czechoslovakia									
Per 1,000 hectares	1,059	1,183	1,267	163	147	128	100	112	120
Per 1,000 workers	7,220	8,463	9,103	249	216	178	100	117	126
German Democratic Republic									
Per 1,000 hectares	1,155	1,312	1,514	178	163	153	100	114	131
Per 1,000 workers	8,503	9,894	11,349	293	253	223	100	116	133
Hungary									
Per 1,000 hectares	520	572	637	80	71	64	100	110	123
Per 1,000 workers	3,398	3,892	4,259	117	99	84	100	115	125
Poland									
Per 1,000 hectares	724	1,001	1,418	111	124	143	100	138	196
Per 1,000 workers	2,799	4,160	6,205	97	106	122	100	149	222
Romania									
Per 1,000 hectares	496	571	634	76	71	64	100	115	128
Per 1,000 workers	1,854	2,448	3,083	64	62	60	100	132	166
Yugoslavia									
Per 1,000 hectares	397	592	763	61	73	77	100	149	192
Per 1,000 workers	1,587	2,489	3,409	55	64	67	100	157	215
Total, Eastern Europe									
Per 1,000 hectares	649	807	992	100	100	100	100	124	153
Per 1,000 workers	2,900	3,917	5,100	100	100	100	100	135	176
Western Europe									
Per 1,000 hectares	1,357	1,601	1,885	209	198	190	100	118	139
Per 1,000 workers	11,740	15,017	19,400	405	383	380	100	128	165

[1]Data for 1982 are preliminary.

Sources: Calculated from statistical yearbooks of respective CMEA countries and FAO yearbooks and monthly statistical bulletins.

Table 21.10

CONSUMPTION OF COMMERCIAL FERTILIZERS PER HECTARE OF
AGRICULTURAL LAND

Pure Nutrients[1]

	in kilograms per hectare			Eastern Europe=100 [2]		
	1973-1976	1976-1979	1979-1982	1973-1976	1976-1979	1979-1982
Bulgaria	105	119	151	75	78	97
Czechoslovakia	218	244	248	156	160	158
German Democratic Rep.	287	273	270	205	179	172
Hungary	201	221	225	143	145	144
Poland	176	189	186	126	124	118
Romania	69	87	91	49	57	58
Yugoslavia	49	57	65	35	37	41
Total, Eastern Europe	140	152	157	100	100	100
Western Europe	176	197	210	126	130	134

[1]Nitrogen (N), phospate (P_2O_6), and potash (K_2O).

[2]Data for 1982 are preliminary.

Sources: Calculated from statistical yearbooks of respective
countries and FAO yearbooks and monthly statistical bulletins,
assuming commensurability of the pure nutrients per kilogram.

Table 21.11

COMBINED FACTOR PRODUCTIVITY, 1965-1983
(Indexes are 3-year moving averages, 1965-1967=100)

	(1) Bulgaria	(2) Czechoslovakia	(3) GDR	(4) Hungary	(5) Poland	(6) Yugoslavia	(7) Eastern Europe
1965-67	100	100	100	100	100	100	100
1967	101	104	103	103	102	104	103
1968	100	105	104	106	98	107	104
1969	100	106	102	103	94	106	103
1970	102	105	100	104	92	109	103
1971	105	106	101	103	95	109	104
1972	107	108	103	108	98	114	107
1973	107	111	107	111	99	119	109
1974	110	112	108	113	98	123	112
1975	113	111	108	111	95	127	111
1976	114	112	107	111	93	131	111
1977	114	113	106	112	94	134	112
1978	114	113	107	114	93	136	113
1979	114	112	106	114	90	137	112
1980	114	110	107	113	85	141	112
1981	114	109	105	115	82	145	112
1982	116	107	104	115	82	149	112
1982-83	118	108	102	115	83	152	113

Sources: Combined factor productivity was calculated by Cobb-
Douglas production function of the form Output=AL^aK^{1-a}, where L represents the labor input index, K the non-labor (capital, land and
expenses) input index, a the percentage share of returns to labor in
total output, (1-a) distributed to non-labor factors of production
valued at adjusted factor cost, and A the combined factor
productivity.
    For output, labor input, and operating expense indexes, see QP-62
and QP-81; for agricultural land and fixed capital indexes, see
statistical yearbooks of respective countries. The percentage shares
of labor and non-labor inputs in total output in 1967-69 period
(depending on country) were estimated from QP-48 and QP-62; these
shares were used to calculate the factor productivity for 1965-1975
period. The percentage shares of labor and non-labor inputs in total
output in 1975-1977 period (depending on country) were estimated from
QP-64 and QP-81; these shares were used to calculate the factor
productivity for 1975-1982 period. These two indexes were linked at
1975 to obtain one consistent series. Eastern Europe: average of six
countries.

Table 21.12

COMPARISONS OF LEVELS OF AGRICULTURAL OUTPUT AND AGRICULTURAL
OUTPUT PER HEAD: EAST EUROPEAN COUNTRIES,
USSR, WESTERN EUROPE, AND UNITED STATES

(In percent, United States = 100)

	Total agricultural output				Agricultural output per head of population			
	1966-1970	1971-1975	1976-1980	1981-1983	1966-1970	1971-1975	1976-1980	1981-1983
Bulgaria	3.3	3.2	3.0	2.9	78.7	76.2	74.6	74.6
Czechoslovakia	4.2	4.4	4.2	4.0	58.8	62.9	61.7	60.4
GDR	5.6	5.7	5.3	5.0	66.1	70.3	70.8	69.8
Hungary	4.2	4.5	4.4	4.3	81.4	91.1	92.0	94.2
Poland	10.6	10.7	9.7	8.2	65.8	67.2	61.5	52.3
Romania	5.5	5.9	6.5	5.6	55.5	59.2	66.8	57.5
Yugoslavia	5.3	5.3	5.3	5.1	53.2	53.7	53.5	52.7
Eastern Europe	38.6	39.6	38.4	35.1	63.5	66.1	65.7	61.3
USSR	74.9	74.3	69.3	62.4	63.1	62.6	59.1	53.4
Western Europe	86.3	86.0	79.8	77.5	52.7	53.3	51.2	51.2
United States	100.0	100.0	100.0	100.0	100.0	100.0	100.0	100.0

[1]Preliminary.

Sources: Physical quantities and population data were taken from
statistical yearbooks of the respective countries. The FAO wheat-
based price relatives for the 1961-65 period were used as weights and
are taken from: United Nations, Food and Agriculture Organization,
Production Yearbook, 1975, Rome, 1976, pp. 470-471, and FAO, Monthly
Bulletin of Statistics, 1983, No. 11, pp. 9-10.

APPENDIX A

Bibliographical Sources to Tables 21.1 to 21.12

Eastern Europe: All quantity series and national prices needed for the construction of tables 21.1–21.12 were taken from publications of the Research Project on National Income in East Central Europe, published in New York by Columbia University, Riverside Research Institute (RRI), and LW International Financial Research (LWIFR), as follows: *Bulgaria*: G. Lazarcik, "Bulgarian Agricultural Production, Output, Expenses, Gross and Net Product, and Productivity at 1968 Prices, 1939, and 1948–1970," OP-39, 1973 (updated to 1983) RRI and LWIFR. *Czechoslovakia*: G. Lazarcik, "Production and Productivity in Czechoslovak Agriculture, 1934–38 and 1946–1967," Ph.D. dissertation (updated to 1983) Columbia University. *East Germany*: G. Lazarcik, "East German Agricultural Production, Expenses, Gross and Net Product, and Productivity, 1934–38 and 1950–1970," OP-36, 1972 (updated 1983) RRI. *Hungary*: L. Czirjak, "Hungarian Agriculture Production and Value Added, 1934–38 and 1946–1965," OP-14, 1967 (updated to 1983) Columbia University. *Poland*: A. Korbonski and G. Lazarcik, "Polish Agricultural Production, Output, Expenses, Gross and Net Product, and Productivity, 1934–38, 1937 and 1946–1970," OP-37, 1972 (updated to 1983). RRI. *Romania*: G. Lazarcik and G. Pall, "Romania: Agricultural Production, Output, Expenses, Gross and Net Product, and Productivity, 1934–38 and 1948–1971," OP-38, 1973 (updated to 1983), RRI and LWIFR. *Yugoslavia*: J. Bombelles, "Yugoslav Agricultural Production and Productivity, Prewar and 1948–1967," OP-31, 1970 (updated to 1983) RRI. *Countries of Eastern Europe*: T.P. Alton, E.M. Bass, L. Czirjak, and G. Lazarcik, "Statistics on East European Structure and Growth," OP-48, 1975 LWIFR. T.P. Alton, E.M. Bass, G. Lazarcik, W. Znayenko, and J.T. Bombelles, "Agricultural Output, Expenses, Gross Product, Depreciation, and Net Product in Eastern Europe, Prewar and 1965-1979," OP-62, 1980 LWIFR. T.P. Alton, E.M. Bass, G. Lazarcik, and Wassyl Znayenko, "The Structure of Gross National Product in Eastern Europe (Deriviation of GNP Weights for 1975–1977)," OP-64, 1981 LWIFR. T.P. Alton, K. Badach, E.M. Bass, J.T. Bombelles, and G. Lazarcik, "Agricultural Output, Expenses and Depreciation, Gross Product, and Net Product in Eastern Europe, 1965, 1970, and 1975–1983," OP-81, 1984 LWIFR. J.T. Bombelles, "The Structure of the Gross National Product of Yugoslavia, 1976," OP-79, 1983 LWIFR. *USA and USSR*: United Nations, Food and Agriculture Organization, "Production Yearbook, 1981," Rome, 1982, FAO, "Monthly Bulletin of Statistics," No. 11, Rome, 1983.

22

Inter-regional and Inter-organizational Differences in Agricultural Efficiency in Czechoslovakia

Josef C. Brada, Jeanne C. Hey, and Arthur E. King

Introduction

Agricultural policy in Czechoslovakia has aimed at three objectives. First, agriculture was to be socialized, with private production replaced by the collective farm or JZD (jednotne zemedelske druztvo), or by the state farm (statni statek). Second, agriculture was to become more productive. In part productivity gains were to come from socialization, but also from the substitution of capital for labor. More recently, the reorganization of state farms and JZDs into larger units has been viewed as an important source of productivity gains. Finally, planners have sought to eliminate regional differences in the productivity of agriculture. This process required the raising of productivity in the Slovak Socialist Republic (SSR) to the level attained in the Czech Socialist Republic (CSR).

The collectivization of agriculture in Czechoslovakia began in 1949 on the basis of the Unified Cooperatives Act of February 23. The pressure exerted on peasants to join collectives eased somewhat in 1953 and a brief period of de-collectivization, particularly intense in Slovakia (Faltus *et al.*, p. 504), ensued. The collectivization effort was renewed in the Summer of 1955 and was effectively completed by 1960. During the same period, state-owned land as well as parcels from large estates that had been nationalized were formed into state farms. These state farms were supposed to serve as models for the collective farm sector in the introduction of new technologies and large scale mechanization. Since the state farm was viewed as a more socialist form of organization than the collective, it was hoped that it would eventually emerge as the dominant form. In the case of Czechoslovakia, this has not come about, largely because state farms do not appear to have developed a significant edge in productivity over collectives.

Once collectivization was completed, attention turned to increasing the productivity of agriculture. This was in part obtained by increasing the level of investment in agriculture, so that, by 1960, agriculture's share in investment surpassed the contribution of agricultural to NMP (Waedekin, pp. 114–5). The supply of fertilizers and agricultural chemicals was also increased (Brada and King, 1983). In addition to increases in capital and material inputs, both state farms and JZDs were amalgamated into larger units, although the relative importance of the two types of organizational form did not change much. Thus, while the number of collective farms decreased from 6,200 in 1970 to 1,722 in 1980, the average size of the collective farms almost quadrupled, and the total membership of JZDs decreased only slightly. During the same period, the number of state farms decreased from 393 to 200 while their share of arable land dropped only marginally from 20.4 percent of the total to 19.9 percent. Also, their share of the agricultural labor force has remained around 16 percent.[1]

While the rationalization of both JZDs and state farms appears to be consistent with the goals of the planners to mechanize agriculture and to create an agro-industrial complex, the relative stability of the share of land, labor and other resources allocated to these two forms of organization is somewhat surprising. Presumably, if the planners have ideological preferences for state farms over JZDs, then a period of amalgamation and organizational restructuring would appear to have been particularly favorable for converting JZDs to state farms. However, if Czechoslovak policy-makers perceived the lower efficiency of state farms, one possible obstacle to such a course would have been the expected decline in output from the shift in resources to state farms. The evidence of the superior efficiency of JZDs is, however, based on rather simple measures of productivity, such as output of milk per hectare of land, etc., that are subject to a number of biases. Thus whether, indeed, the desire to promote the growth of state farms at the expense of JZDs on ideological grounds ought to have been held in check by pragmatic considerations remains an unanswered empirical issue.

The regional allocation of agricultural resources between the two Republics involves both economic and political issues. Slovakia had traditionally been more dependent on agriculture as a source of employment, and thus some disguised underemployment in that sector and the resultant lower labor productivity were to be expected. Moreover, the mountainous nature of Slovakia presumably hindered both crop production and the type of large-scale mechanization being promoted in the Czech Republic. The leveling of incomes and perforce productivity between the two Republics was a political goal. To achieve it, the rapid industrialization of Slovakia appeared as the most practical means. Thus agriculture appeared to be, at best, a source of labor not only for nascent industries in Slovakia but also in the Czech Republic where labor reserves were less abundant. The movement of surplus labor out of Slovak agriculture increased productivity, and labor-saving investments served the same end. These improvements across the agricultural sector of the economy presumably raised important allocational issues for planners. In particular, the Czechs seem to suspect that, due to its topography, Slovakia is less suitable for agriculture than the Czech Republic. If true, the optimal policy, from a national standpoint, would be to wind down agriculture in Slovakia and to employ the workers thus released in industry, either in Slovakia or elsewhere. On the other hand, if the remaining differences in factor productivity between Czech and Slovak agriculture reflect lower levels of capital stock in the latter, then it would make sense to shift investment resources away from Czech agriculture in order to strengthen agriculture in Slovakia.

Thus in their agricultural investment decisions, Czechoslovak planners have faced two allocational issues, the first involving the relative importance of state versus collective farms and the second involving the allocation of investment between the agricultural sectors of the two republics.

Estimating Factor Productivity

To provide some insight on these allocational issues we estimated production functions for state farms and for JZDs each in the Czech and Slovak Republics. Complete data disaggregated by type of agricultural unit and by Republic were only available for the period 1967–80, and consequently we chose to estimate a relatively simple form of the Cobb-Douglas production function of the form:

$$Y = A \ K^a \ L^{1-a} \qquad\qquad \text{(Eq. 1)}$$

One of the difficulties in estimating production functions for agricultural activities is the range of complex possibilities for complimentary or substitution that exist among both inputs and outputs. To overcome these difficulties we chose crop production as our output measure. Since our measure of capital, tractors, is more likely to be related to production of crops than to animals, this should improve the statistical power of our results. The nominal value of crop production, by type of agricultural unit and by Republic, was deflated using a price index derived from national data on crop output in current and fixed prices. Of course, such a procedure is not without problems. Delivery prices may have varied between JZDs and state farms and possibly also between Republics, particularly for the output of private plots that is included in the output of the JZDs. However, this issue of output from private plots should not be very serious as many JZDs eliminated them in the 1970s. Moreover, the share of private plots in total JZD land fell from 6.3 percent to 1.5 percent in the Czech Republic and from 8.0 to 3.5 percent in the Slovak Republic over the sample period. Labor is measured in number of economically active workers with no adjustment for hours worked, since information on the latter was not available for the entire sample period.[2] The most difficult data problem is in the capital stock series. As the proxy for capital, we elected to use number of tractors, as these appeared to be the most appropriate available capital measure for crop production. This is due to the fact that tractors form the primary form of motive power for other types of machinery, and they are also an important means of transporting crops. Thus other machinery should be roughly proportional to the number of tractors. Unfortunately, at the level of disaggregation employed in this study, the Czechoslovak reporting practice switched from tractor equivalent units of 15 horsepower to the number of tractors in 1971. To account for the effects of this change on both the level and rate of change, we included a dummy variable for both intercept and slope. This procedure, by increasing the sample size, also improved the degrees of freedom and hence the power of our results.

We estimated, for JZDs and state farms in each republic, Equation 2 as

$$\ln \left(\frac{Y}{L}\right)_t = A_0 + A_1 \ln \left(\frac{K}{L}\right)_t + A_2 \text{ DUM} + A_3 \text{ DUM} * \ln \left(\frac{K}{L}\right)_t + e_t$$

Y_t = value of crop output in millions of 1967 kcs in year t
L_t = number of workers employed in year t
K_t = tractors in year t; pre-1971 in 15hp. units, post-1971 in number
   of tractors
DUM = 1 for t < 1970, 0 otherwise

Thus, we assume constant returns to scale and, even though we account for change in the measure of capital by intercept A_2 and slope A_3 dummies, no disembodied technological progress.[3] Moreover, the production function implicitly requires two additional assumptions. First, since land is not included, we must assume that land per worker was relatively constant throughout the period. This seems reasonable on the basis of available evidence. Moreover, land is assumed to be of the same quality for all units. Although the Czech literature argues that state farms have poorer land there is no hard evidence to support this. In any case, the poorer land of state farms should be offset by greater use of fertilizer, irrigation etc. on state farms. As between Czech and Slovak farms, quality of land should favor the former. Second, we exclude purchased inputs, despite our use of a gross output measure, again because the ratio of material costs and depreciation to gross agricultural output increased only very slightly from 0.652 in 1965 to 0.673 in 1975 (*Economic Survey of Europe*, p. 33).

Parameter estimates were computed with a maximum likelihood estimator in order to adjust for serial correlation; they are presented in Table 22.1. In terms of variation explained and significance of the estimates the results are reasonably good although the multicollinearity problem (see footnote 3) for the Slovak farms is particularly obvious. The estimates for A_1 imply positive marginal products for capital in all cases save state farms in the Slovak Republic. In the latter, the replacement of small tractors by large ones in recent years may reflect an errors-in-variable problem rather than a true judgement on the productivity of tractors. Nevertheless we take the result at face value for purposes of discussion.

Inter-regional and Inter-unit
Differences in Productivity

Differences in output per worker between JZDs and state farms or between the Czech and Slovak Republics stem from two measurable causes. First there are differences in technology and efficiency. These are reflected in the parameters of the production functions reported in Table 22.1, which reveal significant inter-unit and inter-republic differences in efficiency (A_0) and in the marginal product of capital. The other source of difference in per capita output is the amount of capital per worker available to different units or Republics. These differences, expressed in the measures of capital and labor employed in our regression results, are illustrated in Table 22.2. It is evident that there are significant inter-unit and inter-Republic variations in resource endowments. Nationally, for both years, state farms have more tractors per worker than do JZDs. However, in the Czech Republic, their advantage over JZDs has narrowed much more rapidly than in the Slovak Republic. There is also a large disparity between the two Republics, with the Czech Republic having a large and growing advantage over the Slovak Republic in capital per worker. There has been only a slight improvement in Slovak capital intensity. Thus from Table 22.2 we may conclude that the allocation of capital in Czechoslavakia has favored state farms over collective farms and the Czech Republic over the Slovak Republic.

To determine whether such an allocation of capital was desirable, we calculated the per capita production of the two types of agricultural units on the basis of hypothetical alternative allocations of resources. These resulting estimates of output per worker, in collective and state farms in each Republic, are reported in Table 22.3. Column 1 was calculated from the production function parameters in Table 22.1 with the actual capital-labor ratios that existed in each type of agricultural unit. In 1971, estimated output per worker was highest in state farms in the Czech Republic. Taking this level of output as the base for comparison, in index form, Czech JZDs had per worker output of 8 percent less, followed by Slovak state farms which were 11 percent below this level and Slovak JZDs at 16 percent less. In 1980 the ranking is reversed between Czech JZDs and state farms, the former now 17 percent higher. While Slovak farms were still less productive than Czech ones, the gap between JZDs and state farms had narrowed. In both republics the improvements in JZD productivity per worker, vis a vis state farms, appear to be the result of more equal capital-labor ratios (evident in Table 22.2).

Turning now to a comparison of intra-Republic differences in labor productivity between JZDs and state farms, we examine columns 2 and 3 of Table 22.3. In Column 2 we estimated what the output per worker in Czech JZDs and state farms would have been if both types of units had the same K/L ratio, that being the one obtaining for the entire Czech Republic. For 1971, such a redistribution of capital would have had an appreciable impact and reversed their positions. This would have occurred largely because the K/L ratio for JZDs was nearly the same as for the Republic (see Table 22.2) and collective farms comprise about three times the amount of input or output of state farms. Moreover, in 1980, we can see that an equal distribution of capital between the two types of units would have widened the spread in the productivity between them by 2 percentage points in favor of JZDs (i.e. 119 instead of 117). In the case of Slovakia, the higher productivity of state farms relative to collective farms is diminished when resources are distributed equally between them. With such a reallocation, state farms have virtually no change in the level of productivity, but JZD improvements close the gap. Also, this conclusion holds over time. Even though Slovak state farms become slightly more capital intensive there is no improvement in their estimated output per worker. Thus on an absolute level based on Columns 2 and 3, it is evident that, ceteris paribus, Czech JZDs are more productive than Czech state farms and Slovak JZDs appear to be marginally less productive than Slovak state farms. Over time, the productivity differential betwen JZDs and state farms widened in the Czech Republic but narrowed slightly in Slovakia.[4]

Columns 4 and 5 of Table 22.3 compare the efficiency of each agricultural organization across Republics. In column 4 the K/L ratio for all collective agriculture was used to compute output per worker in Czech and Slovak JZDs. This is equivalent to measuring productivity on the assumption that tractors belonging to Czechoslovak JZDs were redistributed so that JZDs in both the Czech and Slovak Republics had the same K/L ratio. The results clearly indicate that with the same K/L ratio, Slovak collective farms would have had higher output per worker than would Czech ones. The margin was 19 percent in 1971 and 13 percent in 1980. For state farms this finding is reversed. Czech state farms are more efficient, ceteris paribus, than are their counterparts in Slovakia, and the gap is widening.

Finally, column 6 of Table 22.3 reports the estimated output per worker if all tractors in Czechoslovakia were allocated among state and collective farms so as to equalize the K/L ratio across units and Republics. Using the output of Czech JZDs as the basis for our index so as to maintain comparability with Column 1 (reflecting actual resource allocations), we obtain a much altered perspective of agricultural efficiency in Czechoslovakia. The most efficient agricultural units, adjusted for resource endowment, are Slovak collective farms. With this adjustment, projected Slovak JZD output per worker is 31 percent higher than Czech state farms in 1971, and 29 percent higher in 1980. Even if the comparison is made between like units, productivity in Slovak collectives is 22 percent more than in Czech ones in 1971 and 14 percent more in 1980. The ranking does not change over time. Czech collective farms are the second most efficient units, followed by Czech and then Slovak state farms.

Conclusion

From Table 22.2 it is evident that agricultural investment policies have favored Czech over Slovak agriculture. This has made Czech agriculture

340   *Josef C. Brada, Jeanne C. Hey, and Arthur E. King*

appear to be more efficient, and thus provided a rationale for the existing allocation of resources. Our calculations, based on production function estimates, indicate that in the collective sector Slovak farms are more efficient than their Czech counterparts and that, as a result, investment resources have been misallocated. Agricultural output in Czechoslovakia could have been higher had capital been shifted from collective farms in the Czech Republic to those in Slovakia.

We have also shown that, ceteris paribus, state farms are less efficient than collective farms and thus that shifts in capital from the former to the latter would have increased agricultural production. The failure of the Czechoslovak authorities to expand the state sector at the expense of the collective sector would seem to reflect an awareness of these differences in efficiency. At the same time, the maintenance of a large gap between the capital endowments of Czech and Slovak collective farms represents a serious misallocation of resources.

Notes

This paper was written while Brada was a guest at the Osteuropa Institut Munchen. We also gratefully acknowledge the support of the National Council for Soviet and East European Research, Washington, D.C., and the Deutscher Akademischer Austauschdienst.

1. All data from *Statisticka Rocenka Ceskoslovenske Socialisticke Republiky*, various years.
2. The use of workers rather than hours worked does not create much of an error as the correlation between the two for the entire Czechoslovak Republic is over 0.99. Of course, one must assume that the allocation of labor between crop production and animal husbandry was relatively constant over the sample period.
3. As it is, the data present serious problems due to multicollinearity. The correlation coefficients of ln K, ln L, ln Land are all well above .95. The inclusion of land per worker or of a time trend exacerbates these problems without providing much additional information. It is, of course, difficult to differenciate between economies of scale and neutral technological progress. We have chosen a relatively restrictive form of the production function, though our analysis of the errors suggests no serious problem from this specification.
4. Land quality and climate effects may be responsible for some of this, particularly in Slovakia where the mountainous terrain may lead to greater variance in micro climates.

References

Josef C. Brada and Arthur E. King, "Czechoslovak Agriculture: Policies, Performance and Prospects," *East European Quarterly*, Vol. XVII, No. 3 (September, 1983), pp. 343–359.
Josef Faltus, *et al.*, *Strucny hospodarsky vyvoj Ceskoslovenska do roku 1955* (Prague: Svoboda, 1969).
United Nations, *Economic Survey of Europe, 1976*, Part II (New York: United Nations, 1977).
Karl-Eugen Wädekin, *Agrarian Policies in Communist Europe* (Totowa, N.J.: Allanheld, Osumn, 1982).

TABLE 22.1

PARAMETER ESTIMATES FOR EQUATION 2*

	CZECH SOCIALIST REPUBLIC		SLOVAK SOCIALIST REPUBLIC	
COEFFICIENT	STATE FARMS	COLLECTIVE FARMS	STATE FARMS	COLLECTIVE FARMS
A_0 (constant)	-2.401 (0.783)	-1.709 (0.294)	-4.025 (1.715)	-2.308 (2.586)
A_1 (ln (K/L))	0.769 (0.442)	1.059 (0.156)	0.044 (0.780)	0.686 (1.076)
A_2 (DUM)	49.884 (18.249)	31.859 (11.506)	33.596 (32.831)	0.463 (13.937)
A_3 (DUM*ln (K/L))	-4.824 (1.759)	-2.809 (1.003)	-3.653 (3.560)	-0.092 (1.309)
$\bar{R}^2$ **	0.715	0.986	0.938	0.955
F-ratio	11.037	267.764	60.399	84.628
D.W.	1.898	2.054	1.512	1.492
ρ	-0.73 (0.19)	-0.48 (0.31)	0.32 (0.36)	0.48 (0.33)

*standard errors in parentheses below estimates
**statistics based on rho-transformed variables

TABLE 22.2

TRACTORS PER WORKER, 1971 AND 1980

BY REPUBLIC AND BY ORGANIZATIONAL UNIT*

YEAR	CZECHOSLOVAK SOCIALIST REPUBLIC			CZECH SOCIALIST REPUBLIC			SLOVAK SOCIALIST REPUBLIC		
	TOTAL	COLLECTIVE FARMS	STATE FARMS	TOTAL	COLLECTIVE FARMS	STATE FARMS	TOTAL	COLLECTIVE FARMS	STATE FARMS
1971	.1185	.1123	.1458	.1340	.1271	.1606	.0903	.0873	.1077
1980	.1390	.1354	.1541	.1692	.1682	.1728	.0918	.0892	.1082

*Source: Computed from Statistiká Ročenka ČSSR

TABLE 22.3

ESTIMATED OUTPUT PER WORKER BY REPUBLIC AND BY ORGANIZATIONAL UNIT

(IN MILLION 1967 KCS PER WORKER)

REGION & UNIT	(1) ACTUAL K/L RATIOS	INDEX	ESTIMATES BASED ON: (2) CZECH REPUBLIC K/L RATIO	INDEX	(3) SLOVAK REPUBLIC K/L RATIO	INDEX	(4) COLLECTIVE FARM K/L RATIO	INDEX	(5) STATE FARM K/L RATIO	INDEX	(6) CZECHOSLOVAK K/L RATIO	INDEX
1971												
ČSR												
JZD	.0204	92	.0215	111			.0179	81			.0189	107
State Farm	.0222	100	.0193	100					.0206	100	.0176	100
SSR												
JZD	.0187	84			.0191	96	.0222	100			.0230	131
State Farm	.0197	89			.0198	100			.0194	94	.0196	111
1980												
ČSR												
JZD	.0274	117	.0276	119			.0218	87			.0224	113
State Farm	.0235	100	.0231	100					.0215	100	.0199	100
SSR												
JZD	.0189	80			.0193	97	.0252	100			.0256	129
State Farm	.0197	84			.0198	100			.0194	90	.0195	98

23

The USSR:
The Livestock Feed Issue

Barbara Severin

Introduction

Despite long-standing emphasis on the development of the Soviet livestock sector, progress has been hindered by factors such as unsuitability of breeds; lack of adequate veterinary service and supplies, daily care, and sanitation; shortages of skilled labor, machinery, and equipment; and shifting government policies. Probably the most important factor hampering the growth of livestock production, however, is the feed situation—a chronic shortage of sufficient energy feeds and an imbalance among the major feed components, including a serious protein deficit.

Importance of the Livestock Sector

The program to increase supplies of meat has been a centerpiece of Soviet consumer policy since 1965. With good weather and successful grain crops, this commitment was met during the late 1960s and early 1970s (see Table 23.1). In 1975, unusually poor weather caused a grain crop failure. In that year the USSR responded to a sharp drop in grain production by importing record quantities of grain and by reducing herds drastically. Smaller herds led to reduced meat output in 1976. Not until 1978 did meat output again reach trend levels. From 1979 through 1982, average annual meat production lagged below the 1978 peak. With feed supplies reduced as a consequence of four successive poor-to-mediocre grain crops, the regime sacrificed growth in meat production to maintain herd numbers, accepting the lower animal productivity associated with smaller feed rations. Only by importing record quantities of meat, about 900 thousand tons annually during the 1980–82 period, did Moscow keep meat consumption per head from falling more (see Figure 23.1). Because food (excluding tobacco but including all beverages) accounts for nearly half of Soviet household expenditures on consumer

344

goods and services, the quality of the diet, especially the availability of meat, is a key factor by which Soviet consumers judge their well-being.

The shift in emphasis from distress slaughter to herd maintenance was a gamble; disease or bad weather could have killed large numbers of animals weakened by reduced feed rations. The gamble paid off and meat output reached a new record in 1983. Even so, production was almost 4 percent below the 16.6 million ton level indicated by the 1960–82 trend. Combined with a new high in meat imports, availability of meat per person increased by 3 percent.

Because money incomes have grown steadily while the leadership has pursued a policy of maintaining stable, relatively low prices on livestock products in state retail stores, where most meat is sold, demand for meat has grown more rapidly than supply. The extensive queuing that has resulted imposes a drain on time and morale; local rationing and special distribution systems, however, have tended to reduce the problem for workers and other favored groups. To reduce the problems associated with excess demand for meat as well as other goods and services in short supply, Soviet officials have waged a continuing effort to bring consumer incomes into line with the availability of goods and services by holding down growth of income. In 1983, per capita disposable incomes increased by an estimated 3 percent, roughly the increase in meat availability. Consequently, pressures on supplies did not increase.

The Feed Situation

Soviet livestock feed rations remain deficient in both quantity and quality despite long-standing plans to upgrade animal diets. Data on feed balances for the USSR are more limited than for most western countries, including only concentrates and a few categories of roughages fed, an estimate of pasture "fed", and total feed units used by all livestock. In addition, these data are for calendar, not crop, years. Changes over time in the physical relationships between feeds and livestock product output are difficult to determine except at the most aggregate level. The degree of substitutability among feeds, particularly between roughages and concentrates, presents another problem. Nonetheless, the available data combined with anecdotal evidence and scattered references to specific farm performance do provide insight into current Soviet problems in the feed livestock economy.

Goals vs. Attainment

Ambitious plans to increase supplies of livestock feed have consistently fallen far short of target. The Tenth Five-Year Plan (1976–80), for example, called for an increase of almost 30 percent in feed unit availability. Instead feed supplies grew by only 8 percent, even less than the 12 percent growth registered during the previous 5-year plan period. The availability of feed per standard animal unit, however, has increased only slightly since 1965.[1]

Livestock feed comprises concentrates (feeds with high nutritive content such as grain and oilseed meals)[2] and roughages (feeds with high cellulose and/or water content such as hay, silage, and potatoes and other feed roots). Roughages can be further disaggregated into those that are harvested, and thus can be measured, and pasture. Throughout the 1970s Soviet farms have come fairly close to meeting targets for feeding concentrates but have fallen far short of those for roughages. In part this was possible because of the substantial growth in grain production up to 1978 (see Table 23.2). Output of grain nearly doubled from 1965 to 1978. At the same time growth in the production of key roughages has been much slower. These crops have been slighted in allocation of yield-enhancing fertilizers and pesticides and have suffered from a lack of specialized equipment for harvest and storage.

Rations Deficient in Quantity

Overall quantities of energy available in the average livestock feed ration remain about 20 percent below announced standards.[3] The strong emphasis on expanding livestock herds and the length of time farms require to bring animals to acceptable slaughter weight have combined to absorb most of the increase in production of feedstuffs.

In recent years Moscow was forced to import massive quantities of grain and other feedstuffs to keep the calorie deficit from increasing. According to United States Department of Agriculture (USDA) statistics, imports of grain averaged 36 million tons during the 1979–1982 crop years. This equals more than 20 percent of average annual production (standard weight, that is, production less waste and losses) in those years.[4] During this period the USSR also imported about 750 thousand tons of mixed feed and 500 thousand tons of manioc.[5] If all the imported grain had been used for feed, about one-quarter of total concentrates fed during 1979–82 would have been imported.

Imports of soybeans averaged 1.4 million tons annually during calendar years 1979–82 and imports of soybean meal averaged about 650 thousand tons. The soybean meal figure masks a remarkable growth, from 25 thousand tons in 1979 to 1.550 million tons in 1982. Although these imports added a substantial quantity of energy to feed supplies, their effect on average quality was more important (see below).

Rations Deficient in Quality

Animals gain weight more rapidly and require less feed per unit of gain when the feed ration is correctly balanced between concentrates and roughages as well as in terms of nutrients—protein, minerals, vitamins, trace elements, and so on.

For more than a decade, the USSR had stressed the importance of increasing quantities of concentrates fed to livestock, both absolutely and as a share of the ration. The quantity of concentrates fed more than doubled during 1965–80, while feeding of harvested roughages increased by only 40 percent. Feed derived from pasture declined by 3 percent over the period despite an 8-percent increase in total farm pasture area (see Figure 23.2). The share of concentrates increased from about 23 percent in 1965 to 36 percent in 1980 (in terms of feed units). In some areas such as Estonia, the share of grain per standard animal, the major concentrate fed, reportedly reached 60 percent of the feed ration.[6]

The increase in feeding of concentrates was not accompanied by an increase in average animal productivity. During 1971–80 use of grain for milk production rose by 17 percent or nearly twice as fast as milk output increased; the use of grain for cattle-feeding increased by 35 percent, or about 60 percent more than beef production. One Soviet authority noted it took twice as much grain to produce a unit of milk in 1975 as in 1965, and 2.5 times as much for a unit of weight-gain in cattle.[7]

In 1978, the spoken and written emphasis began to shift toward the importance of forage crops and the need to reduce the use of grain. *Pravda* noted on 20 June, that "The use of concentrates to make up for shortages of hay, silage, haylage, and root crops in feed is unacceptable." But the roughage sector had long been neglected.

Roughage Sector Slighted. Slow growth in production of roughages traditionally has been attributed to a number of causes. Among them are:

- lack of yield-enhancing fertilizer and pesticides;
- lack of high-quality seed;
- poor harvesting techniques and delays in harvesting; and
- probably most important, failure to improve pastures.

In the USSR pastures occupy well over 300 million hectares and provide an estimated 18 percent of animal feed (nutrient value). Large resources are being devoted to pasture improvement, particularly to provide water, but to little avail.[8]

A Dramatic Change—Record 1982 and 1983 Forage Output. By the end of October 1982, supplies of harvested forage were running almost 15 percent ahead of the previous year, and a similar increase was achieved in 1983. Three general factors undoubtedly contributed to this suddenly improved performance.

- The Food Program, announced by Brezhnev in May 1982, not only repeated the periodic emphasis on roughages production but also directed some increased resources such as fertilizer and investment in machinery and storage facilities toward the sector;
- The repeated warning to farms not to count on state stocks of grain to cover on-farm feed shortages could have caused farms to concentrate more effort on roughages; and
- Longer, more favorable growing seasons (earlier springs in both years) enabled additional cuttings of hay and other roughage crops as well as better pasture growth.

The Role of Fertilizer. As fertilizer production has steadily increased, quantities used for roughages have also gone up, particularly in recent years. Less than one million tons (nutrient value) of fertilizer, 15 percent of total fertilizer delivered to agriculture, was used on roughages in 1965; by 1982 the quantity had increased to 5.7 million tons, or 30 percent of the total. Even in 1982, however, the quantity of fertilizer applied to feed crops (excluding grain) was only about 60 percent of the quantity needed.[9]

The Role of Storage. The value of forage crops is only as good as their initial quality and the success in maintaining that quality. Storage facilities are limited in the USSR, and physical losses as high as 40 percent have been cited in Soviet literature dealing with agricultural developments. Protein losses of 20 percent are also cited.[10] Annual storage losses for silage and haylage average 20 million tons (8 percent of annual average silage and haylage use) and of hay, 6 million tons (7 percent of annual average hay used in recent years).[11] In 1980, only 40 percent of silage, 80 percent of haylage, 10 percent of root crops, and 8 percent of hay were stored in adequate facilities.[12]

Lack of Protein

In 1980 the average feed ration contained 95 grams of digestible protein per feed unit compared with the long-established Soviet norm of 105 to 110 grams.[13] To have eliminated the protein deficit with soybean meal, a readily available high protein feed, would have required almost 11 million tons of imports in addition to the 438 thousand tons imported in that year. Upgrading the protein content to the norm level would have, in turn, reduced the calorie deficit to 5 percent or less. Western observers have long urged imports of soybean meal or of soybeans as a "simple and quick" solution to the protein deficit.[14] Moscow, however, stubbornly refused to pursue this course of action until recently, perhaps from a realization that the mixed feed industry, with its lack of adequate mixing facilities and trained personnel, would not be able to utilize the meal efficiently.

Although protein is found in nearly all feed, high-protein feeds are generally defined as those containing 20 percent or more of their total weight as crude (total) protein.[15] Protein feeds may also be categorized according to source as non-protein nitrogen, plant, animal, and single cell.[16]

Non-protein Nitrogen. This feed, mainly urea, is used routinely in ruminent rations in the United States and Western Europe to replace limited amounts of plant protein. Western authorities note that the USSR makes little use of this feed because of the risk of poisoning and animal death through over-dosage or by incorrect incorporation into feed rations. In 1980–82 the USSR used an average 100 thousand tons (nutrient value). This is about 15 percent of the quantity used in the United States, which had a 2-percent smaller cattle inventory during the period. Considering that urea is utilized in well-balanced, high-energy rations, not as a supplement to low quality roughages, and that Soviet feed rations are, in general, poorly balanced and deficient in energy, the USSR is probably wise not to pursue substantial increases in urea feeding at this time.

Oilseed Meals. These feeds currently make up about one third of high-protein feeds, down from about 44 percent in 1965 (see Figure 23.3). For most of the period, oilseed meal from sunflower and cotton seed accounted for over 90 percent of total oilseed meal. Since 1978, soybean meal has been increasingly important, providing about 40 percent of oilseed meal in 1982 and nearly 50 percent in 1983.[17]

Animal Sources. These feeds, which supply about half of the estimated protein available from high-protein feeds in the USSR, include whole and skim milk, whey, meat and bone meals, and fish meal. The USSR currently uses roughly 11–12 million tons of whole milk and over 20 million tons of skim milk, buttermilk, and whey annually in feeding livestock, roughly the same quantities used in 1970. Efforts to reduce these quantities, considered unjustifiably large by Soviet specialists, have not been successful. Growth in production of starter feeds and milk substitutes has been slow. In 1983, for example, the USSR produced only 310 thousand tons of milk replacer, equal to 2.4 million tons of milk.

Production of fish meal and of meat and bone meal grew steadily from 1965 to 1975 but has stagnated since then. Fish meal output has been constrained as the Soviet fish catch has been limited by offshore territorial limits in recent years, and meat and bone meal output because of the slowdown in growth of meat output.

Single-Cell Protein. The USSR is by far the world's largest producer of SCP. Although comparatively small amounts are produced in the West, the cost of production, roughly double that for soybean meal, and fears of possible carcinogenic properties have effectively halted growth in output.

The USSR, however, has chosen to develop the industry, primarily to increase self-sufficiency in supplies of high-protein feed supplements (see Figure 23.3).[18] Moreover, raw materials, particularly hydrocarbon and agricultural wastes, were readily available. After rapid growth during 1970–76, production of SCP stagnated during 1977–80 at about 900 thousand tons. In common with most industries in the USSR, development of the microbiological industry has been hindered by failure to commission new plants on time and shortfalls in supplies of raw materials, frequently because of transportation difficulties. Many of the materials, corn cobs, rice husks, straw, wood shavings, and sawdust are comparatively light-weight, so trucking enterprises are unwilling to haul them. In addition, production of SCP has been held back by difficulties with hydrocarbon contamination and problems with corrosion and general wear and tear in existing plants. By 1980, SCP production amounted to nearly one million tons; in terms of protein, SCP accounted for over 16 percent of the protein available from high-protein feeds.[19] Although output grew by over 12 percent annually during 1981–83, the ambitious plans for SCP continue to be unfulfilled.[20]

Prospects for Increasing and Improving
Feed Supplies

Soviet plans call for increasing the supply of feed to 500 million tons of feed units by 1985 and to 540–550 million tons by 1990. This implies an increase of about 25 percent by 1985 from the average quantity used during the 1978–82 period. Total feed use peaked in 1978 at about 410 million tons (of feed units) then fell back to about 400 million tons for the next 4 years. Increased supplies of grain and roughages in 1983 allowed feed use to slightly exceed the 1978 level. Even so, achieving the 1985 target seems unlikely. Availability of feed has consistently fallen far short of five-year-plan targets as the following tabulation in millions of tons of feed units[21] shows:

	Plan	Actual
1975	459	369
1980	475	398
1985	500–509	—

According to G. P. Rudenko, the share of concentrates is to drop to 33 percent by 1985.[22] Plans for the share of grain within concentrates have not been announced. If the share remains constant at about 85 percent, total grain feeding will increase by roughly 15 percent from the 1980 level. This is about 1 percentage point annual growth less than the 1976–80 rate. Barring further poor grain crops, down to the 150–160 million ton range, the implied grain feeding goal is feasible; reducing the share of grain in the ration is less likely.

Plans call for increasing the supply of coarse feeds, primarily hay and haylage, by nearly two-thirds (see Table 23.3). Plans for the third major category, succulent feeds, are difficult to interpret. In planning parlance the category "summer green feed" apparently includes the pasture fed category of feed use. Plans for feed from pasture per se seldom appear, nor, except in rare cases, do actual data on summer green feed appear. Consequently, any statements about meeting plans are highly tentative. The share of succulent and summer green feed in the 1985 plan calls for roughly the same share of feed units as were supplied by succulent feed and pasture in 1980, implying an increase of nearly one-quarter in supply. Supplies of the various roughage crops have consistently fallen far short of plan, however, and targets are likely to continue out of reach. Planned fertilizer deliveries are not sufficient to raise yields to the necessary levels; yield increases from land improvement (irrigation and drainage) are very slow in coming; specialized equipment for harvest continues in short supply; and storage facilities are woefully insufficient for even current production levels. Because some improvement in supplies of crucial inputs will occur, the shortfall may decline from 18 percent in 1980 to about 15 percent. If so, and if targets for feeding grain are achieved, total feed availability would fall about 10 percent short of plan and the share of concentrates would reach a new high of 37 percent.

Reducing the Protein Shortage

The obvious quick answer to the protein shortage is imported soybean meal. As noted above, very large quantities would be required. Such imports would be expensive; imports of 10 million tons, for example, at mid-1984 prices would cost about $1.7 billion and could be difficult to incorporate into feed rations. Indeed, Western authorities speculate that problems with handling the 2.6 million tons of meal imported in 1983 caused Moscow to draw back from such large imports in 1984.

In the longer-term, the Soviet Union plans to increase protein content through three major channels: domestic production of oilseed meals and high protein crops such as pulses and alfalfa and other grasses, and the microbiological industry. Resources to increase the supply of animal-based protein feeds are limited.

Oilseed Meals. Area sown to oilseed crops, including cotton and flax, in the USSR has been fairly constant, averaging 10 million hectares annually during the 1979–83 period. Yields, however, have been disappointing, showing no increase over the period. Plans to produce an average of 6.68 million tons of sunflower seed annually during 1981–85 are well out of reach. Cottonseed availability, the other major domestic oilseed, will remain roughly constant as plans call for cotton production to remain at the current level through 1985.

Soybean production continues to be dismal. The USSR has little farm land with agroclimatic conditions suitable for soybean production, yields are less than one-third yields in the United States, and incentives to emphasize soybean production are lacking. Meeting plans for average annual output of 1.4 million tons during 1981–85 will be impossible; production averaged about 550,000 tons during 1981–83.

Rape is another oilseed crop that has been attracting attention in the USSR recently. Output is planned to increase to 500,000 tons in 1985 and 1.5 million tons in 1990.[23] With production of winter rape pegged at 18,000 tons in 1981, the latest published data, these also appear overly ambitious goals.[24] Even with substantially increased area, and perhaps yield as well, rapeseed supplies will not add large quantities of protein to animal rations for many years.

Pulses and Grasses. Plans to increase the share of pulse crops in grain to 10 percent on average for the country by 1985 and to an even higher percentage in key areas such as the Ukraine will not be achieved. Plans call for sowing 7.0–7.5 million hectares to pulses by 1985. Thus, in order to meet the production target of 12–13 million tons in 1985, yields must increase by 30–40 percent. In fairness, it should be noted that preliminary data for 1983 indicated that sown area was up 30 percent over the 1980 level. The yield, however, as estimated by the USDA, remained at the 1980 level largely because of difficulties in seed selection and purity, problems that are not likely to be overcome soon. Similarly, longer range plans to raise alfalfa area to 10 million hectares and clover to 8–9 million hectares by 1990 compared with 6.8 and 6.2 million hectares currently are likely to go unmet. A key bottleneck to increasing these crops is the shortage of good quality seed and the slow development of high-yielding and disease and pest resistent varieties.

The Microbiological Industry. During the 11th FYP (1981–85) nearly 3 billion rubles were scheduled to be invested in further development of the microbiological industry.[25] Plans call for production of 1.9 million tons of single-cell protein by 1985.[26] This is a downward revision of earlier plans to raise output to 2.3 million tons in that year.[27]

The numerous chronic raw material shortages, particularly of paraffins, and the slowness in commissioning new capacity as well as "acute problems in utilizing available capacity" suggest that in this area plans will also not be achieved. Moveover, because microbiological processes are very material and energy intensive, development is likely to continue at a slower-than-planned pace.

Conclusion

The previous paragraphs highlight the dim prospects for bringing livestock feed rations into concentrate-roughage or protein balance before the end of this decade although some progress will be made. With normal or better weather and continued strong emphasis on the production of roughages, including achieving planned increases in deliveries of fertilizer, pesticides, machinery and equipment, and storage capacity, feed rations per standard animal should increase by some 10–15 percent, permitting substantial improvement in animal productivity.[28] Nonetheless, the ration will still be some 10 percent short of the optimum level.

In the unlikely event that production plans for domestic sources of high-protein feeds are achieved, protein availability per unit of feed will still be 5 to 10 percent short of the Soviet norm. Highly simplified calculations indicate that, in the absence of any imports, protein content will actually decline from the present estimated 96 grams to 94 grams in 1985. By 1990, protein content will have increased to about 100 grams. Nevertheless, the protein deficit is a long-standing problem and is likely to continue well into the next decade.

Notes

1. The USSR aggregates feed supplies in terms of feed units, using oats as the standard, that is, one feed unit contains the nutrient equivalent of one kilogram of oats.

2. Concentrates as reported exclude the animal-based, meat and bone meal, fish meal, milk, and so on.

3. See, for example, *Vestnik sel'skokhozyaystvennoy nauki*, No. 3, 1982, p. 46.

4. The USSR measures grain on a bunker-weight basis, that is, as it comes from the field before cleaning and drying thus including excess moisture, weed seeds, and other non-grain materials.

5. Problems in the use of manioc, as reported in Soviet technical journals, the cessation of the US partial embargo on sales of grain and feedstuffs to the USSR, and the world surplus of grain and consequent favorable grain purchase prices combined to turn Moscow away from continued manioc imports.

6. *Sel'skaya zhizn'*, 23 June 1981, p. 1.

7. *Vestnik sel'skokhozyaystvennoy nauki*, No. 12, 1978, p. 49.

8. *Vestnik sel'skokhozyaystvennoy nauki*, No. 10, 1983, p. 8.

9. On cultivated land. Kormoproizvodstvo, No. 2, 1984, p. 2.

10. *Kormoproizvodstvo*, No. 5, 1983, p. 1.

11. *Sel'skaya zhizn'*, 26 June 1983, p. 2.

12. *Kormoproizvodstvo*, No. 1, 1982, p. 2.

13. *Ekonomika sel'skogo khozyaystvo*, No. 2, 1981, p. 61.

14. D. Gale Johnson, *The Soviet Impact on World Grain Trade*. British–North American Committee, USA, May 1977, pp. 12–19.

15. Crude protein refers to all the nitrogeneous compounds in a feed; digestible protein refers to protein utilized by the animal and is estimated by coefficients derived over time from feeding trials.

16. Single-cell protein (SCP) is a collective term including protein-rich micro-organisms such as algae, yeast, molds, and other fungi grown on byproducts of oil, on methanol, or on organic wastes from agriculture and industry.

17. The increase is, of course, a result of the very large soybean and soybean meal imports in recent years. Despite several campaigns to increase domestic production of soybeans, output has stagnated at around 500 thousand tons since 1975. Imports of soybeans during the early 1970s were more closely related to the need for vegetable oil than to that for oilseed meal.

18. Soviet authorities also note that SCP output has an added advantage because it is factory produced and thus not dependent on weather. The USSR began experimental production of cellulose-based SCP from hydrolysed straw in 1936. A Soviet textbook reports that by 1943 industrial production had begun. Experiments based on the use of liquid paraffin (obtained from crude oil) began in the mid-1960s. In 1966 the Main Administration for the Microbiological Industry, which has responsibility for SCP production, became an independent branch of the economy. The industry also produces numerous other needed feed components, premixes, vitamins, minerals and trace elements, several essential amino acids such as lysine and methionione, antibiotics, and so on, as well as plant "protectants" and other products for agricultural use.

19. Although it is likely that some SCP is being used experimentally to develop foods suitable for human consumption, the amount is negligible.

20. *Pravda*, 3 January 1983, p. 2.

21. See Table 23.3 for sources.

22. Cited in Table 23.3.

23. *Zakupki sel'skokhozyaystvennykh produktov*, No. 6, 1983, p. 16.

24. *Vestnik statistiki*, No. 3, 1982, p. 72.

25. *Ekonomika sel'skogo khozyaystva*, No. 8, 1979, p. 5.

26. *Ekonomicheskaya gazeta,* No. 51, 1983, p. 1.

27. *Pravda,* 2 June 1980, p. 7.

28. The limited plan data that have appeared to date (for January 1986) indicate overall growth in livestock numbers is to slow from earlier rates. To make this calculation, 0.5 percent average annual growth in herds is assumed.

Table 23.1

USSR: PRODUCTION OF LIVESTOCK PRODUCTS[a]

	Meat[b] (million tons)	Milk[c] (million tons)	Eggs (billions)
1965	10.0	72.6	29.1
1970	12.3	83.0	40.7
1975	15.0	90.8	57.4
1976	13.6	89.7	56.2
1977	14.7	94.9	61.2
1978	15.5	94.7	64.5
1979	15.3	93.2	65.8
1980	15.1	90.9	67.9
1981	15.2	88.9	70.0
1982	15.4	91.0	72.4
1983	16.0	96.4	74.7

---

a Official Soviet statistics. SSSR v tsifrakh v 1983 godu, p. 113, Narodnoye khozyaystvo SSSR v 1982 g., p. 189, and earlier editions.

b Meat includes poultry meat and slaughter fat. To be comparable to Western measures, the quantity should be reduced by roughly 18 per cent.

c Milk statistics are not fully understood. Gross output of milk is given in physical weight while marketed milk statistics are in terms of standardized butterfat content--3.6 per cent. Nearly 40 percent of milk, however, is not marketed and must be estimated from survey data and farm accounts using standard conversion factors. Z. G. Tresorukova, Tovarnaya produktsiya sel'skogo khozyaystva, Moscow, 1974, p. 102-103.

356

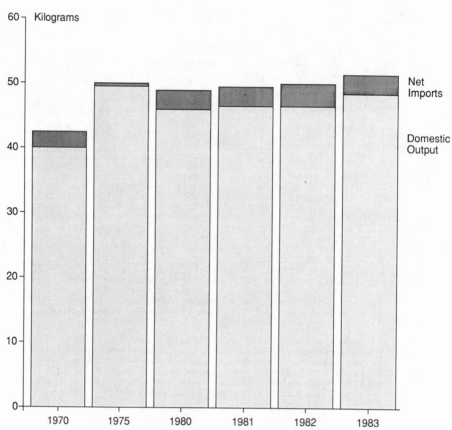

Figure 23.1: USSR: Per Capita Meat Availability

Note: Soviet official statistics on meat production are adjusted to conform
to western definitions (trim, including slaughter fat and bone is removed).

Table 23.2

USSR: PRODUCTION OF GRAIN AND SELECTED FEED CROPS[a]

(Million Tons)

	Grain	Corn for Silage and Green Feed	Feed Roots	Green Feed In Hay Equivalent
1965	121.1	181	23.8	82.5
1970	186.8	212	35.7	110.3
1975	140.1	193	34.4	115.8
1976	223.8	277	50.0	131.2
1977	195.7	247	45.3	135.3
1978	237.4	251	45.7	151.7
1979	179.3	230	38.4	134.4
1980	189.1	266	41.6	148.0
1981	160.0	232	36.6	149.0
1982	180.0	294	45.5	160.0
1983	190.0	298	48.1	177.4

a Narodnoye khozyzystvo SSSR v 1983 g., p. 209, and earlier editions. Because grain statistics have not been published since 1980, the 1981–1983 figures presented are the US Department of Agriculture estimates.

358

FIGURE 23.2: USSR: Production of Selected Feeds

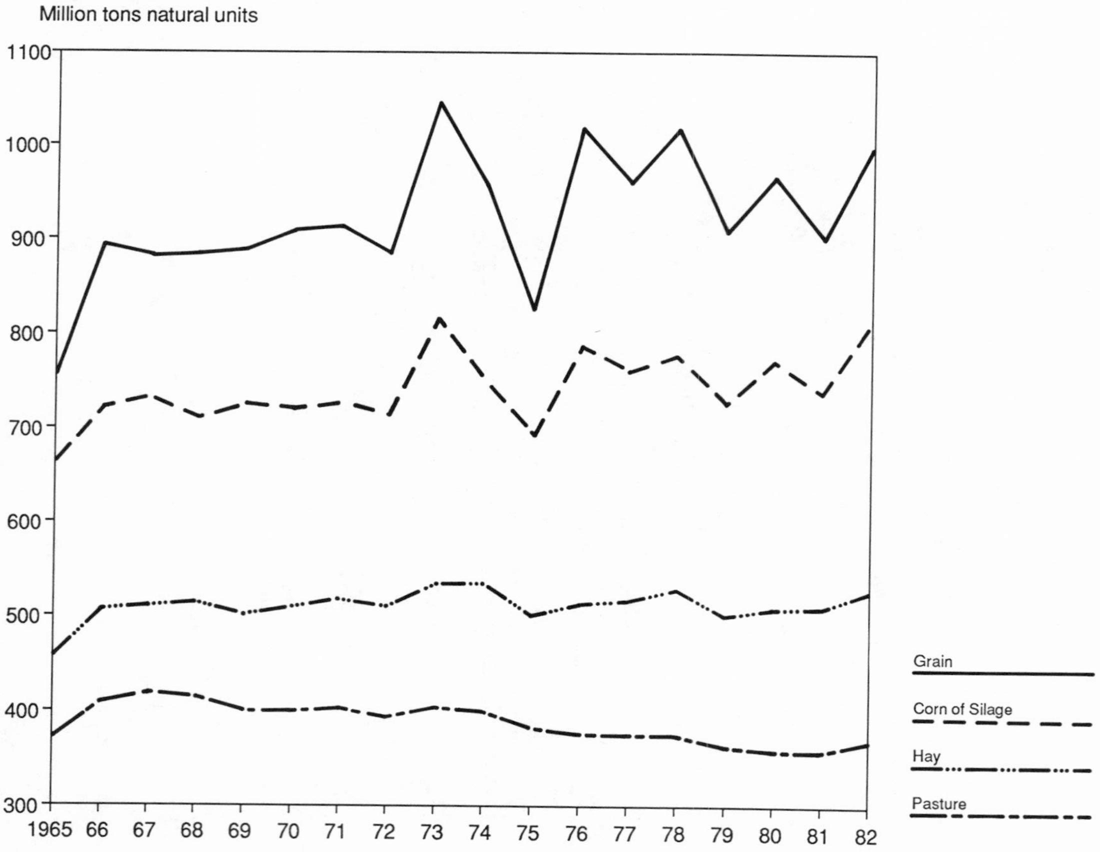

Million tons natural units

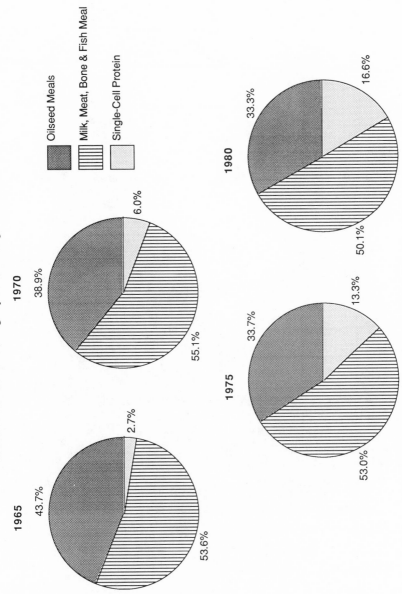

FIGURE 23.3: USSR: Growing Importance of Single-Cell Protein*

* Shares based on digestible protein content of high-protein feeds.

Table 23.3

USSR: ROUGHAGE AVAILABILITY, PLAN AND ACTUAL

(Million Tons, Natural Units)

	1975		1980		1985
	Plan[a]	Actual[b]	Plan[c]	Actual[b]	Plan[d]
Coarse feed	251.4	237.6	248	231.7	NA
Hay and haylage	142.1	NA	159	NA	187-192
Of which hay	NA	78.8	NA	78.8	NA
Succulent feed	449	501.6[e]	436	585.8[e]	NA
Of which silage	258.1	171.1	254	198.9	260-275
Summer green feed	762	NA	747	NA	690
Pasture	NA	386.7[f]	NA	363.1[f]	NA
Succulent and summer green	1211	NA	1183	NA	NA
Succulent and pasture	NA	888.3	NA	948.9	NA

----

a Gosudarstvennyy pyatiletniy plan razvitiy narodnoggo khozyaystvo SSSR na 1971-1975 gody, Moscow, 1972, p. 175.

b Narodnoye khozyaystvo SSSR v 1980 g., p. 253.

c G. C. Gaponenko, Osnovnyye napravleniya razvitiya sel'skoggo khozyaystvo v desyatoy pyatiletke, Moscow, 1976, p. 76.

d G. P. Rudenko, Razvitiye agropromyshlennogo kompleska v odinadtsatoy pyatiletke, Moscow, 1982, pp. 42, 44.
Ya. P. Ryabov, Sotsial'no-ekonomicheskoye razvitiye SSSR v odinadtsatoy pyatiletke, Moscow, 1981, p. 41.

e Includes a portion of summer green feed.

f Includes a portion of summer green feed.

24

Rural Infrastructure in the Soviet Union: Roads and Other Priorities

Elizabeth Clayton

The Need for Infrastructure:
New Marketings

The New Food Program anticipates meeting the demand of consumers by enlarging their supplies of meat, fruits, and vegetables.[1] This policy presents a substantial departure from the past emphasis on food grains in that it emphasizes the increased production of products that are perishable, and timely delivery is absolutely essential. They have a high unit value, so that losses in transit can easily turn a year-end profit into a loss. Sensibly, the Program also recognizes that these products require a large advance in the marketing infrastructure that links consumers to producers.

In common with the marketing of other products, Soviet food marketing has been relatively ignored, demanding of regions that they be relatively self-sufficient in food. Such a policy suffices for guaranteeing a quantity of food, but not its diversity or quality, and it will not capture the advantages of specialized regional production. Further, an imbalance of investment that favors production over marketing eventually increases output only to have it languish on the farm and rot.

The relationship between production and marketing has changed in recent years. Food production has increased, and for most products the marketings have increased faster. Increasingly marketing takes place in the public, not the private, sector. The data in Table 24.1 illustrate recent structure and some trends.

Table 24.1 shows that the marketings generally increased markedly, but with differences between crops and animal products. The marketings of vegetables and potatoes grew faster than production, indicating more for consumers and less left on the farm. But the marketings of animal products grew less than production (and even declined for meat), indicating possible unreported marketings and probable losses between producer and consumer.

The procurements of all products except meat grew faster than marketings, indicating that more was marketed through the state sector and less through private markets. In all cases, the state procurement agencies took a growing share of marketings.

These data indicate that for vegetables and potatoes growth occurred as much, or more, in marketings as in production; product was available and needed to be moved to consumers. In animal husbandry, growth was hampered by deficiencies in both production and marketing; even when product was available, some never reached the consumer, although it is also possible that some reached the consumer but was unreported. In all products, the increased marketings stretched the capacity of existing rural infrastructure, particularly in transport.

The Rural Transport Sector

In the past, agriculture's transportation needs were met primarily by railroads and waterways, which are well suited to hauling grain, which is not perishable or fragile, but poorly suited to today's new priorities, which need timely delivery. The need for timeliness has increased the importance of auto freight, which handles about three-fourths of agricultural marketings. The weakness of Soviet auto freight is that it delivers more to other transport than to final users. Data from the total economy show that trucks deliver more tonnage than railroads, but have a very short average length of haul; only 18 km, in contrast to 434 km by river boat, and 930 km by rail.[2] Symons found that these brief trips ended primarily not at final users, but at rail and water transport centers, where the journey is continued.[3] Using a weight-distance measure in ton-kilometers, auto freight carries only 7 percent of all freight.[4] Of this small share, however, 19 percent is devoted to agricultural products.[5]

Expansion of Soviet agricultural motor freight is limited by the length and condition of roads.[6] In the RSFSR in 1980 only 85 percent of rural raion centers and only 78 percent of central farms were served by all-weather roads.[7] This limits not only product marketings but input purchases that improve agricultural productivity; a Soviet study estimates that on average 2.5 tons of input enters a farm for each 1 ton that leaves as product. It is estimated that these represent each year 21 million tons of fuel, 20 million tons of fertilizer, 10 million tons of construction materials, 20 million cubic meters of wood and 1.7 million agricultural machines.[8]

Lacking too are the all-weather roads that link a farm's outlying areas with its center. Large Soviet farms include many small villages, and half of their transport needs are for intra-farm movements of people to jobs, feed to livestock, and equipment to fields. Only one-fifth of their roads can be used in any weather.[9] The New Food Plan anticipates a fund of 3.3 billion rubles to assist low-profit farms in building intra-farm roads and other infrastructure.[10] The Plan's commitment is important not only for its funding, but for the promise that it holds for claiming scarce construction resources for roads. The capital budget for rural road improvement is 40 percent higher in the 11th Five-Year Plan than in the 10th Five-Year Plan.

The need for on-farm roads can be measured by comparing the official norm of 2.7–3.0 km per thousand hectares of agricultural (*ugod'ya*) land[11] and the actual roads in the *whole* republic. Table 24.2 shows these calculations by region.

Wealthier agricultural republics such as Moldavia, Estonia, and Georgia have a much higher road density than poorer republics. The value per hectare of their production is also higher. Conversely, production value per hectare is low in republics whose road density is low. However, this calculation does not adjust for differences in climate, crop structure, or prices. In a study that compares only Krasnodar farms, the tons harvested from hectares whose road density achieves the national norm (3 km per thousand hectares) is twice as much as the harvest from those that have only half the norm.[12] All weather roads on the farm not only increase output but improve profitability. Some indicators are:

1. overall machine productivity increased 40 percent, gasoline usage fell 35 percent, and repairs decreased by one-third;[13]
2. in Stavropol krai machine productivity increased 40 percent, gasoline usage fell 35 percent, and cost per ton-kilometer decreased 35–40 percent;[14]
3. usable agricultural product increased 10 percent.[15] This in part would be a surplus captured from the 20 percent of fruits and vegetables, 25 percent of sugar beets, and one-third of potatoes now left to rot in the fields;[16]
4. tractors used for transport at 17.5 kopecks per ton-kilometer were replaced by less expensive trucks that cost only 7.5 kopecks.[17]

Although improved roads create savings in use, they cost more. One ton-kilometer of freight costs 2–3 kopecks on a major highway and 15–20 kopecks on a dirt road, but to construct a major highway costs 33 times more and a final evaluation depends on traffic density.[18] These costs are virtually unchanged since the 1960s.[19]

Improved rural roads increase the attractiveness of living in rural areas because people, goods, and services can more easily enter and exit. Rural labor force quality is improved as it acquires access to specialized secondary education and modern medical care. However, the benefits of rural roads for attracting and keeping rural labor are problematic. Soviet authors acknowledge that rural workers use the easy exit on rural roads to bypass agriculture and relocate in cities. Some would offset this tendency by resettlement from small, isolated, "futureless" villages to larger agricultural villages with modern amenities. This program of long standing costs dearly because the state finances rural housing and utilities; without it, most rural housing costs are shifted to the private sector. It is also expensive because resettlement plans may not coordinate with optimal road patterns.[20] At best, rural roads must be accompanied by investments in other amenities to hold rural labor.

The administrative responsibility for road building is shared between the Ministry of Transportation, which builds roads located outside farms, about four-fifths of total length, and the farms and other Ministries, which build the remaining, internal roads. Responsibility for road planning is not necessarily shared. State construction agencies impose some comprehensive planning on the external road network, but the autonomous farms have neither the obligation nor the expertise to follow these plans and can build on-farm roads that are uncoordinated with other farms or with external roads. State agencies impose building standards and methods that are unattainable on farms, which tend to build with local materials that may be cheap but wear away quickly. In addition, a single farm cannot afford large-scale, specialized equipment for this single purpose and it is too small to capture the significant economies of scale available in building all-weather roads.

Other Infrastructure

The avowed benefits of rural road building are threefold: the recoupment of lost product, more effective use of machines, and less migration from the countryside. However, it is important to note that these same goals might be achieved by alternative policies that compete against roads for investment funds.

One alternative is to augment the motor freight sector. Administrative responsibility for trucking itself is shared between farms, the Ministry of Auto Transport, the State Committee on Agricultural Technology, and inter-farm cooperatives. Farms possess their own delivery trucks, but few pieces of specialized equipment, which are allocated to the centralized transportation agencies and inter-farm organizations where machine utilization rates are higher. The centralized agencies handle about half of agricultural auto freight and their share is rising; for some specialized products their share is higher, e.g., they carry 67 percent of marketed meat.[21] Three possible changes to the motor freight sector are considered here: more truck deliveries, reformed tariffs, and containerization.

In the current Five-Year Plan, about 1450 thousand trucks will be added to the agricultural fleet, including refrigerated carriers for cattle, poultry, and live fish; and tank cars for complex liquid fertilizers. This plan sizably increases deliveries over the 1108 thousand trucks delivered to agriculture during the last Five-Year Plan. So far, the truck deliveries have been fewer than planned, but more than in the previous plan. In 1981 and 1982, agricultural truck deliveries (including specialized trucks) achieved a rate for the current plan that equals about 1340 thousand.[22]

The truck tariffs paid by farms to centralized trucking agencies embody poor incentives for timely delivery. They are subsidized by the Ministry of Transportation, but the subsidy share has been falling, which exacerbates their harmful effects. The tariffs are flat fees per ton-kilometer based on total weight; they are higher for under five tons weight, and truckers prefer smaller capacity trucks, so to capture the higher piece rates.[23] There is no adjustment for road quality, so centralized truckers choose pickups and deliveries on good roads and ignore those on poor roads. The most serious deficiency in tariff structure is the lack of responsibility to the receiver— the centralized agents are paid by ton-kilometer and not by the condition of arrived product; the farm and trucker contract for transport; excluded are the receiver and the production brigade.[24]

Tariff reforms have been proposed and tested, but they only shift the burden of the tariffs and do not change the incentive structure. The best known tariff reform proposal was tested in Belorussia in the early 1970s.[25] It is still offered up today. It prices freight only by weight, not distance, and centralizes trucking. This removes a penalty placed on outlying farms, but fails to encourage a high arrival quality.

Containerization protects product quality from farm to consumer but has appeared only recently in the Soviet Union. For vegetables, it costs 3– 12 rubles per ton, and it increases usable potatoes and other root vegetables by 5–6 percent and usable cabbage by 15 percent.[26] About half of the potatoes in the Ukraine, which grows about one-fifth of Soviet potatoes, now are containerized.

Although improvements within the motor freight infrastructure offer cost savings, the greater need within the larger food sector is for storage and handling facilities. Even if there were new rural roads, improved tariffs, better trucks and more containers, consumers would not necessarily benefit because of storage and handling bottlenecks. Storage capacity is satisfied only 66 percent for grain, 32 percent for vegetables and potatoes, 47 percent for fruit, and 40 percent for silage and hay.[27]

Handling facilities are too seldom mechanized. Trucks are often under-utilized because they must wait for handlers. One author estimates that an average truck experiences 40 days waiting time per year.

Benefits and Costs

The economic impact of these alternative investment strategies can be compared. Omitting the inexpensive (containerization) and the unlikely (tariff reform), rural road building and storage provide a comparison most instructive about current rural bottlenecks.

Road building cost varies with road quality; the national average cost of one kilometer is 15 thousand rubles for dirt roads, 60 thousand rubles for asphalt, and 500–2500 thousand rubles for major highways.[28] Regional opportunity costs may be less where there is substantial unemployment, but this will not be considered here. When the national unit cost is multiplied by the low estimate of on-farm need that was developed earlier, the total cost for all-weather roads only on the farms would be 39.4 billion rubles.

The benefits from this cost can be estimated as the sum of:

1. Increased marketed output. This can be estimated at 7.6 billion rubles in 1982.[29]
2. Net costs decreased from improved machine usage, but increased from the transportation costs of increased output; assumed to equal zero.

The net undiscounted rate of return is 19 percent, with a payback period of 5 years.

Storage construction costs are unknown, so that a comparable estimate cannot be made for that. However, the relative economic importance of alternative investments is shown by Soviet estimated payback periods: 3–4 years for storage and capacity, and 8–10 years for roads.[30] My estimate above indicates that the Soviet estimate for roads is possibly low, but still less than that for storage. The priority of storage within the food industry must surely be the higher, and the bottleneck greater.

Notes

1. Reference for the New Food Program is L.I. Brezhnev, "Party Session Approves Food Program," *Pravda*, May 25, 1982, translated in *Current Digest of the Soviet Press*, 34(21–22), June 23 and 30, 1982.

2. *Narodnoe Khoziaistvo SSSR v 1982* (Moscow: 1983).

3. Leslie Symons and Colin White, *Russian Transport: An Historical and Geographical Survey* (G. Bell and Sons, London: 1975), pp. 98–99.

4. *Narodnoe Khoziaistvo, op. cit.,* p. 296.

5. B. Kerblay, "Un handicap de l'agriculture sovietique: l'etat des routes rurales," *Revue d'Etudes Comparative Est-Ouest,* Vol. 14., No. 2 (June, 1983), p. 7.

6. The Russian term *c tverdym pokrytiem* has been translated as "all-weather."

7. P.P. Kobzev, "Transport i realizatsiia prodovol'stvennoi programmy," *EKO*, No. 6 (1982), p. 108.

8. Kerblay, *op. cit.,* p. 7.

9. V. Dobrynin, "Infrastruktura sel'skokhoziaistvennogo proizvodstva i ee ekonomicheskoe znachenie," *Ekonomika Sel'skogo Khoziaistva*, No. 10 (1983), p. 12.

10. A. Arkhipov, "Prodovol'stvennaia programma i razvitie ekonomiki kolkhozov," *Voprosy Ekonomiki,* No. 1 (1983), p. 88.

11. V. Krasovskii, "Problemy sovershenstvovaniia infrastruktury," *Planovoe Khoziaistvo,* No. 10 (1981), p. 62.

12. S.S. Ushakov, *Problemy razvitiia transporta SSSR: Edinaia transportnaia set'* (Moscow: Transport, 1981), p. 115.

13. A.V. Pikul'kin, *Proizvodstvenno-ekonomicheskie sviazi agropromyshlennogo kompleksa* (Moscow: Rossel'khozizdat, 1981), p. 137.

14. V. Em, "Effektivnost' kachestvennogo preobrazovaniia vnutrikhoziaistvennykh dorog," *Ekonomika Sel'skogo Khoziaistva*, No. 8 (1972), p. 37.

15. Dobrynin, *op. cit.,* p. 12.

16. John Scherer, *USSR Facts and Figures Annual*, Vol. 7 (Gulf Breeze, FL: Academic International Press, 1983), p. 162.

17. Pikul'kin, *op. cit.,* p. 136.

18. Dobrynin, *op. cit.,* p. 12.

19. Holland Hunter, *Soviet Transport Experience,* (Washington, D.C.: The Brookings Institution, 1968), p. 96.

20. F. Egorov and G. Shukshin, "Uchot transportnogo faktora pri razmeshchenii sel'skogo naselennogo punkta," *Ekonomika Sel'skogo Khoziaistva,* No. 8 (1982), p. 42.

21. V. Krestovskii, "Razvitie sotsial'noi i proizvodstvennoi infrastruktury sela," *Ekonomika Sel'skogo Khoziaistva,* No. 6 (1982), p. 17.

22. *Narodnoe Khoziaistvo SSSR 1980* (Moscow: 1981), p. 217, and *SSSR v tsifrakh v 1982 g* (Moscow: 1983), p. 127.

23. V. Kotelianetz and A. Pilichenko, "Sovershenstvovanie ekonomicheskikh vzaimootnoshenii transportnykh organizatisi i obsluzhivaemykh imi predpriiatii APK," *Ekonomika Sel'skogo Khoziaistva,* No. 9 (1983), p. 45.

24. *Ibid.,* p. 46.

25. M. Gorskii, "O rabote avtotransporta v sel'skom khoziaistve," *Planovoe Khoziaistvo,* No. 3 (1972), pp. 137–141.

26. G. Elistratov, "Do potrebitelia—bez poter'," *Ekonomika Sel'skogo Khoziaistva,* No. 3 (1982), p. 23.

27. Dobrynin, *op. cit.,* pp. 12–13.

28. *Ibid.,* p. 12.

29. Dobrynin (*op. cit.,* footnote 15) estimates that road improvement both on- and off-farm would add ten percent to gross agricultural output. In 1982 this would have been 12.7 billion rubles (*Narodnoe Khoziaistvo SSSR 1982, op. cit.,* p. 194). Deducting from this total the increment to be attributed to off-farm roads (5.1 billion rubles, or 4 percent of gross agricultural output), the gain from adequate on-farm roads would be 7.6 billion rubles.

30. Dobrynin, *op. cit.,* p. 12; Em, *op. cit.,* p. 41.

TABLE 24.1

PRODUCTION, MARKETINGS, AND PROCUREMENTS

	Average 1971-75	1982	Growth
		(thousands of tons)	
Vegetables			
Production	22,974	29,993	+31%
Marketings	16,100*	22,400	+39%
Marketings/Production	70%	75%	
Procurements	13,073	19,440	+49%
Procurements/Marketings	81%	87%	
Potatoes			
Production	89,782	78,185	-13%
Marketings	20,500*	21,300	+ 4%
Marketings/Production	23%	27%	
Procurements	12,732	15,680	+23%
Procurements/Marketings	62%	74%	
Meat (slaughter weight)			
Production	14,004	15,362	+10%
Marketings	12,200*	11,900	-2.5%
Marketings/Production	87%	77%	
Procurements	9,914	9,959	+0.4%
Procurements/Marketings	81%	84%	
Milk (with milk products in milk equivalents)			
Production	87,446	91,044	+ 4%
Marketings	58,700*	60,100	+ 2%
Marketings/Production	67%	66%	
Procurements	52,113	57,996	+11%
Procurements/Marketings	89%	96%	
Eggs (millions)			
Production	51,408	72,409	+41%
Marketings	36,700*	50,300	+37%
Marketings/Production	71%	69%	
Procurements	27,474	46,419	+69%
Procurements/Marketings	75%	92%	

*1975 only

Source: Narodnoe Khoziaistvo SSSR v 1982 g.,
p. 197,219,220,223-24,246-47,250-51.

TABLE 24.2

NORMATIVE ON-FARM ROADS AND ACTUAL TOTAL ROADS, 1982

Republic	Needed roads (thousand km)	Actual roads	Actual/ needed (Percent)
RSFSR	650	458	70
Ukraine	124	174	140
Belorussia	28	39	139
Moldavia	7	11	157
Georgia	9	31	344
Azerbaidzhan	12	23	192
Armenia	4	9	225
Latvia	7	18	257
Lithuania	12	22	183
Estonia	4	26	650
Kazakhstan	587	80	14
Uzbekistan	79	58	73
Kirghizia	30	19	63
Tadzhikistan	11	15	136
Turkmenistan	90	13	14
TOTAL	1651	995	60

Sources: Needed roads calculated: 3 km x agricultural (ugod'ya) land [Narodnoe Khoziaistvo SSSR v 1982 g., p. 210]. Actual roads are equal to all-weather roads [Narodnoe Khoziaistvo SSSR v 1982 g., p. 309].

International Trade
and the Agrarian Sector

25

Hungary as a Trade Partner for Socialist and Market Economies

Tamas Ujhelyi

Introduction

The volume of Hungarian agricultural exports grew steadily during the last two decades, and there were only a few years, 1968, 1976, 1978, with a small decline (Tables 25.1 and 25.7). This trend was in conformity with the growth targets of the national economy, and the agricultural sector contributed strongly to the progressive development of the country.

The dynamic expansion of agricultural production was a primary reason for the practically unbroken growth of exports, although the world market situation was an important contributing factor. Agricultural products could be fairly easily sold and inputs bought at reasonable conditions. This favourable world market situation in the "golden age" of the Hungarian agricultural transformation led to a development strategy strongly emphasizing animal production combined with rapidly growing imports of feedstuffs, especially protein feed and somewhat neglecting the expansion of domestic protein feed production. The same is true for industrial inputs also; industrial development policies by-passed the creation and modernization of production capacities for agricultural machinery, pesticides, etc. Therefore, imports of these inputs expanded very strongly as a consequence of the industrialization of agricultural production. At the beginning of the 1960s, before the large scale transformation of agriculture, the import of agricultural inputs of industrial origin was one-third, and in the 1980s two-thirds of Hungarian food and beverage imports (Tables 25.7 and 25.11).

Parallel with the very strong growth of agricultural imports, markets were also fundamentally transformed. Before the Second World War Germany and Austria were the most important partners; in 1937, they took 33 and 26 percent of total Hungarian agricultural exports. They were followed by Italy, taking 18 percent; Switzerland, 6 percent; the United Kingdom, 5 percent; and the United States, 4 percent. These six countries completely dominated the export outlets of Hungary, buying more than 90 percent of the exported commodities. After the war, markets profoundly changed. For the first time in history Eastern countries appeared as buyers on the agricultural markets and gained overwhelming importance. At the beginning of the 1980s almost half, 46 percent, of agricultural exports went to the Soviet Union, with Western Germany at 8 percent and Italy at 7.5 percent ranking second and third, followed by Czechoslovakia, 6 percent; the GDR, 5 percent; Poland, 3 percent; and Austria, 3 percent. The six principal importers of 1937 bought only 28 percent of Hungarian agricultural exports in the 1980s.

Socialist countries buy two-thirds of Hungarian agricultural exports and three-quarters of this goes to the Soviet Union (Tables 25.1 and 25.3). The Common Market is the other important trade partner, taking more than half of the exports going to non-socialist countries; other developed market economies and developing countries are not important markets.

A high share, approximately 30 percent, of agricultural products in total exports to developed market economies is a permanent feature of Hungarian foreign trade. Agricultural products have a much smaller share in exports to the Socialist countries, but this share has started to grow in recent years. There is a permanent export surplus both in the ruble and dollar trade of agricultural products, while imports of agricultural inputs are higher than exports.

Production and Export Structure

As the main dimensions of the commodity structure of agricultural production and of crop exports are established by natural conditions, there has been comparatively little change in the traditional composition of crop exports in the post-war years. Changes in recent years mainly occurred among products that could replace each other. Rye and barley were largely replaced by wheat and maize, clover by lucerne, etc. Changes of the yields of different crops had a much greater impact. The high potential of wheat and maize for higher yields stimulated their cultivation, and as a result the basic question was raised of what to do with the increment in output since it could be sold in its original form or transformed into livestock, and ultimately into meat.

Hungarian meat production per head is among the highest in the world. Very considerable exports of animal products were gradually established based on large imports of feedstuffs, especially protein feed. The growth rate of certain types of animal products was very different in the last decades, and this led to different export growth. While pigs and poultry were characterized by continuous and dynamic growth based on the augmentation of the feed base, mainly maize and wheat, production of beef and lamb had to face vagaries of the raw-fodder supply that caused high inconsistency and uncertainty for these activities.

The production of fruit and grapes has been much more stable. Production of horticultural crops is often the only way to utilize bad soils, steep hillsides, etc. Thus there is a pressure for establishing stable export outlets for these products.

Stages of the International
Division of Labor of Hungary

Until the 1960s, post-war agricultural production policy was characterized by a primary emphasis on supplying domestic consumers with food. The entire domestic demand for all agricultural products had to be covered; importation of agricultural products that could be domestically produced was out of question. The strongly autarchic policy was of course detrimental for efficiency, as crops had to be produced for which foreign countries were more competitive. Experimenting with cotton and citrus cultivation was an outgrowth of this mistaken policy. Some remnants of this abortive concept still exist because large scale farming was built on the traditional Middle-European multi-product, mixed farming mode, emphasizing self-supply.

Not only the commodity structure, but choice, quality, etc., of the products offered on the market are very strongly influenced by the tastes of domestic consumers. Preferences and tastes of foreign buyers which differ from those of the traditional domestic customers have difficulty making themselves felt. This situation is increasingly becoming an obstacle to an export-led development strategy. It is becoming evident that a competitive agricultural structure is not consistent with a production structure defined by the demands, preferences, and tastes of domestic consumers. Such a "domestic first" concept has an adverse effect on export prices. The future lies not in selling the surplus on foreign markets, while producing according to the demand of the domestic consumers, but rather by producing for the foreign market with full consideration given to the characteristics, habits, and preferences of foreign buyers.

The Future of the International
Division of Labor

There is a strong case for the further development of Hungarian agricultural exports. The climate, soil, and abundant flatland are favorable for the production of practically all crops and animal species characteristic of the temperate zone. For some crops such as cereals, seeds, and leguminous crops, conditions are among the best in Europe. The amount of land per person is large. Most of the land is suitable for farming. In particular the rich soils of the great plains have a good potential for farming, this advantage being even more important, since flat land facilitates mechanization and thus modernization. There is considerable capital and know-how accumulated in the agro-complex, and agriculture has a lower energy and imported input requirement than industry. It utilizes renewable resources, and this is particularly important in a country where natural resources are scarce.

Hungary's location is favorable for reaching the most important markets in East and West Europe; the landlocked position is, however, a disadvantage for trading bulk-goods and reaching markets on other continents. Marketing efforts largely benefit from long-established contacts; Hungarian traditions of cattle and wheat exports go back for hundreds of years, those of special quality vegetables, such as onion and paprika, some decades.

The wide choice of products offered favors selling on different markets; this can lead to bigger exports and diminishes the risk of adverse market conditions. In recent years considerable efforts were made to transform the management and institutional structure of agriculture in order to make the supply of food products more flexible. Among such measures were the development of small scale production, organization of associations of producers, suppression of "trusts", introduction of multi-channel trading, etc.

There are, however, important factors hampering the expansion of agri-cultural exports. Bad weather often interferes with the basically favorable climate; late frosts in spring and early frosts in autumn, cold spells during the main blossoming time, drought in summer and rainy periods at harvesting time often result in high losses and considerably enhance the risk of some activities. Deficient storage capacity interferes with flexible marketing policy, as there is considerably less freedom of movement both interseasonally and between markets than is necessary for efficient trading.

The engineering, chemical, and construction industries' capacity for pro-ducing inputs for agriculture are largely deficient, and these products have to be imported mainly from hard currency countries. The present scarcity of material resources and unfavorable world market perspective do not warrant a clear-cut concentration of scarce resources on the agricultural sector.

It is obvious that Hungary will be compelled to make the utmost efforts to increase foreign exchange earnings. The ability to expand agricultural production proved to be considerable in recent years; 27 percent of the improvement of the foreign trade balance between 1978 and 1980 resulted from the growth of agricultural exports. A sluggish growth rate of domestic food consumption as a consequence of the low birth-rate and an already well-supplied market contribute to a high potential for the augmentation of exports. The problem is what to do, how to utilize the potential in the best way, taking account of the long and short term pressures facing the national economy.

All indications are that the European CMEA countries will be Hungary's most important agricultural export markets. Oil producing developing coun-tries also seem to provide important outlets for agricultural commodities. Expansion of agricultural exports to some Near- and Middle Eastern markets has started already. It is to be expected that such recourse to distant developing country markets is going to continue. The future of agricultural exports to the developed market economies is most precarious.

What are the most important development issues? It is quite clear that cereals will have an important role in all production strategies for the future. If large foreign currency earnings are indispensable, and most probably this will be the case, some of the growth of cereal production will have to be transformed into livestock, meat and meat products to get value added on export goods. As a consequence, protein imports will grow. There is, of course, always a reason at times of a tight foreign currency situation to produce protein foods domestically, but the results have not yet justified such a strategy as yields of the main cereals are always much higher and more stable than those of soybeans. Thus it is preferable to export cereals and import soybeans. It is rather through a higher utilization of food industry by-products for feeding purposes that an increase in the self-supply of protein feeds can be achieved.

Problems and uncertainty facing the horticultural complex are much greater. The short term foreign market outlook for fruit, vegetables and wine is not good and does not justify a concentration of scarce resources in this sector. The long term outlook, however, is much better and thus it seems to be justified that basic development of new plantations, varieties, modern processing technologies, storage and transportation facilities should not be neglected because of the short-term outlook. There is a distinct likelihood of a demand for these products materializing in East European countries at a later phase of market development.

Higher export earnings by changing from raw to processed products is an almost universal endeavor of agricultural exporting countries. This strategy was much discussed in Hungary also. Some people even declared that not only export earnings but also sales opportunities, better producer and export price relations, etc., could be achieved in this way. Discussion of the problem centered on problems of the grain oilseed livestock complex, whether cereals should be exported where the relation of costs and prices is very favorable, or rather livestock, meat and meat products, etc., where export earnings are much larger but the relation of the costs of production and export prices is much worse. The problem is even more complex, as there are potentially many different sets of costs, prices, risk levels, marketing opportunities, etc. The arguments put forward by the production and marketing specialists boil down to the somewhat disappointing statement that one has to analyse and establish what to do for every basic product and, which form or stage of processing (or a mix of these) has the highest, most stable, etc., export earning potential, considering the present and potential markets of Hungary.

Table 25.1

AGRICULTURAL FOREIGN TRADE OF HUNGARY: 1976-1983
(billions of Forints)

Total of this:

		Socialist countries	Non-socialist countries
Exports			
1976	47.3	27.0	20.3
1977	54.9	29.8	25.1
1978	52.0	24.3	27.7
1979	59.0	30.1	28.9
1980	62.9	34.8	28.2
1981	75.5	46.7	28.8
1982	80.6	51.1	29.5
1983	86.0	-	-
Imports			
1976	23.7	6.7	17.1
1977	29.8	6.0	23.8
1978	26.4	5.2	21.2
1979	25.3	5.2	20.2
1980	25.1	5.7	19.4
1981	28.5	7.3	21.2
1982	22.7	6.2	16.5
1983	26.7	-	-
Export (+) or import (-) surplus			
1976	+23.6	+20.3	+ 3.2
1977	+25.1	+23.8	+ 1.3
1978	+25.6	+19.1	+ 6.5
1979	+33.7	+24.9	+ 8.7
1980	+37.8	+29.1	+ 8.8
1981	+47.0	+39.4	+ 7.6
1982	+57.9	+44.9	+13.0
1983	+59.3	-	-

Source: Kulkereskedelmi Statisztikai Evkonyv, Budapest

Table 25.2

HUNGARIAN AGRICULTURAL FOREIGN TRADE
BY MAIN DESTINATIONS
(in percent)

	Socialist countries	Non-socialist countries
Exports		
1976	57	43
1977	54	46
1978	47	53
1979	51	49
1980	55	45
1981	62	38
1982	63	37
Imports		
1976	28	72
1977	20	80
1978	20	80
1979	20	80
1980	23	77
1981	26	74
1982	27	73

Source: Kulkereskedelmi Statisztikai Evkonyv, Budapest

Table 25.3

DISTRIBUTION OF HUNGARIAN AGRICULTURAL EXPORTS
BY COUNTRY GROUPS 1976-1982
(in percent)

	Socialist countries	of this: Soviet Union	Non-Socialist countries	of this: Developed market economies	European Community	Developing market economies
1976	100	50	100	88	60	12
1977	100	54	100	84	57	16
1978	100	53	100	81	55	19
1979	100	56	100	83	55	17
1980	100	69	100	85	55	15
1981	100	72	100	79	53	21
1982	100	72	100	81	57	19

Source: Kulkereskedelmi Statisztikai Evkonyv, Budapest

Table 25.4

HUNGARIAN AGRICULTURAL IMPORTS BY COUNTRY GROUPS 1976-1982
(percent)

	Socialist countries	of this: Soviet Union	Non-Socialist countries	of this: Developed market economies	European Community	Developing market economies
1976	100	8	100	45	19	55
1977	100	10	100	33	18	67
1978	100	11	100	37	16	63
1979	100	11	100	41	21	59
1980	100	8	100	36	16	64
1981	100	6	100	42	21	58
1982	100	10	100	41	18	59

Source: Kulkereskedelmi Statisztikai Evkonyv, Budapest.

Table 25.5

HUNGARIAN FOREIGN TRADE IN AGRICULTURAL INPUTS
(Billion Forints)

	Agricultural machines	Fertilizers	Pesticides	Total
Exports				
1976	4.0	1.1	0.9	6.0
1977	5.2	1.6	1.3	8.1
1978	5.1	1.3	1.5	7.9
1979	6.1	2.8	1.6	10.5
1980	6.2	3.6	1.7	11.5
1981	5.8	4.9	2.0	12.7
1982	5.8	4.6	2.4	12.8
Imports				
1976	7.0	5.0	2.8	14.8
1977	8.3	5.1	2.3	15.7
1978	9.6	5.4	2.9	17.9
1979	8.8	5.0	3.3	17.1
1980	6.4	5.1	2.4	13.9
1981	6.9	6.5	2.6	16.0
1982	8.7	6.0	2.6	17.3
Export (+) or import (-) surplus				
1976	-3.0	-3.9	-2.0	- 8.8
1977	-3.0	-3.5	-1.0	- 7.6
1978	-4.6	-4.1	-1.5	-10.0
1979	-2.6	-2.2	-1.6	- 6.6
1980	-0.2	-1.5	-0.8	- 2.4
1981	-1.1	-1.6	-0.6	- 3.3
1982	-2.9	-1.4	-0.2	- 4.3

Source: Kulkereskedelmi Statisztikai Evkonyv, Budapest.

Table 25.6

HUNGARIAN FOREIGN TRADE IN AGRICULTURAL INPUTS BY MAIN DESTINATIONS
(percent)

	Agricultural machines		Fertilizers		Pesticides		Total	
	Socialist countries	Market economies	Socialist countries	Market economies	Socialist countries	Market economies	Socialist countries	Market economies
Exports								
1976	85	15	13	87	66	34	55	45
1977	92	8	45	55	68	32	58	42
1978	92	8	47	53	68	32	67	33
1979	85	15	32	68	77	23	59	41
1980	87	13	51	49	81	19	57	43
1981	84	16	65	35	79	21	57	43
1982	84	16	66	34	85	15	60	40
Imports								
1976	69	31	59	41	13	87	69	31
1977	66	34	64	36	11	89	79	21
1978	58	42	71	29	9	91	80	20
1979	67	33	78	22	9	91	70	30
1980	61	39	71	29	16	84	75	25
1981	52	48	80	20	15	85	76	24
1982	62	38	76	24	14	86	78	22

Source: Kulkereskedelmi Statisztikai Evkonyv, Budapest.

Table 25.7

VALUE OF HUNGARIAN AGRICULTURAL TRADE[1]
1962-1981
(million U.S. dollars)

	Exports	Imports	Export Surplus
1962	235.9	144.9	+ 91.0
1963	298.3	168.0	+ 130.3
1964	309.0	176.7	+ 132.3
1965	356.4	194.8	+ 161.6
1966	369.7	184.4	+ 185.3
1967	402.3	214.1	+ 188.2
1968	372.5	197.9	+ 174.6
1969	489.1	215.9	+ 273.2
1970	531.9	277.5	+ 254.4
1971	590.3	335.9	+ 254.4
1972	758.0	322.2	+ 435.8
1973	1088.6	420.3	+ 668.3
1974	1250.5	646.1	+ 604.4
1975	1437.1	643.8	+ 793.3
1976	1440.7	748.4	+ 692.3
1977	1747.6	962.7	+ 784.9
1978	1785.1	904.0	+ 881.1
1979	2102.2	890.4	+1211.8
1980	1990.4	820.9	+1169.5
1981	2250.3	834.2	+1416.1

[1] SITC 0, 1, 4, 22, 29,

Source: FAO Trade Yearbook, Rome.

Table 25.8

HUNGARIAN TRADE IN AGRICULTURAL MACHINERY[1]
1962-1981
(million U.S. dollars)

	Exports	Imports
1962	26.8	32.3
1963	17.2	50.6
1964	12.4	51.2
1965	13.4	44.6
1966	19.9	47.0
1967	21.8	59.9
1968	23.7	49.4
1969	21.1	46.9
1970	19.5	58.8
1971	19.8	132.9
1972	40.2	76.4
1973	71.1	90.5
1974	85.6	156.9
1975	108.2	198.6
1976	115.0	207.2
1977	157.9	234.8
1978	172.0	284.8
1979	216.8	271.4
1980	205.3	182.8
1981	165.9	179.6

[1] SITC 721-722.

Source: FAO Trade Yearbook, Rome.

Table 25.9

HUNGARIAN FOREIGN TRADE IN FERTILIZERS[1]
1962-1981
(million U.S. dollars)

	Exports	Imports
1962	3.1	23.3
1963	2.5	29.9
1964	4.8	38.8
1965	12.9	30.2
1966	12.9	30.8
1967	8.7	31.1
1968	3.9	40.2
1969	2.0	22.6
1970	1.3	49.3
1971	2.7	53.8
1972	10.2	64.9
1973	11.7	97.7
1974	5.4	193.8
1975	5.7	183.1
1976	34.8	187.4
1977	48.4	197.3
1978	44.0	230.5
1979	70.4	233.9
1980	110.3	199.6
1981	144.7	238.2

[1] SITC 56, 271

Source: FAO Trade Yearbook, Rome.

Table 25.10

HUNGARIAN FOREIGN TRADE IN PESTICIDES[1]
1962-1981
(million U.S. dollars)

	Exports	Imports
1962	-	-
1963	-	-
1964	-	-
1965	-	-
1966	1.1	10.5
1967	1.8	14.0
1968	4.3	14.4
1969	6.4	17.5
1970	3.8	18.4
1971	4.4	25.1
1972	4.3	25.0
1973	13.1	34.1
1974	13.2	52.0
1975	13.1	73.2
1976	27.9	94.1
1977	39.0	73.4
1978	48.8	101.5
1979	85.8	118.8
1980	52.0	80.6
1981	58.8	83.1

[1] SITC 591

Source: FAO Trade Yearbook, Rome.

Table 25.11

VALUE OF HUNGARIAN FOREIGN TRADE IN AGRICULTURAL INPUTS[1]
1962-1981
(million U.S. dollars)

	Exports	Imports
1962	29.9	55.6
1963	19.7	80.5
1964	17.2	90.0
1965	26.3	74.8
1966	33.9	88.3
1967	32.3	105.0
1968	31.9	104.0
1969	29.5	87.0
1970	24.6	126.6
1971	26.9	211.8
1972	54.7	166.3
1973	95.9	222.3
1974	104.2	402.7
1975	127.0	454.9
1976	177.7	488.7
1977	245.3	505.3
1978	264.8	616.8
1979	373.0	623.3
1980	367.6	463.0
1981	369.4	500.9

[1] SITC 56, 271, 591, 721, 722

Source: FAO Trade Yearbook, Rome.

26

Current Issues
in East-West Trade Relations

Paul L. Kelley

Strategies of grain exporting nations to maintain or increase their relative market shares will dominate East-West agricultural trading relationships during the mid-1980s. These strategies will be strongly affected by world-wide macroeconomic events, as well as by those primarily endogenous to East-West trade. Major changes in the worldwide economic environment have emerged over the past two decades that act to promote or constrain trade. With increased global interdependence a well intergrated international capital market emerged. The 1970s also brought about a change from fixed to floating exchange rates thus radically changing the impact of trade instability on the agricultural sectors of economies. State trading and the rise of market economies in Third World countries were also highly significant events. Finally, for a number of reasons, there has been a major increase in world monetary and commodity price instability starting in the late 1960s.[1]

Four worldwide macro issues will dominate most trading relationships over the next several years, and particularly East-West agricultural commodity flows. These are the world recession and LDC debt problem; exchange rate effects; agricultural productivity gains; and protectionism.

A set of specific issues relate primarily to East-West trade but will indirectly affect other nations. Of importance here are the magnitude of United States export declines; embargo policy; changing Soviet import strategy; bilateral agreements; European Community and the United States agricultural program budget crises and; likely United States export policy options.

This list of macro and specific issues includes political as well as economic considerations. However, this analysis is limited to the most likely economic effects of these factors on levels of world agricultural trade flows and the resulting general level and instability of agricultural commodity prices. Particular attention is given to their impact on East-West trading relations. Because the United States is the world's largest residual grain supplier, its strategy will greatly influence East-West trading relationships. Therefore, more emphasis will be given to emerging United States policies related to the above macro and specific issue's agenda as they impact East-West trading relationships.

Setting

At the time of the Sixth International Conference on Soviet and East European Agricultural Affairs in June, 1981, at Giessen, there was considerable debate concerning the expected future trend of real prices of grains in world markets. That debate seems partially resolved at the moment with current evidence tending to support the belief that the drift in real world grain prices is primarily flat and even perhaps continuing its long-term downturn, at least for wheat. This outcome is, in general, due to the likely prospect that increasing productivity in world food systems will outstrip gains in demand for food. But given this somewhat tentative consensus concerning the trend in real food prices, great concern still exists for developing analytical mechanisms for predicting large annual variations in prices about the trend, particularly downturns.

Obviously, the state of the art in economic science for predicting price instability in international agricultural commodity markets is still in its infancy. However, two major schools of thought dominate the scene, the so-called capital market-exchange rate group and the market structuralists. Both analytical frames of reference are considered in this analysis.[2]

Worldwide Economic Issues

World Recession and the LDC Debt Problem

The international debt crisis reached acute levels during the fall of 1982 but has eased somewhat since that time. Some 30 developing and East European nations are in some debt difficulty. Emerging LDCs included in this group are the most rapidly growing market for United States exports. Lagging exports for these nations, coupled with a doubling of interest rates since 1980, have created enormous debt servicing problems, reducing their capacity for purchasing grain imports. If these countries resort to widespread currency devaluations to solve their debt problems, major trade impacts will follow:

1. It will cause countries such as Argentina, Brazil, Thailand, and Turkey to become more competitive with their own agricultural exports—which include wheat, feed grains, and soybeans; and/or
2. It will cause countries such as Mexico and Brazil (in the case of corn) to reduce their imports.[3]

The impact on East-West trade of widespread devaluation in debt ridden LDCs would be substantial. Major exporters such as the United States, Canada, and Australia would be faced with a substantial loss of traditional buyers. At the same time, they would face additional competition for Soviet and East European sales from alternative supply sources. The path that is ultimately used to resolve the liquidity problem of the LDCs, therefore, is very important to the evolution of East-West trading relations over the next several years.

A former Federal Reserve official in a recent article candidly summarized a growing United States concern:

> The flash point has shifted from purely financial considerations, which influence the ability to pay, to the political considerations, which might affect the willingness to pay. The fear in the markets now is that one or more countries will be forced by events to flatly repudiate their debts. Such an action is likely to be in a political context in which hard work and skilled negotiations by experts in international finance just won't matter.[4]

Alternatives to devaluation or default include five elements recently outlined by Treasury officials for dealing with the international debt problem. These include (1) adoption of policies by industrialized nations to sustain non-inflationary growth; (2) development of sound economic policies by the LDCs to operate within their budgets; (3) further strengthening the IMF; (4) continuing to encourage commercial bank lending; and (5) keeping bridge financing available. The current deficit in the 200 billion dollar range for the United States does not brighten prospects for continued reduction of inflation in the United States. Also the LDCs, except for one or two nations, do not seem to be on a viable track to bring their economic houses in order.

Most commercial banks are not likely to be strong lenders in the near future for new activities given their recent loan experience. The most viable option appears to be to continue to strengthen the support role of the IMF in the current crisis. In Pardee's words:

> To conclude this discussion of the LDC debt situation, the US Treasury has set forth a useful structure for analyzing the problem but still lacks a comprehensive strategy for solving it.[5]

In any event, assuming the best possible scenario other than widespread devaluation, market potential for large exporters will be curtailed for several years, perhaps to the end of the decade for wheat and corn. This places additional pressure on major grain exporters, such as the United States, to aggressively seek increased levels and market shares of grain exports to the Soviet Union and East Europe.

Exchange Rate Effects

The value of the dollar in international exchange has been a major factor influencing American exports. The trade weighted value of the dollar has been almost inversely related to the value of United States agricultural exports for more than a decade. During the 1970s and early 1980s the value of the dollar declined relative to grain importer currencies. United States grain exports, then relatively cheap to buyers, expanded rapidly. But since 1981 the dollar has risen more than 25 percent relative to grain importer currencies and United States grain exports declined by 21 percent (1980–81 to 1982–83 fiscal years). Since 1980, Canadian wheat export prices have declined about 9 percent, while those of Argentina dropped by more than 30 percent relative to the dollar. The latter decline is, in large part, due to devaluation of the peso, giving Argentina a strong advantage in the international wheat market and, in particular, in sales to the Soviet-East European area. In the short term, there is very little that can be done to modify exchange rate effects. Over the longer term, Schuh and others have proposed new international banking institutions and arrangements that would have as their principal role partial stabilization of exchange rates.[6] Current evidence suggests that, while there will be some limited ups and downs, odds at least up to early 1985 favor a strong dollar over the next several years due to enormous United States budget deficits, which will force up interest rates and stimulate the flight to safe haven dollar denominated investments from international sources. This will place continuing negative pressure on the ability of the United States to export grains and to be a competitive source for Soviet and East European grain imports. Canada and Australia may continue to expand their market shares to the Soviet Union and East Europeans as a result.

Agricultural Productivity Gains

Several basic trends underlie expanded world food output in recent years. These trends have increased pressure on the world's agricultural natural resource base. But this has been offset in part by increased use of irrigation and fertilizers. Agricultural land worldwide expanded less than one half percent per year during 1950–80 with most of the increase concentrated in the first two decades of this period.[7]

> What would otherwise have been downward pressure on agricultural production and upward pressure on commodity prices was successfully countered in the land-tight as well as the more richly-endowed countries by a trend toward intensifying resource use and accelerating growth in productivity.[8]

According to O'Brien, irrigation grew seven times faster than expansion in arable land, while the percentage of irrigated area almost doubled. Worldwide fertilizer use grew from 20 to 80 kilograms per hectare from 1950 to 1980.[9] O'Brien argues that

> growth in ouput related to intensifying resources and augmenting natural resources with man-made inputs such as fertilizer generally accounted for over three-fourths of the growth in supply since 1950.[10]

Other studies tend to confirm O'Brien's conclusion that, for the present, increases in agricultural productivity world-wide seem to provide capacity for world food output gains to outstrip increases in worldwide *commercial* demand for food. These trends suggest that world grain markets over the next several years will be characterized more as a buyers' market rather than a sellers' market, enhancing Soviet and East European nations leverage relative to western grain trading nations.

Protectionism

Congressional discussion and legislative proposals in support of protectionism are on the increase in the United States. These actions arise from concerns in the industrial as well as agricultural sectors of the economy. The closing of steel plants due to technical obsolescence, overcapacity, and foreign competition has resulted in pressures for import quotas on steel. The auto industry, facing stiff foreign competition, is seeking domestic content legislation. Following the success of the textile industry in limiting imports, California wine growers are aggressively proposing increased tariffs on foreign wines, particularly those from Europe.

This new wave of protectionism is strengthened by the effects of the worldwide recession, exchange rate fluctuations and other developments. National agricultural policies in the United States and in the EC have resulted in substantial surpluses that need a "home." This growth of surpluses has led to export subsidization by the EC, particularly of wheat exports. Further, in a partial effort to solve its internal budgetary difficulties, the EC recently proposed restricting imports of United States corn gluten feed and corn based products, affecting nearly $500 million of trade annually.

These developments have led to the formulation of a variety of protectionist legislation such as the "Wine Equity Act" and the "Trade Remedies Reform Act." The former would increase wine import restrictions and is aimed principally at the European Community. If passed and implemented it would certainly result in requests for compensation under the GATT. Depending on level of compensation, if any, the EC would most likely retaliate against US grains.[11] The "Trade Remedies Reform Act" proposal would impose new duties on products such as nitrogen fertilizers. The recent China textile affair, restructuring imports of Chinese finished textiles, resulted in a reduction of United States wheat imports of nearly $700 million by The Peoples Republic of China. This is dramatic evidence of the interrelationship between import restrictions and reduced export opportunities.

Offsetting these negative developments has been a somewhat more optimistic set of discussions held recently with Japan concerning beef imports. Japan increased imports of beef, citrus, and other high-valued agricultural products from the US.[12] This action was not viewed, however, with favor by Japanese farmers. But faced with growing concern in Congress about the inroads the Japanese auto industry is making in the United States, this was a strategic concession made by Japan.

Most countries have not solved the problem of compensating those injured by the short-term negative effects on certain industries of policies that move to a more open trade environment. Clearly movements towards greater protectionism do not benefit most consumers and producers over the long-term. Protectionistic trade policies, in general, have the impact of lowering world trading prices. Whether trade flows are reduced or increased depends on the origin of the protectionistic policy. A move to greater protectionism in world grain markets would tend to benefit the East in terms of lower world prices in the short run. The outcome with respect to quantities of trade flows cannot be estimated at this time.

Specific East-West Trade Issues

Dimensions of the US Export Decline

There was a widespread view among many American farm leaders, expressed in national food policy emerging in the early 1970s, that the phenomenon of expanding grain markets was here to stay, and that it represented a permanent solution to the United States farm problem. This euphoria was sharply reversed in the early 1980s. United States agricultural exports declined by one-fifth from their peak in 1981 of $43.8 billion to $34.8 billion in fiscal 1983. Furthermore, there was a major decline in the relative importance of the United States market shares in export markets. These declines called for a substantial realignment of United States grain export strategy. The magnitude of change in the agricultural export sector since the early 1980s can be expressed by another means, which provides some additional insights to the woes of American farmers and policy makers.

The 22.5 million acres (9.1 million hectares) reduction in United States land capacity alone is more than one-third of the approximately 60 million acres (24 million hectares) of idle land brought back into crop production during the export boom of the 1970s. If one adds to crop land reduction the contractions in variable capital, and the idling of a part of the associated fixed capital asset structure of American agriculture, it is easy to understand why grain export strategies are so high on the current farm policy agenda. This drastic reduction in export sales resulted in one of the most severe farm crises in the United States since the Great Depression. Due to lack of timely administrative implementation of existing policy instruments, grain stocks reached record levels in late 1982 and early 1983. Even in 1982, United States policy makers were still looking for an export solution. Ultimately, the policy response to this dilemma resulted in the most massive land retirement program in history (82 million acres out of a 391 million cropland base in 1983), an expenditure of more than 21 billion dollars for the Payment-in-Kind Program (PIK) and a total budget outlay for federal agricultural programs in the 35 billion dollar range. Although the enormous costs of the PIK program were largely buried in fiscal accounting shell games, there is a growing realization among farm leaders that farm programs requiring expenditures at these levels in the future have small likelihood of Congressional support. There is also a growing realization that the export market is a fragile and highly volatile source of American farm revenue.

Domestic and export farm policies, therefore, are joined today in the United States agricultural policy debate. No longer is export policy the stepchild of domestic food policy. Of importance to East-West trade relations is that the magnitude of the current decline in exports is causing policy makers to seriously appraise possible changes in United States domestic policy to recapture export market shares in the East.[13]

Embargo Policy

Perhaps by now United States policy makers have learned that within the current structure of world grain markets, an embargo generally injures the United States agricultural sector more than it does the embargoed nation. This was certainly the outcome for the Brazilian soybeans case and the January 4, 1980, United States embargo on Soviet grain sales in excess of those guaranteed in the 1975 grain agreement. Soviet net imports for the period July 1980 to June 1981 were 35.5 MMT and increased to 44.5 MMT in the 1981/82 marketing year. At the same time the physical volume of the United States exports peaked in 1980, with dollar volume peaking in 1981. Reduced imports from the United States by the Soviet Union were offset by increased purchases from other countries. Likewise, displaced United States exports found other outlets in the world trading pool. Such offsets, in some instances, do require development of new selling strategies. At any rate, given current evidence, there would be strong political resistance from the Amerian agricultural sector to proposals for future grain embargoes, except in an extremely acute political crisis.

The potential for an embargo strategy on grain exports by the United States or any other western nation does not appear to be a viable factor in reducing the level of grain traded with the East. In fact, lack of such potential on the part of the United States enhances the competitive posture of other western exporters in seeking sales in the East.

Changing Soviet Import Strategy

Perhaps the most important effect of the embargo on the Soviet-American grain trade of the early 1980s was the Soviet counter-strategy of reducing dependence on the United States. In 1979, the Soviet Union imported about 70 percent of its grain from the United States. By 1983, the American share of Soviet imports dropped to less than one-third. Some will argue that in a multilateral trading world these adjustments "wash out." Such an argument does not take into account the imperfect nature of world grain markets. Different pricing strategies are involved when the United States shifts from one major buyer to another, especially when nations have sharply different strategic import characteristics. There does not appear to be much optimism in grain trade circles that the United States will ever regain the dominant share of the Soviet market that it had prior to 1980.

In view of the general tendency for world grain markets to be buyer-dominated for the foreseeable future, we should expect aggressive competition by the United States to attempt to regain some of its lost share of Soviet grain imports. This will probably be resisted by the Soviet Union and East European nations, even if United States prices were more attractive than those of other nations. A more rational United States policy would be to seek a cooperative arrangement among major western exporters.

Bilateral Agreement

Bilateral trade agreements are strongly opposed by most private trade groups in the United States. However, they will likely continue to be an important policy instrument for grain trading between the United States and centrally-planned nations for the near-term future. There are some limited signs of an improvement in the political posture of the United States vis-a-vis the Soviet Union which would suggest a possibility of some relaxation of American pressure for bilateral agreements. Additionally, sharp reductions in the United States share of the Soviet import market is decreasing the overall impact of such agreements in East-West trade affairs.

EC and United States Agricultural Program Budget Crisis

Two major western entities, the United States and the EC, are facing agricultural program budget crises. Resolutions of these crises certainly will affect East-West trading relationships. United States farm income stabilization expenditures increased from $3.5 billion in 1980 to $13.3 billion in 1982, and peaked at $20.6 billion due to PIK in 1983. Estimated cost is $8.9 billion in 1984, with a request for $12.6 billion in 1985. These figures are almost unbelievable coming as they do from one of the most conservative administrations in years.[14]

The EC has similar problems. Expenditures on farm price supports in the Community use two-thirds of its $21.6 billion budget, almost equal to the 1983 US PIK outlay.[15] France and Italy support the view that the budget can be topped up from member state funds in 1984 and 1985 despite strong opposition from Germany and Britain. The budget crisis in the EC has been characterized by various measures to increase revenue and decrease internal expenditure. The strong dollar in late 1984 has relieved pressure on export restitution particularly for wheat. Recently the EC offered to raise a proposed duty-free quota for imported United States maize gluten feed from 3.0 to 3.4 million tons. This was rejected by the United States. If the quota and imports tariffs are imposed, retaliation is likely to follow.[16]

Substantial budget constraints are most likely to be imposed in the United States due to political pressures. As a result, commodity support prices will be under strong pressure. In the near-term they most certainly will be held at near current levels and not allowed to escalate with inflationary pressures. This could result in a more aggressive export posture. Budget pressures on the EC will certainly tend to slow down programs requiring export subsidies such as the recent ones for cereals. This will tend to decrease export shares for their commodities.

Most Likely US Export Policy Options

The principal thrust of this paper has been to analyze strategies that major grain exporting nations will use to maintain or increase their shares, particularly in the Soviet and East European markets. There is little that the United States can do in the short-term to alleviate world recession and exchange rate fluctuations, other than through its policies to reduce inflation and world financial uncertainty. Trends in agricultural productivity gains and protectionism will continue. The most viable short-term options for the United States will emerge from the 1985 Farm Bill. There are already signs that there will be strong pressures to make exports more competitive by lowering or even freezing loan rate levels and reserve release prices. This was illustrated by the amendment to the 1984 Farm Bill signed by President Reagan on April 10, 1984. This legislation lowered the target price for wheat and corn in 1984 and 1985. Diversion payments are offered to wheat producers as an increased incentive for participating in the 30 percent acreage reduction program for the 1984–85 crop year.[17]

It would be hard to devise a policy that would ensure a greater certainty for loss of market shares than the current United States policy of rigid loan and release levels for wheat and feed grains in the face of an increasing value of the dollar. During the boom of the 1970s, loan prices for wheat and feed grains shifted upward but were either generally inoperative or did not increase at a rate seriously impeding export sales. However, there is growing concern that current rigid loan and release levels, coupled with the strong dollar, are reducing export sales. What is needed is some indexing procedure that would vary loan and release levels as the value of the dollar changes relative to currencies of other exporting countries.[18]

Some economists assert that for suppliers such as the United States, the export demand for wheat and feed grains is becoming increasingly more elastic and now may even be in the elastic range. To date, analytical studies to prove this argument have been inconclusive, but it is a notion that must be seriously appraised.

In the short-term, lowering export prices, if it did not invite cut-throat competition from other exporters and if the export elasticity argument is valid, would enhance aggregate export revenue. However, some individual producers who could not compete on the basis of cost in such a scenario would certainly suffer.[19] If the elasticity argument is ultimately verified and accepted, it will certainly reinforce the argument for downward flexibility in the United States loan and reserve release prices.

Another measure that will receive attention in the 1985 Farm Bill will be an expansion in the export credit program. More aggressive "shots over the bow" export subsidies to recapture selective strategic markets will likely emerge. If American policy moves to a greater reliance on private stockholding strategies, then it is most likely that total United States grain stocks will be reduced from present levels, thrusting a greater dependence on stockholding on major buyers, such as the Soviet Union and East Europe.

Attempting to forecast changes that the Congress will make in current farm legislation to recapture grain market shares in the Soviet bloc is a high risk venture. However, the weight of evidence suggests that the United States will become a more aggressive exporter to the Soviet Union and East Europe while at the same time it will develop a diversified sales strategy by seeking expanded markets in other areas, such as China. One of the major difficulties for the United States, however, in seeking alternative markets to offset losses in Soviet and East European exports, is that worldwide macroeconomic events dominate expansion possibilities. These events are not under control of the United States or any of the other western exporting nations.

Notes

1. See Schuh, G. Edward, "International Dimensions of Capital Markets" keynote address, *International Finance Symposium,* International Trade Institute, Kansas State University, April 27, 1984.

2. For a detailed review of the literature see Kelley, Paul L., "Implications for World Food System Strategies with Special Regard for the Role of the United States," in *Current Trends in the Soviet and East European Food Economy,* edited by Karl-Eugen Waedekin (Berlin: Duncker and Humblot, 1982).

3. "Policy Options for Improving the Trade Performance of US Agriculture," *Task Force on Trade Policy Alternatives: National Agricultural Forum,* Washington, D.C. (January, 1984), p. 19.

4. Pardee, Scott E., "Prospects for LDC Debt and the Dollar," *Economic Review*: Federal Reserve Bank of Kansas City (January, 1984), pp. 3–5. The author is executive vice president of Discount Corporation of New York and formerly manager of foreign operations for the Federal Reserve Bank of New York.

5. *Ibid.,* p. 6.

6. Schuh, G. Edward, "The Foreign Trade Linkages," in *Modeling Agriculture for Policy Analysis in the 1980's,* Federal Reserve Bank of Kansas City, Mo. (1981), pp. 83–85.

7. O'Brien, Patrick, "World Market Trends and Prospects: Implications for US Policy," in *Agriculture, Stability, and Growth* (Washington, D.C.: Curry Foundation, 1984), p. 2.

8. *Ibid.,* p. 3.

9. *Ibid.*

10. *Ibid.*

11. Johnson, Robin, "US Agriculture Must Fight Protectionism," *Cargill Bulletin* (April, 1984), p. 2, Minneapolis, Minn.

12. Toner, Ann, "Compromise Saved the Day for US Trade," *The Kansas City Star* (April 15, 1984), p. 5E.

13. A special National Agricultural Export Commission to study United States agricultural export policy was passed by the US House and Senate and approved by President Reagan in the late summer of 1984. "The purpose of the Agricultural Export Commission is to examine the past and present trade policies of the United States, determine whether these policies have either helped or hindered agricultural exports and develop a consistent and stable long-term trade policy conducive toward developing new markets and expanding existing foreign markets," Rep. Doug Bereuter (R-Neb.).

14. See *1985 US Federal Budget in Brief* (Washington, D.C.: US Govt. Printing Office, 1985), p. 40.

15. "Common Market Woes Discussed," *The Kansas City Star,* p. 4A (March 19, 1984).

16. For a view at the time of this writing, see *Agra Europe,* London, Feb. 24, 1984, p. 1, and October 19, 1984, p. 5. The United States policy has been one of strong opposition to imposition of any duty levies on gluten feed. Gluten feed was exempt until the recent duty proposals which were designed as a revenue source to ease EC budget difficulties.

17. See *Doane's Agricultural Report,* Doane Publishing Co., St. Louis, Mo. for details of legislation, April 6, 1984.

18. Target prices do not directly affect export prices but directly affect producers decisions to participate in the loan program. The argument is made however that under certain circumstances target prices act as an export subsidy.

19. Such a policy would be vigorously opposed by many farm groups. See report by the Texas Agricultural Forum, Ad Hoc Committee to Review the National Agricultural Forum Task Force report on International Trade, Dallas, Texas, Feb. 1984. Limited mimeographed copies are available from Mr. Lynn Elrod, Office of the General Manager, Associated Milk Producers, Dallas, Texas 75200.

Table 26.1

United States Export Declines 1980-83

Reductions in Volume of Exports		Decrease in Land Use at Average Yield	
		acres	hectares
Wheat	575 mil. bu.	10.3 mil.	4.17 mil.
Corn	505 mil. bu.	4.5 mil.	1.82 mil.
Soybeans	209 mil. bu.	6.5 mil.	2.63 mil.
Cotton	1.4 mil. bales	1.2 mil.	0.48 mil.
		22.5 mil.	9.10 mil.

Source: Policy Options for Improving the Trade Performance of U.S. Agriculture, Task Force on Trade-Policy Alternatives, National Agricultural Forum Jan. 1984, pp. 5. Washington, D.C. and calculations of the author.

27

Changing Perspectives in East-West Agriculture Trade: United States–Soviet Relations, 1972–84

Joseph Hajda

The uninterrupted prominence of agricultural trade as a major issue in United States–Soviet relations dates to the early 1970s, when the two countries began to shape the pattern of a regular, non-emergency agricultural trade relationship. Soviet wheat and corn imports from the United States took a quantum leap in 1972 and remained at a substantial level during the subsequent years (see Figure 27.1). With the exception of the partial grain embargo of January 1980 to April 1981, this regular relationship was divorced to a remarkable degree from the arduous political competition between the two countries as well as from diplomatic risks and ideological conflict.

Soviet grain import requirements were enormous during the 1972/73–1983/84 marketing years, totaling more than 288 million metric tons, and averaging 24 million tons annually. The Soviet Union imported these huge quantities of grain to offset deficits and to maintain stockpiles. A glance at the 12-year import data reveals that the Soviet market was a large and volatile market (see Table 27.1). Looking at the 1979/80–1983/84 imports, we find that the Soviet Union imported 177 million tons of grain, with an annual average of 35.4 million tons, including a record 46 million tons in 1981/82 and an estimated 33 million tons in 1983/84. The 33 million tons consisted of 20 million tons of wheat, 12 million tons of corn, and 1 million tons of miscellaneous grains.

Compared with the previous five years, the total of 177 metric tons represents a spectacular expansion of grain imports. During 1974/75–1978/79, Soviet grain imports totaled 77 million tons averaging annually slightly over 15 million tons, peaking at 26 million tons in 1975/76. During the previous seven years, 1972/73–1978/79, the annual average had been under 16 million tons.

The evidence vindicates those western policy analysts who in the mid-1970s took a hard look at the Soviet realities and submitted their views and explanations candidly, predicting Soviet grain import expansion up to the mid-1980s. However, nobody anticipated the spectacular import surge, averaging 35 million tons, during 1979/80–1983/84.

Several crucial facts and conditions are related to the massive Soviet grain imports:

- the environmental conditions, with particular emphasis on the misfortune caused by unfavorable weather patterns;
- the level of technological resources, with special emphasis on the difficulties of diffusing a complex and diverse technology throughout the USSR;
- the planning and management system, the quality of the labor force, and the character of rural life, with particular emphasis on the mismanagement of Soviet food and agricultural sectors and the sectors related to the production and marketing of food supplies, together with other shortcomings in the functioning of the economic mechanism;
- the necessity to treat with caution the demand by Soviet consumers for more and better quality of food, especially more meat and animal products: with the help of massive grain imports, per head meat production in the early 1980s was held at a relatively steady level (see Table 27.2).

Changing Perspectives: 1972–79

Starting in 1972/73, when the Soviet grain imports surged from the previous year's 8 million tons to nearly 23 million tons, the Soviet market represented a very attractive export opportunity for the United States and other major grain exporting countries. When it became obvious that this opportunity was a long-term one, the large Soviet import requirements came to play a significant role in shaping the direction and thrust of United States agricultural and trade policies. As the Unites States' share of Soviet grain imports rose to 67 percent in the 1976/77–1978/79 period, the United States Government reconfirmed the view that massive Soviet purchases of grain should continue to be an important element in fashioning United States grain production and marketing strategies. By 1979, the United States perceived the Soviet Union as its best market for grain exports in the years to come, as long as a certain degree of stability was preserved in the overall relationship between the two countries.

Optimistic views regarding the grain trade prospects were generated by the Soviet-American rapprochement in the sphere of agricultural trade relations. The rapprochement evolved in spite of substantial differences in the short-run political goals and long-run ideological interests of the two countries. These differences gave rise to considerable friction and cast a dark cloud over the prospects for commercial relations outside the sphere of agricultural trade. The long-term prospects for a continuing Soviet need to import large quantities of grain, and the readiness of the American private export-marketing system to sell the Soviet Union as much grain as it was willing to purchase, were coupled with a significant degree of negotiating flexibility. This flexibility became an important component in the flow of trade transactions within the broader framework of East-West relations, contributing to the intricate network of bilateral understandings and contractual arrangements, and operating by means of its own elaborate structure of implementing machinery.

From the United State Government's early 1970s perspective, a long-term intergovernmental agreement was not the preferred way to develop a trading relationship. The Government tried to keep a low public profile in regard to the political aspects of agricultural trade and stressed the need to rely on regular market operations, the flexibility of the market, and the efficiency of the private export-marketing system. But the Soviet Union was not an ordinary buyer. Given its import needs and its behavior as a single purchasing unit, with high potential for market disruption, along with the influence of political as well as economic factors in Soviet buying decisions, and the Soviet preference for locking in the long-term trade relationship and the share of the market on political grounds, the United States opted for accommodation. By 1975, a long-term Soviet-American grain agreement was perceived by the United States Government as the best practical way to secure the predominant share of the Soviet grain import market and to minimize the scope for market disruption.

A more stable structure of understanding on agricultural trade issues came into being as a result of this grain agreement, signed in October 1975 to run from October 1976 to September 1981. Under the terms of the agreement, the Soviet Union assumed the commitment to buy a minimum of 6 million tons of wheat and corn in approximately equal amounts each year. The United States agreed to sell to the USSR up to 8 million tons of grain without further consultations. Purchases over 8 million tons could be arranged after consultations, to be held every 6 months or as requested. The 1975 grain agreement provided a significant means of binding the United States and the USSR into a stabilized, longer-term relationship. The agreement and the actual trade dimensions reflected the acceptance by the trade policy makers on both sides of the notion that agricultural trade should be conducted on the basis of mutual satisfaction and reciprocal benefits. In the broadest terms, agricultural trade was perceived as contributing to both countries' development, promoting their national economic growth and creating conditions conducive to the general well-being on both sides. The recognition by both sides of mutually beneficial effects of agricultural trade strengthened the propensity to trade, with definite consequences for the evolution of trade patterns, the modalities of trade relations and the con-figurations of the infrastructure's component parts.

The importance attached by the American trade policy makers to grain exports to the Soviet Union derived from concerns about the dynamic evolution of the American agricultural economy, aggregate farm income, the shape of the various commercial sectors affected by agricultural exports, and the implications of grain exports for the balance of payments. The importance attached by Soviet trade policy makers to grain imports derived from the notion that the imports were not just a stop-gap measure to remedy a short-lived problem, but rather a long-term necessity.

Trade policy makers on both sides were aware of the fact that trade and related activities had to be looked upon as providing channels for transmitting not merely grains and payments but also ideas: ideas about the functioning of production and marketing systems, education and information systems, the application of scientific discoveries and technological advances in farming and related industries, the role of incentives and disincentives, farming systems and infrastructures, standards of living and ways of life, and institutional designs and arrangements. Given the critical importance of food and agricultural issues in public agenda-building, in the long run the total gain from agricultural trade expansion appeared to be both immense and incalculable.

All these developments were accompanied by a vigorous public controversy in the United State over the wisdom of selling huge quantities of agricultural products to the Soviet Union. The segments of American agricultural and business communities directly involved in producing and exporting such products warned about the dangers arising out of attempts to tamper with trading opportunities. Their opponents argued that the massive exports were a means of sustaining and fortifying America's enemies. Meanwhile, the Soviet Union maintained discreet silence about the controversy among its decision makers over the wisdom of massive grain imports from the United States and other western countries. We can assume that at some point it was a mirror image of the controversy in the United States.

A significant by-product of the controversy in the United States was increased awareness of the Soviet agricultural lag in terms of productivity and output, and the reasons for lack of economic efficiency in resource utilization. The controversy also brought into sharp focus the perception of agricultural trade policies as key symbols of general economic policies in both countries and as key ingredients in promoting diverse strategic or political objectives within the context of East-West relations.

The 1980–84 Perspectives

The enormous Soviet grain import needs, the United States' predominant role in meeting the needs, and the locking in of the relationship on political grounds with the help of the long-term intergovernmental grain agreement affected the perception of links between the grain trade and overall bilateral relations between the two countries. During the late 1970s, these perceptions infected the controversy concerning the role of the grain trade in foreign policy considerations and tempted some United States decision makers to use the "food weapon" against the Soviet Union. The temptation became irresistible in January 1980 when the United States decided to "punish" the Soviet Union for its behavior in Afghanistan by imposing restrictions on sales and shipments of agricultural products to the USSR. The restrictions brought about a substantial change in the pattern of Soviet grain imports when Argentina, Canada and other exporting countries used the opportunity to expand their agricultural exports to the Soviet Union (see Figure 27.1). When the United States lifted the restrictions in April 1981, it was faced with the difficult task of reshaping the Soviet-American relationship in agricultural trade.

Miscalculation was at the heart of this predicament: the Soviet Government had not anticipated a strong United States reaction, principally in the form of economic sanctions, to Soviet military action in Afghanistan; and the United States made a misguided unilateral decision to impose a partial embargo for the purpose of "punishing" the Soviet Union. The result was that sales and shipments of specified United States agricultural products to the USSR were suspended, including 17 million tons of grain ordered by the Soviet Union in excess of eight million tons which the United States was committed to sell under the terms of the 1975 grains agreement.

The embargo policy received strong domestic support from those opinion leaders who argued for the limitation of economic links with the Soviet Union, advocating the policy of blocking most economic interactions, or severely restricting trade ties, and using the "food weapon." They assumed that the United States had it in its power to increase enormously the strains under which the Soviet policy must operate, and to force the Soviet leaders to observe a far greater degree of moderation and circumspection than they had observed in the late 1970s.

The critics of the "food weapon" approach felt that the unilateral embargo policy had little impact on Soviet foreign and security policy aims; that it had poor reliability without making sure that the Soviet Union would not be able to obtain needed grains from other sources or to achieve significant adjustment of internal consumption; and that it had considerable threat of backfiring. The controversy sharply focused on the question of using food as a flexible and reliable instrument of foreign and security policies, and a key element of the United States' approach to the Soviet Union. The critics of the embargo policy gained the upper hand when it became evident that the other major grain exporting countries were replacing most of the embargoed amount of grain by additional sales and shipments to the Soviet Union. As Argentina and Canada took advantage of the opportunity to capture bigger and longer-lasting shares of the Soviet import market by means of long-term agreements, the unrealistic scenario became a dead one, and the embargo was lifted.

The lifting of the embargo came at a time when Soviet import needs remained at an unprecedented level, and United States grain traders had high hopes that sales and shipments to the USSR could be expanded significantly soon after restrictions were removed. However, Soviet decision makers were not ready to restore the pre-embargo trade patterns. It appears that the embargo partially contributed to the search in the USSR for updating the structure for food production and marketing. The updating had been on the agenda for several years, but the 15-month long imposition of restrictions by the United States supplied additional urgency to measures intended to ease the problem of reliability of food supplies, respond more effectively to the growing demand for improvements in the sphere of food consumption, put the country beyond the reach of chance, and weaken the effect of world market conditions on the Soviet economy. Food production and marketing was perceived as a vital problem of paramount political, economic and social importance, calling for prompt action. The Food Program up to 1990, announced in May 1982, became the chosen approach to updating a vital segment of the economy and reversing the explosive growth in the Soviet grain imports in the 1980s.

The lifting of the embargo signaled the restoration by the United States of the prudent approach toward exporting grains to the USSR. The approach was reinforced by a flexible stand on the question of readiness to sell massive quantities of grain to the Soviet Union, beyond the 8 million tons provided for by the 1975 grain agreement. In 1981 and 1982, the United States offered to increase Soviet annual purchases of wheat and corn up to 23 million tons. The USSR's response fell far short of these offers. However, in 1982/83, the Soviet Union purchased from the United States 14 million tons of grain indicating interest in fairly substantial grain imports, and simultaneously cultivated close agricultural trade relations with the United States that would justify negotiation of a successor to the 1975 grains agreement. In the meantime, both governments agreed to extend the grain agreement for a year in 1981 and again in 1982.

The United States aimed at restoring its predominance in the Soviet grain import market, but the Soviet Union had strong reservations about the reliability of American grain trade policy. In practical terms the reservations meant that the United States' share of the Soviet market decreased from an average of over two-thirds in the late 1970s to less than one-third in the early 1980s.

After the United States announced, in December 1981, the postponement of the renegotiation of the grain agreement with the Soviet Union in response to the imposition of martial law in Poland, it became clear that it did not close the door to exploratory talks with Soviet officials. Members of Congress from agricultural states, such as Senator Bob Dole from Kansas, and agribusiness spokesmen played a leading role in these talks. Their involvement was crucial in preparing the ground for negotiating a new long-term grain agreement.

American trade negotiators were confronted with an array of problems in early 1983. The most important problem was the Soviet Government's insistence that it must have complete confidence that agreements will not be broken, that without that confidence no deals could be made, and that it was necessary for the United States to renounce once and for all the doctrine of using trade as a weapon against the Soviet Union. The United

States was urged to define more clearly the rules under which bilateral trade was to be conducted, including the guarantee that no action would be taken to restrict or control sales of grain and other agricultural products to the USSR by the private export-marketing system. Such embargo protection or contract sanctity was provided by an Act of Congress (in the form of an amendment to the Commodity Futures Trading Act of 1983), stipulating that if the President declares an embargo, he may no longer cancel shipments of grain or other commodities that have been privately contracted for until 270 days have passed. This restriction is automatically suspended only if the President declares a national emergency or the Congress declares war.

Specific United States guarantees that agreements will not be broken improved the climate for grains negotiations. However, the context of the negotiations was different from the 1975 context. In 1980 and 1981, Soviet agricultural trade policies concentrated on securing steady access for needed commodity imports from several countries. The effort produced a number of long-term trade agreements with Argentina, Brazil, Canada and India for Soviet purchases of grains and soybeans, and with Argentina and New Zealand for meat and dairy products. The Argentine-Soviet grain agreement is a 6-year agreement specifying a 4.5 million ton minimum. The Canadian-Soviet grain agreement is a 5-year agreement containing an escalating minimum level of purchases beginning at 4 million tons in 1981/82 and rising to 6 million tons in 1985/86. The pattern of these long-term agreements suggested that the Soviet drive to secure adequate commodity supplies was to remain in high gear during the first half of the 1980s, but the agreements also reflected the USSR's decision to diversify its suppliers. These agreements, together with short-term bilateral agreements for several other commodities, made it clear that it would be difficult for the United States to recapture the predominant position it had lost as a result of the embargo or to become the supplier of at least 50 percent of Soviet grain import requirements. In fact, actual Soviet purchases of grains and soybeans and products in the early 1980s exceeded the amounts specified in the agreements. However, it was not inconceivable that the United States could be the primary supplier of Soviet grain imports.

Another important circumstance was the USSR's tightening of hard currency use for agricultural imports. For example, the total 1981 agricultural import bill included almost $12 billion for imports from western countries, or about 40 percent of the USSR's total hard currency purchases. Grain imports absorbed a major share of this total. As the demands of the USSR's global involvement became both more complex and intense, the constraints imposed by the Soviet political framework on the use of hard currency earnings became more important.

The negotiation of the 1983 grain agreement was facilitated by the application of the prudent approach. Like the 1975 agreement, the successor agreement locked in the long-term intergovernmental relationship on political grounds and provided for a stable structure of understanding on agricultural trade issues. As in 1975, the United States concluded that regular market operations could not be relied upon to maintain a steady level of grain exports to the Soviet Union. Once again, the consideration of the enormous Soviet import needs, the influence of political as well as economic factors in Soviet buying decisions, and the high potential for market disruption, led the American negotiators to the conclusion that the long-term agreement was the best practical way to lock in a share of the Soviet market by political means, the prime share rather than the preponderant share, and to minimize the possibility for market disruption.

The agreement was signed August 25, 1983, to run from October 1983 to September 1988. Under the terms of the agreement, the Soviet Union assumed the commitment to buy a minimum of 9 million tons of wheat and corn annually, with the option of substituting up to 500,000 tons of soybeans for 1 million tons of wheat and corn. The United States agreed to sell up to 12 million tons of grain without further consultations. Purchases over 12 million tons could be arranged after consultations, to be held every 6 months under the agreement or as requested.

The shooting down of Korean Air Lines Flight 7 by the Soviet air defense forces in August 1983 did not cause a single change in United States agricultural export policy, proclaimed in 1982 when the President said that the "granary door is open." There was no suspension of grain sales and shipments to the Soviet Union.

The effort to revitalize United States grain exports to the Soviet Union, so that the United States would remain the primary supplier of Soviet grain imports, was underscored in January 1984, when the United States informed the USSR that it could purchase up to 22 million tons of grain in the October 1983–September 1984 period. The estimated Soviet purchases amounted to 14.36 million tons of grain, consisting of 7.76 million tons of wheat and 6.6 million tons of corn, plus 416,200 tons of soybeans. The total fell far short of the United States offer.

Future Prospects

Will it be possible to divorce the opportunity to sell the Soviet Union huge quantities of agricultural products on a long-term basis from other Soviet-American concerns? The appraisal of United States–Soviet (and East-West) agricultural trade relations presupposes a given political order, and cannot be profitably undertaken in isolation from politics. The larger configuration of East-West politics and Soviet-American interests determine in large measure the framework of these relations. The United States and Soviet governments seek to organize and maintain the level of agricultural trade relations in terms of their respective economic and security interests. These interests are related to their respective domestic concerns and foreign policy considerations. Each government pursues trade policies that reflect domestic economic and political needs and external considerations. Such considerations are never completely out of the trade picture.

What is a plausible scenario for the mid-1980s? There is no evidence that the slowdown in Soviet economic growth will be reversed in the forseeable future. The United States military buildup is likely to continue to put pressure on the Soviet government to maintain a substantial growth rate in the defense sector (4.5 percent or more in 1984–86 according to Defense Minister Dmitri F. Ustinov) making it difficult to produce sufficiently large growth increments in the civilian sectors so as to accelerate vast improvements in the production and marketing of food.

Based on measures taken to implement the Food Program up to 1990, prospects for hard currency earnings, grain production and marketing trends, large animal herds, and meat output, we can estimate that Soviet grain import requirements for the mid-1980s could average 25–40 million tons per year, with the United States' market share averaging 30–40 percent of Soviet grain imports. Geographic diversification of external economic ties in the sphere of grain trade, a classic risk reduction strategy, can be expected to remain a key component of the USSR's import policy.

FIGURE 27.1

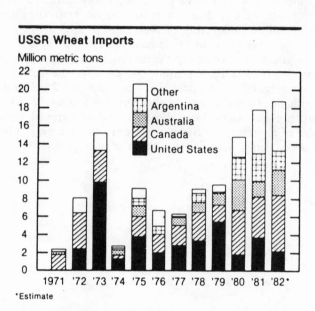

USSR Wheat Imports
Million metric tons

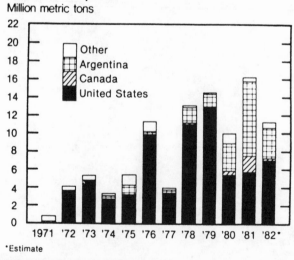

USSR Corn Imports
Million metric tons

Source: U.S. Department of Agriculture.

TABLE 27.1

USSR: Grain Imports, 1972/73-1983/84
(million metric tons)

Year	Imports (July/June)	Year	Imports (July/June)
1972/73	22.8	1979/80	30.5
1973/74	11.3	1980/81	35.0
1974/75	5.7	1981/82	46.0
1975/76	26.1	1982/83	32.5
1976/77	11.0	1983/84	33.0
1977/78	18.9		
1978/79	15.6	5-year annual average	35.4
7-year annual average	15.9		

Source: U.S. Department of Agriculture.   The 1983/84
amount is an estimate of grain imports from all
foreign sources.

TABLE 27.2

USSR: Per Capita Meat Production, 1980-83
(in kilograms, carcass weight)

Year	Beef and Veal	Pork	Poultry	Total
1980	26.4	20.0	8.5	56.9
1981	26.2	19.9	9.5	55.6
1982	26.1	20.1	9.9	56.1
1983	26.2	20.6	10.5	57.3

Source: U.S. Department of Agriculture.   The 1983 amounts are
estimates.

28

Assessing the Significance of the Soviet Market for United States Agricultural Exports

Philip M. Raup

Introduction[1]

The United States entered the 1980s dependent upon exports for just under one-fourth of total cash receipts from farm marketings and for the disposal of production from well over one-third of total crop acres harvested. These percentages were more than double those prevailing in the early 1960s. The largest percentage increases occurred in the proportion of wheat and coarse grain output entering world trade as shown in Table 28.1. In land use terms, exports accounted for the production from 17.0 percent of the crop acres harvested in 1956–60 and for 34.0 percent in 1976–80. In 1980, the peak year in volume, crop exports were equivalent to the production from 38.9 percent of the harvested acres. In dollar terms, agricultural exports accounted for 10.3 percent of total cash receipts from farm marketings in 1956–60 and 21.0 percent in 1976–80. In 1980 this rose to 24.0 percent, as shown in Table 28.2.

Reactions of American farmers to their accelerating involvement in world trade were conditioned by a number of beliefs or forecasts, including:

1. A belief in the finite nature of resource supply, triggered by publication of *The Limits to Growth* in March 1972.
2. Forecasts of an expanded market in the Soviet Union, following the unexpectedly large Soviet grain purchases in 1972/73.
3. A fear of world famine, reinforced by the run-down in carry-over grain stocks, which dropped from 21.2 percent of annual use in 1968/69 to under 12 percent in 1972/73 and 1973/74 and to a low of 10.9 percent in 1974/75.
4. Widespread publicity given to explosive rates of population growth in newly developing countries.

5. The advent of new chemical and genetic technology, promising a new technological revolution in agriculture.
6. The formation of OPEC and its embargo of oil shipments to major customers in 1973, activating a search for agricultural substitutes for fossil fuels.

Each of the fears and forecasts listed above appears in a much different light in 1984 than the light in which they were viewed ten years earlier. The limits to growth have been drastically revised; problems of grain surpluses have reappeared; population growth rates have slowed, in some cases dramatically; the profit potentials of new agricultural technology have not been realized as quickly as hoped; and efforts to develop agricultural substitutes for fossil fuels have been all but abandoned, or are proving to be highly uneconomic. In these circumstances it seems reasonable to conclude that human resources and physical capital were committed to agriculture in the 1970s on the basis of expectations that were unrealistic.

In terms of the psychological impact upon farmers' expectations, one of the most powerful forces at work in the past decade was the prospect of a large new market in the Soviet Union. The strength of this hope was dramatized by the reactions to the sudden imposition of an embargo on grain sales above agreed limits to the Soviet Union on January 4, 1980. The embargo figured prominently in the United States presidential election of 1980, and its termination in April 1981 was highly publicized as a major agricultural policy initiative of the new Reagan administration.

Subsequent negotiations for a new Soviet-American grain agreement were pushed forward in 1982–83 at a time when they seemed to be in head-on conflict with other United States policy postures toward trade with the Soviet Union. The renegotiated grain agreement of August 25, 1983, was presented by the Reagan administration as one of its most successful efforts to expand export markets for United States agriculture.

During the past decade, both farmers and political leaders in the United States have eloquently stressed the importance they attach to access to the Soviet market for agricultural imports. That their emphasis on this particular market may be somewhat misplaced is indicated by the rankings of recent United States agricultural export markets in Table 28.3.

Although the peak export years of 1979–81 bridged the period covered by the partial United States embargo on grain shipments to the USSR, it is important to note that the value of total American agricultural exports to the Soviet Union exceeded $2.0 billion only in 1979, when they totaled $2.85 billion. In most recent years Mexico, Canada, and South Korea have purchased approximately as much as the Soviet Union, and they have been far out-ranked by the Netherlands and Japan. The lure of the Soviet market nevertheless remains. Given this history, it seems appropriate to look critically at available evidence regarding the prospective size and durability of the Soviet market for United States agricultural exports. That market is currently confined almost totally to grains, including soybeans. The discussion that follows will explore some of the trends and shifts in production and consumption patterns that seem likely to guide Soviet demand for grain imports into the 1990s. No attempt will be made to appraise the potential for crop-yield increases. Instead, the emphasis will be on some of the steps that could be taken to improve the utilization of current output.

Some Major Features of the
Soviet Grain Economy

The approach selected is to examine some of the factors that currently limit the effectiveness with which the Soviet Union produces and utilizes grain. In comparison with other industrialized countries, three features of Soviet grain usage stand out:

1. The seeding rate is unusually high, leading to a very low multiple of product when compared to seed used.
2. The feeding rate is high, leading to a high ratio of grain used per ton of meat produced.
3. Waste and dockage are excessive.

The quantities of grain involved are large. Seed usage in the past decade has varied from 27 to 29 million metric tons, and is estimated to equal from one-eighth to one-fifth of total grain production. In five of the ten years from 1973/74 to 1982/83 quantities required for seed obligated 15 percent or more of total grain output.[2] Livestock feeding accounts for the major fraction of grain usage in the USSR, averaging about 120 million metric tons annually in the period since 1977/78. Grain loss through waste and spoilage is large, averaging ten to fifteen percent of bunker-weight production. In five of the ten years from 1973/74 to 1982/83 waste and dockage exceeded 28 million metric tons and averaged 24.2 million tons annually for the 10 years. For the same 10-year period, grain imports averaged 23.3 million metric tons.

Agronomic experience in Canada and the northern portions of the United States wheat belt suggest that USSR seeding rates could be cut in half. If this saving of over 12 million tons annually could be combined with an improvement in livestock feeding efficiency of 10 percent and a reduction in wastage of 20 percent, the grain that could be saved in these ways approaches 30 million tons. For comparison, Soviet grain imports in 1983/84 were 32.4 million tons and are projected to reach a record 49 million tons in 1984/85. Bad weather unquestionably plays a major role in explaining this high level of imports, but that is not the only explanation. What problems of internal utilization contribute to this continuing dependence on imported grain?

Seeding Rates

A. S. Shevchenko has pointed out that wheat-growing peasants of the Altai-region foothills in Kazakhstan used to say that "we must plant enough seed so that at least 16 grains of it would stick to a horse's hoof." Without information about the wetness of the soil or the size of the horse, this poses a nice problem in conversion rates before we can estimate kilograms per hectare. But he goes on to say that the old people always claimed that the proper amount of seed was "5 poods [of 36.11 pounds or 16.38 kilograms] and 3 handfuls" (Shevchenko, 1960, p. 17). Assuming that he was speaking of poods per desyatin (1.093 hectares), this is equivalent to a seeding rate of roughly 75 kg per hectare, or 67 pounds per acre. This is well within the range of currently recommended seeding rates for spring wheat in similar climatic zones in Canada.

Based on a careful review of current Soviet literature on recommended seeding rates, Karen Brooks concluded that for small grains the seeding rate averages approximately 200 kilograms per hectare or roughly 180 pounds per acre (Johnson and Brooks, 1983, p. 161). For wheat, this represents three bushels per acre, or more than double the seeding rate used in comparable spring-wheat growing areas of Canada. What accounts for this seemingly excessive rate of Soviet seeding?

One explanation concerns the predominance of spring-sown wheat and barley in Soviet grain output. Winter grains (fall-sown) tiller or "stool" after emergence and a single grain can result in a multiplication of stalks after the period of winter dormancy. Spring-sown grain often lacks this feature to a comparable degree, requiring a heavier seeding rate to produce a similar plant population.

Weed control also plays a major role. A dense ground cover of sown grain can shade out weeds, thus substituting for control through better tillage or with chemicals. The well-documented shortage of agricultural chemicals in the USSR increases the probability that weed-control is prominent among the reasons for heavy seeding rates.

Some sense of the degree of over-seeding can be gained from Canadian data. A series of experiments from 1960 to 1980 (Guitard, Newman, and Hoyt, 1961; Pelton, 1969; and Baker, 1982) used seeding rates for spring wheat ranging from 22 to 200 kg per hectare. The various locations in Saskatchewan and Alberta represent latitudes and climatic conditions that are roughly comparable to many of the spring grain regions of the USSR.

While great variations were found in the relationships among plant varieties, row spacing, time of seeding, and other variables, in none of the experiments did seeding rates in the range of 150 to 200 kg/hectare (the Soviet range) prove to be desirable. In general, seeding rates in the 90–140 kg/hectare range resulted in the highest yields, with lower rates (ranging down to 40 kg/hectare or below) proving best in areas subject to moisture deficiencies. At the level of generalization used to characterize the USSR seeding rate (200 kg/hectare), the Canadian data suggest a rate at roughly half that level.

One feature of a recent Canadian experiment is revealing (Baker, 1982). While grain yields rose by 16 percent when seeding rates were increased from 36 to 90 kg/hectare, a further increase to 140 kg/hectare added only 3 percent to gross yield. The additional 50 kg of seed produced only 110 kg of additional output, for a net marginal increase in output of only 1.7 percent. This difference must certainly be within the error limits of any field crop experiments.

What may be more important in the Soviet context is that the increase in output of straw was proportional to the increase in grain output. At seeding rates varying from 36 to 140 kg/hectare the straw produced was a constant 53 to 54 percent of the combined weight of grain plus straw, in experiments that included eight different varieties of spring wheat at three different locations in Saskatchewan (Baker, 1982, pp. 287–288). Since the bulk of grain from a Soviet farm goes to the state, while all of the straw stays on the farm, we may be approaching a more understandable explanation for the high seeding rates in the USSR. Straw is a principal feed-stuff on a Soviet farm. Anyone who has traveled in grain-producing regions of the USSR can attest to the care with which it is assembled and removed from the fields. In semi-arid regions it is a major feed reserve for the farm and more particularly for any livestock kept by farm workers on their private plots. If straw yield is a linear function of grain yield, and, if the grain goes to the state while the straw stays at home, it is rational at the farm level to seed heavily, even though the marginal increase in grain output may be very low.

Granting the importance of weed control, and the probability that Soviet seed quality falls short of established norms, it seems likely that a major part of the explanation of high seeding rates in the USSR lies in the institutional defect that values grain in the social sector and straw at the farm level. If true, this helps explain the persistence of high seeding rates in the face of agronomic evidence indicating that they should be cut in half. It also underlines the difficulty involved in achieving a cut of this magnitude.

The separate "markets" in which grain and straw are valued also point up a potential difficulty in securing widespread adoption of modern high-yielding wheat varieties in the USSR. The "miracle wheats" of Green Revolution fame are semi-dwarf in character. Much genetic and agronomic effort has been devoted to an increase in the ratio of grain to straw. If it can be assumed that grain delivery quotas will be increased to reflect the higher grain yields of semi-dwarf varieties, then a shift to these varieties with their short straws will reduce the value of the not-so-fringe benefit represented by straw that stays on the farm. If a Soviet farm manager has a choice, he approaches the problem of maximizing returns from these joint products with a different set of value-weights than those used by central planning authorities.

Converting Feed to Meat

The phenomenal increases in Soviet grain imports after 1971 have been primarily to provide livestock feed. The greatest potential for any reduction in grain imports lies in improvements in feed conversion efficiency. If we deduct quantities used for seed, and estimated waste and loss, then livestock feeding at the beginning of the 1970s was equivalent to approximately two-thirds of net available grain from domestic production and averaged under 100 million tons annually. From 1975/76 through 1979/80, feed use of grain averaged 114 million tons annually and 82 percent of net domestic production. For 1980/81 through 1983/84 annual grain feed usage is estimated at 119 million tons, and 90 percent of net domestic output. In the poor crop year of 1981/82, when gross grain output fell to 160 million tons, feed usage was equal to 99 percent of domestic production, after deducting seed and waste (USDA, 1984B). The Soviet Union entered the 1980s with a feed-livestock economy using the equivalent of nine-tenths or more of total grain supplies from internal sources.

Although the incentive to reduce imports must be very great, the record of success in improving feed conversion efficiency is disappointing. As shown in Table 28.4, feed conversion coefficients in terms of kilograms of output have been unchanged from 1971 to 1982 for pork, and have actually increased for beef and milk.

A major part of the problem is the preoccupation of Soviet authorities with the maintenance of livestock numbers. An overriding focus on the body count is revealed in the ruling from central planning authorities that "farms are ineligible for receipt of the 50% premium for above-plan sales if the previous year's inventory levels for each individual type of animal are not retained to January 1 of the next year" (Gray, 1982, p. 96). One consequence is that the USSR holds too many animals in inventory in relation to the output of meat and milk. While some progress was made in the 1970s and again in 1983 in improving livestock throughout by reducing the ratio of inventory to output, the USSR still remains well above the levels achieved in developed countries, or in those countries in East Europe for which comparable data are available.

Table 28.5 shows for selected countries the number of head of cattle and hogs in inventory (usually as of January 1) per ton of beef and pork produced, for 1972 and 1982. This crude measure throws little light on the efficiency of feed conversion but it does underline the potential for further improvement in using feed to produce meat instead of maintaining body weight for an excessive number of frames. As of 1982, the USSR held approximately fifty percent more cattle in inventory per ton of beef produced than was needed in Western Europe, Canada or the United States. For pork, the ratio has shown more improvement than for beef since 1973, but in 1982 was still roughly fifty percent above the ratios prevailing in Western Europe, the United States or Hungary.

The meat problem in the USSR is similar to that of a supermarket that fails to turn over its inventory at sufficient speed. The carrying costs of excessive stocks diminish profit potentials. It is intriguing to speculate on the possibility that one reason for excessive livestock inventory holdings is the absence of a functional interest rate on capital stock in the USSR. In a country in which inventory holding involves a high opportunity cost of capital, the pressure of high or rising interest costs forces attention upon measures that will improve turnover. This pressure is largely lacking in the USSR. Instead, the official pressure to maintain livestock numbers throws the emphasis on head-counts at the expense of turnover. It seems reasonable to conclude that one step that could improve grain utilization in the USSR would be to adopt realistic interest rates in calculating the farm-level capital costs of producing livestock products. Soviet pricing policies are defective in many dimensions, but one of the most distorting is the absence of an adequate price on time. This is especially so in the use of imported grain to feed livestock.

Pricing policy distorts the pattern of grain use in another dimension. With croplands that lie too far to the north to permit large-volume production of oil-seed crops, the USSR is reduced to animal (and marine) resources for much of its supply of fats and oils. This is abundantly reflected in the retail meat price structure. Fat cuts of meat are the highest priced cuts, are the first to disappear from retail meat counters, and command good premiums in the collective farm markets.

A search for a time-series of retail meat prices in non-state stores (kolkhoz markets) has been fruitless. Alternatively and in connection with study tours in 1958, 1968, and 1978 I assembled meat prices from the same state stores in Moscow, Kiev and Rostov in all three years, together with prices from similarly located collective farm markets. In all cities and in all three periods the premium on fat meat and lard was pronounced. Official prices in the state stores showed the least premium but even there fat cuts of pork including "sow belly" were among the highest priced meats on display.

For comparison, Figure 28.1 shows the long-run trend in the price of lard relative to the liveweight price of hogs in the United States from 1905 to 1981. Prior to the mid-1930s in the U.S., an additional pound of fat put on a hog increased the carcass value of the animal. Beginning in 1946 this relation reversed. Since about 1965 the price of lard has fluctuated around a level of roughly fifty percent of the liveweight price of the hog. This abandonment of a fat standard in valuing pork has contributed directly to changes in feeding practices and to the increased efficiency with which grain is converted into meat.

These price-induced incentives are absent in the USSR. With lard in state stores in the late 1970s at ruble 1.70 per kg and state procurement prices for hogs in the ruble 1.50 per kg range, the fat-price ratio in the USSR is at approximately the trend level of the U.S. in the late 1920s.

Increasing the effectiveness of feed grain use in Soviet meat production by shifting away from the stress on fat will not be easy. It involves cooking, eating, and drinking habits, as anyone who has faced the customary bottle of vodka and quarter-pound of butter at a Soviet banquet can testify. As meat availability and quality improve, the potential for increased efficiency in feed grain conversion through a de-emphasis on fat will increase. At present, procurement pricing policy and the virtual absence of quality differentials at the farm level prevent this shift from occurring.

Waste

Three components of waste are dominant: storage, transport, and prices. The storage problem is endemic in a system in which prices do not move with time. The market-economy incentive to construct storage arises from the prospect of higher prices if supplies are not dumped on the market at harvest time. With fixed state procurement prices this incentive does not exist in the USSR and neither is it available to "first handlers" or local grain procurement agencies. In addition, Soviet authorities have for decades made every effort to get the grain off the farms and into state granaries as quickly as possible. Storage on farms has been distrusted.

As a result, the lack of local or on-farm storage is one of the greatest deficiencies in Soviet agriculture. This is compounded by the relative absence of quality tests for grain at the farm level. There is dockage for excessively wet or dirty grain when farm deliveries are made, but more refined quality testing occurs further up the procurement chain. Farms have no price incentive to construct storage, and no strong price penalty for poor quality. Waste and dockage are also guaranteed by the practice of paying harvest crews on the basis of speed of harvest and tons of grain delivered from the combine (bunker weight). This creates a strong incentive to operate the harvester in a manner that introduces waste matter (weed seed, imperfectly threshed grain) or grain of high-moisture content to increase weight. Much of the waste in the Soviet grain economy is due to the large discrepancy between the bunker weight of grain as it leaves the field and the dry weight of cleaned and storable grain held by state procurement agencies. In effect, harvested tonnage is overstated.

Waste is compounded by the lack of good farm-to-market roads. The basic cause can be traced to a defective structure of local government. Farms are responsible for road construction within the farm. Given their size, they become de facto units of local government. No unit with revenue raising power above the farm level can focus the interest of farms in a given region on the construction of market-access roads. These become the responsibility of governmental units too far removed from the farm-level to be responsive to the need to "get the farmer out of the mud." To this must be added the deeply-rooted preference of Soviet planners for rail transport. Long-distance truck transport is virtually unavailable to farms in many grain producing regions of the USSR. Transport delay is inevitable, and beyond the control of farm managers. Since the grain is a public good, it suffers from lack of care as procured at the farm level. Harvesters and handlers may be penalized for careless work, but they do not have a direct monetary interest in the product.

Any efforts to reduce waste must penetrate the roots of the Soviet system. The seriousness of the problem is apparent in the domestic literature, where editors repeatedly publish letters denouncing spoilage and waste. Some effort is being made to promote the construction of on-farm storage, but it remains a state-sponsored effort in which the farm has primarily a custodial role.

The growing number of automobiles is increasing the demand for better roads. But until the price system is reformed to reflect the importance of time and quality at the farm level, the problem of waste will persist.

Conclusion

The conditions that make massive grain imports necessary in the USSR arise from self-inflicted wounds. The roots of these causal factors are deeply imbedded in the structure of the Soviet system. Comparatively simple steps that could be taken to improve grain utilization would make grain imports unnecessary in all but the most exceptional years. A combination of seeding rates now used in comparable agronomic zones of Canada with grain feeding efficiencies now achieved in Hungary and western Europe plus a reduction in waste to levels only twice as high as in other developed countries would yield savings roughly equal to average grain imports of the past four years.

Given the relative costs of water and rail transport, it will remain advantageous for the USSR to import grain for its Far-Eastern and Pacific regions. Labor costs and transport delays in the heavily industrialized European regions at times will also make water-borne grain cheaper in regions served from Leningrad or Black Sea ports. Given the risk exposure involved in the latitudinal position of the main grain surplus regions of the USSR, it will be rational to rely on grain imports in years of bad weather. For these reasons the Soviet Union can be expected to offer a reliable market for limited grain imports for the rest of this century, perhaps on the order of 5 to 8 million tons per year.

An escalation of imports above these levels will be the result of institutional features and policy decisions that could be changed. In appraising the extent to which the Soviets offer a reliable market for United States grain exports, any hedging of estimates should be toward the low end of the range. In a rational world the Soviet Union should be a grain exporter, not a grain importer. It seems unwisely pessimistic to base United States grain export expectations on the assumption that this level of rationality is beyond the grasp of Soviet leaders.

Notes

1. Paper 1944, Miscellaneous Journal Series, Agricultural Experiment Station, University of Minnesota. I am indebted for suggestions, comments and data to Karen McConnell Brooks, Kenneth Egertson, Anton Malish, Yuri Markish, Donald Rasmusson, and Barbara Severin. Any errors of fact or interpretation are mine.

2. For these and subsequent estimates, U.S. Dept. of Agriculture (FAS) *Foreign Agriculture Circular, Grains,* "The USSR Grain Situation," SG-6-84, April 10, 1984, p. 6.

References

Baker, R. J., 1982. "Effect of Seeding Rate on Grain Yield, Straw Yield and Harvest Index of Eight Spring Wheat Cultivars," *Canadian Journal of Plant Science,* Vol. 62, No. 2 (April, 1982), pp. 285–291.

Brooks, Karen McConnell, 1983. "The Technical Efficiency of Soviet Agriculture," Chapter 9 in D. Gale Johnson and Karen McConnell Brooks, *Prospects for Soviet Agriculture in the 1980s* (Bloomington: Indiana University Press, 1983), pp. 120–164.

Dowell, A. A., R. E. Olson and O. B. Jesness, 1953. *The Export Market for Pork and Lard,* University of Minnesota, Agricultural Experiment Station, Bulletin 418 (June, 1953). *Ekonomika Sel'skogo Khozyaistva,* No. 5, 1972.

Gray, Kenneth, 1982. "Soviet Livestock: Stymied Growth, Increased Cost and Search for Balance," *Soviet Economy in the 1980's: Problems and Prospects,* Part 2, Selected papers submitted to the Joint Economic Committee, Congress of the United States, 97th Congress, 2nd Session (Washington, D.C.: U.S. Government Printing Office, Dec. 31, 1982), pp. 86–108.

Guitard, A. A., J. A. Newman and P. B. Hoyt, 1961. "The Influence of Seeding Rate on the Yield and the Yield Components of Wheat, Oats and Barley," *Canadian Journal of Plant Science,* Vol. 41, No. 4 (October, 1961), pp. 751–758.

Mackie, Arthur B., 1983. *The U.S. Farmer and World Market Development,* U.S. Dept. of Agriculture, ERS, October 1983.

Pelton, W. L., 1969. "Influence of Low Seeding Rates on Wheat Yield in Southwestern Saskatchewan," *Canadian Journal of Plant Science,* Vol. 49, No. 5 (September, 1969), pp. 607–614.

Shevchenko, A. S., 1960. "On the Virgin Lands of Siberia and Kazakhstan," *Sovkhoznoye Proizvodstvo* (Sovkhoz Production), Moscow, No. 12, December 1960. Translation from Joint Publications Research Service, U.S. Dept. of Commerce, JPRS 8450, 13 June 1961, p. 17.

U.S. Dept. of Agriculture, 1960. *Livestock and Meat Statistics, Supplement for 1960,* Statistical Bulletin No. 230, June 1961.

U.S. Dept. of Agriculture, 1974. *Foreign Agriculture Circular, Livestock and Meat,* FLM-7-74, June 1974.

U.S. Dept. of Agriculture, 1983. FAS, *World Livestock and Meat Situation and Outlook,* FL and P-1-83, January 1983.

U.S. Dept. of Agriculture, 1984A. ERS, *Foreign Agricultural Trade of the United States,* January–February 1984.

U.S. Dept. of Agriculture, 1984B. FAS, *Foreign Agriculture Circular, Grains,* "The USSR Grain Situation," SG-6-84, April 10, 1984.

U.S. Dept. of Agriculture, 1984C. FAS, *Foreign Agriculture Circular, Grains,* FG-8, 84, May 1984. *Vestnik Statistiki,* No. 10, 1981, and No. 11, 1983.

Table 28.1

UNITED STATES GRAIN EXPORTS AS PERCENT OF PRODUCTION

Crop Year	Percentage of Production
1969/70	17.6
1979/80	36.7
1980/81	42.0
1981/82	33.0
1982/83	28.4
1983/84	46.1
1984/85 (forecast)	31.1

Source: U.S. Dept. of Agriculture, FAS, Foreign Agriculture
    Circular Grains, FG-29-82, Sept. 15, 1982; FG-8-84, May
    1984.

Table 28.2

United States Agriculture

Period	Exports as a Percent of	
	Crop Acres Harvested	Cash Receipts from Farm Marketings
1951-55	12.2	8.4
1956-60	17.0	10.3
1961-65	23.0	11.6
1966-70	22.0	10.6
1971-75	41.5	12.8
1976-80	34.0	21.0
1980	38.9	24.9

Source: The U.S. Farmer and World Market Development,
    Arthur B. Mackie, U.S. Dept. of Agriculture, ERS,
    October 1983, pp. 5-6.

Table 28.3

Value of United States Agricultural Exports to 20 Leading
Markets, Annual Average, 1979-81 and Calendar Years
1982 and 1983

Country	Annual Average 1979-81	1982	1983
		Billion Dollars	
Japan	5.98	5.56	6.25
Netherlands	3.11	3.08	2.58
Mexico	1.97	1.16	1.94
Canada	1.83	1.82	1.84
South Korea	1.75	1.58	1.84
Germany, F.R.	1.67	1.45	1.53
USSR	1.86	1.87	1.47
Taiwan	1.10	1.16	1.31
Spain	1.11	1.68	1.21
Egypt	.78	.80	.97
Belgium-Luxembourg	.68	.91	.83
United Kingdom	.98	.92	.82
Italy	1.09	.99	.73
India	.35	.35	.70
Venezuela	.70	.67	.66
Portugal	.62	.58	.66
China, P.R.	2.82	1.50	.54
France	.71	.62	.48
Brazil	.64	.53	.48
Saudi Arabia	.39	.50	.45
World Total	39.77	36.62	36.10

Countries ranked by order of importance in 1983.
Sources: The U.S. Farmer and World Market Developments, by
Arthur B. Mackie, U.S. Dept. of Agriculture, ERS,
Washington, D.C., October 1983, Table 13, P. 24.
(Column 1). Foreign Agricultural Trade of the United
States, U.S. Dept. of Agriculture, ERS, Washington, D.C.,
January-February 1984, Table 1, p. 2. (Columns 2, 3).

Table 28.4
USSR Feed-Conversion Coefficients
(Kilogram of Oat Unit Equivalent/ Kilogram of Output)
on State and Collective Farms

Product	1971	1980	1982
Beef	10.3	13.4	13.4
Pork	9.2	9.2	9.2
Milk	1.4	1.5	1.6

Sources: Ekonomika sel'skogo khozyaistva, No. 5, 1972; Vestnik
   Statistiki, No. 10, 1981, and No. 11, 1983. Data include
   all feeds.

Table 28.5

Production of Beef and Pork in Relation to Livestock Numbers
Selected Countries, 1972 and 1982

Country	Number of Head in Inventory Per One Metric Ton of Meat Produced			
	Beef		Pork	
	1972	1982	1972	1982
Canada	13.7	12.1	11.7	11.0
United States	11.4	11.1	10.1	9.1
Argentina	23.9	23.0	20.8	15.6
Brazil	42.1	38.8	51.2	34.5
Mexico	44.0	25.8	27.8	13.8
Australia	20.7	15.1	15.2	10.4
France	14.9	13.3	8.1	7.0
Germany, F.R.	11.3	10.1	8.5	8.4
Italy	8.4	8.4	12.3	9.0
Germany, D.R.	17.2	15.0	15.1	10.3
Hungary	17.9	12.5	18.0	9.1
Poland	21.1	16.0	15.4	12.9
USSR	19.2	17.5	18.7	14.4
World Total*	36.5	23.3	24.4	11.3

*Includes other Reporting Countries not listed above.
Sources: Foreign Agriculture Circular, Livestock and Meat,
      U.S. Dept. of Agriculture, FAS, FLM 7-74, June 1974;
      World Livestock and Meat Situation and Outlook, FL and
      P-1-83, January 1983.

FIGURE 28.1: Price of lard at wholesale relative to the liveweight price of hogs U.S., 1905-1981

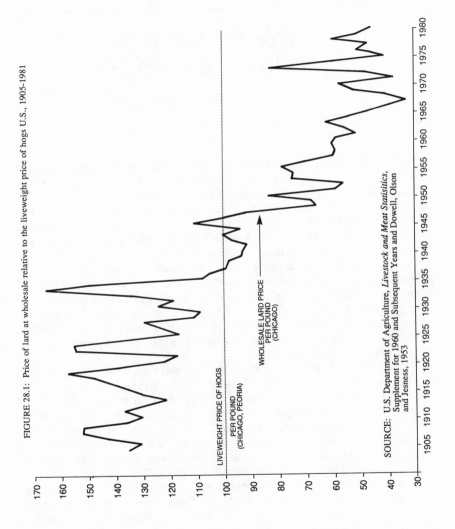

SOURCE: U.S. Department of Agriculture, *Livestock and Meat Statistics,*
Supplement for 1960 and Subsequent Years and Dowell, Olson
and Jesness, 1953

29

East European
Agricultural Trade Policy

Chantal Beaucourt

In centrally planned economies, the volume and structure of agricultural trade depend mostly on the policy choices made by the decisionmakers. The two main aims that in the countries of the CMEA guide these choices were defined in the long-term agricultural cooperation and development programs of these countries in 1978, and since then many times reaffirmed, particularly at the 37th meeting of the CMEA in October of 1983.[1] This program aims to assure the stable production of grains, meat, milk, vegetables, fruits and fish as well as their processed products in order to guarantee as soon as possible a regular supply for the population of all agricultural products and to permit a better structure of consumption of agricultural products. In order to achieve these goals, it has been decided that, countries that are more capable of increasing their output should increase output according to the needs of the area: fruits and vegetables, wine, tobacco, malt and hops are the main products concerned.

Nevertheless it is thought that all the European members of the CMEA can and should cover their "basic" needs. Each of them has, in particular, the means to increase their grain and feed production to the regional level in order to develop livestock herds large enough to meet the needs of the population. The repercussions of this policy on the structure and orientation of trade are important. If one adheres strictly to the directives, trade between CMEA countries should concentrate on those products that are produced in specialized regions. Purchases outside of the CMEA should be limited to those goods which can be obtained only from non-CMEA sources and sales limited to surplus goods. Trade in "basic goods," meaning grains, meat, dairy products, eggs and fish, should gradually decrease until it disappears. The achievement of these goals will therefore have significant effects on the balance of trade in convertible currencies, to the extent that almost all trade in "hard" currencies is with the West, and that these agricultural purchases have a significant impact on the balance of trade and the size of the East European debt to the West. Agriculture being such an uncertain sector in most of the countries, economic conditions can cause the decisionmakers to shift their strategies. In order to appreciate the effects of their choices on the attainment of these objectives and the evolution of trade, and to show the prospects of success, three criteria were chosen and applied to a few typical products: self-sufficiency, the reorientation of trade within CMEA, and the structure of trade outside CMEA. First we briefly characterize the general evolution of agricultural trade during the last decade.

The Tendencies of the Evolutions of Agricultural Trade in the Years 1970–1982: The Inflicted Realities

A Growing Deficit Until 1981–1982: 1982 the Start in the Reversal of This Trend?

In spite of constant progress, agricultural production in East Europe does not meet the needs of these countries, and the deficit in the trade balance for agricultural products of the region worsened notably at the end of the 1970s. As Table 29.1 shows, net imports rose from an average of $4.3 billion over the 1971–1975 period, to $12.6 billion in 1976–1980 and to a record of $22 billion in 1981. At the same time, CMEA purchases play a larger role in the world agricultural trade as their share has risen from 9.7 percent in 1971–1977 to 12.6 percent in 1981. In 1982, there was a spectacular reversal in this trend, with the overall agricultural trade deficit dropping by $3.5 billion. This was totally due to a reduction of imports by $4 billion and reflects the effects of the austerity program that was put into action at the beginning of the 1980s.

Yet these developments had different effects on the countries of the region. Until 1982, the deterioration of the trade deficit was mostly imputable to the USSR. From one billion dollars at the beginning of the decade, net imports reached $6.7 billion in 1975 and $18.3 billion in 1981. But, the northern-tier CMEA countries are also to blame. The deterioration of the agricultural trade balance was particularly pronounced in Poland, but also evident in the GDR and Czechoslovakia. In 1980 and 1981 even Romania, a traditional agricultural exporter, was affected. The significant growth in exports in Hungary, and to a lesser degree in Bulgaria and Romania (except in 1980 and 1981), did not compensate for this trend and the agricultural trade deficit worsened during the decade, in the East European countries taken together. The recovery observed in 1982 is yet very important in these countries where the deficit decreased by $2 billion. The most spectacular decrease took place in Poland. Thanks to an export effort along with a limitation in purchases the deficit dropped $1 billion. At the same time, Romania became a net exporter again. In most of the other countries the improvement in the agricultural trade balance was exclusively due to a limitation on imports. In the zone as a whole, exports dropped by 2.4 percent. In 1983 these evolutions are confirmed, except for Poland, but less pronounced.

The situtation is quite different if we look at food products and agricultural raw materials separately, although they are often put together in the analysis.[2] The overall deficit of the USSR is, in effect, due to its purchases of food products and the USSR has a large surplus in its trade of agricultural raw materials, while the deficit registered in Eastern Europe is mostly due to trade in this second group of products, and all the countries of the region, even the overall net exporters have deficits in this type of trade.[3] This situation is not without importance because the raw materials in question include both exotic products such as natural rubber, and the "specialized" goods of the zone including textiles and wood, while food products are mostly "basic goods".

Western Countries: The Main Beneficiaries of This Unbalanced Trade

Since 1979, the East European trade balance of food products which has been positive with the USSR has been negative with Western countries (Tables 29.3–29.5). Nevertheless, trade has remained relatively balanced with Western Europe, and the deficit is mostly with industrialized countries outside Europe and in 1983 with developing countries. The USSR on the other hand, has had a negative trade balance with all these groups of countries, but the rapid deterioration of this deficit, particularly in 1975, was due mostly to increased imports from the western industrialized countries. Soviet food imports from developing countries have not grown while those from developed countries more than doubled from 1971 to 1981 and the western countries now supply close to four-fifths of the USSR's agricultural imports.

As far as agricultural raw materials are concerned, most trade takes place within CMEA, and a balance exists between the delivery of Soviet agricultural raw materials to its East European partners and the food product that they supply to it.[4] Agricultural raw material exports to the West provide a net surplus for the USSR that reduces its deficit from food goods but does not affect the deficits of Eastern Europe. *The growth of the agricultural deficit is due mostly to grain purchases.*

In the USSR, from 1972 to 1980, grain purchases represented on the average 80 percent of food imports from the western industrialized countries and since then, the increase of grain and meat purchases from developing countries, has more than compensated for the reduction of trade with the West. Thus, almost all grain imports and more than 60 percent of meat come from western countries and in 1983 the cost can be estimated at over $7 billion. Moreover, the East European agricultural trade deficit with the West can all be attributed to grain purchases.

The Criteria for the Evaluation
of the Agricultural Trade Policy

Towards Which Self-sufficiency?

Two goods, grain and meat, are particularly characteristic of the East European policy choices concerning the supply and demand of foodstuffs as well as of the effects of these choices on trade. These products occupy a very important place in the diet and meat remains, in these countries, a good indicator of the improvement in the food structure. The disparity between the supply of meat and the demand for meat conveys the difficulties in adapting to the changes brought by a higher standard of living and increasing urbanization. Because of this, meat is an important factor in economic policy. Furthermore, grains make up the basis of livestock diet. In the USSR over 120 million tons of grains are used to feed animals, and thus, the two goods cannot be treated separately.

We can nevertheless distinguish three phases in trade policy for these products during the period from 1970 to 1982. In the first phase, which continued until the mid 1970s, demand was primary and, with it, livestock raising.[5] In order to satisfy this demand, trade adjusted itself to the inadequate development of grain production and, more generally, to livestock needs. The USSR and three East European countries proceeded to make larger, although irregular, grain purchases. Thus, even though Hungary, Romania and Bulgaria were net exporters, the zone as a whole including the USSR became a net grain importer on the world market. This policy resulted in a net increase of meat consumption in all these countries. Furthermore grain purchases represented less than 9 percent of consumption in Eastern Europe.

The second phase marked a return to a more restrictive consumer policy. While, at the same time, the grain dependency on the western market increased. The difficulties encountered in the execution of their agricultural programs moved the decisionmakers to make a drastic revision of policy. They tolerated massive grain purchases but meat consumption did not increase. In the USSR, where the imports were especially large and were complemented in 1979 by large meat purchases, meat consumption had hardly increased since 1975, nor that of bread grains.[6] In the East European countries, grain purchases also increased rapidly in Poland, Czechoslovakia, and Romania and to a lesser extent in Bulgaria, and the GDR; in Hungary, grain exports decreased. At the same time net meat exports increased for the region as a whole, since a part of imported grain served to produce the meat destined for export. Meat consumption increased moderately in three countries and stagnated in the other three.

From 1980, adhering to this policy became more difficult and planners did not seek to compensate for weak productive performances through trade. *Meat consumption was reduced* in some countries, as in Poland and Czecho-slovakia in 1982, or at best was maintained at the same level. Consumption of meat stagnated in the GDR from 1980 to 1982, and in Hungary in 1982. The massive purchases of the preceeding period weighed heavily on the "hard currency" balance of trade, and agricultural trade was controlled by the same vigorous policy used to eradicate the debt. Grain purchases were reduced starting in 1981 in the GDR, and also in Czechoslovakia where they amounted to $2 million tons in 1979 and 1980 and less than a million tons in 1981: at the same time meat external supplies showed a net surplus of $28 and $56 million, respectively.

The Reorientation of the Trade
in the CMEA

In order to evaluate the effort to reorient food trade towards the CMEA countries, and more particularly towards the European members of the group, two products, fruits and vegetables, are examined. These products played a major role in the restructuring of the food trade advocated within CMEA. With the exception of tropical and subtropical products, they are, furthermore, representative of the type of goods whose production should be specialized to some of these countries, and whose trade should thus develop within the region.[7] Among the agricultural raw materials, textile fibers will also be examined because they fulfill the same criteria.

The growing importance of grain and meat in trade as well as the ambiguity of the concept of self-sufficiency leads to an analysis of the geographical structure of these goods. One can then examine how these developments fit into the geographic redistribution of trade in these agricultural goods.

Fruits and Vegetables

The East European fruit and vegetable trade balance shows a large deficit that, since 1980, has hovered around one billion dollars.

Actually three countries had negative trade balances: total purchases of the USSR, the GDR and Czechoslovakia, were on the 1979–1981 average $2.112 billion, while exports totaled barely $190 million; the other countries show a net surplus of $1.163 billion and this trade plays an important role in food purchases and sales in these countries (Table 29.9). In the meantime, the regional deficit was almost exclusively due to the purchases of tropical and subtropical goods (Table 29.10). These purchases increased rapidly during the decade in most of the countries, especially between 1970–1975, and they made up a large part of fruit and vegetable imports in the deficit countries.

Trade of other fruits and vegetables is just about balanced and shows, depending on the years, a slight deficit, on the average between 1979–1981 $20 million, or a surplus of $25 million in 1982, at the expense, or in favor, of the East European countries. But it appears that the net surplus that the exporting countries have, almost completely covers the import needs of the deficit countries, and that the reorientation of trade has taken place as planned. This balance and reorientation took place also in part at the expense of the consumer. In the surplus countries per head vegetable consumption has not increased between 1975 and 1980 in Bulgaria and Poland, and it even diminished in Hungary until 1982. Only Romanian consumers increased their level of consumption. On the importing countries' side, the purchases barely improved consumers' plight in the GDR and it worsened in Czechoslovakia. On the other hand, the USSR registered a net improvement over the last few years.

Textile Fibers: Cotton

There is a fairly different evolution in textile fibers, particularly cotton. During the 1970s, the USSR had, in effect, become one of the main exporters and in 1981, she furnished over 21 percent of world sales. Deliveries almost doubled between 1970 and 1981, and tripled, from 259.5 to 894.0 metric tons, if net exports are considered; sales to East European countries stagnated, their share dropping from 75 percent in 1970 to 41 percent of Soviet exports in 1981. In that year, Soviet cotton exports covered three-fifths of the import needs of her East European partners, but they did not benefit from the reorientation of her trade. In 1983 and 1984 the production shortfall of cotton in the Soviet Union had a considerable effect on fiber exports which declined abruptly. Exports to East Europe, however, decreased only slightly in absolute terms, thus increasing in relative terms.

Grains and Meat

In 1980, grain and feed made up over half of East European food imports and about 40 percent of those of the USSR, and if animal products are added 61 percent and 52 percent respectively. Thus, these goods whose trade were to be restricted occupied, paradoxically, a large place in imports, and it is worth analyzing how the purchase of these goods was geographically distributed, especially for meat where a redistribution could be made in favor of the USSR while Eastern Europe has an increasingly large overall trade deficit with the Soviet Union.

The situation for grain trade is clear. One country, Hungary, is still a net exporter but her surplus cannot meet the needs of the whole region. However, a complete reversal in the direction of the flows can be observed during the 1970s. At the beginning of the decade almost all Soviet grain deliveries were destined for Eastern Europe, but since 1973, a growing share of her sales have gone to developing countries and more recently to Communist countries in Asia. Thus, in 1981, only 15 percent of Soviet grain exports went to Eastern Europe and they represented 3 percent of the regional import needs (38 percent in 1971–1975). Conversely, in 1970, four-fifths of East European grain exports were delivered to the West, of which 65 percent went to developed countries and only 16 percent to other East European countries. In the last few years, grain trade within the region has increased regularly and most exports have gone to the USSR. In 1981, over 77 percent of sales were to planned economies, of which 33 percent went to Eastern Europe and 44 percent to the USSR. Of course, these purchases made up only 3.3 percent of Soviet grain purchases and the posibilities for trade reorientation appear to be very limited. But this means a fairly heavy burden for some countries.[8]

The situation for meat is quite different. Eastern Europe, and, since 1979 each East European country has become a net exporter with Hungary, Bulgaria, Romania, and Poland (except in 1981 and 1982) predominating. At the same time, exports have increased significantly from 100,000 tons in 1970 to 650–750 thousand tons at the end of the decade. Moreover, the USSR has become an important market. In 1983, her total purchases reached close to a million tons while the trade deficit between Eastern Europe and the USSR increased.[9] According to estimates, except for 1980–1981 when meat purchases from western countries partially compensated for the decrease in grain purchases, planned economies supplied about half of Soviet imports of meat.[10] These deliveries may increase. Hungary, the main exporter of the region, has continued to increase her deliveries to the USSR, especially since 1980; from 32,000 tons in 1971 (about 20 percent of Hungarian sales) they reached, in 1982, 262,000 tons about half of the sales of this type. A rough estimation would show that the same proportion of the region's available meat is sent to the USSR. Thus, it is theoretically possible to enlarge the quantities sent to the Soviet Union. It is especially possible for Romania where, in 1980, only 6.7 percent of the value of meat sales was to CMEA countries. In any case, meat purchased from East Europe is particularly advantageous for the USSR because it permits her to avoid paying for meat and grain purchases in hard currencies and if all meat were imported from the West, it would cost the USSR $1.4 billion. She can be expected to put pressure on the East European countries to increase their sales, in order to improve their overall balance of trade with her. Nevertheless, one should keep in mind, that the livestock and meat are, by far, the largest components of East European food sales in West Europe and thus represent an essential source of the hard currency earnings needed to pay off their debts.

How do these developments fit into the geographical distribution of this food trade as a whole and in the structure of trade outside of the zone? On the whole one notes a reorientation of food exports in the six East European countries towards the USSR. Table 29.4 shows that the share of food exports to the West has fallen during the decade, despite the relative increase in the share of sales to the Third World except in 1983—and that the USSR was the main beneficiary of this re-distribution of trade. At the same time, Soviet food sales to Eastern Europe diminished in relative terms and made up only 7 percent of their imports as opposed to 23 percent in 1970. The USSR remains nevertheless a major supplier of agricultural raw materials and, in spite of the stagnation in the volume of cotton sales, makes up a third of East European purchases of these products. Among the developed countries, West Europe remains the main outlet for East Europe as well as for the USSR but while agricultural raw materials make up 90 percent of Soviet sales in this area, food products are one of the main East European exports and meat products represent approximately a quarter of these exports. Furthermore, the development of the structure of agricultural purchases significantly changed the geographic distribution of East European imports. Market economy countries have become the main supply sources of food products for the USSR as well as for the other East European countries. Among developed countries, those outside of Europe that are the main grain suppliers have increased their share of sales from 6 percent in 1970 to 30 percent in 1979 to the USSR and from 5.5 percent to 18 percent for the six East European countries. Since 1980, some developing countries have won back a part of the East European grain market and in 1982 their share increased quite a bit at the expense of developed countries. West European exports remained weak (except for 1980). The significant increase in the value of West European food sales during the decade is also linked, to a great extent, to that of grain deliveries and feed, which now make up a third of these sales.[11] A further evolution of trade along these lines is uncertain.

The Orientation of Trade Policy in the Medium Term

Three factors will have a large impact on the development of East European agricultural trade: the efficiency with which these countries use their agricultural potential; the relationship between supply and demand; and a "sure" supply. While the first will play a predominant role in the long run, it will have little effect in the next few years: the economic decisionmakers of these countries do not seem to expect significant improvements in the medium term from their efforts to reorganize production and increase its efficiency. The second factor, on the other hand, will be more decisive and many elements permit one to already foresee the policies to be used. These will include:

1. Food and agricultural production will increase moderately in all these countries. Productive resources will increase only a little. The investment situation is the most strained because all these countries are feeling the effects of the deceleration of economic growth and, in some of them, agricultural investments will remain fixed at the same level as that of the preceding five year plan. Furthermore, the modernization of equipment might be slowed by the slowdown of imports from the West.
2. In any case, the restrictive import policy for goods paid in hard currency should continue during the next few years. While in Czechoslovakia it is hoped to reduce the Western debt by 1985, the clearing up of the financial situation can take place only later in the other countries. Poland cannot hope to rebalance western accounts before the end of the decade. This policy will not spare food purchases.
3. In fact, initial forecasts of food consumption were lowered in most of these countries with meat consumption being the most reduced. At the same time, domestic production will not assure a sufficient grain supply and steps have been taken to deal with this.

*The Impact of This Will Be
Expressed in Three Ways:*

1. A moderate progression in trade both within CMEA and with the western market.

Inside the zone, the developments noted for some products do not permit one to foresee a development of trade through a reorientation of flows towards CMEA countries. The reorientation of trade seems to have reached, at least for these goods, a saturation point. Trade between East European countries will only be able to develop at the rate of increase of those goods whose production, we noted, had slowed down. Nevertheless, the increase of purchases from non-European members of CMEA should continue, as far as citrus fruits from Cuba and rice from Vietnam are concerned. And it is possible that the Soviet Union's partners will make up a part of their deficit with the USSR through grain purchases in western markets and reexport them to the USSR either directly or in the form of meat.

On the international market, tropical and subtropical goods purchases will be limited in many of these countries to those that cannot be made inside the CMEA. Thus Poland foresees buying only coffee, tea, rice and pepper. Grain will continue to be the main component of food imports. As low as planned food consumption already is, the decision-makers seem to have taken a realistic approach to foreseeing large purchases: the agreements concluded by the USSR total more than 20 million tons of grain per year; and the GDR made an agreement with Canada for the delivery of 3 million tons from 1981–1985. The combined influence of improved yields, restructuring of feed and limiting of meat consumption, suggest that East European grain purchases could be limited to 8 or 9 million tons between 1985–1990 (5 to 6 million tons of net imports), that is a 50 percent drop compared to 1980.[12] For the USSR the estimates are not as certain if one keeps in mind the extreme fluctuations in harvest. In any case, the goal for the 1990 grain harvest is most ambitious. If it does attain 240 million tons, Soviet net imports needs would be, on the average, about 20–25 million tons. The Soviets seem ready to take advantage of a favorable world market in order to make opportune purchases of certain goods.

2. Diversification of supply sources and long term agreements.

In order to assure a regular and certain supply, which they cannot assure through their own production, two means have been used. The USSR but also other East European countries have attempted these last few years to diversify their supply sources. This was a constraint for the USSR at the beginning of the decade, but the Soviet Union has nevertheless continued to carry out this orientation. Thus, the United States was not able to recapture all of the Soviet grain market. Nevertheless American participation will remain very important to the extent that the United States is the main supplier of corn, although some grain agreements were made by USSR with Argentina, Brazil, Australia, Canada, Thailand, and Hungary. These agreements can also include meat, as does that with Argentina. The GDR has also decreased grain purchases from the United States from 3 million tons in 1980 to 1 million in 1983, and concluded that year an agreement with Canada. At the same time, long term agreements are more and more sought by these countries.

3. The development or a "subsistence" economy as a stop gap measure for the reduction of food imports?

The attention given in the Soviet food program to the private plots and subsidiary holdings of enterprises is fairly characteristic of this orientation of food policy in the region. They need "to create favorable conditions so that each family which lives in the rural area can have a private plot, some poultry and cattle, and that the surplus of their production be bought at opportune time by the consumers cooperative". In the same way "each enterprise, each organization which can do it, should have an auxiliary farm and will be allocated some land to this end".[13] Two figures are characteristic of the potential to be developed and of the hope that it creates. Between 1980 and 1982, private cattle of the population increased by 1.1 million, private cows by 200,000, pigs by 1.8 million and reserves are large enough because over half of sovkhoz and kolkhoz families do not have cows and 70 percent do not have sheep and pigs.[14] In the Rostow Oblast, over 500 enterprises and organizations have created their own auxiliary farm, and their production is expected to give 25–26 kg of meat per worker. Moreover, it is estimated that the whole production furnishes to retail sales and collective and individual, consumption 58 kg of meat per capita, but income levels would permit a consumption of 70–75 kg.[15] Stop-gap measures for a crisis situation? No matter what, these postpone to a poorly defined future the desired goals of the food programs.

Notes

1. *Ekonomiceskoe sotrudnicevstvo stran-clenov SEV,* 1983–1986, p. 51.

2. Table 29.2; UNCTAD. *Handbook of international trade and development statistics* (1983), pp. 110–11, and A. 32, includes fish (03) and forest products (24, 25).

3. Excluding the forest products, Soviet agricultural raw materials trade is, more or less, balanced.

4. Over two third of Soviet exports are destined for Eastern Europe and represent 86 percent of their imports.

5. The policy was defined by L. Brezhnev in 1965 and adopted in other Eastern European countries.

6. Soviet grain imports reached 31 million tons in 1981 and meat imports, 1,138 million tons (Tables 29.6 and 29.7).

7. *Ekonomiceskoe sotrudnicevstvo stran-clenov SEV,* 1984(4) p. 18.

8. Soviet-Hungarian agreement for Hungarian sales of a minimum 400,000 tons in 1981–1985 (principally wheat). In 1982, 163,000 tons were exported.

9. *Vnesnyaya torgovlja,* 1984(5) p. 17, gives the figure for 1984 as 985,000 tons.

10. Minimum 27 percent in 1974, maximum 72 percent in 1978. In 1980, 60 percent of Soviet meat was imported from the west, of which 36 percent from developing countries. Estimated on basis of "Vnesnyaya torgovlja SSS", in rubles.

11. Source: based on data of the Centre d'Etude Prospective et d'Informations Internationales, Paris.

12. E. Cook, R. Cummings, and T. Vankai, "Agricultural production and trade prospects through 1990", USDA, Economic Report, Number 195.

13. *Ekonomiceskaya gazeta,* 1982, No. 22 et 23.

14. *Planovoe khozajstvo,* 1983(8), p. 8.

15. *Voprosy ekonomiki,* 1982(7), p. 4.

TABLE 29.1

Agricultural Trade in Eastern European Countries - 1971-1982
(millions $)

	1971-1975	1976	1977	1978	1979	1980	1981	1982
Net exporters								
Bulgaria	+164	+451	+530	+556	+658	+805	+420	+795
Hungaria	+436	+515	+594	+626	+890	+890	+1.210	+1.503
Rumania	+182	+ 48	+465	+417	+ 29	- 70	- 59	+223
	+782	+1.014	+1.649	+1.599	+1.577	+1.625	+1.571	+2.521
Net importers								
1) GDR	-1.103	-1.510	-1.518	-1.609	-1.756	-1.926	-1.617	-1.643
Czechoslovakia	-834	-1.123	-1.259	-1.246	-1.660	-1.410	-1.286	-1.207
2) Poland	-389	-914	-1.015	-1.214	-1.350	-1.991	-2.452	-1.395
SSSR	-2.800	-7.500	-7.000	-8.300	-11.100	-15.192	-18.307	-16.600
Sub-total	-5.126	-11.047	-10.892	-12.369	-15.866	-20.518	-23.662	-20.845
East Europe excluding SSSR	-1.542	-2.533	-2.243	-2.470	-3.189	-3.702	-3.789	-1.724
TOTAL	-4.342	-10.033	-9.243	-10.770	-14.289	-18.899	-22.091	-18.324

1) Traditional industrial countries
2) Countries with agricultural potentialities

Source: FAO, Trade Yearbook, vols.34 and 35; for 1982: Eastern Europe - Outlook
        Situation Report, USDA 1984. SITC 0, 1, 22, 4 + 21, 23, 26, 29
        (excluding fish and forest products).

TABLE 29.2

East European Agricultural Trade Balance by Commodities and
by Regions (1)

(millions $) - 1980

| | Planned Economies | | | | | | | |
Soviet Union	Total (2)	Eastern Europe (3)	Soviet Union	Asia	Sub Total	Devel- oped	Devel- oping	Sub Total
A - Food products SITC 0, 1, 22, 4								
Export	1.553	454	-	217	671	255	621	876
Import	14.926	2.669	-	368	3.037	5.398	6.154	11.552
Net Import (-)	-13.373	-2.215	-	-151	-2.366	-5.143	-5.533	-10.676
B - Agricultural raw material SITC 2, - (22 + 27 + 28)								
Export	4.862	2.095	-	78	2.173	2.319	359	2.678
Import	1.896	341	-	128	469	725	702	1.427
Net Export (+)	+2.966	+1.754	-	-50	+1.704	+1.594	-343	+1.251
Other Eastern European countries								
A - Food products SITC 0, 1, 22, 4								
Export	8.397	1.495	2.669	110	4.274	2.776	1.326	4.102
Import	8.235	1.495	454	347	2.296	4.017	1.924	5.941
Net Import (+)	+162	-	+2.215	-237	+1.978	-1.241	-598	-1.839
B - Agricultural raw material								
Export	2.362	276	341	182	799	1.258	250	1.508
Import	4.377	276	2.095	126	2.497	1.182	698	1.880
Net Import (-)	-2.015	-	-1.754	+56	-1.698	+76	-448	-372

Source: UNCTAD - Handbook of International Trade and Development Statistics.
1983, pp. A30 et A31.

(1) Including fish and forest products; thus the total differs from Table 29.1

(2) Some adjustments in the total of world export are not distributed by
destination.

(3) Excluding USSR.

TABLE 29.3

Agricultural Trade in Eastern Europe (1)

$(10^6$ $ - FOB)

	World	Market Economies				Planned Economies		
		developed		Deve-				
		Total	Europe	loping	Asia	SSSR	intra	Total
A - Exports								
1970	2.280	992	913	131	20	707	407	1.134
1978	6.308	2.227	1.935	885	75	1.898	1.194	3.167
1979	7.187	2.584	2.228	980	87	2.257	1.268	3.612
1980	8.117	2.646	2.306	1.255	109	2.667	1.419	4.195
1981	7.859	2.214	1.952	1.422	82	3.005	1.126	4.213
1982	8.154	2.082	1.819	1.559	101	3.287	1.100	4.488
B - Imports (2)								
1970	1.811	471	372	465	50	418	407	875
1978	5.175	2.025	1.051	1.392	257	308	1.194	1.758
1979	8.312	2.863	1.354	1.451	271	648	1.268	2.188
1980	7.775	3.770	1.952	1.850	299	437	1.419	2.155
1981	7.363	4.025	-	1.439	247	527	1.126	1.900
1982	5.709	2.176	-	2.007	194	232	1.100	1.526

(1) SITC 0,1. Excluding Soviet Union.

(2) See Table 29.2

Source: United Nations - Monthly Bulletin of Statistics - May 1983 and 1984,
pp. XXXIV et. seq.

TABLE 29.4

Geographical Structure of Agricultural Trade (1)
Eastern Europe (excluding USSR)
Total world = 100

	Market Economies				Planned Economies		
	developed		deve-				
	Total	Europe	loping	Asia	SSSR	Intra	Total
A - East European Exports							
1970	43.5	40.0	5.7	0.9	31.0	17.8	49.7
1978	35.3	30.7	13.5	1.2	30.0	18.9	50.2
1979	35.9	31.0	13.6	1.2	31.4	17.6	50.2
1980	32.5	28.4	15.5	1.3	32.9	17.5	51.7
1981	27.9	24.6	18.1	1.0	38.2	14.3	53.5
1982	25.5	22.3	19.1	1.2	40.2	13.6	55.0
B - East European Imports							
1970	26.0	20.5	25.7	2.7	23.0	22.5	48.3
1978	39.1	20.3	26.9	5.0	23.1	6.0	34.0
1979	34.4	16.3	17.5	3.3	7.8	15.2	26.3
1980	48.5	25.1	23.8	3.8	5.6	18.2	27.7
1981	54.6	-	19.5	3.3	7.1	15.3	25.8
1982	38.1	-	35.1	1.6	4.1	19.3	26.7

(1) SITC 0,1.

Source: Derived from Table 29.3

TABLE 29.5

Geographical structure of agricultural trade - USSR
(Total world = 100) (1)

	Market Economies				Planned Economies		
	developed		deve-			Eastern	
	Total	Europe	loping	Total	Asia	Europe	Total
A - Exports							
1970	15.0	13.3	22.6	37.6	10.6	51.7	62.3
1978	17.6	11.2	40.5	58.1	15.1	26.8	41.9
1979	14.4	9.2	33.8	48.2	13.3	38.4	51.7
1980	16.0	10.0	39.0	55.0	14.8	30.1	44.9
1981	10.0	6.9	40.0	50.0	15.5	34.5	50.0
1982	14.5	10.1	54.0	68.5	13.0	18.5	31.5
B - Imports							
1970	12.8	-	45.3	58.1	3.1	38.8	41.9
	(12.7%) (2)	(6.6) (2)					
1978	25.7	-	49.6	75.3	3.1	21.6	24.7
	(27.3%) (2)	(5.3)					
1979	34.4	-	42.2	76.6	3.0	20.4	23.4
	(36.9%) (2)	(7.1)					
1980	36.2	-	42.9	79.1	2.5	18.4	20.9
	(36.1%) (2)	(15.1)					
1981	38.0	-	42.9	80.9	1.8	17.3	19.1
1982	33.4	-	46.4	79.8	1.7	18.5	20.2

(1) SITC 0, 1. The structure does not vary if SITC 22 + 4 are added.

(2) UNCTAD. 1983 A. 18: SITC 0, 1, 22, 4.

Source: United Nations, Monthly Bulletin of Statistics - May 1984.

TABLE 29.6

Eastern European Grain Trade (1)

$(10^6$ $ FOB)$

| | Total World | Market Economies | | | Planned Economies | | |
		Developed	Developing	Asia	Intra (1)	SSSR	Total
A - Exports							
1970	121	79	19	1	19	3	23
1978	212	54	30	4	62	59	125
1979	311	84	38	4	106	75	185
1980	361	90	49	5	129	89	222
1981	461	47	51	4	153	206	363
1982	486	93	31	2	175	184	361
B - Imports							
1970	507	129	27	2	19	328	351
1978	1.290	1.039	98	71	61	21	153
1979	2.095	1.627	46	75	106	240	422
1980	2.533	2.226	32	83	129	64	276
1981	2.595	2.262	44	69	153	67	289
1982	1.487	1.036	102	51	175	123	349
C - Net Imports							
1970	-386	-50	-8	-1	-	-325	-326
1978	-1.078	-985	-58	-67	-	+38	-29
1979	-1.784		-8	-71	-	-165	-236
1980	-2.171		+17	-78	-	+25	-53
1981	-2.126	-2.215	+7	-65	-	+139	+74
1982	-1.001	-943	-71	-49	-	+61	+12

(1) Excluding USSR.

Source: United Nations, Monthly Bulletin of Statistics, May 1984.

TABLE 29.7

Soviet Grain Trade

(Million $ - FOB)

| | World Total | Market Economies | | Planned Economies | | |
		Developed	Developing	Asia	Eastern Europe	Total
A - Imports						
1970	136	84	37	13	2	15
1971	213	146	49	15	3	18
1972	804	749	26	0	29	29
1973	1.399	1.234	35	0	70	70
1974	681	381	224	23	53	76
1975	2.312	1.728	331	22	230	252
1976	2.583	2.199	230	24	132	155
1977	1.390	1.220	100	46	24	70
1978	2.303	1.889	309	45	59	105
1979	3.244	2.873	243	54	75	128
1980	4.452	3.110	1.192	60	89	149
1981	6.173	3.784	2.121	62	206	268
1982	5.422	3.788	1.371	79	184	264
B - Exports						
1970	422	23	47	24	328	352
1971	608	65	92	12	437	450
1972	328	31	37	15	245	260
1973	490	7	167	24	279	316
1974	825	3	411	18	392	411
1975	509	4	137	22	346	368
1976	218	0	83	59	75	134
1977	518	0	129	84	305	389
1978	214	1	102	90	21	111
1979	569	5	196	129	240	368
1980	320	0	152	99	64	163
1981	438	3	238	130	67	196
1982	431	0	235	72	123	195

Source: United Nations, Monthly Bulletin of Statistics, May 1983 and 1984.

Table 29.8

East European Fruit and Vegetable Trade
(in percent of all food trade)

		1970	1975	1980
1)	Importers (1)			
	SSSR	13.6	8.6	8.0
	GDR	21.0	19.9	18.2
	Czechoslovakia	10.9	13.7	15.5
2)	Exporters (2)			
	Hungary	26.0	24.6	18.0
	Bulgaria	25.0	26.8	22.0
	Poland	17.0	16.4	18.6
	Romania	–	–	(35.0)

(1) Fruits and vegetable imports in percent of food
     imports.

(2) Fruits and vegetable exports in percent of food
     exports.

Source: United Nations Revue du commerce agricole No. 21,
        except for Romania which was estimated from
        national statistics.

TABLE 29.9

Fruit and Vegetable Trade - Eastern Europe and USSR

	Import	Export	Net Import (-)
USSR	1.361	57.5	-1,303.5
GDR	417	34.5	-382.5
Czechoslovakia	334	98.0	-236.0
Hungary	98.5	397.5	+299
Bulgaria	31.5	412.5	+381.0
Poland	164	213.0	+ 49
Rumania	(15)	(449)	(+434)
TOTAL	2.422	1.662	-759

Source: See Table 29.8

Table 29.10

East European Tropical Products Trade
(in percent of fruit and vegetable trade)

	Tropical Products			Other Products			
	A	B	C	A	B	C	TOTAL
Imports	430	310	740	1.682	–	1.682	-2.422
Exports	–	–	–	190	1.472	1.662	+1.662
Trade Balance	-430	-310	-740	-1.492	+1.472	-10	-760

(1)   Million dollar, average 1979-1981.

A =   net importers; B = net exporters, C = East Europe + USSR.

Source: FAO Trade Yearbook and National Statistical Handbooks.

Table 29.11

Soviet Cotton Fibers Exports (1)

	1970	1975	1979	1980	1981
Total exports (metric tonnes)	516.5	800.2	789.0	843.2	915.9(1)
Thousands of which: – to Eastern Europe					
1) in tonnes	402.4	394.9	377.1	431.1	375.5
2) in percent:					
– of Soviet exports	77.9%	49.4%	47.8%	52.2%	41%
– of East European imports	–	–	59.6%	62.2%	60.2%

Sources: FAO, Trade Yearbook Vneshnyaya Torgovlja SSSR

(1)   The value of Soviet exports to Eastern Europe doubled in the
70's but as a percentage of all Soviet exports they diminished
from 78 percent in 1970 to 48.6 percent in 1981 and these
exports represent only 48 percent of East-European purchases.

(2)   Soviet cotton imports reached a maximum of 257 thousand tons
in 1970, but decreased rapidly, to 22-25 thousand tons in
1981-1982.   In 1983, and 1984, they increased again
and exports decreased considerably.   Thus exports to Eastern
Europe increased in relative terms but diminished in absolute
terms.

About the Contributors

Claude Aubert received his education in agronomy at the Institut National Agronomique in Paris. Currently he is director of research at the French National Institute of Agronomic Research, where he specializes in Chinese rural economy and society. He has done extensive field research in both Taiwan and the People's Republic of China. Among his recent publications are a monograph, *Les Greniers de Mancang, Chronique d'un Village Taiwannaise,* coauthored with his wife, Chen Ying, and a book on the People's Republic of China entitled *La Societe Chinoise Après Mao.*

Chantal Beaucourt was educated at the University of Strasbourg and at the Sorbonne. After receiving her doctorate she taught at the Sorbonne before becoming a senior researcher at the Center for International and Perspective Studies, where she specializes in agriculture, the energy sector, and employment issues in the Soviet Union and East Europe. Her work has been published in *Economie Prospective Internationale, Le Courrier des Pays de l'Est,* and by the OECD.

Ivan Benet graduated from the Faculty of Agricultural Economics of the University of Economics in Budapest. He is a research worker and department head at the Institute of Economics of the Hungarian Academy of Sciences where his work centers on agribusiness, links between agriculture and industry, and the policies for developing Hungarian agriculture and agricultural trade. He has published numerous books and articles on these topics. Benet is also a professor at the Agricultural University, Keszthely.

Elizabeth Clayton is professor of economics at the University of Missouri in St. Louis. She received a doctorate in economics at the University of Washington in Seattle and has been a Fellow at Harvard University Law School and at the Kennan Institute for Advanced Russian Studies of the Woodrow Wilson International Center for Scholars in Washington, D.C. She is a former president of the Midwest Economics Association and has written numerous articles on Soviet economic problems, particularly in agriculture.

Edward Cook studied economics and Russian at the State University of New York in Binghamton, The Maurice Thorez Foreign Language Institute in Moscow, and the University of Wisconsin. He is employed by the Economic Research Service of the U.S. Department of Agriculture. His interests include Soviet and East European agricultural policies, especially those relating to finance, organization, and grain and livestock production. His work has appeared in *Soviet Studies,* the *American Journal of Agricultural Economics,* and *Food Policy.*

Michael Ellman studied at the universities of Cambridge, London, and Moscow, receiving his Ph.D. at Cambridge in 1972. He is currently professor of microeconomics at the University of Amsterdam, where his interests include socialist planning and agriculture as well as the economics of the welfare state. He is the author of several books and many journal articles and is a member of the editorial boards of the *Cambridge Journal of Economics,* the *Journal of Comparative Economics,* and *Matekon.*

Zbigniew M. Fallenbuchl is professor of economics and dean of the College of Social Science at the University of Windsor. Educated at the universities of London and Montreal and at McGill University, he has published extensively on Polish economic issues.

Adam Fforde was educated at Oxford University, Birkbeck College, and received his doctorate at Cambridge University. His research is based, in part, on the results of fieldwork conducted during lengthy stays at Hanoi University. He was awarded an ESRC Post-Doctoral Research Fellowship at Birkbeck College and was a Visiting Fellow at the National Economics University, Hanoi.

Joseph Hajda is professor of political science at Kansas State University, where he also served as director of international activities. He received his B.A. and M.A. degrees at Miami University and his Ph.D. degree at Indiana University. Besides writing extensively on East European agriculture and East-West trade, he has served as advisor to U.S. Secretary of Agriculture Orville Freeman and to the U.S. special representative for trade negotiations.

Wiktor Herer has written extensively on the relationship between agriculture and other sectors of the economy and on the effect of agricultural performance on economic growth. Formerly he combined university teaching with work at the Polish central planning organs. He then participated in the drafting of long-term development plans for the Polish economy under the leadership of Michal Kalecki. Currently he is carrying out research at the Institute for National Economy.

Jeanne C. Hey is a doctoral candidate in the College of Business and Economics at Lehigh University. She received her A.B. degree at Bucknell University and her M.B.A. at Lehigh University. Her interests include the application of econometric methods to policy evaluation.

Karl Hohmann studied agricultural economics at Justus Liebig University in Giessen and then joined the Research Institute for German Economic and Social Issues. His work, which has been published in both books and journals, centers on the organization and productivity of the GDR's agriculture.

Paul L. Kelley received his B.S. and M.S. degrees at Kansas State University and his Ph.D. in economics at Iowa State University. He has served on the faculty of Kansas State University as professor and as chair of the Department of Economics, and he has also held visiting appointments at the University of Arizona and Colorado State University. His research, published in numerous journals and books, centers on international agricultural trade and on the policies followed by major agricultural exporting and importing countries. Among his recent works are a chapter in *Economic Analysis and Agricultural Policy,* edited by Richard Day, a study of the Egyptian food system, and an investigation of the decline in U.S. grain exports to Latin America.

Arthur E. King is associate professor of economics and assistant director of the Center for Social Research at Lehigh University. He received his Ph.D. at Ohio State University. The major focus of his research has been econometric studies of East European economies and especially of Czechoslovakia.

Andrzej Korbonski is professor of political science and director of the Center for Russian and East European Studies at the University of California, Los Angeles. He has written extensively on various aspects of Soviet and East European politics and economics.

Betty A. Laird is an independent researcher, writer, and cartographer, an actress who has performed in numerous commercial and educational films, and co-founder and president of Parker-Laird Enterprises. She received her B.A. in theater and English at Hastings College and completed postgraduate work in Soviet studies and statistics at the universities of Washington and Kansas. She has published articles on both Soviet agriculture and the history of Kansas.

Roy D. Laird is professor of political science and Soviet and East European studies at the University of Kansas. He received his Ph.D. from the University of Washington. Most of his books, articles, and book chapters have dealt with various aspects of East European and Soviet agricultural affairs. He is the founder of the International Conference on Soviet and East European Agriculture and organizer of its first meeting, which was held at the University of Kansas in 1962. His most recent book is *The Politburo: Demographic Trends, Gorbachev and the Future* (Westview, 1986).

Gregor Lazarcik received his Ph.D. at Columbia University. He has engaged in university teaching and in research on East European agricultural production, costs, and productivity for the Research Project on National Income in East Central Europe.

Ivan Loncarevic studied agriculture at the universities of Zagreb, Madrid, and Giessen. After receiving his doctorate at the latter institution, he joined the Zentrum fur kontinentale Agrar- und Wirtschaftsforschung at Justus Liebig University, where he has conducted research on, and published articles about, Soviet and Yugoslav agriculture.

Stephan Merl is Wissenschaftlicher Mitarbeiter in social and economic history in the Department of History at the Free University of Berlin. He received his doctorate at the University of Hamburg, having previously studied history, political science, and Russian. His research interests include the social and economic history of the Soviet Union and East Europe and the role of agriculture in industrialization. He has published several books as well as articles on these topics.

Robert F. Miller received his B.A. at the University of Michigan and his M.A. and Ph.D. at Harvard University. He currently teaches at the Australian National University. Previously, he served on the faculties of Washington University, the State University of New York at Stony Brook, and the University of Illinois. His interests include economic administration in the USSR and Yugoslavia, politics of socialist countries, and Soviet foreign policy. Among his books are *One Hundred Thousand Tractors: The MTS and the Development of Controls in Soviet Agriculture* and *Gorbachev at the Helm.*

Alec Nove graduated from the London School of Economics, served in the British Army throughout the war, and then served as a civil servant in London. Subsequently he taught at the University of London and at the University of Glasgow, where he was both professor of economics and director of the Institute of Soviet and East European Studies. He has been a visiting professor at the universities of Kansas, Pennsylvania, Paris, Rennes, Santiago, and Montreal, as well as at Columbia University and UCLA. Among his books are *The Soviet Economic System* and *An Economic History of the USSR.*

Alain Pouliquen received degrees in agriculture at INA-Paris and in economics at the University of Paris. He is currently director of research at the National Agronomic Research Institute's Department of Agricultural Economics and Sociology. While his early interests centered on econometrics and French agriculture, more recently he has turned to East European and Soviet agricultural problems, and he has published numerous articles on agricultural organization in these countries.

Jean Radvanyi holds a Ph.D. from the Sorbonne as well as a Doctorat d'Etat. He teaches courses in geography and the civilization of the USSR at the Institut National des Langues et Civilisations Orientales and is deputy chairman of the Center for Russian and Soviet Studies. He has written numerous books and articles about agricultural modernization and regional policies in the Soviet Union.

Philip M. Raup has served on the faculties of the University of Wisconsin and the University of Minnesota, where he is currently professor of agricultural economics. Educated at the universities of Kansas and Wisconsin, he has published numerous books and articles on a wide range of topics including land economics, structural change in agriculture, and world agricultural development.

Eberhard Schinke studied agriculture at Leipzig and Giessen universities. Since 1971 he has been teaching at Giessen University while conducting research on Soviet and East European agriculture. He has published extensively on agricultural planning, organization, policies, and trade in both the FRG and the GDR as well as in other socialist countries.

Barbara Severin is an economist employed by the U.S. government. She has an undergraduate degree from the University of California at Davis and a graduate degree from Cornell University. Her research interests include the Soviet economy, particularly the consumption and agriculture sectors.

Ihor Stebelsky was educated in geography at the University of Toronto and the University of Washington. He has taught at the University of Windsor since 1968 and is presently professor and chairman of the Department of Geography. He is coauthor of *Eurasia: Its Lands and Peoples* and author of articles in journals, such as the *Journal of Geography* and *Soviet Geography,* and chapters in books, such as *Interpretations of Calamity* and *Russian Historical Geography.* His current research is on the geographic variation of Soviet food consumption.

Franciszek Tomczak is a professor at the Central School of Planning and Statistics in Warsaw. He has also held appointments at Tripoli University and the University of Minnesota. Educated at the University of Warsaw and the Central School of Planning and Statistics, where he received his Ph.D., he has published many books and journal articles on agricultural issues in Poland and on agricultural economics.

Tamas Ujhelyi is a department head at the Hungarian Agricultural Research Institute, where his research interests focus on Hungarian and world trade in agricultural products. He has written numerous articles and books on these topics.

TRENDS IN
Computer Assisted Education

TRENDS IN
Computer Assisted Education

EDITED BY

R. LEWIS
ESRC — Information Technology
and Education Programme
University of Lancaster

E.D. TAGG
formerly the University of Lancaster

Blackwell Scientific Publications

OXFORD LONDON EDINBURGH

BOSTON PALO ALTO MELBOURNE

© 1987 by
Blackwell Scientific Publications
Editorial offices:
Osney Mead, Oxford, OX2 0EL
8 John Street, London, WC1N 2ES
23 Ainslie Place, Edinburgh, EH3 6AJ
52 Beacon Street, Boston
    Massachusetts 02108, USA
667 Lytton Avenue, Palo Alto
    California 94301, USA
107 Barry Street, Carlton
    Victoria 3053, Australia

First published 1987

Set from the authors'
word-processor disk by
Oxford Computer Typesetting
Printed and bound
in Great Britain

DISTRIBUTORS

USA and Canada
  Blackwell Scientific Publications Inc
  P O Box 50009, Palo Alto
  California 94303

Australia
  Blackwell Scientific Publications
  (Australia) Pty Ltd
  107 Barry Street
  Carlton, Victoria 3053

British Library
Cataloguing in Publication Data

Trends in computer assisted education.
  1. Education, Higher — Data processing
  I. Lewis, Robert, *1940 Sept. 27–*
  II. Tagg, E.D.
  378'.0028'5   LB2324

ISBN 0-632-01527-6

Library of Congress
Cataloging-in-Publication Data

Trends in computer assisted education.

  Proceedings of the 1986 Conference in
  Computers in Higher Education, held at Lancaster
  University.
  Bibliography: p.
  Includes index.
  1. Computer-assisted instruction — Congresses.
  2. Education, Higher — Data processing —
  Congresses.
  I. Lewis, R. (Robert), 1940– . II. Tagg, E.D.,
  1913– . III. Conference in the Computers in
  Higher Education (6th : 1986 : Lancaster University)
  LB1028.5.T65 1987   371.3'9445   86-29929
  ISBN 0-632-01527-6

Contents

Editors' Preface

These Proceedings of the 1986 Conference in the Computers in Higher Education series include the invited and submitted papers and, in addition, short reports on the seminar sessions. It is unfortunate that there is no way in which the informal discussions which took place during the workshop sessions could be represented. These sessions were extremely lively with both individual exploration and classroom-style experimentation. It is to be hoped that the papers reflect some of this activity but we are unable to capture the contributions made by Tony Scott, Alan Marsden and others to these sessions. Neither can we provide any feeling of Colin Wells' invited presentation on Computers in Music Education.

We would like to thank the contributors who submitted papers in machine readable form. These came on a variety of disks which, together with JANET files, were transferred onto a Research Machines Nimbus and edited with MS-DOS WORD. These files were transferred to disks in Apricot format for direct typesetting by Blackwell Scientific Publications. The technical support of Mark Bryson and the editorial help of Maureen Boots, both of the ESRC-Information Technology and Education Programme based at Lancaster should not pass without words of thanks from us.

R. Lewis
E. D. Tagg

Foreword

The conference on 'Trends in Computer Assisted Education' was the 6th in the series of Computers in Higher Education conferences and the 4th to be held at Lancaster University. When I attended the first as a very new lecturer in 1974, I did not anticipate that 12 years later I would have the pleasure and privilege of chairing the Conference Steering Committee. As my involvement in the application of computers to education has been limited to the subject of Engineering, so the task of chairing a committee of individuals of much greater direct knowledge and experience than myself presented a particular challenge. The conference was attended by over 100 people, including delegates from Canada, Yugoslavia, Denmark, Norway, Sweden, Australia, New Zealand, and the Netherlands as well as from the UK. One feature, however, was the absence of delegates from secondary education. As these have formed a significant element of past conferences it is hoped that their absence is only temporary.

Being in touch with, but on the fringes of, an area of study does, however, have its advantages, particularly perhaps when assessing the changes that have taken place in any given interval. At the first conference individuals and groups were attempting to produce packages based on largely inadequate hardware and I well remember sitting down to a demonstration given on a chattering teletype. This period represents the hardware limited phase of development.

Since that first conference the development has in hardware terms been staggering with levels of processing power that were largely unimagined at the time now being available at relatively minimal cost. Faced with this increase in computing power the developments in software tools have to a large extent fallen behind. The result is that the production of material for CAL and CAI has now entered a software limited phase in its development. With this is mind, the conference programme included invited papers on Artificial Intelligence to highlight developments in this important area.

Over the same period there has been a tremendous growth in the range and variety of uses to which the computer is being put in education. The conference illustrates just a few of these with papers on Interactive Video, Music and Art included alongside papers on the sciences.

A change from previous conferences was the incorporation into the conference programme of a series of workshops and seminars. These enabled a wide range of topics to be discussed and programs to be demonstrated more effectively than has been the case in previous conferences. It is hoped that this approach will be adopted at future conferences.

The conference also invited three special speakers, Professor B. Penkov from Bulgaria, Colin Wells from the University of Reading and Roger Hartley from the University of Leeds. Unfortunately, Professor Penkov fell ill just before the conference and was unable to attend. Fortunately, an excellent replacement was found in Dr. W. Clancey of Stanford University who was attending a meeting in the Lake District and was able to break his journey to Manchester Airport to give the opening address. Colin Wells' presentation on Music education generated interest, if not agreement, amongst all who heard him. Certainly if learning is to be both interesting and enjoyable than the approach outlined seemed to go a long way towards achieving this. Roger Hartley has been involved in CAL for many years and his closing address provided both a background and a theme for development.

Finally, I would like to thank all those people who contributed to the conference. The members of the Steering Committee who contributed ideas and advice and organised the invited papers. To Bob Lewis and Donovan Tagg for their efforts in editing the papers, Mark Bryson for sorting out the formats of the various submissions and lastly, but by no means least, Maureen Boots who organised everyone, in particular myself, most effectively.

David Bradley

Programme committee

Dr. D.A. Bradley, (Chairman), *University of Lancaster*

Professor A. Bajpai, *Loughborough University of Technology*

Mrs. J. Coates, *Council for Educational Technology*

Professor R. Lewis, *ESRC and University of Lancaster*

Ms. R. Rymaszewski, *University of Lancaster*

Dr. J.A. Self, *University of Lancaster*

Dr. E.D. Tagg, *University of Lancaster*

Mr. J. Turnbull, *National Computing Centre*

Section 1: Keynote Address

1 / Computer-Based Support Systems for Learning and Teaching

J. R. HARTLEY *University of Leeds*

Abstract

A brief analysis of the practical achievements of Computer-Assisted Learning (CAL) shows them to be disparate and low-key. Current CAL designs tend to be restricted in ambition and set well within the compass of present technical and theoretical expertise. Even if current CBL software were utilised more widely and intensively in the classroom, it must cause difficulties for teachers who, directly or indirectly, have to provide a supporting 'intelligence' (i.e. respond to individual ideas and questions as programs are used, give advice on learning from these materials, and superintend student learning of the software packages). Hence, the argument is for designing and providing more 'knowledgeable' materials to give such learning support and for methodologies and software tools to aid their design and implementation. These views on developing the (micro)computer as a learning station are illustrated through two case-studies; one concerns knowledge-based learning advisors (used in conjunction with pre-stored and other materials) for the development of problem-solving skills; the other outlines an intelligent on-line help system which could be extended for use with software laboratories for learning.

Keywords Computer-assisted learning, Artificial intelligence, Learning support, Man-machine interface.

Introduction: the need for learning support

It is twenty-one years since Computer-Assisted Learning (CAL) made its educational debut, so it seems an appropriate time to assess its maturity, to consider the methodologies now available for CAL, and to determine ways in which it might move forward and have an innovative influence on teaching/learning practices.

So far, the achievements of CAL are not particularly encouraging. Of course, since the 1960s there have been large technological advances so that now relatively cheap 16/32-bit microcomputers/workstations are available, with concurrent operating systems and window

Computer Based Learning Unit, University of Leeds, Leeds, LS2 9JT management, and sufficient on-board memory and processing power to permit and encourage greater educational ambitions. Much has been accomplished also in Cognitive Science, in delineating the mental processes which are active, for example, in comprehension and in problem-solving, and in providing various formalisms (such as frame-based or rule-based systems) for representing knowledge structures and student models. However, these developments are not well exploited by current CAL materials which, although better dressed and attractively presented, have changed little in basic design during the last decade.

Some of the reasons for this state of affairs are not hard to find. Few training workshops take place in Higher Education, and those concerned with School Education financed under the National Microelectronics Education Programme (MEP) concentrated on the utilisation of materials rather than on the principles of their design in relation to learning difficulties. Again, teachers themselves have little time to engage in program development, do not have detailed knowledge of implementation languages, and so are not sure whether more ambitious or imaginative ideas can be given a practical format. Further, in the educational sphere it is difficult to make the development of materials economically self-sustaining. Publishing houses, though supportive, cannot afford to be out-of-pocket and few programs sell well enough to recoup the initial outlay. There is a big difference also between homespun local initiatives, and testing, documenting and maintaining such programs to publishers' standards.

Currently, institutions are limited in the hardware and the student access which can be given to CAL. In fact this shortage affords the teacher some protection. Course materials (whether item banks, tutoring/practice exercises, simulation packages, or software laboratories) act in a supplementary role, and for best effects require careful preparation, monitoring and follow-up when used in classes. For example, few of these materials keep or infer an adequate student model (some none at all), so cannot proffer useful advice, or provide explanation and respond to user's questions, or take up comments unless these have been specifically anticipated. This intelligence has to be provided by the teacher. However, CAL materials are most effective when they are allowing or stimulating individuals or groups of students to develop knowledge or ideas using their own experience and perspectives. Given even a moderately sized class, the teacher will not be able to service adequately these demands and so provide the level of learning advice required for a proper utilisation of the material. In short, if CAL is to be more effectively diffused, the learning systems will have to incorporate more supporting 'intelligence' to aid both the student and the teacher.

The problem will be further compounded as software packages

from the 'place of work', but useful for learning, become more available (e.g. database systems, spreadsheet/modelling software, statistics and symbolic algebra laboratories and bespoke packages in engineering design). Even ignoring the need for supporting advice during their educational use, the packages themselves require significant time for their learning — so much so that some teachers are reluctant to demand this amount of 'dead-time' from their students. What is needed is supporting but knowledgeable on-line help which can accommodate the different objectives, styles of use and degrees of experience of the learner.

Many teachers now have preliminary experience in CBL techniques and, from this base, materials could be designed to have an innovative influence on the curriculum. A rationale (theory is too strong a word) for instructional methodology is needed to guide this work, and it is suggested this should be knowledge based. In outline, the primary level could be a representation of the topic domain — its concept networks, relational rule-sets, procedures and plans which make up 'expert' knowledge. To make this understandable to the learner (i.e. to interrelate with previous experience) there are teaching/learning materials

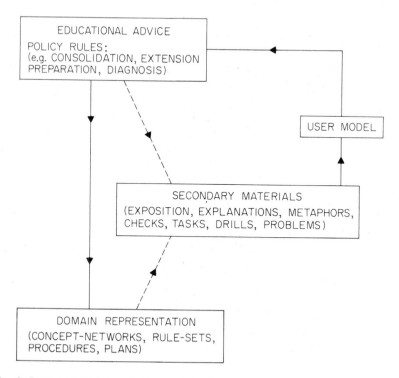

Fig. 1. Data and data-flow in the teaching-learning system.

whose function is to provide these supporting frameworks — various styles of exposition and explanatory schemes, tutorial modules and exercises, experimental and problem solving tasks which relate to the domain knowledge, and which are part of the repertoire of experienced teachers of the domain. Then, given a particular student, selections can be made to suit the knowledge level, learning style and experience. This 'top-level' decision making (which can include some learner control) employs policy rules which relate this user model to the type of materials and the knowledge organisations of the domain. The flow of data is shown in the diagram, while control alternates between the Advisor and the teaching/learning materials selected by the top-level policy rules when a topic area is activated. This system can provide support to the student at the two levels: on learning the knowledge and cognitive skills associated with the domain, and, through the advice provided by the policy rules and their explanation, on learning how to manage the learning process more effectively.

This flexibility is necessary. Some time ago a CAL program on Chemical Thermodynamics was designed at Leeds. Preliminary off-line experiments with students, in which they talked through a series of small problems, showed they followed two broad explanatory schemes. Some made statements about energy in terms of molecular movement, while others used macro-concepts such as work done. For many questions both forms can produce equally valid and effective answers. Thus, the on-line materials had to be capable of making feedback comments and of providing expositions in both these ways. Which should be followed with a particular student (i.e. whether to consolidate or change his/her explanatory scheme) will depend on the question itself, the consistency with which the student uses the type of answer scheme, and the competence of its application. The policy Advisor had to take account of these factors in making its judgments (Butcher 1982).

Systems for supporting problem solving

At Leeds we have been studying the performances of undergraduates in the Biological Sciences with problems which require the application of mathematical methods (such as acidity/pH values, exponential growth and decay). Typically, the problem context yields an equation with two unknowns, one of which can be eliminated by reasoning from the given context (for example, by noting or inferring boundary conditions), and the value of the other variable can then be determined mathematically (for example, by using or evaluating logarithmic functions).

In considering the type of computer-based support systems which might be effective in helping students to improve their performances, it was decided that pre-stored materials might well be useful, particularly as problem solving is usually 'taught' through a sequence of particular examples. In representing the domain, a first step was to devise an organising structure for knowledge by analysing the problem type into a framework of working points. The problem tasks were broken down into AND/OR trees of sub-tasks which determined the size and placing of a working node. Thus problems were made of parts, composed of smaller tasks (stages), built up from smaller steps. The commands (PARTS, STAGES, STEPS, GO ON, GO BACK) allow the student to move freely round the coordinates of this workspace.

The general purpose of the command or query language was not only to accommodate different knowledge levels and preferred learning styles, but to help the student to distinguish the types of knowledge (and their functions) which were being called into play. For example, there is information on the goal/sub-goal connections (WHY-DO that working point goal?) which results in a forward-chaining explanation, (if we find this ... we can find ...) with WHY being asked successively to extend the chain. The student might need help on how to achieve the goal (HOW); this produces a method hint appropriate to the parts/ stages/steps level and further HOW queries can obtain more details. Justifying the method comes from HOW-WHY interchanges, and this knowledge can also be elaborated by consulting FACTS/DEFINITIONS information on concepts and entities. In an attempt to encourage students to hold knowledge in qualitative/quantitative and specific/general forms, the information to answer the HOW/WHY questions was given in both versions.

An important component in problem solving is trying to obtain feedback on progress and errors. In this system student responses at the particular point in the problem are matched using pre-stored criteria and placed in broad categories (CORRECT, SMALL ERROR, PARTLY RIGHT in method, LOGIC/CONCEPTUAL ERROR, MATHS/ METHOD ERROR, CONTEXT ERROR, IRRELEVANT, UNRECOG-NISED). A general hint on the nature of the error is then displayed under this classification, and the user can type WHY-WRONG if he/she needs more specific details.

A further aid is a small file of heuristic hints (e.g. simplifying, making assumptions), with examples which the student can access, but these are not particular to any specific work-point in the problem set.

To organise this material the display screen was divided into windows; these accommodate the problem information, a work space for the task point showing its place in the problem structure, a panel showing the command set (which is cleared and used for the display of

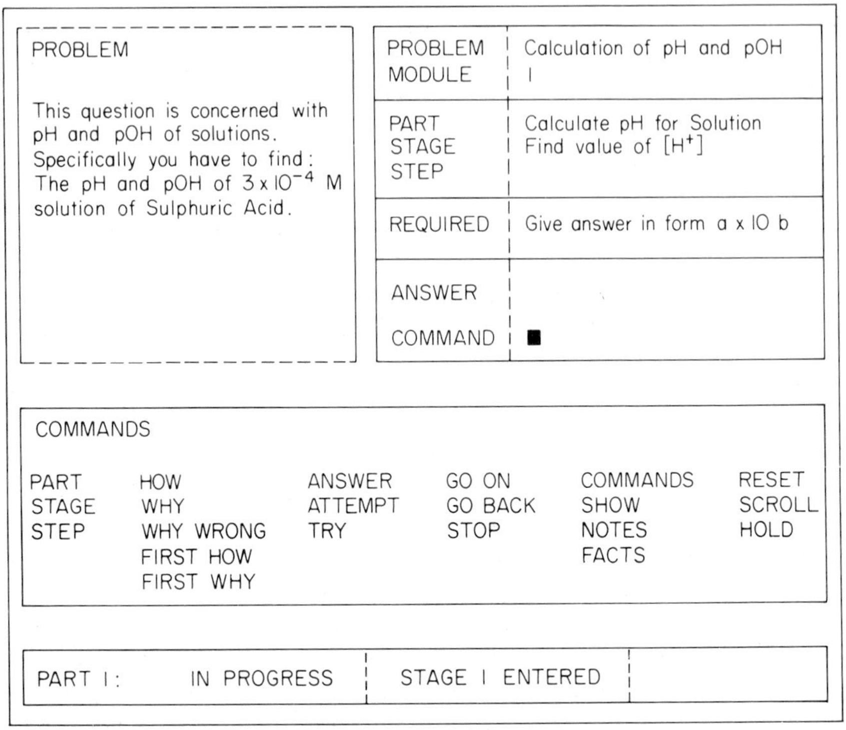

PROBLEM		
	PROBLEM MODULE	Calculation of pH and pOH
This question is concerned with pH and pOH of solutions. Specifically you have to find: The pH and pOH of 3×10^{-4} M solution of Sulphuric Acid.	PART STAGE STEP	Calculate pH for Solution Find value of $[H^+]$
	REQUIRED	Give answer in form $a \times 10\ b$
	ANSWER COMMAND	■

```
COMMANDS

PART        HOW              ANSWER      GO ON      COMMANDS      RESET
STAGE       WHY              ATTEMPT     GO BACK    SHOW          SCROLL
STEP        WHY WRONG        TRY         STOP       NOTES         HOLD
            FIRST HOW                               FACTS
            FIRST WHY
```

```
PART I:      IN PROGRESS  │  STAGE I  ENTERED  │
```

Fig. 2. The division of the display screen into working areas.

help information) and a progress barometer which fills as Parts, Stages and Steps are completed. The arrangement is shown in Figure 2.

To determine if the system and materials were well-liked and effective in improving problem-solving performances, a sample of twenty-five undergraduates worked through a fixed sequence of five problems. Evaluating a learner-controlled system is awkward as students have different and preferred styles of using the programs and so cover different materials with varied degrees of help. As a consequence, post-test comparisons can be misleading. In this experiment, students were asked to work through the same sequence of problems once only though they could use the command set as they chose. All response data at each working point was collected by the system for later analysis.

Overall, there were 1318 responses of which 729 (64%) were first-time answers to the task question of the working point. Additionally, 33% sought help (usually HOW-DO) before answering, and only 2% altered the size of task (the remaining 1% requested the answer). In brief, students regulated the STAGES/STEPS commands so that their working levels of success were approximately 70%. When errors were made students asked for HOW-DO help (32% of responses), altered the task size (32%), consulted WHY-WRONG (15%) or REMIND/REVIEW (15%). Only a small minority of responses referenced FACTS (4%) or WHY-DO justifications (2%), and the heuristic files and were consulted only very infrequently.

The programs themselves were well-liked by the students and are now a part of the working materials of their courses; performances also improved on similar problems with fewer errors, less use of help files, and a moving up of task size from STEPS $->$ STAGES and STAGES $->$ PARTS. However, there were little transfer benefits between similar problems which were set in different contexts or argued to a converse. Students used the system to help them determine particular answers to particular questions, and, in spite of reminders that the structure of work-points and the command vocabulary were to enable them to reflect on the process of solution and the justification for methods, these aspects (e.g. referenced through the WHY-DO and heuristic facilities) were largely ignored (Almazedi, 1985).

Problem solving is a way of learning from experience, since, after working through a task, the performance can be examined, improved and developed. The command vocabulary is useful here; it permits reworking at STAGES and PARTS to develop a larger-step organisation of methods under the goal/sub-goal structure. General heuristic rules can also be replaced by specific, less-redundant procedures appropriate to that class of problem. By asking WHAT-IF questions in which values or features of the task are changed, or WHAT-ABOUT questions comparing method differences between problems, students can become aware of those strategies and procedures which generalise types of tasks.

In order to help the student use the problem solving materials more effectively (i.e. learn how to learn), a top-level knowledge-based Advisor is being designed. The problem exercises are supplemented with other second-level teaching materials deriving from the topic domain representation. These include a bank of diagnostic questions, tutorial/ coaching modules for dealing with basic concepts and mathematical procedures (and misconceptions), and follow-up WHAT-IF questions and comparison WHAT-ABOUT modules between chosen pairs of problems. An Advisor must give supporting suggestions about the curriculum (i.e. the choice/sequence of materials) and for the suggested module the points on which to concentrate, the type of support to seek if in difficulty, and cautionary notes bearing in mind the student's knowledge state. This advice is to enable objectives (which it is inferred the learner requires) to be reached economically. Since the student may not agree with this advice and/or may wish to learn how the suggestions have been worked out, HOW/WHY queries will need to be answered.

For its operation the Advisor has three knowledge bases. First, the concept/procedure network which forms the domain representation, and the name and type of each related secondary material (test items, tutorial modules, specific coaches, problem solving tasks) which supply performance data to the User Model. For the problems, a small database also shows the relations between them (similar/converse/extension/generalisation). A second knowledge base is the User Model showing the topic domains covered by a student, the 'strength' of knowledge on concepts and procedures and, for problem tasks, the performance level (on Part, Stages, Steps), the type of help and categories of error. The third data structure is the Policy Rule system which links the knowledge state of the student (as represented by the User Model) to the secondary materials and to ways of using these materials. The Advisor first determines its educational policy, perhaps to consolidate knowledge, or to extend problem solving performance, or to spend time on preparation by practising mathematical procedures, or to coach out

POLICY		REQUIRED MATERIALS
CONSOLIDATION	1.	Rework same problem (Higher task level, Lower Help)
	2.	Continue with similar problem (Higher task level, Lower Help)
	3.	Work through What-If module (plus problem summary, if necessary)
EXTENSION	1.	Work some problem type with Converse
	2.	Work through problem with Generalisation (not Converse)
	3.	Work through more complex problem (extra components referenced)
DEVELOPMENT		Work through What-About module (plus problem summaries if necessary)
TUTORING	REPAIR	Work through specialised COACHES to clear persistent errors
	PREPARE	Work through appropriate Tutorial modules in given problem solving area
INVESTIGATION		Work through appropriate Diagnostic/Test Items in given problem solving area

Fig. 3. Policy choices of the advisor.

persistent errors, or to collect more diagnostic information about the student's capabilities. Once the policy decision has been made, it points out the type of materials which are needed (Figure 3) and the Advice-Giver then decides on the specific module and prepares comments on the conditions of study and cautionary notes (Almazedi, 1985).

The Advisor is based on teachers' judgements and they have to set out the conditions under which they would decide to follow particular educational policies, and, given those policies, the rules which determine the study materials and the degree/type of support that are appropriate.

On-line help systems

The development of the 16-bit microcomputer as a learning station with software tools running under a concurrent operating system is also proving useful for teaching Applied Statistics where problem solving exercises — and illustrative tutorial materials — making use of a STATLAB (e.g. Minitab) provide the learner with an elementary command language for simulating statistical experiments. Under concurrency the Statlab working can be placed in one window, and supporting material retrieved and placed in other windows alongside.

The problem solving exercises are pre-determined, but the STAT-LAB can be employed in different ways by the student to accomplish the task goals. However, while it is extremely useful to employ software packages such as STATLABS or spreadsheets from Commerce/Industry, the time and effort needed for students to gain experience in their operation and their diverse modes of use might make them unsuitable for large classes within the the limited timespan of an undergraduate course. The symbolic algebra laboratories (e.g. MACSYMA) or some of the CAD/CAM software have similar disadvantages, and there is a need for knowledgeable on-line help systems that can form an interface between the student and the package, take account of the user's own plans and intentions, and so provide appropriate explanation, advice and teaching.

To do this, the Help System must monitor progress and recognise when there is a need to interrupt. Perhaps this is to stop a catastrophic error or give extra comment when it is judged that the feedback supplied by the package is likely to prove inadequate. Further, if the student has made a syntactic or semantic error, remedial instruction is required; also suitable opportunities will arise for introducing related but new knowledge about the facilities of the package. On the other hand, users may wish to put their own questions to the Help System. To respond to these situations with explanations and advice that suit the user's working contexts and levels of knowledge, the Help facility must continuously emulate the state of the base system in reaction to the student's responses, and also update current knowledge held about the student (the user model).

Over the last eighteen months we have been developing and experimenting with such a system for dealing with UNIX-MAIL, though a longer term and more general aim is the design and implementation of software tools for building intelligent on-line Help Systems. [This work is part of a collaborative enterprise funded by the European ESPRIT initiative, and involving ICL (Knowledge Engineering Division), the University of Amsterdam, Courseware Europe, and, in Copenhagen, the Dansk Datamik Corporation and Computer Resources International.] Clearly, the Help System must have knowledge of UNIX-MAIL, stored as domain representation of Objects/entities (e.g. mailbox and message) and command descriptions, (e.g. send, delete) together with a structured taxonomy of Tasks relevant to 'dealing with Mail'. There is also a record of known misconceptions associated with specific commands (e.g. forgetting particular side effects), and a plan grammar which is used in the detection of user-plans. For extending the student's knowledge in a systematic and coherent manner, commands are inter-linked as a structured graph showing increasing specialisation and refinement. The User Model is seen as an overlay of this domain knowledge in which response and performance data is used to estimate a numeric 'strength of understanding' placed against the commands and tasks of the domain. A short introductory quiz also provides information on the user's previous experience of computers and allows comment on the frequency and type of help-interruption the student would prefer. Note that with these types of packages, the curriculum is entirely determined by the tasks of the users who also decide on the balance between objectives of performing mail tasks and of learning about the system facilities.

In order to manage the Help dialogue, interpretations and inferences have to be made from the user's responses with Mail and from knowledge held in the (Mail) domain representation and in the User Model. When the HELP button signals that a question is to be asked by the student, then the EXPLAINER component of the Help System is activated. On the other hand, if the user types a command sequence to the MAIL System, the response is checked, mistakes are classified as syntactic, semantic or mode errors and the TUTOR is then alerted to proffer advice. If the user has typed a valid command instruction, i.e. one which the MAIL System will carry out, the Help System makes several checks. For example, will the systems action lead to a 'catastrophic' result or an awkward side effect? Further, on the basis of command sequences which have been typed, the PLAN RECOGNISER uses the plan grammar to infer those tasks the user might have in mind and to consider if the plans contain redundancies. In this case TUTOR will offer comment. If the student response passes these checks, it is transferred for MAIL action but the Help System also considers whether the resulting feedback supplied by the MAIL System is likely to be sufficiently informative for the particular student. The user model will be consulted here, and this also provides data (through its genetic graph structure) so that the Help System can determine if the occasion is suitable for extending student knowledge. All the resulting interventions are under the control of the TUTOR which is able to construct advice, provide additional feedback, give error coaching and undertake teaching on Mail commands and entities (Breuker and de Greif, 1986).

An important component of Help is the answers and explanations given to questions put by the user. In preparing the design of the Explainer, a sample of students with varying experience were asked to think and talk aloud as they worked through a range of tasks on UNIX-MAIL with the experimenter acting as a reluctant aid when difficulties arose. These subjects engaged in a variety of mental activities such as goal-setting, planning and method specification, interpreting and evaluating system responses, debugging, exploring the Mail facilities, recapping progress and re-orientating and re-organising their plans. From these protocols a set of seven question-types were identified including elaboration (requesting a description of an object or command), enablement (how to carry out a task), justification (why), interpretation (what has ... happened?), exploration (what-if enquiries) and clarification (where am I in the system?). However, the pilot study showed that inexperienced users were not clear in identifying their requirements and the information they needed, and so in order to help them develop these access structures the Help-system Explainer suggests questions which it thinks the student has in mind.

To do this, the probable types of enquiry are chosen by the Explainer from the user's cycle of working. In the plan Formulation phase, the user might well require answers to Enablement (How) and Elaboration (What-is) questions. For Enablement, the Explainer considers which tasks are being undertaken by matching the latest sequence of commands/responses against the task hierarchy. This determines an anchor task which at least spans these responses, and which is likely to require other commands for completion. Within this span completed sub-anchor tasks are identified and the Explainer, omitting the completed sub-tasks, places those remaining and related 'brother' tasks into a selection list. Sub-tasks or commands which the user already knows (indicated by the User Model) are also eliminated from the list since they are unlikely to be asked about, as are sub-tasks which cannot be immediately executed within the working context. The remaining candidates are then sequenced, suitably phrased and displayed in the Help-Menu window; so are components (i.e. entities and commands) which are related to these chosen tasks and which form the What-is (Elaboration) menu (Smith and Hartley, 1986). In case these anticipated questions do not capture the user's intentions, entries to browsers of the complete set of How and What-is questions are also provided and arranged alphabetically, grouped to reflect their task functions and according to the judged experience level for their operation.

When a question has been identified, working out a suitable answer for a particular user in a specific working context is not easy. Clearly, the Help response should be comprehensible, referencing concepts which are familiar to the user or, if not, ensuring they are adequately explained and/or illustrated. Also the answer should be made convincing, perhaps by explaining the way the base system (UNIX-MAIL) will respond to the commands suggested in the Help response. Finally, the answer should be cooperative pointing out misconceptions or difficulties (e.g. particular side effects) which might be encountered, or perhaps noting other variants or facilities which are related to the tasks and which could extend the user's knowledge.

Since asking a question might be the start of a dialogue about the task in hand or the capabilities of the base system, the Explainer prepares an answer database following the requirements noted above. The content is inferred and constructed from the Domain representation (of UNIX-MAIL) and, for Enablement questions, by using a Planner program in collaboration with the Task Taxonomy. The reply to a question is direct in tone with the Explainer using policy rules to take account of user knowledge and experience. To allow the dialogue to develop, continuation menus are chosen, constructed and also displayed with the Help-message. Thus for example, an Enablement answer (which will be a task-command plan to achieve a higher goal) might give the options to ask for more details, for an explanation of what the Mail system will do, for information about commands which have been referenced in the answer, for cautionary notes, for references to extra facilities or for answers to exploratory What-if/How-if questions. The replies to these continuation questions are displayed through a series of overlapping windows from which the user can back-track or exit to the Base (Mail) system.

A pilot demonstrator EUROHELP has now been implemented and is being used in formative evaluation studies.

Conclusions

The argument of this paper has been for Computer-Based Learning to develop systems which support and inform the student's own efforts to learn. This requires a knowledge-based methodology for constructing a representation of the topic domain, an associated user model, together with some provision for on-line help and larger scale advice about managing the learning process. The necessary techniques are becoming available through advances in Artificial Intelligence and Cognitive Science, though the current state of knowledge and the cost of adequate hardware/software systems cause the primary aims to be those of research rather than immediate development. However, such endeavours in CBL should lead to demonstrator projects which can serve as a base for experimentation and for the development of software tools. Hence the requirement is for multi-disciplinary teams involving educational practitioners, cognitive scientists and workers from Artificial Intelligence. Such corporate expertise is unlikely to be available within any one institution, and so the research must be collaborative and concentrated, at least informally, under work plans in which major curriculum organisations (e.g. in engineering, medicine, languages, chemistry) have a prominent input. Indeed, unless the need for such an impetus is recognised, CBL will remain disparate in its efforts and restricted in its educational vision and accomplishments.

References

Almazedi, A. K. (1985) *A study of learned control programs for teaching problem solving.* Unpublished PhD Thesis. University of Leeds.

Breuker, J. and De Greif, P. (1986) *Information processing systems and teaching and coaching in Help systems.* ICAI Research Workshop.

Butcher, P. G. (1982) *A computer based study of the understanding of chemical thermodynamics.* Unpublished MPhil thesis. University of Leeds.

Smith, M. J. and Hartley, J. R. (1986) *Explanation giving in intelligent Help systems.* Internal report: Computer Based Learning Unit. University of Leeds.

Section 2

These three invited papers on Artificial Intellegence have an additional common thread running through them. This concerned getting at what sense a learner made of what they were trying to learn. Each uses interestingly different approaches.

Du Boulay's paper described work aimed at "understanding" novice PROLOG programmers and the difficulties they get into, for a clear pragmatic purpose. Rather than trying to model individual student's competencies the approach is to identify "black spots" in learning PROLOG based on widely occurring misconceptions. This was not as a basis for redesigning the language or arguing for the use of some other language (with a different set of "black spots") but as a potential basis for pinpointing what teaching must tackle.

In Ford's paper a student model is discussed in connection with the intelligent teaching system of which it forms a part. So it is designed to influence tutorial action in a more specific way than the work discussed by Du Boulay. Information gathered by the system about the student's strengths and weaknesses is used along with a representation of what is to be learned to determine aspects of teaching such as the frequency and timing of exposition and remediation. So the conception of student model here has more the flavour of a 'profile'.

Ross's paper pointed out that to talk of user modelling is an oversimplification. In an ITS it is not user beliefs but user/system beliefs which must be captured, a moving target since these are revised through user system dialogues. So the approach he described concentrates on the user model by extricating it from any potential tutorial interaction.

A most salutory reminder may be Ross's observation that the question of what a user model is for is frequently not addressed. I suspect that the utility of the different types of user models discussed by Ross, i.e.

what the user knows/can do (cf. Ford);
what the user misconceives (cf. Du Boulay);
what the user wants to know/do (cf. Ross);

may depend on the sophistication of what is in two of the other components of a conventional ITS — the teaching strategy and the discourse strategies.

Making good use of knowledge of the student in teaching requires the possibility of significantly different teaching actions. Human teachers have a wide range of teaching ploys and tactics, whether or not they are generated from any well-articulated grand strategy. As Ford indicated in discussion this may be an area where much more research is needed.

Ford also held up the ideal of using information from student models to tailor explanations to particular students, and for this the 'discourse strategy' component of an ITS would need to be relatively well-developed. In other words how the system makes use of what it knows about a domain (Ford's expert system component) in conjunction with what it believes a student already believes, what it believes a student wants to know, and why it believes they want to know it (cf. the example in Ross's opening paragraph) to generate an effective explanation.

It should not be forgotten, however, that teaching which was addressed by all these papers at least as an ultimate goal, is not the only application of Artificial Intelligence in education. The use of AI techniques by students as modellers of phenomena they are trying to understand or as 'expert system builders' may be a more fruitful one in the short term for those who were concerned in the discussion with how soon useful applications would be available in their subject areas.

Rachel Rymaszewski

2 / Learning PROLOG: An Introductory Bibliography

BEN DU BOULAY and JOSIE TAYLOR *University of Sussex*

Abstract

PROLOG is being used increasingly in research and development as well as in teaching at both tertiary and secondary levels. All programming languages present difficulties for novice programmers, and PROLOG is no exception. The language and the environments in which it runs are still evolving so studies of user's experiences may have beneficial effects on the direction of its development. At present there seem to be five kinds of "educational" PROLOG-related research study in progress, and it is the purpose of this paper to provide an introductory bibliography for this work. These studies are concerned with:

— teaching issues;
— novice's misconceptions;
— PROLOG environments;
— use of PROLOG in education;
— computer tutors for PROLOG.

   The paper will focus in particular on novices' misconceptions.

Keywords Interface, Man-machine, Declarative languages, Modelling, PROLOG.

Teaching issues

Bundy and his colleagues at Edinburgh (Bundy, 1984; Bundy and Pain, 1985; Pain and Bundy, 1985; Ross, 1982) have concerned themselves with the issue of how the complex symbolic machinery of a PROLOG system should be explained to novices, in particular investigating the merits of different ways of presenting PROLOG search spaces, execution behaviour and answer justification. They have also tabulated a sequence of concepts that need to be tackled in an introductory PROLOG course. The difficulties of introducing PROLOG in school classrooms have been investigated by Cumming (Cumming and Richardson, 1984; Cumming, 1985).

Cognitive Studies Programme, University of Sussex, School of Social Sciences, Falmer, Brighton, BN1 9QN

Novices' misconceptions

At Sussex we are conducting a number of case-studies of novices (Taylor, 1984; Taylor and du Boulay, 1986) with a view to identifying "black spots" that cause difficulties for beginners, such as translating a problem description through the successive representation languages of English, an abstract problem description, an abstract PROLOG description and then an actual PROLOG program. Work with experts is also in progress to attempt to identify exactly what skills PROLOG experts employ in the building and debugging PROLOG programs. Other studies have focused on known areas of difficulty such as backtracking and list-representation (Coombs and Stell, 1985; Ormerod et al., 1984a; Ormerod et al., 1984b) as well as on the kinds of incorrect programming clichés or "mal-rules" (Van Someren, 1984; Van Someren, 1985) that novices are observed to produce.

PROLOG environments

There is much debate about how the user interface to a PROLOG system should behave, concerning such issues as integration with an editor and display of the PROLOG database. This is related to the issue of tracing and debugging tools and their use as explanatory devices. One of the problems of traditional PROLOG tracing tools has been the undiscriminating nature of the information that they present and the difficulty that the user has in identifying crucial episodes in the execution of a program (Ross, 1982; Taylor, 1984; Eisenstadt, 1985).

Use of PROLOG in education

There is increasing interest in the use of PROLOG as a vehicle for teaching such subjects as Logic, History and Science. Here the idea is not primarily to teach PROLOG but to exploit the logical nature of the language to constrain pupils to think with greater precision about, say, an historical incident (Ennals, 1984; Nichol and Dean, 1984).

Computer tutors for PROLOG

Shapiro details an automatic debugging system (Shapiro, 1983) that might be used by an inexperienced PROLOG programmer. The design for a system that could automatically diagnose novice errors is described by Coombs and Alty (1984).

References

Bundy, A. (1984) *Simple PROLOG Prototypes,* work in progress report, University of Edinburgh.

Bundy, A. and Pain, H. (1985) *Evaluating PROLOG Environments,* work in progress report, University of Edinburgh.

Coombs, M. and Alty, J. (1984) *Expert Systems: an Alternative Paradigm,* Int. J. Man-Machine Studies, 20, pp. 21-43.

Coombs, M.J. and Stell, J.G. (1985) *A Model for Debugging PROLOG by Symbolic Execution: The Separation of Specification and Procedure,* Dept of Computer Science, University of Strathclyde, Glasgow.

Cumming, G. and Richardson, J. (1984) *Logic Programming: PROLOG and Education,* in Salvas, A.D. (ed) Computing and Education — 1984 and Beyond (Proceedings of the Sixth Annual Conference of the CEGV) La Trobe University.

Cumming, G. (1985) *Logic Programming and Education: Designing PROLOG to fit children's minds,* Proceedings of the First Pan Pacific Computer Conference.

Eisenstadt, M. (1985) *Tracing and Debugging PROLOG Programs by Retrospective Zooming,* Technical report No.17, Human Cognition Research laboratory, Open University.

Ennals, R. (1984) *Teaching Logic as a Computer Language in Schools. In New Horizons in Educational Computing,* Yazdani M. (ed), Ellis Horwood.

Nichol, J. and Dean, J. (1984) *Pupils, Computers and History Teaching. In New Horizons in Educational Computing,* Yazdani, M (ed), Ellis Horwood.

Ormerod, T.C., Manktelow, K.I., Steward, A.P. and Robson, E.H. (1984a) *Content and Representation with Reasoning Tasks in PROLOG Form,* Occasional Paper, Dept of Mathematics and Computer Studies, Sunderland Polytechnic.

Ormerod, T.C., Manktelow, K.I., Steward, A.P. and Robson, E.H. (1984b) *Reasoning with Hierarchies Written in PROLOG Form,* Occasional paper, Sunderland Polytechnic.

Pain, H. and Bundy, A. (1985) *What Stories should we tell novice PROLOG Programmers?* work in progress report, University of Edinburgh.

Ross, P. (1982) *Teaching PROLOG to Undergraduates* in AISBQ, Autumn 1982.

Shapiro, E.Y. (1983) *Algorithmic Program Debugging,* MIT Press.

Taylor, J. (1984) *Why novices will find learning PROLOG hard,* Procs ECAI, 1984.

Taylor, J. and du Boulay, J.B.H. (1986 forthcoming) *Why novices may find programming in PROLOG hard,* in The Child and the Computer: Issues for Developmental Psychology, J. Rutkowska and C. Crook (eds) Wiley.

Van Someren, M.W. (1984) *Misconceptions of Beginning PROLOG Programmers* Memorandum 30, Dept of Experimental Psychology, University of Amsterdam.

Van Someren, M. (1985) *Beginners' Problems in Learning PROLOG,* Memo 54, Dept of Social Science Informatics and Department of Experimental Psychology, University of Amsterdam.

3 / Anatomy of an ICAI System

LINDSEY FORD *University of Exeter*

Abstract

TUTOR is an experimental intelligent computer-aided instruction system. Its three main components are its instructional strategy, its subject knowledge, and its model of the student receiving instruction. In principle TUTOR can teach a variety of subjects provided they are of the rule-based type e.g. legislation. The architecture of TUTOR is examined and some tentative conclusions about its strengths and weaknesses are drawn.

Keywords Computer-assisted learning, Expert systems.

Introduction

In 1984 Logica began a research and development programme for an Intelligent Computer-Aided Instruction (ICAI) system under contract to the Ministry of Defence. The experimental software resulting from this work has become known as TUTOR (Davies et al., 1985) and although it is an example of only one subclass of systems that could be labelled ICAI, it nevertheless provides a useful case for discussing some of the main components of an ICAI system.

The TUTOR software forms the basis for two important research and development programmes that are unconnected with the original MoD requirement, which suggests that it has some useful general properties. The first of these, entitled 'Knowledge-Based Engineering Training', aims to provide maintenance and programming training for computer Numerical Control milling machines with novel use being made of videodisc and superimposed graphics. The second project uses TUTOR as an adaptive user interface to enable man-machine interaction issues for a space station to be explored. To facilitate the further use of TUTOR, it has been ported to several host environments: VAX 11/750 (VMS, PROLOG-1); ORION (UNIX, CPROLOG); IBM PC/AT (PC-DOS, PROLOG-2); SUN (UNIX, Quintus PROLOG); ICL 2900 (PROLOG X); VAX 11/780 (VMS, POPLOG).

The next section of this paper provides an overview of TUTOR's instructional features. The anatomy of TUTOR — the form and purpose

---

Department of Computer Science, University of Exeter, Exeter EX4 4PT (formerly Logica Cambridge Ltd.)

of its architecture — is discussed in the following section. Some tentative conclusions concerning the appropriateness of TUTOR's anatomy for meeting its original aims are drawn in a final section.

Overview

Three headings (Self, 1974) serve to discuss TUTOR's pedagogy. They relate to TUTOR's knowledge of:
— how to teach;
— what is being taught;
— who is being taught.
Each is discussed below.

The training needs of industry and the MoD are frequently somewhat different from the educational requirements of schools in terms of how something is learned. Whereas a pupil may be required to grasp new concepts and indeed a new body of knowledge for which understanding is a key feature, a trainee will often need to acquire a skill or remember a procedure. Furthermore, unlike education, which tolerates significant differences in students' abilities and learning methods, industry's training programmes assume a high degree of isomorphism in trainees. This it can successfully do since to meet its operational goals cost-effectively, due attention is given to matching staff to tasks. It therefore comes as no surprise that instructional strategies for the two situations are in sharp contrast. Learning by discovery — presently fashionable in schools — is ill-suited to industry for which a formal and regimented training approach is more appropriate. This relies on minimal trainee initiative and provides limited scope for self-organised learning but ample opportunity for practice is usually a necessity. A constraint placed on the teaching strategy for TUTOR was that its repertoire of instructional actions should be expressed in the software independently of the subject to be taught and hence capable of being applied to a variety of subjects. Clearly this is a useful property for any teaching strategy but it severely restricts its patterns of behaviour since only those strategies that are considered to be generic should be included in it. The above factors are reflected in TUTOR's teaching strategy which emphasises orderly presentation of factual material, followed by task-oriented exercises.

The aim for TUTOR is to teach rule-based subjects, examples of which are legislation, emergency procedures, and the Highway Code. Such subjects are often well-defined and lend themselves to being represented as rule-based programs. This is important to TUTOR since it utilises a rule-based representation of the subject expertise in order to impart knowledge of the subject. In this respect TUTOR continues the line of research exemplified in SOPHIE (Brown et al., 1982) and GUIDON (Clancey, 1982). By having a subject's competence knowledge represented in this way TUTOR can, for a given task, 'execute' the set of rules and, on the basis of a comparison of its solution to a student's, provide a critique. It also clarifies the goal of training which is to impart all of the rules to the student.

By imposing a rigid and uniform style of representation on rule-based subjects it becomes clear how a general teaching strategy is practically possible. Since all subjects that TUTOR will teach are com-posed of the same structural material (rules), the teaching strategy can access the structure of a subject without being aware of its content. TUTOR has an explicit syllabus in the form of a tree structure, each node of which represents a topic. This enables TUTOR to introduce new topics appropriately and progress a trainee through the course material in an orderly way.

TUTOR provides individualised tuition by adapting its pattern of behaviour to suit a particular student. This it does only in a rudimentary way and only with respect to what the system believes the student knows of the subject being taught. (It does not attempt to model other, perhaps important, characteristics of a student such as his learning habits.) TUTOR recognises just three states of knowledge a student may have of a rule he is learning: has not been taught a rule (it is assumed he does not know it); has mastered a rule (is aware of it and can use it appropriately); has been taught but not mastered a rule. One of these three states is assigned to each rule and this information constitutes the student model. This type of model falls into the category described as 'overlay' (Goldstein, 1982) i.e. the student model maps onto or overlays the rules being taught. This is in contrast to the mal-rule model (Sleeman, 1982) which recognises that a student may have deviant rule knowledge.

TUTOR architecture

The diagram below shows the main elements of TUTOR's software architecture.

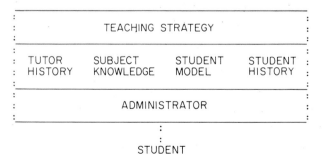

Administrator

Imagine that a student has been presented with a task to perform and has provided a solution. The administrator records the student's response in the student history database (TUTOR may make use of this information later) and then presents the task for the expert system to perform. A comparison of the two solutions — student and expert — enables the student model to be updated appropriately. In the case of a wrong solution, the teaching strategy may decide to invite the student to try again. In this situation the administrator is activated again. It updates the TUTOR history database (to indicate that the student should repeat the same task) and outputs a message to that effect to the student.

In the case of a correct solution, the teaching strategy is again informed but will now have to decide on some other form of action to foster learning, perhaps another but more difficult task.

The decision is communicated to the administrator which performs an update of this information to the TUTOR history database and then outputs a natural language sentence of it to the student. A new dialogue cycle is thus initiated.

At each point in the dialogue with a student, TUTOR enables the student to take the initiative in a number of ways.

He may select any topic from the syllabus and one of four types of training:
— novice
— skilled
— self-test
— examination.

Novice training consists of exposition followed by tasks and, where appropriate, remedial feedback. Skilled training assumes that the student has already received novice training either from TUTOR or some alternate source and provides tasks and remedial information. The self-test mode of training is useful to the student using the system for the first time since it enables him (and TUTOR) to assess the level of training required during subsequent use of the system. TUTOR can set formal examinations, the results of which are made available to a human course administrator.

Other options available to the student include: WHY (or what is the justification or explanation of exposition or task answer); I DON'T KNOW (the answer to a task); ANSWER (the task yourself); CONTEXT (of the present situation i.e repeat the task or exposition); and HELP (indicate the options available to me and explain them).

So the purpose of the administrator is to: validate a student's input; check a student's solution where appropriate and update the student model; update the student history; pass control and relevant information to the teaching strategy. The teaching strategy will then decide what has to be done and send its decision to the administrator. The administrator records the decision in the TUTOR history and then relays it to the student.

Student history, TUTOR history

From what has been stated it can be appreciated that the history files form TUTOR's memory. They allow TUTOR to 'remember' what a student has done and what decisions TUTOR itself has taken. The 'memory' lasts for one interactive session only although key information, such as the type of training and the last task the student was given, is retained for the following session. This enables TUTOR to commence a session from where the previous one terminated.

Each history is a chronological ordering of actions. The student history has recorded in it the responses a student makes to tasks, the type of training that has been requested, what topic has been selected, and so on. TUTOR's history has details of what tasks, exams and tests have been presented, for example. Such information enables the teaching strategy to:

— avoid re-presenting a recently given task
— determine how many responses a student has given for a task
— determine whether the student has responded to a task or decided to take his own initiative.

Subject knowledge

Central to TUTOR is a knowledge base of rules and an interpreter of them. These rules represent the subject expertise that TUTOR attempts to impart to a student. A typical rule from the Highway Code is:

IF the intention is to overtake and you have checked your mirror THEN indicate to overtake

TUTOR uses rules such as this in two ways.

Firstly, it uses them to provide a solution to a task given to a student which it compares with the student's solution in order to verify its correctness and, where appropriate, to provide a critique.

Secondly, TUTOR uses the rules in a consultation mode to provide students with task competence information about the subject domain.

In other words a student may simply ask TUTOR for its solution and a justification of it.

Each rule has an internal and external form. The internal form is executable (expressed as a PROLOG clause) and contains preconditions, prerequisite actions, and an action part. The precondition of the rule above is the intention to overtake. If a student is given a task requiring knowledge of this rule but his solution does not require the rule to fire, then a comparison with his solution rule may indicate a misunderstanding or misconception of the precondition. Similarly, the prerequisite action (you have checked your mirror) may indicate a student's lack of knowledge of an earlier step in the overtaking procedure. Both types of information are used to construct a critique of a student's incorrect response. The external form of the rule consists of two strings of text. One is a description of the rule, the other is a justification of the rule, e.g. you must make your intentions clear to other road users. Each is used for expository purposes.

TUTOR does not generate tasks but instead selects from a library of them. As with rules, each task has an internal form (containing preconditions and prerequisite actions for the task) and an external text form.

An explicit syllabus completes TUTOR's subject knowledge. As mentioned before, this is a tree structure which reflects the decomposition of the subject into topics and sub-topics. The 'leaves' of the tree represent discrete pieces of specific knowledge such as how to overtake on a motorway. The tree is organised such that a depth-first traversal provides a sensible instructional sequence, but since the learner can control this process if he wishes, TUTOR uses prerequisite node labelling to ensure that the student does not attempt a topic for which he lacks any prerequisite skill. Rules in the knowledge base are linked to leaf nodes to enable TUTOR to associate expertise with topics.

Student model

TUTOR maintains, for each student, a model of his knowledge of the subject he is learning. The model is used to influence tutorial action (of which more later) and to provide the course administrator with a profile of the student. Typically a profile will indicate the strengths and weaknesses of a student and his coverage of the syllabus.

At the lowest level the model has recorded in it details of rule learning. We regard a rule as a simple piece of declarative knowledge e.g. a motorway is a dual carriageway, or a step of a procedure e.g. indicate after checking mirror when overtaking, for which three types of learning evidence are recorded in the model:
— the number of times the student has received exposition for the rule,
— an aggregate task score,
— a chronological history of correct and incorrect use of the rule in task performance.

TUTOR uses this information to build up its belief picture of a student's state of knowledge for each rule.

Teaching strategy

The three types of learning evidence in the student model are used by TUTOR's teaching strategy component.

The first of them it uses to control the frequency of exposition, and the last, the timing of exposition and presentation of remedial information. The aggregate task score is a function of the number of tasks performed requiring knowledge of a rule, the task performance (correct or incorrect), and the task difficulty. Each rule has a threshold associated with it which, when compared with the task score, indicates whether the student has met some pre-established criterion. When a student's score hits the threshold no further training will be provided for the rule unless some subsequent task performance causes the score to drop below the threshold.

Now each rule is associated with a particular topic in the syllabus, thus an 'interpretation' of the model allows TUTOR to draw conclusions about a student's mastery of a particular topic. The teaching strategy of TUTOR is therefore able, by reference to the model and the interpretation of it, to determine on which topic a student needs further tuition and, in particular, on which rules of the topic. It then draws on the subject knowledge to provide an appropriate piece of text or task.

The teaching strategy is itself a set of rules — there are about 20 of them. A small number of rules are concerned with managing a student's task responses which involves deciding whether to allow the student more than one attempt at a task for example. But its main function is to draw from its repertoire of actions concerned with exposition and task selection:
— providing (remedial) exposition
— setting another task (perhaps related to the previous one)
— progressing the student to a new sub-topic
— regressing the student to a previously taught sub-topic (where this is appropriate).

The important point to note is that the teaching strategy uses all the information available to it to reach a decision, and that decisions are taken not at the end of some preconceived lesson plan, but on each interaction cycle. Sensitivity to a situation (which includes historical information as well as the current state of the student model) and immediacy of response to it, both characteristics of human tutor-student interaction, are features of this approach.

Conclusions

Comments in this section are restricted to TUTOR's architecture.

The main criticism of TUTOR's administrator component is the severe restriction it places on students' inputs. These are limited in scope. An earlier TUTOR prototype had a creditable natural language interface which allowed a student considerable freedom to: respond to a task in his own words; ask a question about his own defined task; conjecture about a set task (what if?); provide conditional responses to ·a task. Without such freedom, a student may feel the system is too overbearing and react accordingly. The system itself is also handicapped since it must rely on constrained patterns of behaviour on the part of the student but still attempt to construct an accurate student model. A natural language interface, perhaps with speech, is desirable for teaching many subjects and would enhance the administrator.

TUTOR's memory, the two history files, would benefit from restructuring. Presently the list form of its entries does not easily allow the teaching strategy to quickly focus on key entries. Memory searching time increases during a session. Also only minimal inter-session information is saved, allowing a new session to pick up only from where the previous one left off. A restructuring of memory could allow TUTOR to review previous sessions at the start of a new session and facilitate reminding the student of his specific past activities where they relate to his current ones.

TUTOR's subject knowledge is confined to a rule-based view of competence and a rigid syllabus. Each could be augmented by other views of the subject. Rivers (1986) has suggested using a semantic net in TUTOR where nodes could represent individual rules and arcs their relationships. This would help overcome one objection to the rule-based approach that it does not reflect how rules fit together (Clancey, 1984). The syllabus in TUTOR permits only one relationship between two ·related topics — namely, decomposition — yet analysis of human teaching protocols for the Highway Code shows that there are at least two other types of relationship that a teacher distinguishes — generalisation and specialisation. The semantic net scheme may well be the most convenient way to express these relationships.

We have already mentioned one weakness in TUTOR's student modelling capability inherent in the overlay approach, that it cannot model a student's misconceptions of rules. But there are a range of other student variables unconnected with the subject, per se, that could be used to improve TUTOR's overall performance. These include learning style and intellectual factors such as memorising. Many of these variables could be modelled directly by TUTOR from its present knowledge sources.

Given the possibilities already mentioned, a more enlightened view of what is possible for the teaching strategy can be envisaged. For example, a comparison of arcs from nodes in the subject knowledge semantic net may enable some nodes to be regarded as analogous to others. This, combined with TUTOR's better organised memory and richer student model, may allow the strategy to refer the student to a previously learnt and analogous concept. Apart from the learning possibilities of this approach it would relieve the student from the present routine doses of drill and practice given by TUTOR. A feature of human teaching missing from TUTOR is the ability to outline what is planned for a teaching session. The plan may of course change during a session but a student can be made aware of this. TUTOR's rule-based strategy focuses only on recent interactions to determine what single step it should next take. There is no reason in principle why it should not use its historical information and what it knows of the subject and student to provide its plan for several steps ahead. In this case, as with our other conclusions, it is not TUTOR's basic architecture that is lacking but the richness of information within individual components.

Acknowledgements

A number of people have contributed to the TUTOR programme in a variety of ways. The team at Logica Cambridge has included Nigel Davies, Simon Dickens, Rod Rivers, and Helen Tang. From the Ministry of Defence we are indebted to Steve Bevan, Dave Lowry, and Philip Wetherall. Much invaluable advice has been provided by Bran Boguraev, Rod Johnson, Tim O'Shea, and John Self.

References

Brown, J.S., Burton, R.R. and de Kleer, J. (1982) *Pedagogical, natural language and knowledge engineering techniques in SOPHIE I,II, and III.* In Intelligent Tutoring Systems (eds D. Sleeman and J.S. Brown), Academic Press.

Clancey, W.J. (1982) *Tutoring rules for guiding a case method dialogue.* In Intelligent Tutoring Systems (eds D. Sleeman and J.S. Brown), Academic Press.

Clancey, W.J. (1984) *Methodology for building an intelligent tutoring system.* In Methods and Tactics in Cognitive Science (ed. W. Kintsch), Lawrence Erlbaum.

Davies, N.G., Dickens, S.L. and Ford, L. (1985) *TUTOR — A Prototype ICAI System.* In Research and Development in Expert Systems (ed. M. Bramer), Cambridge University Press.

Goldstein, I.P. (1982) *The genetic graph: a representation for the evolution of procedural knowledge.* In Intelligent Tutoring Systems (eds D. Sleeman and J.S. Brown), Academic Press.

Rivers, R. (1986) *Personal communication.*

Self, J.A. (1974) *Student models in computer-aided instruction.* Int J Man-Mach Stud, 6, pp. 261-276.

Sleeman, D.H. (1982) *Assessing aspects of competence in basic algebra.* In Intelligent Tutoring Systems (eds D. Sleeman and J.S. Brown), Academic Press.

4 / User Modelling in Intelligent Teaching and Tutoring

PETER ROSS, JOHN JONES and MARK MILLINGTON
University of Edinburgh

Abstract

User modelling is the general name given to the task of gathering relevant information about an individual user, that can be used to guide the behaviour of an intelligent teaching, tutoring or monitoring system. The paper describes the problems of this task, surveys the existing ideas and outlines an experimental approach based on using a blackboard system.

Keywords User modelling, ICAI, Blackboard systems.

Introduction

Many kinds of intelligent system, not just ICAI software, need to gather information about the user in order to adapt to his needs. For example, in natural language interfaces and in expert systems there is a need to do more than respond correctly and in detail to the user's questions. Consider a hypothetical information system:

> User: How do I get to lecture room 8?
> System: Sorry, the seminar has been postponed till Friday.

The reply depends on assumptions; the system needs reasons for making them. Although the default strategy is to make default assumptions, it may be possible to get specific information about the user by analysing the dialogue as it proceeds. However, the user also draws conclusions from the dialogue, both about the content and the system with which he is conversing. In general it is a very difficult task to formalise users' behaviour patterns and predict what information they will extract from what they are told — see Joshi et al. (1981; 1984) and Allen (1982) for examples of recent research on this.

In intelligent teaching, training and monitoring systems it is particularly important for a system to try to form some model of the user's state of knowledge, and of his skills. In many dialogue systems or expert systems it is possible to ask the user for clarification. A user who

---

Department of Artificial Intelligence, 80 South Bridge, Edinburgh EH1 1HN

is just learning some new idea or skill may not yet be able to explain what he knows, and may not understand some types of question from the system. The purpose of a user model, in the context of intelligent computer-assisted instruction (ICAI), is thus to provide information about the user's knowledge and skills, whether correct or not, so that the system's long-term decisions about planning his learning and the short-term decisions about what to do and say next can be tailored to his advantage. It is beyond the state of the art to tailor these decisions to his best advantage; at present there are not even any established techniques of user modelling, as such. All that exists is a collection of promising prototypes, and it is not clear how far they can be generalised beyond the few domains in which they have been shown to work. Some of these are outlined below.

There is one kind of system where it might be possible to avoid some of the more complicated problems of user modelling, namely a monitoring system. The function of such a system is only to watch what a user is doing, and stop him if he tries to do something that would be wrong for him. For instance, imagine a system that watches over novice users of a computer operating system and tries to deduce what they know and can do. Novices' actions are often catastrophic for them, such as deleting a file that they have just spent an hour editing, even though such an action is legal and could be arguably sensible in certain circumstances. A system that only resisted those errors which arise from inaccurate knowledge or inexperience would still have obvious educational benefits, and would not have to cope with issues of dialogue management. A monitoring system might also be useful to experienced users, if it could recognise the user's intentions without pestering him with questions and lend a hand at appropriate moments. For instance, consider the task of text generation. Spelling checkers often take a while to run, and often need to be told to make use of an additional private dictionary. It might be nice to have an automated assistant that noticed when you had made major changes to a text file, and at least offered to run the spelling checker on it for you. In each such case, the saving for the user is small, but the collective saving of effort might be large. However, such a monitoring system would need to have a way of recognising the user's plans, given only the sequence of his actions so far. This is, even by itself, an interesting research problem.

General points

An ICAI system ought to fit Hartley's framework (Hartley, 1973) for adaptive CAI which says that such a program needs, in some form or another:

— knowledge of the subject to be taught;
— knowledge of the user, and his performance;
— knowledge of suitable teaching skills;
— a theory of how to apply those skills in particular cases.

The task of user modelling is heavily dependent on what subject knowledge is available and in what forms it is represented. The simplest kind of user model is merely a record of facts about the user's input — that he has or has not shown knowledge of certain facts, that his accuracy is of a certain level and so on. Even this is open to abuse, it is all too easy to get into the habit of believing that because a user has not shown some knowledge, he does not have it. In other contexts such an assumption may be tolerable, having no bad consequences; in teaching and tutoring it can lead to trying to teach the student what he already knows, risking alienation.

If trying to design some more sophisticated user modelling system, there are several questions to answer.

1. What is the user model to be for? This is the key design issue. For example, if the model is to be used to predict responses, the prediction being used for making teaching decisions, then Self (1974) argues strongly in favour of procedural types of model. These can be conveniently run, whereas a fact-based model is likely to need a special-purpose theorem prover to make predictions. Experience suggests that such theorem provers are likely to have limited power unless very carefully designed. A procedural approach also seems to be the easiest way to capture knowledge of skills. As Sparck-Jones (1985) points out, there is possibly a moral dimension too. If a user modelling system deduces a certain lack of knowledge, and the ICAI system reports that to a teacher, then the temptation is to believe such a report however it is phrased. When another party, such as a teacher, is involved then the user ought to be told what the system is deducing about him. If the computer is only used for unassessed, unmonitored teaching then this issue is less important.

2. What is the initial model to be? An assumption of total ignorance usually means that the system has much work to do before it can stabilise to a model of any individual. The other extreme is as awkward. Starting from a single prototype of any user can also be too general, although this is probably the most common method. In any case, it will be necessary to do some research about the intended group of users. Aiming at too broad a spectrum is a mistake.

3. What is to be the representation language of the model? In the most naive model, a set of variables suffices. In any complex model, it must be possible to represent all the kinds of faulty knowledge of facts or skills that users might reasonably be expected to have.

4. When are deductions from the model to be made? In particular, is the model to contain predictions about the user's knowledge and likely next actions? If the user of an arithmetic tutor has shown good ability at multiplying small numbers, is it sensible to modify the model to assert that there is some chance of proficiency at general multiplication as soon as that first ability is recognised. On the other hand, is the deduction only to be made when the need for it is seen by the ICAI system?

5. How is 'noise' from the user to be handled? Everyone makes typing mistakes and other silly slips. They need to be distinguished from genuine misconceptions somehow, perhaps by giving the model some kind of inertia to being changed. Also, a user's knowledge rarely expands monotonically — he forgets too.

6. If the model is to capture incorrect as well as incomplete knowledge, how is the blame to be assigned? For instance, if a person cannot spell well, is it because they are dyslexic or because they haven't yet learned much English, or because they cannot type well? The need to distinguish will of course depend on the application.

As a simple experiment for getting to grips with these issues, consider the game known as Indian Poker. Each player gets a playing card, but does not look at it. Instead he holds it to his forehead so that all other players can see it. Players then bid against each other that their own card is the highest; a good bluff often wins. It would be straightforward to create a kind of system to play according to a fixed strategy. There is not much information to handle: the other players' cards, the size of the pot, the financial reserves of all the players, whose turn it is. However, a program to emulate a good player would need to form models of the strategies of the other players and how they varied. Imagine six copies of such a program playing against each other. After the first game the models would differ, because one won. Would the models converge, in time, to the same thing? Why, or why not? Would the answer be the same if one of the copies were replaced by a human?

Some existing ideas

This section outlines some of the existing ideas. A more detailed survey with a recent bibliography can be found in Jones (1984). None of the ideas can claim much psychological validity; at best they are only a step or two removed from behavioural emulation, taking no account of such phenomenological features as boredom or motivation. The ultimate aim is not a performance model, but a competence model that captures only idealised aspects of individuals' knowledge and skills. It is likely that, even were it possible to build up a performance model, it would be too hard to make use of.

The existing prototypes being so diverse, it is hard to categorise them well. Perhaps the simplest division is between user models that take a behaviourist or predictive approach, and those that take an analytic approach. The former consider a number of possible models at any stage, perhaps generated or perhaps explicitly provided, and select the model that best fits the actual user's input. The latter try to analyse the user's input to see which of a range of features it has. The division between these is not very sharp. All the existing models are, to some degree, overlay models. An overlay model is one that supposes the student's knowledge to be a subset of the system's knowledge of the subject. As the student learns, the subset grows, and the modeller's job is to keep track of the subset. Usually a pure overlay model does not try to capture a user's misconceptions, only his lack of knowledge or his degree of confidence in it. Predictive and analytic methods both build on the framework of an overlay model, in attempting to capture misconceptions too.

Overlay models

The best-known examples are probably GUIDON (Clancey, 1979a; 1979b; 1982) and the IMAGE student modeller in GUIDON2 (Clancey and Letsinger, 1981; London and Clancey, 1982). GUIDON tries to teach the medical knowledge in the MYCIN expert system. There are three main parts to the student model, which is initialised by asking the student at the start to indicate his level of expertise. The model is used to guide the application of a set of teaching rules. The three parts are:
— a record of what rules the student knows, qualified by certainty factors to express the degree of belief that each is known. This is gathered directly from answers to questions about particular rules and indirectly from requests for help and from student commentary.
— a record indicating beliefs in the student's ability to apply rules to particular cases.
— a record indicating beliefs in the student's ability to use rules in giving explanations.

As GUIDON is to MYCIN, so GUIDON2 is to NEOMYCIN. The IMAGE modeller within it tries to explain a student's behaviour first by considering the choices that NEOMYCIN itself might make in that situation. If any matches the student's choice, the behaviour is deemed explained. Otherwise a bottom-up search is done to determine what phase of the diagnosis the student is in, and hence which of the rules he might be using. The bottom-up search is tightly controlled by special heuristics; by itself it cannot produce alternative explanations of behaviour. The top-down search can, and so the IMAGE modeller does maintain a set of predictions about what particular diagnostic activity the student has in mind.

Predictive methods

Typically, such models are used when trying to identify particular misconceptions, as opposed to careless errors, in the learning of a single skill such as addition. One method is to represent the skill by some kind of procedure, and then damage the procedure in credible ways to produce models that may emulate the user's input. For example, in the work of Brown and others on BUGGY, DEBUGGY and IDEBUGGY (see for example Brown and Burton, 1978; Burton, 1982; VanLehn, 1982; VanLehn and Friend, 1980) the skills of addition and subtraction are represented in the form of a procedural network. Each node represents a component skill, and has a conceptual part which expresses the intention of that node and an operational part which describes ways of carrying out that intent, including incorrect ways. Links between nodes indicate how each method is implemented in terms of lower-level skills. In the original form of BUGGY, the incorrect methods were built in, and described all the basic simple bugs and a few of the common compound ones. The model was essentially static and was used to generate problems for training teachers to identify bugs. DEBUGGY and IDEBUGGY analysed student answers to set problems to determine which bugs were present, by first finding which incorrect methods could produce at least one of the student's answers and then pruning the set according to various heuristics. In IDEBUGGY the set of hypotheses could be searched by generating problems that would split the set.

Brown and VanLehn later produced a way of generating incorrect methods for a procedural network, called 'repair theory'. Missing methods could be filled by an incorrect method generated by some heuristics that were domain-dependent but not specific to any instance of a problem, and then vetted by others for credibility in the specific case. The theory was able to explain some kinds of phenomena. (See Brown and VanLehn, 1980; 1982; VanLehn, 1980; 1982; VanLehn et al., 1982 for details.)

LMS, the Leeds Modelling System (Sleeman, 1979; 1981; 1982a; 1982b; 1983a; 1983b; 1983c; Sleeman and Smith, 1981), was designed to investigate student learning in the domains of arithmetic and simple algebra. The idea was to have a sequence of generic models representing an ordered sequence of levels of ability. Each model was represented in production rule form. For each rule, in any model, the system had information about which other rules it subsumed and had a set of mal-rules (incorrect forms of the rule) to draw on. Given that a student knew all the rules at one level, say of model M(i), LMS would set problems appropriate for M(i+1). It would try to model the student at that level by adding rules to M(i), either selected from the correct ones needed to extend M(i) to M(i+1) or from the sets of associated mal-rules, in an attempt to find a model that would mimic the student's answers. Various heuristics were needed to control how new rules could be added to those in M(i) to maintain consistency. Some enhancements have been proposed, such as the automatic generation of mal-rules rather than requiring them to be built in at the start or the automatic generation of diagnostic problems by running candidate models backwards.

Yet another predictive method is based on Goldstein's 'genetic graph' (Carr and Goldstein, 1977; Goldstein, 1976; 1978a; 1978b; 1979; Goldstein and Carr, 1977). The graph contains procedural nodes representing rules that the user might have. Links between the nodes represent expressions of how the rules evolve from one another. For example,

— rules are analogous if there is a mapping between the explicit constants in the two rules;
— a rule is a generalisation of another if it involves quantification over some constants. The inverse is specialisation;
— a rule is a refinement of another if it involves extra preconditions. The inverse is simplification.

The genetic graph depends on the notion that student learning progresses by rule modification according to the links. Modelling is done by having a number of 'experts', each associated with an area of the graph. These try to emulate the student's responses using only the rules from that area. Experts that draw on the more complex rules receive less weight when comparing performance at emulating a succession of responses, and this makes the process naturally conservative. Goldstein proposed various extensions to the basic idea of the genetic graph that might help in trying to model a student's confidence in his beliefs. However, this style of modelling is limited by the fact that the graph must be complete, that the graph has to be explicit rather than generated at need and by the assumption about learning stated above.

Analytic methods

Typically, such models are used when there is more than one top-level skill to be modelled, or when the system must be able to model the complete lack of a skill too. One approach, 'differential modelling', is exemplified by Burton and Brown's WEST (Brown et al., 1975; Burton and Brown, 1976; Burton and Brown, 1979). The assumption is that a student's response is determined by his knowledge and by the situation which he is being asked to respond to, and that possible responses can be ordered by merit. A procedural expert generates all the possible responses to the known situation, and those which are better than the student's are analysed in comparison with it to determine which skills and knowledge were not used by the student. This differential suggests his weaknesses. However, the approach depends on being able to describe the set of requisite skills, and is sensitive to the 'assignment of blame' issue described earlier.

Another approach that fits loosely under this heading is that of Genesereth's MACSYMA Advisor (Genesereth, 1977; 1978; 1979; 1982). It tries to debug the user's faulty sequence of MACSYMA commands. For this purpose it employs a plan recognition system that works both from bottom up and top down. From bottom up it tries to recognise plan fragments, which can suggest what ought to precede and follow the fragment. A top down search can try to mesh with this to get confirmation of the overall plan, and the mismatches are where the user's plan went wrong. The system assumes that all the user's misconceptions are about what particular MACSYMA commands do. The MACSYMA Advisor can be said to take an analytic approach because it works on complete command sequences. In a sense, the entire command sequence can be thought of as a single student input.

Rich's program GRUNDY (Rich, 1979a; 1979b; 1979c; 1983) combines the predictive and analytic approaches; user modelling is its main task. It tries to advise a user on the choice of a suitable library book. To this end it has a number of stereotype readers represented by a hierarchy of frames. As in most frame-based systems, there is an agenda of frames activated by finding evidence of a fit between the slot values and the information provided by the user. GRUNDY can blend frames to make up a 'stereotype of the user', and once the user has accepted a recommendation, the system modifies its original stereotypes as necessary to try to keep a reasonable degree of correspondence between the stereotypes and the real users.

A framework for an analytic approach

Consider the problems of user modelling within one fairly general area, namely command-driven systems such as computer operating systems. All the applications for modelling outlined in the first section are represented within this area. Moreover, there are some convenient generalisations about the kinds of knowledge involved.

— There is a defined set of commands, each with its own semantics. The basic concepts of the system provide the vocabulary for trying to express such semantics. Often, the existence of command options makes the semantics interestingly complex and is a source of problems for beginners. In many instances this alone might be a reason for wanting to produce some kind of ICAI system.

— There is often a command language grammar, for composing new commands from the basic set. This too can be a source of trouble.

— The system has a purpose, and it is often possible to characterise, in an informal way, what the users want to do with the system and the ways in which they tend to do it. Since there is always a trade-off between structure and function in the design of a command-driven system, not every aim can be achieved by a single command. Usually there are several ways, each with their advantages and disadvantages. What they are will depend on the individual users knowledge and competence, and so some kind of personal monitoring system might well be useful. In a sense, the useful command sequences are the skills of the domain.

There are various important aspects to the problem of user modelling in this area. Besides that of determining his knowledge of the system, there is the problem of detecting his intention, the problem of detecting how he thinks he will achieve it, and of assessing the adequacy of that in the light of his basic knowledge and the 'common knowledge' about the system. There are also aspects not tackled by any of the existing ideas mentioned in the third section. For instance, it is possible for the user to have several independent goals in mind simultaneously. An example might be that of a computer user who logs on in order to finish some text preparation, tidy his filespace and read his mail. A single command may serve the purposes of more than one of these goals.

Another aspect of the problem is that the basic unit of input is the command. As each new command is given, the system has to make what deductions it can. This means that the user model has to maintain competing hypotheses about various aspects of the user's knowledge and intentions with confidence and support information about each. It also means that plan recognition is difficult.

All this suggests that some kind of blackboard system is needed for building and maintaining a user model in this kind of domain. The model then takes the form of a subset of the hypotheses entered on the blackboard, perhaps with associated procedures driven by this data. A further reason for using a blackboard system is that a user modelling system of any complexity will need to be able to reason about its use of computing resources, if the response time is to be adequate, since processing can be done asynchronously only to a limited extent. The user modeller will need to devote most of its efforts to confirming its picture of the user's basic knowledge to start with. Once that has stabilised (and experience suggests that most users' knowledge at this level does not often change fast), the modeller can build on it to spend more effort on investigating the user's intentions and command habits. Barbara Hayes-Roth's OPM (Hayes-Roth, 1985) has shown that it is feasible for a blackboard system to reason about its own control. The penalty for all this is that such systems are normally very inefficient, but this mainly matters in application systems. It is not a serious drawback at the experimental stage, when the need is for a flexible means of testing ideas.

Using a blackboard for the user model also suggests some convenient if nonspecific answers to the questions asked in the second section. In particular, following the numbering of those questions:

2. It should be possible to procrastinate by having several initial models. The one that stabilises quickest might later be chosen as the one to keep.

3. The support information recording how hypotheses depend on each other and the uncertainty handling provided by all but the simplest such systems ought to provide the basis for an elaborate representation scheme.

4. The availability of support information and the fact that the system permits competing hypotheses ought to make this question unimportant, at least during the development of the modelling system.

5,6. Having competing hypotheses allows the system to use a least commitment strategy in making decisions about the causes of errors. We are currently experimenting with such an approach, using the UNIX operating system as our target. Some of the special features of the task of modelling novice UNIX users are described in Ross et al. (1985). The blackboard system itself is written in PROLOG, and has a simple windowing system for monitoring purposes. Within it we have been designing and building knowledge sources for such tasks as command knowledge and plan recognition and for hypothesising causes of errors such as simple typing mistakes. For example one of the existing knowledge sources can, if a user's command seems wrong, try to see whether any of the commonest kinds of typing mistake could account for the problem.

Although we expect this work to be part of a long-term effort, it looks promising. By starting with the user modelling component, rather than leaving it till last or at least by investigating it before the specific objectives of any ICAI system have been defined in detail, we feel that we will be able to acquire a better understanding of what kinds of ICAI system might be possible in the future.

Acknowledgement

The work is currently supported by SERC grant GR/C/35967

References

Allen, J. (1982) *Recognizing intentions from natural language utterances,* In Computational Models of Discourse, M. Brady (Ed.), MIT Press, Cambridge, Mass. Mass.

Brown, J.S., Burton, R.R., Miller, M., DeKleer, J., Purcell, S., Hausman, C. and Bobrow, R. (1975) *Steps towards a theoretical foundation for complex knowledge-based CAI,* BBN report 3135 (ICAI report 2).

Brown, J.S. and Burton, R.R. (1978) *Diagnostic models for procedural bugs in basic mathematical skills,* Cognitive Science, **2**, pp. 155-192 (also BBN report no. 3669, ICAI report no. 8).

Brown, J.S. and VanLehn, K. (1980) *Repair theory: a generative theory of bugs in procedural skills,* Cognitive Science, **4**, pp. 379-426 (also Xerox report CIS 4(SSI-80-8),1980).

Brown, J.S. and VanLehn, K. (1982) *Towards a generative theory of bugs,* In Addition and Subtraction: a cognitive perspective, Carpenter, T.P., J.M. Moser and T.A. Romberg (Eds.), Erlbaum, N.J., pp. 117-135 (see also Xerox PARC report CIS-2 (SSL-80-6), 1980, and Proc. Wingspread Conference, University of Wisconsin, 1980).

Burton, R.R. (1982) *Diagnosing bugs in simple procedural skills,* In Intelligent Tutoring Systems, Sleeman and Brown (Eds.), Academic Press, pp. 157-183 (also Xerox PARC report CIS-8 (SSL-80-10), 1981).

Burton, R.R. and Brown, J.S. (1976) *A tutoring and student modeling paradigm for gaming environments,* In Computer Science and Education, Coleman, R. & Lorton, P. (Eds.), ACM SIGCSE bulletin **8**, pp. 236-247.

Burton, R.R. and Brown, J.S. (1982) *An investigation of computer coaching for informal learning activities,* In Intelligent Tutoring Systems, Sleeman & Brown (Eds), Academic Press, pp. 78-98 (also IJMMS **11** (1979), pp. 5-14).

Carr, B. and Goldstein, I.P. (1977) *Overlays: a theory of modeling for computer aided instruction,* MIT AI memo 406.

Clancey, W.J. (1979a) *Transfer of rule-based expertise through a tutorial dialogue,* Ph.D. Thesis, Dept. of Computer Science, Stanford University (also report STAN-CS-769).

Clancey, W.J. (1979b) *Dialogue management for rule-based tutorials,* IJCAI **79**, pp. 155-161.

Clancey, W.J. (1982) *Tutoring rules for guiding a case method dialogue,* In Intelligent Tutoring Systems, Sleeman & Brown (Eds.), Academic Press, pp. 201-225 (also IJMMS **11** (1979), pp. 25-49).

Clancey, W.J. and Letsinger, R. (1981) *Neomycin: reconfiguring a rule-based expert system for application to teaching,* IJCAI **81,** pp. 829-836 (also report STAN-CS-82-908, Stanford University).

Genesereth, M.R. (1977) *An automated consultant for MACSYMA,* IJCAI **77,** p. 789.

Genesereth, M.R. (1978) *Automated consultation for complex computer systems,* Ph.D. Thesis, Harvard University.

Genesereth, M.R. (1979) *The role of plans in automated consultation,* IJCAI **79,** pp. 311-319.

Genesereth, M.R. (1982) *The role of plans in intelligent teaching systems,* In Intelligent Tutoring Systems, Sleeman & Brown (Eds.), Academic Press, pp. 137-155 (also Report no. STAN — CS-81-842, HPP-80-4, Stanford University, 1980).

Goldstein, I.P. (1976) *The computer as coach: an athletic paradigm for intellectual education,* MIT memo 389.

Goldstein, I.P. (1978a) *The genetic graph, a representation for the evolution of procedural knowledge,* Proc. Canadian Soc. for Computational studies of intelligence, 2nd annual conf.

Goldstein, I.P. (1978b) *Developing a computational representation for problem solving skills,* MIT AI memo 495.

Goldstein, I.P. (1982) *The genetic graph: a representation for the evolution of procedural knowledge,* In Intelligent Tutoring Systems, Sleeman & Brown (Eds.), Academic Press, pp. 51-77 (also IJMMS **11** (1979), pp. 51-77).

Goldstein, I.P and Carr, B. (1977) *The computer as coach: an athletic paradigm for intellectual education,* Proc. Annual Conf. ACM, pp. 227-233.

Hartley, J.R. (1973) *The design and evaluation of an adaptive teaching system,* IJMMS, 5, pp. 421-436.

Hayes-Roth, B. (1985) *A blackboard architecture for control,* Journal of AI, 26, pp. 251-321.

Jones, J. (1984) *A review of some user modelling techniques,* Edinburgh University Dept. of AI Working Paper 177.

Joshi, A., Webber, B. and Sag, I. (1981) *Elements of discourse understanding,* Cambridge University Press.

Joshi, A., Webber, B. and Weischedel, R.M. (1984) *Living up to expectations: computing expert responses,* AAAI-84, pp. 169-175.

London, B. and Clancey, W.J. (1982) *Plan recognition strategies in student modeling: prediction and description,* AAAI 82, pp. 335-338.

Rich, E. (1979a) *Building and exploiting user models,* Ph.D. Thesis, CMU-CS-79-119, Carnegie-Mellon Univ.

Rich, E. (1979b) *Building and exploiting user models,* IJCAI **79,** pp. 720-722.

Rich, E. (1979c) *User modeling via stereotypes,* Cognitive Science, **3,** pp. 329-354.

Rich, E. (1983) *Users are individuals: individualising user models,* IJMMS **18,** pp. 199-214.

Ross, P.M., Jones, J. and Millington, M. *User modelling in command-driven systems,* to appear in K. Gill (Ed.), AI For Society, John Wiley (see also Edinburgh University Dept. of AI Research Report 264, 1985).

Self, J.A. (1974) *Student models in computer-aided instruction,* IJMMS **6,** pp. 261-276.

Sleeman, D.H. (1979) *Some current topics in intelligent teaching systems,* AISB quarterly **33,** pp. 22-27.

Sleeman, D.H. (1981) *A rule-based task generation system,* IJCAI **81,** pp. 882-887.

Sleeman, D.H. (1982a) *Assessing aspects of competence in basic algebra,* In Intelligent Tutoring Systems, Sleeman & Brown (Eds.), Academic Press, pp. 185-199.

Sleeman, D.H. (1982b) *Inferring student models for intelligent computer-aided instruction,* In Machine Learning, Michalski, R.S., J.G. Carbonnel and T.M. Mitchell (Eds.), Tiago Press, Palo Alto, pp. 483-509.

Sleeman, D.H. (1983a) *Inferring (mal) rules from pupil's protocols,* Proc. Machine learning workshop (ML 83), pp. 221-227, Illinois.

Sleeman, D.H. (1983b) *Basic algebra revisited: a study with 14 year olds,* Stanford HPP, report HPP-83-9.

Sleeman, D.H. (1983c) *An attempt to understand pupils' understanding of basic algebra,* Stanford HPP, report HPP-83-11.

Sleeman, D.H. and Smith, M.J. (1981) *Modelling student's problem solving,* A.I. **16,** pp. 171-188.

Sparck-Jones, K. (1985) *Issues in user modelling for expert systems,* In Proceedings of AISB **85,** pp. 177-186.

VanLehn, K. (1980) *On the representation of procedures in repair theory,* University of Pittsburgh, Learning Research and Development Lab., Technical report.

VanLehn, K. (1982) *Bugs are not enough: empirical studies of bugs, impasses and repairs in procedural skills,* Xerox PARC report, CIS-11 (SSL-81-2), 1981 (see also Jnl. of Mathematical Behaviour, **3,** 3-72).

VanLehn, K., Brown, J.S. and Greeno, J. (1982) *Competitive argumentation in computational theories of cognition,* Xerox PARC report, CIS-14 (to appear in Methods and Tactics in Cognitive Science, Kinsch, W., J. Miller and P. Polson (Eds.), Erlbaum, N.Y.).

VanLehn, K. and Friend, J. (1980) *Results from Debuggy: an analysis of systematic subtraction errors,* Xerox PARC technical report.

Section 3: Invited Papers on Interactive Video

5 / Interactive Video: Research into its Potential for Management Education

DON BINSTED *University of Lancaster*

Abstract

This paper describes a research strategy for investigating the potential of interactive video systems for developing managers and supervisors. Two prongs of this strategy are field studies and laboratory studies. This paper deals with the latter and outlines what the work currently being carried out at the Centre for the Study of Management Learning, sets out to accomplish. This includes how the research was set up and some of the factors which are peculiar to management education and training.

Keywords Interactive Video, Management Education.

Introduction

The Centre for the Study of Management Learning is a research and postgraduate teaching department of the University of Lancaster. As its name implies, our field of study is management education and development, the primary underlying process being *learning*. Our stance from the start (we were originally funded by the Foundation for Management Education in 1974) has been that a fundamental understanding of learning processes would enable understanding of how to facilitate learning. In this field 'facilitation' includes teaching, training, developing, etc. Our students, colleagues and clients have these roles in educational and a wide variety of other organisations.

Over the years we have carried out both research and teaching activities which have focused on face-to-face facilitation. This has ranged from traditional lecture room activities to the formation of learning sets (Casey and Position, 1977) and learning communities. Latterly we have built on this work to do research into both open and distance learning. It is this new thrust which, among other things, has led us into computer based learning and interactive video.

Our first piece of research resulted in preparing a position paper for the Manpower Services Commission (Binsted and Hodgson, 1984) which reported on the then current position regarding the application of

Centre for the Study of Management Learning, University of Lancaster, LA1 4YX

open and distance learning in management and supervisory education and development. Some of the conclusions we arrived at, relevant to the use of computer based technology were:
— there was then very little courseware available (suitable for management);
— there was very little evidence of research, although there were some groups who were producing limited but interesting examples of computer based packages suitable for management;
— interactive video offered new and, to a great extent, unexplored potential.

This led us to draw up a modest research programme to investigate the application of open and distance learning in the management field, including both high and low tech applications. It should be appreciated that in open and distance learning the learner is generally solo with the tutor absent.

Research projects

Two types of project are being undertaken:
— field studies;
— laboratory studies.

Field studies

These focus on the experience of the learner in interacting with educational packages. Laboratory studies involve designing and testing packages which include specific innovations introduced for research purposes. In this paper I shall confine myself to the laboratory studies which involve interactive video (IV) systems.

Laboratory studies

The overall aims of these studies are as follows.
— Explore the technology and evaluate its usefulness for generating the sort of IV packages suitable for management. One particular issue is whether or not the authoring system or language is usable by people with little or no programming experience or computer literacy.
— Define the boundaries of what sorts of learning can be facilitated with interactive video packages.
— Test out specific designs to see if they can be accommodated within an IV system; in some instances to see if designs developed for face-to-face facilitation can be translated into IV format.

All the foregoing are in the context of use within employing organisations. This certainly implies delivery of courseware within the
organisation and generally implies at least a desire to produce within
the organisation as well.

The clients

Since we set up a distance learning facility within CSML we have had a
constant stream of visitors to look over what we have collected and get
some hands-on experience of using IV and CBL packages. This has
revealed a very high degree of interest and in many cases an urgent
need to improve understanding. Most of our visitors are senior management development people who are responding to a combination of
pressures to do *something*. Some of these pressures stem from a feeling
that IV has something to offer, may solve training problems, save
money and anyway should be experimented with. At this point they
generally meet a bewildering set of problems. What courseware to buy
(if they can find it, and get some evaluation of it), whether to consider
producing themselves, which IV hardware to buy and which authoring
language or system will match.

It seemed sensible to support this research by gathering together a
group of organisations who would act as co-sponsors for the project, by
each contributing £5000 per annum for two years. This proved to be a
very time consuming and difficult task and took approximately one year
to organise. The difficulty stemmed from getting a number of large
organisations to the starting gate at one time. Such an arrangement has
many significant advantages, one of which is that they feed in research
topics which are of the most significance to them. Such a group can also
make available 'real' learners (managers or supervisors) for the testing
stage.

What is special about management?

Learning is often required in areas unique to management, and needs
to be set in an organisational context. Examples are problem solving
and decision making abilities, a wide range of interpersonal skills,
attitudinal learning, planning etc. Such learning may involve three
types of learning in various combinations. The three types of learning
can be described as:

> COGNITIVE
>
> SKILL
>
> AFFECTIVE

Some types of management learning require combinations of these as shown in Figure 1.

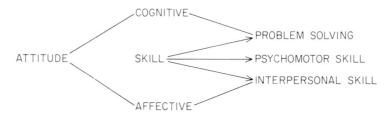

Fig. 1. Combinations of types of learning.

Earlier research in a face-to-face situation has indicated that different facilitation is required for different types of learning (Binsted and Snell, 1981-82). The question is whether designs for IV packages can achieve such learning, particularly of the deeper cognitive, skill or affective sort. Answers to these questions will greatly influence the application in the management field.

The research

In our research we set out to test a number of principles, to build in things we had not seen before and avoid other things we had seen. Examples are as follows.

— Avoiding designs based on conditioning theories of learning. This implies non-judgmental responses to the learner, and allowing them to make their own judgments against various criteria.

— Getting the more difficult processes to occur in the learner's head.

— Giving the learner maximum choice about how to respond and proceed.

— Using the video sequences to communicate in the sorts of ways a manager must be able to operate with, e.g. problems often manifest themselves from conversation and do not arrive as carefully written case studies

— Building in whole cycles of learning, including receiving input, discovery and reflection, though not necessarily in that order.

— Generating feedback from characters in video sequences.

— Using camera input into programmes so that two or more learners can look at their own behaviour for interpersonal skill development. This can be integrated into the programme together with pre-recorded models.

For the purpose of our research we decided to use tape-based systems only, since these could easily be made and modified.

Problems

Our plans to do this posed several practical problems.

— To find an authoring language or system which was flexible enough to allow us to implement the innovations in design which would form the basis of our experimentation. When evaluating systems, a key issue was not only would they do the things which we wanted them to do, but whether or not we could stop them doing what we did not want them to do.

  For example, systems based on instructional techniques which involved pre-test, instruction, and post-test and involving a scoring system which fed back scores to learners, posed particular problems. Although such a facility could obviously be of use in certain types of learning design, in one instance we could find no way of defeating it. Since avoidance of designs based on conditioning theories was one of our research goals such a system was of no use to us.

— To find an interface for integrating into a tape-based interactive video system which was compatible with the cheaper micros, in our case the BBC B+, Apple IIe and Ferranti 86b (which is IBM PC compatible). Additionally, the vital issue was that the interface had to be compatible with the authoring language or system.

— To select a combination of authoring language/system and interface which would allow easy and flexible logging of video sequences which did not require pre-editing of the video tape.

Some solutions

We found considerable difficulty in solving all three elements of this problem, although it was not too difficult to find solutions to two elements at a time. The two systems which we are currently working with are as follows.

— 'Take Five'; which is a very easy to learn and use authoring system with interface, based on a BBC B+ and Betamax domestic VCR (this also makes it comparatively cheap).

— A system based on a Ferranti 86b (which is IBM PC compatible) using the BCD VIPc interface and using the version of 'Pilot' suitable for the IBM PC as the authoring language.

  It should be noted that people wishing to make instructional type programmes will find other combinations possible. The two systems we are using could of course be used in this way if required, but these two systems met the particular requirements of our research goals.

Evaluation

The research methodology requires that we make experimental packages containing innovation and principles which we want to test. These are then evaluated by inviting the client organisations to provide learners who are managers or supervisors (or potentially so) to use the packages, after which they are asked to provide data via questionnaires and interviews. This step is vital since evaluation by trainers and educators could provide misleading results.

The client view

There is little doubt that there is a certain seduction about interactive video technology and as a facilitation for learning it is undoubtedly both novel and involving at the least. To these can be added elements which can legitimately be described as fascinating, entertaining and fun. The realisation of this becomes apparent in my experience when trainers sit down and run through a programme for themselves, rather than read about IV.

Having become aware of the potential of IV systems the trainer within a organisation is faced with a number of decisions, about which it is difficult to get reliable guidance. For example, whether to buy-in generic courseware or contemplate making their own IV packages. The buy-in option has two constraints. First there is currently very little available in the management field with notable exception of the 18 packages from Felix (now available from Wirey Systems) and the 'Expert' packages (available from Personnel Development Projects Ltd). Such a decision also implies the need to acquire the hardware and interface necessary for delivery, which at the time of writing is unique to the courseware.

The decision to make one's own courseware is even more problematical. This involves choosing the appropriate authoring system or language and compatible interface which may or may not be compatible with the existing hardware (micro or VCR) that the trainer may have. Having got a workable system the questions of design and production have to be solved, which require considerable resources, both human and money.

The current scenario

Overall my perception of interactive video for the facilitating of learning in the management field is that developments are at a very early stage, and are not backed by adequate research, nor is there significant operating experience or evaluation. There are a few exceptions but by and large this is the situation. However, there is considerable interest and curiosity and in many organisations a need to get something going. The potential of IV is recognised. In the management field the interaction provided by the computer and the video element can provide vital components of the educational design. Some examples are:

— presenting a rich context to some area of learning, with which the learner can identify;
— using dramatised case studies which can have much more impact than written ones;
— simulating management communication and data gathering (managers often acquire information about problems from phone calls, interviews etc which can be presented in short video sequences);
— presenting visual information which would be inadequately conveyed by graphics.

The video component is particularly vital in areas such as problem solving, interpersonal skill development and attitude change, which are key areas in management development.

A future scenario

The potential for using IV systems for management education and training is recognised. The problem at the moment for those working as trainers and educators in organisations is how to become operational. Some of the factors which will convert the potential into reality are in my view:-

— the availability of high quality generic courseware;
— a choice of easy-to-use authoring systems which do not restrict packages to conditioning based designs;
— interfaces which will link the most frequently found micros and VCRs and preferably will link more than one combination of hardware;
— low cost systems when taken as a whole, i.e. courseware, authoring system, interface and new hardware not already held in the organisation.

Personally, I am optimistic and enthusiastic about the future. The potential is there but the conversion of that into reality will in the end depend on the reaction of the learners. In turn that will depend on three factors.

— The quality of the courseware. This will include not only content but the effectiveness of the design of the learning process.
— The reliability of the total hard and software system.
— The support structure which creates the learning environment (Hodgson, 1986).

That is why I believe that research which focuses on learner experience is so important, and why both field studies and laboratory studies are two prongs of research strategy for developing effective IV for us in the field of management training and development.

The bad scenario is that learners find the packages available to them unsatisfactory. The whole approach may then be written off as a 9 day wonder and be added to the heap of management bandwagons whose wheels have come off.

There is, I believe, some urgency to establish high quality IV as a workable and effective contribution to management development.

References

Casey, D. and Position, D. (eds) (1977) *More than management development.* Gower Press.

Binsted, D. and Hodgson, V. (1984) *Open and Distance Learning in Management Education and Training A Position Paper.* Manpower Services Commission.

Binsted, D. and Snell, R. (1981-82) *The Tutor Learner: Interaction in Management Development* Parts 1-5 Personnel Review **10**, 3, 1981 and **11**, 4, 1982.

Hodgson, V. (1986) *The interrelationship between support and learning materials.* Journal of Programmed Learning and Educational Technology **23**, 1.

6 / What's In It for Us?

Co-operation between Industry and Higher Education

TONY GRAY *Director, Loughborough University of Technology*

Abstract

We are an inventive nation. However, to benefit from this natural inventiveness, there is a need for academics and industrialists to collaborate not only in invention, but also in spotting potential, developing ideas and producing products. However, this is not always straight-forward. Drawing upon the experience of Loughborough Micro Project (one group working with industry in the field of IT), some advantages and disadvantages of working together are described.

Keywords Computer-Assisted Learning, Interactive Video, Information Technology.

Introduction

The Japanese equivalent of the Department of Trade and Industry, MITI, has published a report which concludes that of products currently making large sums of money in world markets, 55% of them result from British innovations. This compares with figures of the order of 3% for other European countries and about 11% for the US. Profit from these products is being made, needless to say, by non-British companies. Regardless of what you believe should be done with commercial profits once they have been made, ordinary citizens cannot benefit if the profits from our ideas are largely going abroad.

Of specific concern to this conference is the fact that these profits are not available to be ploughed back into British research. Grants for pure and applied academic research are going to foreign universities. Industrial research and development is slowly being starved of funds, making it less likely that work will be commissioned in institutions of higher education. This in turn slows down the process of understanding IT and its applications in Computer-Aided Learning (CAL).

It is irrelevant whether work is 'pure' research, development, applications or devising ways of improving production; we all depend on

---

Loughborough Micro Project, University of Technology, Loughborough, Leicestershire, LE11 3TU

this process as the only means of creating resources to continue. The (much-simplified) cycle shown below (Figure 1) is failing if our research is not turned into re-investment after successful selling at home and abroad.

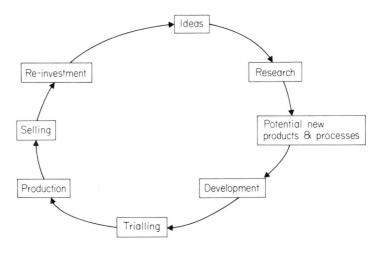

Fig. 1. Turning ideas into money for more ideas.

Of course, it is tempting and popular to blame our failure on a British lack of selling skills. But it is not so simple. At a recent conference on long-term unemployment, the Managing Director of a successful British company pointed to the situation in the car industry:

'The Japanese are not brilliant at selling. They don't even advertise much. Look at the new Austin Rover campaign — ''Now we're motoring''. The Japanese don't do all that macho stuff. Instead they research the market, design a good product and build it cheaply by using efficient production methods. Then they say ''This is it. Take it or leave it. It's got everything you want and it'll cost you two grand less than anyone else's.'' And they still have a flourishing dealer network, despite the self-imposed quota systems which operate against them.'

Now this was not an entirely serious comment. However, you can see the point: if, as a nation, we are to benefit from our natural inventiveness, there is a need for us to be as skilled at spotting potential, developing ideas and producing products as we are at innovation. If academics, researchers and industrialists recognised their mutual inter-dependence and worked together on these aspects of the creative process, funds would be available to help everyone.

With the IT industry in particular, we have a major opportunity because many 'traditional' areas of knowledge wait to be applied in this new area of study.

For example: reading research might tell us about optimising screen layout; applying existing knowledge of learning theory could help us decide the most effective modes of learning in CAL environments. What is the most effective way of monitoring a CBT student's progress? Perhaps those who already know about assessment of performance and progress could help. What is the best way of employing synthetic speech in CAL? Work needs to be done in this area because high quality speech synthesis is with us now and quality speech recognition is just around the corner. Phoneticists, Psychologists, Educationalists and Graphic Designers might all have something to offer by way of addressing these issues.

There is no shortage of work for "non-technical" academic disciplines. The speed of developments in hardware has fast outstripped the speed of others to find and fully explore applications. Much of the CAL material produced in early years was based on little more than a hunch or two. More recently work has been embarked upon to look carefully at the impact and effectiveness of CAL, but even as this work progresses, new hardware developments are arriving. Faster processors with cheap storage for huge amounts of data on interactive read/write video discs, new input devices, speech recognition and synthesis, access to national networks and email, sophisticated imaging systems, artificial intelligence, authoring systems ... the list is endless. Discovering how to apply all this in such a way that the learner is not swamped by a torrent of audio-visual information presents a major challenge to educationalists and institutions.

Loughborough Micro Project (LMP) is one group working in this area. The rest of this paper will describe the project and its work with industry, illustrating some of the features of this type of research and the need for collaboration particularly in the field of CAL.

Loughborough Micro Project

The simplest way to introduce the project is to look at our press/ industry handout:

> "LMP is a research group of the University of Technology, Loughborough, and is housed in the Education Department. There are five permanent staff, other assistance being engaged as the need arises.
>
> The Project's aim is to understand how information technology can be used to enhance learning and teaching.

This involves the team in:

— creating new software and hardware;
— designing, producing and evaluating materials for computer-aided learning (CAL) and computer-based training (CBT);
— managing research and development projects for government and industry;
— contract research and consultancy work for organisations involved in CAL and CBT;
— disseminating findings by publications, lectures and courses.
    At present LMP is working in four main areas:
— the development of educational software packages (for Longman, Europe's largest publisher of educational software);
— the application of talking computers in education (for the UK Council for Educational Technology);
— the application of interactive video in education and training; and
— the Project has been engaged by the National Coal Board and the Manpower Services Commission as consultants to guide and implement the introduction of CBT into the mining industry's £70M a year training operation.

Loughborough is a Technological University used to the pressures of commercial, industrial and government sponsors. Loughborough Micro Project realises that resources are too precious to put into projects which have only marginal outcomes. A two-year research project which yields only a vague report is not our style. We are interested in work which has positive and obvious application; work which will not only help us in our research, but also lead to genuine benefits for our sponsors.

If you are interested in our work, have a project you wish to discuss, or would simply like to find out more about LMP, please call; we would be happy to meet you."

Using a process which often begins with such a handout, LMP has attracted £350,000 in industrial sponsorship during the last four years. The project staff are not in Established Posts.

Working with industry

A cynic might say that the main goal of most research projects is to ensure continued funding. A realist will acknowledge that this is certainly one goal. If a team feels that their work is valuable (beyond avoiding their being added to the unemployment statistics) they must attract further funding. In contract research particularly, the work stops if the money stops coming in. In this respect running a group engaged in contract research is like running a small business: industry too depends upon continued cash flow.

An obvious point worth making is that industry and academic institutions have similar fundamental interests. Worth making because it has been our experience that many industrialists do not regard academics with much respect and that there are stereotypes used by academics in retaliation.

For example, there is the industrialist's stereotype image of the academic ivory tower occupied by those who think that over-running agreed deadlines has no real effect; those who are unconcerned with tangible outcomes and those who are careless with other people's money. I was once told that "burning tenners in your office" was better than funding university research because at least this had an impact on the company's bill for heat, light and power.

On the other side, there are some academics who seem to believe that working with industry is close to prostitution. They have the notion that taking industrial money by way of the Exchequer and Research Council is somehow cleaner than getting cash directly. Equally, there are those who think that anything other than 'pure' research is somehow demeaning. They forget the cycle presented at the start of this paper: 'pure' research depends upon those who are prepared to get their hands dirty in the hurly-burly of development and production. The British attitude towards engineers is another manifestation of this perception.

Plainly, such attitudes must change if essential collaboration between industry and higher education is to succeed. So, what are the benefits of working together? To explore this, we shall look at some of our work.

Examples of working with industry

In the field of CAL, which for us includes educational applications in the context of both initial schooling and industrial training, one is dealing with companies which survive either by selling products or by improving productivity as a result of CAL. The benefits for the company therefore need to be tangible.

An example of the first type of company is the publishing group Longman, with whom LMP have been working since 1982. In this case we are in a position to describe actual outcomes and benefits to the company.

As a result of working with LMP, Longman have been able to develop a list of educational software for schools which is rooted in the best of current practice. This was done cheaper than could have been done by a software house or in-house, even assuming Longman had the staff, the time and the technical knowledge. Further, LMP has a large network of close contacts capable of helping with evaluation and software design. The fact that there are Pre-service students and In-service Training courses for teachers taking place in the department is also valuable to Longman. LMP have helped Longman with their staff training; given advice on production and marketing based on information from field trials; and helped the company maintain contacts with national bodies such as the Micro-electronics Education Programme (RIP).

The above paragraph gives a flavour of the benefit accruing to Longman. For the project, there were different advantages:

Longman is a large company with many contacts and we have been able to meet authors who would not otherwise have been so accessible. In addition, Longman have been very open and prepared to share their experience. We delivered material on time and they responded by helping us learn more about the process of producing software, information which was helpful when submitting proposals for other contracts.

This exchange of ideas and suggestions resulted in a discipline which was good for the project. On the whole we worked on the material we wanted. However, from time to time our sponsors made suggestions which forced us to think about different perceptions and ideas, ideas which have resulted in both new material and material better than it would have been otherwise.

Finally, Longman have kept us in touch with those who purchase our software and we have been able to glean much from these people. One example of this is our video, which was paid for by Longman, produced by the University AVS unit and is available (free of charge) for viewing and use on courses from Longman at Harlow.

Therefore, in this example of academic collaboration with industry, there were tangible benefits to the company and ourselves. Collaborative work is not simply about squeezing cash out of industry to do what you fancy.

The second type of company is exemplified by the National Coal Board, for whom CAL is perhaps a means to increased productivity.

In this case, the Board has recently engaged LMP to help introduce CBT. The pilot project began in September 1985, so at the time of writing (November 1985) it is not yet possible to describe actual outcomes. However, looking at this project will illustrate some other aspects of working with an industrial partner.

The desired outcome of the work is an improvement in productivity. The Board is moving from time-based to standards-based training and part of this move will be to monitor progress using microcomputer technology, an interesting problem in itself. Further to this however, the Board wishes to create a large amount of CAL material. Some of this will use interactive video; fast, high-resolution, real-time graphics overlaid on these video images; a variety of non-keyboard input devices; complex simulations of underground situations; access to NCB CAD files; and other forward-looking CBT/CAL technologies. In addition, the whole area of managing this change will need to be looked at, as will the in-service training of existing teaching staff.

Initially, this work will involve LMP in selecting hardware and system software. Following this, the team will be adapting or creating an authoring system for the NCB which must be capable of being used both by those new to computing and also by more experienced users. The system must control a range of peripherals, powerful graphic facilities and be capable of 'talking' to the NCB mainframe and Colliery Training Record systems.

This sketch of the project illustrates the very wide range of work being undertaken and hopefully demonstrates why the partners need one another: the Board requires an independent adviser with a much greater range of skills and resources than could be found in industry; and the project team has the opportunity to explore a fascinating and demanding application which will have positive and tangible feedback into future work in CAL.

Problems and prizes

Having looked at these examples, what are the advantages and disadvantages, problems and prizes in such collaborations? Here is a personal selection.

Problems: for academics

— Researchers are not just interested in products. They are most interested in research and development. Some companies may have problems understanding that academic consultants cannot/should not be treated just like an in-house production facility.
— Getting into the social network of a company is a delicate business. This is particularly true of large bureaucratic organisations.
— Overcoming stereotypes.
— These problems however fade into insignificance beside the problem of managing project continuity when sponsors often offer only short-term contracts of, say, one year.
  It is wasteful and inefficient to build a new team for each contract.

Good work arises from good relationships between talented people who know one another well, who are involved in project decision-making, and who enjoy what they're doing. All of this, in turn, depends upon continuity of staffing. Consequently, if a team is to be viable and working at its peak of ability, staff turnover must be kept low and one member of the team must be more or less constantly engaged in seeking future contracts. I spend at least half my time looking for contracts instead of getting on with my research.

Problems: for industrialists

— Researchers may lack an awareness of commercial reality. Academics will need to be made aware of company pressures and policies.
— The cost of a project almost always rises. However, it is necessary to recognise that some increases in cost will be justified because development involves working with the unexpected. Knowing which increases are justified and which are not is difficult.
— Unexpected outcomes are hard to ignore. This may be either a problem or a blessing. Sometimes real advantage may be made of exploring such gifts. At other times temptation will lead to expensive excursions down interesting but not very fruitful avenues.
— Innovation is risky and those engaged in such work must be allowed to make mistakes from time to time. This is costly. The trick for managers is to ensure that the success rate is higher than the failure rate. Doing this indirectly when employing academic consultants may be difficult.
— Employing researchers alongside in-house staff is one way of training the company's people. However, this may not be successful: staff may resent external academic consultants or see them as a threat. In turn, academics may see such staff as a nuisance.

Benefits: for academics

— The discipline of working with industry has advantages. The imposition of mutually agreed deadlines focuses activity, and team members know precisely where they stand. Constraints upon the work may also act as a stimulus.
— Discussions with sponsors can lead to the team exploration of fruitful avenues not previously considered. This broadens perspectives and the team's experience. This in turn gives the project director an edge when selling the team's skills to potential future sponsors.
— Sponsored research results in improved contacts with industry, in-

creased knowledge of new equipment and services, and a heightened awareness of what is happening to CAL users in general.

— It is interesting, satisfying and challenging to make something that will be of value to your sponsor. This includes creating something which you know is better than it would have been had you worked alone.

Benefits: for industry

— Research teams in academic environments tend to have a much broader base than those found in industry. This view has often been offered to us as one reason for employing academic researchers. This seems to mean that the mix of educational background, experience and interests of those involved is not as restricted as in industry because of differences in recruiting policy. Since innovation often involves seeing new perspectives, breadth of vision is an advantage.

— Library and other support facilities, contact with colleagues not directly involved in the project and access to the academic community.

— Price: institutions can afford to be competitive in terms of overheads charged on salaries. Consequently, academic consultancy can be cheaper than other forms of advice.

— Objectivity and an institutional guarantee can make a sponsor feel more secure than perhaps would be the case with a commercial consultancy who may have an axe to grind. (Remembering of course that academics are also capable of grinding axes.)

Conclusion

I hope that the foregoing illustrates that although there are difficulties to be overcome, working with industry is interesting and worthwhile.

The best deals are those in which all benefit: the project, the industrial or commercial concern and the community at large. IT and CAL in particular need the advantages which flow when successful collaboration occurs between industrial and academic partners. There is too much to be learned, too quickly, to leave developments solely to the manufacturers and others involved in the IT industry. These enterprises need the guidance which we can give them by way of our work. We need their sponsorship to do the work and their insight into what should be done. Together we can plot a course which will lead to further resources and further development.

If this happens, a MITI report in 1996 will still be able say that 55% of all successful contemporary innovations are British. The difference will be that we will also be reaping the benefits.

7 / What Can Higher Education Do for Industry?
With special reference to Interactive Video

GRAEME KEIRLE *Media Services Centre for Educational Resources for the Construction Industry*

Abstract

This paper outlines the growing need for collaboration between Higher Education and Industry. An outline is given of basic requirements in the use of interactive video and also those for programme and system design and evaluation. An account is given of the work in this field at the Centre for Educational Resources for the Construction Industry (CERCI). Developments are suggested for a strong flexible input from Higher Education working alongside the commercial sector.

Keywords Computer-assisted learning, Interactive Video, Information Technology, Industrial Applications.

Background

Five years ago the simple answer to the question posed in the title of this paper might commonly have been "very little". In the area of the production of media learning resources, which has come to include video and computer assisted learning, an effective coverage has traditionally been provided by the individual company's own in-house staff, or by turning to a commercial production agency specialising in the appropriate area. Whilst facilities have existed within UK Universities and Polytechnics for the production of learning materials, in general they did not attract a significant level of work from, or encourage collaboration with, the great majority of British industry. What we have witnessed over the last five years, however, has been a radical change in attitudes towards post-institutional education. This, in turn, has brought about a shift in the perceived standing of HE from the industry point of view. The most important factors influential upon this change have been the following.
— The spread in the range of industrial areas where education is now seen as important.

The Building Centre, Store Street, London, on behalf of The National Interactive Video Centre, Marylebone Road, London

— The push being provided by central government for industry to update its work force, at all levels, to stay competitive.
— The promotion of principles of distance and open learning. The emergence of the Open University, with the quality of their broadcast and package material so obvious to all.
— The lowering of the distinction between training and education, as the industry's information needs become more sophisticated and diverse.
— The increasing need to provide an improved level and quality of information to customer, specifiers and clients on companies products and services.
— The proliferation of industry-based higher degrees and diplomas.

Within Higher Education (HE), over the same period, there have also been pressures and incentives to forge better links with industry; using many of the channels listed above. Probably most noticeable, in this connection has been the recent Alvey initiative encouraging HE to go out and adopt industrial "uncles" in support of their application for information technology research funding. The PICKUP scheme, although less well received, is another clear example. Universities and polytechnics can indeed gain a great deal from a closer association with industrially-based projects. But it's not only money. The wider benefits of collaborative working can be far more importantly measured in terms of improved IV programmes and an enhanced level of understanding of the principles of information design.

The need for specialist skills

The underlying reasons given above, suggesting an increased incentive for industry and HE to combine their efforts, might not in themselves serve as a complete justification for collaboration. Stronger reasons can be found when one looks at the requirement for new specialist skills. To service the emerging information technologies, such as computer assisted learning and interactive video (IV), traditional education and training methodologies will not suffice. The effective creation of these new media resources, furthermore, calls for a range of development techniques which are still little understood. The translation of an instructional ideal into a product (as industry is apt to consider the origination of educational material) has, quite simply, become more complicated. It now involves more people, calls for a wider range of skills and demands of the designer a far higher level of knowledge and experience. At least for the time being, industry is deficient in many of these areas. The provision of this expertise in a flexible and responsive manner, as a contractual service, will provide the main focus for the proposition advanced in this paper.

Interactive video is the area of activity chosen to illustrate this argument. Interactive video, in fact, serves as a very clear example of where a technical improvement in the delivery mechanism (for information and learning) can awake in the minds of those industrial clients who select to use it a realization (previously dormant) of the fundamental importance of sound educational theory and principles. This now includes an enthusiastic interest in different learning styles and assessment procedures such as discovery learning, role play/simulation, selective route, performance regulated progression, free word selection, etc. This is accompanied by a growing realization of the importance of testing and evaluation. All are areas which were previously (if ever) considered as purely academic. Interactive video, in a way that television never wholly tolerated, has legitimised the role of the information/education designer (scientist, technologist, call them what you will) and in that capacity HE is particularly well placed to provide a valuable, and valued, service. An input of highly specialised skills is something which educational units in industry, consumer information agencies and production companies themselves (albeit to a lesser extent) are currently lacking.

Early days

The first wave of IV development in the U.K. saw the medium used for two main purposes: tutorial style training programmes and large scale visual databases. To call many of these early programmes interactive, in the literal sense of the word, was rather like calling a parrot an interactive pet. They could better be described as "reactive", leaving it all too likely that the user, at the terminal, would rapidly acquire the feeling that it was not the information displayed on the screen to which he was responding but the intelligence (or otherwise) invested in the computer controlware representing the programmer. Simple nodal branching, with reiterative "remedial" loops, would frequently leave the viewer stuck in a comprehensive cul-de-sac. From this sad situation the only "break-out" option available would return you to the start of the program. Other "interactive" structures would repetitively gate you through the same single performance-based branch which demanded, as the operating mechanism, that you input precisely "the correct response". There is nothing self-paced about a question you cannot answer. Just as in the early days of television we witnessed producers pointing their cameras at existing stage plays, the first phase of IV development, driven by the technology, presented familiar patterns of learning through novel devices. The means of delivery might have been different, but the styles of learning or information retrieval which were encouraged remained fundamentally the same.

Progress

The last year or so, however, has seen the emergence of a number of interesting IV programmes which I firmly believe represent the beginnings of a more imaginative and ambitious approach to "free route accessed" visual information design. This marks the start of what can be seen as phase 2 in the chain of IV development. To progress still further, that is to establish IV as a "familiar" presentation form, requires a research input directed at three main areas.

— Improving our understanding of branching structures, indexes, menus and "help" devices.
— Evaluating the performance of users, in terms of the logic of progression, level of control, challenge, contentment and popularity.
— Developing the user-control hardware such as keyboards, touch screens, mice and the essential improvement in screen handling information which must accompany it.

Here, HE can make a substantial contribution; and in a manner which the production houses or the industrial client are at a disadvantage to consider. The value of good research and development in information and educational technology is increasingly becoming recognised by industry as an area to be afforded some priority. The climate for collaboration, in developing this contract use of specialist "outside" skills, is currently very good.

Main areas for research and development input

The following lists show some of the areas where the need for research and development work can most clearly be identified. First, it might help to establish the broad boundaries of our ambitions in this connection.

Basic aims

— To understand better where the use of IV is appropriate.
— To increase our knowledge on how to design and display it.
— To increase the ease with which the user can freely access the information in relation to his own individual needs and circumstances.

Basic requirements

— Improved feedback of information on the production and use of existing programmes. These to be published as design studies and evaluation reports.
— Improved pre-planning and design "tools". A "human language" notational form to be used at the decision-making stage of branching structure design. A "kit of parts" or "design shells" approach looks promising here.
— Improved screen handling facilities featuring the use of visual iconics, together with more cross-referencing of interrelated material and improved user support facilities.

A more detailed examination of areas where a strong research and development input would appear likely to yield rewards reveals three main areas of work.

Programme design

— Studies of the grammar of television incorporating: the role of chronology, visual association, matching, anchoring, analogy, metaphor and symbols.
— Studies into the positive use of subliminal image effects and visual iconics to encourage: the "short circuiting" of knowledge structures, accelerated learning, parallel associative learning and memory and "tripping" devices for revision purposes.
— Studies into the human logic of database "front ends": covering indexes, menus and user support facilities.
— Studies into IV programming structures: to progress from basic nodal branching to totally free (and manageable) break-out and re-entry options from and to any part of an instructional programme. This represents the important middle ground between databases and guided delivery programmes.

System design

— Improved user terminals, mice, touchscreens, etc.
— Improved screen handling information, proportionally presented, in relation to available options of related material or available search and viewing strategies.
— Electronic note pads for retaining and rationalising temporary "thought-process" information, in support of later higher level accessing of material.
— Expansion of the audio capacity over "still frame" visuals using digital sound store or interlinked random access tape players.

— Performance data collection on users, or (with exhibition display/point-of-sales use) the registering of customers' interests categorised to products.
— Duplication "take-away". Copying of selected material as viewed onto video tape, slides or print as a "dump", individually tailored to the user's future requirements.

Evaluation

— Pre-evaluation. Of the "appropriateness" of IV for specific purposes, and the best design strategy to pursue.
— Mid-term evaluation, following flow charting, at the final vision edit stage, or following the computer programming.
— Post evaluation. Surveys and reports on the applicational use of the material in the field.

Many HE institutions, of course, have production capacity of their own and will continue to undertake valuable original work in the areas of programme design and production. We also see a legitimate extended role for these centres, as well as a role for departments without the support of in-house production capacity, to work as consultants in the areas of learning/information design, testing and evaluation. The particular skills required would come from across a wide range of disciplines including education, computers, psychology, information science and visual display; selected as appropriate for the job in hand.

CERCI, for the construction industry, and the National Interactive Video Centre (NIVC) more generally across all industries, have a positive, identifiable role to act as co-ordinators in the management and organisation of such work. The list which follows shows some of the areas of activity in which CERCI is currently involved (in producing IV) on behalf of the construction industry. In each case a team approach, drawing on the best available skill, is to be adopted.

CERCI interactive video projects

Which brick?

— A product finder, providing two levels of user access by technical specification or by visual matching for the "expert" architect and "novice" householder respectively.

Effective briefing

— A resource disc to be used by an inexperienced client, as a dry run simulation, before he enters the building design phase for real. This is a tutorial style educational disc, not a large scale visual database but a combination of the two: — in fact a communication disc. The aim is to provide common analogous examples of the main aspects of building design and technology. These to be used by the novice client:

(a) in advance of the actual briefing process;

(b) at meetings with the expert architect to respond to "what if" questions or to be used to explain "that's what if" lines of association and repercussion.

— The use of the resource will be entirely dependent upon the current individual needs of the users. The exciting possibility exists here that from what was in the mind of the user and what was seen on the screen, a previously unexplored or unconsidered design idea could be created. This catalytic use of IV to explain and expand the potential for design creativity is an area that CERCI is particularly keen to explore.

Generic health and safety disc

— Generic discs would appear to be one of the most positive ways to gain awareness within the IV industry. Construction is the second most dangerous occupation in Britain. Approved safe working practices and procedures are ideally demonstrated by a visual medium. IV will add the ability of selective viewing, knowledge pre-test, simulation demonstration, situation recreation, post-testing and revision. This vital area for improved information and training is both large enough and homogeneous enough to easily support a generic approach.

Building materials product directory

— There already exists a large print directory with accompanying colour photographs. Visual aesthetics are often of paramount importance in the accurate and creative specifying of building products and materials. An interesting opportunity exists here for developing the concept of space selling on the disc (as stills and moving footage) to a range of manufacturers who wish to exhibit their products.

Tape-based information terminal

— At its simplest a visual (with audio) juke box of building products, materials and services. Additional enhancements to this simple basic information terminal could include:

— The provision of a visual matching facility. This would allow complementary materials and products such as baths, tiles, paints etc. to be brought together for visual comparison.

— Estimation sub-routines. To help the user in calculating required lengths, areas and volumes of building materials.

— Collection of "leads". An important aspect of product marketing and display already provided, manually, within the Building Centre. On this occasion the user, at the terminal, could register a request for further information on a product (or range of products) and type in his name and address for further information to be sent. These "leads" would be collected and passed on to the appropriate companies at the end of each week.

— Survey research. The use of the interactive information terminal to gain feedback from the users on the popularity and appeal of new or prototype products.

For many interested parties the financial commitment and risk of disc based projects is seen as far too high. For many purposes the facilities offered by tape-based systems if used in a flexible and creative manner are adequate. Tape-based system hardware and software has improved rapidly over the past year. For many purposes (especially point-of-sales or exhibition display) tape-based IV is often the most appropriate technology currently available.

There can be few industries that had more to gain from developing and using the full potential of IV than the construction industry. Building products are bulky, heavy, difficult and costly to transport, stock, store and, most importantly, to display. Architects are visually literate people. There is already an extensive use of slides, films and videos in undergraduate teaching of building design. The Building Centre, in London, offers four floors of permanent exhibition display on building products and materials backed up by a comprehensive advice and information service. Not surprisingly therefore IV is seen as an ideal method of increasing and improving upon these services. Outline proposals and design reports are available for all the above projects from the CERCI offices.

Achieving a flexible approach

Industry is familiar with higher education providing valuable contract research expertise, most notably in the sciences and engineering, in relation to product development. There are, no doubt, some equally good examples of collaboration in the information and communication sciences but the full potential of the Universities and Polytechnics in this area are still, I believe, undervalued. What this paper seeks to advocate is that the possibilities for, and increased productivity from, collaborative working will only be improved upon by changes to the mechanism of engagement. An extension of the range of "common working" options available is required to provide a more flexible, more responsive ability (as an extension of a University or Polytechnic's own facilities) to work in conjunction with external industry-based projects. The key features of this provision will be demonstrated by the willingness to work as follows:

— as part of, or as input tó, a commercially based production venture;
— with a specialization in the areas of IV planning, design and evaluation;
— freely outside of the HE environment;
— reporting back to both the project manager and their own departments where necessary;
— publishing and promoting their findings both within the "trade" (IV) and, if appropriate, in academic journals.

This list represents a model for response which industry would welcome seeing from HE in Britain.

What are the chances though that this can be achieved and, perhaps more importantly, which factors from collective past experience might have a bearing on the likelihood of success? The most frequently mentioned areas of significance are the following.

— The need for improved information and advice on available skills and expertise available within HE, sub-divided into areas of activity.
— The need for improved updating material on relevant projects being undertaken within the universities and polytechnics, presented in a more digestible form. (Video Disc Newsletter has now gone a long way towards filling this gap.) Better crossover of information between the academic journals, which industry does not read, and the "trade" magazines, which the academic community does not always receive.
— The need for an awareness that research must, in the industrial environment, be application based. Much of this work will be "downstream" of the origination stage, directed specifically at providing alternatives and solutions for known areas of design difficulty or weakness.
— The level of empirical detail and accuracy necessitated by an academic discipline is higher than commonly required in information technology fields in the industrial sector. The requirement is for an appropriate level of verification in line with the decision-making abilities of production management.
— The publication of results or recommendations should be in a form which allows their immediate use in support of proposals, as a basis

for design, or as evidence of comparative success or failure.

It is only fair to point out that a similar list of requirements for collaborative working could be produced by HE for improvements in the working practices found in industry. "What does HE want from industry?" is an equally valid question, but one which must remain the subject of another paper.

What are the future chances for IV?

The big banks, motor manufacturers and leading computer companies have all used IV in an accomplished yet largely predictable manner. The quality and reliability of the equipment is now beyond doubt. The range of options and opportunities it can provide is truly impressive. Interactive video however, I would advance, has reached a sticking point; right on the threshold of what could become a great leap forward or a gradual backslide into obscurity. The equipment manufacturers acknowledge this problem but see it to be demand based: a classic chicken and egg situation of too few players in use to attract would-be programme makers. I believe the market is shrewder than that, and the real problem lies on the side of design. Too few IV designs so far have demonstrated sufficient comparable advantage over the other methods of presentation to persuade those with an education or information need (and a budget to spend) to elect to use this particular medium. The capacity of a single IV disc is awesome. The quality of programme production in Britain, both on the video and computer side, is impressive and readily available. The most appropriate design development skills required to "show" IV at its best have yet to be fully harnessed. A strong and flexible input from HE, working alongside the commercial sector, is an important first step in gaining this improved level of performance. No less a person than Marx himself, when talking about television (Groucho Marx that is), once said "I find television very educational. Every time someone switches on the television I go into the next room and read a good book." IV, if used creatively, can provide the advantages and qualities of both.

Conclusion

The creation of good IV is expensive, time consuming, and requires a wide diversity of skills. Universities and Polytechnics which have the technical capacity for their own disc production (to pre-master stage) will remain a most important element in advancing our knowledge of IV design techniques. Industry in this instance would welcome a more coherent and usable output of information in the form of design reports and evaluation studies on their work. Outside of these "chosen few" institutions there clearly exists a great depth of specialised expertise, in many fields, with relevance to IV development. If an appropriate mechanism can be found to "release" this talent on a more flexible contract basis then industrial clients (for IV production) and the production agencies themselves could move closer to realising the full potential of this wonderful resource. A few steps forward together, on the design side, could provide that giant leap in terms of IV's universal usefulness that I for one am greatly looking forward to.

Section 4

This session contained four dissimilar but related papers in fields as diverse as Art, Medicine and Engineering. The opening paper by Gardner and Paisley concentrated on developments in both hardware and software which have contributed to the applications of computers in Art and Design education. Of particular note was the low cost of the system and the use of a mouse as an input device. In questions two particular points were raised relating to the place of computers in Art Education, the tactile aspects and the concept that 'The artist is no longer a true artist and a bad artist is only as good as the machine'. In response the authors recognised that there are many aspects to art and what was required was a proper integration of the whole.

Goodyear then dealt with an approach to system modelling using an aspect of Environmental Science as a base. In particular the development of a toolkit to simplfy the construction of the model was described and its use illustrated. Discussion concentrated on the development of the toolkit and the need to integrate experiments with the simulation.

The following paper by Taylor covered clinical simulation. Unfortunately the presentation was handicapped by the inability of the projector to handle the slides provided, a difficulty the author capably surmounted. The paper concentrated on the use of a BBC computer to simulate the events that take place on admitting a patient into a hospital emergency department. Operation is at a number of levels from hospital elapsed time to simulation elapsed time. Questions centred on the language used to write the simulation package.

The final paper by Pountney and Richmond dealt with the provision of a front end for a numerical analysis library to protect an inexperienced user from the complexities of the library. The presentation set out the principles and problems involved in developing the front end and discussion centred on the use of mainframes or PC's for this purpose.

David Bradley

8 / Microcomputer Graphics in Art and Design Education

JOHN GARDNER and ROBERT PAISLEY *Queen's University, Belfast*

Abstract

Recent developments in software and hardware are combining to make computer based imagery more viable, relevant and attractive for art educators. The most notable of these developments has been the use of a roller-ball mouse interface to drive painting software which incorporates icons and graphics painting effects. For some time the systems which were available were relatively expensive but the costs have now decreased to a level at which a larger group of art educators can begin to explore their potential. This paper considers the educational viability of such systems in terms of their flexibility and attractiveness for teachers and students and their relevance to the aims and objectives of formal art and design education.

Keywords Art and Design, CAL, Icons, Mouse, Education

Introduction

Until recently teachers of art and design, who wish to avail themselves of computer based media and tools, have been restricted to complex yet limited packages which require a significant amount of both teacher and student preparation time for effective use (Gardner, 1986). To date, therefore, computer assisted learning (CAL) in art classrooms has been based mainly on the use of relatively inexpensive packages to illustrate rather than realise the possibilities for computer graphics in art and design. With the advent of mouse-driven icon and painting software computer based imagery is now, however, a more viable, relevant and attractive component of art and design education.

The possibilities for mouse-driven graphics packages were first heralded by the launch of the Apple Macintosh and its associated MacPaint package. For most users, outside of Higher Education perhaps, the costs of this hardware have proven prohibitive despite attractive educational schemes promoted by Apple. Aside from funding constraints, the reluctance to purchasing the Mac has probably been

Department of Education, The Queen's University of Belfast, 69/71 University Street, Belfast, BT7 1NN

due to the relatively standard equipping of UK schools, further education colleges and teacher education institutions with Research Machines and/or Acorn BBC microcomputers. The development of "friendly" mouse-interfaced graphics packages for these machines is well advanced with the Advanced Memory Systems Ltd. AMX Super Art package for the Acorn BBC B and the Paint software running under Microsoft Windows for the Research Machines Nimbus. As the BBC B is so widespread in UK education it is likely that the use of packages similar to the AMX system, at under £90 complete with painting software, will have, for the foreseeable future, the greater impact in art and design education.

Although the improving quality of art-oriented software is likely to weaken the barriers to the more widespread use of computer based graphics in art education, many hardware and software problems still remain to hinder progress. Such problems include the high cost of quality monochrome and colour printers and plotters and also the lack of integrated control software for use between existing packages and printing/plotting equipment. Whilst economic viability is necessary to encourage the wider acceptance of the computer perhaps the most important consideration is its educational viability. This educational viability must be based on two factors:

— the attractiveness of the techniques to both teachers and students and

— the relevance of the techniques to art and design education.

The task of making software convenient, clear and attractive is the subject of much research and in the UK a number of groups have been concerned with the presentation and control of educational software. Chelsea College (Alderson and DeWolf, 1984) has produced guidelines for screen design while the various control methods include the Drivechart from ITMA (Fraser, 1984), the Command Standard from AUCBE (Tagg, 1980) and the Control Interface from Homerton College (Daly, 1984). Of these only the Homerton Control Interface has been designed specifically to include control by a mouse but since most CAL requires some form of textual expression it is not surprising to note a predominance of keyboard entry. Art CAL by contrast is based on visual expression and for this a mouse-driven control is much more appropriate and attractive.

Mouse-driven painting software owes much of its attractiveness to three main attributes. Firstly the input method is much more pleasing than keyboard entry. The movement of the mouse is similar to the sweep of the artist's hand, more so even than in the case of joystick input. Secondly the use of pull-down menus, pattern and colour palette windows with icons for the various tools, makes the screen presentation and driving method much more attractive than conventional menu or command driven systems. Thirdly the fast and simple manipulation of colour, pattern and shape makes a variety of conventional and even new applications and styles available to the user.

In considering the relevance of any artistic medium, technique or instrument to art education, a useful basis for discussion is the National Criteria for Art and Design published by the Department of Education and Science (DES) in 1985. Although aimed at standardising, to some extent, examinations in art and design for 15-16 year olds at the new General Certificate of Secondary Education (GCSE) level, the criteria should be valid for all levels of art and design education.

Aims of art and design education

"... The words or the language as they are written or spoken do not seem to play any role in my mechanism of thought. The physical entities which seem to serve as elements in thought are certain signs and more or less clear images which can be voluntarily reproduced and combined ... (these) elements are, in my case, of visual and some of muscular type. ..."

When Einstein wrote these words (Rowland, 1976) he was attributing a fundamental importance to the role of visual and tactile imagery in his own thought processes. In a similar vein art educators in general and the authors of the DES GCSE document in particular, consider art and design to be primarily concerned with the visual and tactile modes of expression ... "a unique vehicle for communication and self-expression equivalent in importance to literacy and numeracy". In this work the potential of mouse-driven software to stimulate, develop, manipulate and reproduce such images for this mode of communication and self-expression will be illustrated by examples and discussed in terms of the aims of art and design education.

Computer graphics can be shown to offer opportunities for visual expression but tactile expression is only achievable when the computer is linked to a physical extension such as a lathe or other machine-tool or perhaps an animated sculpture or drawing device. This is not a particularly serious drawback since every medium has its specific limitations which the artist must accept. In the same manner in which the photographer who takes advantage of a zoom lens must also accept the limitations which the lens imposes in terms of aperture and depth of field, so the artist must adapt to the limitations of computer based imagery.

The GCSE aims recognise that the output from art and design

activity derives from a synthesising process involving either intuitive and/or analytical approaches. Mouse-driven software can accommodate both by allowing the user to be as imprecise or as exact as s/he chooses in reproducing any image the hand may create. Figures 1 and 2 illustrate the different approaches.

Fig. 1. Ulster farm house (Macintosh).

In Figure 1 the farm house, although it still retains its representational quality, was in fact created in a freehand style.

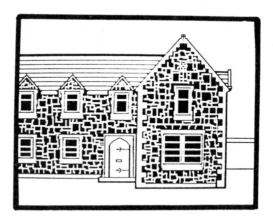

Fig. 2. Old primary school (AMX).

Figure 2 on the other hand is a more precise representation of an old primary school with Figures 3 and 4 indicating how the software facilities were used to complete the detail.

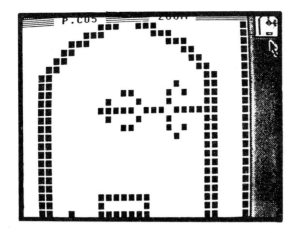

Fig. 3. Using "zoom" facility (AMX).

In Figure 3 the use of the pull-down menu system is shown with the mouse pointer confirming the "Zoom". Figure 4 shows how the door-hinge may be completed by filling in the square in the lower curve. This pixel level precision is extremely useful for representational work.

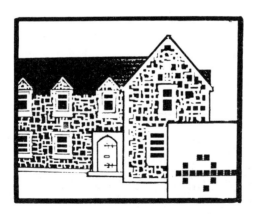

Fig. 4. Alteration at pixel-level (AMX).

In addition to the general aims discussed above the National Criteria identify 12 main aims and 8 associated assessment objectives for art and design education. A selection of these aims is reproduced below along with comment detailing the relevance of computer based art and in particular mouse-driven painting packages.

Art and design education should stimulate, encourage and develop the following aims:

(a) the ability to perceive, understand and express concepts and feelings in visual and tactile form.

Aside from the problems associated with tactile expression noted
earlier, it should be obvious that computer generated images are as
open to the normal criteria of visual acceptability as images produced
by any other means. The perception, understanding and visual expression of concepts and feelings should be just as valid and the student's
personal response should be accommodated just as subjectively in a
computer medium as in any conventional media.

(b) the ability to record from direct observation and personal experience.

Mouse-driven software is particularly suited to the recording of
direct observations and personal experiences. The facility and speed of
representational recording like that exemplified by Figure 1 is bettered
by few techniques outside of photography and as such must be viewed
as a considerable encouragement to this type of activity. An example of
direct recording from observation is illustrated by Figure 5 in which the
"Petite Double Face" of Soto (Lucie-Smith, 1975) was the inspiration.

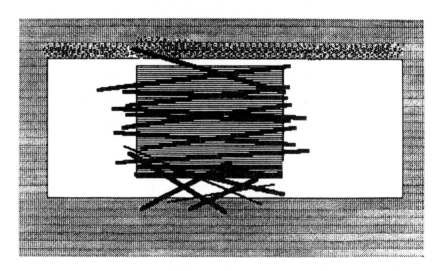

Fig. 5. "Soto" observation (Macintosh).

(c) the ability to form, compose and communicate in two and three
dimensions by the use of materials in a systematic and "disciplined" way.

(d) the acquisition and understanding of technical competence and
manipulative skills, which will enable individuals to realise their
creative intentions.

Aside from the limitations imposed by the use of a two-dimensional medium (a limitation shared by conventional painting) computer based art offers the same opportunities to achieve these aims as most conventional media. Even though mouse-driven software is very user-friendly, through the use of pull-down menus and icons, the driving method is still inherently systematic and logical.

The user is actively encouraged to adopt a disciplined approach to the work both in the creative development of an image (e.g. picture framing, brush or tool size and shape and so on) and in the technical management (e.g. file naming, disk management and so on). Learning all the possibilities a package has for creative application in, for example, the use of patterning to simulate the visual texture of Aboriginal art in Figure 6 (Edwards and Guerin, 1976) is comparable to the acquisition of technical and manipulative competence in any aspect of a conventional medium such as clay or oils.

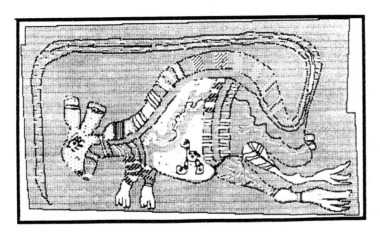

Fig. 6. Aboriginal bark art (Macintosh).

(e) experimentation and innovation through the inventive use of materials and techniques.

Much imaginative and innovative work has been carried out by ''computer'' artists such as Em, Mandelbrot, Julich and Hall (Michie and Johnston, 1984) on mainframe computers but the power of even today's microcomputers makes creative computer based work available to a much wider user base. The speed at which the computer can handle repetitive, complicated and often tedious detail encourages experimentation to such an extent that very often new and totally innovative images may be created in a fraction of the time necessary with conventional media. Figures 7 and 8 serve to illustrate the opportunities for experimentation.

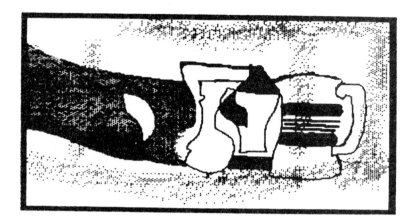

Fig. 7. Visual experimentation on Nicholson-type image (AMX).

In Figure 7 a still-life inspired by Nicholson (1978) can be subjected repeatedly to colour and tone experimentation literally by the push of a button. Figure 8 is an example of visual experimentation on the theme of an observed group of horse parsley stalks.

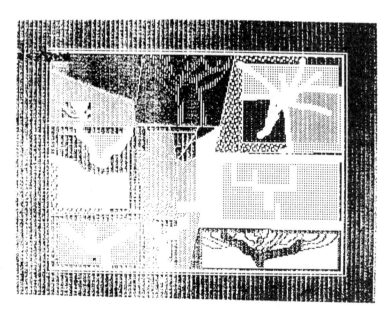

Fig. 8. Visual experimentation on theme of "Horse Parsley" (AMX).

(f) intuitive and imaginative abilities, and critical and analytical faculties.

The ease of use of mouse-driven software encourages experimentation and readily draws out intuitive and imaginative ability. Even those who would claim to have little artistic ability can quickly produce stimulating images which in turn engender more confidence in themselves and their ability to be creative. A natural consequence of this process will be the enhancement of their own critical and analytical faculties. In more formal settings the machine can effectively contribute to critical and appreciative studies in which major works may be selected for analysis and recreation. Figure 9 illustrates how the brush strokes in van Gogh's "Self-Portrait in a Soft Hat" may be replicated using the spray-can tool as a paint-brush with small brush size selected.

Fig. 9. Brush-stroke analysis in Van Gogh study (Macintosh).

One particular area in art and design, which requires that aspect of imagination which enables outcomes to be predicted, is Relief Printing. The concept is difficult for some students to grasp as the technique involves creating "in the negative" so to speak. The mouse can be used to flood an area of screen with a particular colour and then "cut-out" with the "eraser" or a variety of cutting shapes in another colour. In this manner it is possible not only to create relief images as finished products (Figure 10) but also to use the technique as preparation for studies in wood-cuts and lino-cuts.

(g) the ability to identify and solve problems in visual and tactile form: to research, select, make and evaluate in a continuum.

Fig. 10. Relief printing imagery (Macintosh).

The main tools in the artist/designer's problem solving kit are those elements of visual language such as line, tone, colour, pattern and texture, which allow the creation of shape, form and space. The speed and convenience of selection of these tools, in combination with the ability to alter, erase, zoom into/out of, re-orient or replicate the visual information, make the research into and evaluation of computer based solutions of art/design problems attractively effective and, in terms of time at least, economical.

Conclusions

There is little doubt that the full potential of computers in art and design still remains to be explored. Already several schools of thought on the subject exist and these range from those who cannot bring themselves to accept computer output as a valid art form at all to those who believe computer art should be exactly that ... artistic output generated solely by a computer which, with the aid of artificial intelligence techniques, "knows" the rules of "art". Somewhere in between are that large group of artists and art educators who feel the computer can and will contribute to art and design either as another art form or another tool for the artist. Most of these people do not want to program or code their work (what percentage of painters manufacture their own oils and canvasses?) ... they prefer to use tools and media which are readily available to express their creativity. In this manner the advent of friendly mouse-driven graphics software, with icons and various graphics painting effects, now brings the power of computer graphics attractively within the grasp of those artists who do want to use it as a tool and/or medium for artistic self-expression.

References

Alderson, G. and DeWolf, M. (Eds), (1984) *Guide to effective screen design,* Computers in the Curriculum, Chelsea College, University of London.

Daly, F. (1984) *Software Design: the User-Machine Interface in CAL,* Computing and Curriculum Development Centre, Homerton College, Cambridge.

Edwards, R. and Guerin, B. (1976) *Aboriginal Bark Paintings,* Rigby, Sydney.

Fraser, R. (1984) *Drivecharts* — various publications from Investigations into Teaching with Microcomputers as an Aid (ITMA), College of St. Mark & St. John, Plymouth.

Gardner, J. R. (1986) *CAL In-service and the Visual Arts.* J. Comp. Asst. Learning **2,** 1.

Lucie-Smith, E. (1975) *Movements in Art Since 1945,* Thames and Hudson, London.

Michie, D. and Johnston, R. (1984) *The Creative Computer,* Viking-Penguin, Middlesex.

Nicholson, B. (1978) In *Recent Paintings on Paper,* Waddington and Galleries Ltd., London.

Rowland, K. (1976) *Visual Education and Beyond,* Ginn, London.

Tagg, W. (1980) *A Standard for CAL Dialogue,* Advisory Unit for Computer Based Education (AUCBE), Hatfield.

9 / A Toolkit Approach to Computer-Aided Systems Modelling

PETER GOODYEAR *University of Lancaster*

Abstract

This paper describes the development of a "toolkit" of LOGO procedures for use in a course on ecosystem modelling. The toolkit approach requires a distinction to be drawn between computer programming activities which are central to the learning exercise and those which can be delegated to the teacher. The modularity and natural extensibility of the LOGO language allow learner-defined and teacher-defined procedures to be used in combination. The approach should be applicable in other domains concerned with systems modelling.

Keywords LOGO, Computer-Assisted Learning, Modelling, Earth Sciences.

Introduction

Packages or systems to support CAE differ from each other in many ways, but two dimensions of variation are particularly important. These are: (a) the learning effort demanded of students before they master the operation of a system — what might be called its "incidental learning cost" — and (b) the degree of learner-control (or user-control) embedded in the system's design.

More often than not, these characteristics are in direct proportion. The more autonomy a system provides for the learner, the greater the incidental learning cost. Achieving a workable balance between learning cost and user control is a key issue when selecting appropriate software, especially when there is a high level of curriculum or timetable constraint — where the students' time is a scarce resource — and also when there is a considerable diversity of skill levels and experience among the student group.

This paper derives from the design and operation of two course components in Environmental Systems Modelling. It discusses some of the pedagogic issues involved in providing software for this activity, focusing particularly on the "problem" of having a diversity of skill levels, experience and learning styles within a student group. It also describes the software solution adopted — that of providing the stu-

Department of Educational Research, University of Lancaster, Lancaster, LA1 4YL

dents with a "toolkit" of modelling procedures in the high level language LOGO. Such toolkits are inherently malleable things and since computer-aided systems modelling (in its many forms) is found in a large number of disciplines (Tawney, 1976), it is hoped that educators from most subject areas will find this approach of interest.

The course concerned is a two year DipHE (CNAA) programme in Environmental Studies. Over the last four years it has included a one-term (20 hour) introduction to computing, which is now followed by a similar length component in computer-aided environmental systems modelling (CAESM). Like other DipHE courses, it tends to have a more mature and diverse intake than conventional degrees, with a substantial number of students arriving through an "exceptional entry" route. Computing experience will vary from nil (the majority), through owning a home microcomputer, to previous work in systems analysis or programming. A number of students will have a deep mistrust of computer technology.

Software for modelling and simulation

The selection of an appropriate system to support the modelling work has to be made from the range of solutions summarised in Table 1. To an extent, the sets (A–E) overlap but, in essence, they offer a continuum of decreasing learner control and decreasing "incidental learning cost" as one moves towards (E).

HIGH LEVEL OF
USER CONTROL

LOW LEVEL OF
USER CONTROL

A	B	C	D	E
General Purpose High Level Languages	Simulation Languages	Simulation/ Modelling "Toolkits"	Fixed-Format Modelling Packages	One-Off Topic Specific Simulations
e.g. FORTRAN Pascal LISP/LOGO	e.g. SIMULA GPSS	e.g. DEMOS EDSIM	e.g. Spreadsheets DIFGLE, GRIPS MODL	e.g. Longman's "Pond" Ecology

HIGH INCIDENTAL
LEARNING COST

LOW INCIDENTAL
LEARNING COST

Table 1: Software options for computer-aided modelling

The common high level languages (A) place a great deal of control in the hands of the user or learner; principal limitations being those of the computer itself, and the accessibility of its features from the language concerned. The learning cost is correspondingly high, however, and can probably only be justified if a substantial amount of later programming work is envisaged.

The complexity of the programming task, and the entailed learning, can be reduced to a certain extent by using one of the purpose-built simulation languages, e.g. SIMULA (Dahl, Myhrhaug and Nygaard, 1970), GPSS (O'Donovan, 1979) or ECSL (Clementson, 1966). These provide a variety of programming constructs which render the task of systems modelling more natural than is the case with more conventional programming languages such as FORTRAN. Languages like SIMULA or SMALLTALK, with their notions of "processes" and "activities" or "objects" and "classes", provide a much better grammar in which to construct representations of environmental phenomena (see Jackson, 1980, p.341; Goldberg and Robson, 1983; O'Shea and Self, 1983). However, they still entail a much greater learning commitment than can be afforded in short non-specialist computing courses.

At the other end of the scale, in terms of ease of learning, one finds increasing use being made of topic-specific simulation packages (type E). A major problem with such packages, apart from the subject-specificity which circumscribes their appeal, is their limited capacity for user-control. They are "simulation packages", which incorporate and execute a computer model, rather than "modelling packages", which help the learner create her own models. The user is limited to altering the input parameters of the model and observing its outputs (Self, 1985, p.42). Any learning that takes place is consequent upon repeated examination of the external behaviour of a "black box" system, and observation would suggest that the evolution of the learner's mental model of the black box is slow and far from guaranteed (Dekkers and Donatti, 1981; Goodyear, 1985). This is in contrast to model-building activities, where thorough understanding of the system being modelled is integral to the task.

Intermediate between simulation languages (B) and simulation packages (E) are products aimed at facilitating model-building. These may be programs into which one inserts sets of differential equations — e.g. DIFGLE (Wedekind, 1982) or MODL (Hartley and Lewis, 1982) — or more sophisticated packages which use graphical interfaces or knowledge-based front-ends to aid model specification — e.g. IBM's CSMP-1130, GRIPS (Wedekind, 1982) or ECO (Uschold et al., 1984). While such systems can be of great assistance in a number of modelling domains, none of the available products was flexible enough to meet the needs of the CAESM course.

A modelling toolkit

Consequently it was decided to pursue a "toolkit" approach, using the high level language LOGO (Papert, 1980; Goodyear, 1984). The LOGO language has a core vocabulary of "primitive" instructions, which can be extended through the addition of user-defined procedures. The "toolkit" consists of a number of such procedures, designed to facilitate the modelling task. A decision to use LOGO as the base language was made on the following grounds.

— It is modular, allowing systematic program construction using hierarchical procedures and localisation of variables. (This is critically important in avoiding the cognitive overload involved in writing/ understanding long unstructured quantities of code.)
— It allows meaningful variable and procedure names, encouraging the collaborative creation of self-documenting programs.
— Its natural extensibility allows for "seamless" incorporation of teacher and learner-provided procedures
— Its list data type provides flexible and powerful data structuring capabilities.
— It has an excellent programming environment, with integral screen-editor, clear error-messages and good debugging aids.
— It is available in powerful, full implementations with good fast graphics on MS-DOS/PC-DOS systems.

The remainder of this paper outlines the construction of a toolkit for the CAESM exercise, expanding on a number of these features. The example given involves modelling the effect of applications of agricultural nitrates in a catchment upon the quality of the water in the stream draining the catchment. Figure 1 is a graphical model of part of such a system and is derived from work on water quality in the Darent Valley catchment undertaken by members of the Environmental Studies course team.

Converting this graphical representation into a runnable computer model is an intimidating task if it has to be expressed in the vocabulary of a "raw" programming language. A LOGO toolkit, intended to help overcome this difficulty, needs to provide the following capabilities:

(I) an easy, natural method of representing the components of the system and their linkages, and of modifying these;

(II) straightforward methods for entering data defining the input parameters of the model;

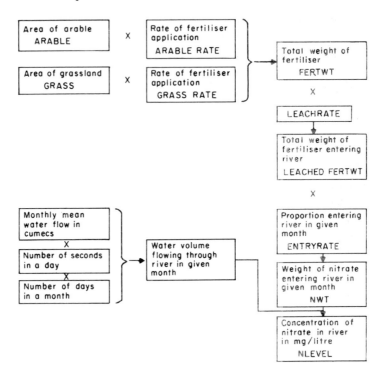

Fig. 1. Graphical model of nitrate flow in the Darent Valley (after McPhee, 1985).

(III) adaptable methods for displaying, examining and storing output data — including mechanisms for re-scaling or transforming data and alternative means of graphical display.

Fundamental to the "toolkit" philosophy is that the LOGO procedures comprising the final model are of three kinds.

(a) Procedures that the students should write themselves as an integral part of the modelling process.

(b) "Service" procedures that facilitate routine tasks (such as saving to disk or graphing) which are peripheral to the learning task. These will usually be treated as "black boxes" or as if they were primitives.

(c) "Service" procedures such as those in (b) but which a significant proportion of the students will wish to examine, and perhaps modify.

It is procedures of types (b) and (c) that make up the modelling toolkit.

Task I, the representation of systems components and their linkages, is at the heart of the modelling exercise. Hence the procedures required here should be written by the students themselves. This task is made easier by a readily apprehended similarity between the graphical representation of systems components and the syntax of

LOGO procedures. Components in the environmental system can be thought of as processes with one or more inputs and one or more outputs (see Figure 1). Similarly, many LOGO procedures are written as information transforming "functions", which take one or more inputs and produce an output. For example, the following RM LOGO procedure (sumsq) takes two inputs, and outputs the some of their squares.

    sumsq number1 number2
    result (:number1 * :number1) + (:number2 * :number2)

(Note: the LOGO primitives include a large set of mathematical functions — SQT, LOG, TAN etc.)

As part of the modelling exercise, students will write, among others, a procedure to represent the process of nitrate leaching. This might, at its simplest, take the form:

    leach weight
    result : weight * 0.5

where the input is the total weight of nitrate applied in time period (t) and the output is the weight of nitrate leached into the river. A more detailed procedure might take a larger number of inputs, while still producing a single output. For example:

    leach weight time.since.application soil.type crop.type
    ... ...
    ... ...
    result ....

Another representational symmetry, which aids the transformation of the graphical model into a runnable LOGO program, is that both representations allow hierarchical decomposition of structure. For example, each process component in Figure 1 might be unpacked to portray a more complex internal structure, or indeed the whole system might be rendered as just one component of a much larger system. Similarly, individual LOGO procedures may be built from other LOGO procedures ... which may be built from other LOGO procedures, to arbitrary levels of complexity. This facilitates a "top-down" or "stepwise refinement" approach to both systems modelling and program construction.

Most of the remaining procedures needed in the modelling exercise (for tasks II and III) are "service procedures" which make up the modelling toolkit. Because of the natural extensibility of LOGO, these can be treated by the students exactly as if they were inbuilt LOGO primitives. To use them, they need only know their input-output behaviour, or what inputs create what effects. Indeed, the toolkit designers can choose to "bury" the definitions of some toolkit procedures so that their internal structure is concealed from the students. Although this reduces their autonomy, it also serves to reduce the surface complexity of the programming task.

An example of such a "service procedure" is TRANSFORM. This teacher-defined procedure is used to transform each of the elements in a LOGO list of data. The procedure takes two inputs — a list and the name of a "function" which is to be applied to each of the elements in the list. Its output is the transformed list:

```
transform func list
if emptyq :list [result []]
result pf (first eval se :func first :list)
                    (transform :func bf :list).
```

This is a very useful tool for manipulating the individual numbers in a list of data according to a primitive or user-defined "function". It is just the sort of procedure which will intimidate novice computer users. Consequently there is a strong pedagogic argument for turning it into a black-box by "burying" its definition.

Other procedures in the toolbox, particularly those concerned with displaying outputs from the model, are best treated as "grey" boxes. Some students will view these as "black", others will want to look inside and try to modify them. This flexibility, which is not easily attainable in other high level languages, is of great educational significance. Firstly, it allows students to tune the display of model outputs to suit their own investigative learning strategy. In addition, it helps cope with the diversity of learning styles found among the students. Some need to establish a firm understanding of (and trust in) the workings of each procedure before progressing to the next. Others prefer to treat many procedures as black boxes until they have an overall, if superficial, grasp of the system (cf. Pask's serialist and holist learners).

This diversity of cognitive style, coupled with the diversity of programming skills and computing experience in the group, could be seen as a difficulty to be overcome, particularly in a rigid curriculum which could not be shaped to meet diverse student needs. In the more flexible LOGO modelling environment, however, our initial observations suggest that this diversity is less a problem than a positive advantage — allowing us to capitalise on the variety of learner confidence and expertise through a considerable degree of peer-teaching.

Appendix — The toolkit

A brief annotated list of some of the toolkit procedures developed for the nitrate/water-quality modelling exercise. (The toolkit runs on a 16-bit Research Machines Nimbus, using RM LOGO; further details available from the author.)

(I) Procedures to represent the system components and their linkages: written by students themselves.

(II) Procedures for data entry

SETUP	a user-modifiable procedure which establishes input values for the model as global-level variables.

Additionally, students can use EDLIST which allows the screen-editor to manipulate data lists. SETUP may use a number of primitive and toolkit functions to automatically establish data lists (e.g. of random values with certain distributional characteristics).

(III) Procedures for examination and storage of data output, for example:

GRAPH	takes two input lists and plots pairs of values; makes use of toolkit subprocedures such as AXES, PLOT.CHAR, LABEL.AXIS; allows one or more plots at user-selected screen locations. ARCHIVE/FETCH service procedures for saving the model (or data from the model) to disk, or loading from disk.
TRANSFORM	enables transformation of input, output or intermediate data lists (e.g. LOG conversion prior to graphing)

References

Clementson, A.T. (1966) *Extended Control and Simulation Language.* Computer Journal **9**, 3, pp. 215-220.

Dahl, O-J., Myhrhaug, B. and Nygaard, K. (1970) *SIMULA 67 Common Base Language.* NCC Publication S-52, Norwegian Computer Center, Oslo.

Dekkers, J. and Donatti, S. (1981) *The Integration of Research Studies on the use of Simulation as an Instructional Strategy.* Journal of Educational Research **74**, 6, pp. 424-7.

Goldberg, A. and Robson, D. (1983) *SMALLTALK-80: the Language and its Implementation.* Addison-Wesley, Reading, Mass.

Goodyear, P.M. (1984) *LOGO: a Guide to Learning Through Programming.* Ellis Horwood, Chichester/Heinemann, London.

Goodyear, P.M. (1985) *Computer Aided Learning, Computer Based Guidance and the Teaching of Educational Research Methods.* British Educational Research Journal **11**, 3, pp. 93-102.

Hartley, R.J. and Lewis, R. (1982) *A Computer Language System for Model Building and Experimentation.* Int. J. Math. Educ. Sci. Technol. **5,** pp. 391-400.

Jackson, M.A. (1980) *The Design and Use of Conventional Programming Languages* In Smith, H. and Green, T. (eds) Human Interaction with Computers, Academic Press, London.

McPhee, E. (1985) *The Movement of Nitrates in the Darent Valley.* Darent Valley Research Report 3, Thames Polytechnic.

O'Donovan, T. (1979) *GPSS Simulation made Simple.* Wiley, Chichester.

O'Shea, T. and Self, J. (1983) *Learning and Teaching with Computers.* Harvester, Brighton.

Papert, S. (1980) *Mindstorms: Children Computers and Powerful Ideas.* Harvester, Brighton.

Self, J. (1985) *Microcomputers in Education.* Harvester, Brighton.

Tawney, D.A. (1976) *Simulation and Modelling in Science Computer Assisted Learning.* CET, London.

Uschold, M. et al. (1984) *An Intelligent Front-End for Ecological Modelling.* DAI Research Paper 223, Edinburgh University.

Wedekind, J.P.E. (1982) *Computer Aided Model Building and CAL.* Computers and Education **6,** pp. 145-151.

10 / System Design Features for Clinical Simulations

M. J. TAYLOR, W. A. CORBETT*, P. R. EDWARDS* and
J. R. COUGHLAN *University of Liverpool*

Abstract

Simulations of medical emergencies using the dialogue programming
language MICROTEXT have been developed on the BBC microcomputer. The medical emergencies are presented as a series of
sequential layers and interaction with the simulation allows decisions
to be made from both within and between the layers. The simulations
are realistic and experience has been gained by their use at both
undergraduate and postgraduate level.

Keywords Computer-assisted Learning, Simulation, Medicine.

Introduction

Medical teaching encompasses a wide variety of modalities from formal
lectures through to small group tutorials and bedside tuition with
patients. Despite comprehensive planning it is not always possible to
expose students to all the clinical situations that illustrate important
principles in patient management. There is therefore a requirement to
produce a means by which gaps in experience may be filled or failures
in understanding corrected. Computer-assisted learning (CAL) should
be valuable in this context when the full potential of the computer is
realised and is not solely used for 'turning pages' (Zemper, 1973). Early
CAL programs did not achieve this in that they provided little more
than a simple pencil and paper approach, often requiring the student to
refer to an accompanying book. Interactive programs have been produced which include as a principal feature a time-base so that the
patient's condition deteriorates with time and this is an important
factor to consider in the management of emergency conditions (Dugdale et al., 1982). Further programs have failed to develop the interactive aspects of CAL and have usually only required the student to select
an answer from a menu supplied on screen (Geddes et al., 1983) or in

---

Departments of Computer Science and *Surgery, PO Box 147, Liverpool, L69 3BX

an accompanying folder (Murray et al., 1976). Recently, new programming environments have been applied to facilitate the presentation of patient information and enhance the interaction with the student (Lakhani et al., 1984; Puntis and Hughes, 1984).

In the present study it was considered essential that interactive CAL programs be developed (Corbett and Taylor, 1985). The major requirements are that the student responses should be without external assistance or undue menu prompting against a time limit set by the program which would respond by changing the state of the simulation in accordance with the students' actions. We have applied the dialogue programming language MICROTEXT (Bevan and Watson, 1983) as the basis for the development of interactive clinical simulations which fully utilise the colour, sound and graphics capabilities of the BBC microcomputer.

Simulation structure

The clinical simulations chosen could be represented in three well defined levels (Figure 1) that reflect both the sequence of the problem and its management. Each level has to be negotiated separately and in turn, with medical decisions taken at one level influencing the progress at a subsequent level. Similarly, options or strategies adopted within a level need to have both immediate and delayed effects on the response of the simulated patient. Within a particular level, options can either follow the optimal pathway, deviate from it and return successfully, or leave the pathway completely resulting in failure to progress to the next level of the simulation. Failure is manifested by the demise of the simulated patient and success by the recovery of the patient at the end of the simulation.

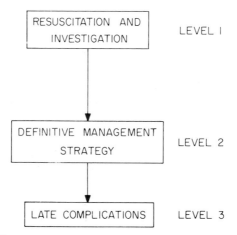

Fig. 1. Outline of program sequence.

Level One — Resuscitation and investigation

— Entry Module. Serves as an introduction for the student and initialises the various data structures used within the system.
— Control Module. Is responsible for accepting free text entry or, alternatively, for presenting menus for option or strategy selection and finally for transferring control to the selected module. The module also evaluates hospital time (real elapsed treatment time) as a function of the simulation system time and treatment time penalties that are encountered within other modules.This facilitates the display of a hospital time clock on the screen and the storage of the patient physiological evaluations on a time base of fixed increments of hospital time.
— Option/Strategy Modules. They are based on specific actions relating to either the investigation of or the intervention in the clinical problem (Figure 2). For each clinical scenario the modules may be specified as either:

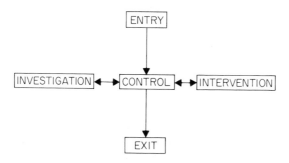

Fig. 2. LEVEL ONE: Problem definition and initial management.

— Essential. Successful negotiation of these modules is essential to meet the predefined medical criteria required to complete this level of the simulation and pass on to the next.
— Unnecessary. Several of the options or strategies may not contribute directly to the management of the patient in the simulation, though they may provide corroboratory information. These selections represent deviations from the optimal pathway without necessarily leading to failure within the simulation, and are in essence a measure of time wasted in the management of the simulated patient.
— Detrimental. Under certain conditions plausible options or strategies may adversely interfere with the progress of the simulation in a manner disproportionate to the apparent work or time involved. These modules are very likely to lead to failure within the level.

The completion of LEVEL ONE requires all essential modules to be negotiated and for the simulated patient to be maintained in a satisfactory condition as shown by the current physiological status. These parameters are finally checked by an exit module before the transfer of control to the next level.

Level Two — Definitive management strategy

Successful entry into this level should reflect an understanding of the clinical problems encountered in the simulation, so the logic of the situation can be assessed by an evaluation of the management strategies adopted. All modules at this level are interconnected, so that incorrect or inappropriate actions taken at this level, or the previous one, can be related to the circumscribed problem which is revealed (Figure 3). In this way the management strategies adopted by the student can be modified and channelled back towards the correct pathway where necessary.

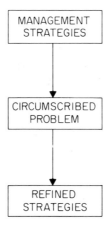

Fig. 3. LEVEL TWO: Development of management strategies.

Level Three — Late complications

Although the immediate situation has been dealt with, accommodation must be made for late problems associated with both the clinical problem itself and with its management, in a manner that reflects the possible clinical pathways. These are restricted, yet allow for both success and failure, either as an early or a late event after reoperation (Figure 4).

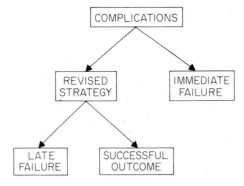

Fig. 4. LEVEL THREE: Final pathways.

Ultimately, failure within the simulation results in the options of either trying again from the start, or by viewing a summary of the problem with an explanation.

Clinical scenarios

Two simulations have been developed within the described structure: one for trauma, the other for gastrointestinal haemorrhage. The screen displays show personal information and clinical details as they are discovered, and comments appropriate to the last selected option, together with elapsed hospital time and patient physiological status. Decisions on options and strategies are made either as free text (Figure 5), or by menus that provide a means of prompting the student should difficulties arise (Figure 6).

To illustrate the problem use is made of the computer's graphics to display physiological parameters such as pulse and blood pressure (Figure 7), and to represent investigative actions such as fibre-optic gastrointestinal endoscopy or chest X-rays (Figure 8). These colour displays, together with sound, are used to enhance the realism of the simulation and to maintain the interest of the student.

Experience

These simulations have been tested at both undergraduate and post-graduate level, and they have been found to be both realistic and absorbing. Formal evaluation under routine teaching conditions in hospital is currently underway and early results have shown a significant improvement in performance on multiple choice question (MCQ) examination by students allowed access to the computer simulations.

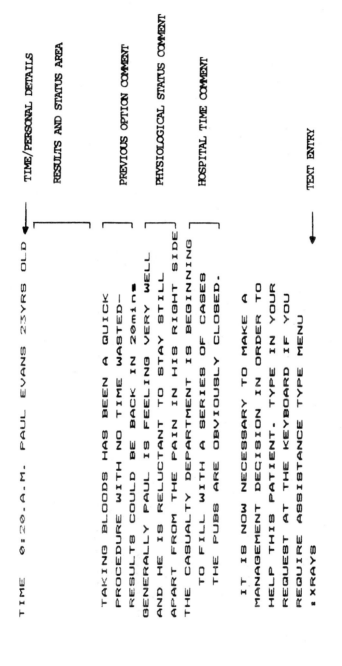

Fig. 5. Monochrome screen dump of colour display for the selection of options by free text input.

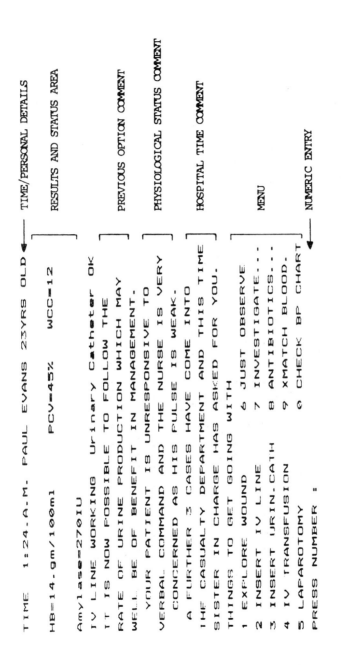

Fig. 6. Monochrome screen dump of colour display for option selection using a menu.

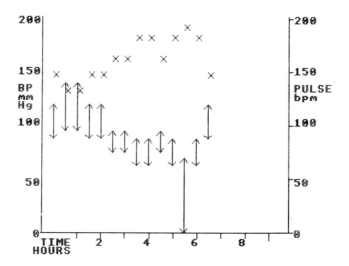

Fig. 7. Graphical representation of pulse and blood pressure (BP) chart reflecting patient's progress.

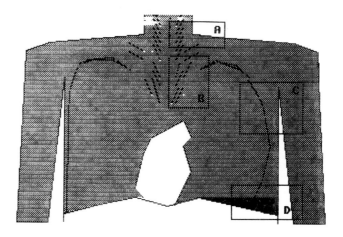

Fig. 8. Screen representation of a chest X-ray. Areas of interest are highlighted by boxes and lettered to enable further explanation to be given.

References

Bevan, N. and Watson, R. (Eds.) (1983) *Microtext for the BBC Microcomputer,* Acornsoft Limited, Cambridge.

Corbett, W.A. and Taylor, M.J. (1985) *A microcomputer simulated interactive clinical problem,* Lecture Notes in Medical Informatics, **25,** pp. 113-117. Springer-Verlag.

Dugdale, A.E., Chandler, D. and Best, G. (1982) *Teaching the management of medical emergencies using an interactive computer terminal,* Medical Education, **16,** pp. 27-30.

Geddes, C., Kendle, K.E., Selkirk, A.B. and Walker, W. (1983) *KEKEPI: A computer program for simulating the therapeutic responses of patients suffering from idiopathic epilepsy,* Medical Education, **17,** pp. 325-330.

Lakhani, A., Goldschmidt, J. and Clayden, G. (1984) *Computer aided learning-the development of interactive microcomputer based medical teaching programs,* Journal of Microcomputer Applications, **7,** pp. 345-348.

Murray, T.S., Cupples, R.W., Barber, J.H., Hannay, D.R. and Scott, D.B. (1976) *Computer assisted learning in undergraduate medical teaching,* Lancet, **1,** pp. 474-476.

Puntis, M.C.A. and Hughes, M.M. (1984) *The use of a BBC microcomputer in computer-aided learning,* Journal of Microcomputer Applications, **7,** pp. 353-356.

Zemper, E.D. (1973) *Computer assisted instruction in medical education.* Office Paper No 1973-1, Michigan State University, East Lansing.

11 / Front-Ends for Software Libraries — A Case Study

D. C. POUNTNEY and A. N. RICHMOND *Liverpool Polytechnic*

Abstract

The need for the front-ending of subprogram libraries for use in Higher Education Engineering and Science courses is outlined. A particular front-end is discussed for the specific case of solving simultaneous equations using the NAG FORTRAN library. The difficulties highlighted and desiderata for front-ends in general are considered. Finally, a sketch of a more ambitious scheme is given.

Keywords Front-ends, Software libraries, Numerical methods.

Introduction

The problems associated with the teaching of 'numerical methods and computation' to Engineers and Scientists in Higher Education are numerous. Discussions on syllabuses and teaching requirements for such Engineering and Science courses often centre around certain questions.

— Do Engineers/Scientists need to know a computing language? If so, which one is appropriate? Is a short intensive programming course satisfactory?

— Do Engineers/Scientists need to know any underlying theory behind numerical methods? Should they be more concerned with using software which incorporates sophisticated techniques to produce answers which can be analysed?

The answers to the above questions appear to vary across Higher Education establishments. From the authors' own experience, it would seem that many Engineering and Science Degree courses still require a computing language to be taught for use in the more specialist Engineering/Science topics and for research purposes, but it seems that in general the need for the language (whichever is chosen) is becoming less significant as more reliable teaching software becomes available. The growth of such software has been considerable in recent years and

---

Department of Mathematics, Statistics and Computing, Liverpool Polytechnic, Liverpool, L3 3AF

a catalogue of computer-assisted learning software for areas of numerical analysis has recently been compiled (Burkhardt and McLone, 1984).

If it is decided, however, that Engineers and Scientists need only numerical answers, it would seem more appropriate to develop user-friendly software, using current, sophisticated numerical techniques, that produces not only numerical answers (where possible) but also comments on these results (or lack of results). Such an approach can be adopted in part by teaching students how to access numerical subprogram libraries such as NAG, I.M.S.L., PORT, HARWELL etc.

The principal difficulties in accessing such libraries are:
— the user must be able to program in a language compatible with that of the library, e.g. FORTRAN when using the NAG library;
— the user must be able to select the appropriate routine;
— the user must be able to understand how to invoke the routine and relate it to the particular problem;
— even if on-line aid is available, it may be too technically sophisticated for the novice and anyway the user will often need to consult the library manuals which may be at too high a level.

The experiences gained in surmounting the above difficulties can be beneficial to some users but can also be unnecessarily arduous for those who require only to solve a problem involving a straightforward application of a particular numerical technique. A practical solution is to attach a 'front-end' to the library which will:
— select the appropriate routine after a question/answer session with the user;
— advise the user if no appropriate routine is available;
— if requested, execute the routine with data supplied by the user;
— display results and/or interpret any error messages.

Such a front-end could dramatically influence the amount of use of computational methods by non-specialists. The need for such a front-end for industrial use of large software libraries has already been outlined (Moralee, 1984).

In an attempt to formulate more fully the difficulties involved, Chapter F04 of the NAG FORTRAN library was chosen for a pilot scheme, with the front-end for the Chapter being written using the interface tool SYNICS (Guest and Edmunds, 1983). Details of this case study are discussed below together with the implications.

Solution of simultaneous linear equations — a case study

The NAG Fortran Library comprises a set of about 600 primary routines that solve mathematical and statistical problems. It is divided into chapters, each of which refers to a particular class of problem, e.g. the F04 chapter consists of a set of black box and other routines that deal with the solution of simultaneous linear equations.

There is an error reporting mechanism common to the library namely that an output parameter called IFAIL is set to a value that indicates the success or failure of the routine and reasons for failure in the latter case.

Chapter F04 was chosen for this study because it seemed likely at the outset to illustrate and highlight the problems involved in front-ending routine libraries whilst at the same time producing a suitably limited problem definition, when restricted to the black-box routines, such that the case study could readily be completed.

The systems tool SYNICS is a suite of FORTRAN programs which enables an expert to easily construct dialogue in a front-end so that a user can readily converse with the system. SYNICS also has the facility to interact with FORTRAN subroutines which is an obvious necessity in the present study.

A dialogue flow-chart is presented in Figure 1. A clear, concise introduction informs the user how the package works, what can be achieved and what help is available. The initial dialogue enables the user to either:
— find and execute a NAG routine;
— find and not execute a NAG routine;
— execute a NAG routine nominated by the user.

Whichever option is taken, once the appropriate NAG routine has been determined by the system, the data is requested. Matrix coefficients can be input either directly from the terminal or from named data files. Once data input is complete, the selected routine is called and the IFAIL parameter is examined on exit from the routine. If IFAIL = 0, the system informs the user that a solution has been determined and outputs the solution to either the terminal or a named file as desired. If IFAIL is not 0, an appropriate error message is passed to the user and possible remedial action is suggested. In either event the user then has the option of solving another problem or quitting the package.

At each stage, the construction of the system and dialogue was made with the convenience of the user in mind. Optional HELP facilities are available, both to aid passage through the package and to explain technical terms. Where appropriate, the data input by the user is validated by the system and the user is allowed to correct the input data. In the case of matrix input, the data is echoed by the system for user validation. The dialogue questions were designed so as to obtain the maximum amount of information with the least number of questions, subject to the requirements of clarity and data vetting.

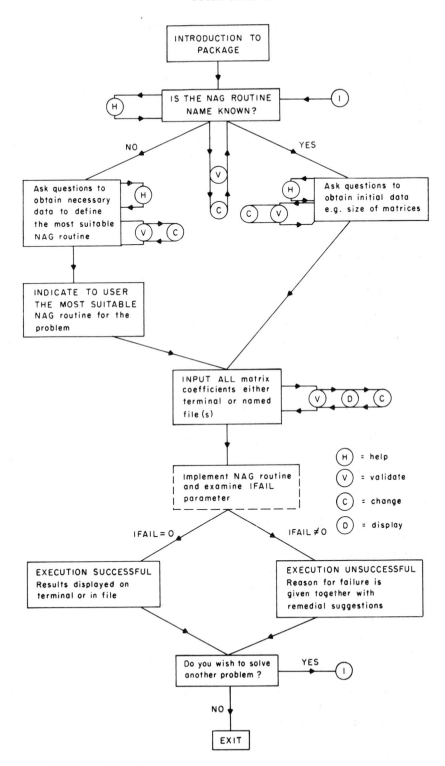

Fig. 1. Dialogue flow chart.

A typical system/user dialogue interaction is listed below.

Overview of this program

The program eases the use of "black-box routines" in chapter F04 of the NAG FORTRAN subroutine library, which are concerned with the solving of linear algebraic equations. Press any key to continue.

You may either select the NAG routine yourself or leave it to this program to select an appropriate routine.

After the questions of the dialogue have been answered and the data read in, from files or terminal, the program will call the selected NAG routine and report on its success or failure with details of the latter.

Help is available in the dialogue with selected technical terms.

Press any key to continue.

This program will attempt the solution of the equations Ax = b (or if there is more than one right-hand side vector, AX = B).

If A is square then its elements can be real or complex. Further if A is real there are routines to take advantage of its structure; for example when A is banded or symmetric positive definite. If A is rectangular then it must be real. Further the number of rows is assumed to be at least as large as the number of columns and the rank of A to be equal to the latter.

Press any key to continue.

This package solves a system of linear equations written in matrix form as AX = B. The solution is found using a NAG routine.

Do you know the name of the appropriate NAG routine? (YES/NO) (Type H for help)
N

Enter number of rows of matrix A. (Type H for help)
3

Change it? (YES/NO)
N

Enter number of columns of matrix A. (Type H for help)
3

Change it? (YES/NO)
N

Enter number of rhs vectors. (Type H for help)
2

Change it? (YES/NO)
N

Is your matrix real? (YES/NO) (Type H for help)
Y

Is A a real symmetric matrix? (YES/NO) (Type H for help)
N

Will an approximate solution suffice? (YES/NO)
(Type H for help)
H

Crout's method of factorisation is used to give either an approximate solution, saving computer time and storage, or an accurate solution, using the iterative improvement technique.

Will an approximate solution suffice? (YES/NO)
(Type H for help)
Y

THE ROUTINE BEING USED IS F04AAF

If matrix A is to be read from a file, type its name (XXXX.XXX).
If not, type NO
SING.TXT

Display matrix A? (YES/NO)
Y

TITLE OF MATRIX: MATRIX OF COEFFICIENTS

	COL 1	COL 2	COL 3
ROW 1	0.5000000E+01	−0.3000000E+01	0.4000000E+01
ROW 2	0.1000000E+01	0.1000000E+02	0.6000000E+01
ROW 3	0.1100000E+02	0.4000000E+01	0.1400000E+02

If the vectors B are to be read from a file, type its name (XXXX.XXX).
If not, type NO.
SING.TXT

Display matrix B? (YES/NO)
Y

TITLE OF MATRIX: MATRIX OF RHS

	COL 1	COL 2
ROW 1	0.2000000E+01	0.1000000E+01
ROW 2	0.1000000E+01	0.0000000E+01
ROW 3	0.4000000E+01	0.0000000E+01

STARTING EXECUTION OF F04AAF

A unique solution could not be found. This may be because
(a) the equations really do not have such a solution or
(b) they do have a unique solution but it was not found because of the limits of the computer arithmetic.

Perhaps a re-examination of the source of the equations might be beneficial.

A more technical explanation? (YES/NO)
Y

The NAG routine found that the matrix of coefficients was singular, possibly due to rounding errors.

Do you wish to solve another problem? (YES/NO)
N

We hope you have found the package useful. Good-bye.

Discussion and future developments

This final section contains a discussion of two problems common to the front-ending of any set of numerical routines as well as a problem common to an extensive and vital subset of such routines. An outline of a much grander scheme meeting the needs of both education and industry is also presented.

The first problem is what knowledge base to assume for the user. Even in this limited case study whose subject matter is relatively easy and well-understood and where users are well defined, the problem still arose. After some deliberation the user was assumed to understand the formulation and terminology of linear equations when expressed in matrix form, the concept of real and complex numbers and the meaning of matrix symmetry.

Those assumptions are reasonable but what about the meaning of a positive definite matrix, the condition of a problem, least squares solution, for example, all of which are fundamental to the subject? These concepts are not easy to explain in an elementary but succinct manner.

The second problem concerns the amount of data the user should be requested to supply. For instance, in the case study, the user could first supply the matrix and the program could deduce its order and structure. However, if a minimum data set is supplied, that implies that data validation is necessarily limited. For example only if the order and elements of the matrix are supplied can the user be prompted for the data and its completeness checked. The authors consider that prompting and validation are desirable and so opted not to use the minimum data set. It is worth noting that in other areas of numerical methods numerical experiments on the data prior to the selection of a routine may be essential; for example to determine whether a system of differential equations is stiff.

The SYNICS system eases the writing of dialogue and allows data to be entered and the results returned in an uncomplicated way. However, an efficient solution to a problem that did not arise in the case study has yet to be found. Many numerical methods operate on functions, e.g. numerical quadrature. How are these to be entered? Before NAG-SYNICS can be run it must be compiled but it is at run-time that data, including the function, must be entered. There is an associated problem: how is the user to specify the function if he does not know how to program?

The scheme outlined above is still being developed so although no results can be reported it is reasonably certain to be of use to the limited class of user for whom it is intended. However if one goes beyond that and considers its use for researchers or in industry it suffers from a major drawback. Although it is true that some numerical problems can be isolated from the application area e.g. quadrature, differential equations, optimisation (NAG/SYNICS Seminar, 1985), most often the numerical problem is subsidiary and embedded in an application and for these the scheme would be of limited value.

The software package is one answer to the contextual problem and although the approach requires little or no programming from the user and although the package is application-orientated, it does not possess the wide applicability of the subroutine library nor is it so easy to maintain and port.

What is needed is a system that combines the two approaches: an intelligent knowledge-based numerical software system which will cover a wide range of problems, converse in a language tailored to the problem area, have an inbuilt numerical consultant package, be able to build the program that attempts to solve the larger problem, store results and programs for later use and modifications, advise on the validity of results and have a variety of input and output devices. A proposal for such a scheme has been made to the Alvey Directorate by the Universities of Liverpool and Manchester, NAG Ltd., and Liverpool Polytechnic (Intelligent Knowledge Based Numerical Software Packages) in 1985.

It would take a considerable amount of of money and manpower just to develop a basic version of this scheme and to test its reliability. Meanwhile, front-ending libraries such as NAG is a worthwhile exercise both to ease the use of such libraries and to gain experience for the grander scheme.

References

Burkhardt, D. and McLone, R. (Editors) (1984) *Undergraduate Mathematics Teaching Conference,* Software Information Service, University of Nottingham.

Guest, S. and Edmunds, E. (1983) *Synics 1.5 — A Software Tool for Front-ending Applications,* In 'Intelligent Front-End Workshop 1', Bundy, Sharpe, Uschold and Harding (editors).

Moralee, S. (1983) *Intelligent Front-Ends,* In 'Intelligent Front-End Workshop 1', Bundy, Sharpe, Uschold and Harding (editors).

NAG/SYNICS Seminar held at Liverpool Polytechnic, February 1985.

Section 5

The papers in this session concerned the teaching of science subjects at undergraduate level where a computer is used to augment the process in the laboratory and in the classroom.

Professor Ogborn's opening paper set the scene for the first three papers in describing modelling techniques and the use of the relevant software. The essential feature, expressed in various ways by all the speakers was to separate out the conceptual thinking of the student from the routine mechanics involved in the initiation of the methods and the production of tabular or graphical results.

Dr. Borcherds brought out another interesting dichotomy of analytical and numerical methods, pointing out that, whilst much earlier pre-computer teaching involved the former simply because of the time factor involved in working out of numerical results, this limitation is now removed by the use of computers. Hence it is possible to deal with complex multi-body problems in physics not amenable to analytical solution.

The calculation and graphical abilities of the computer applied to engineering teaching were also demonstrated by Dr. Loader. He showed that CADCAM engineering teaching can be directed towards relevant commercial engineering experience through prepared programs and exercises leading to the solution of real engineering problems.

The question sessions reflected this interest in using the computer as a learning tool for modelling and design for science-based students where the emphasis lies in the results of such application to the learning ability and achievement of the student. In answer to one question Dr. Manning expressed a view supported by statistical study, that the success of a student's work in other areas can also follow from his achievement in grasping successfully the principle of computer-aid applied to mathematics.

Dr. Loader also confirmed the efficiency of this approach in answer to several questions on the application of his CADCAM design work for the engineering student.

An extensive study of the design language CAMTEK was not found essential for the initial learning stage; the ability to apply demonstration examples through a 'Help' resource proved adequate for project work.

Some general interest was shown by delegates in the viability of computer aided instruction of mathematics in a 'stand-alone' laboratory session. Dr. Borcherds answered this by confirming that the laboratory work is always associated with classroom work.

In his lecture Professor Ogborn introduced the advantages of cellular-modelling, relating this to spread-sheet operation but containing functions and graphics capabilities. This aroused interest amongst some delegates who saw this as a medium suitable for wide application, possibly reaching a lower age group; but the lecturer could not be specific on this point. He did however discuss a new possibility of block schematic development software in answer to one question, but stated that this type of facility is not yet generally available.

Ken Beauchamp

12 / Computational Physics for Undergraduates

PETER H. BORCHERDS *University of Birmingham*

Abstract

The increasing availability of computers, particularly of those with graphics displays, is having an impact on the teaching of physics: not just on how it is taught but also on what is taught. Until recently a number of conceptually simple topics have been excluded from undergraduate physics courses owing to their analytical intractability. With the availability of computers this exclusion need no longer apply.

Keywords Physics, Computer-assisted learning, Three-body problem, Chaos.

Introduction

For the past few years we have offered an optional course on Computational Physics to our undergraduate students (Borcherds, 1986). This course has been under continuous development to take advantage of developments in microcomputers with their excellent graphics facilities. In its current form the course comprises both lectures and laboratory work: the laboratory work is carried out on BBC microcomputers with colour graphics displays.

To some extent the topics which have been studied by physicists have been determined by the availability of suitable mathematical tools; this consideration has also strongly influenced the topics covered in undergraduate courses. Since the 17th century we have had available the powerful analytical calculus, which has enabled us to write down the differential equations describing a wide variety of systems. Calculus shows us how to write down such equations, but does not enable us to solve more than a very few of them analytically.

That a problem cannot be solved analytically does not mean that it cannot be solved at all: almost all such problems are capable of numerical solution, and numerical methods of solving differential equations were developed simultaneously with the invention of calculus. Such methods involve a large amount of computation, and yield less insight than an analytic solution, unless a large number of cases are solved.

This requirement of a lot of computing for a single solution, and a

---

Department of Physics, University of Birmingham, B15 2TT

lot of solutions for insight has considerably limited the coverage of numerical work in undergraduate physics courses. The easy availability of computers and particularly computers with graphical displays has made these considerations less restrictive, and we may in the future expect to see many topics of this nature entering mainstream physics teaching.

At the present we are witnessing a period of rapid change in the development and use of computers, and special courses on computational physics are needed to increase the awareness of the powerful tools now becoming increasingly available, and also an awareness of the limitations on their use: we have in mind here particularly the need to be aware of the various types of error term inherent in all numerical methods.

We omit from our definition of computational physics the on-line use of computers: the control of experiments and the collection of data. This use is extremely important, but involves different techniques from those we are considering here.

The course

The course has two aspects: it provides an introduction both to numerical methods and to the use of such methods in physics. The traditional teaching of mathematics to physicists concentrates on analytic methods: in the future there is likely to be emphasis on numerical methods as well.

We believe that physicists must not only be able to use ''library'' programs but that they must also have an appreciation of the methods those programs use. Such an appreciation will enable them better to interpret the results of such programs, and to assess their validity, and to decide whether a program needs modification to suit their needs. Most physicists are involved at some stage in their career in the writing of programs, and we believe that with a knowledge of numerical methods they will write better programs. We shall not here further discuss the numerical methods aspect of the course.

The second aspect of the course, namely the use of numerical methods in physics, covers a wide range of techniques and topics. Since we are here not primarily concerned with numerical methods, we shall attempt to classify the applications on the basis of the way the computer is used rather than on the numerical method being used. It is easier to provide examples than to classify them, but the following classification seems to the author to have some validity:
— direct solution;
— approximation methods;

— Monte Carlo methods;
— repetitive calculations;
— data processing.

We shall briefly explain what we mean by each class and then proceed to give illustrative examples of some of the classes.

Direct solution

Here the problem is solved as though the appropriate analytic tools were available, but numerical methods are used instead. We discuss an example in more detail below.

Approximation methods

An example is the perturbation method, where we "find" an analytic problem similar to the non-analytic one we wish to solve. Solutions of the non-analytic problems are then developed from those of the analytic one: usually this involves computation, but less than in a direct solution.

Monte Carlo methods

Monte Carlo methods involve the use of pseudo-random numbers and are analogous to public opinion surveys based on random samples. The use of such methods enables approximate solutions to be obtained for otherwise intractable problems: intractable because they would require an impossibly large amount of computing. The Ising model of ferromagnetism provides a suitable introduction to the method (Mouritsen, 1984).

Repetitive calculations

In repetitive calculations, which may be iterative or recursive, a simple calculation is repeated many times, perhaps a million times. There is no precedent for such calculations, and they are at present perhaps more of an art than a science, but hold promise of some exciting developments. We discuss an example in more detail below.

Data processing

This is a portmanteau heading for a number of methods, such as least squares fitting (regression) and the fast Fourier transform. Using computers to gather experimental data can swamp our comprehension: it is necessary to have methods of processing the data to reduce the quantity to a manageable amount.

Direct solution: the gravitational two-body and three-body problems

The formulation of these two problems is straightforward: the forces acting are the inverse square law gravitational forces between pairs of bodies and it is straightforward to write down the differential equations describing the motions of all the bodies.

The two-body problem, e.g. the motion of the earth and the sun (neglecting all the other bodies of the solar system, and indeed of the universe) can be solved analytically. The three-body problem cannot.

The two-body problem (Earth-Sun)

The solution of the earth-sun problem is that both describe elliptical orbits about their centre of mass, which is close to the centre of the sun, so that it is a good approximation to say the earth orbits the sun.

If an orbit is circular, the rate of rotation is uniform. In the case of an elliptic orbit, the rate of the rotation is determined by the "law of equal areas" due to Kepler: the effect of this is that the rate of rotation is greatest when the earth is closest to the sun. In the case of the earth its orbit is almost circular and this effect is small, but in the case of more elliptic orbits (e.g. Halley's Comet) the effect is very marked.

This law is familar to physicists and is learned early in an undergraduate course.

It is not possible to carry out laboratory exercises on gravitational two-body motions, so there is no direct way of demonstrating the law of equal areas. However, a simple program can simulate this, and the author still remembers with pleasure "discovering" this law by observing the orbit being plotted on a display: the rate at which the orbit was plotted gave the impression of continuous motion!

Thus, even in the case of a fully understood system, there may be pedagogic merit in a direct computer solution of the problem.

The three-body problem

The full three-body problem is intractable. A lot of effort has gone into the solution of what is called the restricted three-body problem, defined as follows.

— Two of the bodies, the primary and secondary, are massive, the third, the satellite of negligible mass.

— The primary and secondary move in circular orbits about their centre of mass.

— The motion of all three bodies is coplanar, i.e. the satellite moves in the plane of the circular orbit.

Even with these simplifying assumptions, the problem is not capable of analytic solution. The method of solution is to write down the differential equations describing the motions of the bodies (in the restricted problem, the motion of the third body only) and to solve them numerically.

What this involves, to describe the process loosely, is finding out at some instant where the three bodies are, and how they are moving, and from this to calculate the forces acting. This enables us to calculate the changes in the velocities, and to deduce where each body will be a short interval of time later. At this new instant the whole process is repeated, and from this repetitive calculation the motions of the bodies can be found. At each step the time interval has to be small enough that the truncation errors are kept within bounds.

The strength of this method is that it permits the solution of any such problem: its weakness is that it provides only a numerical answer, and if the same problem has to be solved with different starting conditions, it is necessary to repeat the full calculation.

The availability of graphics displays of solutions does help to increase the insight into the nature of the solution, as in the two-body example mentioned above.

The sling shot effect (Sun, Jupiter, Spacecraft). When a spacecraft passes close to a large body (Jupiter) its orbit is considerably perturbed. This effect has been used to give extra energy to all the spacecraft which have so far visited the outer planets.

Such a perturbation is easily modelled on a computer and provides a useful demonstration of the need to be able to control the size of the time interval at each step. Midway between the Sun and Jupiter a time interval of many "days" is acceptable, but close to Jupiter a time interval of a small fraction of a "second" may be required.

Repetitive calculations: playing with computers

Some of the ways in which computers are being used in physics could have been predicted, for example the direct solution of the three-body problem, but some of the ways would not have been predicted: they have arisen from people playing with computers. (NOT playing games on computers: that is a different story altogether!)

Playing with computers has a respectable precedent in recreational mathematics: mathematics done largely for fun, such as searching for big prime numbers, where there is no obvious application, and where the knowledge that some enormous number is a prime is of little theoretical interest.

Playing with computers can take a variety of forms: one of the simplest, and one which has proved surprisingly fruitful, is the endless repetition of a very simple calculation: this has led to such cases as the Henon attractor (Henon, 1976), cellular automata (Wolfram, 1984), the game of life (Berlekamp et al., 1982) and Mandlbrot's fractals (Mandlbrot, 1982).

One feature all of these have in common is their ability to generate attractive graphical displays: at present their relevance to physics is not always obvious, and their usefulness may turn out to be in biological rather than physical science.

In most of the cases, while the individual calculations are simple, they generate irrational numbers, so are unsuitable for mental arithmetic, and furthermore to obtain an interesting result involves between ten and a million repetitive calculations. Such calculations are feasible only with a computer (or a programmable calculator, which was used in at least one case).

Onset of chaos: turbulence

The flow of fluids at low speeds is known as streamline, and is relatively well understood. At high speeds fluid flow becomes chaotic, disordered or turbulent and is not well understood, the onset of turbulence is also not understood.

There has recently been the beginning of an understanding of the onset of chaos through studying the simple iterative relation (Kadanoff, 1983)

$$x_{n+1} = 4Qx_n(1 - x_n)$$

In this relation, we guess an initial value x_0, substitute it into the right hand side and thus calculate x_1. That value of x_1 is used to calculate x_2, and so on.

The ultimate behaviour of this calculation depends upon the value of Q. If Q lies between 0 and 0.25 the iteration rapidly converges to zero, while if it lies between 0.25 and 0.75, the iteration converges to $(1 - 1/4Q)$. For larger values of Q the behaviour is surprising.

If Q is slightly more than 0.75, instead of the iteration converging to a single value, the series jumps between two values, one less, the other greater than the predicted limiting value of $(1 - 1/4Q)$: we say that a bifurcation has occurred. At a slightly larger value of Q the series hops cyclically around four values: a further bifurcation is said to have occurred. As Q increases further, more and more doublings occur, but the values of Q at which this happens get progressively closer together and converge to a critical value, 0.8925. If Q is greater than this the pattern appears to be entirely chaotic, except at a few special values.

The connection between this simple iterative procedure and the onset of turbulence in fluid flow appears rather tenuous. However, it has been found that a similar sequence of bifurcations occurs in other cases, and that the values of the equivalent parameter (Q) at which such bifurcations occur are the same as for the above relation. Some of the cases displaying this sequence are other mathematical relations, but there are also physical systems behaving in this way too.

A physical system displaying this behaviour is a non-linear oscillator circuit, consisting of a choke and a diode: the diode behaves like a capacitor. The behaviour of a resonant circuit consisting of a choke and a simple capacitor is well known: if it is driven at its resonant frequency large voltages are generated across the components at the same frequency as the driving voltage. In the case of the non-linear circuit, the behaviour at small values of driving voltage are exactly as expected. However, as the driving voltage increases period doubling occurs: alternate voltage peaks in the circuit are large or small. As the driving voltage increases further, a further period doubling occurs: every fourth peak is the same height, and yet further period doubling occurs until eventually chaos sets in and there is no obvious relation between any peak heights. What is remarkable is that the ratios of the voltages at which the transitions occur are the same as those for Q in the simple mathematical relation above.

What is perhaps equally remarkable is that both the physical and mathematical systems display "windows of order" in the chaos: at certain values of the parameter (voltage) there is a three-fold pattern which is remarkably stable: other windows exist too, but their stability is less marked.

In this case we have an example of playing with a computer yielding a bonus of insight in an entirely unexpected field.

Iterative relations like the one we started with are sometimes used to solve non-linear equations. It was well known that such iterative methods worked only for certain ranges of parameters (e.g. Q less than 0.75 in the example). It took someone playing with a computer to realise that there was something of interest in the region of misbehaviour, Q greater than 0.75.

It is almost certain that observations of the period doubling effect of non-linear circuits had been observed many times before they were formally reported, but that, because there was no understanding, they were ignored.

There is a lesson in all this: that until some level of understanding of a phenomenon exists, the phenomenon will be ignored or discarded as undesirable. This particular example is a case where playing with the computer has led to insight into a problem which is analytically intractable.

Discussion

The increasing availability of computers with graphics displays is making a considerable impact on the teaching of undergraduate physics: not just in the way it is taught, but also in what is taught.

In this paper we have identified several ways in which computers are used in physics, and also identified a number of areas in physics in which a computational approach will result in qualitative changes in teaching, and, indeed, in our whole approach. We have attempted to demonstrate this with two very different examples: the direct numerical solution of the three-body problem and the iterative approach to chaos.

The first example uses a computer in an entirely predictable way: in the second the solution was found by an observant owner when playing with his pocket calculator (Feigenbaum, 1978).

References

Berlekamp, E.R., Conway, J.H. and Guy, R.K. (1982) *Winning Ways for your Mathematical Plays,* pp. 817-850. Academic Press.

Borcherds, P.H. (1986) *Physics Education* **21**.

Feigenbaum, M.J. (1978) *J. Stat. Phys.* **19,** pp. 29-52.

Henon, M. (1976) *Commun. Mathematical Phys.* **50,** pp. 69-77.

Kadanoff, L.P. (1983) *Fifth International School of Mathematical Physics,* Erice, Sicily: pp. 27-44.

Mandlbrot, B.B. (1983) *The Fractal Geometry of Nature.* Freeman.

Mouritsen, O.G. (1984) *Computer Studies of Phase Transitions and Critical Phenomena.* Springer-Verlag.

Wolfram, S. (1984) *Physica* **D 10,** pp. 1-35.

13 / Microcomputers in University Mathematics Teaching

ROBERT D. HARDING *University of Cambridge*

Abstract

Computer Aided Teaching of Applied Mathematics (CATAM) has been used in Cambridge since 1968. The computer is used in two principle roles, illustrative and investigatory. The distinctive feature of CATAM is its emphasis on the latter, requiring students to learn both programming and some numerical methods and to use these skills to undertake various computational projects. The benefits claimed are that the doing of these projects and the interpretation of the results lead to a thorough understanding of the topic concerned. Results of an evaluation study support this claim showing a significant improvement in examination performance. For many years the courses have not assumed any prior computing skills in students, but the advent of microcomputers has changed this assumption and led to a complete redesign of the courses. It is shown that projects which used to be done on a powerful minicomputer can be done on a standard BBC Micro. Examples are given from dynamics, electromagnetic theory, fluid dynamics and quantum mechanics. Software has been written to reduce the proportion of inauthentic labour required by students when programming, in particular graphics and numerical methods packages have been written. Use of this software on the BBC Microcomputer is described with examples.

Keywords Microcomputer, University Mathematics, Problem Solving, Project, Graphics, Modelling.

Introduction

At DAMTP (Dept of Applied Mathematics and Theoretical Physics), computing activities by students have been a significant part of our undergraduate courses since 1968. The name given to the project to develop these activities is CATAM (Computer Aided Teaching of Applied Mathematics).

CATAM has been fully described in various publications, the most recent being Harding (1984). This paper describes the work that has been done to adapt CATAM courses to using microcomputers, taking

Department of Applied Mathematics and Theoretical Physics, Silver Street, Cambridge CB3 9EW

account of the new degree of computing experience found amongst university students.

For completeness, and in order to make the arguments clearer to readers who have not heard of CATAM before, sections 2, 3 and 4 give a brief survey of the mathematics degree courses structure at Cambridge, the way that CATAM fits into this structure, and the objectives and justification of CATAM.

Relation of CATAM to other courses

The Mathematics Faculty offers a 3 year degree course, taught mostly in the traditional style using lectures and tutorials. In common with most British universities, students are not graded continuously during the year, but instead take an examination at the end of each academic year (May or June). The Mathematics examination always has 4 papers lasting 3 hours, each paper containing questions drawn from a wide variety of courses.

There are two mathematics departments at Cambridge, Pure and Applied. The CATAM courses are available in the second and third years and consist mostly of practical computing projects on topics chosen for their relevance to the other applied maths courses. In a typical project, students are given a resume of relevant theory and sometimes a few hints on how to proceed, and asked to write programs and get results which must be interpreted and discussed in a written report. The idea is that by undertaking this work students acquire a better understanding of these courses. Associated with the practicals there is a lecture course in each year whose purpose is to teach any numerical methods required for the projects, but the teaching of numerical methods is regarded as a means to an end. The lecture courses bear much the same relationship to Numerical Analysis as service mathematics courses for engineers (say) do to courses for a full degree in mathematics.

The CATAM courses are not compulsory. Ideally, a recommendation to the students that doing CATAM coursework would improve their preparation for the examination should be sufficient, but in practice it has been found necessary to offer more of an incentive. This takes the form of marks to be added to those obtained on the written papers, based on an assessment of the written reports.

Justification for computing

In the computing project work mentioned above the computer is being used in an investigatory role. Another role is the illustrative role, where the computer is used with prepared programs either by a lecturer during class, or by students in their own time. Typically these programs would be run several times with various parameters allowing the properties of the system represented by the program to be explored.

The most distinctive feature of CATAM is the prominence given to the investigatory role. It is far more demanding on time and concentration than the illustrative role and requires the student to learn both programming and some numerical analysis. However it can hardly be said that it is a disadvantage for an aspiring applied mathematician to learn these skills; in terms of career they may be amongst the most important taught.

CATAM is aiming to go beyond teaching these skills to using them to improve a student's understanding of certain topics through "Investigatory computing". For the justification, look at the purpose of applied mathematics, whether practised by engineers, scientists or applied mathematicians. It is to gain insight into, and therefore to be able to make predictions about, the real world. We may be talking about suspension bridges, aero-engines or black holes, but in this sense our objectives are the same. Mathematical models are built, whose usefulness is judged by how well they predict actual behaviour. Contrast the steps needed to do this using a computer to those needed when the model is purely analytic.

Computing approach

— devise mathematical model;
— decide on numerical technique;
— devise an algorithm and write program;
— run program, observe results, debug;
— interpret results, relate to real world;
— perhaps change the model and repeat.

Analytic approach:

— devise mathematical model;
— decide on mathematical techniques;
— carry out algebraic manipulations to get solution;
— investigate properties of the solution;
— interpret results, relate to real world;
— perhaps change the model and repeat.

The computer-based approach has two important advantages. First it allows greater freedom of choice for the model, as many well-posed mathematical problems have no closed form solution. Second, with the help of graphics the computer solution can directly supply the kind of qualitative information needed to help with interpretation.

There are disadvantages of course. Computing is time-consuming; as already mentioned, numerical and programming expertise are needed; and finally there is always the question of the validity of a computed solution.

The time needed for programming is one of the most important influences on the design of projects and of the software environment to be provided to help the student tackle them. The distinction between authentic and inauthentic labour (MacDonald et al., 1977) is a very useful one when projects are being designed. CATAM has adopted the policy that the detailed programming needed to produce graphs, for instance, is inauthentic labour, whereas the setting up of differential equations is authentic labour. This is a fairly general policy, but in other cases the distinction may well depend on the individual project. Another general policy is that the programming of standard numerical algorithms is considered inauthentic labour unless the subject of the project is that numerical method itself. A software environment is provided which reduces the inauthentic labour to a minimum; the two most important components are graphics routines and numerical routines, and a brief description of these is given in section 'Changing to Microcomputers'.

Returning to the subject of the validity of computed solutions, it should be noted that the same question should also be asked about results obtained by a traditional analytic approach, but over the years courses in applied maths have tended to avoid this question because natural limitations on time and the knowledge of the students forces lecturers to simplify problems enormously in order to deal with them at all. One advantage of numerical techniques is that many methods will work with a variety of similar problems: so that for example if it was felt that a non-linear term should be introduced into some differential equation to make it more realistic, then that is easily done on a computer.

There are two questions of validity: one is the question of the model itself, and the other is whether a solution, numerical or analytic, is the correct solution of the model. Both of these should combine to force the investigator to think very carefully about the solution, whether its features were expected and how they relate to the original model. The steps labelled 4, 5 and 6 tend to run into each other to produce a thorough understanding of what is going on.

The main educational purpose of CATAM is to exploit this effect: the projects cover a wide variety of topics and we think that each will help to reinforce the students' understanding of each subject in which a project is undertaken.

Evaluation

A certain amount of informal evaluation has been done, such as using questionnaires and interviewing a selection of students, and some of the results have been published (Harding, 1976). There has also been a more rigorous statistical approach (Johnson and Harding, 1979). The main conclusion was that the extra time students devoted to doing investigatory project work (learning the programming and numerical analysis needed, and doing the projects) had a positive correlation with their examination results. Students doing CATAM coursework were significantly better off; there was a consistent statistically significant difference in the examination performance favouring this group over the other students who had not chosen to do CATAM coursework. This was particularly apparent when the project work was included in the examination marks, but the effect was present even without including this work.

Some further questions of interest remain to be answered, and it could not be said that evaluation was complete. For example, one might ask if any type of sufficiently mathematical programming was beneficial, or whether the educational benefit was linked to the subject areas of the projects that a student attempted. It would be interesting to know which projects contributed most to a student's development and further how much of the contribution was due to the student having to write the program, or alternatively whether a complete program which the student only had to run would be just as effective.

What can be done with a microcomputer

At present the need to teach some programming and numerical analysis means that the first CATAM course (second year) is numerical method oriented. However the second course can assume these skills and so a wider selection of projects is available. Although in recent years the course has used a time-sharing minicomputer, all of the projects have turned out to be feasible on microcomputers. The next sections describe projects for both second and third years; the list is not exhaustive but it gives an idea of the range of the projects.

Solving the Schrödinger equation

This is a rich hunting ground for CAL and many program packages have been written (see for example, McKenzie, 1979). The CATAM approach is to describe the problem in sufficient detail to remind the student of his course notes, set up the actual equation to be solved, and leave the student to construct and test the program, often including graphics. An actual student solution for a one-dimensional potential well was given in Harding (1984). This used only 30 lines of simple BASIC, including comment, showing that such a problem does not place impossible demands on programming or numerical expertise. Other projects that have successfully been used include S-wave scattering, and searching for allowed energy bands in a periodic potential such as for an electron in a crystal lattice. Many other projects are possible, and many more are described in a recent book by Killingbeck (1983).

Differential equations

There is hardly a subject in applied maths that does not eventually require the solution of an ordinary differential equation. Even in fluid dynamics where the governing equations are partial differential equations in space and time, there are many special cases of interest where after some approximations the problem can be reduced to an ordinary differential equation. One example is the Falkner-Skan equation, which describes the behaviour in a boundary layer; this equation is third order and non-linear and analytical treatment is difficult. The essential behaviour of the equation can easily be discovered numerically. An example from dynamics theory is to simulate the motion of a spinning top; its equations of motion do not have explicit solutions as functions of time, but again the qualitative behaviour is easily reproduced numerically. In other subjects differential equations are of interest in themselves; for example the non-linear Van der Pol equation

$$y'' + \mu y' (y^2 - 1) + y = 0$$

for which a typical program is shown in Table 1 and the results in Figure 1. Other examples are shown in Figures 5, 6 and 7.

```
10 REM   Solve the Van der Pol equation
20 :
30 REM   Graphics routines L1-2D from
40 REM      "Graphs & Charts"
50 REM   Runge-Kutta ODE solver P.RK4
60 REM      from "Maths Toolkit"
70 :
```

```
 80 REM   Dimension arrays
 90 DIM   Y(1),y(1),f(1),k(1) 100 :
110 REM   set initial values
120 Y(0)=0: Y(1)=1: T=0
130 :
140 REM   ask for values
150 INPUT "mu = "mu
160 INPUT "stopping value of T = "Tend
170 INPUT "stepsize dT = "dT
180 :
190 REM   set ranges and draw axes
200 MODE 4: PROC#INIT(4)
210 ¢XL=−3: ¢YL=−3: ¢XH=3: ¢YH=3
220 PROC#AXES(0)
230 REM   move to first point
240 PROC¢MOVE(Y(0),Y(1))
250 :
260 REM headings
270 PRINT TAB(0,0);"Van der Pol"
280 PRINT TAB(0,3);"Plot y vs y'"
290 PRINT TAB(0,5);"mu=";mu
300 PRINT TAB(0,6);"Tend=";Tend
310 PRINT TAB(0,7);"dT=";dT
320 :
330 REM   loop with until T>=Tend
340 REPEAT
350    PROCRK4(1,dT) : REM order=2
360    PROC¢DRAW(Y(0),Y(1))
370    UNTIL T>=Tend
380 END
390 :
400 REM ----------------------------------------------------------
410 REM PROCfn defines derivatives for
420 REM   y" + mu*y'*(y ↑ 2−1) +y = 0
430 REM Variables: y(0) is y,
440 REM            y(1) is y'.
450 DEF PROCfn
460   f(0) = y(1): REM y'=y(1)
470   f(1) = −y(0) −mu*y(1)*(y(0) ↑ 2−1)
480 ENDPROC
```

Table 1. Program to solve Van der Pol's equation.

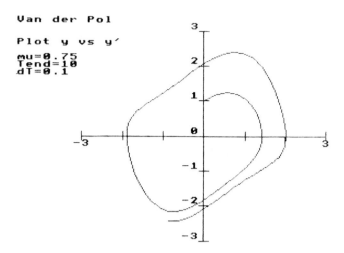

Fig. 1. Phase plane plot of solution to Van der Pol's equation.

Electromagnetic theory

Many problems in elementary electromagnetic theory are potential problems, often requiring the solution of Laplace's equation. Table 2 is a program for the parallel plate capacitor, and the solution in Figure 2 shows the field lines. Solutions like this help students to understand the validity of approximations which are often not fully justified in standard text books. Analytic techniques can describe the far field of a radiation source, and the near field; Fourier techniques allow the intermediate field to be obtained, showing how the transition occurs.

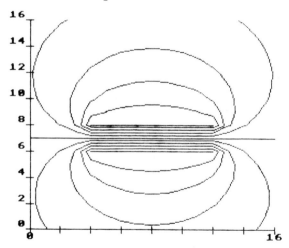

Fig. 2. Equipotentials produced by the program in Table 2. Notice that between the plates the equipotentials are virtually parallel to the plates, justifying the usual approximation which ignores the field in the rest of the region.

```
10 REM    Program PLATES
20 REM    uses L1-2D and L1-CNTR from "Graphs & Charts"
30 :
40 DIM    ¢W(32,32): IM%=32: JM%=32
50 K=1.7: REM    Gauss-Seidel acceleration parameter
60 :
70 REM    zero the mesh
80 FOR J%=0 TO JM%: FOR I%=0 TO IM%
90        ¢W(I%,J%)=0: NEXT:NEXT
100 :
110 REM    set potentials of +1 and -1 on plates
120 REM    plates are at J=J1%, J2%, between I=I1%, I2%
130 J1%=14: J2%=16: I1%=12: I2%=20
140 FOR I%=I1% TO I2%
150     ¢W(I%,J1%)=-1: W(I%,J2%)=1: NEXT
160 :
170 REM    dW is max change in values each sweep
180 REM    do Gauss-Seidel sweep until dW small
190 it=0: REPEAT: it=it+1
200   dW=0: PROCgauss: PRINT it;"   ";dW
210   UNTIL dW1E-4
220 :
230 REM    then plot contours of central area
240 FOR J%=0 TO 16: FOR I%=0 TO 16
250     ¢W(I%,J%)=¢W(I%+8,J%+8): NEXT:NEXT
260 MODE 4: PROC#CN2D(4,16,16,8)
270 END
280 :
290 REM --------------------------------------------------------
300 REM    Gauss-Seidel routine
310 DEF PROCgauss
320 FOR J%=1 TO J1%-1:FOR I%=1 TO IM%-1
330      PROCpt: NEXT:NEXT
340 J%=J1%:FOR I%=1 TO I1%-1: PROCpt: NEXT
350          FOR I%=I2%+1 TO IM%-1: PROCpt: NEXT
360 FOR J%=J1%+1 TO J2%-1:FOR I%=1 TO IM%-1
370      PROCpt: NEXT:NEXT
380 J%=J2%:FOR I%=1 TO I1%-1: PROCpt: NEXT
390          FOR I%=I2%+1 TO IM%-1: PROCpt: NEXT
400 FOR J%=J2%+1 TO JM%-1:FOR I%=1 TO IM%-1
410      PROCpt: NEXT:NEXT
420 ENDPROC
430 :
```

```
440  DEF PROCpt: LOCAL D
450  D= ¢W(I%,J%−1)+¢W(I%+1,J%)+¢W(I%,J%+1)
                                          +¢W(I%−1,J%)
460  D= D/4 − ¢W(I%,J%)
470  IF ABS(D)>dW THEN dW=ABS(D)
480  ¢W(I%,J%)=¢W(I%,J%)+K*D
490  ENDPROC
```

Table 2. Program for the parallel plate capacitor.

Linear systems

Fourier series and Fourier transforms can be done numerically, illustrating for example the Gibbs phenomenon and allowing students to obtain a qualitative feel for the relation between a function and its transform, as shown in Figures 3 and 4. Although investigative projects on these subjects have been devised, they are also suitable for the illustrative approach, and the author has recently published a book and software on this subject (Harding, 1985).

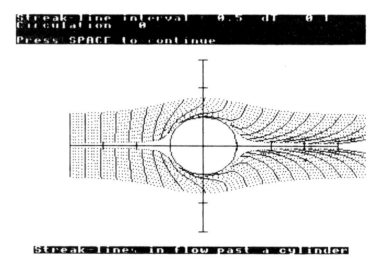

Fig. 3. Fourier transform of a function.

There are many other subjects for projects, and further examples are shown in Figures 5, 6 & 7.

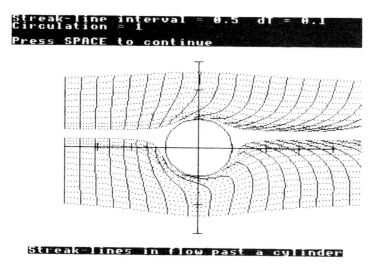

Fig. 4. Discrete Fourier transform of a periodic function. These results are proceeding to a limit in which the top function will be periodic. Notice that the transform shows a discrete structure, which in the limit will become a sequence of delta functions, corresponding to the Fourier series for the periodic function.

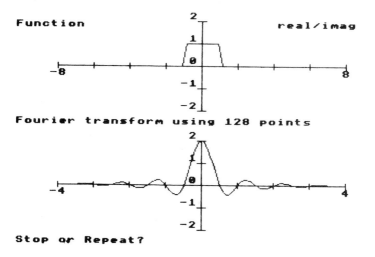

Fig. 5. Steady two dimensional flow past a cylinder (1). A number of fluid particles (dots) are tracked to follow the evolution of a dye-line or streak-line (lines). Flow is from left to right. In this case there is no circulation around the cylinder. Notice how an initially straight streak-line is distorted permanently, even though the flow is symmetrical.

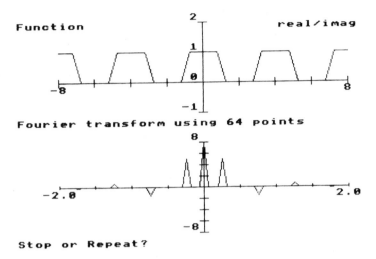

Stop or Repeat?

Fig. 6. Steady two dimensional flow past a cylinder (2). This shows a similar situation to Figure 3, but this time there is circulation round the cylinder. Notice that symmetry about the x-axis has been lost, and that the two stagnation points, which were at $y = 0$, $x = -1$ and $x = 1$, have now moved upwards along the cylinder boundary.

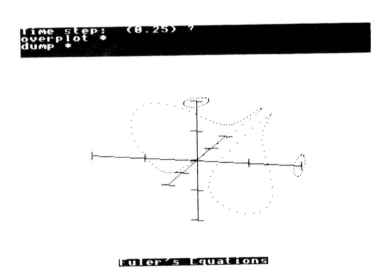

Fig. 7. Rotation of a rigid body under no forces. There are four trajectories in this figure. Each dot represents the orientation of the angular momentum of the body with respect to the principle axes of inertia of the body, which are parallel to the coordinate axes shown. Note that in Newtonian dynamics the angular momentum remains constant and the axes rotate.

The importance of microcomputers

In this paper microcomputer means a machine costing under £1000, thus distinguishing it from a personal computer. The most obvious advantage of microcomputers over larger machines is their cheapness, and in that narrow sense it could be said that they will make little difference to teaching in those institutions that are already well provided with equipment, where costs have not been a barrier. At first sight it might even seem that micros are a backward step in these circumstances, because they are far less powerful and often have rather primitive operating software. (This has been true up to date, but of course better and cheaper products are being produced all the time.) However, present day micros have adequate power even for degree level mathematics teaching purposes, as shown.

The really significant effects of microcomputers in university teaching are side-effects of the price. They are:

(a) user oriented design;

(b) increased availability including personal ownership;

(c) increased student familiarity with programming.

(a) User oriented design comes about partly through marketing considerations and partly through the capabilities of micro technology. Manufacturers of microcomputers and personal computers have made this one of their major sales lines: "user-friendliness" is the keyword. In the simpler types of home micro where only one programming language is supported, usually BASIC, there is close integration between the operating system and the programming language. From the user's point of view this is excellent; it leads to unified documentation for the system as a whole, and makes the whole process of writing and editing programs very much simpler to a degree that can seldom if ever have been reached in say a typical university time-sharing system. An excellent example of this is the cursor copy/edit feature of the BBC Microcomputer. When used with BASIC, a line with a simple mistake can quickly be corrected. We have some evidence that features like this raised expectations amongst users. For the five years up to 1985 the CATAM time-sharing system had used Tektronix terminals, whose construction did not allow a backspace/delete style of editing. Until the 1983/84 year, student questionnaire responses never produced any criticism of the editing features that we used, but in that year there were several complaints on this score. It would seem that the commercial pressures of designing computers has achieved a far better product from an educational point of view than years of conventional mainframe development.

(b) Increased availability is a consequence not just of price but of suitability. The BBC Micro has all the features needed for school computing apart from training with standard commercial packages, and is perceived in many universities as a useful general purpose system. It makes a versatile and cost effective graphics terminal for a mainframe, and DAMTP now has at least 10 apart from any being bought for use with CATAM. This micro seems to be in widespread use in the higher education sector generally, in the author's experience. This phenomenon makes a welcome change from previous patterns in higher education: de facto standardisation will obviously make it much easier to exchange software and ideas.

Personal ownership is high too. In DAMTP over 80% of the academic staff have a micro, mostly BBCs; it has long been realised that significant research computing does not always need megabytes of memory, and that it is much more convenient to leave a program running overnight on a micro if necessary than to come into the Department at midnight in order to log on to the mainframe. Nor is one subject to service schedules which may not be arranged for your convenience. In DAMTP many of the teaching staff use exactly the same computing equipment as their students, and there is every reason to hope that this will lead to much greater use of computers in teaching. Many students too have their own micro or easy access to one, at home for example. From shows of hands in lectures, fewer than 5% have BBCs and perhaps 20% have a Sinclair Spectrum or equivalent. This is personal ownership, but a very large proportion have some experience of BBC Micros from their schools. If these numbers grow, then in themselves they are a very strong argument for basing coursework on microcomputers. A survey of previous experience and personal microcomputer ownership amongst our mathematics undergraduates is being carried out in 1985/86.

(c) Increased student familiarity with programming is coming about as more schools install micros and teach programming; personal ownership is contributing to this too of course. At present nearly all our students have some minimal programming experience before coming to university, and we anticipate that within the next two or three years we will be able to rely on over 75% being fairly experienced. For CATAM this is very good, because it means that the students can do investigative projects at an earlier stage. The high proportion who have had previous experience of using a BBC Micro also has important implications for our courses.

Changing to microcomputers

Software for investigative computing on BBC Microcomputers has already been written and published. The following two publications are important components of the software environment, and as discussed in the section 'Justification for computing' they help to reduce some of the inauthentic labour involved in doing the projects. The graphics routines (Harding, 1982) cater for all usual mathematical needs such as $x-y$ plotting, contour maps, and wireframe views of functions of two variables. The mathematical routines (Harding, 1986) include finding roots, finding maxima and minima, spline interpolation, numerical integration, solving ODEs (as used in Table 1), Fourier transforms, solution of linear equations, and matrix eigenvalues and decomposition. Examples of their use are shown in Figures 1–7.

A microcomputer laboratory with 24 networked BBC Microcomputers was installed in DAMTP during 1985 and from October 1985 it has been the main resource for CATAM coursework. The third year course was subjected to careful review but kept its previous form. The second year course was considerably changed, and now contains only two compulsory exercises (on numerical methods), and eight investigative projects of similar style to those used in the third year from which four must be chosen. Some programming skills will be assumed; to cater for those who have no previous programming experience, a voluntary course will be available in the first year, requiring at most 10 hours work, enabling newcomers to learn BBC BASIC and familiarise themselves with the system.

The educational value of CATAM is clearly established. Thanks to the advance of technology CATAM's equipment needs can be satisfied very cheaply; our students are starting courses from a higher level of computer literacy than ever before, and our lecturers are more closely in touch with the software that students are using. This means that many of the obstacles to learning more about applied mathematics through computer projects are being overcome, and so it is hoped that more time can be devoted to the projects. CATAM should be able to look forward to an important step forward in effectiveness.

References

Harding, R.D. (1976) *Evaluative development of a computer assisted learning project.* Int. J. Math. Educ. Sci. Technol. **7**, pp. 475-483.

Harding, R.D. (1982) *Graphs and Charts on the BBC Microcomputer,* Acornsoft Ltd, Cambridge.

Harding, R.D. (1984) *CATAM Revisited.* Comput. Educ. **8**, pp. 113-125.

Harding, R.D. (1985) *Fourier Series and Transforms,* Adam Hilger Ltd, Bristol.

Harding, R.D. (1986) *A Mathematical Toolkit: Numerical Routines with Applications in Engineering, Mathematics and the Sciences,* Ellis Horwood Limited, Chichester (publication due 1986).

Johnson, D.C. and Harding, R.D. (1979) *University level computing and mathematical problem solving ability.* J. Res. Math. Educ. **10**.

Killingbeck, J.P. (1983) *Microcomputer Quantum Mechanics,* Adam Hilger Ltd, Bristol.

MacDonald, B. et al. (1977) *Computer Assisted Learning: its educational potential* — Chapter 3 in Final Report of the National Development Program in Computer Assisted Learning, ed R. Hooper, CET.

McKenzie, J. (1979) *CAL in Physics: Simulations,* in Chapter 6 of "Learning Through Computers", Tawney D.A. (Ed.), Macmillan, London.

14 / Undergraduate Use of CADCAM

ALAN J. LOADER and STUART R. TURNBULL
University of Lancaster

Abstract

This paper outlines a scheme of work used in the Lancaster University Engineering Department, which incorporates the use of a CADCAM package within a ten week design-build-test project. Within this scheme, the learning curve is shortened by using the facilities of the package itself to perform interactive computer tutoring of its commands and capabilities.

Keywords Computer-assisted instruction, Simulation, Learning Pace Acceleration.

Introduction

Historically, engineering undergraduates have been taught to program in one of the high level languages, such as FORTRAN, ALGOL etc. In their careers as engineers, they have then been responsible for using these languages to build mathematical models of particular processes, solve problems and analyse data. Increasingly, however, computer manufacturers and third party software houses are supplying software packages to carry out many of the problem solving and analysis tasks required by engineers. With the advent of high resolution graphics in the early 1970's, computer aided design (CAD) and later, computer aided manufacture (CAM) packages started to become available. Initially, these ran on mainframe computers and were very expensive. However, with the introduction of mini — and micro-computers, the price of individual packages has fallen to match the price of hardware.

The required engineers' skills have thus moved from software writing, to the effective use of software packages. So how can undergraduates be taught to use these packages and with what aims and objectives? Commercial CADCAM packages often require a long learning curve, and this is usually acceptable where they are in daily use in industry. However, student exposure to these packages is usually 2-3 hours per week and students often forget detail from one week to the next. Thus, a student cannot be expected to become fully conversant with a package; instead the intention must be to instil a feel for the capabilities of such packages, together with some computer literacy.

Department of Engineering, University of Lancaster, Lancaster LA1 4YR

The CADCAM facility

The Department has a number of Olivetti M24 personal computers, each with 10 Mbyte hard disc drive, 8087 maths co-processor, colour graphics and digitiser tablet. These are networked together (Clearway) and to a printer, colour plotter and tape punch. The software installed in each computer includes BASIC, FORTRAN and PASCAL compilers, AUTOCAD (2D draughting), ANSYS (2D finite element stress analysis), CAMTEK (2½D Numerical Control machine tape preparation) and some CAL packages, e.g. visual vibrations.

The installation was chosen having drawn on our experience gained over the previous five years. For the first three of these, the students wrote the Numerical Control programming codes and directly entered them into the Numerical Control milling machine used. Later, students used a version of PATHTRACE, running on Commodore PET computers, to aid the production of the codes. The decision to use PCs rather than the department's VAX 11/750 computer was based on requirements of accessibility and response time.

The design-build-test project

The Engineering degree course at Lancaster bases its practical work on design-build-test projects, each of one term duration. In addition, there are a limited number of single afternoon, self-drive demonstrations. During their first year the students, in small groups, undertake a structures project, an electronics project and a fluid mechanics project. In their second year they undertake a heat transfer project and either a microprocessor or pre-stressed bridge project, depending on their intended third year specialism (civil/mechanical/electronics). In their third year each student undertakes a major individual project of his/her own choice.

The heat transfer project consists of the design of a staggered tube heat exchanger, as in Figure 1.

This is followed by the generation of the program to drive the department's Beaver Numerical Control milling machine, which is used to machine the header tanks. The final stage is the assembly and test of the complete unit. The students are given a specification which the design has to achieve, given the air/water input temperatures and flow rates. They are required to calculate the size of the tube array and the number of water passes across the heat exchanger. This then determines the hole array, and the number and shape of pockets in each header tank.

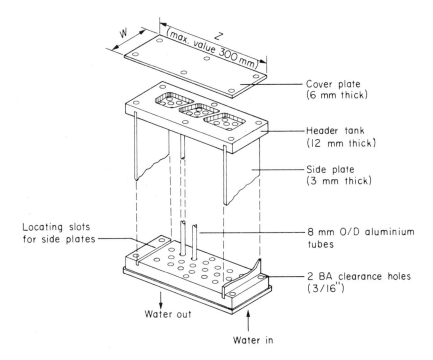

Fig. 1. Heat exchanger assembly.

The CADCAM package

CAMTEK (Malvern) produce industrial software packages for the preparation of programs to drive Numerical Control lathes, milling machines, flamecutting machines, punch presses etc. The user writes in a high level language and the program is converted to BS 3635 code by 'post-processing' software.

Initially, the user inputs commands to create the geometry of the component. As each command is entered, the resulting geometry is displayed in the large graphics window, as shown in Figure 2.

Eventually, it is intended to eliminate this stage by transferring the geometry from the AUTOCAD package, which allows for faster generation of the geometry. The user then inputs the machining parameters such as cutting speed, feed rates and tool diameters. These are followed by machining commands such as PROFILE and DRILL. These powerful single commands will drive the cutting tool around the outside/inside profile of a component or drill a large array of holes. The

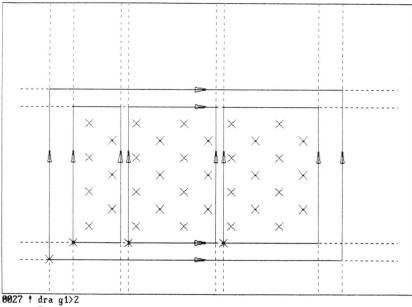

0027 ! dra g1>2
0027 !

Fig. 2. Header tank geometry.

cutter path is displayed on the screen together with the component, as in Figure 3. The user can view the cutter path from various directions to check for clashes with fixtures holding the component. Once satisfied with the tool path, the user calls the post-processing software to automatically generate the machine code to drive the NC machine. This can be transferred electronically or by punched paper tape.

The criteria used in selecting the CAMTEK package were based on experience of using PATHTRACE and Olivetti's GTL3V CAM software (in consultancy work). The latter used unbounded geometry to create the component's shape, and we have found this to be easier to teach than the former's sequential line/curve method. It was considered essential to have in-program editing and part program execution, so that mistakes could be identified and corrected without having to terminate program generation. CAMTEK met all of these requirements and had the added bonus of allowing the user to re-write standard machining commands and modify the post-processing software to suit particular requirements. It is also possible to create additional commands, by writing a named macro/subroutine, and store them in the macro library file. This last capability has been used by the authors to create a POCKET command, which causes the cutting tool to remove all the material from a pocket or cavity in a component, as in Figure 3.

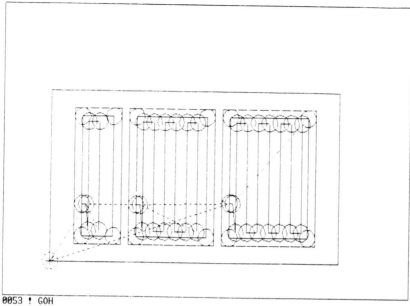

0053 ! GOH
0054 * ▌

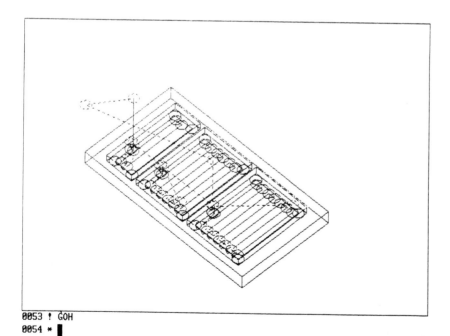

0053 ! GOH
0054 * ▌

Fig. 3. Geometry and cutter path.

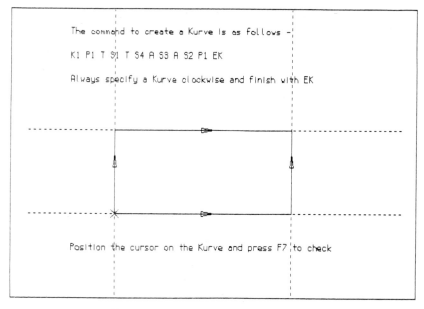

Press CR to continue

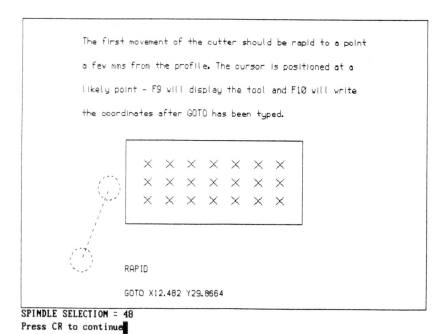

SPINDLE SELECTION = 48
Press CR to continue

Fig. 4. Tutorial program pages.

This macro is 110 lines long and generates cutting tool movements by searching for the edge of the pocket, in a direction determined by the aspect ratio. The tool is then driven from side to side within the pocket, leaving excess material on the periphery for a final profiling cut. Despite the power and user-friendliness of the software, the user manual leaves a lot to be desired, as is often the case with proprietary packages.

Application

The seventy second year students work in pairs on the project, for one afternoon session of three hours per week. It was decided to teach the students how to use the package by hands-on instruction, rather than by lectures. Once this decision was made, individual tutoring by members of staff was ruled out because of student numbers. A handout was considered but, because of the package's facilities of creating text on the graphics screen (used for dimensioning) and asking for input from the user (used for parametric geometry), it was decided to use interactive tutoring on the computer.

Two tutorial programs were written by the authors. One describes geometry creation and the other the machining commands. Pages of text and graphics are displayed in sequence to illustrate the commands input in a typical programming run. Figure 4 shows two such pages.

The student responds to the instructions on the screen by the use of the cursor on the digitiser tablet and the keyboard function keys. The student is then invited to write his/her own program. At any time the student can re-run the tutorial to check the use of commands. This computer based instruction is supported by a much reduced version of the user manual, produced in the department, to enable the parameters of each command to be checked. Using this method of instruction, students have been able to write programs to machine the header tanks after about five hours tuition/practice.

Conclusions

The use of interactive computer tutoring has proved very successful. The students enjoyed the project and were motivated to use the computers outside timetabled periods. They quickly learnt to use the system and could rapidly revise at the beginning of each session using the tutor programs. The loading on members of staff was correspondingly reduced. It was found that the students tended to refer to the tutor programs rather than use the manual. As a development, it is intended to incorporate the tutor programs within the package via a HELP macro, which the student can call up from within his/her own program.

15 / Computational Modelling in Science

JON OGBORN *Institute of Education, University of London*

Abstract

Three programs and their uses for computational modelling as part of science education are discussed. Two are special purpose educational modelling packages; the third is the commercial spreadsheet. It is argued that iterative (dynamic) models have a particular value in teaching theoretical structures and concepts in science. Examples given include population growth, dynamics, electric circuits, optics, chemical equilibrium and homeostasis.

Keywords Micro-computer, Utilities, Modelling, Learning Process, Problem Solving, Science Education, Model construction, Spreadsheet.

Programs for making models on computers

This paper discusses some programs which have the potential to ease an important problem in science education, namely getting pupils into theoretical thinking. We have not done too badly in getting them into empirical ways of thinking, into having pupils contribute to the planning and carrying out of experiments. But theory tends to remain the sole province of the teacher: for pupils something to be learned, not something to be thought about, let alone invented.

One of these programs is the Dynamic Modelling System (Ogborn, 1985), which was developed initially for use in the Revised Nuffield Advanced Physics course (Nuffield, 1985-6), but which is now finding uses in other subjects. Another is the group of commercial programs usually called Spreadsheets, of which Visicalc was the first and perhaps best known. A third is a new system which is rather like a spreadsheet, but designed for educational use. We call this the Cellular Modelling System and it is being developed in our Department by David Holland.

All have several things in common. All look at computational modelling as calculating in steps, with a model being a sequence of steps which is repeated as necessary. Thus they deal with a wide class of problems: most differential equations and finite difference models. Such models may be called dynamic models. Secondly, all are tool-like

Institute of Education, 20 Bedford Way, London WC2 0AL

programs, which provide the user, whether pupil or teacher, with a powerful set of possibilities, but which do not tell the user what to do with these possibilities. In particular, this feature encourages the gradual building up of models from simple and inevitably inadequate beginnings, to more complex and less inadequate later versions, so that the pupil may play some part in the actual development of theory, being less a passive spectator as theory is unfolded.

Such programs should be seen in the context of the existence of a number of computer modelling languages, which may offer more power at the cost of greater complexity. One which can be regarded as a direct precursor is the MODL system (Hartley and Lewis, 1982), developed for use in secondary and higher education.

What is a computational model?

Consider rabbits breeding on an island, having babies which themselves grow up to have more babies. To compute the new number of rabbits in one generation we need something like:

RABBITS = RABBITS + BIRTHS
GENERATION = GENERATION + 1

The model is dynamic because it repeats the same calculation generation after generation, taking the previous values through to the next step. We need to work out the number of births in each generation: one possibility is simply

BIRTHS = FERTILITY * RABBITS
RABBITS = RABBITS + BIRTHS
GENERATION = GENERATION + 1

With its constant fertility, this model gives exponential growth. Figure 1 shows how this model can be set up on the Dynamic Modelling System, to be discussed in the next section, the points on the graph showing the values at each iteration. Notice that because the model is formulated in step by step terms there is no need for any explicit use of exponential or logarithmic functions, so that what is usually considered rather difficult mathematics may become more easily accessible. An obvious improvement is to introduce deaths:

BIRTHS = FERTILITY * RABBITS
DEATHS = MORTALITY * RABBITS
RABBITS = RABBITS + BIRTHS − DEATHS

giving exponential decay if mortality exceeds fertility. However, if the population grows, it cannot grow indefinitely, as the rabbits will run out of food. We can model a maximum carrying capacity by making the fertility (or mortality) depend on the rabbit population. Adding

FERTILITY = (1 − RABBITS/MAXIMUM) * FO

gives the familiar logistic population growth curve, as shown in Figure 2. Seen as a sequence of differential equations with analytic solutions, the models discussed so far present considerable difficulties. Seen as step by step computational models, their difficulty arguably increases more slowly with increasing complexity. Furthermore, if the fertility FO is made greater than unity, we see a new effect, with the model bifurcating as the population oscillates above and below the maximum. Larger values of FO give further bifurcations and then chaos, as shown in Figures 3 and 4. Such fluctuations between generations of insect populations are not unknown.

The point of these examples is to show what dynamic models are, and to emphasise how from simple starting points we can, without great increase in difficulty, quickly reach rather sophisticated models. Adopting the computational point of view can alter one's perception of the difficulty of building theoretical models.

The dynamic modelling system

The dynamic modelling system is designed to be a flexible and general purpose 'model processor'. Models are written in BASIC, but without line numbers, as seen in Figure 1 or 2. The system attaches line numbers and programs itself to run the model, automatically placing it in a loop. Initial values are similarly written as lines of BASIC, as seen in Figure 3 or 4, and can thus include computations such as X=SIN(ANGLE) or N=RND() as well as assigning numerical values.

For writing models and giving initial values a simple but powerful screen editor is provided. Values are changed just by erasing a number and entering another. Models can be similarly modified at will; in addition lines can be reordered by moving them up or down on the screen. Models or parts of models stored on disc can be read in to the current model at the screen cursor position.

The names of models stored on disc can be called up on the screen. The current model can be saved, or stored models can be inspected or deleted. Models on disc store graph or table parameters as well as model and initial values.

When a model is run, results can be presented graphically as in Figures 1 to 4. Quantities to be plotted can include functions of vari-

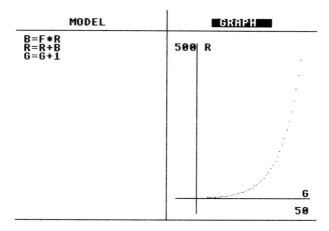

Fig. 1. DMS: Exponential growth of a population.

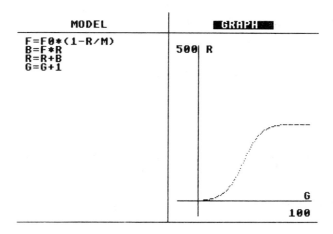

Fig. 2. DMS: Limited population growth (logistic).

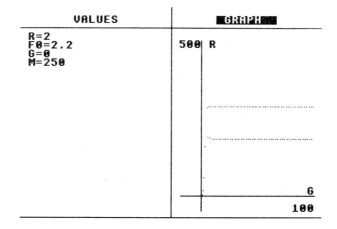

Fig. 3. DMS: Limited population growth, showing bifurcation.

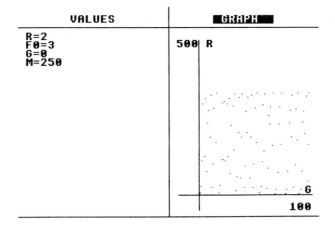

Fig. 4. DMS: Limited population growth, developing chaotic variation.

ables (e.g. LOG(R)) as well as any specified variable. The graph axes can be moved around the screen and their scales altered. Alternatively, results can be presented as numerical tables.

The system presents two 'scratch pads' on the screen. Either pad can be employed at any stage for any of the various system uses as described above. In summary, these uses are:

MODEL	writing a model
	changing a model
	reading a model stored on disc
VALUES	giving initial values to variables
	changing initial values
GRAPH	plotting graph
	setting graph axes and scales
TABLE	tabulating numerical output
DISC	directory of models on disc
	saving models to disc
	inspecting models on disc
STATUS	reports existence of model, values,
	graph scales and variables.

The user thus has the option to display side by side at any time model and values, model and graph, values and graph, pairs of graphs with different initial values, etc. Another possibility is to edit a model whilst showing the original. A single pad option is available if one wants a larger simpler display.

Errors are trapped and an error message is displayed, showing the line of the model or values where the error occurred. One can exit from the program at any time, with the option to start afresh or continue with the present model.

The system requires at least a single disc drive. The system disc contains the system programmes and help files, being supplied with a user guide appropriate to a wide variety of users. Models are stored on model discs, either supplied by the user, or bought for a specific subject together with a teachers' guide. A model disc and guide is available for Advanced Level Physics, and others for Chemistry, Biology, Economics, and Geography are in progress. The system was published in Spring 1985 by Longmans for the Nuffield-Chelsea Curriculum Development Trust, in versions for the BBC microcomputer, Apple II and IIE, and RML 380Z and 480Z.

Dynamic models in physics

Radioactive decay and decay of stored charge

Clearly, radioactive decay is not unlike a dying rabbit population in the previous example. We might write

```
D = L * dT * R
R = R - D
T = T + dT
```

where R is the number of "surviving" radioactive nuclei, D is the number that decay in time dT, and L dT is their "mortality rate". To reflect the random nature of the decay, we could try

```
P = L * dT
D = 0
FOR I = 1 TO R: IF RND(1)<P THEN D = D + 1: NEXT I
R = R - D
T = T + dT
```

which gives each of the remaining nuclei a probability P to decay in time dT. Figure 5 shows this model and its output.

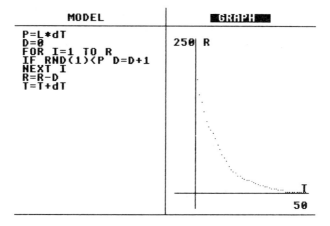

Fig. 5. DMS: Random decay.

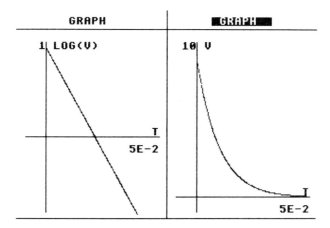

Fig. 6. DMS: Decay of potential difference across a capacitor with additional logarithmic plot.

The decay of charge on a capacitor is very much the same:

V = Q / C
I = V / R
Q = Q − I * dT
T = T + dT

Figure 6 shows how the system can give a logarithmic plot, comparing it side by side with a direct plot of voltage against time.

Through such examples, it would be important to bring out that quite generally one gets exponential change if the rate of change of a quantity is proportional to its present value, in the cases discussed above but also for problems of cooling, viscous damping, or of resource depletion. What is brought out in teaching using analytic solutions by the repeated appearance of the same function needs to be shown by comparing families of models, if one uses computational models.

Dynamics

If a ball is at position X, then

$$X = X + V * dT$$

just increases X at each step in proportion to the velocity. Acceleration A increases the velocity:

$$V = V + A * dT$$

Thus

$$V = V + A * dT$$
$$X = X + V * dT$$
$$T = T + dT$$

gives the Euler approximation to the solution of the second order differential equation of motion. If our problem is that of free fall, we compute the force and then the acceleration:

$$F = -g * m$$
$$A = F / m$$
$$V = V + A * dT$$
$$X = X + V * dT$$
$$T = T + dT$$

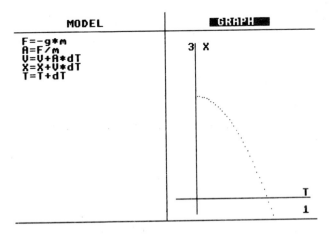

Fig. 7. DMS: Free fall.

Figure 7 shows the model of free fall, plotting X against T. It is easy, and instructive, to define kinetic and potential energies and plot them, or to plot V against T. Figure 8 shows the effect of replacing the first line by the new force law

F = −k * X

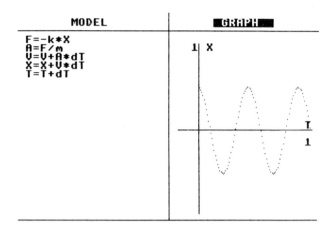

Fig. 8. DMS: Harmonic oscillator.

This gives, with no other change, a model of a harmonic oscillator. One may point the moral that all dynamics problems are the same, except for their force laws. Damped motion can now be studied, adding a frictional term such as −FR*V to the force law. Frequently the difficulty of integrating equations containing damping terms prevents any serious study of friction; here the emphasis can be on the physical nature of the frictional term in the force law.

Models in two dimensions are longer but perhaps not very much harder. Thus a projectile could be written as:

FX = 0 : FY = −g * m
AX = FX / m : AY = FY / m
VX = VX + AX * dT : VY = VY + AY * dT
X = X + VX * dT : Y = Y + VY * dT
T = T + dT

To get a gravitational orbit, the radial distance R is given by

R = SQR(X ↑ 2 + Y ↑ 2)

and the radial force F by

    F = −G * M * m / R ↑ 2

so that X and Y components of force can be found from

    FX = F * X/R: FY = F * Y/R

(X/R and Y/R being cos0 and sin0 respectively). The rest proceeds exactly as for the projectile. To go over to alpha scattering requires a change of only the force law, now written

    F = Q * q / (4 * PI * E0 * R ↑ 2)

with a positive sign indicating a repulsive force.

Such examples could help to bring out some of the essential unity of classical dynamics, in which the same equations with variations on the force laws produce a wide variety of behaviour from the same underlying structure. It should help in attaining such a perspective that the computational models require no knowledge of (for example) equations for conic sections.

More circuit problems

The simple capacitor discharge model can also be used to show the effects of a sinusoidal or square driving voltage on an RC circuit, for example:

    V = V0 * COS(w * T)
    VC = Q / C
    VR = V − VC
    I = VR / R
    Q = Q − I * dT
    T = T + dT

The phase difference between VR (across R) and VC (across C) is readily shown. If inductance is added, as in the model shown in Figure 9, the solution oscillates.

Optics

The diffraction pattern of a single slit may be modelled by dividing the slit into a number of small slices, and adding waves with correct phase for each slice, at a given point on the screen. The summation of waves can be written in a loop inside the model, with the iteration of the model itself moving from point to point across the screen.

The diffraction grating with infinitesimal slits is essentially the

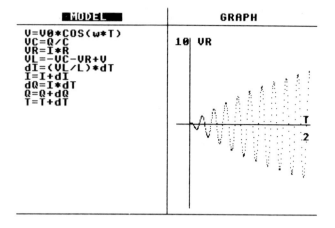

Fig. 9. DMS: Driven LCR circuit, showing resonance.

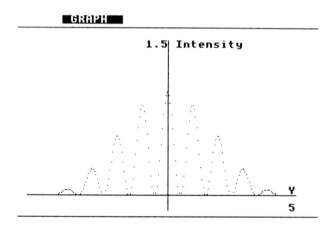

Fig. 10. DMS: Interference from a double slit.

same problem. The two ideas combine in a model for a number of slits each of finite width. Figure 10 shows output for a model of two finite slits.

From decay to chemical equilibrium

A simple approach to chemical equilibrium might first consider the decay of species A into species B:

    dA = rate * A
    A = A − dA
    B = B + dA

Then B can be made to decay into C:

```
dA = rate1 * A
A = A - dA
dB = rate2 * dB
B = B + dA - dB
C = C + dB
```

This is the problem of a radioactive series, and we can watch B first rise and then fall. We approach equilibrium if we make the product C the original species A, so that A converts to B and B is then converted back to A:

```
dA = rate1 * A
dB = rate2 * B
A = A - dA + dB
B = B + dA - dB
```

This last model reaches an equilibrium which depends on the two rates, the amounts of A and B at equilibrium being such that equal amounts go in each direction. More realistic chemical models with several reactant and product species can then be introduced, the equilibrium principle remaining the same.

Uses of spreadsheets in science teaching

The spreadsheet has become one of the most popular business tools, being used for financial modelling. However, the idea can readily be exploited in teaching science.*

A spreadsheet is an array of cells, in each of which there may be a numerical value, which may be calculated from the values of other cells. The sheet is calculated row by row in sequence, so that the pattern of cells is an implied program. Thus the rabbit population model could look like:

```
Fertility
0.1
Rabbits        Births
100            10
New Rabbits
110
```

Initially, the cell containing the number of rabbits would be set to an initial value. The cell for births is told to calculate the product of fertility and number of rabbits, and the cell for the new number of rabbits to add births to rabbits. When the new number of rabbits from the first

---

* [see also Catterall and Lewis, *J. Comp. Asst. Learn.* **1**, 3 (1985) Ed.]

iteration is known, the cell for the number of rabbits is altered to take on the value of the cell holding the new number, thus making a loop in the model. From then on, every recalculation of the sheet will make a further iteration.

Clearly, all the foregoing examples can be implemented on a spreadsheet in this way. An advantage over the Dynamic Modelling System is that one can watch the values of all the variables all the time; if this would be distracting it may be possible to place just those which are wanted in one or more display windows. A disadvantage is that few spreadsheets have any real graphic capability, so that one has to watch numbers changing, not the form of a curve developing. This may partially be overcome by using a system in which the spreadsheet is integrated with a graphics package, though it will not generally be possible to watch both at the same time.

Another, more complex, iterative use of a spreadsheet might be the body's sugar — insulin system, as suggested in Figure 11. If the blood sugar level is greater than some fasting level, insulin is secreted at a rate proportional to the difference. Sugar in the blood is metabolised at a rate proportional to the product of the insulin and sugar levels. Some insulin also naturally degrades, at a rate proportional to its level. With suitable values the system returns to equilibrium after a sugar feed.

If the sugar level falls below the fasting level (as it does when running, for example), sugar is secreted from the liver (the pathway is not represented here). Thus the system also comes to equilibrium from below. Effects of feeding sugar or injecting insulin can be studied, and

```
INSULIN          AND       BLOOD      SUGAR      LEVELS

        0.00 SUGAR FED

    fasting                 sugar                insulin
     level                  level                 level
    100.00                 141.13                  0.48

    insulin                insulin               insulin
   injected               secreted              degraded
     0.00                   0.04                   0.05

                           sugar                 sugar
                          secreted               metab
                            0.00                   0.67

      new                   new
     sugar                insulin
     level                 level
    140.46                  0.47
```

Fig. 11. Spreadsheet: Insulin and blood sugar.

instabilities corresponding to diabetes can be modelled. Thus we see how rather complex systems, which (unlike the dynamic modelling system) can easily accommodate arbitrary inputs at any step of the computation, can be modelled. Similar examples from totally different fields would be water accumulation and runoff with variable rainfall, or models of economic production and consumption.

A spreadsheet can also be used as an equation solving tool. Thus for example finding the values of concentrations which satisfy an equilibrium constant,

$$K = [A]^a \, [B]^b \, / \, [C]^c \, [D]^d$$

starting from initial values of the concentrations is analytically non-trivial. One alternative is to find the values by trial and error on a spreadsheet set out as below:

amount to react

x

stoichiometry:	a	b	c	d
concentrations	A	B	C	D
correct	current			
equilibrium	calculated			
constant	constant			
K	K'			

Starting with initial values of concentrations A, B, C and D, their values are then set to A − ax, B − bx, C + cx, and D + dx, where x is the amount chosen to be reacted. The value K' which these concentrations give is then immediately visible, and one can react more, or reverse the reaction, to get nearer the correct value K. It is helpful to show calculated values of ln K and ln K', and for acid-base equilibria, the pH, as in Figure 12.

A final example of chemical uses of the spreadsheet is for calculations of chemical equilibrium. A classic example is the Haber process.

Figure 13 shows a calculation for a temperature of 298 K, total pressure 1 atmosphere. Column D, rows 13-15 show the entropy changes to the chemicals as one mole of nitrogen combines with 3 moles of hydrogen to make 2 moles of ammonia, calculated from the standard molar entropies in column C. The net entropy change for the chemicals is negative (cell D19), but the entropy change of the surroundings (D21) is positive, the total entropy change in the standard state (D24) being positive. However, if the partial pressure of one of the species differs from one atmosphere, its entropy per mole has added to it −Lk ln p, and cells F13 to 15 contain these corrections, calculated from partial pressures entered by the user in cells E13 to 15. By

```
ACID - BASE    EQUILIBRIUM

    Amount to
     React:
     0.000

                           ACID          HION          ANION

    stoichiometry            1             1              1


    concentration          1.956         0.044          0.044

       ln Concn            0.671        -3.119         -3.119



            Ka                 K (for current  values)
         0.001             0.001

          ln Ka            ln K             pH
         -6.908           -6.909          1.355
```

Fig. 12. Spreadsheet: Acid–base equilibrium.

```
.........A.........B.........C.........D.........E.........F
..1       HABER PROCESS
..2
..3
..4    Enthalpy                              L      6.02E23
..5     change       92000                   k      1.38E-23
..6      Temp          298                   Lk     8.3076
..7
..8
..9                          Standard   Standard   Partial    Further
.10                          entropy    entropy    pressure   entropy
.11    Event      moles      per mole   change     atm        change
.12
.13    Lose N2     -1        191.4      -191.4     0.0153     -34.74
.14    Lose H2     -3        130.6      -391.8     0.0458     -76.83
.15    Gain NH3     2        192.5       385       0.9389      1.05
.16
.17
.18            Standard State:           ------   Alter by:    ------
.19    entropy change of  chemicals     -198.2               -110.52
.20
.21    entropy change of  surrounds      308.72
.22
.23    total change of  entropy          ------    total      ------
.24            (standard state)          110.52    entropy      0.00
.25                                      ------    change     ------
.26
.27
.28                                    equilib constant K      599560
.29
.30                                            ln K            13.30
.31
.32    Gibbs' free                            Lk ln K         110.52
.33    energy change
.34    (standard state)        -32936         LkT ln K        32936
```

Fig. 13. Spreadsheet: Chemical equilibrium Haber process at 298 K, 1 atmosphere total pressure.

adjusting the partial pressures of the three gases, one can search out values which make the total entropy change zero, that is, which are equilibrium values. In Figure 13, the ratio of nitrogen to hydrogen is held at 1 to 3, and the total pressure at 1 atmosphere. The equilibrium constant is then given by

$$K_{p=pNH_3}^{\,2} / p_{N_2} \, p_{H_2}^{\,3}$$

Here is a case where one can experiment quickly, using the spread-sheet, with a variety of values, in a way which would be much too tedious for hand calculation.

The Cellular Modelling System

The Cellular Modelling System is one we are currently developing, in the hope of making modelling accessible to younger pupils than those for whom the Dynamic Modelling System is suitable. It can be thought of as like a spreadsheet, in that the contents of an array of cells are calculated in a fixed sequence, displaying the results.

In most spreadsheets, however, one must refer to a cell by its coordinates and calculate cells by expressions such as "A2*B3" which do not at once convey the meaning of the calculation. In the Cellular System each cell can be given a name which labels its value, so that a cell called "speed" would be calculated by "distance/time", where "distance" and "time" refer to other cells. In effect, the system is an array of functions (in the computational sense), each having a name, parameters and yielding a numerical value.

In practice, this is much more elementary than it sounds. A model is built up by asking what one needs to calculate, and how, making a cell for each step. The cells each have four slots:

name	for	CLOCK
method of calculation	example	CLOCK + 1
comment		seconds
present value		60

In this example, a cell has been called "CLOCK". A clock ticks, adding 1 to its value in each unit of time, so its output is entered as "CLOCK + 1". Units can be put in the comment slot. Initial values are just entered as numbers in the output value slot.

A cell can be asked to display its value graphically as well as numerically. Thus the example of products of decay or of chemical equilibrium discussed above can be set up so as to show the amounts of all the reactants and products simultaneously (Figures 14 and 15 show these two models).

Model name: DRAUGHT

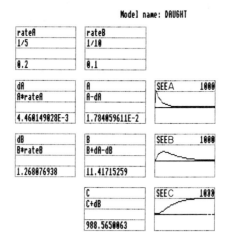

rateA	rateB	
1/5	1/10	
0.2	0.1	

dA	A	SEEA 1000
A*rateA	A-dA	
4.460149028E-3	1.784059611E-2	

dB	B	SEEB 1000
B*rateB	B+dA-dB	
1.268076938	11.41715259	

	C	SEEC 1000
	C+dB	
	988.5650863	

Fig. 14. Cellular Modelling System: Radioactive decay with a decaying daughter product.

Model name: CHEM

rateA	rateB	
1/5	1/10	
0.2	0.1	

dA	A	SEEA 1000
A*rateA	A-dA+dB	
62.5000006	312.5000019	

dB	B	SEEB 1000
B*rateB	B+dA-dB	
62.49999964	624.9999974	

Fig. 15. Cellular Modelling System: Elementary case of approach to chemical equilibrium.

A very simple example of its use is to watch random numbers being averaged and coming to a steady mean as more and more are taken, using an array of cells such as:

COUNT	NUMBER
COUNT + 1	RND(10)
counter	random number
500	7

TOTAL	MEAN
TOTAL+NUMBER	TOTAL/COUNT
total so far	present average
2580	5.16

The array can be calculated cell by cell in 'slow motion', or can be made to pause after each calculation of the whole array, as well as running continuously. Cells can also be designated to take their values from keyboard entry at each iteration.

It is too soon to say much about the system's possible classroom uses, but it is hoped that the combination of meaningful names and graphic output will make it easy to use for elementary work. It is currently restricted to sixteen cells, but even so manages to run in the highest resolution mode on the BBC microcomputer. On a 16-bit machine with more memory it could be made much more powerful still.

Conclusions

The present article is concerned simply to illustrate some of the range and variety of things which can be done with various modelling programs, whether 'educational' or 'commercial'.

We do have some limited experience of their use in schools. One research study (Wong and Robson, 1985) has shown that A-level Physics students in England can quickly learn to use the Dynamic Modelling System, even if they know no BASIC beforehand, and shows some evidence of clearer thinking and of willingness to tackle questions about differential equations. In research just starting we are looking at the possibility of using this system, and the Cellular Modelling System, with younger pupils. Teachers seem to welcome the systems, and to find them easy to use; we have examples of teachers without previous computer experience writing their own models within an hour or so of starting to learn the system.

New developments include attempts to involve teachers of other disciplines, particularly Chemistry, Biology, Geography and Economics. We think we have noticed here an important problem: where a school subject (such as Economics, but also Chemistry) has traditionally relied as little as possible on formal mathematics, the possibilities of mathematical representations have become 'hidden' from teachers — one does not consider what seems impossible. So we are told that modelling of this kind, while accessible to pupils, and while part of the subject itself, does not 'belong in the subject at this level'. Perhaps Physics was the easy subject in which to start to try to reinstate the value of theory.

References

Hartley, R.J. and Lewis, R. (1982) *A computer language system for model building and experimentation,* Int. J. Math. Ed. Sci. and Techn., **13,** 4, pp. 391-400.

Nuffield (1985-86) *Revised Nuffield Advanced Physics Teachers Guide 1; Students Guide 1,* Longman 1985; *Teachers Guide 2; Students Guide 2,* Longman 1986.

Ogborn, J. (1985) *Dynamic Modelling System* (System disc and Physics Models disc), Longman Micro Software.

Wong, D. and Robson, K. (1985) *School Science Review,* Summer 1985.

Section 6

The first two papers in this session addressed issues of managing computer-based learning. That of Beer concerned some of the administrative problems encountered in teaching computer science when one moves from a mainframe to a microcomputer environment. The motivation behind this development is associated with parallel trends in the commercial world. Where students are to be given direct experience of popular commercial PC packages, such as Lotus 1-2-3, there are attendant problems of managing copies of the software and project data files. The solution adopted in the pilot study at Liverpool was one intended to reflect principles of database management, with data files being stored in hierarchically organised directories on a host VAX computer, to which the students' PCs were connected.

Beilby's paper concerned the establishment of a supportive environment within which mathematically-oriented programming could be nurtured. The context was that of a relatively traditional Mathematics Department attempting to integrate a new micro-computer laboratory into its undergraduate teaching programme. This integration was assisted by a concurrent review of undergraduate teaching generally. A striking feature of this development was the fostering of collaborative programming, investigative and problem-solving work among the students, as a result of their perception of the lab as a resource which was theirs alone. Also noteworthy was the speed with which students rejected CAL materials that they saw as too didactic or patronising (or which stifled their own initiative).

The paper of Makinson and Morarji described the design of a new CAL authoring system, KAS, which paid clear testimony to the principles of good software engineering one associates with the University of Kent. Considerable emphasis was placed on the portability of the system. This was facilitated by writing a component to translate KAS statements into C sourse code, by selecting Unix as an operating environment, and by handling output (including graphics) in a device independent manner. A second feature of the system was the ease with which external subroutines could be attached to the KAS teaching programme; a benefit to mathematical users in particular. On-going enhancements to the system included the incorporation of prepared teletext frames, three-dimensional plot files and the handling of non-standard mathematical or scientific symbols.

In discussion it was recognised that the coding of a tutorial programme is only a small part of the CAL design task. The best authoring language will not improve poor educational decisions. One might hope for higher-level software tools to become available, which might assist in the design and specification phases of CAL software creation.

Peter Goodyear

16 / File Management In Practical Classes Using Microcomputers

MARTIN D. BEER *University of Liverpool*

Abstract

This paper describes some of the experiences of managing an intensive set of practical classes in a microcomputer laboratory. As practicals have become more sophisticated, it has been found necessary to provide students with both programs and data at the start of each practical.

Suitable methods of managing and maintaining the material that the students require have to be developed, as do arrangements for collecting in the completed work so that it can be accessed. Some of the experiences in running this type of course are discussed, together with the measures now being implemented to overcome previous limitations.

A logical arrangement of personal computers is described, where the programs and data that are required for an individual practical are transferred to the students' microcomputers, as required. Communication is provided to other computer facilities, so that if data is better stored elsewhere, it can be collected automatically, and passed on to the student without his necessarily knowing where it has come from.

Keywords Microcomputer, Practical, File Management.

Introduction

The widespread use of microcomputers has made a significant change in Computer Science teaching. Students now expect an immediate response from the computers that are available for their use, rather than queueing up to use a single teletype, or worse still waiting for a batch monitor to compile and run their program before returning the output to them.

This has allowed course organisers to arrange a far wider range of practicals than was previously the case, when the majority of practical time had to be used for programming practice. At the same time, industry has taken to using microcomputers for small-scale computing

Department of Computer Science, University of Liverpool, PO Box 147, Liverpool, L69 3BX

activities, which were previously either performed manually, or were undertaken by the data processing department as a low priority or only after a long delay. This has led to the development of simple, easy-to-use but highly sophisticated general-purpose applications packages which can be used as a basis for practical work, which will introduce many of the topics that will be covered in depth in later courses.

Until recently both the microcomputers designed for the commercial market, and the packages themselves were far too expensive for classroom use. This was because it is necessary to equip a classroom with several systems, each with the same software, which will be used for only a few hours a week, whereas both the computers and the packages were priced for the office market, where the same program would be run for the majority of the working day.

Recent price changes in the sixteen-bit microcomputer marketplace caused by a fall in demand and consequent overproduction, together with a more enlightened approach to the education market by the larger software suppliers has changed this.

The use of microcomputers in commerce can be broadly divided into the following applications:
— word processing,
— spreadsheets,
— small database applications, and
— small-scale accounting.

This limited number of different applications, together with the emergence of a few highly-successful standard hardware configurations has allowed independent software suppliers to design sophisticated program packages which allow computer users to develop their own applications without having to write programs.

Considerable effort has been expended in developing training materials which are designed to teach students and office workers how to use the packages available (Lotus, 1984). Little has however been reported so far on how these packages can be integrated into computer science courses. This is unfortunate since particularly in the areas of data analysis and databases introductory practicals at an early stage in the course would allow quite complex concepts to take root and grow over a much longer period than is usually the case.

The current situation

Extensive use has been made of microcomputers within the Department of Computer Science at Liverpool for a number of years. This has included both using them as individual computers and as quite sophisticated teaching workstations attached to central computers providing a specialised teaching service (Charlton, 1985).

All this work has been based on the Acorn BBC microcomputer, of which there are about eighty within the department. Whilst this was a highly appropriate choice at the time, the design has not developed as expected, and is therefore now looking very dated. The choice of a non-standard hardware configuration and operating system mean that the software packages under discussion are not available for this machine, and the substitutes offered have neither the facilities required, nor the backup in terms of teaching materials, books and manuals. Also, as memory prices have fallen, it has become possible to provide microcomputers which can handle realistic amounts of data at an economic price for classroom use.

The developments already discussed have allowed the Department to institute a pilot study to investigate how these objectives can be achieved. Even with the reduced prices now ruling, it is not possible to provide enough microcomputers and software for the first year honours Computer Science practical classes. A smaller joint honours group has therefore been chosen. This is the Accountancy/Business Studies/Economics and Computer Science group, as the class size of about twelve students can be sensibly split into two groups. Each of these groups spends about half the classroom time working on the new practicals, whilst the other works on a suitable selection of problem taken from the associated class for single honours Computer Science students.

The microcomputers chosen for the pilot study were IBM Personal Computers running:
— a spreadsheet (Lotus 1-2-3) and
— a database package (DBase III).

It is intended that the students will eventually analyse data that has been collected for administrative purposes, and which is stored on the University's central computers. The exact data that will be used has currently not been finally decided since there are problems of confidentiality. These will be solved by extracting the required information before it is made available to the students. In the meantime, special datafiles have been generated, that contain dummy information.

The use of information that is already available in machine-readable form means that an effective method of file transfer is required. In addition to the transfer of data, the main computers can be used to store the majority of the programs that will be required by the students. Whilst this cannot be done completely because of the software suppliers' attempts to limit piracy, much of the disc copying, that has formerly been a necessary preparation for this type of practical, can be avoided.

File transfer facilities

Early attempts at providing the file management facilities required involved the use of commercial personal computer networks (specifically BBC microcomputers connected by means of ECONET) or an advanced terminal emulator, which includes downloading and file transfer facilities (Acorn, 1982). Considerable difficulties were experienced with the simple network because of:

— the lack of facilities to manage and backup file servers;
— problems with maintaining appropriate levels of file security. Files are available to everyone, or just one workstation. This was not what was required as several practicals might share a number of files. This led to the maintenance of several copies of the same file, since it was felt highly desirable that directories should be kept small, containing only relevant files;
— it was found necessary to connect each workstation to both the file server and the general asynchronous communications network because appropriate bridges were not available;
— as different microcomputers are purchased to perform specific tasks, they cannot be connected to the current proprietary network. They must be connected to new networks (with their own file servers) or only with asynchronous lines.

It has therefore often been found that it is necessary to provide each student with a disk containing the programs and data that he or she needs for a particular practical. This is a time consuming process, since each student normally needs a copy of a different disk for each practical. It was found however, that if a standard disk could be produced, a copy of which would be issued to each student at the start of the series of practicals, most of the problems were eliminated.

The solution adopted has been to attach each of the personal computers to a multi-user microcomputer system running Unix. Most of the files required for the practicals are held on this microcomputer, and can be accessed or copied as required. If it is more appropriate to hold a particular file on a mainframe computer, it can be collected by the information server (Beer and Walsh, 1985) logging in to the appropriate machine automatically, running the appropriate service job. The student need not know where the information is normally stored. It is automatically collected and transferred to his disk when he requests it.

The current file transfer facilities are based on the Kermit (da Cruz and Catchings, 1984) file transfer software, developed by the University of Columbia. This provides a convenient open-architecture transfer facility over asynchronous terminal lines between a comprehensive range of mainframe, mini and micro computers. The use of terminal lines allows microcomputers to be connected to their hosts over local and campus terminal networks without regard to the particular technology involved.

Future plans

The current system is an effective means of distributing quite complex collections of program and data files to students when they need them. The problems of copying different disks for each practical has been eliminated, allowing staff and demonstrators to concentrate on the work that the students are actually doing. The file store is currently managed as a Unix tree structure, with files used in several practicals 'linked' together. The files required for each practical are then grouped together in a single directory.

The student's profile is used to set the appropriate directory, using a menu script, and to start up the file transfer process. This then proceeds under student control once he or she has escaped back to the personal computer. Certain files contain instructions on how to collect information from other computers. These are marked by special file names at present, and the file transfer process is intercepted to issue the relevant transfer job. This is unsatisfactory at present, and it is expected that further progress will be made in this area over the summer.

No attempt has been made so far to collect completed work in a similar fashion. A student is still expected to hand in a report, together with appropriate printouts and a floppy disk containing his programs and data. This in itself causes marking difficulties since all the material has to be cross-referenced for assessment. In practice the information on floppy disk is rarely accessed unless there is some query in the report or printout. In the case of a large class, the value of the disks held within the assessment procedure can be quite large. It is intended to look at this area and see how the files needed for marking can be collected.

References

Acorn Computers Ltd. (1982) *The Econet User Guide.*

Beer, M.D. and Walsh, B.C. (1985) *An Intelligent Information Server,* Internal Report No CSR 85/5, Department of Computer Science, University of Liverpool.

Charlton, C.C. (1985) *Liverpool University's Soft Terminal for the BBC,* Internal Report No CSR 85/215, Department of Computer Science, University of Liverpool.

da Cruz, F. and Catchings, W. (1984) *Kermit: A File Transfer Protocol for Universities,* Byte.

Lotus Development Corporation (1984) *1-2-3 Introduction Manual.*

17 / Experience of Computer-Assisted Education in a University Department

MICHAEL BEILBY *University of Birmingham*

Abstract

The microcomputer laboratory in the Department of Mathematics has been operating for three academic sessions. Students are taught to use it to develop investigative skills. Laboratory conventions have been standardised, and provide access to demonstrations, coursework and library programs and procedures. Staff have been encouraged to present material through the medium of the laboratory and students show a willingness to take the initiative in experiments.

Keywords Computer-assisted learning, Mathematics.

Introduction

In September 1983 a microcomputer laboratory was established in the Mathematics Department. It was to be a deliberate step towards the integration of computing methods into a B.Sc. Mathematics programme. It was an attempt to take aspects of a subject, in which there is a large amount of conceptual material, away from the lecture-room mode of teaching. Students were to be expected to broaden their understanding of mathematics by experimenting with mathematical ideas.

Over the last three years the teaching method has developed. All undergraduates in the Department now participate in a first-year laboratory course which introduces the facilities and encourages students to accept the principle of computer-based investigation. During this course, practical exercises are set with scenarios taken from other first-year lecture courses. Subsequently, undergraduate courses draw on laboratory material, and lecturers can expect students to be able to follow up and develop class-room examples.

Working environment — main considerations

Setting up the student/laboratory and staff/laboratory interfaces has been guided by two main considerations.

The first is that the laboratory material should initially be available

---

Department of Mathematics, University of Birmingham, Birmingham, B15 2TT

for courses without assuming a pre-knowledge of computer programming on the part of student or lecturer.

The introduction of microcomputers into schools has equipped almost all (in Mathematics apparently about 95%) undergraduates with keyboard experience, but only few (about 10%) seem to have the confidence to write programs themselves. Equally, only a small proportion of staff are likely to write their own software, but a significant number will obtain useful programs from colleagues, from contacts, or from commercial sources.

Therefore some coursework (typically demonstration packages) should be capable of being selected by the student 'pressing buttons'. Further, there should be a standard procedure for placing this software within the system.

The second major consideration is that the student should be encouraged to write and modify programs, but this process should be incidental and must not dominate the subject material.

The ideal is that it would be possible, during a lecture course, to say to a student 'Go to the Lab, write a program to measure phenomenon xxx, and tell me what you find'. This question might just as well arise in an English or History course (for example, in the study of text constructions, or in a data-base search) as it might in Mathematics, Engineering, Physics or Biology. Bearing in mind the unpreparedness and reluctance of most students to undertake lengthy programming tasks, and the sophistication required to access files, draw diagrams and perform numerical and algebraic manipulations, an involvement of students with the technicalities of computing is only generally practicable if there is substantial support, in terms of standard program constructions and libraries of routines (in addition to library programs).

Hence, there should be a central structure by which programming aids and library software is available. Further, the library should contain data sets available for study in different contexts.

Working environment — practice

Our situation at Birmingham led us to install BBC micros. They had obvious advantages in terms of graphics capability and a structured BASIC. At present there are 45 machines in total, networked using Econet Level III, and there are two main hard-disc file-servers, with a total 40Mbyte capacity. There are 24 student machines in the laboratory (serving a population of 250), and the remaining micros are distributed in staff offices round the Department. The staff machines also use floppy disc media.

Connection of the micros in a network has been an important

feature of the Laboratory and the user interface has been designed with this in mind. As it has happened, communication of files on the network has been found to be fast and reliable, and has therefore been accepted by users.

The network file-servers provide a central source of software organised in the following way:

— user files;

— demonstrations;

— libraries of programs and procedures grouped in subjects e.g. 'graphics', 'numerical', 'statistics', etc. Following the convention of Harding (e.g. in 'Graphs and Charts', Acornsoft) there are three levels requiring different stages of involvement in the 'technicalities' of computing; 1) raw procedures, 2) functional procedures, and 3) stand-alone programs.

— Course Units comprising read-only menus and programs related to specific undergraduate courses.

The user's working environment is presented in a standard format. When logging into the network the function keys on the BBC micro are automatically set to provide three types of service.

— A search through a directory tree for course units. This is within the capability of a 'button presser'. Lecture courses have their own directories on the file-servers. A press of the 'Course Unit' function key presents a list of course identification codes. When a code is selected, a catalogue of course units is displayed. When a unit is selected a menu of programs is offered. The search proceeds down a simple tree:

  Course Unit Mode
  Which course?
  Which unit?
  Which program?

— A search through a directory tree for library programs and procedures. A 'button presser' will be able to run a library program, but if a user writes a BASIC program he can also append library procedures. The library is divided into subject categories, e.g. 'graphics', 'matrix theory' and 'statistics', each having its own sub-directories. Pressing the 'CHAIN library' or 'APPEND library' function keys presents a list of sub-libraries. When one is selected, a catalogue of files is displayed. Further selection results in either a program being run, or a routine being appended to the user's program statements. The file names can be referenced against documentation available in the laboratory and include a code digit to indicate the level of applicability. (It is easy to envisage 'help' files being available in this respect.) Thus, the search proceeds down a

tree:
   Library Mode? CHAIN or APPEND
   Which sub-library?
   Which file?
— Certain aids to BASIC programming are available from other function keys. These include diagnostics and text editing.

These facilities are achieved with a bootstrap resident in the micro. Access over the network is sufficiently fast that downloading the system programs to implement the tree searches is transparent. There are 15 courses each with up to 10 units in the coursework tree. There are 5 sub-libraries in the library tree.

Implications about syllabus

One of the advantages of the above structure is that it provides facilities for integration of computer-based teaching into an on-going teaching programme with a relatively small amount of disruption.

In the Mathematics Department it was decided to include an introductory course at the beginning of the first year. This would equip students to use the Laboratory and encourage them to experiment. To some extent the course displaced some conventional computer programming material, and anyway is kept separate from a formal approach to computing itself.

The introductory course includes 10 lectures which explain use of the machines and the networked library, and describe suitable BASIC 'cookbook' constructions. Each student also attends at least 10 out of 15 accompanying 2-hour practical sessions of graded difficulty in a variety of scenarios based on first-year undergraduate material. Students are assessed on the basis of the practical work.

Thereafter, the student is referred to the Laboratory from within the normal teaching programme. The computer-based teaching method is expected to evolve naturally in the aspects to which it is best suited.

Staff response

It must be remembered that the teaching staff are specialists in their own subjects, not necessarily in computing, and will be asked to make adjustments to adapt to a style of presentation using an unfamiliar teaching medium. Furthermore, the department has to be prepared for some changes of syllabuses, teaching practices and examination procedures. The facility must be seen to be worth the disruption its introduction might cause. The students will only be convinced of its importance when they see the staff as a whole prepared to accept it.

In the Department we have embarked on a policy whereby machines are fairly freely available to staff, and are now used by them in the preparation of teaching material. To some extent the machines have to become a feature of departmental life. The argument is simple. If they slot into a lecturer's lifestyle, they will be introduced quite naturally into his, or her, thinking and into presentation of subject material.

Prominent questions in our case have been 'Will there be an erosion of the time spent teaching the discipline subject?', 'How should the lab be scheduled?', 'How much staff time will be required in supervising computer labs, or answering queries in 'clinic' sessions?' and 'How are the computer exercises to be assessed?'.

Some pleasing positive responses have been in relation to the ease with which it is possible to prepare examples and notes, the willingness of some students to experiment, and the better staff/student relationship encouraged through contact in the Laboratory.

Student response

Although in the main the undergraduates come with a familiarity with keyboards, it must be realised that a significant proportion of students do not feel an affinity for computational devices.

In consequence, considering *all* the students, the reaction has varied. There is considerable enthusiasm at the beginning, and an overall readiness to commit time and effort to work in the lab. There is plenty of evidence of constructive co-operation, and a willingness amongst some to pursue work outside the prescribed exercises.

On the other hand, it is often difficult to gauge the right degree of structure to the exercises, and thereby encourage the less enthusiastic for whom the sole attraction is the mathematics. A pervading defensive comment has been 'We should either do maths or computing, but not both at the same time!'.

Setting this initial reaction to one side, probably the most useful, and most widely stated comment is surprising. It can be paraphrased, 'We find the partly- and pre-prepared demonstrations boring, and prefer to write our own programs'. Certainly, the exercises that require the student to write a program and, in our case, to explore some mathematics in their own terms have been better received than those in which the students follow an investigative path through a pre-prepared set of programs. The tendency over the two years has been away from more conventional computer-aided teaching.

Computer resources and logistics

Clearly, considerable resources are required if a year's intake are all to be provided with frequently available computer facilities. It is not often appreciated how difficult it is to provide these resources within a discipline away from computer studies.

It is interesting to examine the logistics of lab organisation in some detail. At Birmingham one computational course with a weekly afternoon laboratory session for each student requires four sittings for a 75-student course. Bearing in mind lecture timetables, and setting aside mornings for class demonstrations and private study, it will only be possible to run two full computational lab courses in the three-year undergraduate programme.

The capital outlay for our 24-student laboratory, plus supporting staff micros, is of the order of £40,000, the direct running costs are about £3000 per year, and there is substantial staff involvement in software, but relatively little in operation.

The exercise is just about acceptable using the BBC micros. Even though there are substantial mainframe facilities available at Birmingham, it has so far not proved practical to consider using them for this style of teaching.

A development that is practicable and under consideration is the use of the microcomputer laboratory as a 'front-end' on a link to the main-frames. In this respect the micros could call for mainframe support, introducing and preparing data for computational packages and data searches. This is particularly relevant when a subject, like Mathematics, is taught in a service role. The micro then takes on the task of local communicator, providing an interface between discipline and generalised package. An experiment along these lines is being conducted with respect to mathematical programming, a set of techniques that appear in different user situations in teaching and industry. Yet the techniques might all be implemented by access to the same programs in, say, the NAG library. When used by students in the Mechanical Engineering Department, in the Engineering Production Department, in the Economics Department, etc. the micros would help interpret the problem as appropriate locally and assemble the data; the mainframe would undertake the computation centrally.

Related reference

Beilby, M. H. and McCauley, G. P. (1986) *Introduction to Computational Mathematics*, Scottish Academic Press.

18 / Experiences of a New Authoring System for Computer-Assisted Learning

G. J. MAKINSON and H. L. MORARJI *University of Kent at Canterbury*

Abstract

KAS, Kent Authoring System, has been designed and implemented at the University of Kent at Canterbury. It provides an effective framework for the teacher to construct a student-computer dialogue with the facility of calling routines for computation, simulation, file handling, and, in particular, generating graphical output.

Keywords Computer-assisted learning, Student-computer interface, Author language.

Introduction

A project on Computing Facilities for teaching in Universities, conducted at the University of Kent, has been used to develop an authoring system (Makinson and Morarji, in press). A key feature of this system is the student-computer interface. It is common for teaching packages to be either menu driven or command driven. The menu driven approach presents the student with a set of choices at each level of activity. It is very well suited to the inexperienced user, because it eliminates the need to remember, or to rely on a manual for the proper input of responses. However, the menu driven approach has its drawbacks. The time needed to display the menu, combined with the time it takes to read information on the menu delays the student response and hence the overall speed. The inconvenience, for an experienced user, of reading through menus and possibly having to traverse several menus to perform a single function is the most commonly expressed complaint against a menu system being the sole interface to a computer system (Martin, 1973; Robertson et al., 1979). In the command driven approach the user is not presented with instructions or structures that have to be read or negotiated, except at the user's request (Heffler, 1982). This is a convenient interface for more skilled users who expect speed and efficiency. The main difficulty with command languages is

School of Mathematical Studies, University of Kent at Canterbury, Canterbury, Kent, CT2 7NF the complexity of the commands, the potentially large number of commands, and the variety of command formats (Grimes, 1979).

Authoring systems currently available on small, medium and large computers are surveyed and described by Barker and Singh (1982). Most of the languages listed provide authors of CAI with facilities which include
— presentation of text via frames;
— student testing;
— receiving and analysing student responses;
— provision of remedial and reinforcement material, and
— branching facilities which enable the presentation of material to depend on the nature of the student responses.

These facilities are reminiscent of what was available on teaching machines, and fall far short of a full CAL authoring system.

The multiplicity of author languages has always made the exchange of teaching packages a difficult task. In order to resolve this problem, the National Research Council of Canada commissioned the development of a National Author Language (NATAL-74) (Brahan et al., 1980). Four goals were considered: (i) ease of use, (ii) language portability, (iii) terminal independence, and (iv) computational, logical and file handling functions. The Kent Authoring System (KAS) has been developed with these four goals in mind and has, we believe, been successful in achieving these goals. KAS has its origin in the Leeds Authoring Language and CALCHEM, a project of the UK National Development Programme in CAL. The new design is based on experience gained from a project at the University of Canterbury in New Zealand. It is dialogue driven; this intermediate approach is more flexible than either a solely menu driven approach or a single command language. The dialogue is organised in a tree structure with various nodes, each node performing a specific function. It moves towards the use of a simple dialogue and the user responses can be in English-like or mathematical-like form as preferred.

Features of the Authoring System

The Kent Authoring System provides the following capabilities:
— Output of teaching material, instructions and questions to the student.
— Recognition of textual and numerical input from the student.
— Control of dialogue between the student and the computer system using a "branching tree" structure.

— Interface into external routines which include numerical computations, graphics and library routines.
— Interface into external routines which handle the input of user-defined functions (Makinson and Morarji, in press) and data, and command routines.

The teaching programme

The teaching programme is divided into a number of nodes forming the basis of a branching tree structure. These nodes must contain a unique identifier which assigns a name to the node and routing instructions which route the student to other nodes of the tree structure, and any one of the following:
— Text which is to be printed at the terminal, and which may include questions or messages to the student.
— Anticipated responses to cover as many interpretations of the student responses as possible.
— Calls to external routines and subsequent routing to other nodes.

Implementation of KAS

KAS is currently implemented on an Orion Supermicro with the UNIX 4.1 BSD Operating System. A Teaching Programme Compiler (TPCOMPILER) has been designed and developed using the C language at Kent. Its function is to convert the teaching programme written using KAS to a C source code consisting of a table of nodes forming the structure of the student computer dialogue. Since UNIX* and C are available on a very wide range of computers KAS is portable to other machines with a similar operating system environment. Initially KAS was implemented on a VAX11/780 at Kent and the transfer to the Orion Supermicro required no change to the authoring system. The output, including the graphics, is generated in a device independent format and could drive different terminals or plotters.

In the development of the teaching programme the following methodology has been used:
— Specification by the teacher of pedagogic material to be covered and the numerical algorithms within these topics to be made available to the student.

---

* UNIX is a trademark of Bell Laboratories, Murray Hill, New Jersey.

— Establishment of a tree structure consisting of a sequence of questions, answers and messages to assist in teaching.

— Concise formulation, in plain English, of the sequence of questions in the above and various anticipated responses from the student.

The teaching programme is then coded according to the syntax of KAS. The TPCOMPILER then generates a C source code and appends the code to the Numerical and Graphical routines. On compilation of the combined code, the executable code for the teaching package is created.

Syntax of the language

The main features of the Kent Authoring System are described here. A full description of the language is available in the UKC Computing Laboratory Report (Makinson and Morarji, 1982). The following conventions are used in this section:

a is a single alphabetic character;

d is a single decimal digit;

is a command character which indicates the beginning of a node identifier;

! is a command character which indicates the start of a routing instruction;

@ is a command character which indicates that the user response is to be input and compared with an anticipated response;

$ is a command character which marks a call to an external routine.

Node identifier

Format : #add

No spaces should occur in this character string, and nothing else should appear on the same line.

Text

Any teaching material such as questions, solutions or explanations which is to be printed at the terminal is included in the text part of the node.

Routing to other nodes

The name of the destination node follows the control character !

Response matching

Format : @anticipated response!add

The response matching and routing part of the node includes the following functions:
— input of the student response;
— comparison of student response with an 'anticipated' response;
— routing to other nodes depending on the response;
— recording of the student responses to provide the feed-back to the teacher on the suitability of the communication.

Calls to external routines

Format : $nameofroutine!addadd

The name is terminated by a pointer on the same line to two nodes. Control passes to the first node after a normal termination of a procedure or because of a certain condition set by the procedure. If there is an abnormal termination of a procedure or if a different condition is set by the procedure, the control passes to the second node.

Command routines

KAS also provides the teacher with standard routines which are designed to help in the development of the teaching programme. The following are examples of a few routines which are currently available and are being used by the Kent system.

Routines	Function
clearscreen	clears the screen
waitroutine	waits at the current screen until user responds
center	prints text near center of the screen
userresponse	accepts the user's response from the keyboard
readdata	accepts numerical data from the user
setwindow	sets the window for the graphics

Example of a typical teaching programme

A part of a typical teaching programme as prepared by the teacher is shown below:

```
#a00
$clearscreen!a01a00
#a01
$center!a02a01
#a02
```

You are linked to the Optimization package for functions of one variable only.

This package illustrates unconstrained optimization of a function f(x) using univariate search methods.

Do you need any guidance on the use of the package?
Enter yes or no and then press the RETURN key.
?
!a05
#a05
@yes!a10
@y!a10
@no!a20
@n!a20!
!a00
#a10
$clearscreen!a12a10
#a12
$center!a14a12
#a14

You should input your response on receiving a ? from the system.

You may keep your response as English-like as you want.

Enter your response in lower case letters terminating each response by pressing the RETURN key.

If you need to find out what is available in the package or how to answer a particular question, enter help and press RETURN.

To prevent any ambiguity you will be guided by the system on what to enter; this will be enclosed in single
quotes ' '.

Enter all your numerical data separated by SPACE.

For graphical output you will have to provide the dimensions of the graphics window (i.e. xmin, xmax, ymin, ymax) which you can change to get a ZOOMING effect.

```
!a16
#a16
$waitroutine!a20a16
#a20
$clearscreen!a21a20
#a21
$center!a22a21
#a22
```

Will you provide your own function or do you want to use one of the functions provided in the package, which illustrates the methods?

Enter 'p' for package function or 'o' for own functions.
```
?
!a25
#a25
@o!b05
@p!a30
!a20
#a30
$setstdfn!a35a20
#a35
$choosefn!a40a20
```

Use of KAS

As part of the Kent project, teaching packages in the topics of nonlinear equations, interpolation and nonlinear optimization (single and multivariable functions) have been developed using the Kent Authoring System. They have been used effectively in numerical analysis courses at first and third year level for 100 students and 15 students respectively.

Reactions to the teaching packages have been very favourable. The dialogue driven approach requires minimal user input and the students have found the packages convenient to use. The tree structure used within the dialogue provides the students with a number of paths which they can follow. Some of the options which are available to the students include:

— providing their own functions during the running of the teaching package;
— choosing one of the standard functions specially chosen to illustrate particular features;

— trying any or all of the numerical methods available in the package to solve a particular problem;

— choosing and modifying the necessary parameters for the numerical method to study the effect on the solution;

— displaying graphically the numerical results;

— obtaining hard copy output for numerical results and/or graphical displays.

For cases where the student response does not match with any of the anticipated responses or if the student requests help, the teaching package assists the student with how to respond to a particular question or gives a list of options which are available to the student. The students have found this facility highly satisfactory. Provision is also made for input of user comment which is stored for analysis.

From the teacher's viewpoint, KAS provides the mechanism by which the teaching packages can be modified and updated easily. New numerical algorithms can be incorporated without any difficulty into the existing packages. The recording of the student responses at each node during the running of the teaching package enables the teacher to extend the list of anticipated responses to include the most commonly used student responses in the teaching programme, thus improving the effectiveness of the communication.

Conclusions

For the authors of teaching packages KAS fulfills the many requirements of an authoring system. It has been found to be easy to use and provides the facilities that are required without the need for undue effort on the part of the author. With its development in a UNIX environment, it is generally portable and provides terminal independence through a device independent implementation. It also fulfills the computational, logical and file handling functions through the medium of the C language. Computation routines may be written in other languages such as FORTRAN.

The use of KAS has provided both a friendly user environment for the student and has served the purpose of providing the teacher with a development tool admirably. Work is still in progress to add further facilities and refinements to the system.

References

Barker, P.G. and Singh, R. (1982) *Author Languages for Computer-Based Learning*, British Journal of Educational Technology, **13**, 3, pp. 167-196.

Brahan, J.W., Henneker, W.H. and Hlady, A.M. (1980) *NATAL-74-Concept to Reality,* Proc. of the Third Canadian Symposium on Instructional Technology, Vancouver, pp. 230-240.

Grimes, J.D. (1979) *A Knowledge Oriented View of User Interfaces,* Proc. 12th Hawaii International Conf. on System Sciences, pp. 158-163.

Heffler, M.J. (1982) *A Human-Computer Interface that Provides Access to a Diverse User Community,* Proc. 14th Hawaii International Conf. on System Science, Vol. 2, Section 2, pp. 601-610.

Makinson, G.J. and Morarji, H.L. (1982) *KAS — A new authoring system for computer-assisted learning,* University of Kent at Canterbury Computing Laboratory Report No. 32.

Makinson, G.J. and Morarji, H.L. (in press) *Computation with Graphics in Mathematics Teaching Initiative,* Int. J. Math. Educ. Sci. Technol.

Makinson, G.L. and Morarji, H.L. (in press) *The input of user-defined functions during execution of CAL programs.* Int. J. Math. Educ. Sci. Technol.

Martin, J. (1973) *Design of Man-Computer Dialogues,* Academic Press.

Robertson, G., McCracken, D. and Newell, A. (1979) *The ZOG Approach to Man-Machine Communication,* Technical Report 10, Computer Science Dept., Carnegie-Mellon Univ.

Section 7

In addition to the formal presentations reported earlier in these proceedings, we include, in this final part, some of the contributions to the seminars and workshop sessions.

The papers by Stratil and Burkhardt, and by Veljkovic, et al., introduced demonstrations by Diana Burkhardt and Bogdan Jankovic. Donald Gillies and Jim Ridgway introduced seminars on 'Higher Education and Industry' and 'CAL Development and Evaluation', respectively. Finally, a group of students, supported by the ESRC-ITE Programme, reported on the early parts of their research in the field of Information Technology and Education.

Bob Lewis

19 / A Content-free CALL Multimedia Package Incorporating Speech Synthesis and Interactive Video

MARIE STRATIL and DIANA BURKHARDT *University of Birmingham*

Abstract

A content-free software package is described. The system is designed to enable university lecturers to create CALL (Computer Aided Language Learning) modules exploiting the technology of interactive video, speech generation and optical character reading of printed texts. Although initial work has been in collaboration with the University Spanish and French departments, the system is applicable to a wide range of languages and will also have potential outside CALL. A modular approach has been adopted allowing the lecturer to choose at any one time from a number of courseware-building tools and circumventing the need to learn a specific author language. The design draws upon the methods of artificial intelligence using, for example, an expert system approach for the production of suitable phonemes in the speech synthesis. The aim is to provide software which enables lecturers to enter their own material and to modify the resulting courseware with the minimum of effort and computer expertise.

Keywords Computer aided language learning, Authoring system, Interactive video.

The hardware configuration

The diagram (Figure 1) shows the hardware links between the various components of the mainframe prototype multimedia system. The software system resides on a DEC 2060 to which is linked an IMS microcomputer.

Overview of the software structure

The package design is based on a modular concept of loosely interlinked segments of program (Figure 2). The grammar modules and the video, speech, dictation and exerciser can be accessed via the main menu. To create or extend a teaching package the lecturer uses the

Centre for Computing and Computing Science, University of Birmingham, P.O. Box 363, Birmingham, B15 2TT

package building tools to build lessons and link in existing modules, for example, the video module which may be used in any package for any language.

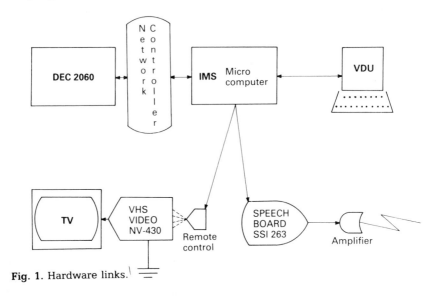

Fig. 1. Hardware links.

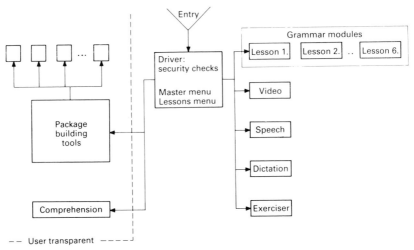

Fig. 2. An overview of the package design.

In order to test the package-creation software, a book of Spanish grammar and a book of Spanish exercises was read into the University's Kurtzweil optical character reader. This material was successfully converted into a CALL package intended for students who have just started to learn the Spanish language.

A speech chip, an SSI 263, was installed with the terminal. It accepts phonemes which may be manipulated via five registers each modifying different speech parameters. The sound section in the package uses an expert system approach for analysing text into phonemes. These can be spoken immediately as the text is typed in, or for fixed messages, the coded sound may be embedded in the lesson text in the form of phonemes and spoken at execution time. The rulebase includes both rules of accentuation and of pronunciation. In future developments, a sentence marker such as the comma, question mark, full stop etc. may form a part of the program-recognised set of characters and be linked to some production rules which will modify the sentential voice inflection.

Future work

The user model is to be expanded providing the opportunity to move towards an Intelligent Tutoring System (ITS). For successful CAL the authoring environment is quite as important as the tutoring environment. A poor environment will almost certainly restrict the quality of the teaching material. An Intelligent Authoring System (IAS) which monitors the author's use of the system and provides appropriate advice for the individual user is a long term aim.

20 / The System Software of the New Yugoslav School Micro TIM-010

DUSAN VELJKOVIC, BOGDAN JANKOVIC,
NEDELJKO PAREZANOVIC and VELJKO SPASIC
University of Beograd

Abstract

This paper considers the concept of system software for the school microcomputer. The system software consists of the operating system, the system interpreter and the language processors. The proposed system software is designed to achieve two main goals. The first is to provide a software environment for education in programming and problem solving, and the second is to offer an example of school system software. The unique system interpreter facilitates the implementation of several languages which can be mixed within the same program.

Keywords Micro-computer, Operating systems, problem solving, BASIC, input/output, interface

Introduction

The microcomputer TIM-010 is intended to be used for computer science teaching as well as to support other curriculum subjects. It is based on the 8-bit microprocessor INTEL 8085. In the basic configuration, the system supports the following peripherals: keyboard, VDU (monitor or TV), cassette recorder and printer. There is an additional possibility of expansion with a floppy disc drive, A/D and D/A converters. The screen displays text in 24 rows and 40 columns each. In the expanded configuration the system has 320×240 high resolution colour graphics.

The present paper describes system software aspects of the TIM-010 microcomputer.

Preliminary considerations

Before we started to develop the operating system, it had been neces-

Centre for Multidisciplinary Studies, Penezica-Kreuna, 35/IV, Slobodana, 11001 Belgrade, Yugoslavia

sary to decide how much of it would be "visible" from the user's point of view, and which would be the "visible" functions. It is not easy to answer this question for a school microcomputer. It is clear that if the operating system is visible to the user, such as in the case of CP/M — a frequently used operating system for microcomputers — then it is necessary for the user to know and understand the basic concepts and functions of it, which means additional learning and efforts. On the other hand, if the accepted concept is complete embedding of all the operating system functions into the commands of the language interpreter (such as a BASIC interpreter for example), then it is impossible to expand the system with a new language processor; also this is not good practice. We decided to have an operating system with the minimum number of functions available to the user, and for which (s)he easily realises why they are necessary in the system.

Support of the peripherals

One of the operating system's basic functions is to support the communication between the central processor and the peripheral devices. The system has several peripherals: keyboard, VDU (monitor or domestic TV), cassette recorder, printer, and optional floppy disc drive, A/D and D/A converters. In addition, it is necessary to have program support for the high resolution colour graphics and the tone generator. The basic concept in the implementation of the programs for the peripherals support is based on the following:
— the usage of the interrupt system for peripherals support, including keyboard;
— the modular approach which enables the maximum number of program modules to be used in the future development of the system.
  It should be noted that the text can be displayed on the screen in several different ways by adding the various attributes to the text.

Screen editor

For flexibility in program editing, a screen editor is adopted for the school computer. Using the cursor keys, it is possible to position the cursor at any place on the screen, and modify the screen's content via pressing keys using editor commands which can:
— insert a new string;
— move the cursor to points such as the beginning of the next word, the end of the current program line, the top of the screen etc.;
— erase a symbol, part of the program line, the whole program line or the whole screen.

The change is made in the program zone only after the <RETURN> is pressed.

When in insert mode, the graphics symbol for the cursor is changed in order to mark the inserting mode of operation. The screen editor is active all the time, so that a data input, for example, in BASIC INPUT statements, goes through it.

System interpreter (SI)

In order to meet the educational requirements in full, the interpreter, built into the operating system, supports all the commands from three different levels.
— operating system level — base level of communication;
— BASIC language level — programming in the higher level language;
— user defined statements — extension of the BASIC language with a new statement, or definition of the new language processor (PAS-CAL, LOGO, symbolic language, text processors ...).

The main functions of SI are to recognise and execute the commands and statements in the immediate mode or program mode, and to form the program by entering program lines (Brown, 1979). The program is held in the internally coded form, which is developed in such a way that the maximum execution speed is achieved, and the use of memory is reduced.

The set of instructions which the interpreter can understand, is divided into two groups.

Resident part:
— commands for program zone manipulation: LIST, DELETE, RENUM, NEW, AUTO;
— command for the program execution: RUN;
— utility commands: SYNTAX, TRACE;
— commands for entering the operating system: SYSTEM, BYE;

Transient part:
— operating system statements: IN, OUT, CHECK, START, BASIC, USER;
— BASIC language statements;
— user defined statements.

Resident commands are present at each of the levels of operation. Each of the levels possesses a particular set of transient statements. The basic level is the operating system level which is entered when the computer is switched on, or the RESET pressed. It is then possible to enter either the BASIC language level or the level of user defined statements. Direct connection of these two levels is not possible, but can be done by the operating system using the command SYSTEM from the resident part. This command does not interfere with the program entered or results, but makes it possible to use the operating system level commands, including BASIC and USER, which provide for the activation of another level or the reactivation of the previous one (see Figure 1.) In that way, it is possible to have the operating system commands, BASIC language statements and the user statements in the same program. The interpreter can handle up to the 240 different statements and commands.

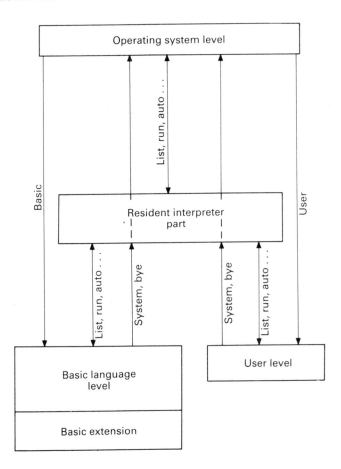

Fig. 1. Interpreter level to level switching.

Command BYE from the resident part, reinitialises SI, erasing all the interpreter zones, and switching to the operating system level.

Programming is possible at each of the levels in the usual BASIC language manner. There is a decimal line number at the beginning of each program line ranging from 1 to 65535. At the operating system level it is possible to write only simple programs without branching.

Multi-statement lines are allowed with the colon ":" as a separator. One of the specific characteristics of this interpreter is the possibility of having one program line within another program line. The execution of such a line is equivalent to the entering of a new line from the keyboard which provides program modification at the the level of a higher programming language. This modification can be used recursively.

Listing the program on the screen is formatted in such a way that the first five places in the program line are reserved for the line number and then the statement follows. There is always one space to the left and to the right of each statement keyword.

The user can place n spaces to the right of the separator sign. SI will then generate a corresponding number of TAB symbols shown in the listing. In that way, all the lines inside the FOR-NEXT loop, for example, can be shown one TAB indented, loops embedded in the first one, two tab indented etc.

A syntax error report can be given immediately after the program line has been entered, or after an attempt to execute that program line. SYNTAX command parameter 0 or 1 determines which will be the case.

The operating system language

The user sees the operating system through the commands by which functions of the system are activated. Each of the commands has its syntax and semantics, and altogether they make the operating system language. Therefore, the user relates to the operating system through the operating system language. That was the reason for trying to achieve the following:

— simple syntax with semantics that is obvious to the user;
— the user insight to the existence of the operating system and the language processor, and
— the extension of the commands for the machine and symbolic level users.

The first task is realised by the commands generated from the following syntax definitions:

    <function>"<device>[:<name>]"[<address>[,<address>]]
    where
    <function>::=OUT IN CHECK
    <device>;;=C[ASSETTE RECORDER] S[CREEN] K[EYBOARD]
    P[RINTER]
    <name>::=<letter> <letter> <digit>

As can be seen, commands provide for the communication between the computer and the peripherals: sending the information from the computer (OUT) to the peripherals; sending from the peripheral to the computer (IN), as well as the check of the transmission (CHECK) in case of tape recording. In the commands, <name> should be used only when dealing with the tape; in other cases it has no meaning.

Entering the language processor and leaving the operating system is done by simply stating the name of the language processor. At the moment, only the BASIC interpreter is implemented, and switching to it is done by the command BASIC. Two different prompt symbols serve for differentiating between the language processor and the operating system control.

The concept of the operating system allows all main operations on the microcomputer:
— dealing with user written BASIC programs;
— dealing with machine level programs;
— possibly expanding the system with a new language processor.

The last stated possibility is very interesting having in mind the necessity of developing different language processors for the different levels of education in school.

Specific characteristics of the BASIC language

School BASIC should enable the user to implement his knowledge in other computers as well. Because there is no widely accepted BASIC detailed standard, TIM-010 BASIC is constructed in such a manner that the most frequently used BASIC elements are present. All the commands of the resident parts of the interpreter are included; all the commands for manipulating the program zone are the same as in the majority of other BASIC languages. The following language commands are also the same as in most commonly used BASIC languages.
— Input/Output commands: GET, INPUT, PRINT.
— Assignment statements: LET (which can be left out).
— Conditional branching statement is structured: IF-THEN-ELSE.
— Unconditional branching statements: GOTO, GOSUB, RETURN.
— Statements for loop programming: FOR-TO-STEP and NEXT.
— Command for clearing the zone of variables: CLEAR.
— Commands for data within the program: DATA, READ, RESTORE.
— Command for array dimensioning: DIM.
— Commands for direct memory access: POKE, CALL.
— Commands for the program termination: STOP, END.
— High resolution graphics commands: PLOT, LINE.
— Sound support command: BEEP.

— Screen commands: SCROLL, CLS.
— Cassette recorder commands: LOAD, SAVE, VERIFY.

The program accepts two usual types of data, numeric and string. Variable names can be up to six other symbols long, and all are significant. String variables have a dollar sign appended to them. Arrays cannot have more than two dimensions.

The full set of numeric and string functions is implemented, as well as the functions for conversion from one type to another.

— String functions SEG$, TIME$, CHR$.
— Numeric functions: SIN, COS, TAN, ATN, EXP, INT, SQR, ABS, SGN, RND.
— Conversion functions: ASC, VAL, POS, LEN, STR$.

Reference

Brown, P.J. (1979) *Writing Interactive Compilers and Interpreters,* John Wiley and Sons, London.

21 / Higher Education and the High Technology Industry

DONALD J. GILLIES *Ryerson Polytechnical Institute, Toronto*

The revolution in informatics and telematics has produced the information society. The information society depends for its existence on the high technology industry. Industry depends on higher education for scientists, engineers, technologists and managers. Is higher education meeting the demands of the high technology industry for such personnel? Is the high technology industry depending on higher education for such personnel? The answers to these questions are neither clear, simple nor direct.

In this seminar we examine these questions and the context which makes it difficult to answer them. We address such matters as:

— patterns of relationships between higher education and the high technology industry;

— high technology products, services and expertise available to higher education;

— examples of computer-assisted learning, computer-aided instruction, computer-based training, computer-directed learning and computer-managed learning;

— in-house high technology industrial training for employees and customers and its extension to the private and public sectors;

— integrating new technologies into the curriculum; issues of faculty resistance or inertia, governance and affordability;

— informal individualised learning versus formal centralised mass education;

— higher education; net user or net supplier of high technology teaching and learning;

— higher education as the conserver of learning and wisdom in the information society.

The papers in the bibliography reflect some of my thoughts for discussion.

Film and Photography Department, Ryerson Polytechnical Institute, 350 Victoria Street, Toronto, Ontario, M5B 2K3

Bibliography

Gillies, D.J. and Nash, D.C. (1983) *The Future of Videotex/Teletext: A view from Silicon Valley,* Videotex Canada, **2,** 1.

Gillies, D.J. (1984) *Videotex and Teletext; Teaching and Learning.* In Proceedings of the Fourth Symposium, National Research Council of Canada, Associate Committee on Instructional Technology, Ottawa, 1983.

Gillies, D.J. (1984) *Video: Broadening Our Perspectives,* Videotex World, **1,** 1.

Gillies, D.J. (1985) *Videotex in Education — What's Happening in Canada,* Videotex World, **2,** 2.

Gillies, D.J. (1986) *CAL in Canada: Innovations and their Sources in Teaching and Learning,* Computers and Education, **10,** 1.

22 / Development and Evaluation of CAL Materials

JIM RIDGWAY *Department of Psychology, University of Lancaster*

Abstract

Evaluation is always problematic. Here it will be argued that: the methods of evaluation should be tailored to the purposes for which CAL has been developed; and that evaluation should be an integral part of software development, not something to be applied after the software development process has been completed. A process of formative evaluation can be quite expensive in terms of time and the allocation of scarce resources. However, these resources are essential if software is to be developed which works robustly in the hands of the target group for whom it is intended.

Keywords Computer-assisted learning, Curriculum development, Evaluation, Research needs.

Issues in evaluation

There is a variety of purposes which evaluation can serve and a complex range of issues which can be involved in any evaluation project. We can illustrate some of these themes in Figure 1.

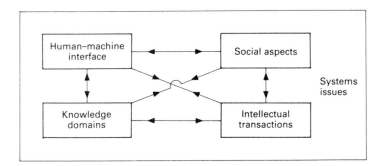

Fig. 1. Topics for evaluation.

Human–machine interface refers to all aspects of the interactions between the user and the computer. Most systems need fine tuning, if not

Department of Psychology, University of Lancaster, LA1 4YF

a major re-working between the stages of writing software which works robustly, and the development of software which can be driven smoothly by users. One might summarise initiatives in this area as a desire for the production of a transparent machine; that is to say a machine in which the users' intentions can be translated immediately and naturally into commands to drive the machine in particular ways. One can identify several research projects whose aim is to achieve such transparency. An example has been provided at the Conference by Roger Hartley and his co-workers on the EUROHELP project (Hartley et al., 1985) which aims to provide intelligent help systems for UNIX users. An illuminative example of the problems which one can encounter with HMI design has recently been provided by Thomas Green. He reported an editor which would obey the command <4U> by moving the cursor up 4 lines, try to predict how the editor responds to a user input of <4D>. Well, of course the editor deletes 4 lines!

Knowledge domains refers to the many issues concerned with knowledge representation:
— knowledge representation within the machine — for example, the way the machine chooses to represent knowledge via, say, semantic nets, or genetic graphs, list structures and the like;
— the knowledge with which the machine imbues the user;
— the knowledge which the user possesses before the interaction;
— the knowledge which the user possesses after the interaction.
    'Knowledge' should never be viewed in a simplistic fashion as consisting simply of a set of skills. Users' knowledge representation should certainly include descriptions of process variables such as discovery skills, problem solving strategies, and the ability and willingness to reflect upon current processes. It should also include the learner's mental model of the machine, and machine-mediated learning.

Intellectual transactions refers to the flow of commands between the user and the machine, and indeed, teachers and other users. These are often likely to be a central focus for CAL evaluation.

Social aspects are critically important in the evaluation of CAL yet are often neglected. In our studies (e.g. Ridgway et al., 1984) the microcomputer has been shown to play a major role in enabling teachers to shift the social dynamics of classrooms. At a more parochial level, it is clear that quite different kinds of interaction take place when pairs or groups of users, interact with a computer, compared to individual, tutorial CAL. The development of CAL which fosters and exploits this potential for the enrichment of human-human intellectual transactions, should certainly be one of our major goals (e.g. Fraser et al., in press).

Systems issues relate to the whole environment within which CAL takes place. If we are talking about a school environment, then systems issues will involve the provision and deployment of computers, booking procedures, and the personal dynamics which determine priorities amongst users. At a higher level still, systems issues will include LEA policies on such matters as the total computer provision, arrangements for maintenance, software provision, teacher-training and the like. In University contexts, systems issues will include: times of access to staff and students; levels of machine provision; staff support during tutorials; and decisions about whether CAL is compulsory or optional.

On the state of the nation's CAL

The quality of educational software in schools is often decried. The Cockcroft Report in 1982 commented in para 407:

> There is at present relatively little software ... available ...much ...
> is of poor quality ... badly written and documented, and sometimes
> inaccurate and sometimes merely 'gimmicks'.

Studies in America have produced evidence which shows that this is not just a local problem. For example, Bialo and Erickson (1985) examined 163 evaluations conducted in the Educational Products Information Exchange in December 1983. Of these programs: 80% provided no evidence that the programs had been developed in any systematic way; 65% had no defined objectives, either educational or otherwise; 20% had spelling or language errors; 70% had no coursework support; and 60% had no facility for assessing pupil performance (this is quite dramatic, given that over 70% programs focussed on drill and practice): 75% of these programs made no use of branching!

This picture is really rather gloomy. How might things be improved?

A model for CAL development

The model described here is used in our work in developing CAL for classroom use. The model has been used extensively by the ITMA collaboration throughout our work. It is illustrated in schematic form in Figure 2.

The initial stage of the creation of a piece of software depends on some ideas about the kinds of activities which are likely to be useful in

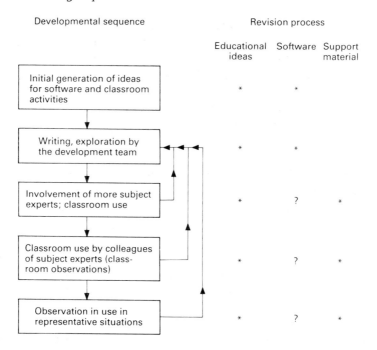

Fig. 2. The idealised ITMA development process.

the classroom, which the computer can support. Writing software is often considered to be a time-consuming, arduous task. While we have some sympathy with this view, we take the more radical view that the time spent in coding computer programs, and the intellectual challenges posed by coding, are rather small compared to the challenges we face when we try to produce packages of software which work with the target audience for whom they are intended.

The first stage in our development is to write software and explore its uses amongst ourselves. In this context, "ourselves" can refer to an individual author, a sub-set of the research team, or a developmental group which includes practising teachers. This stage of writing and exploration usually leads to suggestions for enhanced software facilities, consideration of easier ways in which software can be driven, and some suggestions for classroom use.

The next stage of development involves use of the software in class by subject experts. The subject experts are people who are confident within their domain, and who are confident that they can use microcomputers to aid education. This phase of work results in two new sorts of knowledge: first, we often gather more ideas about the educational uses to which a particular piece of software can be put; second, we often use our observations of subject experts as the basis for the generation of support materials, commonly presented in the form of lesson-plans, which less expert teachers might choose to use. Of course, it is always possible that at this stage extensions to the facilities offered by a particular piece of software can be made; for example, changes can be made to the way the system is controlled.

The next stage of the formative evaluation process usually involves teachers within the same school as our computing using subject specialists, who try out ideas in their own classrooms. These teachers are working in a supportive environment and are aware that help is to hand with problems which may arise, and that they are contributing to the development process. This stage of development can lead to revisions of the kind of support materials which are provided, and can yield further educational ideas about uses of software. Again,the possibilities that the software itself may need revision are always entertained.

A final, and more radical form of evaluation, is to observe a piece of software in use in representative situations. By this we mean teachers: who do not necessarily use the computer regularly in their teaching; whose teaching is, in most respects, unexceptional; and who are, by and large, unsullied by contact with enthusiasts, experts, and people desirous of educational change. Evaluation with this group has broken many a heart! Most of us have had the experience that our own particular brilliant idea, which can produce marvellous and dramatic results in some people's classrooms, turns to ashes in the hands of teachers who face the day-to-day realities of classroom life. This group too, can provide insights into new ways of using particular pieces of software, and often are able to suggest different kinds of support material, or helpful modifications to support material which is already written.

Observation and evaluation

What kinds of observation are appropriate to this development process? Before one can begin to design methods for systematic observation, one needs to construct:

— an educational story about the kinds of activities one is trying to foster, and the reasons why such activities might be useful to students and teachers;

— ideas about the goals which are to be attained and the processes to be enacted;

— ways of describing teaching and learning;

— some means of capturing these descriptions economically, yet in a way which provides data of sufficient reliability to be used for research purposes and which can serve as a means of communication within the research team.

An exemplar: the mathematics trial

In 1982 and 1983, we set out to observe a large number of lessons in secondary mathematics classrooms in which teachers agreed to use microcomputers. Many of our aims and objectives are neatly captured in para 243 in the Cockcroft Report (1982). This paragraph states that "Mathematics teaching at all levels should include opportunities for:

— exposition by the teacher;
— discussion between teacher and pupils and between pupils themselves;
— appropriate practical work;
— consolidation and practice of fundamental skills and routines;
— problem-solving, including the application of mathematics to everyday situations;
— investigational work."

In our study we wished to take an open-eyed view of the way in which educational software would be used in representative classrooms. Teachers were supplied with a large collection of software suitable for secondary mathematics, and some suggestions about use in class. They attended a weekend training course which introduced them to the use of the equipment and some of the software. In exchange, each teacher agreed to use the computer for one lesson per week, and to have an observer present while the lesson took place.

Observers made a number of records, namely:
— a systematic behavioural description of the lesson, as it took place;
— an essay, which described the most notable features of the lesson from the observer's viewpoint, in an open-ended way;
— a summary sheet, which consisted of a brief questionnaire, and a global assessment of the usefulness of the CAL used during the lesson.

The behaviour schedule used was called SCAN (Beeby, et al., 1979). This provides codes for many of the events of interest. The summary sheet of the lesson addressed items of central interest to us; for example:
— whether the documentation provided was satisfactory;
— whether teachers felt under pressure from the level of demand expected of them;
— whether the classroom atmosphere was such that pupils were able to pay attention to the task in hand, etc.

In all we observed about 170 mathematics lessons and were able to, draw a wide range of conclusions about the impact of the computer on the classroom, in particular on its ability to shift teacher style dramatically, supported by evidence provided by behavioural descriptions of lessons captured by SCAN. A general conclusion was that more teacher support was desirable to help them use CAL effectively; that teachers seemed to prefer software packages which were rich enough to permit use in a variety of different ways, as opposed to using a large collection of programs, each of which had a single function. We also identified a surprisingly large number of technical and managerial problems which had to be overcome. (These are described more fully in Phillips et al., 1984.)

Lessons from the exemplar

The purpose of the exemplar is not to review our earlier studies of CAL in mathematical education; rather it is to highlight some important development principles which have arisen from these studies. Perhaps the most important lesson is that one should begin with some statement about the goals one wishes to achieve, together with a description of the behavioural correlates of these goals. The next task is to develop evaluative methods which are geared to the analysis of these behavioural goals. For example, if our focus is to change the balance of classroom activities, as in the exemplar above, then we need to develop an observational schedule geared to describing different patterns of classroom activities. If our intention is to improve reasoning skills, then we need to develop some measures of the sort of reasoning skills in which we are interested. (We might also develop a different observation schedule to describe lessons aimed to foster these reasoning skills.) If we want to shift pupils' perceptions of the usefulness of computers in social affairs, we need some methods for assessing these conceptions. If we are seeking to use a computer to increase pupils' composition skills in creative writing, or in art work, we need to develop some exemplar tasks which can illustrate these improvements.

Studying the processes associated with CAL is critically important. We need to be able to tell a story about the processes by which specific objectives might be achieved, in order to illuminate our general understanding of knowledge acquisition processes.

Watching other people using software in a variety of ways has, in our experience, proved to be invaluable it two respects: first it highlights weaknesses in the sorts of support being provided; and second it suggests valuable CAL based activities. Aspects of software design which lead to user difficulties are a rich source of useful ideas for receptive observers; observation of difficulties often lead to development in particular software packages, or in support materials which accompany software. By far the most salutary aspect of this sort of CAL evaluation is the observation of "robust" software in ordinary use. One's assumptions about what "everyone" knows are quickly shaken; more positively, one can often discover exciting possibilities for CAL use which even the design team, and experienced teachers, had not thought of.

Beyond CAL evaluation

Earlier we described the need to take account of the general systems in which CAL use is embedded. The control of CAL varies a good deal depending on the context in which one is working; to use our examples earlier, if one is working in an engineering department where computer-aided design is an essential part of the syllabus, then it is highly likely that all students will take a course which involves some computer-aided design. If one works in a mathematics department where students are strongly encouraged to explore a software library to facilitate their mathematical skills, then again, a significant proportion of students are likely to explore CAL for themselves. As the locus of control moves further away from the author, the problems of introducing CAL increases. Software development teams have little control of when and how CAL will be used in classrooms. Similarly outside agencies making recommendations about computer-based learning in industry are unlikely to have a final say about how and where such CBL will finally be deployed. These systems are all worthy of exploration. The successful introduction of CAL will depend critically on an understanding of the organisational structure in which CAL is to be used.

In our own work we have developed a number of themes which take account of such systems perspectives. For example, in the area of secondary mathematics we have collaborated with the Joint Matriculation Board in the introduction of a course on problem-solving which supports part of the revised 'O' Level syllabus set by the JMB. A major determinant of classroom behaviour in secondary school is the range of tasks which pupils will face in their examinations at O-level, CSE, or the new GCSE. We took the view that, if classroom behaviour is to be shifted to reflect the goals in the Cockcroft Report listed earlier, then these examinations must be changed. We set ourselves the task of bringing about some necessary changes in collaboration with the JMB. This involved a large scale exercise in curriculum development, involving:
— the production of curriculum materials;
— evaluation in class to observe the behavioural effects of these materials (following the development model outline in Figure 2);
— and the development of examination materials.

This process is described elsewhere (Ridgway et al., in press). The product of this research is a curriculum package (Shell Centre, 1984) which provides a 200 page teacher guide; video and supporting notes which describe different patterns of classroom style; pupil materials; and of course, a disk with supporting documentation which helps to provide the basis for classroom problem solving. After a similar process of curriculum research and development in the area of Functions and Graphs we have produced a module (Shell Centre, 1986) which supports a coherent package of work intended for the new GCSE examination. Again, CAL forms an integral part of this material. This work has convinced us of the need to treat seriously broad systems issues, i.e. those beyond the initial narrow range of questions which face one as a developer of CAL and other curriculum materials.

Concluding remarks

There are many pressing needs for research into IT in education (Ridgway, 1986). Evaluation of CAL is problematic. There are relatively few systematic studies of CAL in use; far more are needed. CAL evaluation should primarily be of a formative nature — we know rather little about the potential uses of CAL, and need to find out a good deal more — including trawling for new uses and new ideas by observing CAL in use — rather than simply producing summary statements about the global impact of a particular piece of software, as if it had already reached some zenith of perfection. CAL evaluation is likely to depend on the development of purpose-built, observational techniques. These in turn require a good deal of development work, but are likely to provide rich rewards if used appropriately. Fostering CAL throughout the educational system is likely to require a yet broader range of evaluative techniques, if systems issues are to be addressed adequately.

References

Beeby, T., Burkhardt, H. and Fraser, R. (1979). *SCAN — A Systematic Classroom Analysis Notation*. Shell Centre for Mathematical Education, University of Nottingham.

Bialo, E.R. and Erickson, L.B. (1985). *Microcomputer Courseware: Characteristics and Design Trends*. Journal of Computers in Mathematics and Science Teaching. Summer, pp. 27-32.

Cockcroft, W.H. (1982). *Mathematics Counts*. HMSO: London.

Fraser, R., Burkhardt, H., Coupland, J., Phillips, R., Pimm, D. and Ridgway, J. (in press). *Learning Activities and Classroom Roles*. Abacus.

Hartley, J.R., Carr, I.G. and Hijne, H. (1985). *Human Factors Experiments: experiences with EUROHELP.PO prototype*. Document CBLU-ULE/EUROHELP/022 (available from authors).

Phillips, R., Burkhardt, H., Coupland, J., Fraser, R., Pimm, D. and Ridgway, J. (1984). *Computer Aided Teaching*. Ergonomics, **27**, pp. 243-258.

Ridgway, J., Benzie, D., Burkhardt, H., Coupland, J., Field, G., Fraser, R. and Phillips, R. (1984). *Investigating CAL?* Computers and Education, **8**, 1, pp. 85-92.

Ridgway, J., Swan, M., Haworth, A. and Coupland J. (in press). *Innovation in Mathematical Education — The TSS Approach.* Proceedings of ICME **5**.

Ridgway, J. (1986). *Research Needs for Educational Uses of Information Technology.* ESRC-ITE Programme, Occasional Paper, ITE/9/86.

Shell Centre for Mathematical Education (1984). *Problems with Patterns and Numbers,* Joint Matriculation Board: Manchester.

Shell Centre for Mathematical Education (1986). *Language of Functions and Graphs,* Joint Matriculation Board: Manchester.

23 / Research in Progress

The design and evaluation of a knowledge-based adviser for learning materials

F. N. Arshad *Computer Based Learning Unit, University of Leeds**

Introduction

The long term goal of this project is to develop a learning aid for undergraduates in the Biological Sciences. The project is particularly concerned with developing problem solving skills that initially tend to demand specific knowledge of a domain, but which may develop into more general knowledge for applying the skill to similar types of problems in other domains. We are exploring the potential of the workstation as a "study desk" for students. As well as providing the student with a supportive environment, in the form of a knowledgeable Adviser to guide study tasks, the student is able to manipulate and manage the information in whatever way seems desirable. This provides students with a certain amount of control over what they learn, the rate at which they learn it, and how they learn it, whilst all the time having access to advice that takes these preferences into account.

Stages of the project

It is hoped to achieve the above goals by:
— conducting a pilot study to collect information about student conceptualisations, plan/methods, formulations, their use of heuristics, type of help requested and how this degree of support and patterns of work alter through experience;
— designing and evaluating a knowledgeable rule-based Learning Adviser to guide students with:
— preparation for the study of material;
— choice of problem task size and degree/type of support needed;
— follow up contrasts and similarities between types of related examples;
— developing graphical and other software tools.

*An ESRC Linked Studentship supervised by J. R. Hartley.

Learning adviser

The aim of the Learning Adviser is to provide minimum, but sufficient support to allow students to work and acquire problem solving skill, initially in the area of Pharmacology. We feel that such a system must fulfill at least five functions:

— to collect information about the student by asking direct questions and monitoring student activity during problem solving;
— to use this knowledge to build a representation of the student's knowledge;
— to provide feedback in response to the student's action;
— to provide advice on what should be done;
— to support and justify its statements.

These advisory functions are dependent upon the Adviser module having a set of pre-stored Policies which can be used as the basis for providing the student with appropriate support.

The Policies may be to:

— diagnose (assess/check the student's knowledge about concepts and relations);
— prepare (repair any misconceptions the student may have);
— consolidate (strengthen the student's knowledge of the topic by initiating greater use);
— generalise (get them to extend their knowledge, i.e. by comparing and contrasting problems).

The choice of policy made depends on the information available about the domain and about how it should be taught. The domain holds information about the curriculum material (e.g. Physiology, Pharmacology) and the possible teaching and application methods that experts in the respective subject area use. Further, just as experts or teachers are aware of things that can go wrong, it is necessary to include information about types of difficulties likely to arise in acquiring the necessary concepts and problem solving skills. Also of importance is the different learning styles students bring to the problem domain.

We cannot see this Learning Adviser working appropriately unless it can reference some form of user model or user representation. The user representation can provide such information about student capabilities as preferred style and rate of working, as well as student's domain knowledge etc. This can be used by the Adviser to organise and reorganise its knowledge about the level and size of task to be taught and policies to adopt.

Progress

The first few months have been concerned with a literature review of human problem solving, learning to use and evaluate various software tools used in the teaching of undergraduates at Leeds, and learning about the domain in which the Learning Adviser is to be applied. The domain of application chosen is Pharmacology, particularly the area of advice on learning about drugs and understanding the functionality of drugs in terms of some basic principles and mechanisms. Work on the first stage has been started and is at the stage of attempting to develop an understanding of the nature of Advice and Explanation, two issues important to the success of our Learning Adviser. We are also working on the second stage, trying to decide what our Learning Adviser should be composed of and what it should do.

Bibliography

Anderson, J.R. (1981) *Cognitive Skills and their Acquisition,* Lawrence Erlbaum Associates, USA.

Craik, K. (1943) *The Nature of Explanation,* Cambridge University Press.

Mayer, R.E. (1977) *Thinking and Problem Solving: An Introduction to Human Cognition and Learning,* Scott, Foreman and Co., USA.

Newell, A. and Simon, H.A. (1972) *Human Problem Solving,* Prentice-Hall, Englewood Cliffs.

A knowledge-based system to provide advice and explanation in the context of post-operative care

J. J. Bailey *Computer Based Learning Unit, University of Leeds**

History and research background

There has been interest within Leeds University for many years in providing computer-based teaching systems in the medical domain. Attempts have been made to provide supporting knowledge in these programs so that they can work out responses to students' 'help' requests. So far efforts have used only statistically-based (Bayes Theorem) methods.

DIAGNOSE is one such teaching system. It consists of a database of relative frequencies of diseases and symptoms and from this (statisti-

*An ESRC Linked Studentship supervised by J. R. Hartley.

cally) generates a 'patient', i.e. a profile of symptoms. It is limited in the help it can give the user but it will provide suggestions (from Bayesian expectations) as to which symptoms or signs are statistically most significant to the case, and what support levels the symptoms contribute to a differential diagnosis. However these data are numeric and qualitative — the user cannot ask why- or how- type questions for further explanations. This is a typical problem with statistically-based systems, for practitioners generally do not think in terms of numerical probabilities although they have an idea of likelihood and risks. In contrast, rule-based systems, of which MYCIN is the archetype in the medical area, work from a corpus of knowledge rules that has potential to be used in consultation dialogue mode for explanation and advice giving (Shortliffe, 1976).

MYCIN's domain knowledge, which is concerned with bacterial infections and their treatment, is represented by domain specific rules of the type:

IF premise (set), THEN action (set).

These rules are used not only to work out inferences and conclusions but for consultation and explanation purposes. Explanation is available in two forms, either by examining the reasoning goals assumed during a consultation (using WHY questions) or by examining the knowledge which was used during this process (using a HOW command). However there are two important kinds of explanation that MYCIN cannot give:
— it cannot explain or justify why a particular is rule correct, and
— it cannot explain or justify the strategy behind the design of its goal structure.

Johnson and Keravnou (1985) state that "human experts derive their flexibility as problem solvers from their ability to violate a rule in difficult "non-standard" situations, by being able to reason with the knowledge involved in the inference steps that tie antecedents to consequents".

MYCIN is just one example of a system in the medical domain — there are many others, including derivatives of MYCIN, e.g. GUIDON, NEOMYCIN, but it is fair to point out that in designing these programs there has been inadequate study of the types of human dialogue which are used when giving explanation and advice. Differing aims and viewpoints of users tend to be ignored, and explanations are usually pruned traces of the working of the program, not its interpretation into the knowledge structures and types of arguments which are given in human discourse. Further they have no clear rationale of learning processes and hence the ways information on students knowledge levels and experience can be used to individualise answers to the same questions and provide more general educational advice on learning from tasks.

Aims of research

The aim of the current research is to overcome these inadequacies. The overall objective is to produce a knowledgeable adviser which is able to give explanation and advice from differing viewpoints and which will be useful in training. The work is therefore:

— studying 'expert' decision-making through talk aloud protocols, using case-study and simulation techniques.

— examining the types of explanation and advice which experts give to those less-experienced, together with the circumstances and reasons why such advice is given.

We are also representing and using these data to design a knowledge-based system capable of making conclusions/decisions, of providing explanation and of giving advice to learners. A later stage of the research will evaluate the performance of this software and examine the ways it is used by practitioners in improving decision-making skills.

The research context

The working domain is post-operative care in hospitals. Patients are monitored regularly but deciding when signs are at variance with diagnostic expectation, and perceiving the implications for treatment is a difficult task not only for students, but also for junior practitioners. Characteristic features of this scenario are the temporal reasoning that is required for identifying patterns and trends, and the variety of human expertise available and on duty at anyone time.

Two common patient problems frequently encountered involve temperature fluctuations and fluid balance and this study will initially concentrate on these problems.

Outline of the system

The research is in collaboration with surgeons from St. James Hospital, Leeds and at present patient cases are being studied and analysed with these surgeons to identify how they interpret data and make diagnoses. From the results of these investigations so far, we have formulated some ideas of the decision/monitoring process. These include:

— identification of problems through interpretations of data — specifically through value-bounds, trends and patterns of data to identify signs of variance from 'normal' ranges, referenced through pre-operation data of the patient;

— setting up differential diagnostic candidates, some of which can be eliminated by cross-checking and by inference and causal reasoning;

— determining which actions of monitoring (data and frequency) to resolve or to eliminate hypotheses and/or treatment decisions which are judged necessary. Both these judgments involve expectations, assessment of seriousness and other patient factors (e.g. elderly/young).

Explanation

Once the domain representation and data structures have been defined, interest will turn to the explanation-giving capability of this system. The Adviser should be able to provide explanation through responding to users' questions and should take account of users' level of knowledge, intentions and purposes. Thus the Adviser will have to be able to consider a variety of viewpoints in its comments, and answer:

— elaboration queries (e.g. tell more), give

— clarifications (e.g. what conclusions) or differential diagnoses under consideration, provide

— justification (e.g. why?), and

— exploration questions (e.g. what-if? how-if?).

The answer comments, as well as referencing user knowledge and adjusting differing levels of detail, may use various perspectives e.g. physiological views, diagnosis and treatment dialogue and case-management principles.

References

Johnson, L. and Keravnou, E.T. (1985) *Expert Systems Technology: A Guide,* Abacus Press.

Shortliffe, E.H. (1976) *Computer-Based Medical Consultations: MYCIN,* New York: American Elsevier.

An intelligent knowledge based system as an aid to chemical problem solving

David Bateman *King's College (KQC), London**

Introduction

The purpose of this study is to investigate the potential of a knowledge based system as a tool for use by school pupils engaged in chemical problem solving. Such a system is a computer program capable of giving the user access to stored information in the form of facts and relationships but it is more powerful than conventional data bases because it is able to use its stored knowledge to infer new knowledge. The most powerful feature of a knowledge based system is its facility for revealing the inferencing process to the user. This study originated from classroom experiences in trying to engage pupils in chemical problem solving. Problem solving is an important activity in any chemistry course but experience was that pupils did not find it particularly easy and that adequate individual assistance was hard to provide given the diverse demands of teaching in the classroom.

Individual differences between problem solvers lead to large differences between the problem solving abilities of pupils. It is particularly difficult to offer individual assistance to pupils in groups where ability differences are such that some pupils gain grade "A" at O-level and some grade 5 at CSE. Individualised tuition would be helpful but tutorial assistance does not appear in the literature as a significant feature of secondary school work. Reference can be found to investigations into the benefit of this type of education at the tertiary level (Ogborn, 1977; Webb, 1983; Giles and Gilbert, 1981).

Individualised learning is generally catered for by the provision of non-interactive resources such as in the Independent Learning Project in Advanced Chemistry. The main resource in this scheme is a series of units which sets out a programme of work for the students to follow including problems to be solved. The solutions to these problems are available in the units along with a single solution pathway. The starting point for the present study is the suggestion that an interactive resource can provide individualised assistance to problem solvers.

The development of intelligent tutoring systems is one response to pupils' need for interactive assistance. These systems have been con-

*An ESRC Linked Studentship supervised by Dr. John Harris in the Centre for Educational Studies.

structed for research purposes but are not in regular use in teaching. They have had features such as domain competence, student models, tutoring strategies, and user interfaces. Tutoring strategies may be described as active or passive. Most systems have used active strategies but these depend on student models and sophisticated interfaces. Active strategies involve intervention in the pupil actions and place the tutor in control. A passive tutoring strategy is a strategy for conducting a dialogue between a tutor and a pupil which puts the pupil in control. Its major features are pupil initiated questions and tutor provided information and explanation based on the questions asked and knowledge of the domain.

The domain chosen for this work is that of physical separating techniques as would be dealt with in a chemistry course leading to CSE or O-level examinations. This topic is dealt with at an early stage in these courses and covers concepts such as "pure substance" which are fundamental to later work. The domain is likely to remain an important part of school science well into the future and is part of all the proposed GCSE syllabuses in chemistry. Three sets of hypotheses form the focus of the investigation. Each set covers different issues in the construction and use of an interactive resource in the form of an Intelligent Knowledge Based System.

— A knowledge based system can be constructed using hardware and software tools available in schools. The system will be capable of solving problems in the specified domain, of providing information about the domain, and of providing explanation of solutions to problems it has solved.
— Components of a passive tutoring strategy can be identified in the dialogue between a pupil and a human tutor when the pupil is engaged in assisted chemical problem solving.
— The interaction between a pupil engaged in chemical problem solving and a knowledge based system which the pupil can ask for assistance, can be described in terms of a passive tutoring strategy.

Background

Work in the field of artificial intelligence (AI), which generally adopts an information processing view of cognition, has led to descriptions of problems in terms of states of the world. The world in this sense is the problem domain of interest and the states represent snapshots of that world. All problems would therefore have an initial state, a goal state and a set of operators which can transform one state into another. A typical problem in the separating techniques domain would have a list of components in a mixture as an initial state and a single pure substance as a final state. Various separating techniques such as filtration are the operators which are used alone or in combination to transform the initial state into the goal state. Problem solving as viewed from this position is therefore the use of domain knowledge to discover a suitable path from the initial state to the goal state.

Representing domain knowledge is a vital step in constructing IKBS. Formalisms which have been used for this purpose include procedural formalism, analogical systems, frames, production systems, semantic networks, and logic. A combination of the last two has been used in this work. The nodes and links in the network map easily into arguments and predicates in the computer language PROLOG which is based on predicate logic.

Explanation produced by machine is currently little more than the revealing of rules used to infer a conclusion. The explanation facility used in this work is of the same type. The facility used is a commercially available expert system shell written in PROLOG. Although there does not appear to be a philosophical base to the explanation produced, it does match scientific explanation as described by the covering law model. Various categorisations of intelligent tutoring systems exist but one by Sleeman and Brown (1982) describes four research areas in which these systems have been investigated, namely;
— protocol analysis,
— computer-based coaches,
— artificial intelligence techniques, and
— self-improving teaching systems.
A fifth category seems to have developed recently which Cabrol (1986) describes as problem solving partners. This last category most closely describes the work under discussion in this paper.

Methodology

Space does not permit a full description of the methods used in constructing the IKBS. In general terms it was a process of increasing formalisation of textbook knowledge to the point where its description was such that it could be run as a computer program in PROLOG to solve problems. The initial descriptions in English and the final descriptions in PROLOG were bridged by intermediate descriptions such as a semantic network. The network was approached by both a bottom-up and a top-down process. The bottom-up process started with representational primitives in the domain, e.g. "suspension", and entailed describing the relationships between these primitives. The top-down approach started with problems which might be posed in the domain, e.g. "How do you separate sodium chloride from a solution of sodium chloride and water?". Rules needed to solve such problems resulted in an extended semantic network.

The work involving the second hypothesis study will concentrate on the tutoring of one pupil at a time attempting to solve chemical problems in the domain of separating techniques in the presence of a human tutor. The pupils chosen will be about age 15 and be studying chemistry as part of some examination course. It will be assumed they have some knowledge of the domain before the study begins and have some motivation to solve the problems presented to them. In the region of ten pupils will be investigated allowing about 20 minutes for each. It is envisaged that the pupils will be selected at random but will come from schools with pupils of both sexes, of varying abilities and from a variety of ethnic, social and economic backgrounds. The tutor and the investigator are likely to be the same person. This may give rise to some problems. For example, the use of only one tutor may result in tutoring sessions which hide aspects of tutoring which could be observed in other tutors and knowledge of the research programme may influence the tutoring.

As the pupil attempts to solve each problem in turn the tutor will offer such assistance as is necessary to enable the pupil to write down a solution. This assistance will extend to information and explanation but not to the solution of the problem. The pupil will be able to ask for information or explanation at any time during the process. A complete set of about five problems will be solved in this way. The problems will be of increasing complexity in terms of the minimum number of steps needed for a solution to be found. They will all require knowledge of different parts of the domain. The final part of the investigation will look at the use pupils make of the knowledge based system. The last hypothesis will be tested by asking the following sorts of question about the interaction between the pupil and the machine:

— What types of questions, information and explanation are interchanged?
— What are the links between the questions, information and explanation interchanged?
— Are all possible types of question used by pupils?
— What are the major differences between the pupil/human and the pupil/machine dialogue?
— Are there questions which pupils wish to ask but which the system prevents?
— What features of the systems use can be observed but are not recorded via the keyboard?
— How far into explanations do pupils proceed?

A similar selection of pupils will be used for this work as for the previous part of the study. Each pupil in turn will be invited to solve the set of problems. During the process of solving each problem the pupil will have access to the system. The system will provide information or explanation on demand but stop short of providing a solution to any of the problems. The pupils will write down their solutions when they are satisfied that they have found out enough from the system to solve the problem. The use of the system will be observed and significant aspects of its use noted including the pupils verbalised difficulties and comments. The pupil/machine interaction will be echoed to a printer or stored on disc to provide a record. A uniform description of both cases of tutoring will then provide a language for describing strengths and weaknesses in each case.

References

Cabrol, D. (1986) *Some examples of the use of artificial intelligence techniques in chemical education,* 8th International Conference on Chemical Education, Tokyo, Blackwell Scientific Publications (in press).

Giles, E.J. and Gilbert, J.K. (1981) *Prompting in one-to-one problem solving situations,* International Journal of Mathematics Education and Science Technology, **12**, 1, pp. 125.

Ogborn, J. (ed) (1977) *Small Group Teaching in Undergraduate Science,* Heinemann.

Sleeman, D. and Brown, J.S. (1982) *Intelligent Tutoring Systems,* Academic Press.

Webb, G. (1983) *The tutorial method, learning strategies and student participation in tutorials,* Programmed Learning and Educational Technology, **20**, 2, pp. 117.

Students' creation and interaction with computational representation of their own knowledge structure

Nancy Law *Institute of Education, University of London**

Introduction

Computational models of knowledge structures have been used in research both in the field of Artificial Intelligence and in Education. Such models require all features involved to be made explicit in the process of construction, and in turn offer a unique possibility for hypotheses to be tested out on them. Larkin and Rainard's work (1984)

*A British Council Studentship supervised by Professor Jon Ogborn in the Department of Science Education.

is an example where such techniques have been used to great advantage in investigating problem solving skills of novices and experts in Physics.

This paper describes research into children's intuitive ideas of motion through the conscious participation of students in building up of expert systems based on self-inspection of their own conceptions of motion. A basic attitude in this research is that the students are treated as experts in their own right. Techniques employed in AI work on knowledge elicitation and representation are used for probing the possible existence of a 'common sense theory of motion' which underlies the rich collection of pupils' misconceptions/alternative conceptions in mechanics that various research workers have gathered. (See Ogborn, 1985 for one view of what such a theory may look like.)

Problems encountered in the teaching of physics

Researches in Science Education over the last 10 to 15 years have given much emphasis to the investigation of children's conceptions in various content areas before and after instruction. It is evident from the abundant existing literature that students do not come to science classes empty-minded. Instead, they bring with them a whole lot of concepts and ideas of varying degrees of sophistication that they developed through their own personal experience. These conceptual structures are very often different from the accepted scientific views, and yet are extremely persistent in spite of formal instruction. Thus they have been referred to variously as children's ideas, misconceptions and alternative frameworks, by different research groups. (Driver and Erickson (1983) gives a good overview of the scene; see also Gilbert and Watts (1983)).

The existence of widespread alternative conceptions does not mean that students learn nothing at all. Anzai and Yokoyama's work (1984) in problem solving showed that many students who failed to solve a problem because of an initial, naive representation may be helped to develop a scientific representation and subsequently to solve the problem when given suitable cues. This indicates some form of incorporation of the knowledge learnt from Physics lessons into students' original naive conceptions of the Physical world. Apparently, formal instruction has not replaced students' common sense conceptions of the world, but results in an inconsistent, complex hybrid of knowledge obtained from different sources.

Why is learning physics difficult?

According to Kelly (1955), each person constructs for him/herself representational models of the world which enable that person to chart a course of behaviour in relation to it. This model is subject to change over time, adjusting to discrepancies so as to allow for better predictions in the future. Now since both scientists and novices construct their own understanding of the world, we may ask why it is so difficult for novices to arrive at the scientists' construction? Are there fundamental differences in the nature of these two constructions? Wartofsky gave a good exposition:

> In our basic conception of the relation of things to each other we take certain things to be the cause of others, appealing to some general concept of cause and effect, or causality.... Such a conceptual framework therefore, is the way in which we rationally order our knowledge.... [and] serves also to order our actions and expectations. Science has achieved a remarkable rigor in its construction of such a conceptual framework which goes beyond the ordinary requirements of common sense, common language and common activity. (Wartofsky, 1968, p.7)

To clarify the difficulty ahead of a learner of science, the difference between science and common sense warrants analysis at both the epistemological and metaphysical levels. Though no attempt will be made to discuss these important issues here, a brief examination of the structural difference between science and common sense is in place.

Nagel (1961) suggested the distinguishing of scientific laws into two types: experimental laws and theories. The former are basically empirical findings, which could in principle be proposed and asserted as inductive generalisations based on relations found to hold in observed data. Theories, by contrast, may be likened to sets of mathematical axioms. They are free inventions of the human mind to make sense of the world, to relate the diverse results from experimental laws through a model based on the theory. Thus theories are fallible and experimental laws would persist, but the former are much more powerful tools with which to describe and understand the world. In a scientist's mental model, the most general comprehensive theory should have the highest priority, and the hierarchy of theories form salient features in his reasoning.

Common sense knowledge of the world around us is developed through rather different processes. It is shaped by our interactions with our physical environment as a response to the need to order our actions and expectations for everyday activities and also by the language and social practices of our culture. As common sense knowledge will not stand up to stringent demands on rigor or comprehensive applicability, its effect on a person's subsequent formal learning has been neglected until very recently.

Results from researches on problem solving behaviour of experts and novices (Larkin, 1983; Chi, Feltovitch and Glaser, 1981) showed that experts and novices used different mental representations. Experts' representations contain 'fictitious' imagined entities such as forces and momenta; the operators which they use on these entities, to relate them and make inferences about them, correspond to the laws of Physics. Novices, on the other hand, use naive problem representations composed of objects that exist in the real world; the operators which they use for solving problems correspond to developments that occur in real time. Such results would be an expected, logical consequence if there are structural differences between scientists' knowledge and common sense knowledge.

Learning as a change in both the database and datastructure of the learner's memory

The increasing number of researches into children's spontaneous reasoning (Viennot, 1979) or alternative conceptions (Driver and Erickson, 1983) is a healthy trend showing the increased recognition of the effect of preconceptions on learning. Yet, all the researches that have been carried out can be described as having a starting point from the scientific view, and trying to find out where and how the students' view departs from that. This results in a rich crop of data on children's ideas in the form of the possible contents of their knowledge base, with little information on what children's knowledge structures are like. Any attempts at teaching claiming reference to the learner's conceptual framework is not really faithful to the claim unless both factors are taken into account. The lack of significant progress in the direction of developing better teaching strategies may be due to our lopsided attention to the children's knowledge base only.

Rost (1983) proposed learning as the process of changing a learner's knowledge structure to a desired goal structure. Yet what is the learner's knowledge structure like? What is the goal structure like? How may it be possible for a person's knowledge structure to change? What characterises such a process? These are important questions for which we have little idea even of the form of an answer.

The present research

The present research attempts to address the above four questions. The interpretation of the first question differs from Rost's (op cit) which is to find the pre-instructional knowledge structure of the learner. The subjects chosen for this research are Advanced Level Physics students and no attempt will be made to stop abstract terms learnt from Physics entering into the initial representation of their knowledge structure. To insist on starting from a knowledge structure 'untouched' by formal instruction would mean that the subjects would have to be young children, who would not have sufficient intellectual maturity to participate in the processes involved in learning formal physics. By involving students of varying ability, it is hoped that the resulting initial knowledge structures will show interesting differences.

The main task for the students participating in the research is to build an expert system of their own understanding of motion in micro-Prolog (McCabe et al., 1985) using the front-end APES (Hammond and Sergot, 1984). They participate in the actual construction of the initial computational representation, interact with and assess the model built and modify it as they think fit. A representation of the student's knowledge in the form of an expert system has the advantages of being explicit, explorable and capable of offering explanations for deduction paths. This conscious involvement of the students in the model building process is seen mainly as a tool for probing deeper into their knowledge structure. It also offers a good opportunity to explore the possible outcomes of confronting students with explicit representations of their own knowledge.

This research is still in the piloting stage and it is anticipated that many difficulties are likely to arise not the least of which would be of a technical nature. Taylor (1985) pointed out that programming in Prolog has many hidden difficulties for the novice. A major concern in this research is to ensure that the actual coding of the students' ideas in the form of a Prolog program will not distract the students from the main theme of the exercise.

References

Anzai, Y. and Yokoyama, T. (1984) *Internal Models in Physics Problem Solving*, Cognition and Instruction, **1**, 4, pp. 397-450.

Chi, M.T.H., Feltovitch, P.J. and Glaser, R. (1981) *Categorization and Representation of Physics Problems by Experts and Novices*, Cognitive Science, **5**, pp. 121-152.

Driver, R. and Erickson, G. (1983) *Theories in Action: Some Theoretical and Empirical Issues in the Study of Students' Conceptual Frameworks in Science*, Studies in Science Education, **10**, pp. 37-60.

Gilbert, J.K. and Watts, D.M. (1983) *Concepts, Misconceptions and Alternative Conceptions: Changing Perspectives in Science Education*, Studies in Science Education, **10**, pp. 61-98.

Hammond, P. and Sergot, M. (1984) *APES: Augmented Prolog of Expert Systems Reference Manual*, Logic Based Systems Ltd., England.

Kelly, G.S. (1955) *The Psychology of Personal Constructs,* N.Y., Norton.

Larkin, J.H. and Rainard, B. (1984) *A Research Methodology for Studying How People Think,* Journal of Research in Science Teaching, **21**, 3, pp. 235-254.

Larkin, J.H. (1983) *The Role of Problem Representation in Physics,* Mental Models, Gentner, D. and Stevens, A. (eds), Lawrence Erlbaum Associates, London.

McCabe, F.R. et al. (1985) *Micro-Prolog Professional Programmer's Reference Manual,* Logic Programming Associates Ltd., London.

Nagal, E. (1961) *The Structure of Science,* Harcourt, Brace, N.Y.

Ogborn, J.M. (1985) *Understanding Students' Understandings: An example from dynamics,* European Journal of Science Education, **7**, 2, pp. 141-150.

Rost, J. (1983) *Network Theories of Semantic Memory and their Implications for Teaching Physics,* Research on Physics education: Proceedings of the First International Workshop, La Londe Les Maures.

Taylor, J. (1984) *Why Novices Will Find Learning Prolog Hard,* Cognitive Studies Programme, University of Sussex.

Viennot, L. (1979) *Spontaneous Reasoning in Elementary Dynamics,* European Journal of Science Education, **1**, 2, pp. 205-221.

Wartofsky, M.W. (1968) *Conceptual Foundations of Scientific Thought,* The Macmillan Co., N.Y.

The penetration and effectiveness of information technology (IT) in and through teacher education

Mary T. Megarity *The Queen's University, Belfast**

Background

There is a considerable amount of literature available dealing with the broad issue of IT in education. The purpose of this study however is to focus on the factors which contribute to effective in-service teacher education in the field of IT.

Since the mid-1970s it has been increasingly apparent that pupils should be educated about computer technology. Whilst it may be argued that computer awareness can be arrived at by passive means — books, lectures, etc — computer literacy can only be arrived at through practice.

It can be argued that the provision of educational computing resources in schools has attracted insufficient funding with the result that resources are patchy. Where a need for training or formal computing qualifications has been recognised appropriate hardware has been provided. Development therefore has varied primarily according to geographical and institutional location and to the levels of available

*An ESRC Award to Dr. J. Gardner, Department of Education.

expertise and only secondarily as a result of any national objective to train and educate people to exploit the new technology.

The pace of development has not been regular. During the mid-1970s the Government funded National Development Programme for Computer-Assisted Learning (NDPCAL) highlighted the potential of interactive terminal work and the application of computers across the curriculum in higher education. Many University departments participated in the Programme and provided some of the first resources for undergraduate work in the University sector. Often the learning curve on these projects was slow and at least one year was spent by some of the project staff becoming familiar with hardware and software aspects of their proposed CAL work. However those staff remaining within the educational sector were a potential valuable nucleus of expertise for subsequent development work. There is still however, a need for qualified, educationally experienced staff.

It has been suggested that the influence of that Programme could have been extended if the funded projects had been able to foster collaboration across disciplines and between institutions during the post NDPCAL years. However it is the micro-chip revolution and availability of cheap hardware which is influencing and motivating developments now.

With the impact of micro-electronics during the last few years, the Government has focussed its activities in several areas:

Department of Trade and Industry schemes:
— 'Micros in Schools' scheme (1980-1982)
— 'Initial Teacher Training' scheme (1982-1983)
— 'Micros in Primary Schools' scheme (1982-1985)
— 'Peripherals' scheme (1983-1984)
— 'CNC Machine Tools in Further Education' scheme (1983-1984)
— 'Supported Software' scheme (1985-1988).

Department of Education and Science
— Microelectronics in Education Programme, MEP (1981-1986)
— Microelectronics Support Unit, (MeSU) (1986-1987).

The work of the MEP covered three main areas as set out in the Programme strategy document (DES, 1981):
— curriculum development;
— teacher training;
— organisation and support of resources.

In the area of teacher training in new technological education, Fothergill (1983) noted that existing courses "are not evenly spread throughout the country and their range and content vary considerably".

One aim of the programme therefore was "to stimulate an effective pattern of provision and develop materials for training in order to strengthen what already exists and assist the training institutions to make appropriate provision". The follow-on from MEP is the establishment of the MeSU which has the following main aims:

— to act as a central source of information for LEAs and schools;
— to provide training for teacher educators;
— to support the development of curriculum materials.

In-service education of teachers

Purposeful in-service education may have a variety of guises and as the James Committee (1972) suggested, it can cover a wide spectrum ranging from evening meetings and discussions, weekend conferences and other short-term activities to long-term education, for example 1-year fellowships. The following are some examples of different patterns of study which exist:

(i) short courses and short sandwich courses, normally non award-bearing;

(ii) engagement, possibly on secondment, in curriculum development project work at local, regional or national level;

(iii) in-service work involving groups of professionally related, or geographically adjacent, schools;

(iv) schoolteacher fellowships or associateships at universities and colleges;

(v) long-term courses e.g. M.Ed., M.A. (Eds), DASE.

Traditionally, INSET has centred on individual teachers who select which activities they participate in from the menu of courses, workshops, lectures, curriculum groups and so on that are offered by the various providing agencies. However, recent research (e.g. DES, 1978) has suggested that this may not be a very effective means of in-service education and that the school should be the basic unit for INSET rather than the individual teacher. This has been termed school-focussed INSET and may be defined as that which is targeted on the needs of a particular school or group within the school. The actual activity may take place on-site (school-based) or off-site and equally importantly may be internally provided by certain school staff or externally provided by an outside agency (Baker, 1980). It is inevitable that specialist training will centre around the equipment and computer applications of the moment; but ultimately it is important to provide the subject teacher with confidence to use the equipment in a classroom situation. The purpose of this work is to focus on the factors which influence the achievement of this goal. Generally positive support from the Principal or Head of Department is necessary. This includes good inter-staff relationships, appropriate in-service education, and research projects. This theory will be investigated. Teachers' attitudes towards computers will also be examined.

Different interpretations of computer literacy exist and to this extent, the various international efforts in IT education will also be investigated in this work. At the national level the ESRC 'IT and Education' Programme is concerned with the needs of education in relation to IT. This particular piece of research is concerned with investigating IT in teacher education with reference to courses being provided for teachers and teacher educators — using interviews, Delphi enquiries and questionnaires. An attempt at classification of in-service education has also been started in an endeavour to categorise national and local provision.

References

Baker, K. (1980) *Planning school policies for INSET: the SITE Project.* In Hoyle, E. and Megarry, J. (eds) World Yearbook of Education 1980: Professional Development of Teachers, Kogan Page, London.

Department of Education and Science (1978) *Making INSET Work,* HMSO, London.

Department of Education and Science (1981) *MEP: the Strategy,* London.

Fothergill, R., Anderson, J.S.A., Aston, M., Bevis, G., Irving, A., Russell, P. and Wheeler, P. (1983) *MEP Policy and Guidelines Information Guide 4,* Council for Educational Technology, London.

James Committee (1972) in Department of Education and Science report, *Teacher Education and Training,* HMSO, London.

Further reading

Fernig, L.R. (1980) *The Place of Information in Educational Development,* Paris, UNESCO.

Gwyn, R. (1982) *Information Technology and Education: The Approach to Policy in England, Wales and Northern Ireland,* European Journal of Education, **17** (4), 355-368.

Hoyle, E. and Megarry, J. (eds) (1980) *World Yearbook of Education 1980: Professional Development of Teachers,* Kogan Page, London.

Weindling, D., Reid, M.I. and Davis, P. (1983) *Teachers' Centres: A Focus for In-service Education?,* Metheun Educational, London.

What does the student know? Investigating a commonsense theory of motion

Denise Whitelock *Institute of Education, University of London**

Background

It has long been recognised by science teachers that students experience difficulties with the dynamics section of a physics syllabus and that responses to questions which are designed to test understanding reveal a confusion and lack of comprehension which inhibits the correct manipulation of the relevant scientific principles.

However, it is not only practising teachers who are aware of this problem. There is a growing body of research interested in students' intuitive ideas about science. This includes a considerable number of investigations which support the view that pupils have their own conceptions about natural phenomena.

There are a widespread number of findings related to pupils' notions about dynamics and several different types of written assignments have been used to probe students' understanding of force and motion. These studies have been reviewed by Driver and Erickson (1983) and Gilbert and Watts (1983) and although attempts have been made to define common frameworks it is often difficult to fit a descriptive pattern to the results obtained.

The literature not only reveals the abundance of pupils' prior beliefs in the area of dynamics but that the mismatch between students' understanding of science and formal science can persist even through to undergraduate level MacDermott (1984). This suggests that some naive notions could be more permanent than others and that it might prove useful to construct a more formal description of how motion is perceived in a common sense way. A preliminary sketch of a common sense theory of motion (Ogborn, 1985) was derived from ideas presented by Hayes (1984) who wished to devise a computer program which could reason about the world in a natural way and part of his original model was concerned with motion.

Aims of the research

This piece of research aims to investigate how these common sense

---

*An ESRC Linked Studentship supervised by Professor Jon Ogborn in the Department of Science Education.

ideas are utilised by students and raises two methodological questions:
— How can we find out what the student knows?
— How can we represent that knowledge formally?

Since common sense knowledge is so strongly taken for granted and not made explicit, it is difficult to probe. Situations where the subject feels it is both possible and reasonable to explain things which normally need no explanation have to be found.

Research methods

The approach we adopted was to conduct a number of individual interviews with a group of 11-14 year olds. The interview was focussed around a series of events illustrated in children's comics. The comics were chosen because characters from comic strips can be involved in a lot of action which is often fantastic or ridiculous and such movements are often parodies of more natural actions. Hence a joke is created. Since comics are read by many younger pupils their characters need little introduction and are remembered by older pupils and even adults with some affection. During the course of the interview, each subject was asked to describe what was happening in each comic strip and then asked whether it was feasible for these actions to take place in "real life" and to offer explanations as to why these actions could or could not happen. The pupils' intuitive ideas were probed in this way and developed as they arose during the course of the interview.

It was found that pupils perceived falling as a natural motion which occurred through lack of support. The support however, needed to be strong and made of the correct material otherwise it would break and the object would fall. Some students emphasise the fact that adequate support needed to be beneath an object, as with brackets below shelves, or more air under the wings of a bird to maintain its position above ground. Gravity appeared to be an optional extra to the core notion of falling and was not used consistently, but other types of motion required an effort of some kind. The words force and effort were used simultaneously in this context but force or effort had to run out for motion to stop.

The way students classify motions was not investigated in this study but the use of another probe to elicit this type of knowledge has been explored using a Repertory Grid Analysis. This technique focusses upon the individual's construction of knowledge and its theoretical strength (derived from Kelly's Personal Construct Theory). It is an attempt to stand in the subject's shoes and view the world as they see it and should aid the understanding of their perspective.

Another pilot series of individual interviews with a group of 11 year olds and then 17 year olds was conducted. The students were presented with fourteen cards depicting types of motion. Constructs were elicited by asking them to choose a pair of cards alike in some respect and then a third one unlike in the same respect. A preliminary analysis of the results suggests that students tend to group actions in terms of whether they are deliberate or controllable and focus on the direction, source and type of action causing the particular motion.

Representing the findings

Although we are currently assessing the results of the empirical studies we are also concerned with the question of how we can represent this collection of common sense ideas. What would be an appropriate vehicle for the description of such problems as support and movement in a non-scientific manner? Since a PROLOG program offers a description of a "world" made up of facts and rules which generates the consequences of that chosen description, we have tried to capture some of the common sense thinking about support in a PROLOG program employed within the expert system shell APES. The resulting interaction with APES not only reveals, as one would expect, flaws in a less than rigorous description but also provides clues as to where this description is incomplete and, perhaps more importantly, quickly provides feedback about the appropriateness and reliability of any representation which is constructed. Hence our research is currently addressing the methodological problems of knowledge elicitation and representation while attempting to construct and formalise a model of the students' own thinking in the area of dynamics.

References

Driver, R. and Erickson, G. (1983) *Theories in Action: Some Theoretical and Empirical Issues in the Study of Students' Conceptual Frameworks in Science,* Studies in Science Education, **10**, p. 60.

Gilbert, J.K. and Watts, M.D. (1983) *Concepts, Misconceptions and Alternative Conceptions: Changing Perspectives in Science Education,* Studies in Science Education, **10**, pp. 61-98.

Hayes, P. (1979) *The Naive Physics Manifesto,* in Michie, D. (ed) Expert Systems in a Micro-Electronic Age, Edinburgh University press.

McDermott, L. (1984) *An Overview of Research on Conceptual Understanding of Mechanics,* Physics Today, July 1984, pp. 22-32.

Ogborn, J. (1985) *Understanding Students' Understandings: An Example from Dynamics,* European Journal of Science Education, **7**, pp. 141-150.

List of Participants

Miss Jane Aarons, *(student) Leeds Girls' High School.*

Dr. L. Acker, *University of Victoria, Canada.*

Fara Arshad, *University of Leeds.*

Paula Askew, *Education Dept, Hounslow.*

David Bateman, *Kings' College, London.*

Dr. K. Beauchamp, *University of Lancaster.*

Dr. M. Beer, *University of Liverpool.*

Dr. M. Beilby, *University of Birmingham.*

D. Benton, *Craig Dunain Hospital.*

Dr. D. Binsted, *University of Lancaster.*

Dr. P. Borcherds, *University of Birmingham.*

Dr. B. du Boulay, *University of Sussex.*

Prof. G. Boyd, *Concordia University, Quebec.*

Dr. D. A. Bradley, *University of Lancaster.*

Ian Brown, *Education Department, Ipswich.*

Dr. I. C. Brown, *City of London Polytechnic.*

M. Bryson, *ESRC-ITE Programme and University of Lancaster.*

Mrs. L. Burdekin, *Bradford & Ilkley Community College.*

Mrs. D. Burkhardt, *University of Birmingham.*

D. H. Callear, *HCIRU, Loughborough University.*

Nick Campbell, *University of Lancaster.*

Mrs. C. D. Cleverley, *Leeds Girls' High School.*

Jill Coates, *Council for Educational Technology, London.*

Dr. R. Cole, *Glasgow College of Technology.*

Dr. R. Coleman, *University of Sheffield.*

Dr. J. Cook, *Glasgow College of Technology.*

Susan Coote, *University of Lancaster.*

Jonathan Darby, *University of Oxford.*

Dr. Nicki Davies, *University of Ulster.*

Peter Dovey, *Worcester College of Higher Education.*

Dr. P. Duce, *University of Liverpool.*

Nicola Eaton, *University of Wales College of Nursing.*

Dr. L. Ford, *University of Exeter.*

Dr. P. Forer, *University of Canterbury, New Zealand.*

P. Freakley, *Acorn Computers.*

R. Furlong, *Stourbridge College of Technology & Art.*

Dr. J. Gardner, *The Queen's University, Belfast.*

Prof. D. Gillies, *Ryerson Polytechnical Institute, Canada.*

Dr. P. Goodyear, *University of Lancaster.*

Dr. A. Gray, *University of Technology, Loughborough.*

Ms. S. Haigh, *Bradford & Ilkley Community College.*

Dr. R. Harding, *University of Cambridge.*

Roger Hartley, *University of Leeds.*

P. Hindley, *Tresham College.*

R. Hine, *Polytechnic of the South Bank.*

Dr. T. Hinton, *University of Surrey.*

Dr. C Hole, *University of Bristol.*

M. Humpage, *Kingston Polytechnic.*

Rolf Ingvaldsen, *Norwegian Institute of Adult Education.*

Dr. T. Jackson, *University of York.*

D. James, *Leeds Polytechnic.*

Bogdan Jankovic, *University of Belgrade, Yugoslavia.*

Z. Jeniec, *St Mary's College, London.*

Miss C. Johnson, *University of Liverpool.*

G. Keirle, *Educational Resources Unit, The Building Centre,London.*

R. Kitchen, *The Polytechnic, Wolverhampton.*

Mrs. N. Law, *Institute of Education, University of London.*

Prof. R. Lewis, *ESRC-ITE Programme and University of Lancaster.*

Prof. B. Lindstrom, *University of Göteborg.*

Dr. A. Loader, *University of Lancaster.*

Mrs D. Mackie, *Napier College, Edinburgh.*

Dr. G. Makinson, *University of Kent at Canterbury.*

Dr. M. Manning, *University of Cambridge.*

Dr. A. Marsden, *University of Lancaster.*

A. R. Mason, *University of London Computer Centre.*

Ms. Mary Megarity, *The Queen's University, Belfast.*

Dr. N. Millar, *Computer Centre, Edinburgh University.*

H. Morarji, *University of Kent at Canterbury.*

Judith Morris, *Council for Educational Technology, London.*

Dr. P. Murphy, *Open University.*

Miss Louise Murray, *(student) Leeds Girls' High Sshool.*

P. Oates, *MacMillan Ltd.*

Prof. J. Ogborn, *Institute of Education, University of London.*

A. M. Pagie, *Technical University Delft.*

R. Paisley, *Carrickfergus Grammar School.*

J. Patrick, *University of Strathclyde.*

M. J-J. Pauleau, *French Embassy, London.*

F. S. Pederson, *Danish Ministry of Education.*

Dr. J. Pickett, *Brighton Polytechnic.*

William Pollard, *Hyde Sixth Form College, Tameside.*

Dr. D. Pountney, *Liverpool Polytechnic.*

Dr. E. Reed, *Leeds Polytechnic.*

Miss V. Reid, *Polytechnic of the South Bank.*

B. Richards, *Avon Information Technology Unit.*

Dr. A. Richmond, *Liverpool Polytechnic.*

Dr. J. Ridgway, *University of Lancaster.*

D. Rogers, *Harrow College of Further Education.*

Wenche Ronning, *Norwegian Institute of Adult Education.*

Dr. Peter Ross, *University of Edinburgh.*

Ms. R. Rymaszewski, *University of Lancaster.*

T. Scott, *Napier College, Edinburgh.*

Dr. J. Self, *University of Lancaster.*

Dr. E. Shiv, *Glasgow College of Technology.*

C. Sparkes, *Royal Military College of Science.*

Dr. P. Stephen, *Manchester Polytechnic.*

J. Steer, *ILECC, London.*

Dr. A. P. Steward, *Sunderland Polytechnic.*

Mrs. G. Stewart, *Glasgow College of Technology.*

Dr. E. D. Tagg, *University of Lancaster.*

E. Taylor, *Lancashire Polytechnic.*

Dr. M. Taylor, *University of Liverpool.*

D. Unwin, *Queensland Institute of Technology, Australia.*

D. Vaughan, *Blackwell Scientific Publications Ltd.*

Ms. N. Vongsirojgul, *West Hill College, Birmingham.*

Dr. T. Walton, *University of Liverpool.*

Dr. D. Webber, *University of Glasgow.*

Dr. C. Wells, *University of Reading.*

Mrs. D. Whitelock, *Institute of Education, University of London.*

Dr. C. S. Williams, *The Queen's College, Glasgow.*

Keyword Index